Proceedings of the 1993 Connectionist Models Summer School

Edited by:

Michael C. Mozer, University of Colorado, Boulder
Paul Smolensky, University of Colorado, Boulder
David S. Touretzky, Carnegie Mellon University
Jeffrey L. Elman, University of California, San Diego
Andreas S. Weigend, Xerox PARC and
                        University of Colorado, Boulder

LEA LAWRENCE ERLBAUM ASSOCIATES, PUBLISHERS
1994 Hillsdale, New Jersey   Hove and London

Lawrence Erlbaum Associates, Inc., Publishers
365 Broadway
Hillsdale, New Jersey 07642

Books published by Lawrence Erlbaum Associates are printed
on acid-free paper, and their bindings are chosen
for strength and durability.

10 9 8 7 6 5 4 3 2 1

ISBN 0-8058-1590-2

CONTENTS

NEUROSCIENCE

VISION

COGNITIVE MODELING

LANGUAGE

SYMBOLIC COMPUTATION AND RULES

RECURRENT NETWORKS AND TEMPORAL PATTERN PROCESSING

CONTROL

LEARNING ALGORITHMS AND ARCHITECTURES

LEARNING THEORY

SIMULATION TOOLS

FOREWORD

The Connectionist Models Summer School has become somewhat of a tradition. The first Summer School, held at Carnegie Mellon in 1986 and organized by Geoff Hinton, Terry Sejnowski, and Dave Touretzky, took place at the dawn of the modern neural net era. Researchers from diverse academic backgrounds were working in relative isolation, without many opportunities to interact with one another. The Summer School provided the first chance for many graduate students to make contact with their colleagues. The bottled up energy and enthusiasm propelled students through an intense two-week program of lectures, workshops, and informal discussion.

Following the 1986 Summer School, the scene changed dramatically. Commander Data and the Terminator were endowed with neural network brains, a plot line in the Dick Tracy comic strip revolved around an evil neural network computer, several popular press books were written about the field, and the number of neural net journals and conferences seemed to be growing exponentially for a while. Through this explosion, two more Summer Schools were held, one in 1988 at Carnegie Mellon and one in 1990 at UC San Diego. Each time, the organizers questioned whether another Summer School was necessary, given the variety of forums for communication that sprung up within the field (and the agony of raising funds for the event). The Summer School appears to be here to stay, though. It has evolved from an outlet for the downtrodden outsiders to a mainstay of the community. What the Summer School has lost in pioneering spirit, it makes up for in increasing sophistication and maturity of its participants.

The 1993 Summer School was held in Boulder, Colorado, which provided a spectacular geographic locale with the Rocky Mountains as the backdrop and clear, sunny days throughout the duration of the event. The program was intense and demanding, with three 1-2 hour lectures per day, smaller group workshops in the afternoons, and informal sessions in the evening, sometimes continuing well past midnight—for twelve full days.

The 1993 Summer School began a second generation: Two of the organizers were former Summer School students, as were ten of the faculty. Many former Summer School participants view the experience as a critical point in their careers, and indeed, many of the successful recent Ph.D.s in the field today participated in earlier Summer Schools. The students in attendance this year were equally talented and enthusiastic. Over 200 applied for the fifty places available. However, the one-in-four acceptance ratio does not reflect the true intensity of the competition because only the very top Ph.D. students applied to the program in the first place; essentially every applicant was well qualified and of the highest caliber. The accepted students and invited faculty had diverse scientific backgrounds and research interests, reflecting the broad spectrum of areas contributing to neural networks, including artificial intelligence, cognitive science, computer science, engineering, mathematics, neuroscience, and physics, although the slant of the Summer School has always leaned toward cognitive science and artificial intelligence.

The papers in this volume are by Summer School students and faculty, and they exemplify the tremendous breadth and depth of research underway in the field. Each student paper was carefully reviewed by one of the Summer

School faculty or organizers. Indeed, the review and revision process has come to be a significant opportunity for further student-faculty interaction. About a fifth of the papers were conceived or developed during the Summer School, including several that involve collaboration among students who first met in Boulder. This is an impressive feat considering that the final paper drafts were due only two months following the Summer School. As in the past, we feel that the Proceedings contain timely and high-quality work by the best and the brightest in the neural nets game, and it provides an accurate picture of the state of the art in this fast-moving field.

Despite the intellectual energy and intensity that went into the Summer School, the students and faculty found time for a variety of extracurricular activities—volleyball in Chautauqua Park at the base of the Flatirons, our own neural net rave at the Marquee Club, with Sara Solla leading the frenetic dancing until the club closed, a hike through the July snow at Rocky Mountain National Park, and a late afternoon bolt to Water World. Photos documenting some of these activities are included in the back of the volume.

We express our deep appreciation to the National Science Foundation (Human Cognition and Perception Program, Knowledge Models and Cognitive Systems Program, and Linguistics Program), the American Association for Artificial Intelligence, Siemens Research Center, and the University of Colorado Institute of Cognitive Science for their sponsorship of this event. In particular, Steve Hanson of Siemens and Joe Young of NSF gave us the initial encouragement crucial to convincing us to that we could raise the necessary support. We also thank the local student hosts whose heroic efforts allowed the Summer School to run without a hitch, and David Ascher and Brian Bonnlander for creating the text formatting macros used by many contributors to this volume. Finally, the Summer School would not have been possible without the participation and dedication of the faculty. We hope that the experience was as enriching and rewarding for them as it was for the students and organizers.

MICHAEL C. MOZER
University of Colorado, Boulder

DAVID S. TOURETZKY
Carnegie Mellon University

ANDREAS S. WEIGEND
Xerox PARC and
University of Colorado, Boulder

PAUL SMOLENSKY
University of Colorado, Boulder

JEFFREY L. ELMAN
University of California, San Diego

PARTICIPANTS IN THE 1993
CONNECTIONIST MODELS SUMMER SCHOOL

ORGANIZERS

Jeff Elman, University of California, San Diego
Mike Mozer, University of Colorado, Boulder
Dave Touretzky, Carnegie Mellon University
Paul Smolensky, University of Colorado, Boulder
Andreas Weigend, Xerox PARC / University of Colorado, Boulder

FACULTY

Yaser Abu-Mostafa, California Institute of Technology
Dana Anderson, University of Colorado, Boulder
Marijke Augusteijn, University of Colorado, Colorado Springs
Sue Becker, McMaster University
Peter Dayan, Salk Institute
Peter Földiak, Oxford
Mary Hare, Birkbeck College
Cathy Harris, Boston University
David Haussler, University of California, Santa Cruz
Geoff Hinton, University of Toronto
Kristina Johnson, University of Colorado, Boulder
Mike Jordan, Massachusetts Institute of Technology
John Kruschke, Indiana University
Jay McClelland, Carnegie Mellon University
Ennio Mingolla, Boston University
Steve Nowlan, Synaptics
Dave Plaut, Carnegie Mellon University
Jordan Pollack, Ohio State Univeristy
Dean Pomerleau, Carnegie Mellon University
Dave Rumelhart, Stanford University
Terry Sejnowski, University of California, San Diego / Salk Institute
Patrice Simard, AT&T Bell Labs
Sara Solla, AT&T Bell Labs
Janet Wiles, University of Queensland

STUDENTS

Amit Almor, Brown University
David Ascher, Brown University
Loisa Bennetto, Denver University
Anoop Bhattacharjya, Rensselaer Polytechnic Institute
Tad Blair, Yale University
Richard Caruana, Carnegie Mellon University
Mark Craven, University of Wisconsin
Mihail Crucianu, University of Paris
Fred Cummins, Indiana University
Kim Gary Daugherty, USC
Virginia de Sa, Rochester
Valentin Dragoi, Duke University
Itiel Dror, Harvard University
James Eisenhart, University of Georgia
Michael Finke, University of Karlsruhe
Rodrigo Garcés, University of California, Santa Cruz
Zoubin Ghahramani, Massachusetts Institute of Technology
Thea Ghiselli-Crippa, University of Pittsburgh
Anita Govindjee, University of Illinois
Prahlad Gupta, Carnegie Mellon University
Arun Jagoda, State University of New York, Buffalo
John Kolen, Ohio State University
Matthew Kurbat, University of Michigan
Kenneth Kurtz, Stanford University
Margrethe Lindemann, Johns Hopkins University
Alexander Linden, University of Bonn
Thomas Lund, University of Iowa
Devin McAuley, Indiana University
Jennifer Myers, Northwestern University
Lars Niklasson, University of Exeter
Sageev Oore, University of Toronto
Randall O'Reilly, Carnegie Mellon University
Genevieve Orr, Oregon Graduate Institute
Michael Perrone, Brown University
Karl Pfleger, Stanford University
Michael Potts, University of Aston
Thomas Rebotier, University of California, San Diego
Michael Rindner, City University of New York
Philip Sabes, Massachusetts Institute of Technology
Hinrich Schütze, Stanford University
Yoram Singer, Hebrew University
Joseph Sirosh, University of Texas
Michael Spivey-Knowlton, University of Rochester
Catherine Stevens, University of Queensland
Ah-Hwee Tan, Boston University
Anya Tascillo, State University of New York, Binghamton
Irina Tchoumatchenko, University of Paris
Sebastian Thrun, University of Bonn
Hank Wan, Carnegie Mellon University
Michael Young, University of Minnesota

LOCAL STUDENT HOSTS

John Allison, University of Colorado, Boulder
Brian Bonnlander, University of Colorado, Boulder
Franco Callari, University of Colorado, Boulder
Sreerupa Das, University of Colorado, Boulder
Robert Dodier, University of Colorado, Boulder
Kelvin Fedrick, University of Colorado, Boulder
Evelyn Ferstl, University of Colorado, Boulder
Audrey Guzik, University of Colorado, Boulder
Stefanie Lindstaedt, University of Colorado, Boulder
Patrick Lynn, University of Colorado, Boulder
Kevin Markey, University of Colorado, Boulder
Don Mathis, University of Colorado, Boulder
David Nix, University of Colorado, Boulder
Pablo Olmos-Gallo, Denver University
Michael Peacock, Denver University
Carol Siegel, Denver University
Bruce Tesar, University of Colorado, Boulder

NEUROSCIENCE

Sigma vs Pi Properties of Spiking Neurons

Thomas P. Rebotier & Jacques Droulez
UCSD, dept. of Cognitive Science & College de France, LPPA
rebotier@cogsci.ucsd.edu

This study compares two neural mechanisms producing multiplicative rather than additive output: coincidence detection and graded disinhibition. These mechanisms are studied using elementary spiking neurons. Both mecanisms are found to implement multiplication of spiking rates. Coincidence detection has a weaker biological plausibility but an excellent response, and graded disinhibition has a stronger plausibility and response still more multiplicative than additive over reasonible (5-80) spiking rates.

INTRODUCTION

In the PDP litterature, most models of neurons look alike: they have continuous activation values, and transmit without delay a sigmoid function (or other differentiable function) of the sum of their weighted inputs. However, to implement gating, neurons taking the weighted sum of the product of activations within an input group have been introduced as Sigma-Pi neurons. (Rumelhart & McClelland 1986).

The biological plausibility of the neuron model used is often irrelevant to connectionnist modeling. However, there is some plausibility in the behavior of classical sigmoid neuron: in a steady state, the output firing rate is a monotonic continuous function of somatic current influx; when normalized by the maximal firing rate it is bounded in [0,1]. This does not support the Sigma-Pi version of neuron. Yet, multiplicative properties can be obtained by various mechanisms when considering spiking neurons.

Most actual biological neurons are more complex than any model. However, since the initial modeling of nerve influx by Hodgkin and Huxley (1952), various models have described neurons at different levels of complexity. Many modelists are currently using the compartimental model generator GENESIS developed at CalTech (Koch & Seguev 1989), which enables to build a neuron or a small group of neurons with compartments having specified density of various ions channels.

This study uses an even simpler model of neuron, and compares two neural mechanisms producing multiplicative rather than additive output.

Important features in the models presented in this paper are besides the spiking behavior the arrangement of neurons to get a multiplicative response. Two types of such neurons were tested, using spike coincidence detection, and graded disinhibition.

MODEL OF NEURON USED

The neurons used are "integrate, leak and fire" neurons. They sum their inputs and display a spiking, rather than graded, output. These neurons have two main state variables: potential and threshold. The potential increases or decreases according to synaptic input, slowly comes back exponentially to the rest value, is submitted to a small gaussian noise, and bounces to a slight hyperpolarization just after each spike. The threshold increases with each spike, and comes back exponentially to a rest threshold value. Mathematically, when the neuron is not spiking, the potential and threshold obey finite differences equations approximating the following equations:

$$dP/dt = -a.P + input(t) + noise(t)$$

$$dT/dt = -b.(T-T_0)$$

when the neuron is spiking, potential and threshold are clamped:

$$P = P_{post-spike}$$

$$T = T_{post-spike}$$

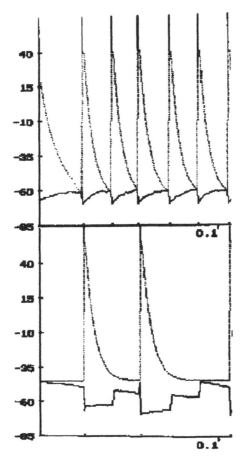

Figure 1: Example of two neurons. The first neuron has a negative rest threshold, i.e. it fires spontaneously. The second neuron receives input from the first one. The lower line is the potential, the upper line (dotted line) is the threshold. Spikes are indicated by a long vertical bar above the threshold peak, and by a small dot at the bottom of the graph for that neuron. Coordinates are seconds and milivolts. One can notice that very small variations in the firing rate of the first neuron (owed to the gaussian noise) are amplified at the level of the second neuron, which reacts to either two or three inputs according to the delay between input # 1 and input # 2.

Synapses are defined with a weight and a delay. The presynaptic neural spike is given a decreasing triangular shape, and the postsynaptic increment of potential occurs after the delay has passed, and is proportionnal to the spike envelope times the synaptic weight. The resulting behavior can range from sudden potential changes to accumulation of smoother PSP's. (see Figure 1) Weights can be positive and negative and the effect of inhibition is symmetrical to that of excitation.

4

MULTIPLICATIVE NEURONS

Two types of multiplicatory neurons have been used. The first type are neurons which act as coincidence detectors. The multiplicative response is excellent, but these neurons have extreme parameters, especially time constants. The second type is by graded disinhibition. This still has a fairly multiplicative response, and is much more plausible, expecially since disinhibition is known to be used in the brain (e.g, in the cortical saccadic command circuit, from Frontal Eye Field via Substancia Nigra Pars Reticulata to Colliculus Superior).

Coincidence Detection:

This simple model of neuron can implement a multiplicative law. When decay time constants are very short, the neuron cannot cumulate inputs across time. If the threshold is high enough, the neuron will only respond when two input spikes are simultanous. Because of the gaussian noise, the inputs are fairly uncorrelated functions, and the output spike rate follows therefore a multiplicative law. The shorter the time constants, the closer the neuron can be made to follow a multiplicative function.

If a neuron's transitions between rest and firing state are infinitely short, the firing rate is proportionnal to the probability of the neuron being in the firing state. When two such neurons affer onto a third one whose threshold demands simultaneous input to fire, the firing rate of that third neuron is the probability of simultaneous firing of the two input neurons, which is the product of the probabilities of firing for each of these. Mathematically, at the limit, the output rates verify:

$$O_j = a.P(j \text{ is firing})$$

$$P(3 \text{ fires}) = P(1 \text{ fires}) . P(2 \text{ fires})$$

hence

$$1/a. O_3 = 1/a. O_1 . 1/a . O_2$$

that is

$$O_3 = 1/a. O_1 . O_2$$

Graded Disinhibition

Graded disinhibition proceeds from the idea of gating. Gating allows an all-or-none multiplication of two signals. Here, the gating is set at a partially efficient level, so that the response is gradual rather than all-or-none. Because we want actual multiplication by the speed signal, rather than suppression, there has to be an intermediary inhibitory stage with a high spontaneous activity, which is inhibited by the speed signal, hence the disinhibition. Figure 2 shows the basic circuit.

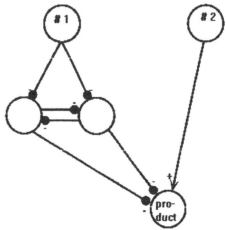

Figure 2: Schema of graded disinhibition. Arrows indicate excitatory connections, circle-ended lines represent inhibitory connections. The middle layer fires tonically (spontaneously).

5

A major feature in this circuit is the feedback within the inhibitory intermediary stage. This feedback actually allows the dynamical properties of the disinhibition to vary widely. For biological reasons (such neurons being inhibitory, and this feedback being local), it is reasonable to restrain to negative feedback only. The feedback allows to "stretch" the response of the intermediary layer as a whole. For example, at moderately high speed signal, only one out of two neurons will remain active in this intermediary stage - which one does not matter, it is set by a symmetry breaking, and we see the dominance flip, but the layer's total output remains steady. Without the feedback, the whole intermediary layer would reflect the dynamical properties of an isolated neuron, i.e. it would spike agressively regardless of the inhibitory speed signal, until the latter reaches a certain threshold, above which the intermediary layer would become silent. Thus, this feedback allows to linearize the response of the intermediate stage, thereby allowing the gating to be effectively progressive.

RESULTS

Coincidence Detection:

Table 1 and Figure 3 show the response of a coincidence detection neuron with extremely short time constants (.5 msec). Because of these very short TC, the multiplicative response is maintained at very high firing rates. Such firing rates are irrealistic for cortical neurons, but not for brainstem neurons, e.g. in the oculomotor system. Note that at small firing rates, coincidence detection has a high variation.

Table 1: Firing rate of a Coincidence Detection Neuron, as a function of the firing rates of its two afferent neurons.

neuron 1	23,0	47,5	65,0	102,5	144,0	238,0
neuron 2						
18,0	3,0	5,0	6,0	9,0	13,0	18,0
23,0	2,0	4,0	8,0	16,0	21,0	23,0
31,0	2,0	11,0	15,0	20,0	22,0	30,0
37,5	4,0	9,0	16,0	19,0	29,0	37,0
47,5	7,0	8,0	19,0	32,0	33,0	47,0
55,0	8,0	15,0	23,0	30,0	46,0	55,0
65,0	7,0	20,0	20,0	42,0	45,0	62,0
79,5	8,0	29,0	32,0	45,0	65,0	80,0
102,5	12,0	27,0	42,0	56,0	75,0	98,0
144,0	19,0	36,0	56,0	80,0	106,0	140,0
238,0	34,0	60,0	95,0	133,0	194,0	234,0

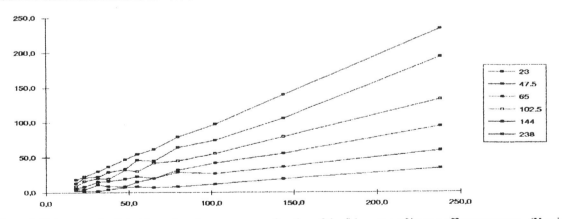

Figure 3: Firing rate of a Coincidence detection neuron, as a function of the firing rates of its two afferent neurons. (X-axis: FR of neuron 1, Y-axis: FR of Coincidence Detector; Each curve stands for a different FR of neuron 2).

6

Graded Disinhibition

Table 2 and Figure 4 show the results for graded disinhibition. Here the neural parameters are in natural ranges, and the response is limited to lower firing rates. In that range, the response is of even higher order than multiplicative; that trend is mostly seen in the last two points.

Table 2: Firing rate of Graded Disinhibition, as a function of the firing rates of its two input neurons.

neuron 1	0	11	20	31	41	55
neuron 2						
0	0	0	0	0	0,1	1
11	0	0	0,5	1	2,2	4,8
20	0	0,2	0,75	2,5	5,5	8,4
31	0	0,7	1,9	4,8	8,5	16
41	0	1	3,7	7,5	13,5	22
55	0	1,75	6	13,5	20	32
70	0	5,4	12	24	33	45
86	0,25	14,4	29	42	55	69

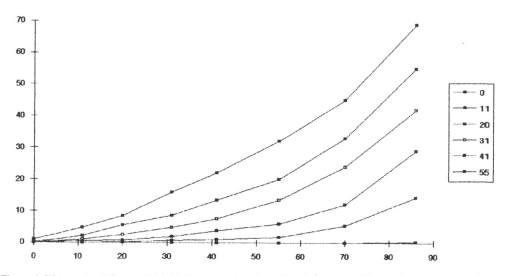

Figure 4: Firing rate of Graded Disinhibition, as a function of the firing rates of its two input neurons. (X-axis: FR of neuron 1, Y-axis: FR of output neuron; Each curve stands for a different FR of neuron 2).

The use of feedback within the inhibitory interlayer is demonstrated by Figure 5. The response curve of the inhibitory layer without feedback is compared to that with FB (shown at its own size, or normalized to the no-FB size). The non-linearity is obviously reduced. More negative feedback produces an even straighter response. Positive feedback would sharpen the non-linearity.

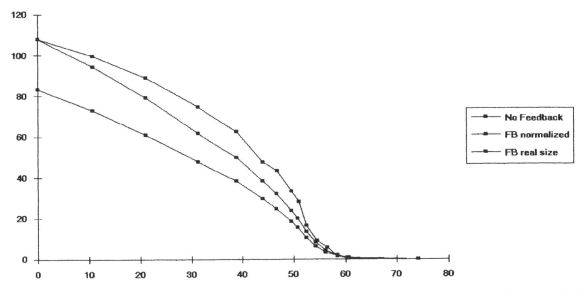

Figure 5: Compared responses (firing rate) of the inhibitory interlayer with or without intra-layer inhibitory feedback, as a function of the inhibitory input firing rate. Top curve: response without feedback; second curve: response with feedback, sized to curve # 1; third curve: response without feedback, real size.

INTERPRETATION OF RESULTS

What it means to have a multiplicative law:

At first, we want the output spiking rate to be as close as possible to the product rather than the sum of input spiking rates. At a deeper level, however, "to follow an additive (respectively multiplicative) law" means more than this, it refers to how well the output could be *any function* of the sum, (respectively product), of the inputs. Thus, if we want to analyze the response of the neurons by themselves, there are two degrees of interpretation: (1) Neurons can spike at total (or product) rate of input rates, or (2) they can spike at a rate depending only on the total (or product) of input rates.

Table 3 (below) enables to compare additive and multiplicative models for both kind of neurons, and according to both possible approaches. For comparison, the same treatment is also applied to the actual sum and to the actual product of the input frequencies, scaled to insure equal maximum output. Table 3 calls for a few comments. First, we see that the Coincidence Detection line differs little from the pure multiplication line; the former actually almost equal to the latter plus noise. Graded disinhibition is not such a clear-cut case, but comparison with the attempt to modelize multiplicatively the sum of input frequencies show that G.D. is an intermediary, compounded response rather than an additive response. Altogether, Coincidence Detection is a better approximation of plain multiplication, but Graded Disinhibiton still shows a multiplicative behavior.

Table 3: The standard deviation of various models fit to the data for Coincidence Detection and Graded Disinhibition. Pure addition and multiplication are also submitted to this modeling. Note how little the standard deviation is (4.7) when approximating multiplication by a non-linear function of addition. Unit: spikes per second. Input range considered: CD: [18-144]x[23-144], GD, addition and multiplication: [0-55]x[0-55].

	prorata of sum	any function of sum	prorata of product	function of product
CD	**12.5**	**6.4**	**3.2**	**3**
GD	**11.3**	**3.8**	**5.6**	**3.6**
addition	0	0	16.4	11.8
multiplication	10.7	4.7	0	0

DISCUSSION AND CONCLUSION

Comparison of these mechanisms

Coincidence detection proceeds from spiking behavior and local neural properties (membrane capacitance properties). On the other hand, graded disinhibition is already a small network phenomenon.

Coincidence detection has a very wide response range, but a high variability at low firing rates. Graded disinhibition is true at low firing rates, but has a smaller range; it amplifies the response untill the output neuron reaches it maximal firing rate. Both mechanisms would be smoothed and regularized if implemented by a large number of neurons.

Are these mechanisms biologically realistic ?

Because of the very short time constants involved, Coincidence Detection is not likely to happen at the level of the soma, but may be very relevant inside the dendritic tree, as show the simulations led by Rall (1977,1989 in Koch & Segev). Also, cortical dendritic transmission turns out to be faster than predicted by classical cable theory (Nowlan, private communication), hinting at non-linearities within the dendritic tree, where Coincidence Detection could be implemented at dendrite junctions.

Graded Disinhibition is a more likely mechanism. Most cortical inhibition is local, but non-local disinhibition is already known to play a role in the saccadic system, during the trigger of voluntary saccades, with disinhibition of the Colliculus Superior by the Frontal Eye Fields via the Substancia Nigra Pars Reticulata (Hikosaka & Wurtz 1983). Just as inhibition is graded, disinhibition could be. Compared with the results of this model, graded disinhibition also should improve with the number of neurons because of the effect of negative feed-back, and thus its response in vivo should be even better than those of the simulations.

Are these sigma-pi neurons ?

No. The CD neurons are pure "pi" neurons, and the GD have a somewhat less rigorous law. Sigma-pi *units* could be obtained by collecting the output of such neurons by a classical "sigma" neuron; these units would then consist of two or three levels. In the case where coincidence detection would be implemented within the dendritic tree, then we would have complicated sigma-pi neurons, but these would not resemble the clear-cut case used by the modelists: these neurons would have a variety of responses to their various inputs, depending on how these inputs spread over the dendritic tree, some interactions would be almost multiplicative, and some would be quite additive, depending upon the time constants and linearity of behavior of the junctions in the dendritic tree where the interacting inputs meet. Therefore, the modelist's sigma-pi neuron is at best an idealisation of a range of continuous interactions where the response varies between pure sum and pure gating.

What use for such "product" mechanisms ?

Products can be used in a variety of cybernetical mechanisms. The main general mechanism using product is gain control. Gain control must be used in most motor tasks, where the motor command must be adapted for the immediate conditions of muscular fatigue and of load; it may also be used in attention. Other mechanisms include the dynamic memory phenomena, whereby a spatial representation is updated by integrating a velocity signal (Droulez & Berthoz 1988).

Conclusion

Product neurons, or small systems for effecting product are biologically plausible. As often, the same function (here, a product) can be assumed by pure neural properties (short time constants leading to coincidence detection) or by the right arrangement of several neurons (graded disinhibition). It is possible that both mechanisms are actually at work in different systems.

Spiking neurons, even very simple, demonstrate qualitatively different phenomena than the classical PDP automata. Yet at this level, these phenomena can still be described functionnally, and modeled by simple -though not classical- automata. The key question for modelist : "can the high-level behavior emerging from low-level properties be modeled per se, at a functional level, or are low-level models necessary to account for high-level behavior ?" still remains open.

References:

[1] Droulez & Berthoz, 1988, Spatial and temporal transformations in visuomotor coordination, in Eckmiller & von der Marlsburg: *Neural Computers*, Springer-Verlag, pp 345-358

[2] Droulez, 1992, Multiplication by Spiking Neurons, communication in MUCOM conference (MUltisensory COntrol of Movement).

[3] Goldberg, Eggers, Gouras, 1991 in Kandell & Schwartz: *Principles of Neural Science*, Elsevier

[4] Hikosaka & Wurtz, 1983, Visual and oculomotor function of monkey substancia nigra pars reticulata, *J.Neurophysiol.* 49: 1230-1301

[5] Hodgkin & Huxley, 1952, a quantitative description of membrane current and its application to conduction and excitation in nerve, *J.Physiol.London* 117:500-544

[6] Koch & Segev, 1989, Methods in Neuronal Modeling, from synapses to networks, MIT Press

[7] McCulloch & Pitts, 1943, a logical caculus of the ideas immanent in logical activity, *Bulletin of Mathematical Biophysics* 5: 115-133

[8] Rall, 1977, Core conductor theory and cable properties of neurons, in Kandel, Brookhart & Mountcastle: *Handbook of Physiology: The Nervous System*, William & Wilkins, Baltimore, pp 39-98

[8] Rumelhart, McClelland & the PDP Research Group, 1986, *Parallel distributed processing, explorations in the microstructure of cognition*, MIT Press

Towards a Computational Theory of Rat Navigation

Hank S. Wan,* David S. Touretzky, A. David Redish
Computer Science Department
Carnegie Mellon University
Pittsburgh, PA 15213–3891

A century of behavioral studies has generated an abundance of proposals for how animals represent and navigate through space. Recently, neurophysiological recording in freely-behaving animals has begun to reveal cellular correlates of these cognitive processes, such as the existence of place cells in hippocampus and head direction cells in postsubiculum and parietal cortex. We propose computational mechanisms to explain these phenomena.

A variety of computer models have demonstrated place cell-like responses, given inputs that encode distance and/or bearing to one or more landmarks. These models utilize machine learning algorithms such as competitive learning [Sharp 1991], recurrent backpropagation/Elman nets [Shapiro & Hetherington 1993, Hetherington & Shapiro 1993], genetic algorithms [Treves et al. 1992], competitive learning with radial basis units [Burgess et al. 1993], and specialized architectures employing a combination of delta rule and radial basis units [Schmajuk & Blair 1993].

The problem with all of these models is that their processing is mainly a function of visual input. The experimental literature clearly shows that hippocampal processing is not that simple. Specifically, although place fields *are* sensitive to visual input (they rotate in agreement with rotation of distal visual cues), place cells remain active when the lights are turned out, and place fields can form when the animal explores novel environments in the dark. Place cells also continue to fire when distal landmarks are removed, but permutation of landmarks causes the animal to behave as if it were in an unfamiliar environment. Finally, place cell firing may be dependent on head direction, at least under certain conditions. An acceptable model of place memory must allow the "current place" to be updated by non-visual means such as motor feedback, and must be both sensitive to visual cues and robust in their absence.

We propose a computational theory of the core of rat navigation abilities, based on coupled mechanisms for path integration, place recognition, and maintenance of head direction. We assume the rat has a path integration system (see [Etienne 1987, Mittelstaedt & Mittelstaedt 1980]) that is able to keep track of its current position relative to selected reference points. We postulate that hippocampal pyramidal cells form place descriptions by learning correlations between perceptual inputs and the rat's internal states, which include the output of the path integrator. Place codes are associated with landmark bearings, so that visual cues can recall previously stored directional information in a manner similar to McNaughton's local view hypothesis [McNaughton 1989].

We describe a connectionist implementation of this theory. Our model reproduces a variety of experimental observations, including reset of head direction in response to visual input, persistence of place fields in the absence of visual input, and modulation of place cell directional sensitivity. We compare our theory with other theories of hippocampal function and offer some predictions based on the model.

Behavioral and Biological Data

Place Cells

Over two decades ago, O'Keefe & Conway [1978] discovered pyramidal cells in the hippocampus that fire maximally when the rat occupies a particular location in the environment. They called these cells *place cells*. Numerous studies have since been performed to elucidate the characteristics of these cells [O'Keefe & Speakman 1987, Muller & Kubie 1987, McNaughton et al. 1989, Sharp et al. 1990, Quirk et al. 1990, Muller et al. 1991, Quirk et al. 1992].

---

*Address all correspondence to the first author. Electronic mail address: hsw@cs.cmu.edu.

When a rat is deposited in a novel arena, place cells are rapidly recruited to code for locations in that environment [Quirk et al. 1990]. They develop a sensitivity to defining characteristics of the environment. In two visually similar but geometrically distinct arenas (one round and one rectangular), mostly disjoint sets of place cells are recruited [Muller & Kubie 1987]. Although each cell's place specificity is broadly tuned and varies depending on the available perceptual cues [Muller & Kubie 1987], their ensemble activity is sufficient to localize the rat's position to within a few centimeters [Wilson & McNaughton 1993]. Quantitative analysis further shows that when the animal is moving, the place code predicts its future position by about 120 milliseconds [Muller & Kubie 1989].

Once the rat has a notion of where it is, place cells continue to respond even when the lights are turned off [Quirk et al. 1990]. Most place cells also continue their activity when some of the visual cues are removed, although some fraction become inactive [O'Keefe & Conway 1978, O'Keefe & Speakman 1987, Markus et al. 1993]. This suggests that place cells are influenced by but not solely driven by visual input.

In open arenas, the most readily observable correlate to place cell activity is the rat's physical location. However, experimenters have observed activity being modulated by other aspects of behavior. For example, Eichenbaum [1987] reports correlates of hippocampal cell activity with task segments in an open arena where the rat is to repeat a sequence of actions: run to an odor-sampling port on one side of the room, discriminate the odor cue, and then, depending on the valence of the odor, run to the opposite side of the room to receive a reward. Some place cell responses were modulated by whether the rat was traveling to the odor port or the reward site as it crossed the place field.

Place cells are normally non-directional [Muller et al. 1991]. But in experiments where the rat is restricted to a corridor environment, such as an eight-arm maze, place cells readily become directionally tuned [McNaughton et al. 1989]. O'Keefe (personal communication) has observed that when rats are trained to run back and forth on a one dimensional track, place cells are initially non-directional, but after they become familiar with the task the cells develop directionality. However, when a food pellet is placed at the center of the track so the rat encounters it unexpectedly, there is preliminary indication that the ensuing arousal response is accompanied by place cells again becoming non-directional. This suggests that place fields may be modulated by attention.

McNaughton (personal communication) reports experiments by Gothard which begin with a rat performing a navigation task in a tightly controlled, cue-restricted environment where the primary visual cues are two cylinders. Additional, non-salient cues are gradually added until the environment is cue-rich. Place cells were observed to follow the position of the cylindrical landmarks (which can be moved about), ignoring the non-salient cues. This demonstrates that hippocampal place cells respond to a *cue set* that can be influenced by the animal's past experience.

Path Integration

Behavioral studies [Etienne 1987, Mittelstaedt & Mittelstaedt 1980] demonstrate that rats are able to wander randomly in the dark and then follow a direct path back to their starting point. They do so by integrating vestibular and kinesthetic cues along the path.

Although hippocampal lesions produce severe deficits in spatial tasks involving exteroceptive cues [O'Keefe & Nadel 1978], lesioned rats can continue to perform tasks that admit alternative strategies, such as path integration [Schacter & Nadel 1991]. For example, in a task where rats were passively transported from a reward site and then had to return without the use of visual or other cues, hippocampal lesions did not produce a deficit, whereas lesion of the caudate nucleus did [Abraham et al. 1983]. This suggests that the path integration system functions independently of the hippocampus.

Head direction

Taube et al. [1990a, 1990b] report cells in postsubiculum and related areas that fire maximally when the animal's head is facing in a particular direction. They are thus called *head direction cells*. The *preferred direction* for such a cell (i.e., the direction eliciting maximal response) is constant throughout an environment. In addition, the difference in preferred direction for any pair of cells is constant across all environments. But cells' preferred directions measured with respect to *true* North may differ across environments. Thus, the set of head direction cells in a rat defines a *directional framework* for each environment to which the animal is exposed.

Head direction cells continue to respond in the dark, but the animal's directional sense will eventually drift if no sensory input is available. In a familiar environment, if visual cues rotate while the rat is in the arena, preferred directions rotate by a corresponding amount. On the other hand, rotation of an unfamiliar environment does not change the head direction cells' preferred directions; the animal's vestibular sense, telling it that nothing has changed, overrides its visual experience (McNaughton, personal communication). When a rat has been disoriented by having been vigorously turned while blindfolded, upon re-entering a familiar environment with eyes uncovered, its cells sometimes revert back to their previously established preferred directions.

Thus, the rat learns a particular alignment of its directional framework with each environment. When disoriented, it restores this alignment by reference to visual landmarks.

A Computational Theory of Rat Navigation

Based on the above and other experimental observations, our theory of rat navigation postulates coupled mechanisms for path integration, place recognition, and maintenance of head direction, as shown in figure 1.

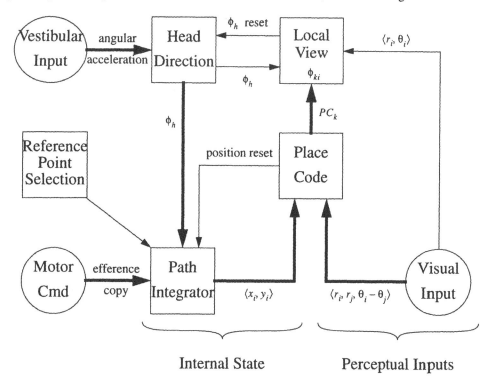

Figure 1: Suggested functional organization of orientation and recognition mechanisms in the rat. Circles are input quantities, boxes are computational modules; they do not necessarily correspond to disjoint or unique brain areas. Thick lines denote main information pathways.

Path integration and place recognition

As noted earlier, a variety of computer models have demonstrated responses similar to place cells. Because the focus of most of these models is on demonstrating formation of place fields from visual inputs, with a few exceptions [McNaughton et al. 1989, Hetherington & Shapiro 1993], none explain how place fields could remain when rats navigate in the dark.

In the model of Hetherington et al. [1993], an Elman net is trained with input sequences from paths to goal locations. This strengthens the recurrent connections between hidden units with nearby place fields. The appropriate place cell can then activate in sequence along paths to a goal without visual input. However, this scheme cannot account for acquisition and maintenance of place fields in the dark in tasks that do not have explicit goal locations [Quirk et al. 1990].

McNaughton et al. [1989] proposes that place cells associate motor actions with transitions between places, so that when visual inputs are unavailable, motor actions can drive the appropriate transitions in hippocampal activity. In effect, this proposes that hippocampus maintains its activity by performing path integration, but it can only do so for familiar regions of the environment. As discussed above, there is data suggesting that rats have a path integration module separate from hippocampus. It therefore seems more likely that efferents from the path integrator to hippocampus are responsible for place cell activity in the dark.

We hypothesize that the rat's path integration module maintains current position relative to a select set of *reference points* by integrating proprioceptive (vestibular) and kinesthetic (motor efference copy) cues. Reference points may be perceptually significant locations such as a corner of the room or a place with distinct odor or texture, but they might also be sensorily nondescript locations distinguished only by the past occurrence of some event, such as the spot in the arena where the rat was released to begin its first exposure to that environment.

The distinction between landmarks and reference points is important. Landmarks are distal cues that generate perceptual input, primarily bearing and distance information. Place cells learn to associate these cues with specific locations, so to be most useful, landmarks should be visible over a substantial portion of the environment. Reference points, on the other hand, are internally-defined locations tracked by the path integrator. They need not have any distinctive sensory attributes. In particular they do not need to be visible at a distance, as in the case of a nest site or burrow entrance.

A central claim of our theory is that the path integrator can maintain position simultaneously with respect to at least two reference points. The selection of "active" reference points is controlled by the animal's goals and attentional state. Place cells are associated with specific reference points, and so their activity is modulated by the active reference point set. Every time this set changes, such as when the animal turns around at the end of a corridor, one set of place cells becomes enabled while another set is disabled. The result is an apparent sensitivity of place cells to head direction. When arousal causes the animal to enlarge the active set to include reference points at both ends of the corridor, head direction sensitivity disappears.

Place recognition and head direction

McNaughton [1989] proposes that hippocampus encodes *local views* tuned to the perceptual features available at a location *with the head facing in a particular direction.* McNaughton et al. [1991] then describe a scheme where place cells encoding local-views are associated with the activity of head direction cells, so that when the rat is disoriented, head direction can be reset based on place cell activity.

We agree with the suggestion that place encodings should include landmark bearings to facilitate realignment of the head direction sense. However, place cells are mostly non-directional in open arenas [Muller et al. 1991]. We therefore think that place cell directional selectivity is unlikely to be the source of head direction realignment. Instead, we offer the following scheme for reconstructing head direction from nondirectional place cell activity.

Since place cells code for locations in a familiar environment, and the reference alignment of a familiar environment is fixed, a place cell activity pattern corresponds to a unique set of allocentric bearings to perceivable landmarks. We therefore suggest that as a rat familiarizes itself with the environment, it learns, in some area external to hippocampus, the correspondence between place codes and allocentric landmark bearings, which is equivalent to the "local view." Later, when the head direction sense is confused, the remembered allocentric bearings (retrieved via place cell activity) can be combined with egocentric bearings to reconstruct head direction. This retrieval process is shown schematically in figure 2.

While place cells are not tuned to allocentric bearings, they can use the differences in bearing between pairs of landmarks to localize points in space. This is because angular difference is constant regardless of head direction. Thus, animals can recognize locations based on landmark cues no matter what direction they are facing. In situations where place cells show directional selectivity [McNaughton et al. 1989], we suggest that the animal has limited its reference point set, e.g., it may only be tracking the reference point corresponding to the current goal location. Shifts in the choice of reference points when the animal reaches ends of corridor segments would result in place cells appearing directional.

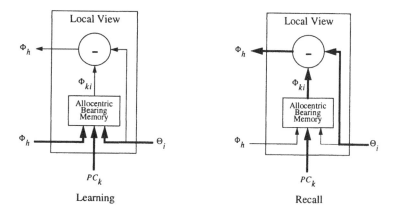

Figure 2: Computational structure of local view association. PC_k is activity of place cell k. Φ_h is head direction, and Θ_i is the current egocentric bearing of landmark i. Φ_{ki} is the allocentric bearing of landmark i at place k. During learning, PC_k is active and Φ_{ki} is recorded as $\Phi_h + \Theta_i$. To realign head direction, PC_k is used to recall Φ_{ki}, and Φ_h is computed as $\Phi_{ki} - \Theta_i$.

A Computer Model

Our place cells are radial basis units tuned to a conjunction of sensory and path integration inputs. Several units are recruited for each location in the environment. Each unit tunes itself to values present in the sensory and path integration systems for two landmarks and one reference point, chosen at random from the set available. The connectivity of these units is shown schematically in figure 3. Such use of radial basis units to model place cells is similar to those described in [Burgess et al. 1993, McNaughton et al. 1993]. In our current simulations, recruitment is done deterministically, but in principle it could be achieved using a Hebbian competitive network similar to those described in [Sharp 1991].

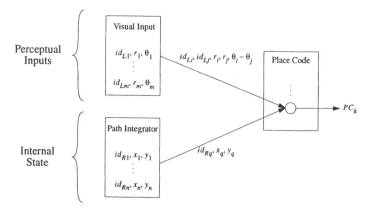

Figure 3: A modeled place cell is a radial-basis unit that tunes to the inputs at a particular location from two perceptual landmarks and one set of path integrator coordinates. id_L denotes an encoding of the identity of a visual landmark, r is the landmark's distance, and θ is its egocentric bearing. Similarly, id_R, x, and y are respectively the identity and Cartesian coordinates of a reference point.

Similar to the model in [Burgess et al. 1993] and unlike [McNaughton et al. 1993], we choose to combine sensory inputs from two landmarks rather than one. When the direction sense is lost, knowing distance to a single landmark only localizes position to a circle; using just egocentric bearing differences between two landmarks localizes to constant angle circular arcs [Levitt et al. 1987]; whereas distances to two landmarks localizes to two points. Thus, we use the combination of distances to and bearing differences between two identified landmarks to model localization to a unique location.

As discussed above, unlike previous computer models, we also include state information from the path integrator as part of the hippocampal input. The animal keeps track of its position in a set of Cartesian reference frames, each centered at an active reference point. For simplicity of exposition we align the x and y axes with East and North, respectively, when computing Cartesian coordinates. The reason for performing path integration in Cartesian rather than polar coordinates is computational stability, as discussed in [Gallistel 1990, p. 76].

The path integrator maintains position with respect to several reference points simultaneously. During exploration and learning, the maximum number of reference points may be active; each newly recruited unit would select one at random to tune to. When the environment has become familiar, a smaller number of reference points might be tracked, and position information is only available with respect to these active reference points. Thus, when a reference point is inactive, the place cells tuned to that point would be silent throughout the environment due to lack of appropriate input. An exception is that when the rat is disoriented, no information may be available from the path integrator, yet retrieval of an appropriate place code is needed. This is resolved by temporarily lowering place cells' dependence on the path integrator so that perceptual inputs alone can trigger place cell activity. In other situations, visual inputs may become unavailable. The dependence of place cells on input from the path integrator then needs to be increased. Mechanisms for such modulations on the extent in which the path integrator drive place cells are external to the present model.

In our simulation, we represent landmark and reference point identities by 1-of-n codes. Distances to landmarks use a distributed code implemented as of an array of radial basis units; differences in bearing are encoded similarly.

Results

Place cells associated with an active reference point are driven by a combination of path integrator and visual cues; they fire if the animal is within the cell's learned place field. For a wide range of parameter values, these cells produce place fields that are similar to those observed in real rats (see figure 4).

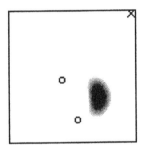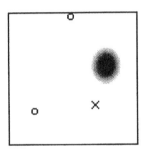

Figure 4: Receptive field of some simulated place cells. Each place cell tunes to a reference point denoted by an 'X' and two visual landmarks shown as circles.

If the rat is deposited in a random spot in the environment, the influence of the path integrator is momentarily reduced, and place units can be driven by visual inputs alone to determine the animal's present location. The path integrator could then be reset accordingly. When the lights are turned out, the path integrator continues to track the rat's position and trigger place cells. This qualitatively accounts for observations in [Quirk et al. 1990].

After disorientation, the animal needs to reestablish its head direction. Active place cell PC_k initiates recall of learned allocentric bearings Φ_{ki} for all visible landmarks i. The difference between Φ_{ki} and the current egocentric bearing Θ_i of the ith landmark gives the current head direction, Φ_h, as shown in figure 2. This reproduces the observations of Taube et al. [1990a, 1990b]

When only a few landmarks are removed, most radial basis place cells continue to receive input. For example, with eight landmarks there are 28 distinct pairings. Assume one place cell is allocated to each. When two landmarks are deleted, 15 of 28 cells continue to receive full input and are unaffected. One place cell receives no perceptual input while 12 cells receive input from one landmark instead of two. These cells can no longer localize positions based on perceptual inputs alone. But by also tuning to valid information from path integration, they could still maintain

16

useful place fields. This is qualitatively similar to the experimental observations in [O'Keefe & Conway 1978, O'Keefe & Speakman 1987]. In contrast, a random transposition of all landmarks would cause most units recruited to code for the environment to become silent because most distances and differences in bearings would change. Other radial units might then be recruited to code for this new arrangement, as would be expected if the animal perceived the modified environment as novel. This would reflect the behavior observed in [Suzuki et al. 1980].

We simulate O'Keefe's one-dimensional track experiment using a reference point at each end of the track. Initially the animal maintains its position simultaneously with respect to both reference points, recruiting two sets of place cells to code for the environment. After becoming thoroughly familiar with the task, it only activates whichever reference point is ahead as it travels down the track. This externally provided attentional input to our model drives direction selectivity in the simulated place cells. Arousal in response to novelty (e.g., a food pellet encountered unexpectedly) results in simultaneous activation of both reference points and loss of direction sensitivity. A similar account can be given for the data in [Eichenbaum et al. 1987].

Discussion, future work, and predictions

As Gallistel points out [1990, p. 76], the accuracy of path integration is sensitive to the choice of representation. In polar coordinates, each update is dependent on the current position estimate, which magnifies cumulative errors. Cartesian systems do not have this problem, because calculation of Δx and Δy does not depend on x and y. We therefore model the states of the path integrator in a Cartesian representation. While the alignment of the Cartesian axes with North and East may seem arbitrary, the sinusoidal array [Touretzky et al. 1993], a spatially distributed phasor encoding, would be a plausible generalization.

In our simulations, the path integrator keeps track of the animal's current position. Instead, if it were to use the motor efference copy to anticipate the rat's position some 120 milliseconds in the future, the resulting place code would then predict the future position of the rat, as described in [Muller & Kubie 1989]. This would not be possible if place cells were driven by perceptual inputs alone.

Given two or more landmarks, a variety of combinations of distance and bearings can be used to localize points in space. For example, Sharp's model uses the conjunction of distances to multiple identified landmarks to reproduce place fields [Sharp 1991]. Similarly, Burgess et al. [1993] use distances to two landmarks.

Most models use fixed combinations of cues to determine location. However, we suggest that the information content in different cue types varies based on landmark properties. For example, while the estimate of distance to a landmark may be very precise when the landmark is nearby, the angles between landmarks can be more informative when the landmarks are farther away. The Hebbian rule has been shown to be closely related to an information maximization principle [Linsker 1987]. Hippocampal associative Hebbian synapses might perhaps be dynamically choosing those spatial primitives with the maximal information content.

We also believe this principle can be applied to the task of retrieving head direction based on perceptual input and place codes. First, to allow for Hebbian learning, the encoding used in the present model for allocentric bearings of landmarks would have to be changed to a distributed pattern of activation rather than a single analog value. Then, we suggest that a Hebbian scheme may establish the appropriate correlations between head direction and perceptual/hippocampal inputs. This way, the module could also make use of compass points (landmarks at an infinite distance; thus their allocentric bearing never changes) when available.

Another natural extension to the model is to allow flexiblity in choice of landmarks and reference point for newly recruited units. The selection could be modulated by factors such as the landmark's perceptual salience, and its stability across trials. This way, more place units would be allocated to code for more informative landmarks. We believe this will allow us to provide a computational account of the "cue set" phenomenon.

Although not addressed in the present model, we believe that tactile and other sensory cues may take the place of visual input to place cells, allowing the place cells to check the path integrator's results and make corrections if needed. For example, a corner in a maze will have geometric qualities apparent to the animal via its whiskers. Upon recognizing this corner, the place system could adjust the path integrator output to more precisely match the learned coordinates of the corner in the active reference frame.

While corners and walls can be viewed as salient landmarks, they are not necessarily uniquely identifiable. The current model requires perceptual inputs to be distinct. Thus, it is unable to cope with any potential ambiguity. The hippocampus might be providing the contextual encoding that enables such configural discrimination [Sutherland & Rudy 1989]. Providing a computational account of this process remains an open problem.

Our model leads to the following prediction: place cells should briefly lose their direction sensitivity when an animal is first released at a random spot in a familiar environment. The reason is that the path integrator is not producing valid output, so place cells must be controlled by visual inputs alone. Only after the animal recognizes its location and resets its path integrator can place cells again become controlled by an active reference point set. While some preliminary observations are consonant with this conjecture (O'Keefe, see above), quantitative experimental data are needed to validate this prediction.

Conclusion

We have proposed a computational theory of rat navigation based on coupled mechanisms for path integration, place recognition, and maintenance of head direction. Our theory accounts for the following phenomena: (1) place cell activity reflects location in the environment; (2) place cell activity anticipates position during locomotion (3) place cells continue their activity in the dark; (4) reset of head direction is dependent on visual cues; (5) place cells are robust against deletion of landmarks; (6) disruption of place cell response occurs after transposition of landmarks; (7) place cells can develop direction sensitivity in routine contexts; and (8) loss of direction sensitivity occurs as a response to novelty.

A variety of problems remain to be addressed. Although our theory makes frequent reference to place cells and the hippocampus, it is not yet a neural-level theory. We have not proposed a specific location for the Local View module, for example, nor speculated on why head direction sensitive cells are found in at least five separate locations in the rat brain (Taube, personal communication). Before tackling these questions, additional computational issues need to be settled. Chief among these are the role of geometric and tactile properties of the environment in determining place codes, the influence of a learned *cue set* on perception, and the mechanism by which cue sets are shaped by experience.

References

[Abraham et al. 1983] L. Abraham, M. Potegal, and S. Miller. Evidence for caudate nucleus involvement in an egocentric spatial task: Return from passive transport. *Physiological Psychology*, 11(1):11–17, 1983.

[Burgess et al. 1993] N. Burgess, J. O'Keefe, and M. Recce. Toward a mechanism for navigation by the rat hippocampus. In *Proceedings of the 2nd Annual Computation and Neural Systems Meeting CNS*93*. Kluwer Academic Publishers, 1993. In press.

[Eichenbaum et al. 1987] H. Eichenbaum, M. Kuperstein, A. Fagan, and J. Nagode. Cue-sampling and goal-approach correlates of hippocampal unit activity in rats performing an odor-discrimination task. *Journal of Neuroscience*, 7(3):716–732, 1987.

[Etienne 1987] A. S. Etienne. The control of short-distance homing in the golden hamster. In P. Ellen and C. Thinus-Blanc, eds., *Cognitive Processes and Spatial Orientation in Animals and Man*, pp. 233–251. Martinus Nijhoff Publishers, Boston, 1987.

[Gallistel 1990] C. R. Gallistel. *The Organization of Learning*. MIT Press, Cambridge, MA, 1990.

[Hetherington & Shapiro 1993] P. A. Hetherington and M. L. Shapiro. A simple network model simulates hippocampal place fields: 2. computing goal-directed trajectories and memory fields. *Behavioral Neuroscience*, 107(3):434–443, 1993.

[Levitt et al. 1987] T. Levitt, D. Lawton, D. Chelberg, and P. Nelson. Qualitative navigation. In *Proceedings of the DARPA Image Understanding Workshop*, pp. 447–465, Los Altos, 1987. Morgan Kaufmann.

[Linsker 1987] R. Linsker. Toward an organizing principle for perception: Hebbian synapses and the principle of optimal neural encoding. Tech. Rep. RC 12830, IBM Research Division, Watson Research Center, Yorktown Heights, June 1987.

[Markus et al. 1993] E. J. Markus, C. A. Barnes, B. L. McNaughton, V. L. Gladden, and W. E. Skaggs. Spatial information content and reliability of hippocampal ca1 neurons: Effects of visual input. manuscript, 1993.

[McNaughton et al. 1989] B. L. McNaughton, B. Leonard, and L. Chen. Cortical-hippocampal interactions and cognitive mapping: A hypothesis based on reintegration of the parietal and inferotemporal pathways for visual processing. *Psychobiology*, 17(3):230–235, 1989.

[McNaughton et al. 1991] B. L. McNaughton, L. L. Chen, and E. J. Markus. "dead reckoning," landmark learning, and the sense of direction: A neurophysiological and computational hypothesis. *Journal of Cognitive Neuroscience*, 3(2):190–202, 1991.

[McNaughton et al. 1993] B. L. McNaughton, J. J. Knierim, and M. A. Wilson. Vector encoding and the vestibular foundations of spatial cognition: Neurophysiological and computational mechanisms. In M. Gazzaniga, ed., *The Cognitive Neurosicences*. MIT Press, Boston, 1993.

[McNaughton 1989] B. L. McNaughton. Neuronal mechanisms for spatial computation and information storage. In L. Nadel, L. Cooper, P. Culicover, and R. M. Harnish, eds., *Neural Connections, Mental Computation*, ch. 9, pp. 285–350. MIT Press, Cambridge, MA, 1989.

[Mittelstaedt & Mittelstaedt 1980] M. L. Mittelstaedt and H. Mittelstaedt. Homing by path integration in a mammal. *Naturwissenschaften*, 67:566–567, 1980.

[Muller & Kubie 1987] R. U. Muller and J. L. Kubie. The effects of changes in the environment on the spatial firing of hippocampal complex-spike cells. *Journal of Neuroscience*, 7:1951–1968, 1987.

[Muller & Kubie 1989] R. U. Muller and J. L. Kubie. The firing of hippocampal place cells predicts the future position of freely moving rats. *Journal of Neuroscience*, 9(12):4101–4110, 1989.

[Muller et al. 1991] R. U. Muller, J. L. Kubie, E. M. Bostock, J. S. Taube, and G. J. Quirk. Spatial firing correlates of neurons in the hippocampal formation of freely moving rats. In J. Paillard, ed., *Brain and Space*, ch. 17, pp. 296–333. Oxford University Press, New York, 1991.

[O'Keefe & Conway 1978] J. O'Keefe and D. H. Conway. Hippocampal place units in the freely moving rat: Why they fire where they fire. *Experimental Brain Research*, 31:573–590, 1978.

[O'Keefe & Nadel 1978] J. O'Keefe and L. Nadel. *The hippocampus as a cognitive map*. Clarendon Press, Oxford, 1978.

[O'Keefe & Speakman 1987] J. O'Keefe and A. Speakman. Single unit activity in the rat hippocampus during a spatial memory task. *Experimental Brain Research*, 68:1–27, 1987.

[Quirk et al. 1990] G. J. Quirk, R. U. Muller, and J. L. Kubie. The firing of hippocampal place cells in the dark depends on the rat's recent experience. *Journal of Neuroscience*, 10(6):2008–2017, June 1990.

[Quirk et al. 1992] G. J. Quirk, R. U. Muller, J. L. Kubie, and J. B. Ranck, Jr. The positional firing properties of medial entohinal neurons: Description and comparison with hippocampal place cells. *Journal of Neuroscience*, 12(5):1945–1963, May 1992.

[Schacter & Nadel 1991] D. L. Schacter and L. Nadel. Varieties of spatial memory: A problem for cognitive neuroscience. In R. G. Lister and H. J. Weingartner, eds., *Perspectives on Cognitive Neuroscience*, ch. 10, pp. 165–185. Oxford University Press, New York, Oxford, 1991.

[Schmajuk & Blair 1993] N. A. Schmajuk and H. T. Blair. Place learning and the dynamics of spatial navigation: A neural network approach. *Adaptive Behavior*, 1:355–387, 1993.

[Shapiro & Hetherington 1993] M. L. Shapiro and P. A. Hetherington. A simple network model simulates hippocampal place fields: Parametric analyses and physiological predictions. *Behavioral Neuroscience*, 107(1):34–50, 1993.

[Sharp et al. 1990] P. E. Sharp, J. L. Kubie, and R. U. Muller. Firing properties of hippocampal neurons in a visually symmetrical environment: Contributions of multiple sensory cues and mnemonic processes. *Journal of Neuroscience*, 10(9):3093–3105, Sep 1990.

[Sharp 1991] P. E. Sharp. Computer simulation of hippocampal place cells. *Psychobiology*, 19(2):103–115, 1991.

[Sutherland & Rudy 1989] R. J. Sutherland and J. W. Rudy. Configural association theory: The role of the hippocampal formation in learning, memory, and amnesia. *Psychobiology*, 17(2):129–144, 1989.

[Suzuki et al. 1980] S. Suzuki, G. Augerinos, and A. H. Black. Stimulus control of spatial behavior on the eight-arm maze in rats. *Learning and Motivation*, 11:1–18, 1980.

[Taube et al. 1990a] J. S. Taube, R. I. Muller, and J. B. Ranck, Jr. Head direction cells recorded from the postsubiculum in freely moving rats. i. description and quantitative analysis. *Journal of Neuroscience*, 10:420–435, 1990.

[Taube et al. 1990b] J. S. Taube, R. I. Muller, and J. B. Ranck, Jr. Head direction cells recorded from the postsubiculum in freely moving rats. ii. effects of environmental manipulations. *Journal of Neuroscience*, 10:436–447, 1990.

[Touretzky et al. 1993] D. S. Touretzky, A. D. Redish, and H. S. Wan. Neural representation of space using sinusoidal arrays. *Neural Computation*, 5(6):869–884, 1993.

[Treves et al. 1992] A. Treves, O. Miglino, and D. Parisi. Rats, nets, maps, and the emergence of place cells. *Psychobiology*, 20(1):1–8, 1992.

[Wilson & McNaughton 1993] M. A. Wilson and B. L. McNaughton. Dynamics of the hippocampal ensemble code for space. *Science*, 1993. In press.

Evaluating Connectionist Models in Psychology and Neuroscience

H.T. Blair
Yale University
Department of Psychology
P.O. Box 208205
New Haven, CT 06520-8205
tadb@minerva.cis.yale.edu

A standard sales pitch for connectionism says that network models share elementary properties in common with the brain, such as massive parallelism, neuron-like computing units, synapse-like weights, fault tolerance, and adaptability [1, 2, 3]. Connectionists have been keen to stress these similarities, and extol connectionism as a potentially powerful tool for studying the nervous system. However, if connectionist models are to help us understand the brain, they must be applied in a manner that is consistent with the methods and goals of neuroscience. In particular, connectionist modeling techniques must be integrated with anatomical, physiological, and behavioral research to develop plausible theories of how the nervous system functions.

But what constitutes a "plausible" model? The answer to this question depends upon a model's stated goals, and upon the level of investigation [4] at which it is specified. Connectionist models are very heterogeneous, and have been applied to address a broad range of phenomena, including vision, speech, language, planning, attention, inference, motor control, learning, memory, and neural disorders. Clearly, it would be impossible to evaluate all connectionist theories by exactly the same set of standards. Yet, I believe that a basic evaluation of most models can be obtained by asking three separate but related questions: (1) Are connectionist techniques appropriate for addressing the chosen problem? (2) Does the model wield predictive power by accounting for some body of empirical evidence? (3) Does the model comprehensibly implement a sensible theory?

In this paper, I wish to explore guidelines for answering these questions. To provide a background for this discussion, I will first introduce some relevant concepts and terms. Because many connectionist networks are not explicitly intended to model cognitive phenomena, it is necessary to begin by specifying a class of networks to which this discussion is intended to apply.

Models Versus Machines

Parallel distributed processing (PDP) networks are generically referred to as "connectionist models." This appellation tends to addle the distinction between *models* and *machines*; a model implements a theory of how something works, whereas a machine solves a problem or performs a task. A connectionist network may fall into either category, or lie somewhere in between, depending on its design and purpose. Although there is no clear division between connectionist models and connectionist machines, it should always be possible to make two separate evaluations of a network, depending on whether it is regarded as a model or as a machine.

Strongly Versus Weakly Predictive Theories

Sejnowski and Churchland [4] have introduced a further distinction, between "strongly" and "weakly" predictive theories. A strongly predictive theory is one which asserts that, at some level of detail, a model is structurally or functionally isomorphic to the nervous system. By contrast, a weakly predictive theory merely demonstrates that information processing in the nervous system could be governed by certain principles. A well-known example of a weakly predictive connectionist model is Rumelhart and McClelland's [5] "Interactive Activation Model," which shows how representations for words might emerge from initial representations that only encode the features of letters in the alphabet. This model is intended to demonstrate how a hierarchically organized network can account for certain aspects of visual word and pattern recognition, but it does not claim to show exactly how such recognition is accomplished in the nervous system [6]. According to Sejnowski and Churchland [4], a connectionist network which implements a strongly predictive theory should properly be called a "model," whereas implementations of weakly predictive theories are better referred to as "demonstrations."[1]

Summarizing, connectionist networks may be classified into three broad categories: machines, models, and demonstrations. Of these three network classes, connectionist machines are the easiest to evaluate, because they are judged only according to their performance and efficiency. By contrast, connectionist models and demonstrations are judged according to their plausibility. There are quantitative methods for defining and measuring performance, but evaluating plausibility is a far more intuitive exercise. Demonstrations present a particular challenge, because their weak assertions tend to be broad and hard to test. Often, as in the case of the Interactive Activation Model, a demonstration's purpose is to elucidate certain principles, or propose novel ways of thinking about a problem. Trying to judge such a creative effort by a set of rules might be criticized as a totalitarian enterprise. The discussion in this paper applies primarily to connectionist models, as distinguished from connectionist machines or demonstrations. Henceforth, unless noted otherwise, the term *connectionist model* shall refer to a network that is explicitly intended to make strong, testable claims about how some function is performed by the nervous system.

LEVELS OF INVESTIGATION

The connectionist literature is rife with discussions about levels, not all of which are compatible or consistent with one another. In this paper, I shall adopt the notion of investigation levels outlined by Sejnowski and Churchland [4]. These authors have distinguished between two types of investigation levels: *levels of analysis* and *levels of organization*. Both empirical data and theoretical assumptions can be classified according to the levels of analysis and organization that they address.

Levels of Analysis

Marr [7] proposed three levels of analysis for understanding information processing tasks. First, the "computational theory" level, which involves formally defining the task and its components. Second, the "representation and algorithm" level, which specifies input and output representations, as well as algorithms for performing the various components of the task. Third, the "hardware implementation" level, which determines the physical substrate for representations and algorithms. It was Marr's contention that higher levels of analysis are independent of the levels below them. Thus, one may formally define a task without concern for exactly how it is performed, or one may specify representations and algorithms without worrying about how they will be physically implemented. This is an attractive view, because it states that lower-level details can be safely deferred, in top-down fashion, until higher-level details have been worked out.

Churchland and Sejnowski [3] have captiously referred to this doctrine of independence as "Marr's dream," deeming it inappropriate for studying the nervous system. In the brain, higher levels of analysis are very dependent upon lower levels. For example, physical implementation details (e.g., cytochemistry, morphology, connectivity) have great consequence for what representations and algorithms can be supported by networks of

---

[1]   Sejnowski and Churchland [4] credit Francis Crick for the distinction between models and demonstrations.

neurons. Marr's highest levels of analysis--the task decomposition level--is poorly defined for the nervous system, because it is rarely clear whether some formal description of what the brain does, or what some part of it does, is complete or correct. Much effort in theory and modeling is directed at formulating and testing such descriptions, but this process is greatly influenced by assumptions made at lower levels of analysis.

Connectionist models inherit some of this level dependence from the nervous system. However, it is not obvious what Marr's hardware implementation level corresponds to in a connectionist network. On the one hand, the same network simulation may be run on a PC, a workstation, or a solid-state electrical circuit, suggesting that independence from hardware is preserved in connectionist networks. On the other hand, a network's connections are analogous to connections in the brain, and brain connectivity is a hardware-level detail of the nervous system that has great functional significance. What is clear is that a for connectionist model--or any system intended to model cognitive function--task descriptions are greatly influenced by choice of algorithms and representations. By opening the connectionist toolbox, a theorist automatically commits to certain formal ideas about *what* the nervous system does, not just about how it does it.

If Marr's levels of analysis are not independent of one another, are they still worth recognizing? Or should they be replaced altogether, with new levels that are better suited to the study of the nervous system?

Levels of Organization

Sejnowski and Churchland [4] have criticized Marr's three-level approach on the grounds that it treats computation "monolithically," ignoring the many structural and physiological levels of organization at which the nervous system functions. Examples of structural organization levels include molecules, synapses, neurons, networks, maps, and systems. Physiological organization levels include ion movement, ion channel configurations, excitatory and inhibitory postsynaptic potentials, action potentials, and evoked response potentials. There may be multiple levels of analysis to consider at each level of organization. In neuroscience, most experimental techniques are specialized to explore one organization level at a time, or at most a few. Indeed, as Sejnowski and Churchland [4] have pointed out, the recognition of different structural and physiological organization levels is largely dependent upon the research methods that are available. As new techniques for studying the nervous system are developed, new organization levels may become apparent.

Connectionist models must also confine their assertions to specific levels of structural and physiological organization. Churchland and Sejnowski [3] have said that connectionist models "should properly be considered a class of algorithms specified at various levels of organization--in some cases at the small-circuit level, in other cases at the system level." Similarly, Rumelhart and McClelland asserted that connectionist models are specified primarily at Marr's level of algorithms [8]. However, one might question why Marr chose to lump algorithms and representations together as a single level of analysis. Perhaps it was because he was committed to the independence doctrine, and he clearly recognized that algorithms and representations were intimately related. However, having dispensed with the independence doctrine, I feel it is useful to recognize representations and algorithms as separate levels of analysis, with representation being the "lower" of the two levels (insofar as such stratification is meaningful, in the absence of the independence doctrine). Furthermore, I think it is more accurate to say that connectionist models are specified primarily at the *representation* level, and that they should be considered a class of *representations* specified at various levels of organization.

REPRESENTATION

In a neural network (or any machine), the way information is represented determines how it can be manipulated. Connectionist learning algorithms, such as back propagation, allow networks some freedom to develop their own internal representations. However, the designer of a connectionist network is always faced with the initial choice of how to represent the network's input and output information. This decision places major constraints upon a network's capabilities, regardless of its architecture or what learning algorithm it uses. In psychology and neuroscience, representation issues crop up at every structural and physiological organization level. For these reasons, I believe that representation may properly be regarded as a level of analysis unto itself.

The representation level is perhaps the lowest relevant level of analysis to consider in connectionist modeling, given the ill-defined nature of the physical implementation level (see above). Because higher levels of analysis are heavily influenced by the representation level, there is a sense in which a connectionist model emerges from its initial representational assumptions. If these assumptions are wrong, the entire model is destined to be wrong. Hence, it is very dangerous to build a model on top of shaky representational assumptions. Furthermore, representational issues must be considered at many different organization levels. For example, at the level of individual neurons, information might reside in mean firing probabilities [2, 8], or in the precise timing of individual action potentials [9]. At the circuit and system levels, information might be encoded by the activity of a single neural unit (local representation), or by a pattern of activity over many units (distributed representation) [10, 11]. Although these questions deal with different levels of organization, they both address the same abstract level of analysis: the representation level.

CHOOSING A PROBLEM

Not all problems in psychology and neuroscience are equally amenable to connectionist modeling techniques. A good connectionist model begins with the selection of an appropriate theoretical problem. Given the nature of connectionist algorithms and our current state of knowledge about the nervous system, connectionist techniques are best suited to address questions at certain levels of organization and analysis. Further constraints are imposed by the availability of empirical evidence.

Organization Level Constraints

Most connectionist networks employ neural units that are defined by an activation function and an output function [13]. Depending on the model, these functions may assume discreet or continuous values. Some models assume that the activity of a processing unit is analogous to the mean firing rate of a single neuron. Others assume that unit activation represents the mean activity of a population of neurons. Since connectionism is all about connecting elementary processing units together into networks that exhibit complex and interesting behavior, individual processing units are supposed to be simple. By trying to relate them to something that is correspondingly simple in the nervous system, upper and lower bounds are placed on the levels of structural and physiological organization at which connectionist models can sensibly be specified.

Due to the simplicity of their processing elements, traditional connectionist models are not well suited to address detailed questions posed at or below the level of the single neuron (e.g., questions regarding membrane time constants, the gating of ion channels, synaptic organization, second messenger systems, etc.). Other modeling techniques, such as cable models [14] and compartmental models [15], are more appropriate for studying these problems. However, because extremely detailed models of individual neurons are computationally intensive (sometimes requiring the simultaneous integration of hundreds of nonlinear differential equations), it is usually impractical to interconnect many such neurons in large networks. Thus, there may be benefits to developing "hybrid" models, which embed cable or compartmental neurons inside of connectionist networks [16]. Such models might allow simultaneous investigation of both network architectures and single neuron computation.

As mentioned, the activity of single units in connectionist models is sometimes interpreted as the average activity of a population of neurons. This is acceptable, so long as the assumed population is relatively small and homogeneous. However, some models (particularly those specified at higher levels of investigation) be may forced to assume that processing units represent large populations of neurons, or even entire brain regions. It is generally undesirable to assume that large, inhomogeneous populations of neurons perform a function so simple that it can be described by a single processing unit in a model, unless such a claim can be well supported by empirical evidence. Likewise, it is undesirable to attribute a complicated function to some neural population, and then represent that population by a single unit in a model. To avoid these pitfalls, it is sometimes helpful to divide a model up into functional subnetworks, and make theoretical assertions at the level of these subnetworks, rather than the level of individual neural units. Subnetworks might correspond either to neural circuits, or to functional systems in the brain. However, dividing a model into subnetworks often constricts it at one or more levels of analysis, by forcing a commitment to some scheme of representation, set of algorithms, or method of task decomposition.

Analysis Level Constraints

Feldman [17] has stated that, "When one combines the constraints from biology, computation, and psychology, the range of possible encodings of conceptual knowledge is relatively small." If this statement were true, studying the nervous system would be much easier than it is. But this statement is not true. The range of possible encodings for conceptual knowledge is tremendous, an exponential function of the range of possible encodings for the sensory perceptions that conceptual knowledge is based on.

A great deal more is currently known about how the nervous system represents sensory and motor information than about how it represents conceptual knowledge. For example, it is fairly well understood how the early visual system extracts certain features from a visual image [18], how frequency is encoded along the basilar membrane in the early auditory system [19], how somatosensory information is organized into topographic maps in the brain [20], and how parts of the brain encode directional information for generating motor movements [21]. Because representations at these stages of processing are well understood, connectionist models of sensory and motor processes can focus on higher levels of analysis, such as the algorithmic and task description levels. However, for higher cognitive functions such as language, planning, and conceptual memory, much less is known about how the nervous system represents information. Therefore, it is very difficult to develop model theories of these functions without resorting to tenuous representational assumptions. Consequently, higher cognitive functions remain largely the domain of weakly predictive connectionist "demonstrations." It is likely that strongly predictive models will be instrumental in elucidating high-level representations from the bottom up, by helping to discover ways of manipulating the lower level representations they are based on.

Empirical Constraints

For connectionist networks in general, Rumelhart [12] has suggested that it is wise to choose problems for which there is an abundance of empirical data, but a relative paucity of good theory to explain that data. However, not all experimental results provide helpful constraints for designing a connectionist model. In psychology and neuroscience, there are three major types of empirical data: anatomical, physiological, and behavioral evidence. Ideally, all three types of evidence should be available to constrain the design and implementation of a model. Special emphasis should be placed on data which addresses the level of investigation at which the model makes major assertions. Often, targeting certain data for comparison with model performance is a key consideration in choosing a modeling problem. As outlined above, the availability of data about neural representations is important for deciding the levels of analysis a model should be concerned with. If a model's output is to be interpreted as a behavioral response, then the model might be applied to simulate certain behavioral experiments. If the activity of a model's processing units is intended to represent activity of single neurons, then it may be important to consult cellular recording data. If parts of the model correspond to neural populations, or entire brain regions, it may be beneficial to "drug" or "lesion" the model, and compare resulting performance with lesion and drug data from the literature.

FITTING THE DATA

A plausible model is one with a fair chance of being correct. But what constitutes a "correct" model? When can it be said that a model is psychologically or biologically real? A model's strengths and weaknesses can best be ascertained by comparing model predictions with experimental data. When model simulations are inconsistent with empirical evidence, there can be only two possible reasons: the model is incomplete, or the model is wrong.

No model is a perfect replica of the system it describes. It simply isn't possible to depict any process or phenomenon down to an arbitrarily minute level of detail. A model must focus on certain investigation levels, and make simplifying assumptions at other levels. Incompleteness is not a shortcoming of a model, it is an inevitability. It is sometimes even desirable, because when a theory accounts for some data but not others, a hypothesis is born: this data is different from that data. But how can an incomplete model be distinguished from an incorrect model? This is where it becomes important to integrate modeling with experimentation. The burden is on the modeler to clearly separate a model's assumptions from its assertions, and make certain that the assertions are experimentally testable.

Success Versus Correctness

A successful model is more than just a machine that has been carefully engineered to perform the task of fitting experimental data. A model might agree with experimental data to the twenty-eighth decimal place, but if it is laden with opaque mechanisms and obstruse parameters, it is of little use to anyone. A model should be *compact*; it should account for many experimental results using relatively few mechanisms, rather than having a separate mechanism for each experimental paradigm it addresses. Above all else, a model should comprehensibly implement a sensible theory. Even if subsequent evidence shows a model theory to be wrong, a punctilious implementation of the model may help to clarify why the theory fails, and thus serve to constrain future theories. A model does not have to be correct to be successful.

SUMMARY AND CONCLUSIONS

At the beginning of this paper, I suggested that a rudimentary evaluation of a connectionist model could be obtained by answering three questions: (1) Are connectionist techniques appropriate for addressing the chosen problem? (2) Does the model wield predictive power by accounting for some body of empirical evidence? (3) Does the model comprehensibly implement a sensible theory? This section translates the preceding discussion into guidelines for answering these questions.

When to Use Connectionist Models

Given the nature of connectionist algorithms and our current state of knowledge about the nervous system, connectionist techniques are better suited for addressing some problems than others. For example, strongly predictive theories are more easily developed at "intermediate" levels of structural organization, since this allows network processing units to be naturally be compared with individual neurons, or with small, homogeneous populations of neurons. Lower levels of organization are better addressed by cable models and compartmental models [15, 16], and higher levels are better suited for weakly predictive connectionist "demonstrations" [4]. Unless good evidence is available about how the nervous system represents the information it uses to perform a task, models should not make sweeping assumptions at the representation level in order to make assertions at higher levels of analysis, such as the algorithmic or task decomposition levels. The availability of empirical constrains is also an important factor in selecting a modeling problem.

Why to Use Connectionist Models

Understanding the brain is a complex undertaking, to say the least. Complex problems necessitate complex theories, and such theories can be difficult to state and understand. By implementing a theory in the form of a connectionist model, two important goals can be achieved. First, the theory becomes formalized by the mathematical equations that govern the behavior of the model. This imposes a rigor upon cognitive theories that is not always obtainable with purely anecdotal theories. Implementing a model may allow unexpected strengths and/or weaknesses of the theory to emerge, which would otherwise have gone undiscovered. Second, if the model's behavior agrees well with empirical evidence, then the model demonstrates that the theory could, in principle, be correct. If the theory fails to account for some portion of the evidence, a well-implemented model may help to indicate whether the theory is completely wrong, or whether it needs to be amended in some way.

In conclusion, models are becoming increasingly important for integrating large amounts of anatomical, physiological, and behavioral evidence into cogent theories of how the brain works. Connectionist models are well suited for addressing certain questions about the nervous system, and provide an invaluable tool for exploring many important issues in psychology and neuroscience.

Acknowledgments

This paper was inspired by discussions with faculty and students at the 1993 Connectionist Models Summer School. It was especially influenced by the lectures and workshops of Terrence Sejnowski, Peter Dayan, Jay

McClelland, and Paul Smolensky. I would like to thank Mike Mozer for his helpful comments on an earlier version of the manuscript.

References

[1] J.L McClelland, D.E. Rumelhart, and G.E. Hinton, "The appeal of parallel distributed processing," in *Parallel Distributed Processing. Explorations in the Microstructure of Cognition. Vol 1: Foundations* (D.E. Rumelhart and J.L. McClelland, eds.), Cambridge: MIT Press, 1986, ch. 1, pp. 3-44.

[2] J.A. Feldman and D.H. Ballard, "Connectionist models and their properties," *Cognitive Science*, vol. 6, pp. 205-254, 1982.

[3] P.S. Churchland and T.J. Sejnowski, "Neural representation and neural computation," in *Neural Connections and Mental Computations* (L. Nadel, L. Cooper, P. Culicover, and R.M. Harnish, eds.), Cambridge: MIT Press, 1989.

[4] T.J. Sejnowski and P.S. Churchland, "Brain and cognition," in *Foundations of Cognitive Science* (M.I. Posner, ed.), Cambridge: MIT Press, 1990, pp. 301-356.

[5] D.E. Rumelhart and J.L. McClelland, "An interactive activation model of context effects in letter perception: Part 1. An account of basic findings," *Psychological Review*, vol. 88, pp. 375-407, 1981.

[6] J.L. McClelland, "Putting knowledge in its place: A scheme for programming parallel processing structures on the fly," *Cognitive Science*, vol. 9, pp. 113-146, 1985.

[7] D. Marr, *Vision*, San Francisco: Freeman, 1982.

[8] D.E. Rumelhart and J.L. McClelland, " PDP models and general issues in cognitive science," in *Parallel Distributed Processing. Explorations in the Microstructure of Cognition. Vol 1: Foundations* (D.E. Rumelhart and J.L. McClelland, eds.), Cambridge: MIT Press, 1986, ch. 4, pp. 110-149.

[9] T.J. Sejnowski, "Open questions about computation in cerebral cortex," in *Parallel Distributed Processing. Explorations in the Microstructure of Cognition. Vol 2: Psychological and Biological Models* (D.E. Rumelhart and J.L. McClelland, eds.), Cambridge: MIT Press, 1986, ch. 21, pp. 372-389.

[10] J.A. Feldman, "A connectionist model of visual memory," in *Parallel models of associative memory* (G.E. Hinton and J.A. Anderson, eds.), Hillsdale: Erlebaum, 1981, pp. 49-81.

[11] G.E. Hinton, J.L. McClelland, and D.E. Rumelhart, "Distributed Representations," in *Parallel Distributed Processing. Explorations in the Microstructure of Cognition. Vol 1: Foundations* (D.E. Rumelhart and J.L. McClelland, eds.), Cambridge: MIT Press, 1986, ch. 3, pp. 77-109.

[12] D.E. Rumelhart, "Theory of backpropagation," presented at the Connectionist Models Summer School, Boulder, Colorado, June 21-July 2, 1993.

[13] D.E. Rumelhart, G.E. Hinton, and J.L. McClelland, "A general framework for parallel distributed processing," in *Parallel Distributed Processing. Explorations in the Microstructure of Cognition. Vol 1: Foundations* (D.E. Rumelhart and J.L. McClelland, eds.), Cambridge: MIT Press, 1986, ch. 2, pp. 45-76.

[14] W. Rall, "Branching dendritic trees and motoneuron membrane resistivity," *Experimental Neurology*, vol. 2, pp. 503-532, 1960.

[15] W. Rall, "Theoretical significance of dendritic tree for input-output relation," in *Neural Theory and Modeling* (R.F. Reiss, ed.), Stanford: Stanford University Press, pp. 73-97, 1964.

[16] T.H. Brown, personal communication.

[17] J.A. Feldman, "Connectionist Representation of Concepts," in *Connectionist Models and Their Implications: Readings from Cognitive Science* (D. Waltz and J.A. Feldman, eds.), Norwood: Ablex Publishing Corporation, ch. 13, pp. 341-363, 1988.

[18] D.H. Hubel and T.N. Wiesel, "Receptive fields, binocular interaction, and functional architecture in the cat's visual cortex," *Journal of Physiology*, vol. 160, pp. 106-154.

[19] G. von Bekesy, *Experiments in Hearing*, New York: McGraw-Hill, 1960.

[20] V.B. Mountcastle, "Modality and topographic properties of single neurons of cat's somatic sensory cortex," *Journal of Neurophysiology*, vol. 20, pp. 408-434, 1957.

[21] A.P. Georgopoulos, J.F. Kalaska, R. Caminiti, and J.T. Massey, "On the relations between the direction of two-dimensional arm movements and cell discharge in primate motor cortex," *Journal of Neuroscience*, vol. 2, pp. 1527-1537, 1982.

VISION

Self-Organizing Feature Maps with Lateral Connections: Modeling Ocular Dominance

Joseph Sirosh and Risto Miikkulainen
Department of Computer Sciences
University of Texas at Austin, Austin, Texas-78712, USA.
sirosh,risto@cs.utexas.edu

The neocortex is the largest part of the mammalian brain, and appears to be the least genetically determined. Much of its structure and connectivity depends on electrical activity during development. Because various neocortical areas are very similar in anatomical structure and exhibit similar developmental phenomena, it has been suggested that a common organizing mechanism underlies their ontogeny [18]. By modeling the development of a well-understood substructure such as the primary visual cortex, it might be possible to elucidate this common mechanism.

The primary visual cortex, like many other regions of the neocortex, is a topographic map, and is organized such that adjacent neurons respond to adjacent regions of the retina. This retinotopic map, as well as finer structures within it such as ocular dominance columns, forms by the self-organization of the afferent (input) connections to the cortex. The self-organizing process is driven by external input [4, 20, 19], and appears to be based on correlated (i.e. cooccurring) neuronal activity and the resulting cooperation and competition between neurons [19, 18].

In addition to the afferent connections, the neocortex contains a dense network of long-range lateral connections parallel to the cortical surface [3, 15]. These connections are reciprocal and are believed to mediate the cooperation and competition. They grow exuberantly after birth and reach their full extent in a short period. During subsequent development, they get automatically pruned into well-defined clusters [2, 5]. Pruning happens at the same time as the afferent connections organize into topographic maps. The final clustered distribution corresponds closely to the distribution of afferent connections in the map. For example, in the mature visual cortex, lateral connections primarily run between areas with similar afferent connection structure, such as iso-orientation columns [3]. The structural correspondence and their simultaneous development indicate that the ontogeny of lateral and afferent connections are interdependent.

The development of lateral connections, like that of afferent connections, depends on cortical activity caused by external input. Three observations support this notion: (1) When the primary visual cortex (of the cat) is deprived of visual input during early development, the lateral connectivity remains crude and unrefined [1]. (2) The pattern of lateral connection clusters can be altered by changing the input to the developing cortex. The resulting patterns reflect the correlations in the input [8]. (3) In the mouse somatosensory barrel cortex, sensory deprivation (by sectioning the input nerve) causes drastic decreases in the extent and density of lateral connections [9]. These three observations suggest that the lateral connection structure is not defined genetically, but is acquired.

Lateral connections do not just modulate cortical activity – their development is essential for the self-organization of afferent connections as well. Every neuron receives a large number of lateral connections. Although each individual connection is weak, their total effect on neural activity can be substantial [3], and thereby affect the development of afferent connections. Changes in afferent connections then change the activity patterns on the cortex, which in turn influence the development of lateral connections. The development of both sets of connections thus appears to proceed synergetically and simultaneously, eventually evolving to a state of equilibrium in the adult animal.

The lateral connection structure plays a significant role also in cortical function: (1) by integrating information over large parts of the cortex, lateral connections mediate context-dependent processing of input stimuli [3]; (2) lateral connections may also mediate the synchronization of activity over long distances of the cortex, and thereby help form dynamic representations of coherent input areas [16]; (3) by learning correlations in input during development, they can potentially form long-term representations of input regularities such as gestalt rules [19]; and (4) by combining such representations with input activity, they may also perform feature grouping and segmentation during perception [19]. Therefore, to understand cortical function one must discover not only the structure and function of the afferent connections but also that of the lateral connections. By modeling how lateral connections develop along with the other aspects of cortical structure, a more fundamental understanding of neocortical processes can be achieved.

Several models have been proposed to explain various aspects of afferent connection structure, such as retinotopy, ocular dominance and orientation preference in the visual cortex [20, 12, 11]. The simultaneous development of these three properties has recently been modeled by the Self-Organizing Map (SOM, [6]) algorithm [14, 13]. These models usually assume that the strength of lateral interaction falls off with distance as a Gaussian function, and is uniform throughout the network. The models do not address the development of lateral connections and how they affect the self-organization of afferent connections.

In this paper, a computational model for the synergetic development of the afferent and lateral connections in cortical feature maps is presented. The model is called LISSOM, for Laterally Interconnected Synergetically Self-Organizing Map. LISSOM is based on a simulated network of neurons with afferent connections from the external world and reciprocal lateral connections. Connections adapt based on correlated activity between neurons. The result is a self-organized structure with (1) afferent connection weights that form a map of the input space and (2) lateral connections that store long-term correlations in neuronal activity.

Although LISSOM can be utilized as an abstract self-organizing algorithm, its most promising application is in modeling the development of the neocortex. This paper addresses how ocular dominance and lateral connections develop simultaneously in the visual cortex. The results of these experiments hold promise for substantial insights into cortical development.

The LISSOM Model

Each neuron in a LISSOM network (figure 1) has a set of afferent input connections (from the external input to the map) and a set of lateral input connections (from the other neurons in the map). Each neuron develops an initial response as a weighted sum of the activation in its afferent input connections. The lateral interactions between neurons then focus the initial activation pattern into a localized response on the map. After the pattern has stabilized, all connection weights are modified. As the self-organization progresses, the neurons grow more nonlinear and weak connections die off. Below, these general structures and mechanisms of LISSOM are described in detail, and illustrated in forming a map of a uniform distribution on a square (figures 2, 3 and 4).

The LISSOM network is a sheet of interconnected neurons (figure 1). Through the excitatory afferent connections, every neuron receives the same vector of external input values. In addition, each neuron has reciprocal excitatory and inhibitory lateral connections with other neurons. Lateral excitatory connections are short-range, connecting only close neighbors in the map. Lateral inhibitory connections run for long distances, and may even implement full connectivity between neurons in the map. Each connection has a characteristic strength (or weight), which may be any value between zero and a prescribed limit that depends on the synaptic resources of the neuron.

Input vectors to the network are normalized so that vectors with large norms do not dominate the self-organizing process. In the normalization, the original n-dimensional input distribution is mapped on the surface of an $(n+1)$-dimensional unit hypersphere [10]. The $(n+1)$th-dimension becomes the radius of the hypersphere, and the original set of n dimensions become angles specifying the input point on the surface of the hypersphere. For example, in forming a 2D map as in figure 2, the square area was laid on the surface of a 3D sphere of radius 1.0. In effect, inputs from this area are still 2-dimensional in spherical coordinates because the radius is constant. Each spherical input vector $(x_1, x_2, 1)$, was then transformed into a 3-dimensional cartesian vector $x = (\xi_1, \xi_2, \xi_3)$:

$$\begin{cases} \xi_1 = 1 \cdot \cos(x_1)\cos(x_2), \\ \xi_2 = 1 \cdot \sin(x_1)\cos(x_2), \\ \xi_3 = 1 \cdot \sin(x_2). \end{cases} \tag{1}$$

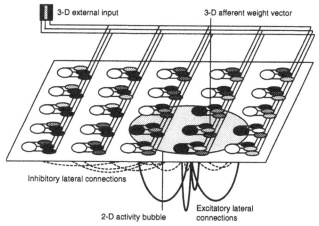

3-D external input   3-D afferent weight vector

Inhibitory lateral connections

2-D activity bubble   Excitatory lateral connections

Figure 1: **The LISSOM architecture.** Each neuron receives the same afferent input vector and computes an initial response based on a measure of similarity of the input to the corresponding weight vector. The responses then repeatedly propagate through the lateral connections (only a few connections of the most strongly active unit are shown) and evolve into an activity "bubble". After the activity stabilizes, weights of the active neurons are adapted.

The external and lateral weights are organized through a purely unsupervised learning process. Input items are randomly drawn from the input distribution and presented to the network one at a time. At each training step, the neurons in the network start out with zero activity. The initial response of each neuron η_{ij} in the map is based on the scalar product:

$$\eta_{ij} = \sigma \left(\sum_h \xi_h \mu_{ij,h} \right), \tag{2}$$

where ξ_h are the inputs to the network and $\mu_{ij,h}$ are the corresponding afferent weights. The afferent weights $\mu_{ij,h}$ can be positive or negative. The function σ is a piecewise linear approximation to the sigmoid activation function:

$$\sigma(x) = \begin{cases} 0 & x \leq \delta \\ (x-\delta)/(\beta-\delta) & \delta < x < \beta \\ 1 & x \geq \beta \end{cases}, \tag{3}$$

where δ and β are the lower and upper thresholds. The sigmoid introduces a nonlinearity into the response, and makes the neuron selective to a small range of input vectors that are close to the afferent weight vector.

The response evolves over time through the lateral interaction. At each time step, the neuron combines external activation with lateral excitation and inhibition:

$$\eta_{ij}(t) = \sigma \left(\sum_h \xi_h \mu_{ij,h} + \gamma_e \sum_{k,l} E_{ij,kl} \eta_{kl}(t-1) - \gamma_i \sum_{k,l} I_{ij,kl} \eta_{kl}(t-1) \right), \tag{4}$$

where $E_{ij,kl}$ is the excitatory lateral connection weight on the connection from unit (k, l) to unit (i, j), $I_{ij,kl}$ is the inhibitory connection weight, and $\eta_{kl}(t-1)$ is the activity of unit (k, l) during the previous time step. The lateral connection weights are all positive. The constants γ_e and γ_i are scaling factors on the excitatory and inhibitory weights and determine the strength of lateral interaction. The activity pattern starts out diffuse and spread over a substantial part of the map, and converges iteratively into a stable focused patch of activity, or activity bubble [17, 10]. After the activity has settled, typically in a few iterations, the connection weights of each neuron are modified.

The lateral weights are modified by the Hebb rule, but keeping the sum of the weights constant:

$$\gamma_{ij,kl}(t + \delta t) = \frac{\gamma_{ij,kl}(t) + \alpha_L \eta_{ij} \eta_{kl}}{\sum_{kl} [\gamma_{ij,kl}(t) + \alpha_L \eta_{ij} \eta_{kl}]}, \tag{5}$$

where η_{ij} stands for the activity of the unit (i, j) in the settled activity bubble, the γs are the lateral interaction weights ($E_{ij,kl}$ or $I_{ij,kl}$) and α_L is the learning rate for the lateral interaction (α_E for excitatory

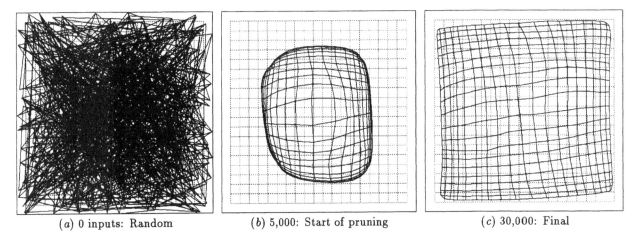

| (a) 0 inputs: Random | (b) 5,000: Start of pruning | (c) 30,000: Final |

Figure 2: **Self-organization of the afferent input weights in a 2D map.** The weight vector of each neuron in the 20×20 map is transformed back to the original spherical coordinates and plotted as a point in the input space (represented by the square). Each weight vector is connected to those of the four immediate neighbors by a line. The resulting dark grid depicts the topological organization of the map. The dotted grid shows the best possible approximation of the input space by a 20×20 network. The afferent weight vectors are initially uniformly distributed on the input square (a). Input vectors are randomly drawn from the input area and presented to the network, and the weights are modified according to equations 5 and 6. As the self-organization progresses, the network unfolds and the weight vectors spread out to form a regular topological map of the input space. Before connection pruning, the map is stable, but contracted into the center of the input distribution (b). After connections begin to die off, the map expands and eventually covers the entire input space (c).

weights and α_I for inhibitory). The larger the product of the pre- and post-synaptic activity $\eta_{ij}\eta_{kl}$, the larger the weight change.

The external input weights are modified according to the normalized Hebbian rule:

$$\mu_{ij,h}(t + \delta t) = \frac{\mu_{ij,h}(t) + \alpha\eta_{ij}\xi_h}{\left\{\sum_h \left[\mu_{ij,h}(t) + \alpha\eta_{ij}\xi_h\right]^2\right\}^{1/2}}, \tag{6}$$

which is otherwise similar to (5), but maintains the sum of squares of external weights constant.

The above processes of lateral interaction and weight adaptation are sufficient to form ordered afferent and lateral input connections (figure 2b). However, in order to develop a good coverage of the input space, it is necessary that these processes gradually become more focused and local. As self-organization proceeds in LISSOM, neuronal responses grow more nonlinear and weak lateral connections die off, which results in more focused activity bubbles and weight changes.

The lower threshold of the sigmoidal activation function specifies the minimum input required for a neuron to produce output, and its slope determines how much the neuron amplifies changes in the input. Therefore, neurons can be made more selective and sensitive by increasing the lower threshold, δ, and decreasing the upper threshold, β, resulting in smaller and more refined activity bubbles. In LISSOM, δ is increased and β decreased proportional to the activity of the neuron at each input presentation, up to prescribed maximum and minimum limits:

$$\begin{aligned}
\delta_{ij}(t+1) &= \min(\delta_{ij}(t) + \alpha_\delta\eta_{ij}, \delta_{\max}), \\
\beta_{ij}(t+1) &= \max(\beta_{ij}(t) - \alpha_\beta\eta_{ij}, \beta_{\min}).
\end{aligned} \tag{7}$$

As a result, the neurons grow nonlinear faster at those parts of the map that see more activity. Such modification automatically takes into account the level of organization around the neuron, and results in regular final maps (figure 2c).

Once the map has organized partially, most of the long-range lateral connections join areas that are almost never active simultaneously. Their weights become small, and they can be pruned without disrupting self-organization. Most long-range inhibitory connections are eliminated this way (figure 3 and 4). Since the total synaptic weight is kept constant, inhibition concentrates in the immediate neighborhood of the

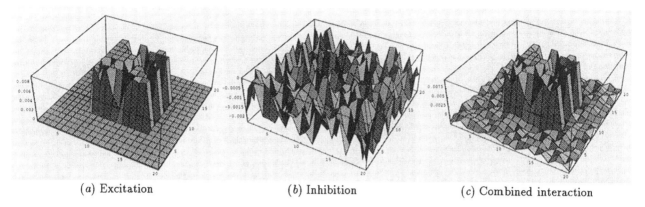

(a) Excitation   (b) Inhibition   (c) Combined interaction

Figure 3: **Initial lateral interaction in the 2D map.** The lateral excitation and inhibition weights and the combined interaction profile are plotted for the neuron at position $(10, 10)$ in the 20×20 map. The excitation weights (a) are initially randomly distributed within a radius $d = 4$, and zero outside. The inhibition weights (b) are randomly distributed within $d' = 12$, and for neuron $(10, 10)$, cover the entire map. The combined interaction (c) is the sum of the excitatory and inhibitory weights and illustrates the total effect of the lateral connections.

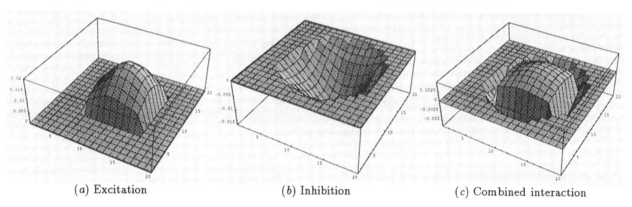

(a) Excitation   (b) Inhibition   (c) Combined interaction

Figure 4: **Final lateral interaction in the 2D map.** The long-range connections have died off (indicated by zero strength in the figure), resulting in more concentrated and deeper inhibition around the neuron. The combined interaction has a "Mexican hat" shape. Such interaction resulted in smaller activity bubbles, allowing the map to expand as in figure 2c.

neuron. The short-range excitatory connections join neurons that are often part of the same bubble. They have relatively large weights and survive.

Before connection death, activity bubbles are large and weights change in large neighborhoods. Each adaptation makes neighboring weight vectors more parallel, which means that the map contracts to the center of the input space (figure 2b). However, as connections die off, the lateral interaction tends to form smaller, higher-contrast activity bubbles. Weights change in smaller neighborhoods, which allows the map to expand and become a better approximation of the input space (figure 2c).

The afferent connections in LISSOM organize very much like in Kohonen's Self-Organizing Map algorithm. However, in the SOM process, the maximally responding unit is chosen through global supervision, and adaptation neighborhoods are reduced according to a predetermined schedule. In contrast, the LISSOM process is based on purely local rules and the network self-organizes completely without global supervision. Even the shape of the lateral interaction is automatically extracted from the statistical properties of the external input. The self-organization thus "bootstraps" by using external input information to establish the necessary cooperative and competive interactions.

MODELING OCULAR DOMINANCE

The LISSOM process models cortical development at a new level, namely that of explicit activity-based cooperation and competition and developing lateral connections. At this level, it is possible to investigate

 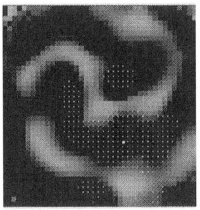 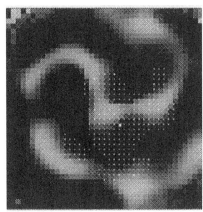

(a) Initial: Random
ocular dominance

(b) Final: Mature ocular
dominance & connections

(c) Final: Connections of
a binocular neuron

Figure 5: **Emergence of ocular dominance and corresponding lateral connection patterns.** In this experiment, the primary visual cortex was modeled by a 40×40 network of neurons. Each neuron is labeled with a grey-scale value corresponding to its ocular dominance. Brightness varying from *black* to *white* represents continuously changing eye preference from exclusive left through binocular to exclusive right. Small white dots indicate the surviving lateral input connections to the neuron marked with a big white dot. (a) The initial state of the network. Neurons have randomly distributed ocular dominance and random-weight lateral connections covering a wide area. (b) After the critical period, weak lateral inhibitory connections die away and the surviving connections predominantly link areas of the same ocular dominance. As simulation proceeds, both the ocular dominance patterns and the lateral connection patterns refine and eventually stabilize. (c) The lateral connections of a binocular neuron come from both eye regions. Note that in (b) and (c), neurons that are physical neighbors do not necessarily influence each other because of the nontopographically distributed lateral connections.

how lateral interaction affects input activity in the cortex as well. As a first step, a model for the development of ocular dominance columns and lateral connections in the primary visual cortex was built.

The inputs to the LISSOM network consisted of three values (x,y,z), (x,y) representing the retinotopic position of the current visual input and $z \in [-Z, +Z]$ representing the ocular dominance. The values $-Z$ and $+Z$ indicate the extremes of left and right dominance, and $z = 0$ that the input comes equally from both eyes. Each neuron had three afferent weights corresponding to the three input values. Initially, the afferent weights were set up with a random ocular dominance $z \in [-Z, +Z]$ and with roughly retinotopic x and y coordinates within $[0, 1]$. The network was trained using input vectors with uniformly distributed random values for x, y and z within these same ranges.

Figure 5 demonstrates the evolution of ocular dominance in the self-organizing process. At the start of the simulation, each input initially results in a rough pattern of activity, which focuses into a single localized activity bubble. As the self-organization progresses, the initial activity patterns begin to split into multiple bubbles. This happens because the map self-organizes like a crumpled sheet in the (original) 3D input space, and cannot completely cover it. Therefore, several areas of the network respond equally well to the inputs falling between folds. Through lateral excitation and inhibition, each of these areas forms a localized bubble. These areas are likely to have similar ocular dominance values. As a result, activity is highly correlated between similar ocular dominance patches and less correlated between those with different ocular dominance. Lateral connections learn to represent such correlations. As afferent connections change and ocular dominance patterns refine, weak lateral connections die away and the surviving connections become clustered around the ocular dominance areas for the same eye. The process continues until a stable equilibrium is reached. The final network has (1) retinotopic afferent weights, (2) well-defined ocular dominance columns, and (3) lateral connections that link areas with the same ocular dominance.

Very similar development was observed by Lowel and Singer [8] in cats. They found that if a newborn kitten is raised with divergent squint-eyes (strabismus), which decorrelates the visual input to the cortex from the two eyes, lateral connections develop preferentially between ocular dominance columns of the same eye. However, binocular neurons at the border of two ocular dominance columns had connections to neurons in both the right and left eye areas. As can be seen from figure 5b and 5c, the LISSOM simulation results

36

match both observations.

Even based on this simple model of ocular dominance formation, interesting functional predictions can be made. For example, divergent squinters cannot achieve binocular vision even if the visual stimulus is completely binocular [7, 21]. Such impairment is puzzling because most squinting people still have some neurons responsive to input from both eyes, and these neurons should be able to perform binocular integration. The LISSOM model suggests an explanation: If only a few binocular neurons exist, the lateral interactions may override the binocular response. Activity bubbles that initially form in binocular areas tend to break up and move into nearby monocular areas. The resulting activity patterns are disjoint and spatially separated, and therefore cannot be recognized as a single and coherent binocular percept.

Standard feature maps represent the topology of the input space by the network's grid-like layout, so that units close by in the map represent nearby input vectors. In the LISSOM model, the neighborhood relations are mediated by the lateral connections, and the model is not limited to strictly 2-dimensional topology. Units that are far apart on the map grid may still belong to the same neighborhood if they are strongly connected laterally as in figure 5. Such topologies are automatically learned as part of the self-organizing process. If several areas of the map are simultaneously active, long-range connections between them remain strong enough to survive connection pruning. These connections cause the units to behave as if they were neighbors on the map.

This property of LISSOM is potentially very significant in representing complex high-dimensional input spaces. While low-level sensory representation in the brain seems to be physically organized in 2-dimensional maps (such as retinotopic maps), it is possible that the functional representations make use of long-range lateral connections to represent more complex similarity relationships [19, 16]. LISSOM provides computational evidence that such maps can form by input-driven self-organization.

CONCLUSION

The LISSOM model demonstrates how lateral interaction and topological organization of cortical maps can be learned simultaneously from correlations in the input information. The model is biologically motivated, and its predictions agree well with experimental observations on cortical development. LISSOM is potentially capable of explaining various aspects of lateral and afferent connection development in the cortex, as well as the nature of lateral interactions in the cortex. The model delineates a functional role for connection death and demonstrates how it can result in nontopographically organized lateral connectivity. These results suggest that a single, general self-organizing process might underlie the development of most aspects of the structure and function of the neocortex. In future research, the model of the visual cortex shall be extended to the development of orientation columns, and used to investigate how lateral connections assist feature grouping and segmentation during perception.

Acknowledgments

This research was supported in part by National Science Foundation under grant #IRI-9309273. The simulations were performed on a Cray Y-MP 8/864 at the University of Texas Center for High-Performance Computing.

References

[1] E. M. Callaway and L. C. Katz, "Effects of binocular deprivation on the development of clustered horizontal connections in cat striate cortex," *Proceedings of the National Academy of Sciences, USA*, vol. 88, pp. 745–749, 1991.

[2] E. M. Callaway and L. C. Katz, "Emergence and refinement of clustered horizontal connections in cat striate cortex," *Journal of Neuroscience*, vol. 10, pp. 1134–1153, 1990.

[3] C. D. Gilbert, J. A. Hirsch, and T. N. Wiesel, "Lateral interactions in visual cortex," in *Cold Spring Harbor Symposia on Quantitative Biology, Volume LV*, pp. 663–677, Cold Spring Harbor Laboratory Press, 1990.

[4] D. H. Hubel and T. N. Wiesel, "Receptive fields and functional architecture in two nonstriate visual areas (18 and 19) of the cat," *Journal of Neurophysiology*, vol. 28, pp. 229–289, 1965.

[5] L. C. Katz and E. M. Callaway, "Development of local circuits in mammalian visual cortex," *Annual Review of Neuroscience*, vol. 15, pp. 31–56, 1992.

[6] T. Kohonen, "The self-organizing map," *Proceedings of the IEEE*, vol. 78, pp. 1464–1480, 1990.

[7] P. König, A. K. Engel, S. Löwel, and W. Singer, "Squint affects synchronization of oscillatory responses in cat visual cortex," *European Journal of Neuroscience*, vol. 5, pp. 501–508, 1993.

[8] S. Löwel and W. Singer, "Selection of intrinsic horizontal connections in the visual cortex by correlated neuronal activity," *Science*, vol. 255, pp. 209–212, 1992.

[9] J. S. McCasland, K. L. Bernardo, K. L. Probst, and T. A. Woolsey, "Cortical local circuit axons do not mature after early deafferentation," *Proceedings of the National Academy of Sciences, USA*, vol. 89, pp. 1832–1836, March 1992.

[10] R. Miikkulainen, "Self-organizing process based on lateral inhibition and synaptic resource redistribution," in *Proceedings of the International Conference on Artificial Neural Networks* (Espoo, Finland), (Amsterdam; New York), pp. 415–420, North-Holland, 1991.

[11] K. D. Miller, "Development of orientation columns via competition between on- and off-center inputs," *NeuroReport*, vol. 3, pp. 73–76, 1992.

[12] K. D. Miller, J. B. Keller, and M. P. Stryker, "Ocular dominance column development: Analysis and simulation," *Science*, vol. 245, pp. 605–615, 1989.

[13] K. Obermayer, G. G. Blasdel, and K. J. Schulten, "Statistical-mechanical analysis of self-organization and pattern formation during the development of visual maps," *Physical Review A*, vol. 45, pp. 7568–7589, 1992.

[14] K. Obermayer, H. J. Ritter, and K. J. Schulten, "A principle for the formation of the spatial structure of cortical feature maps," *Proceedings of the National Academy of Sciences, USA*, vol. 87, pp. 8345–8349, 1990.

[15] H. Schwark and E. Jones, "The distribution of intrinsic cortical axons in area 3b of cat primary somatosensory cortex," *Experimental Brain Research*, vol. 78, pp. 501–513, 1989.

[16] W. Singer, C. Gray, A. Engel, P. König, A. Artola, and S. Bröcher, "Formation of cortical cell assemblies," in *Cold Spring Harbor Symposia on Quantitative Biology, Vol. LV*, (Cold Spring Harbor, NY), pp. 939–952, Cold Spring Harbor Laboratory, 1990.

[17] J. Sirosh and R. Miikkulainen, "How lateral interaction develops in a self-organizing feature map," in *Proceedings of the IEEE International Conference on Neural Networks* (San Francisco, CA), (Piscataway, NJ), IEEE, 1993.

[18] M. Stryker, J. Allman, C. Blakemore, J. Gruel, J. Kaas, M. Merzenich, P. Rakic, W. Singer, G. Stent, H. van der Loos, and T. Wiesel, "Group report. Principles of cortical self-organization," in *Neurobiology of Neocortex* (P. Rakic and W. Singer, eds.), (New York), pp. 115–136, Wiley, 1988.

[19] C. von der Malsburg and W. Singer, "Principles of cortical network organization," in *Neurobiology of Neocortex* (P. Rakic and W. Singer, eds.), pp. 69–99, New York: Wiley, 1988.

[20] C. von der Malsburg, "Self-organization of orientation-sensitive cells in the striate cortex," *Kybernetik*, vol. 15, pp. 85–100, 1973.

[21] G. K. von Noorden, *Binocular Vision and Ocular Motility. Theory and Management of Strabismus*. Baltimore: Mosby, 1990.

Joint Solution of Low, Intermediate and High-Level Vision Tasks by Global Optimization: Application to Computer Vision at Low SNR

Anoop K. Bhattacharjya, Badrinath Roysam

Department of Electrical, Computer, and Systems Engineering

Rensselaer Polytechnic Institute, Troy, New York 12180, USA

anoop@ecse.rpi.edu, roysam@ecse.rpi.edu

Methods for conducting model-based computer vision from low-SNR ($\leq$1dB) image data are presented. Conventional algorithms break down in this regime due to a cascading of noise artifacts, and inconsistencies arising from the lack of optimal interaction between high and low-level processing. These problems are addressed by solving low-level problems such as intensity estimation, segmentation, and boundary estimation *jointly* (synergistically) with intermediate-level problems such as the estimation of position, magnification, and orientation, and high-level problems such as object identification and scene interpretation. This is achieved by formulating a single objective function that incorporates all the data and object models, and a hierarchy of constraints in a Bayesian framework. All image-processing operations, including those that exploit the low and high-level variables to satisfy multi-level pattern constraints, result directly from a parallel multi-trajectory global optimization algorithm.

Experiments with simulated low-count (7-9 photons/pixel) 2-D Poisson images demonstrate that compared to non-joint methods, a joint solution not only results in more reliable scene interpretation, but also a superior estimation of low-level imaging variables. Typically, most object parameters are estimated to within a 5% accuracy even with overlap and partial occlusion.

INTRODUCTION

This paper presents a broadly applicable technique for the construction of computer vision and intelligent imaging systems that can operate robustly and rapidly with very noisy ($\leq$1dB SNR) sensor data. Of interest are applications in which the need to operate with low-SNR data is compelling. Examples include radar systems that are operated at minimum power for stealth, at maximum range, or in the presence of interference, and medical imaging systems that are operated at minimum radiation dosage. Of particular interest to this work are vision systems in which the processing begins with raw sensor data, and culminates in high-level inferences such as object recognition, and scene interpretation. The currently-used processing approach in such systems is mostly an adaptation of the classical paradigm for computer vision [1] that proceeds in the following sequence:

39

$$\text{sensor data} \rightarrow \text{signal reconstruction} \rightarrow \text{segmentation} \rightarrow \text{feature extraction} \rightarrow \text{model matching} \rightarrow \text{scene interpretation}$$

Although successful in a variety of applications, the above approach breaks down when the sensor data is noisy. Noise in the sensor data degrades the computed features (e.g., segmentation labels, boundary features, moments of inertia), that are required for subsequent processing. The use of noisy features inevitably results in secondary artifacts and inconsistencies that tend to accumulate and cascade, resulting in a massive breakdown.

Figure 1A shows a typical noisy imaging scenario of interest. This simulated scene contains three objects, two of which overlap, and one is partially-occluded. The observed image data is a realization from an inhomogeneous Poisson point process with mean intensities of nine and seven photons/pixel over the foreground and background regions, respectively. For reference, the true image intensity profile and the scene interpretation are displayed in Figures 1C and 1D, respectively. The noisy nature of this data can be appreciated by examining Figure 1E that shows plots of Row 80 in the noisy image and the true intensity profile, and from the maximum-likelihood segmentation in Figure 1B.

Figure 2 shows a simple example illustrating the difficulty of conducting computer vision at low SNR using a traditional sequential approach [1]. Figure 2A shows simulated sensor data corresponding to the true scene interpretation displayed in Figure 2B, at a signal-to-noise ratio of 1dB. Figures 2(C, D and E) show the intensity estimate, segmentation labels and edge sites respectively, obtained using a sophisticated maximum a posteriori (MAP) segmentation algorithm [2] that incorporates spatially-varying region process models, and a variety of pattern constraints over segmentation labels and edge sites. These low-level variables are then processed to recognize the object and estimate its position, orientation and scale. The relative match coefficients with the models in the library are displayed as a bar chart in Figure 2F. The longest bar corresponds to the model with the best match. This model and its parameters are displayed in Figure 2G. Note that the model has been recognized incorrectly. The high-level recognition process was misled by the loss of crucial information regarding the nose and tail of the imaged aircraft in the segmentation.

The above example illustrates an important source of processing inconsistencies in conventional vision systems: the lack of optimal feedback from the high-level processing stages to the low-level stages. A major reason for this situation is the reliance of conventional vision systems on syntactic processing at the higher levels. For proper feedback, the syntactic processing must somehow be interfaced consistently with the low-level numeric processing stages. This is difficult because syntactic representations are inherently inflexible in the sense that they do not admit incremental changes.

This work overcomes the above-mentioned limitations by adopting an alternate approach. *Low-level* problems such as intensity estimation, segmentation, and boundary estimation are solved *jointly*, i.e., synergistically, with *intermediate-level* problems such as the estimation of position, magnification, and orientation, and *high-level* problems such as object identification and scene interpretation. This is achieved by formulating the overall vision problem, which includes the low, intermediate and high-level estimation problems, as the minimization of a single objective function. This objective function incorporates all the data and object models, and a hierarchy of stochastic and symbolic constraints [2]. All the image-processing operations are then realized naturally and consistently by a large-scale stochastic optimization process with respect to the above objective function. The optimization results in the optimal interaction of low and high-level variables, satisfaction of pattern constraints at multiple levels of representation, and feedback of high-level modelling information.

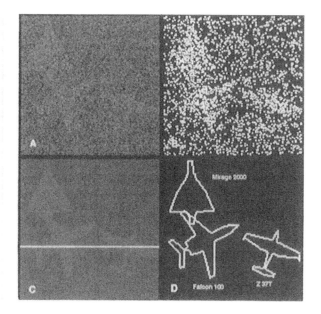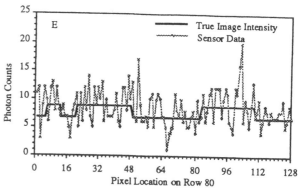

Figure 1: Showing a scene with overlapping and partially-occluded objects at a signal to background ratio of 1dB: (A) simulated Poisson sensor data; (B) maximum-likelihood segmentation; (C) true image intensity; (D) true scene interpretation; (E) plots of Row 80 (indicated by the line in panel C) in the noisy image (panel A) and the true intensity (panel C).

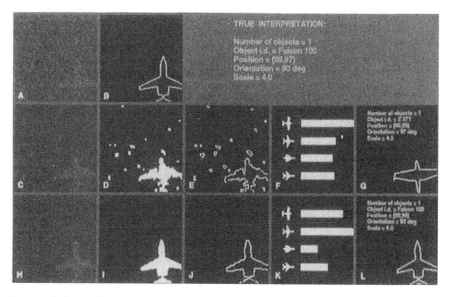

Figure 2: Illustrating breakdown of conventional vision approaches even with sophisticated MAP segmentation, and the impact of a full joint solution: (A) The sensor data; (B) True scene interpretation; (C, D and E) Estimates of the intensity profile, segmentation labels and edge sites obtained from MAP segmentation; (F) Bar chart showing the relative match coefficients based on the MAP segmentation. The resulting (incorrect) scene interpretation is displayed in Panel G. The recognition was misled by the segmentation that lost crucial information relating to the nose and tail of the imaged aircraft. The correct estimates obtained by a joint estimation of both the low and high-level variables are displayed in panels (H-L).

41

The potential improvement resulting from a joint solution is illustrated in the third row of Figure 2. From left to right (H-L), the panels in the third row show the estimated pixel intensities, segmentation labels, edge sites, relative match coefficients with the models in the library, and the recognized model, together with its estimated position, scale and orientation. It is seen that a joint solution achieves correct object recognition, estimates position, orientation and scale parameters to within 5% accuracy, and leads to superior estimation of low-level variables.

IMAGE VARIABLES AND MATHEMATICAL MODELS

The mathematical models and assumptions described in this section will form the components of the overall objective function (14) to be developed in the next section. The optimization of this objective function leads to a joint solution of the following list of problems: (i) image intensity estimation with region-dependent regularization constraints; (ii) segmentation and boundary estimation with syntactic label constraints; (iii) estimation of multiple object locations, orientations and magnifications; (iv) identification of multiple objects from a finite model library; (v) disambiguation of overlapping objects; and (vi) scene interpretation.

The imaged scene is modelled as being composed of an unknown number N of 2-D rigid objects. They can appear at arbitrary locations r_n, orientations θ_n, and magnifications γ_n, in the scene, where $n = 0, \cdots, N\text{-}1$. Parts of objects can be obscured by other objects, or by the boundary of the image field. An organized collection of such polygonal object representations constitutes the *model library* of the recognition system [3].

The observed image data is modelled as a realization of a random process characterized by spatially-varying parameters. In the reported experiments, an inhomogeneous Poisson point process model with spatially-varying parameter $\lambda(i,j)$ is used, where (i,j) denotes a pixel location. The observed sensor data is denoted $s(i,j)$. The overall sensed image array is denoted s. The parameter $\lambda(i,j)$ is expressed as a cut-and-paste function of several unknown region-dependent parameters $\lambda_m(i,j)$, $m = 0, \cdots, M\text{-}1$, as follows:

$$\lambda(i,j) = \sum_{m=0}^{M-1} c_m(i,j)\, \lambda_m(i,j), \tag{1}$$

where, $c_m(i,j)$ is an unknown soft segmentation label that assumes an extreme value of 1 if the pixel (i,j) belongs to region model m, and is close to 0 otherwise. The labels $c_m(i,j)$ are constrained to a unit simplex, i.e., they are allowed to vary in the interval $(0,1)$, and constrained to sum to unity, $\sum_{m=0}^{M-1} c_m(i,j) = 1$, at each pixel location. These constraints are implemented using the hierarchical transformation method of [4]. This transformation expresses each of the M coefficients $c_m(i,j)$ in terms of a vector with only $(M\text{-}1)$ real-valued components. The image background is represented by $\lambda_0(i,j)$. The region-dependent parameters $\lambda_m(i,j)$, are allowed to vary within known region-specific intervals:

$$\lambda_m^l < \lambda_m(i,j) < \lambda_m^h, \ m = 0, \cdots, M\text{-}1, \tag{2}$$

where, the number of regions M can be specified, or estimated by cluster analysis [3]. The above interval constraints are realized by the following sigmoidal change of variables:

$$\lambda_m(i,j) = \lambda_m^l + \frac{\lambda_m^h - \lambda_m^l}{1 + exp\left[-\alpha_\lambda u_m(i,j)\right]}, \tag{3}$$

42

where, $u_m(i,j) \in R$, is the transformed variable with respect to which numerical optimizations are implemented. The parameter α_λ, is a small positive constant (between 1.0 and 3.0, typically).

The region intensity parameters $\lambda_m(i,j)$, are constrained to vary smoothly. This constraint is incorporated into the overall objective function by introducing the following form of Good's rotationally-invariant roughness penalty [2]:

$$H_1(\lambda_m) = \sum_{ij} \left| \sqrt{\lambda_m(i+1,j)} - \sqrt{\lambda_m(i,j)} \right|^2 + \left| \sqrt{\lambda_m(i,j+1)} - \sqrt{\lambda_m(i,j)} \right|^2. \tag{4}$$

For each region type m, the array of segmentation labels is syntactically constrained to be free of single-pixel "holes" and "islands." This can be expressed using finite-state grammars and translated to the following energy representation by the methods presented in [2]:

$$H_2(c_m) = \sum_{ij} c_m(i-1,j)\left[1 - c_m(i,j)\right] c_m(i+1,j) + \left[1 - c_m(i-1,j)\right] c_m(i,j)\left[1 - c_m(i+1,j)\right]$$
$$+ \sum_{ij} c_m(i,j-1)\left[1 - c_m(i,j)\right] c_m(i,j+1) + \left[1 - c_m(i,j-1)\right] c_m(i,j)\left[1 - c_m(i,j+1)\right]. \tag{5}$$

In addition to the above local-neighborhood constraint, the labels are also subject to non-local, high-level region shape priors. Specifically, any hypothesis representing the presence of an object drawn from the model library at a given location, orientation and magnification in the image translates to a specific expected configuration of segmentation labels. Every such hypothesis partitions the image space into two or more regions. For simplicity, suppose that the hypothesized object is composed entirely of pixels corresponding to region type m. Denote the set of points that are interior to this hypothesized object as $\mathbf{M}$, and the points exterior to this object as $\mathbf{M}^c$. Then, the conditional expectation of the segmentation label array given this hypothesis is given by an array with elements $c_m^I(i,j)$, defined as:

$$c_m^I(i,j) = \begin{cases} 1 & \text{if } (i,j) \in \mathbf{M} \\ 0 & \text{if } (i,j) \in \mathbf{M}^c. \end{cases} \tag{6}$$

We term the label array defined in equation (6) above the *instantiated* segmentation label array corresponding to the object hypothesis. Ideally, if the object hypothesis is true, then $c_m^I(i,j) = c_m(i,j)$. The discrepancy between the bottom-up sensor data based segmentation $c_m(i,j)$, and the expected value of the segmentation $c_m^I(i,j)$ corresponding to a hypothesized interpretation of the scene as a specific object with a particular position, orientation and scale, results in a penalty of the form:

$$H_3(c_m^I, c_m) = \sum_{ij} \left(c_m^I(i,j) - c_m(i,j) \right)^2. \tag{7}$$

Every adjacent pair of segmentation labels is punctuated by soft edge site variables [2] in the horizontal and vertical directions, and denoted $h_m(i,j)$ and $v_m(i,j)$ respectively. Like the segmentation labels, edge sites are constrained to the unit interval by a transformation similar to (3). The variable $h_m(i,j)$ is defined as the exclusive-OR of $c_m(i,j)$ and $c_m(i+1,j)$. Likewise, the variable $v_m(i,j)$ is the exclusive-OR of $c_m(i,j)$ and $c_m(i,j+1)$. Following the methods outlined in [2], these Boolean relations can be expressed as the minima of a energy term of the form:

43

$$H_4(h_m, c_m) = \sum_{ij} (1 - h_m(i,j)) \left[c_m(i,j) (1 - c_m(i+1,j)) + (1 - c_m(i,j)) c_m(i+1,j) \right]$$
$$+ \sum_{ij} h_m(i,j) \left[c_m(i,j) c_m(i+1,j) + (1 - c_m(i,j)) (1 - c_m(i+1,j)) \right]. \tag{8}$$

The corresponding expression for $v_m(i,j)$ is written analogously, and denoted $H_5(v_m, c_m)$. Edge sites are syntactically constrained [2] and the corresponding energy term is given by:

$$H_6(h_m, v_m) = \sum_{ij} h_m(i,j) h_m(i+1,j) + v_m(i,j) v_m(i,j+1). \tag{9}$$

As with segmentation labels, we define a set of instantiated edge-site arrays [3] representing the conditional expectations of the edge-site values given a high-level object hypothesis. These arrays are denoted $h_m^I(i,j)$ and $v_m^I(i,j)$ respectively. Edge sites are not only constrained by the local-neighborhood priors (9), but also by non-local model-specific constraints similar to (7). Specifically, the following penalty term is used:

$$H_7(h_m^I, v_m^I, h_m, v_m) = \sum_{ij} \left(h_m^I(i,j) - h_m(i,j) \right)^2 + \sum_{ij} \left(v_m^I(i,j) - v_m(i,j) \right)^2 \tag{10}$$

The overall imaging problem can be defined in terms of the above-described variables and models as follows. Given a sensed noisy image array s of a scene with an unknown number of 2-D objects, the set of prior constraints and an object library as described above, it is desired to estimate the following list of parameters: (i) Pixel intensities $\lambda_m(i,j)$; (ii) Segmentation labels $c_m(i,j)$; (iii) Edge Sites $h_m(i,j)$ and $v_m(i,j)$; (iv) Number of objects in the scene N; (v) For each object in the scene, an identification label O_n that associates it with a specific stored library model, along with a measure of the quality of the recognition; (vi) If the quality measure falls below a preset threshold, an indication that the object being sensed cannot be reliably associated with a stored model other than *none of the rest*; and (vii) For each object in the scene, its location r_n, orientation θ_n, and magnification γ_n.

FORMULATION OF THE GLOBAL OBJECTIVE FUNCTION

The models, relationships and constraints outlined in the previous section can be incorporated into a global objective function as follows.

The pixel segmentation labels $c_m(i,j)$ are cast as outcomes of generalized Bayesian hypothesis tests conducted at each pixel location with respect to probabilistic models characterizing each of the M possible image regions. Each region model can be specified by a likelihood term of the form $P(s(i,j) \mid \lambda_m(i,j))$ where the parameters $\lambda_m(i,j)$ are constrained to known intervals as in (3), and the form of the likelihood term is determined by the assumed noise/texture model. These generalized hypothesis tests can be collectively realized by minimization of the following objective function [2]:

$$H_0(c, \lambda ; s) = - \sum_{ij} \sum_{m=0}^{M-1} (c_m(i,j) + \varepsilon) P(s(i,j) \mid \lambda_m(i,j)), \tag{11}$$

where, ε is an arbitrary, but finite positive bias that prevents the gradient of the above energy function with respect to $\lambda_m(i,j)$ from going to zero ("freezing") if $c_m(i,j)$ is zero during optimization. Using (11), the objective function for the joint solution of the subset of problems corresponding to segmentation, boundary estimation and intensity estimation may be written as [2]:

$$
\begin{aligned}
H_L(c, \lambda, h, v\, ; s) = H_0(c, \lambda; s) + \sum_{m=0}^{M-1} & \left\{ \beta_1(m)\, H_1(\lambda_m) + \beta_2(m)\, H_2(c_m) + \beta_4(m)\, H_4(h_m, c_m) \right. \\
& \left. + \beta_5(m)\, H_5(v_m, c_m) + \beta_6(m)\, H_6(h_m, v_m) \right\},
\end{aligned} \tag{12}
$$

where, $\beta_1(m)$, $\beta_2(m)$, $\cdots$, $\beta_6(m)$, are arrays of Lagrange multipliers. These constants can be chosen differently for each region. The experiments reported in this paper exploit this feature to incorporate a high roughness penalty over the image background while incorporating a negligible penalty over foreground regions. *Prima facie*, the choice of these multipliers appears to be a forbidding task. The situation in practice is much simpler. The "penalty" interpretation allows the following empirical scheme for obtaining these parameters. First, the multipliers β_4, β_5 and β_6 are set to zero. The multipliers β_1 and β_2 are then set to small values and adjusted upward to get acceptably smooth sets of segmentation labels and estimated intensities. Next, the remaining multipliers are adjusted to obtain further improvement in the segmentation labels and edge sites by the incorporation of label-continuity and boundary constraints. Experiments have shown that the algorithm is not very sensitive to these parameters, so approximate values are acceptable.

The objective function in (12) above is augmented with several high-level vision terms. For simplicity, we consider a simple scene with a single object. The problem of estimating the model identification O, location r, orientation θ, and magnification γ, of the object in the scene can be formulated as the minimization of:

$$
H_8(r, \theta, \gamma, O\,; s) = -\mu_c(r, \theta, \gamma, O\,; s)\left(1 + \mu_f(r, \theta, \gamma, O\,; s)\right), \tag{13}
$$

where, $\mu_c(r, \theta, \gamma, O\,; s)$ is termed the *coverage merit*, and $\mu_f(r, \theta, \gamma, O\,; s)$ is termed the *merit of fit*. The reader is referred to [3] for a derivation of these terms and their generalization to a scene containing multiple objects.

The number of objects in the scene N cannot be predicted in advance, and must be estimated jointly with all other parameters. A reasonable prior on N is motivated by a minimum-complexity-based logarithmic penalty term. With this, the overall objective function for the multiple-object case is given by:

$$
\begin{aligned}
H(c, \lambda, h, v, & \left\{(r_n, \theta_n, \gamma_n, O_n)\right\}_{n=0}^{N-1}; s) = H_L(c, \lambda, h, v\,; s) \\
& + \sum_{m=0}^{M-1} \left\{ \beta_3(m)\, H_3(c^I, c) + \beta_7(m)\, H_7(e^I, e) \right\} + \beta_8\, H_8(\left\{ r_n, \theta_n, \gamma_n, O_n \right\}_{n=0}^{N-1}; s) + \beta_9\, \ln(N),
\end{aligned} \tag{14}
$$

where, β_9 is an additional Lagrange multiplier.

PARALLEL MULTI-TRAJECTORY OPTIMIZATION ALGORITHM

The minimization of the nonlinear objective function (14) is a daunting task. The dimensionality of the search space is extremely high, and the function has potential local extrema along every dimension. Direct application of an optimization method such as simulated annealing was found to be unacceptably slow as it performed an essentially serial and random search of the solution space.

In [3] we present a superior strategy that replaces the single search path of a conventional optimization algorithm by a cooperating set of parallel search trajectories. The technique combines evolutionary algorithms [5] with stochastic gradient descent strategies over portions of the search space. Other features that make it an attractive optimization technique are: (i) the ability to optimize objective functions that are non-differentiable, consisting of local extrema, and defined over a mixture of discrete and real-valued variables; and (ii) amenability to asynchronous parallel computation.

SIMULATION RESULTS

Figures 3(i) and (ii) show the initial and final stages in the global optimization of (14) representing the first and fortieth iterations (generations) respectively. The model library for this example is comprised of eight models. The corresponding panels in each of these figures depict the same set of variables at different iterations of the hybrid evolutionary algorithm. Panel A of each figure shows the simulated sensor data. Note that there are two region types ($M = 2$), and three objects ($N = 3$). Panels B and C show the values of the current label and edge-site estimates. The current intensity estimate is displayed in Panel D. Panel E shows all the candidates present in the candidate-solution pool. Each candidate solution is shown in white outline, depicting a hypothesized model at a particular location, orientation and scale. In this example, a population of 40 candidate solutions was used. The current-best interpretation is shown in Panel F. Between Figures 3(i) and 3(ii) we see a refinement of the intensity, segmentation-label and edge-site estimates, and correct determination of the objects in the scene. These results took about 15 minutes to compute on an Intel i860 multiprocessor described in [3].

References

[1] Baird, H. S., *Model-Based Image Matching Using Location*, MIT Press, 1984.

[2] Roysam, B., Bhattacharjya, A. K., Srinivas, C., and Turner, J. N., "Unsupervised Noise Removal Algorithms For 3-D Confocal Fluorescence Microscopy," *Micron and Microscopica Acta*, vol. 23, no. 4, pp. 447-461, 1992.

[3] Bhattacharjya, A. K., Roysam, B., "Joint Solution of Low, Intermediate, and High-Level Vision Tasks by Evolutionary Optimization: Application to Computer Vision at Low SNR," to appear in *IEEE Transactions on Neural Networks,* September, 1993.

[4] Roysam, B., and Bhattacharjya, A. K., "Hierarchically-Structured Unit Simplex Transformations for Parallel Distributed Optimization Problems," *IEEE Transactions on Neural Networks*, vol.3, no. 1, pp. 108-114, 1992.

[5] Fogel, D. B., *System Identification through Simulated Evolution: A Machine Learning Approach to Modeling*, Ginn Press, Needham Heights, MA, 1991.

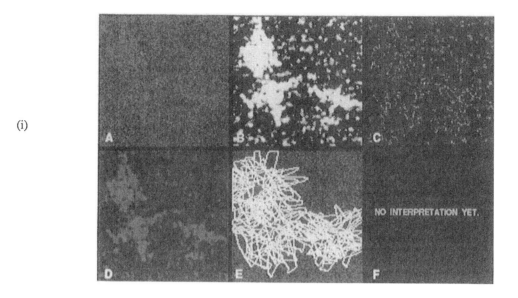

(i)

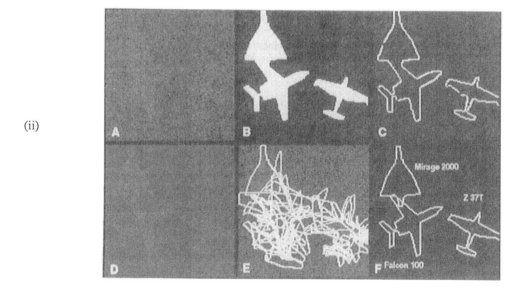

(ii)

Figure 3: Showing two stages in the evolutionary optimization. The panels in (i) and (ii), depict the first, and 40th iterations (generations). For each generation, Panel A shows the noisy scene. Panels B, C and D show the current segmentation-label and edge-site and intensity estimates. Panel E shows in white outline, all the candidates present in the candidate-solution pool. The current-best interpretation is displayed in Panel F.

47

Learning Global Spatial Structures From Local Associations

Thea B. Ghiselli-Crippa and Paul W. Munro
Department of Information Science
University of Pittsburgh
Pittsburgh, PA 15260
tbgst@lis.pitt.edu, munro@lis.pitt.edu

A variant of the encoder architecture, where units at the input and output layers represent nodes on a graph, is applied to the task of mapping locations to sets of neighboring locations. The degree to which the resulting internal (i.e. hidden unit) representations reflect global properties of the environment depends upon several parameters of the learning procedure. Architectural bottlenecks, noise, and incremental learning of landmarks are shown to be important factors in maintaining topographic relationships at a global scale.

INTRODUCTION

The acquisition of spatial knowledge by exploration of an environment has been the subject of several recent experimental studies, investigating such phenomena as the relationship between distance estimation and priming (e.g. [1]) and the influence of route information [2]. Specifically, Clayton and Habibi [3] have gathered data suggesting that temporal contiguity during exploration is an important factor in determining associations between spatially distinct sites. This data supports the notion that *spatial* associations are built by a *temporal* process that is active during exploration and by extension supports Hebb's [4] neurophysiological postulate that temporal associations underlie mechanisms of synaptic learning. This scheme for spatial learning implies local continuity at a scale that is subject to the interrelationship of such variables as speed of exploration (this can vary over orders of magnitude if map scanning is considered a form of exploration) and synaptic learning (which depends on neurobiological factors). Local spatial information acquired during the exploration process is continuously integrated into a global representation of the environment (cognitive map), which is typically arrived at by also considering global constraints, such as low dimensionality, not explicitly represented in the local relationships.

NETWORK ARCHITECTURE AND TRAINING

The goal of this network design is to reveal structure among the internal representations that emerges solely from integration of local spatial associations; in other words, to show how a network trained to learn only local spatial associations characteristic of an environment can develop internal representations which capture global spatial properties. A variant of the encoder architecture [5] is used to associate each node on a 2-D graph with the set of its neighboring nodes, as defined by the arcs in the graph. This 2-D neighborhood mapping task is similar to the 1-D task explored by Wiles [6] using an N-2-N architecture, which can be characterized in terms of a graph environment as a circular chain with broad neighborhoods.

In the neighborhood mapping experiments described in the following, the graph nodes are visited at random: at each iteration, a training pair (node-neighborhood) is selected at random from the training set. As in the standard encoder task, the input patterns are all orthogonal, so that there is no structure in the input domain that the network could exploit in constructing the internal representations; the only information about the structure of the environment comes from the local associations that the network is shown during training.

N-H-N Networks

The neighborhood mapping task was first studied using a strictly layered feed-forward N-H-N architecture, where N is the number of input and output units, corresponding to the number nodes in the environment, and H is the number of units in the hidden layer. Neighborhood mapping experiments were done using square grid environments with wraparound at the edges. Since the neighborhood definitions for the 2-D grid environments identify regions which are not linearly separable, values of H greater than 2 were used. Although the task proved learnable for networks with H>3, the high dimensionality of the hidden unit space did not allow a readily available interpretation of the internal representations, to verify correspondences between their global structure and the spatial structure of the original 2-D environment. Also, a study of the relationship between distances in the 2-D grid environment and distances in the hidden unit space shows that, while the set of representations exhibits global aspects of the environment, it does not capture them fully.

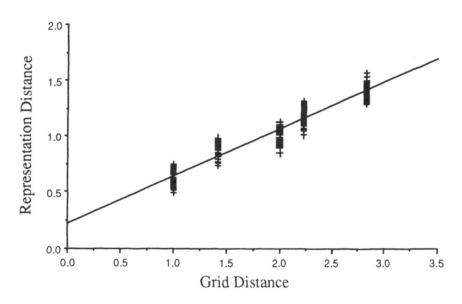

Figure 1: Relationship Between Distances in the Environment and Distances in the Hidden Unit Representation Space.

This situation is illustrated in Figure 1, which represents the relationship between grid distance and hidden unit space distance for all possible pairs of nodes in a 5x5 grid with wraparound at the edges. Each data point in the Figure represents a pair of nodes, which is characterized by its distance in the grid environment (x-axis) and in the hidden unit space (y-axis). Also shown in the Figure is the least-squares regression line through the data points, with correlation coefficient 0.958. Despite the high correlation, note that pairs which have different distance values in the grid environment (as, for example, 1.4 and 2.0 in the Figure) can have very similar distance values in the hidden unit space (in the range 0.7 to 1.0 for the first case and in the range 0.8 to 1.1 for the second case).

To promote the preservation of distance relationships and to improve the interpretability of the internal representations developed by the network, the neighborhood mapping task was then studied using an architecture with two hidden layers: a "topographic layer" (T-layer), with just two units, forces the representations into a 2-D space, which matches the dimensionality of the environment; however, since the neighborhoods in a 2-D representation are not linearly separable regions, another layer (H-layer) is introduced between the two-unit layer and the output (see Figure 2). Thus, the network has a strictly layered feed-forward N-2-H-N architecture, where the N units at the input and output layers correspond to the N nodes in the environment, two units make up the topographic layer, and H is the number of units chosen for the other hidden layer (H is estimated according to the complexity of the graph). Responses for the hidden units (in both the T- and H-layer) are computed using the hyperbolic tangent (which ranges from -1 to +1), while the standard sigmoid (0 to +1) is used for the output units, to promote orthogonality between representations [7]. Instead of the squared error, the cross entropy function [8] was used to avoid problems with low derivatives observed in early versions of the network.

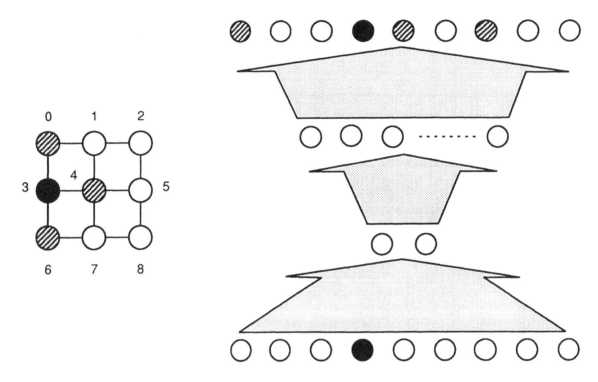

Figure 2: A 3x3 Environment and the Corresponding Network.
When Input Unit 3 is Activated, the Network Responds by Activating the Same Unit and All Its Neighbors.

RESULTS

Neighborhood mapping experiments were done using non-wrapping square grid environments with horizontal and vertical links. The topographic unit activities corresponding to each of the N possible inputs can be plotted, with connecting lines representing the arcs from the environment (see Figure 3). Each axis in the Figure represents the activity of one of the T-units. These maps can be readily examined to study the relationship between their global structure and the structure of the environment. The receptive fields of the T-units give an alternative representation of the same data: the response of each T-unit to all N inputs is represented by circles arranged in the same configuration as the nodes in the grid environment. Circle size is proportional to the absolute value of the unit

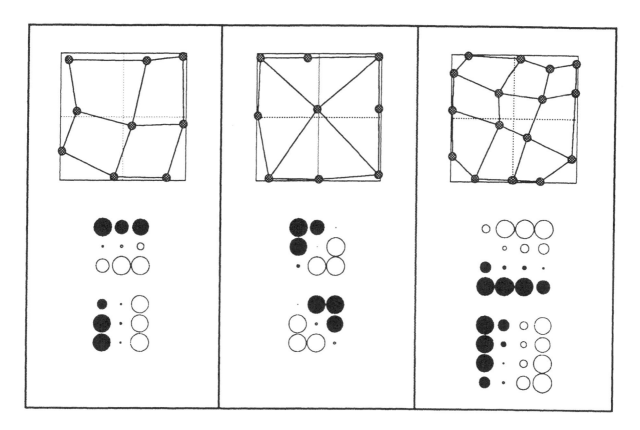

Figure 3: Representations at the Topographic Layer.
Activity Plots and Receptive Fields for Two 3x3 Grids (left and middle) and a 4x4 Grid (right).

activity; filled circles indicate negative values, open circles indicate positive values. The receptive field represents the T-unit's sensitivity with respect to the environment.

The two 3x3 cases shown in Figure 3 illustrate alternative solutions that are each locally consistent, but have different global structure. In the first case, it is evident how the first unit is sensitive to changes in the vertical location of the grid nodes, while the second unit is sensitive to their horizontal location. The axes are essentially rotated 45 degrees in the second case. Except for this rotation of the reference axes, both representations captured the global structure of the 3x3 environment. Larger grids, like the 4x4 case on the right, show a tendency toward the horizontal-vertical orientation.

Noise in the Hidden Units

While networks tended to form maps in the T-layer that reflect the global structure of the environment, in some cases the maps showed correspondences that were less obvious: i.e., the grid lines crossed, even though the network converged. Various techniques have proven valuable for promoting global correspondence between the topographic representations and the environment, including Judd and Munro's [9] introduction of noise as pressure to separate representations. The noise is implemented as a small probability for reversing the sign of individual H-unit outputs. The presence of noise causes the network to develop topographic representations which are more separated, and therefore more robust, so that the correct output units can be activated even if one or more of the H-units provides an incorrect output. From another point of view, the noise can be seen as causing the network to behave as if it had an effective number of hidden units which is smaller than the given number H. The effect of noise as a means to promote robust topographic representations can be appreciated by examining Figure 4, which illustrates the representations of a 5x5 grid developed by a 25-2-20-25 network trained without noise (left) and with noise (middle) (the network was initialized with the same set of small random weights in all cases). As illustrated in the Figure, the representations developed by the network subject to noise are more separated and exhibit the same global

51

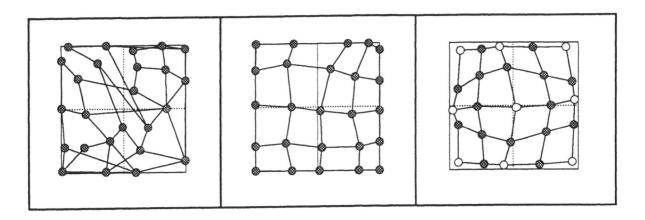

Figure 4: Representations at the Topographic Layer.
Training with No Noise (left) and with Noise in the Hidden Units (middle); Training Using Landmarks (right).

structure as the environment. The drawback for the use of noise in the H-units is an increase in the number of iterations required by the network to converge; for the example considered, the increase was on the order of a factor of 10. A similar technique currently under investigation is the use of low-level Gaussian noise injected in the topographic units, to directly promote the formation of well-separated representations.

Landmark Learning

Another method that has proven effective involves the organization of training in 2 separate phases, to model the acquisition of landmark information followed by the development of route and/or survey knowledge [10], [11]. This method is implemented by manipulating the training set during learning, using coarse spatial resolution at the outset and introducing features at a finer spatial resolution as learning progresses to the second phase. The first phase involves training the network only on a subset of the possible N patterns (landmarks). Once the landmarks have been learned, the remaining patterns are added to the training set. In the second phase, training proceeds as usual with the full set of training patterns; the only restriction is applied to the landmark points, whose topographical representations are not allowed to change (the corresponding weights between input units and T-units are frozen), thus modeling the use of landmarks as stable reference points when learning the details of a new environment. The right pane of Figure 4 illustrates the representations developed for a 5x5 grid using landmark training; the same 25-2-20-25 network mentioned above was trained in 2 phases, first on a subset of 9 patterns (landmarks) and then on the full set of 25 patterns (the landmarks are indicated as white circles in the activity plot).

Noise in Landmark Learning

The techniques described above (noise and landmark learning) can be combined together to better promote the emergence of well-structured representation spaces. In particular, noise can be used during the first phase of landmark learning to encourage a robust representation of the landmarks: Figure 5 illustrates the representations obtained for a 5x5 grid using landmark training with two different levels of noise during the first phase. The effect of noise is evident when comparing the 4 corner landmarks in the right pane of Figure 4 (landmark learning with no noise) with those in Figure 5. With increasing levels of noise, the T-unit activities corresponding to the 4 corner landmarks approach the asymptotic values of +1 and -1; the activity plots illustrate this effect by showing how the corner landmark representations move toward the corners of T-space, reaching a configuration which provides more resistance to noise. During the second phase of training, the landmarks function as reference points for the additional features of the environment and their positioning in the representational space therefore becomes very important. A well-formed, robust representation of the landmarks at the end of the first phase is crucial for the formation of a map in T-space that reflects global structure, and the use of noise can help promote this.

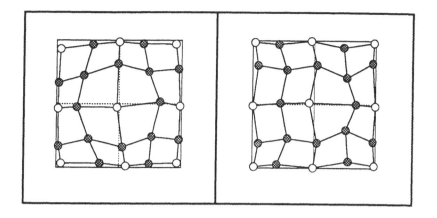

Figure 5: Representations at the Topographic Layer.
Landmark Training Using Noise in Phase 1: Low Noise Level (left), High Noise Level (right).

SUMMARY

Large scale constraints intrinsic to natural environments, such as low dimensionality, are not necessarily reflected in local neighborhood relations, but they constitute information which is essential to the successful development of useful representations of the environment. In our model, some of the constraints imposed on the network architecture effectively reduce the dimensionality of the representational space. Constraints have been introduced several ways: bottlenecks, noise, and landmark learning; in all cases, these constraints have had constructive influences on the emergence of globally consistent representation spaces. The approach described presents an alternative to Kohonen's [12] scheme for capturing topography; here, topographic relations emerge in the representational space, rather than in the weights between directly connected units.

The experiments described thus far have focused on how global spatial structure can emerge from the integration of local associations and how it is affected by the introduction of global constraints. As mentioned in the introduction, one additional factor influencing the process of acquisition of spatial knowledge needs to be considered: temporal contiguity during exploration, that is, how temporal associations of spatially adjacent locations can influence the representation of the environment.

To address this issue, the method used to select each training pair (node-neighborhood) will be changed, from the current method of selecting the next node to be visited from all the available graph nodes, to a more realistic exploratory method. For example, a random type of exploration ("wandering") can be considered, where the next node to be visited is selected at random from the neighbors of the current node. An additional factor can also be introduced: for each node, the complete set of its neighboring nodes can be activated at each visit (as for all the experiments described in this paper), or only one of the neighboring nodes, which in turn will become the next node to be visited, can. In both cases, we expect results similar to the ones presented in this paper, perhaps with longer training times for the latter case. Alternatively, more directed exploration methods can be studied, with a systematic pattern guiding the choice of the next node to be visited. The main purpose of these studies will be to show how different exploration strategies can affect the formation and the characteristics of cognitive maps of the environment.

Higher order effects of temporal and spatial contiguity can also be considered. However, in order to capture regularities in the training process that span several exploration steps, simple feed-forward networks may no longer be sufficient; partially recurrent networks [13] are a likely candidate for the study of such processes.

53

Acknowledgments

We wish to thank Stephen Hirtle, whose expertise in the area of spatial cognition greatly benefitted our research. We are also grateful for the insightful editorial comments of Janet Wiles.

References

[1]   T. P. McNamara, J. K. Hardy, and S. C. Hirtle, "Subjective hierarchies in spatial memory," *Journal of Experimental Psychology: Learning, Memory, and Cognition,* vol. 15, pp. 211-227, 1989.

[2]   T. P. McNamara, R. Ratcliff, and G. McKoon, "The mental representation of knowledge acquired from maps," *Journal of Experimental Psychology: Learning, Memory, and Cognition,* vol. 10, pp. 723-732, 1984.

[3]   K. Clayton and A. Habibi, "The contribution of temporal contiguity to the spatial priming effect," *Journal of Experimental Psychology: Learning, Memory, and Cognition,* vol. 17, pp. 263-271, 1991.

[4]   D. O. Hebb, *The Organization of Behavior,* New York, NY: Wiley, 1949.

[5]   D. H. Ackley, G. E. Hinton, and T. J. Sejnowski, "A learning algorithm for Boltzmann machines," *Cognitive Science,* vol. 9, pp. 147-169, 1985.

[6]   J. Wiles, "Representation of variables and their values in neural networks," in *Proceedings of the Fifteenth Annual Conference of the Cognitive Science Society,* 1993, pp. 1077-1082.

[7]   P. W. Munro, "Conjectures on representations in backpropagation networks," *Technical Report TR-89-035,* Berkeley, CA: International Computer Science Institute, 1989.

[8]   G. E. Hinton, "Connectionist learning procedures," *Technical Report CMU-CS-87-115,* version 2, Pittsburgh, PA: Carnegie-Mellon University, Computer Science Department, 1987.

[9]   S. Judd and P. W. Munro, "Nets with unreliable hidden nodes learn error-correcting codes," in C. L. Giles, S. J. Hanson, and J. D. Cowan, *Advances in Neural Information Processing Systems 5,* San Mateo, CA: Morgan Kaufmann, 1993.

[10]   R. A. Hart and G. T. Moore, "The development of spatial cognition: A review," in R. M. Downs and D. Stea (Eds.), *Image and Environment,* Chicago, IL: Aldine, 1973.

[11]   A. W. Siegel and S. H. White, "The development of spatial representations of large-scale environments," in H. W. Reese (Ed.), *Advances in Child Development and Behavior,* New York, NY: Academic Press, 1975.

[12]   T. Kohonen, "Self-organized formation of topologically correct feature maps," *Biological Cybernetics,* vol. 43, pp. 59-69, 1982.

[13]   J. L. Elman, "Finding structure in time," *Cognitive Science,* vol. 14, pp. 179-211, 1990.

COGNITIVE MODELING

A Connectionist Model of Auditory Morse Code Perception

David Ascher
Department of Cognitive and Linguistic Sciences
Brown University, Box 1978
Providence, RI 02912 USA
david_ascher@brown.edu

The psychological phenomena involved in the task of auditory Morse Code perception are outlined. The relevant auditory neurophysiology is then briefly outlined, suggesting a representation for use in a model of the task. A connectionist model of Morse Code perception based on physiological data is then presented, along with some preliminary results.

INTRODUCTION

One of the appeals of connectionist models in cognitive science is that simplified models of the brain should be able to aid understanding of human behaviors. One of these behaviors is the ability to learn associations between complex low-level *percepts* and high-level *concepts*, as in language acquisition and object recognition research. This paper presents a model of the simpler perceptual task of Morse Code perception that is based both on psychological data to define the performance goals and physiological data to guide the modeling decisions.

As Marr pointed out in *Vision* [9], perception can be understood in terms of successive stages performing specific computations on information. When dealing with processing in the visual domain, Marr presented a model with several stages, each of which had a specific computational role to play, and each of which operated on a different representation of the same input generated by the previous level).

In our case, three stages are considered: the first stage is a rerepresentation of the auditory input, whose only role is the extraction from the signal of the features relevant to the task. The second stage combines these features, providing the final stage an input designed to make its task, classification, as easy as possible.

Defining the three stages of processing (feature extraction, feature combination, and classification) at a computational level provides us with the first level of description for this system. In addition, a description of the algorithms, representations and implementations used is needed. This article assumes the computational roles just defined and describes the first two stages of processing at the algorithm/representation and implementation levels. Work on the third stage is still preliminary.

In contrast to Marr's computer metaphor of the brain, my modeling is guided by neurophysiological evidence. This results in algorithms which, although harder to implement in a computer, are more realistic as models of brain processes.

Outline

The psychological task of Morse Code perception is described, along with various effects which have been identified in this task. The relevant neurophysiology is then briefly surveyed. Drawing from these two areas, a connectionist model of Morse Code perception based on recognizing feature combinations is presented. Finally, preliminary results are outlined.

MORSE CODE PERCEPTION

Morse code is an encoding of the 26 characters of the alphabet and the 10 digits by a predefined set of sequences of "beeps" of one of two durations. For example, an "A" is coded as a short tone (colloquially called a "dot") followed by a longer tone (a "dash") (also represented as [· —]), whereas a "B" is [— · · ·], a "C" is [— · — ·], etc. The psychological task modeled is auditory Morse code perception (or alternatively auditory Morse code character recognition). In psychological studies of Morse code learning, subjects are trained over a period of several weeks to recognize each character and to decode a stream of characters and write them down as quickly and accurately as possible. As training progresses, the time between successive characters is shortened. Advanced students can reach a decoding rate of 60–70 characters per minute with very high accuracy.

Psychological Facts about Morse Code Recognition

Out of the vast array of data on temporal pattern recognition in general, and Morse code in particular, several key points emerge that must be accounted for by a model:

- For temporal patterns of a certain duration (less than 100 msec/item in the pattern), humans seem to be using a very specific pattern recognition system called "holistic pattern recognition" (e.g. Warren [22]). In this range, people perceive the sound pattern as a whole, and do not require sequential perception of its component parts to recognize the complete pattern. Rather, it is the holistic "impression" of the pattern which is perceived.

- Morse code students were very highly trained. This means that the recognition process involves not only the perceptual but the memory systems as well, unlike most auditory experiments which tend to avoid training of the subjects [21].

- Several studies have examined the types of errors that Morse code students make while training. These errors follow specific patterns which are due mostly to the similarity between two characters' encodings [8, 18, 15]. Notably, subjects seem to confuse characters which have the same number of segments[1]; in particular they confuse letters with Morse code representations which differ only in the final or penultimate segment (e.g. a character with a final dot will be mistaken as the character with the same pattern, but with a final dash).

- Experienced Morse code receivers can decode the signal over a very wide range of signal speeds, as long as the relationships between the parts of the signal (the durations of the dot, dash, inter-segment and inter-character silences) are preserved [2].

- Morse code students are able to effectively process very noisy inputs and inputs with a carrier frequency which varies broadly [2].

A MODEL GUIDED BY PHYSIOLOGY

Feature Extraction

The physiology of the auditory system is clearly very complex. Several studies have investigated the feature-extracting capabilities of neurons in the three major areas of the auditory system—the ear, the auditory brain stem nuclei, and the auditory cortical areas. Of these, the physiology of the brain stem nuclei and auditory cortex is the most relevant to Morse code perception. Some auditory cortical cells have been categorized as fitting one of five clearly defined frequency-independent cell response types [5]:

- **Sustained excitation cells:** These cells fire only when a tone is being heard.

- **Sustained inhibition cells:** These cells decrease their firing rate when a tone is being heard.

---

[1]The word segment is used to describe either a dot or a dash.

- **ON response cells:** These cells fire at the onset of tones.

- **OFF response cells:** These cells fire at the offset of tones for a short period of time.

- **ON-OFF response cells:** These cells fire at the onset and offset of the tones.

Similar cell responses (cells which respond to the onset or presence of a tone, and not to its frequency) are found in the auditory brain stem nuclei [13].

These observations suggested that the feature extraction stage of the model encodes the signal not as a set of dots and dashes, but as a temporal sequence of onsets and offsets.

This representational choice has two advantages. Not only does it have considerable physiological grounding, but it also has characteristics which allow a good fit with the psychological data. Because it only encodes the onset and offset of tones, it is independent of the carrier frequency used. It is also noise-tolerant within reasonable limits. Both of these are found in behavioral studies [2]. Moreover, a dot/dash representation cannot easily account for the signal-speed independence shown by subjects, in that a dot could have the same duration as a dash in two Morse streams with different coding speeds. In the onset/offset representation, this issue is not problematic, as it assumes that the encoding of the temporal structure of the signal is performed by a later stage of processing.

As an example of this representation, the time courses of the envelope of the sound signal and of the activations of idealized onset- and offset-sensitive cells are plotted in Figure 1.

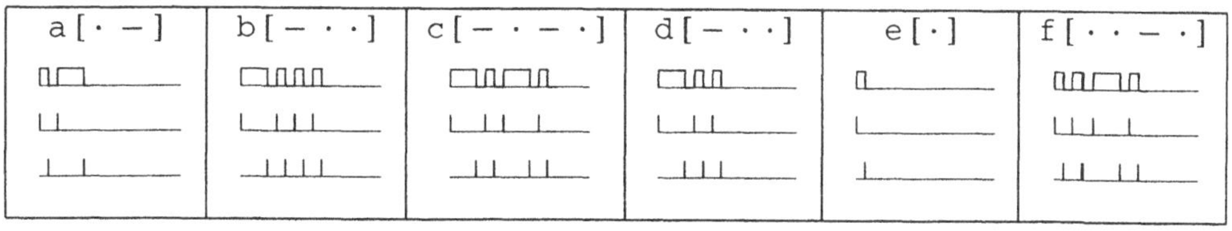

Figure 1: Onsets and offsets for the first few characters. The first line in each box represents the envelope of the signal, the second line the schedule of onsets, the third line the schedule of offsets.

Feature Combination

The physiological data on auditory cortex provides little direction when it comes to the organization of a feature-combination stage such as the one posited above. However, neurophysiology suggests a set of general organizational principles which constrain modeling, namely the use of distributed representations and maps as computational tools. The higher cortical centers tend to show evidence for distributed rather than localist representations [4]. Analyses of the sensory cortices also seem to indicate that a common organizational scheme used by the brain is that of maps, where spatially nearby neurons have functionally similar behaviors. Such maps have been found in somatosensory and motor cortex [12] as well as visual cortex [10]. Auditory cortex in non-mammalian species has also shown topographic organization [19]. Some studies show that even olfactory cortex might be using the topography of the cortical layout to organize "multidimensional overlapping spaces of odor features" [17].

These observations led to the design of a map-based model of auditory feature combinations which constructs distributed representations of the relationships between tone onsets and offsets.

As the structure of the Morse stream is a temporal sequence of onsets and offsets, and the structure of the cortex is a complex three-dimensional spatial network, a mapping from the former onto the latter is clearly needed. Since most neural maps described to date seem to rely on the two-dimensional layout of the outer cortical layers rather than three-dimensional networks, the feature-combination stage is limited to a two-dimensional arrangement of a large number of modules, each of which is posited to perform a sophisticated signal detection process, much like cortical columns in the visual cortex. These modules are assumed to be connected to their neighbors, thus creating a topographic map.

The use of topographic maps as computational tools has been presented in connectionist work [1, 6, 11], but it is more commonplace as an engineering solution [3], or in the cellular automaton literature [14]. Although the type of network presented below has been suggested as a pattern classifier [6], it has not actually been applied to a specific task before.

The most novel feature of this net is that a module is postulated to have an internal state which it propagates to its unexcited neighbors as they reach threshold. When two spreading waves of activation reach a module simultaneously, this module adopts a third state which is the result of the interaction of the two interacting waves. This results in the creation of "interference patterns" of activation, localized in the array at locations dependent both on the topographical relation between the two sources of initial activity, and on the chronological relation between their times of activation. Just as it seems that the olfactory system uses its neural space to code non-spatial attributes of the odor space [17], it is reasonable to argue that the spatial organization of the neural substrate are used in the auditory system to code for the temporal relationships between events. In our model of Morse code perception, the features being detected are the tone onsets and tone offets. Thus some modules in the map are assigned the role of tone onset detection, some are assigned the role of tone offset detection, and most are left unassigned. The latter will allow the transmission of the wave as well as the detection of wave collisions, which represent temporal relationships between onsets and offsets.

MODEL IMPLEMENTATION

Two simplifications of the model were necessary to make the computational requirements of the model fit available computer resources. The first simplification is that the Morse signal is assumed to be perfect—dots, dashes, and pauses are perfectly timed. This allows us to discretize the signal and not lose information[2]. The resulting discrete implementation is functionally equivalent to an analog implementation based on continuous representations and analog processing units.

A second simplification of the model is that instead of the complex modules which compose the feature-combination map described above, we limit ourselves to computationally much more tractable multistable units. Some of these units are assumed to be 'tuned' to detect tone onset, some are tuned to detect tone offset, and most aren't tuned before learning occurs.

In this network, the connectivity of a module to its neighbors is determined by a gaussian probability function of unit height and of adjustable width σ, so that the further away two units are, the less likely they are to be connected. In the runs presented, the width of the gaussian σ was chosen to be equal to 2 (measured in inter-module distances on the array), resulting in an mean ($\pm$ SD) number of connections to a module of 10.2 ($\pm$ 2.8)

The connections between two modules are unidirectional. Each module has a firing threshold, an inhibitory period, and a set of nearby modules connected to it. When the sum of the activation values of the "afferent" modules surpasses a given module's firing threshold, the module's activity is set to a maximum (it "fires"), from which it will decrease geometrically until it reaches its resting value. At the same time, the cell's threshold is also raised to a high level from which it decreases geometrically to its resting value, thus making the module temporarily refractory to further firing. Its high activity is then transmitted through its efferent connections, and if any of those modules' activity surpass their threshold, they will fire, etc. ad infinitum.

Mathematically, this can be expressed in the following way. Let $A_i(t)$ be the activity of module c_i at time t, $\eta_i(t)$ be its firing threshold, and $\mathcal{N}$ the set of modules from which it receives connections. The activation and threshold functions are then given by:

$$\text{the module } c_i \text{ will fire at time } t+1 \quad \text{if} \quad \sum_{j/c_j \in \mathcal{N}} A_j(t) > \eta_i(t) \tag{1}$$

$$A_i(t+1) = \begin{cases} \lambda & \text{if the module is firing} \\ max(\delta A_i(t), A_i^0) & \text{otherwise} \end{cases} \tag{2}$$

$$\eta_i(t+1) = \begin{cases} \gamma & \text{if the module is firing} \\ max(\alpha \eta_i(t), \eta_i^0) & \text{otherwise} \end{cases} \tag{3}$$

The decay terms for the activation and the threshold are δ and α respectively, and the maximum values for the activation

---

[2]Indeed, by sampling at regular intervals defined by the duration of a dot, one does not lose any timing information

and threshold are λ and γ respectively. A_i^0 and η_i^0 are the resting activation and resting thresholds respectively. In this specific model, A_i^0 is set to 0, thus a steady state for a module is that of zero activation.

Spreading: One Feature Activation

The first aspect of the network dynamics that one can examine is the local behavior around an assigned onset- or offset-module. These can be adequately studied in relatively small (100x100) networks.

Depending on the values chosen for the various parameters of the network (η_i^0, γ, λ, δ, α), qualitatively different network behaviors are observed. Apart from the trivial case of no spreading at all in an overly refractory system, there are three types of spreading patterns. Figure 2 shows activation spread as a sequence of snapshots of the dynamical process.

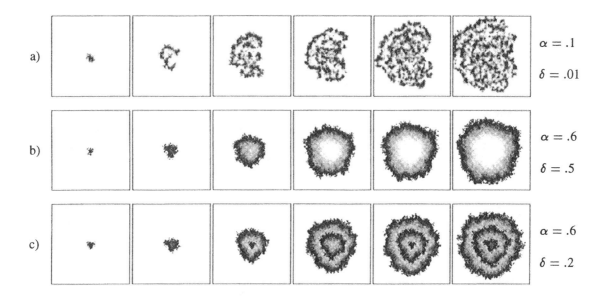

Figure 2: The three basic firing pattern wave types shown in a 100x100 network with the following parameters: $A_i^0 = 0$, $\eta_i^0 = 1.5$, $\sigma = 2.0$, $\lambda = 1$, $\gamma = 100$. α and δ were varied (see the end of each row for their values). These are selected snapshots from the first 15 iterations of each network.

In the first row, the first type of outgoing wave breaks up into smaller waves, each of which spreads from its current location, recursively. Shortly, the pattern loses information about the location and time of initial activation. The second type of spreading pattern, shown in the second row, consists of an outgoing roughly circular activation wave emanating from the locus of initial activation. The final type of activation, in the last row, behaves like the previous type except that the spreading activity from firing modules to modules which have recently fired overcome the latter modules' inhibitory thresholds, and the system thus generates from a single module activation at a single point in time a self-regenerating oscillatory outgoing wave.

The parameters corresponding to the middle row were used subsequently, as the resulting waves are estimated to have the highest information content of the three types described. The first pattern seems to lose the information relating to the point and time of original activation quickly, whereas the last pattern loses information pertaining to the exact time of that activation.

Interferences

Let us now look at how these waves interact when processing a sequence of successive features (tone onsets and offsets). Clearly, the patterns of activation that spread and interact across the array will depend on the locations of these modules and on the timing of the tone onsets and offsets (see Figure 3 for a map with a large number of onset- and offset-sensitive modules).

One of the key aspects of this model is that although the assignment of onset and offset selectivities to modules is random, it is fixed throughout a simulation. That is, for the network to discriminate between the schedules of onsets and offsets that correspond to the different characters, the spatial layout of the onset- and offset-selective cells has to be fixed. The spatial layout of the interference patterns then corresponds to the chronological relations between onsets and offsets.

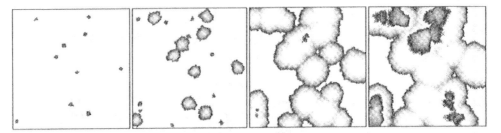

Figure 3: Response of a 400x400 network with 10 randomly located onset-sensitive modules and 10 randomly located offset-sensitive modules to the beginning of a signal. Selected snapshots from the first 20 iterations of the network. In the first box, an onset has been received, and the onset modules have been activated. In the second box, the first offset has been received and the offset waves are starting. In the third and fourth boxes, the interference patterns are visible, emanating from the loci of collision of the onset and offset waves.

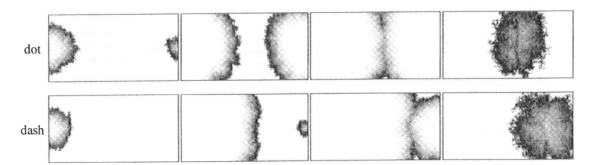

Figure 4: Interference patterns in a 200x100 networks initially seeded with a single pair of onset- and offset-sensitive sources originating at the left and right side respectively, and processing a dot input and a dash input.

For illustrative purposes, let us focus on the area between any one pair of onset and offset modules, and their neighborhood. As can be seen in Figure 4, the interference pattern corresponding to a dot and that corresponding to a dash will be different for a given pair of onset and offset modules, due to the nature of the temporal to topographical mapping performed by this network.

Running simulations on sequences of more than one segment has proven to be difficult because the interference patterns that result are hard to interpret. If one requires interference patterns which are visually identifiable, it seems that the longer sequences need to be run on very large networks, which are very computationally intensive. Some qualitative results can still be outlined. The interference patterns do correspond to the timing relationships between the onsets and the offsets, and the parameters of the network can at least theoretically be tuned so that each character results in a unique interference pattern. Speed-independence can easily be obtained in this model by the use of a global speed-control mechanism. For example, if the gross coding speed is obtained by analyzing the first few characters in a Morse stream, the firing thresholds of the modules can be modified so that the ratio between the duration of a dot and the speed of propagation of the activation waves is constant. This will result in a function which maps the same characters input at different speeds to a character-specific but speed-independent interference map.

A final result is that the psychological effect of high confusability between characters with differences in the last part of their codings is at least qualitatively met by the model. As the interference between onset and offset waves generates new waves of activation (onset-offset waves), second and higher order interactions are generated by the interaction between the onset-offset waves and other onset or offset waves. A complete Morse code character is thus a sequence of first-order interactions between onset and offset waves and of higher-order interactions between the resulting waves. The interference patterns between two characters are most different if the location of the first interaction is different between the two characters (i.e. one starts with a dot and the other with a dash), and least different if the differences lie in the final interferences, which correspond to the final part of the character's Morse code representation. Simulations demonstrating this are in progress.

CONCLUSION

As the theoretical model presented has not yet been fully implemented, it is still early to give a critical evaluation of the model as a cognitive model of Morse code perception. Still, certain methodological insights can be gleaned from this project.

The first conclusion is that auditory perception appears to be a rich field where connectionist modelers will find rich problems which are likely to suggest models different than those developed for other cognitive modalities. Audition relies at its core on the processing of time-varying information, which is something traditional neural network architectures still have a hard time processing adequately.

A second conclusion is that the study of audition can gain considerable insight from physiological data. Indeed, it seems that perception in general, and audition in particular, is the most likely area of inquiry into the mind which is likely to see a true bridge between physiology and psychology. To quote Shepherd,

> "There is [...] a critical need to build bridges between the bottom-up approach of experimentalists and the top-down approach of network modelers, so that one can construct more realistic neural networks for simulating cognitive functions." [16, p. 82]

A final conclusion is that the network of interacting modules presented above appears to have potential as an architecture specialized in processing temporal information and extracting feature combinations from an input.

FUTURE WORK

Clearly, the network as it currently stands is not powerful enough to give interpretable patterns of interactions for sequences of many segments, let alone produce the type of simulation results which would allow a critical quantitative comparison of model results and human performance. Several important steps are required before that point can be reached.

This model is committed to letting physiology guide the modelling decisions. As a direct result, it relies on computations performed by large ensembles of simple units. It appears that for processing patterns such as the Morse code signals, very large networks of several hundred thousand modules are needed. A straightforward step to better the model therefore is to increase the size of the network.

The classification process has yet to be implemented. This is clearly an important requirement before the network can be said to be classifying inputs. Once the model is made to classify patterns, the issue of learning can finally be tackled. As these are enormous nets by the conventional connectionist standards, the conventional training algorithms will not be appropriate. Some work has already been done in the formal study of the mathematics of hierarchical networks such as this one [20], and several training schemes are being investigated. One of these is based on the idea of spatially localized modifications of the network parameters. For example, increasing the firing threshold in an area of the network results in waves which tend to avoid that area. Equivalently, areas with lower firing thresholds tend to attract waves. In another potential training method, related to Hebbian learning, a module might learn to preferentially be in a specific state, learning to be "assigned" to a combination of features just like the "assigned" modules referred to above were associated with single features.

Acknowledgments

Work on this network architecture has been done in collaboration with Jim Anderson, with support from grants from the National Science Foundation (BNS-90-23283) and the Office of Naval Research (NR00014-91-J-4032). I'd also like to thank the following for stimulating conversations at the summer school and since then: Fred Cummins, Devin McAuley, Mike Mozer, Kate Stevens, Andreas Weigend, and Janet Wiles. Finally, special thanks to Mike Mozer, Paul Smolensky and Andreas Weigend for a very enriching summer school.

References

[1] R. L. Beurle, "Properties of a mass of cells capable of regenerating pulses," *Transactions of the Royal Society of London*, vol. 240, no. B, pp. 55–94, 1956.

[2] W. L. Bryan and N. Harter, "Studies in the physiology and psychology of the telegraphic language," *The Psychological Review*, vol. 4, no. 1, pp. 27–53, January 1897. Reprinted in *Psychology of a life occupation* by Bryan.

[3] L. O. Chua and L. Yang, "Cellular neural networks: Theory," *IEEE Transactions on Circuits and Systems*, vol. 35, no. 10, pp. 1257–1272, October 1988.

[4] H. Eichenbaum, "Thinking about brain cell assemblies," *Science*, vol. 261, pp. 993–994, 1993.

[5] E. Evans, Basic physics and psychophysics of sound, in *The Senses* (H. Barlowe and J. Molton, eds.), pp. 251–305. Cambridge, UK: Cambridge University Press, 1982.

[6] B. G. Farley and W. A. Clark, *Activity in networks of neuron-like elements*, ch. 19, pp. 242–251. Washington: Butterworths, 1961.

[7] A. Georgopoulos, M. Taira, and A. Lukashin, "Cognitive neurophysiology of the motor cortex," *Science*, vol. 260, pp. 47–52, 1993.

[8] F. S. Keller and R. E. Taubman, "Studies in international morse code – 2. errors made in code reception," *J. Applied Psychology*, vol. 27, pp. 504–509, 1943.

[9] D. Marr, *Vision*. Freeman, 1982.

[10] W. H. Marshall, C. N. Woolsey, and P. Bard, "Observations on cortical somatic sensory mechanisms of cat and monkey," *J. Neurophysiol.*, vol. 4, pp. 1–24, 1941.

[11] J. G. Milton, P. H. Chu, , and J. D. Cowan, "Spiral waves in integrate-and-fire neural networks," in *Advances in Neural Information Processing Systems 5* (S. J. Hanson, J. Cowan, and C. L. Giles, eds.), pp. 1001–1006, Morgan Kaufman, 1993.

[12] W. Penfield and R. Rasmussen, *The Cerebral Cortex of Man: A Clinical Study of Localization of Function*. New York: Macmillan, 1940.

[13] J. O. Pickles, *An Introduction to the Physiology of Hearing*. London: Academic Press, 1982.

[14] K. Preston and M. Duff, *Modern Cellular Automata, Theory and Applications*. Plenum Press, 1984.

[15] H. Seashore and A. Kurtz, "Analysis of errors in copying code," Tech. Rep. 4010, Office of Scientific Research and Development, 1944.

[16] G. M. Shepherd, The Significance of Real Neuron Architectures for Neural Network Simulators, in *Computational Neuroscience*, (E.L. Schwartz, ed.). The MIT Press, 1990.

[17] G. M. Shepherd, "Toward a molecular basis for sensory perception," To appear in: *Cognitive Neuroscience*, 1993.

[18] S. D. S. Spragg, "The relative difficulty of morse code alphabet characters learned by the whole method," *Journal of Experimental Psychology*, vol. 33, pp. 108–114, 1943.

[19] N. Suga, *The extent to which biosonar information is represented in the bat auditory cortex*, pp. 653–695. Wiley-Interscience, 1985.

[20] J. P. Sutton, J. S. Beis, and L. E. H. Trainor, "A hierarchical model of neocortical synaptic organization," *Matheml Comput. Modelling*, vol. 11, pp. 346–350, 1988.

[21] R. M. Warren, *Auditory perception — a new synthesis*. Elmsford, NY: Pergamon Press, 1982.

[22] R. M. Warren and J. M. Ackroff, "Two types of auditory sequence perception," *Perception and Psychophysics*, vol. 20, no. 5, pp. 387–394, 1976.

A Competitive Neural Network Model for
the Process of Recurrent Choice

Valentin Dragoi, J.E.R. Staddon

Dept. of Psychology: Experimental, Duke University, Durham, NC 27708

A competitive neural network model for the process of recurrent choice is described and a possible explanation for the associated adaptive effects of reinforcement learning is offered. We review a set of relevant experiments that characterize the framework. A minimum set of functional units and a mechanism that links them are proposed. The way in which the model reacts while exposed to various experimental conditions is carefully examined and its specific behavioral patterns are emphasized. The model shows remarkably complex behavior that resembles the general features of the behavior of pigeons and rats under several different choice-procedures.

Introduction

There has been much research interest in studying the process of recurrent choice for the past 30 years. Almost all the performed choice experiments assume the presence of at least two keys, left and right, which pressed (humans and rats) or pecked (pigeons). A variety of procedures in which repetitive responses are intermittently rewarded according to specific schedules have been designed in order to emphasize their adaptive effects. The behavior observed after performing different choice experiments, as will be discussed in some detail in section 2, is extremely complex and full of puzzling results.

The theoretical emphasis regarding these experiments has been based largely on molar equilibrium principles such as the *matching law*, [4], [6], which states that under appropriate steady-state conditions the ratio of response rates, x/y, is approximately equal to the ratio of obtained reinforcement rates, $R(x)/R(y)$. Despite their popularity, the static matching relations do not investigate the specific processes underlying the process of choice on a moment-by-moment basis (real time) or at least on a response-by-response basis.

In their analysis of choice behavior, Davis, Staddon, Machado & Palmer, [3], propose the *cumulative-effects model* (CE), a molar dynamic model designed to characterize the process of recurrent choice. They assume that the subject calculates the overall probability of reinforcement for each response from the entire history of training. The choice alternative with the higher probability of reinforcement is then selected on a winner-take-all basis. Even though the CE model is remarkably simple for its effectiveness in accounting for a large range of data it has difficulties with effects dependent on rates of occurence, such as the partial reinforcement extinction effect (PREE).

This paper deals with a symmetric competitive neural network model designed to describe adaptive effects of reinforcement learning as applied in studies of choice. It proposes to identify the essential properties of recurrent choice and to explain them at the behavioral level. In section 2 we discuss briefly the process of recurrent choice pointing out which are the most important effects a good model should be able to characterize qualitatively. Section 3 presents the proposed competitive neural network model and analyzes its global behavior. In section 4 we discuss how our model can fit a large number of adaptive effects and behaviors similar to the ones presented in section 2. Section 5 contains a brief conclusion summarizing the main findings of this paper.

65

Recurrent Choice

In order to understand behavioral phenomena through explanatory theories we need to set up an isomorphic relationship between sets of experimental results and theoretical models. The experimental situations to which we will refer in this paper are two-choice probabilistic reinforcement schedules with animal subjects and food reinforcement. The data set is the pattern of responses under all possible manipulations of reward probabilities as a function of time. Time has two aspects in choice experiments: (a) the effective time, i.e., when the subject is under experimental conditions and the reinforcement is effective; (b) the intersession time in which even though the subject is not run, indirect effects like spontaneous recovery occur. It is worth mentioning the properties of data we are attempting to explain, i.e., qualitative patterns of change in real-time responding. The subset of data we are dealing with in this paper emerges from the following relevant experiments:

(a) *reversal learning* - reinforcement conditions are changed frequently between the left and right key. *Fig.*1 presents data from a two-armed-bandit experiment, [2], in which hungry pigeons chose between two response keys, each paid off with food reinforcement according to probabilistic schedules. The pigeons were rewarded each day (probability=1/8) for pecking one key, the other one being not rewarded. The "hot" key varied from day to day in an irregular fashion. Some days only forced alternation (*F*) was rewarded. On a few days neither response was rewarded (*E*) or the animal was not run (*O*).

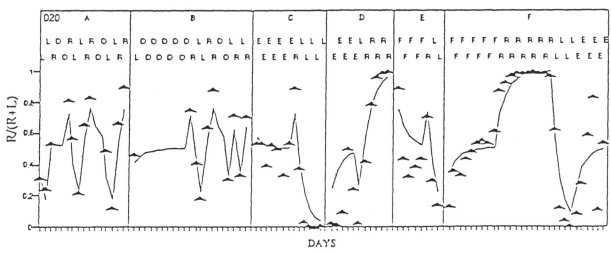

Figure 1: *The entire course (Phases A-F) of a discrimination-reversal experiment with a single pigeon. The solid triangles show the proportion of total responses to the right key each day when reinforcement conditions (shown by the staggered letters at the top) are changed frequently. The conditions were L, i.e., pecks on the left key paid off with probability $\frac{1}{8}$, R, i.e., pecks on the right key paid off with probability $\frac{1}{8}$, E (extinction), F (alternations only), i.e., L → R or R → L, paid off with probability 1, or O (animal not run that day). [Data from [2] which should be consulted for experimental details].*

We can observe in *fig.*1 the following typical behaviors:
- panel *A*: when the "hot" key is alternated the winner response oscillates according to the schedule of reinforcement.
- panel *B*: even though the pigeon was not run for several days it starts responding at a nonzero proportion (see also *regression*)
- panels *C-D*: extinguishing one key and rewarding the other one the pigeon will pay exclusive attention to the reinforced key
- panel *E*: if the schedule of reinforcement is such that only the alternations *L → R* or *R → L* are rewarded the pigeon oscillates its responses between the two keys in a quite regular fashion
- panel *F*: although the pigeon deals with simple alternations followed by successive daily discrimination reversals, after the schedule of reinforcement suppresses the rewards for both keys there is a reversion to a less extreme preference in extinction, i.e., regression, an apparently spontaneous recovery of an earlier preference.

(b) *successive daily discrimination reversal* - conditions that normally lead to improvement in the rate of acquisition each day. *Fig.*2 shows data from daily discrimination reversal in the two-armed-bandit situation. After two or three reversals pigeons show progressive improvement in performance indicating faster discrimination learning each day.

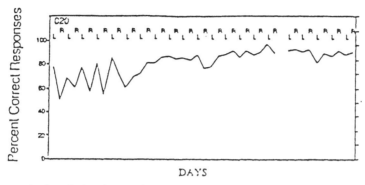

Figure 2: *Improvement in discrimination performance across successive discrimination reversals in pigeons [Data from [2]]. The rewarded response is shown by the staggered letters, R (right), L (left), and so forth.*

(c) *reversal after blocks of N days* - conditions that lead to slower reversal performance after longer training blocks. Pigeons reverse faster after exposure to daily reversals than to reversals in blocks of two or four days.

(d) *partial reinforcement extinction effect (PREE)* - effect observed under experimental conditions which has two main aspects: (i) Subjects trained to respond to infrequent reinforcement stabilize at a performance value, i.e., rate of responding, generally lower than subjects trained with a more frequent reinforcement. (ii) When reinforcement is discontinued (extinction) partially reinforced subjects persist longer in responding than subjects that have been reinforced more frequently, even though they begin extinction responding at a lower rate.

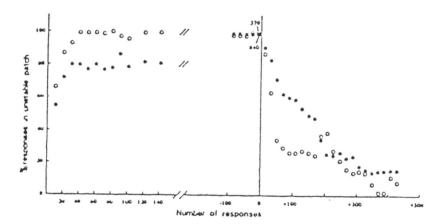

Figure 3: *Partial reinforcement extinction effect - the effects of the concurrent schedules of reinforcement in probabilistic environment are analyzed: the higher the probability of reward the faster the subject will stabilize for the "winner" key; during extinction the switch in preference is more rapid in the 0.75 treatement than in the 0.25 treatement. [Data from [7]].*

*Fig.*3 refers to a PREE experiment, [7], in which a concurrent schedule is run. We can distinguish between two phases: (a) acquisition: reinforcers are provided using a response-based stochastic rule with different reward probabilities for the two keys. The subject is able to figure out the rule of the game in such a way that the higher the probability of reward, the faster the convergence toward stabilizing for the key more frequently reinforced. (b) extinction: the subjects decrease faster the number of responses for the key that has been more frequently reinforced. The actual experiment refers to the effect of varying the probability of reinforcement for the most rewarded key from .75 to .25.

The Competitive Neural Network Model

The model attempts to be a general framework in treating adaptive effects of recurrent choice. Its first version has been used to account for the PREE problem, [5]. It is a time-based neural network which proved to be a powerful tool in trying to offer a unitary view over a large range of experimental situations. The model is sensitive to the whole history of reinforcement training characterizing the subject's overall behavior by means of distinct internal states.

The neural network topology is symmetric with respect to each key (see $fig.4$).

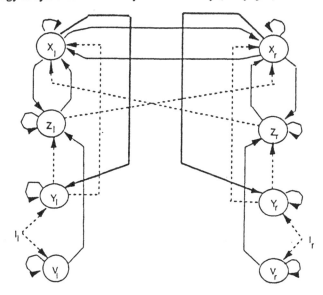

Figure 4: *The diagram of the model: the dashed lines represent excitatory connections whereas the solid lines represent inhibitory connections. The double lines refer to bipolar connections.*

The architecture relies on the competition (mutual inhibition) between the two response units (left and right), X_l and X_r, that compete in order to reach fixation for the most rewarded key. An essential role is played by the "frustration" units, Z_l and Z_r, that compare every moment the short and long-term expectations, Y_l and Y_r. Whenever the long-term effect is more effective than the short-term one, e.g., during extinction, the animal's "frustration" increases determining the decrease in responding for the extinguished key. We can thus imagine the cooperation between short and long-term expectations, V_i and Y_i, that actually supervises the whole process of choice. Another cooperative effect is at the level of the "frustration" units that control the recovery of responses under extinction.

The behavioral mechanism at the level of each key is proposed to be modelled as a four-order nonlinear dependence (see eqns $(1) - (4)$) among the following coupled variables:

- $X_i(t)$ - probability of response for key i, i.e., output unit, where i can be either left or right.
- $Y_i(t)$ - expectation for the coming rewards at the level of key i, i.e., an internal variable designed to estimate dynamically the rule of providing reward, i.e., the probability of reinforcement. This unit is associated to the long-term effect of reward (LT expectation).
- $Z_i(t)$ - "frustration" for not receiving rewards even though the subject activates the key i, i.e., an inhibitory unit which increases its activity only during extinction.
- $I_i(t)$ - reward provided with probability $< I_i >$ for responding the key i.
- V_i - the content of a short-term memory (ST expectation), implemented as a leaky integrator with fixed time constant, associated with short-term reward accumulation (see eqn (4)).
- all X_i, Y_i, Z_i, V_i are neuron-type units satisfying the relation $X = max(\theta, X)$, where θ is a positive threshold (in the present simulations $\theta = 0$).
- $\alpha, \beta, \gamma, \delta, \eta, \epsilon, \phi$ are fixed and small (time scale control).

The LT expectation, Y_i, behaves as a rate constant of X_i's time evolution (see eqn (1)) allowing thus for the response to stabilize faster when Y_i is higher, i.e., key i has been reinforced more frequently. The "frustration" units,

68

Z_i and Z_j, play the prominent role during extinction when they gradually diminish the response strength (see eqns (1), (3)).

$$\frac{dX_i}{dt} + \alpha X_i + \beta Y_i X_i = \beta Y_i - w_{ij} X_j - \gamma(Z_i - Z_j) \tag{1}$$

$$\frac{dY_i}{dt} = (1 - X_i)(I_i - Y_i) \tag{2}$$

$$\frac{dZ_i}{dt} + \delta Z_i + \eta(Y_i - V_i)Z_i = \eta(Y_i - V_i) - \epsilon X_i \tag{3}$$

$$\frac{dV_i}{dt} = (1 - \phi)(I_i - V_i) \tag{4}$$

The process of competition is modulated by the synaptic weights, $w_{ij} = w_{ji}$, that express actually how strong the connection between the two responses is. These weights are updated according to a correlational type rule, i.e.,

$$\Delta w_{ij} = \Delta w_{ji} \sim -min(0, \frac{dX_i}{dt}\frac{dX_j}{dt}) \tag{5}$$

We can observe that the more often the forced transitions $L \to R$ or $R \to L$ occur, the larger the values of the two weights.

The reinforcer, I_i, apply directly to the short and long-term expectation units. Y_i is updated according to eqn (2), where the coming reward, i.e., I_i, is compared to what was in fact expected to come. Since the output X_i varies between 0 and 1, before the stabilization occurs an increased reward sensitivity of the LT expectation unit is expected (see eqn (2)), or, in other words, Y_i will fluctuate. As time goes by and $X_i \to 1$ the variance in LT expectation will be rejected and a stable state reached. This effect might account for the role the experience plays in learning, i.e., the more the subject will be exposed to stimuli, the less the surprise of receiving reward, and consequently the faster the fixation for the corresponding key. Z_i remains inactive during acquisition because of the play between the short and long-term effects, i.e., the term $Y_i - V_i$ in eqn (3). The presence of the difference between the activities of Z_i and Z_j in eqn (1) can account for the phenomena of regression, i.e., spontaneous recovery during extinction (see the next section). The "frustration" units are forced to relax by both the activity of response units and as an effect of their own gradual decay (see eqn (3)).

During extinction, i.e., $I_i = 0$, the ST expectation, V_i, rapidly discharges (see eqn (4)), thus assuring the increase of Z_i, (see $fig.6$). Therefore the "frustration" unit will send more inhibition to the corresponding response unit thus decreasing the probability of the i response (left response in $fig.6$). This drop in response decreases the LT expectation unit's activity according to eqn (2). After Y_i becomes small enough, the relaxation term of eqn (3) decreases toward 0 the state of the "frustration" unit. As a preview, $fig.6$ displays simulation results qualitatively similar to those obtained in experiments, i.e., the longer persistence in responses with the decrease of the probability of reinforcement.

What the Competitive Model Predicts

The proposed model will be evaluated based on a series of experiments, as indicated in the subsections below. We present computer simulations for most of the effects encountered in the experimental situations of section 2. The model uses small values for all free parameters because we think that the adaptive processes characterizing the choice situations should have gradual changes and smooth variations at the level of their internal states in order to describe accurately the whole history of reinforcement training.

Reversal Learning

Suppose that initially both response probabilities are equal, $X_l(0) = X_r(0) = 0.5$, i.e., the subject responds the same amount to both keys. We reinforce the left key for 100 trials (units of time in our model) with probability 1/8 and then change the "hot" key by reinforcing the right responses with the same probability, i.e., 1/8, for another

100 trials, and so forth. This procedure is repeated for several sessions followed by total extinction at both keys to observe regression. The results are shown in $fig.5$. The free parameters have been used with the following values: $\alpha = 0.01, \beta = 0.04, \gamma = 0.055, \delta = 0.01, \epsilon = 0.1, \phi = 0.3$ (these values hold for all the performed simulations).

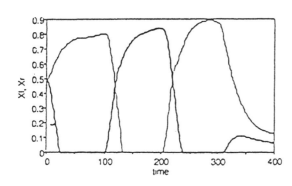 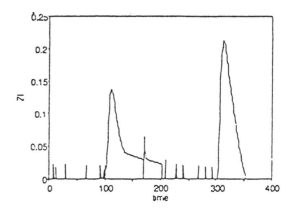

Figure 5: *Simulation results - reversal learning; left: the two response probabilities in a single alternation schedule of reinforcement. Note an improvement in performance (a jump from $X_l = 0.8$ to $X_l = 0.9$) for the left responses. After total extinction a small "bump" of responding for the left key (spontaneous recovery) can be observed; right: the corresponding activity of the "frustration" unit (left) (activated when the corresponding reward is extinguished).*

In order to understand the behavior behind $figs.5 - 6$ let us separate from eqn (1) the variation described by the following equation:

$$\frac{dX_i}{dt} + \beta Y_i X_i = \beta Y_i$$

The typical behavior of such differential equation is to reach the asymptote at 1 (probability 1 for key i means fixation) with a time constant modulated by βY_i. The larger the LT expectation the faster the convergence process. The other remaining members of eqn (1) refer to the set of constraints associated to the choice process, especially the constraints imposed by competition. The term αX_i expresses the gradual self-decay of the response in the absence of any reward. The term $-w_{ij}X_j$ from eqn (1) characterizes the mutual inhibition between responses, being modulated by the frequency of switching between the two keys.

Supposing that only key L receives rewards in time, I_l, the LT expectation gradually increases its activity despite the large fluctuations during the first tens of trials. Following eqn (2), Y_r stays on zero. An increased expectation gives a gradual increase of X_l and, by virtue of the competition, a gradual decrease of X_r which relaxes toward 0 (see eqns $(1) - (2)$). All this time the "frustration" units are not active because the member $Y_l - V_l$ is less than zero (since the subject receives reinforcers the ST expectation is always greater than the LT expectation). In these conditions Z_l tends to decrease up to negative values but the nonlinearity (function max) prevents this from happening and limits the decrease to 0.

After switching the "hot" key (a $L \rightarrow R$ transition), i.e., extinction for key L and $1/8$ probability of reinforcement for key R, V_l will discharge faster than Y_l (see eqn (4)) such that the rate constant of Z_l becomes positive. The more Z_l grows the more the inhibition it sends to X_l, thus driving the response unit to gradually decrease its activity (see $fig.(6)$). As soon as I_r becomes nonzero (the effect of reward), Y_r starts increasing correspondingly. This will determine the increase of X_r on the expense of the decay of X_l (the competition between responses). While X_r is nonzero (but decaying) the response unit inhibits Z_l that finally becomes zero (also due to its own relaxation process). This global behavior is repeated indefinitely as long as reversals continue.

Regression

The competitive model can account for spontaneous recovery. Suppose that right before the onset of extinction of both responses the situation were $X_l = 1, X_r = 0$. Since I_l becomes zero, Z_l gradually increases determining on the one hand the decay of X_l and on the other hand a small bump of activity toward X_r (see eqn (1): the term $Z_l - Z_r$). This pulse of excitation increases for a while the state of the response unit associated to key R, thus accounting for the phenomena of regression, as shown in $fig.6$.

Successive Daily Reversal (SDR)

In order to explain our model's performance in the SDR task we have to investigate whether successive alternations in the reinforcement schedule lead to an improvement in performance, i.e., the speed of reversing the target key. Eqn (1) describes the competition between the two responses via the inhibitory term $-w_{ij}X_j$. According to the update rule the weights will have greater values with the number of exposure trials to reversals. Big weights ease the competition between responses and thus it will take less for the R responses, say, to overcome the L responses (the weights will have a more consistent contribution to the inhibition process) - see also $fig.5$ where a higher level of performance is observed for the left responses after only two sessions.

Reversal in Blocks

The competitive model can explain reversal in blocks in two ways: the more often the subject is exposed to reversals (a) the larger the weights w_{ij} and w_{ji} and consequently (see eqn (1)) the faster the subject reverses the key; and (b) the LT expectation does not have time to stabilize, its average level being less than the situation in which reversals come less frequently (allowing for the expectation to fully charge to the steady state).

Partial Reinforcement Extinction Effect (PREE)

The PREE experiment, [7], is performed on a response-by-response basis. In order to refer to the PREE with our real time dynamical model, it is reasonable to consider that during the experiment the subject can do one out of three activities: responding left, responding right or waiting, for every moment of time. Our model analyzes the effects of the PREE under four different experimental conditions, with the following set of reinforcement probabilities: $P_l = 0.9/P_r = 0.15$; $P_l = 0.75/P_r = 0.3$; $P_l = 0.6/P_r = 0.45$; $P_l = 0.45/P_r = 0.6$, where P_l and P_r represent probabilities of reward for the two responses. The way in which our model fits Kacelnik et al's data, [7], can be estimated from the analysis of $fig.6$.

During the first phase, i.e., acquisition, the rate of convergence for the winner response is proportional to the level of expectation to which the subject stabilizes, i.e., (see eqn (2) and $fig.6$). The expectation stops increasing as soon as the subject pays the whole attention to the "hot" key, i.e., when $X_l = 1$ ($fig.6$). During extinction, the increase of the activity level of the "frustration" units is modulated by the level of LT expectation. The higher the stabilization value of the LT expectation units, the higher the "frustration" level (see eqn (3)) and consequently the more inhibition sent to the response units (see eqn (1)). The effect is a faster decay of the responses with the probability of reward during the acquisition phase. The subject's level of frustration is thus proportional to the rate of extinction (see $fig.6$).

Conclusion

We have discussed a competitive neural network model for characterizing the process of recurrent choice. We have shown that our model provides a good description of relevant individual-animal data from choice discrimination-reversal experiments as well as PREE experiments attempting to give an explanation at the behavioral level.

Three features of the competitive model seem to be critical to the predictions advanced in this paper: dealing with time-by-time dynamics rather than response-by-response dynamics seems to be a good way of looking at choice processes in particular and reinforcement learning in general; the competition between responses offers an elegant method of estimating the time dynamics of the probability of response; each moment the subject compares the short-term expectation to the long-term expectation, thus updating its "frustration" toward the coming events.

Future work will attempt to extend the present network formalism in order to set up a powerful framework for studies in complex choice situations as well as other adaptive effects related to reinforcement learning. Then, a broader interest would be to look for the associated neural structures in order to identify the underlying mechanisms of reinforcement learning in vertebrates.

71

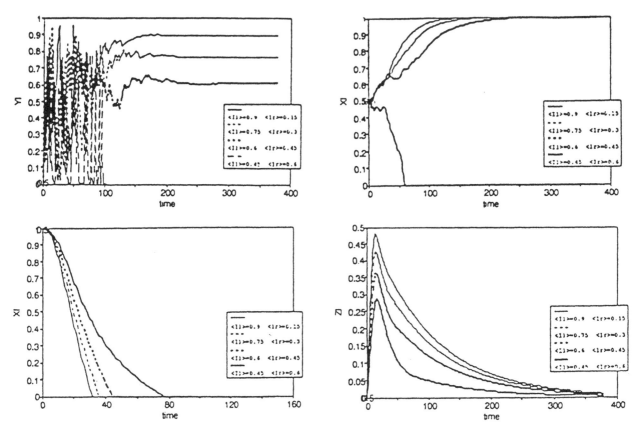

Figure 6: *Simulation results: PREE under different reinforcement conditions; left top: the activity of the expectation unit (left) during acquisition; right top: the activity of the response unit (left) during acquisition; left bottom: the activity of the response unit (left) during extinction; right bottom: the activity of the "frustration" unit (left) during extinction*

Acknowledgements

We are grateful to Terry Sejnowski and Peter Dayan for their valuable comments leading to improvements in the manuscript.

References

[1] R.R. Bush and F. Mosteller, *Stochastic Models for Learning*, New York: Wiley, 1955

[2] D.G.S. Davis and J.E.R. Staddon, "Memory for Reward in Probabilistic Choice: Markovian and non-Markovian Properties", *Behaviour*, 114, pp. 37-64, 1990

[3] D.G.S. Davis, J.E.R. Staddon, A. Machado and R. Palmer, "The Process of Recurrent Choice", *Psychological Review*, 100, No. 2, pp. 320-341, 1993

[4] M. Davison and D. McCarthy, *The Matching Law: A Research Review*, Hillsdale, NJ: Erlbaum, 1988

[5] V. Dragoi and J.E.R. Staddon, "A Neural Network Model for the Partial-Reinforcement Effect", presented at the *Triangle Area Neural Network Society (TANNS) Symposium*, Research Triangle Park, North Carolina, 1993

[6] R.J. Herrnstein, "Relative and Absolute Strength of Response as a Function of Frequency of Reinforcement", *Journal of Experimental Analysis and Behavior*, 4, pp. 267-272, 1981

[7] A. Kacelnik, J.R. Krebs and B. Ens, "Foraging in a Changing Environment: An Experiment with Starlings (Sturnus vulgaris)", in *M.L. Commons, A. Kacelnik & S.J. Shettleworth (Eds.), Quantitative Analyses of Behavior VI: Foraging*, pp. 63-87, Hillsdale, NJ: Erlbaum, 1987

A Neural Network Simulation of Numerical Verbal-to-Arabic Transcoding

A. Margrethe Lindemann
Cognitive Science Department
Johns Hopkins University
Baltimore MD 21218
linde_am@jhuvms.hcf.jhu.edu

Several theories have emerged in the last decade that attempt to explicate the basic cognitive mechanisms underlying human numerical abilities [1-7]. Central to these theories is consideration of the comprehension and production of arabic and verbal numerals. The various explanations differentially implicate semantic and/or asemantic processes in performing basic numerical transcoding (i.e., translating numerals from one form to another, such as arabic *27* to verbal *twenty seven*). Moreover, the various theories also differ in their claims relating to the nature of the internal representations underlying numerical processing in general, and numerical transcoding in particular [8-15].

A MODULAR THEORY OF NUMERICAL PROCESSING

A theory of numerical processing put forth by McCloskey and colleagues [1-2] holds that "numerical transcoding ... is accomplished by a comprehension process that converts the input form into an internal semantic representation, followed by a production process that converts the semantic representation into the output numeral form." ([1], p.119) Moreover, these comprehension and production processes are believed to be functionally independent. As an example, producing an arabic numeral in response to a stimulus in verbal form (e.g., *nine thousand three hundred ten*) is conceived to involve a verbal numeral comprehension process that maps the verbal numeral to an internal semantic representation, followed by an arabic numeral production process that converts the (abstract) semantic representation into a sequence of arabic digit representations (e.g., *9310*).

Lexical and Syntactic Numerical Elements

McCloskey's theory argues that the numeral comprehension and production mechanisms each contain components for processing lexical and syntactic numerical elements. Specifically, "lexical processing involves comprehension or production of the individual elements of a numeral (e.g., the digit *3* or the word *three*), whereas syntactic processing involves processing of relations among elements (e.g., word order) in order to comprehend or produce a numeral as a whole." The theory elaborates the content of the internal semantic representations by hypothesizing that such representations "specify in abstract form the basic quantities in a number, and the power of ten associated with each

73

([1], p.114)."[1] Again, taking the example of the verbal numeral stimulus *nine thousand three hundred ten*, the posited mechanisms of lexical and syntactic processing ultimately assemble from the stimulus:

$$\textit{nine} \, ; \quad \textit{thousand} \, ; \quad \textit{three} \, ; \quad \textit{hundred} \, ; \quad \textit{ten}$$

an internal semantic representation hypothetically specifying:

$$\{9\} \, 10 \, \text{Exp3} \, ; \quad \{3\} \, 10 \, \text{Exp2} \, ; \quad \{1\} \, 10 \, \text{Exp1}$$

which associates the individual quantities {9}, {3} and {1} with their respective powers of ten.

Empirical Evidence from Acquired Dyscalculia

McCloskey's general theoretical claims for the organization of the cognitive mechanisms underlying numerical transcoding processes are largely motivated by empirical data from single-patient studies of brain damaged adults [1-4, 11-13]. McCloskey's view posits independent comprehension and production mechanisms, each with lexical and syntactic processes. Impairment to each mechanism should result in characteristic error types. Thus, in impaired verbal-to-arabic numeral transcoding, errors may be traceable specifically to impairment of the lexical or syntactic processes operating at the verbal comprehension or arabic production stages.

A principal type of transcoding error produced by brain-damaged adults is the lexical error [1-4, 7-15, 18-20]. A lexical error is simply one in which one or more elements within a numeral is substituted with an incorrect element (e.g., a patient might say "*three* thousand eighty *one*" when the correct target response is "five thousand eighty two", or might write the digits 75 instead of the correct response 74). However, syntactic errors have also been identified, with mis-ordered numerals, and deleted or inserted "zero" elements. Syntactic errors may or may not co-occur with lexical errors [1-4, 7-17]. Both lexical and syntactic errors are thought to arise from a variety of possible origins; for example, the hypothetical syntactic errors such as those in Table 1 could result from comprehension or production impairment. Note that these examples are idealized illustrations of some of the less obvious types of syntactic errors documented from brain-damaged individuals [1-4, 7-20]. Typically, more detailed performance data than those simply listed in the table are required to disambiguate which processes are impaired in a given individual.

Table 1: Idealized Syntactic Verbal-to-Arabic Transcoding Errors

nine thousand three hundred ten	*one hundred thirty three*
931	100303
900030010	10033
900310	1303
9301	1033

THE CONNECTIONIST SIMULATIONS

The networks presented here are a preliminary effort to simulate the cognitive processes of numerical transcoding by mapping verbal morphemes to arabic digits in three-layer attractor networks. The attractor paradigm lends itself well to probing the internal representations that emerge through the course of learning. Therefore, one avenue to explore is comparing the network's hidden unit representations with those internal semantic representations claimed in McCloskey's theory. Do the nets develop canonical representations of number quantities, which are associated with canonical representations of the powers of ten? It is also relevant to compare and contrast the performance of normal and impaired nets with normal and brain-damaged humans. Do impaired networks produce errors of the type and frequency that brain-damaged patients make? Similar comparisons may relate the errors and reaction times of intact

---

[1] The cognitive salience of the power of ten is thought to emerge for individuals who, as children, learn base-10 number systems.

nets to normal adults in speeded trials. Such exercises may reveal that those human data which could enable comparative evaluations of these sorts have not yet been obtained. Ultimately, the most productive purpose of comparing simulation performance to theoretical prediction and to empirical data is to judge the merit of the underlying theory or to recommend or even guide its replacement. However, it is inappropriate to wield transcoding networks such as those presented here in assessing the validity of McCloskey's theoretical claims unless the simulation may be defended as a veridical instantiation of the motivating theory.

Representing "Verbal" and "Arabic" Numerals

For the network architectures explored, the input "verbal" representations consisted of 7 fields, each of which might be empty or set to one of up to twenty-two patterns. Each of these patterns was randomly assigned to signify one of the basic morphemes of English verbal number words:

> *zero, one, two, three, four, five, six, seven, eight, nine, ten, eleven*
> *twelve, thir, fif, teen, ty, twen, for, hundred, thousand, (null)*

An assembled verbal numeral input is constructed from the concatenation of these "morphemes". The assembled verbal representations were justified (usually to the left) with respect to the 7 fields (however, experimentation showed that the choice of left or right-justification for verbal or arabic representations did not significantly affect training performance, or results). Fields that were not required were set to "null". Typical corresponding verbal and arabic constructions used for training and/or testing could be:

one null null null null null null	*null null null*	*1*
eleven null null null null null null	*null null 1*	*1*
thir ty nine null null null null	*null null 3*	*9*
three thousand nine hundred thir teen null	*3 9 1*	*3*

The representation of "null" was handled in two different ways. For some networks, the "null" fields were simply empty fields. For these nets, the total activation associated with the composite input or output directly correlated with the number of morphemes or digits making up that input or output. Other networks treated "null" as representationally equivalent to any other verbal morpheme or digit. In this approach, the total activation associated with any complete number did not vary as a function of how many morphemes or digits it included. The general results elaborated below proved to be largely independent of the particular "null" representation implemented in a given network.

Both local and distributed input representations were explored in separate networks. In the local scheme for example, the width of each verbal field equalled the number of morphemes used (e.g., 22). Thus, for a field to signify a verbal numerical morpheme, the unit arbitrarily assigned to that morpheme was activated, while the remaining units were turned off. Local encoding of individual morphemes in a verbal field might look like:

zero	[+ - - - - - - - - - ... - -]
one	[- + - - - - - - - - ... - -]
ten	[- - - - - - - - - + ... - -]

For the distributed representation scheme, each verbal element was represented by a field of 8 units: approximately half of the units were always active, with two of these shared between morphemes. Consider:

five	[+ - - - + - + +]
nine	[- - + + + - + -]
hundred	[+ - + + - - - +]

It should be noted that neither the local nor the distributed representations as implemented thus far capture similarities (i.e., phonological, articulatory, letter identity, visual feature, syllabic, consonant/vowel structure, etc.) which may be shared between morphemes or digits. However, it is certainly the case that morphemes (or syllables) such as *five* and *fif* are more phonologically and orthographically similar than are *five* and *three*. It is also the case that the arabic digits *3* and *8* are more visually similar than are the digits *3* and *1*. A goal for future work will be to enhance the simulations' distributed representations so that they may capture more of the featural similarities and regularities typifying number words (oral or written) and arabic digits. At this preliminary stage of the simulation effort, however, it appears that those aspects of network performance most closely examined thus far (such as error patterns, and gross features extracted at the hidden unit level) are not strongly dependent upon the choice of representation or architecture.

Coding the output arabic digits, while similar conceptually to coding the verbal input morphemes, differed depending upon a network's architecture. These differences are described below.

Architectures

Every verbal-to-arabic transcoding network utilized those input representations just discussed. Each net's input and output units were fully connected via bi-directional, symmetric connections to a single level of hidden units. The numbers of hidden units for the various nets were chosen after some empirical exploration. Typically, however, the number of hidden units required to solve the task was between 15 and 30.

The networks of the "standard" architecture encoded arabic output across 4 positional fields, each of which could be set to a representation of a digit (0-9), or "null". Both local and distributed coding schemes similar to those described for the verbal inputs were implemented for encoding each positional arabic field. Figure 1 illustrates the standard architecture for a verbal-to-arabic transcoding network with distributed input and output representations, and empty null fields.

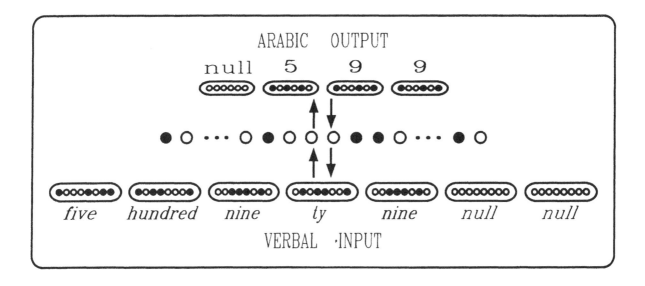

Figure 1: Standard Transcoding Architecture with Distributed Representations and Empty Null Fields

Two additional network architectures were explored on a preliminary basis, and warrant further study. In the first variant, the output consisted of one field only, capable of representing 0-9, or "null". Accordingly, the 7 input verbal morpheme fields were complemented by an additional input context field used to designate that single column of the arabic response the network was to output. The second variant allocated 11 fields for the arabic output, each field representing one of the digits 0-9, or "null". A digit or null field in this architecture comprised local units each representing an output position. For example, a network designed for numbers no larger than the "thousands" would have 4 positional units in each digit and null field. The first and second architectural variants make possible a type of error that cannot be addressed by the standard architecture because these variants do not inherently prevent the assignment of the same output position to more than one digit. Thus the appeal of both of these variants is that they afford the opportunity to produce errors as dramatic in length as the (900030010) example of Table 1.

Training and Testing

The full corpus of training vectors (up to about 300 unique patterns) consisted of: a) the numbers 1-99 (0-99 for some nets); b) the nine numbers *x00*; c) the nine numbers *x000*; d) a subset of the remaining numbers 100-9999. These vectors were selected such that every verbal morpheme, and every arabic digit occupied each possible legal field position an approximately equal number of times. The goal was to provide a minimum number of exemplars while encouraging generalization. For example, a net trained on 1-99, 100, 221, 750, and 3094, ideally should produce "null 1 4 0" when presented with "one hundred for ty" as input even though it may not have been explicitly trained on that pattern. Performance on test sets composed exclusively of patterns on which the nets were not trained was somewhat poorer than training set performance. Networks that had achieved 95-100% accuracy on their training sets, averaged on the test sets 78% accuracy for non-null output fields, but correctly allocated null fields 96% of the time. It was observed, however, that adding more unique patterns to the training corpus appeared to improve generalization.

The network training regimen was not intended to reproduce the exact learning conditions and sequences (order and frequency) that children are thought to experience [15, 21-22]. Some nets were subjected to order and frequency manipulations (earlier and/or more frequent presentation of "small" numbers [e.g., under 100] and more frequent numbers [e.g., *x000*]), however such variations did not significantly affect the primary results.

All nets were trained with the *mean field theory* learning algorithm [23-25], with a simulator developed by McCloskey and associates. Details of the learning algorithm, with explication of the primary parameter settings, are described in [26]. Activation values spanned the range of 0.0 to 1.0. Weights were updated after the random presentation of each training vector. The learning rate typically was initialized to 0.2, and gradually reduced over the course of training. The annealing schedule during settling had 16 steps, starting at a temperature of 30.0. Each subsequent temperature assumed a value equal to 75% of the immediately preceding temperature, with a final temperature step of 0.5. Shortened annealing schedules were used to subject trained nets to time pressure. These were constructed by eliminating steps from the beginning of the normal annealing schedule (i.e., removing steps beginning from that end with the high temperature of 30). Successive temperatures were removed from the normal schedule until each network produced a significant number of errors (typically leaving accuracy at 75-90%).

RESULTS

The various nets were trained until they maintained 95-100% accuracy over 10 test trials. Once training was complete, the nets were subjected to time pressure or to random, asymmetric, or selective damage (manifested as connection weight decrement or addition of noise, or the removal of hidden units or connections). The errors reported below are limited to those committed in response to patterns for which 100% performance had already been established *before* subjecting the fully trained nets to stress of any sort. It is not yet possible to undertake a comprehensive comparison between human performance and the performance of intact and damaged transcoding networks tested under a variety of circumstances because transcoding data are limited, and current theories of numerical transcoding are generally not articulated in enough detail to make clear predictions about error types and distributions.

Lexical Errors

The predominant error type (over 90% of errors) made by most of the stressed nets was the "lexical" substitution error (i.e., one digit appeared in the place of another). Otherwise, nulls were correctly allocated and the correct digits were properly ordered. Lexical errors were always induced by speeded testing, by "non-selective" damage in the form of general linear and non-linear weight decrement, and also by the addition of noise to random subsets of input-to-hidden, and hidden-to-output connections. Some examples from different networks follow (in the form TARGET: *RESPONSE*):

 7: *6;*   62: *82;*   185: *155;*   306: *806;*   3909: *3409*

Of interest is the fact that, if a network erred by making a single-digit substitution at a particular position, it tended to make the same substitution at other positions as well. As an example in this case, a likely multi-digit error made

77

by the net which above produced "**6**" for "**7**" would be producing "**563**" for "**573**". The brain-damaged patient HY reported in [12] evidences similar error patterns.

Syntactic Errors

Far less frequently (less than 10% of errors), the networks also made errors that, with differing degrees of certainty, may be classed as "power-of-ten", or more generally, syntactic errors (see below for some examples). Some of these responses occurred as mixed lexical-and-syntactic errors. Ultimately, a hidden unit analysis must be undertaken to clarify these and other error assignments.

90: *9*;   1101: ***111***;   12: *21*;   3: ***300***;   419: *41*;   56: ***503***

Non-selective network damage and speeded testing generally induced syntactic errors only when overall accuracies were reduced to well below 50% correct. In such cases, virtually all the syntactic errors took the form of mixed lexical-and-syntactic errors. Truly, the nets were very resistant to producing syntactic errors in isolation.

In contrast, syntactic errors not also accompanied by lexical errors were easily induced when connections to certain hidden units identified by a variety of analytical techniques were selectively damaged. For each transcoding network examined, cluster analyses of hidden unit activations, as well as simple inspection allowed the hidden units to be coarsely classified into two groups that either encoded "quantity" information (e.g., a unit in this class might reveal itself as encoding the quantity {6} by being active only in transcoding the numbers 6, 16, 63, 650, 6000, etc.), or what will vaguely be referred to here as "syntactic" information (e.g., a unit in this class might be active in transcoding only those numbers between 100-999). Damaging the connections to one or more of these "syntactic" hidden units in a network produced errors that were reminiscent of the errors illustrated earlier in Table 1 (e.g., producing "**13**" for "**103**", and "**1001**" for "**1100**"). However, the biological plausibility of requiring such selective damage to account for an error type is questionable when victims of brain damage (strokes, etc.) rarely can be said to suffer such specific damage. In fact, cerebrovascular accidents typically cause pervasive damage. Nonetheless, some of these patients produce only syntactic errors.

Some insight may be offered by considering network connection weights. A representative example is presented of a fully trained transcoding network. This network used distributed input and output representations in the "standard" architecture, with empty null fields. A consensus of cluster analyses (using different methods and distance metrics) of that network's hidden unit activation patterns divided the net's 30 hidden units into 2 groups: the "quantity" group containing 16 of the hidden units, with the "syntactic" group containing the remaining 14. Results from a variety of statistical measures indicate that the normalized distributions of weights for the two hidden unit groups differ significantly ($\chi^2(1, N=110)=304.4$, p<0.005; F(32)=179.6, p<0.005). The cumulative weight distributions of the two groups also differ significantly ("quantity" mean: 50.6 vs. "syntax" mean: 51.2, t(110)=3.28, p<0.001). In this network, the "syntactic" hidden units developed the largest-magnitude weights (both positive and negative). On the other hand, weights to the "quantity" hidden units tended to be less extreme and slightly negative. Reducing the magnitude of the strongest inhibitory weights (e.g., those inhibitory weights greater in magnitude than -7.0) indeed induced predominantly syntactic errors. Likewise, reducing the magnitude of only the weakest inhibitory weights (inhibitory weights smaller in magnitude than -0.75) induced only lexical, or quantity errors. In contrast, decrementing the analogous excitatory weight ranges did not result in similarly dissociable errors. The weight distributions therefore may provide a clue about how "biologically plausible" damage could be imposed which effectively impairs one process while sparing another.

CONCLUSIONS

What is repeatedly observed for all nets examined, whether or not they had local or distributed representations, or were order or frequency-manipulated during training, and also irrespective of architecture, is that the verbal-to-arabic transcoding networks differentially encode unitary number quantities, and the ordering of those individual quantities. Such an assessment is made after examining the networks' hidden unit activation patterns, their weights, and the dissociation of error types. To the extent that the networks differentiate quantity information from syntactic information, the simulation results are consistent with theoretical claims that distinct lexical and syntactic processes emerge in numerical transcoding. It is not yet clear how the encoding at the hidden layer mediates syntactic processing, and it remains to be determined whether the networks explicitly encode number quantity and powers of ten strictly and only in the form of McCloskey's posited abstract semantic representations. The scope of the present work is too limited to offer stronger statements in support of or in denial of this or any theory of numerical transcoding. Accordingly, future efforts will expand the current simulations by enabling both verbal and arabic inputs as well as outputs. The verbal and arabic representations themselves will be designed to capture regularities (e.g., visual, phonological, etc.) which are shared between morphemes, and between digits.

The simulation exercise revealed that the motivating theory is not sufficiently articulated with respect to detailed error production to compare theoretical predictions with network performance. It also revealed that more empirical transcoding data must be collected to validate the simulation. It remains to be determined to what extent the simulation results are dependent upon certain parameters (e.g., the cognitive salience of morphemes in verbal representations) about which the motivating theory is silent. While more definite conclusions cannot be offered at this time, the present work illustrates the fruitfulness of an approach to cognitive investigation which embraces data collection, theorizing, and the constrained generation of predictions via simulation.

Acknowledgments

The author is supported under NIMH Graduate Fellowship Training Grant MH18215-07, and by NIH grant NS21047. I am grateful to my editor, Dr. David Plaut, for his careful critique, and constructive suggestions. This paper is stronger, and I am the wiser thanks to Dave's generous guidance. I also wish to thank Dr. Michael McCloskey for providing me a thorough grounding in many aspects of cognitive neuropsychological research, and for thoughtfully reviewing this work.

References

[1]	M. McCloskey, "Cognitive mechanisms in numerical processing: Evidence from acquired dyscalculia," *Cognition*, Vol. 44, pp. 107-157, 1992.

[2]	M. McCloskey, A. Caramazza and A.G. Basili, "Cognitive mechanisms in number processing and calculation: Evidence from dyscalculia," *Brain & Cognition*, Vol. 4, pp. 171-196, 1985.

[3]	S.M. Sokol, M. McCloskey, N.J. Cohen and D. Aliminosa, "Cognitive representations and processes in arithmetic: Inferences from the performance of brain-damaged patients," *J. Exp. Psych.: L,M&C*, Vol. 17, pp. 355-376, 1991.

[4]	M. McCloskey and A. Caramazza, "Cognitive mechanisms in normal and impaired number processing," in G. Deloche & X. Seron (Eds.), *Mathematical Disabilities: A Cognitive Neuropsychological Perspective*, Hillsdale, N.J.: Erlbaum, 1987, pp.201-219.

[5]	J.M. Clark and J.I.D. Campbell, "Integrated versus modular theories of number skills and acalculia," *Brain & Cognition*, Vol. 17, pp.204-239, 1991.

[6]	J.I.D. Campbell and J.M. Clark, "An encoding complex view of cognitive number processing: Comment on McCloskey, Sokol and Goodman (1986)," *J. Exp. Psych.: Gen*, Vol. 117, pp. 204-214, 1988.

[7]	S. Dehaene, "Varieties of numerical abilities," *Cognition*, Vol. 44, pp. 1-42, 1992.

[8]	G. Deloche and X. Seron, "Numerical transcoding: A general production model," In G. Deloche & X. Seron (Eds.), *Mathematical Disabilities: A Cognitive Neuropsychological Perspective*, Hillsdale, N.J.: Erlbaum, 1987, pp.137-170.

[9]	G. Deloche and X. Seron, "From one to 1: An analysis of a transcoding process by means of neuropsychological data," *Cognition*, Vol. 12(2), pp. 119-149, Sep 1982.

[10]   E.G. Gonzalez and P.A. Kolers, "Notational constraints on mental operations," in G. Deloche & X. Seron (Eds.), *Mathematical Disabilities: A Cognitive Neuropsychological Perspective*, Hillsdale, N.J.: Erlbaum, 1987, pp.27-42.

[11]   M. McCloskey, S.M. Sokol, R. Goodman-Schulman and A. Caramazza, "Cognitive representations and processes in number production: Evidence from cases of dyscalculia," In A. Caramazza (Ed.), *Cognitive Neuropsychology and Neurolinguistics: Advances in Models of Cognitive Function and Impairment*, Hillsdale, N.J.: Erlbaum, 1990, pp. 1-32.

[12]   M. McCloskey, S.M. Sokol, and R.A. Goodman, "Cognitive processes in verbal-number production: Inferences from the performance of brain-damaged subjects," *J. Exp. Psych.: Gen.*, Vol. 115, pp. 307-330, 1986.

[13]   S.M. Sokol and M. McCloskey, "Levels of representation in verbal number production," *Appl. Psycholing.*, Vol. 9, pp. 267-281, 1988.

[14]   X. Seron and G. Deloche, "From 2 to two: An analysis of a transcoding process by means of neuropsychological evidence," *J. Psycholing. Res.*, Vol. 13(3), pp. 215-236, May 1984.

[15]   M.P. Noel, "Influence des systemes de notation des nombres sur les mecanisms d'encodage et de traitements numeriques," *Annee Psychologique*, Vol. 91(4), pp. 581-607, Dec 1991.

[16]   M.P. Noel and X. Seron, "Arabic number reading deficit: A single-case study, or When 236 is read [2306] and judged superior to 1258," *Cogn. Neuropsych.*, Vol. 10(4), pp. 317-339, 1993.

[17]   H.D. Singer and A.A. Low, "Acalculia (Henschen): A clinical study," *Archives of Neurol. & Psychiatry*, Vol. 29, pp. 476-498, 1933.

[18]   L. Cohen and S. Dehaene, "Neglect dyslexia for numbers? A case report," *Cogn. Neuropsych.*, Vol. 8, pp. 39-58, 1991.

[19]   C.M. Temple, "Digit dyslexia: A category-specific disorder in development dyscalculia," *Cogn. Neuropsych.*, Vol. 6(1), pp. 93-116, Feb 1989.

[20]   R.A. Weddell, "A dyscalculic patient with selectively impaired processing of the numbers 7, 9, and 0," *Brain & Cognition*, Vol. 17(2), pp. 240-271, Nov 1991.

[21]   R.J. Power and M.F. dal Martello, "The dictation of Italian numerals," *Lang. & Cogn. Processes*, Vol. 5(3), pp. 237-254, 1990.

[22]   X. Seron, and M. Fayol, "Transcoding of numbers by children: A cognitive and cross-linguistic analysis," *Br. J. Develop. Psych.*, (in press).

[23]   C. Peterson and E. Hartman, "Explorations of the mean field theory learning algorithm," *Neural Networks*, Vol. 2, pp. 475-494, 1989.

[24]   C. Peterson and J.R. Anderson, "A mean field theory learning algorithm for neural networks," *Complex Systems*, Vol. 1, pp. 995-1019, 1987.

[25]   G.E. Hinton, "Deterministic Boltzmann learning performs steepest descent in weight-space," *Neural Computation*, Vol. 1, pp.143-150, 1989.

[26]   M. McCloskey and A.M. Lindemann, "Mathnet: Preliminary results from a distributed model of arithmetic fact retrieval," in J.I.D. Campbell (Ed.), *The Nature and Origins of Mathematical Skills*, Amsterdam: Elsevier, 1992, ch. 10, pp. 365-409.

Combining Models of Single-Digit Arithmetic and Magnitude Comparison

Thomas R. Lund
The University of Iowa
Department of Psychology
Iowa City, IA 52242
tlund@umaxc.weeg.uiowa.edu

Elementary school children are usually taught to do single-digit addition problems by repeatedly counting up from one of the two addends. Assuming people actually use this mental algorithm one would predict that the time it would take to solve a simple addition problem would be proportional to the magnitude of the addends. This prediction holds for children, but adults' performance in mental arithmetic shows something less like a counting algorithm and more like memory lookup (see Ashcraft [1] for a review). A similar prediction discrepancy occurs in the task of comparing numbers based on magnitude (i.e. choosing the larger or smaller number). A simple counting algorithm for comparing single digit numbers would predict a linear increase of reaction time as the magnitude of the difference between the two numbers increases. This mental algorithm, again, does not hold for adult performance on the task [15] which shows greater reaction times for small differences and a nonlinear decrease as distance increases.

Because of its obvious educational significance, a great deal of developmental research has addressed childrens' and adults' performance with the basic arithmetic operations such as addition and multiplication. On the other hand, number comparison has been generally overlooked in educational literature. Instead, number comparison has been more closely studied by psychophysicists interested in its similarities with sensory discrimination. Therefore, the literature on arithmetic and number comparison has followed generally nonintersecting paths. Models for each phenomenon have very little in common.

Since models of both arithmetic and number comparison require basic assumptions about how numbers are mentally represented and processed, it would be desirable for models of mental arithmetic were also able to account for number comparison, and vice versa. The present study considers whether representational assumptions used in one class of models of arithmetic skill, Ashcraft's network models, can be used in modeling number comparison.

NETWORK MODELS OF ARITHMETIC

Ashcraft and Stazyk [1],[2] proposed a network model of the development of mental addition that uses a process of spreading activation much like the semantic processing model of Collins and Loftus [6]. In the arithmetic model, a network of nodes was organized in a structure resembling an addition table, as in figure 1. Activation starts in one parent node along each axis of the table; these nodes represent the addends. Activation then spreads to a family of related nodes horizontally and vertically across the table. For example, in figure 1 parent nodes 4 and 7

81

have been activated as in the problem 4+7=11; activation spreads downward from parent node 4 and across from parent node 7. Each node in the selected row and column will receive activation proportional to its connection strength with the parent node; connection strength is a weighting term determined by the frequency of occurrence of various addition errors by grade school students [16]. At the intersection of the row and column of the parents, the proper sum receives activation from both parent nodes, making it the most activated node in the table. The predicted reaction time (RT) to finish an addition problem is negatively proportional to the activation level of the sum.

	1	2	3	4	5	6	7	8	9
1	2	3	4	5	6	7	8	9	10
2	3	4	5	6	7	8	9	10	11
3	4	5	6	7	8	9	10	11	12
4	5	6	7	8	9	10	11	12	13
5	6	7	8	9	10	11	12	13	14
6	7	8	9	10	11	12	13	14	15
7	8	9	10	**11**	12	13	14	15	16
8	9	10	11	12	13	14	15	16	17
9	10	11	12	13	14	15	16	17	18

Figure 1: Architecture of Ashcraft and Stazyk's [2] Network Model of Addition. The example problem, 4 + 7, is highlighted.

The model is equivalent to a linear perceptron with no hidden layers. Two sets of ten parent nodes comprise the input, and a ten by ten matrix comprises the output. The only nonzero input layer to output layer weights are between the top row inputs and the outputs within that input's column; the only nonzero weights between the left column inputs and the outputs are within the corresponding row.

The model also works with verification tasks. In verification, the addends are presented along with a proposed sum. The network proceeds to calculate the sum as above, but simultaneously, all nodes containing the value of the proposed sum are activated as well. The activation of the proposed sum is then added to any activation of that node brought about by spreading activation. If the proposed sum and the activated (calculated) sum are incongruous, then the competition between them increases RT proportional to the ratio between the two numbers' activation levels.

Converging evidence has been gathered in support of this network model of addition. Primarily, Ashcraft's model predicts the increase in response time as the problem size (sum) increases [1],[2], which it was designed to do. Similar success with a multiplication model [17] strongly argues for generalized network models of arithmetic. Further evidence for both models comes from lengthened reaction times in the multiplication modes to reject a false equation where the proposed sum or product is arithmetically related to the addends, such as 3+4=12, 3*4=7, or 8*3=32 [4],[17],[18]. The model explains these phenomena as the effect of competition between false proposed sums and products and computed sums and products: a false sum receiving additional activation either because it is within one of the parent node's family or because it is highly activated by another arithmetic operation association will compete more strongly than a node without additional activation.

Other compelling evidence for network models comes from a study by LeFevre et.al. [10] that specifically tested whether spread of activation from addends to sum was automatic as has been found in semantic memory [6]. They showed subjects a set of two digits, and then simply asked if a third digit was a member of the previous set. When the third digit presented was the sum of the previous two digits, subjects took longer to say no than when the digit was unrelated to the previous set. Since no instruction was given to sum the two numbers (experiment 2), this increase in RT showed that activity did indeed spread automatically.

Evidence of the success of these network models of arithmetic facts encourages one to believe that network representations would be appropriate for numerical comparison as well. I will now describe a network model of digit comparison based on Ashcraft's arithmetic models.

NUMBER COMPARISON

The data that must be described in modeling numerical comparison come from skilled adults' performance on timed comparison tasks. The usual tasks are selection and classification [7]. In selection, the task is to choose the greater (or lesser) of two simultaneously presented numbers, while in classification, members of a sequence of numbers must be individually classified as being greater than or less than a known standard such as 55. The basic dependant measure for numerical comparison is RT in milliseconds.

The most basic result in both selection and classification tasks is the distance effect [14],[7]. This effect refers to the fact that RT decreases nonlinearly as the numerical distance between comparators increases. Specifically, RT in single digit comparisons correlates well with both the so-called Welford function:

$$RT = a \log L - a \log (L-S) + b \qquad (1)$$

[14] and two-digit comparison correlates well with the log difference between comparators:

$$RT = - (c \log |L-S|) + d \qquad (2)$$

[8] where L is the magnitude of the larger digit and S is the magnitude of the smaller digit, and a, b, c, and d are positive constants. Since both of these models were originally used to describe sensory discrimination data, some researchers (eg. [14]) have used the distance effect to argue that adults compare numbers by converting each number into a logarithmic internal analogue and then discriminating the two analogues much like a psychophysical discrimination task.

Although adults may use more than one representation in the processing of numerical information, it would be advantageous to consider a system with only one representation. In order to extend models of either arithmetic or comparison to include the other phenomenon, it would be necessary to either consider analogue models of addition or network models of number comparison.

Miller et. al. [13] tested the viability of each of these modeling combinations. They predicted that with models using analogue representations, both addition and comparison are one-step operations and should be highly related in processing speed. Analogue multiplication, however, would require extra transformation steps and would therefore be less closely related in processing speed. By correlating subjects' RT in solving simple addition, multiplication, and comparison problems, they were able to show a closer relationship in processing speed between addition and multiplication than between addition and comparison. These results argue against using analogue models to unify arithmetic and comparison, but are consistent with using network models like those discussed above.

Given this finding, the next task in unifying models of arithmetic and comparison is to use a network model to simulate the main results of number comparison, especially the distance effect. In the next section, I will present a preliminary version of a network model of numerical comparison based on Ashcraft's model of addition. Included in the discussion are a simulation of the model, an analysis of its strengths and weaknesses, and suggestions for improving its performance.

A NETWORK MODEL OF DIGIT COMPARISON

The proposed model of digit comparison is based on Ashcraft's models of arithmetic. As such, it is composed of a network of nodes organized in a table structure (see figure 2) where the elements in the table represent the greater of two digits in each possible comparison (i.e., choose greater). Activation starts at the two parent nodes representing the digits to be compared and then spreads horizontally and vertically across the table. The amount of activation should be related to the frequency of the individual comparisons, as in Ashcraft's model. In the absence of such information, all connection weights are assumed to be equal to one. The decision mechanism is similar to Ashcraft's, but a few changes must be made. Since the same number nodes appear multiple times in the cells, the decision will be made by summing the activation of equal cells. The decision rule is based on Ashcraft's verification procedure in which the reaction time is proportional to the ratio of the node with more activation to the node with less activation.

	1	2	3	4	5	6	7	8	9
1	1	2	3	4	5	6	7	8	9
2	2	2	3	4	5	6	7	8	9
3	3	3	3	4	5	6	7	8	9
4	4	4	4	4	5	6	7	8	9
5	5	5	5	5	5	6	7	8	9
6	6	6	6	6	6	6	7	8	9
7	7	7	7	7	7	7	7	8	9
8	8	8	8	8	8	8	8	8	9
9	9	9	9	9	9	9	9	9	9

Figure 2. Structure of proposed model of digit comparison (greater than comparisons). The decision is based on the ratio of the summed activations of each digit.

Analysis of the Model

A preliminary version of this model was applied to the selection task, and its predicted RTs are shown in Table 1. Judging from Table 1 we see a distance effect in the proper direction: decreasing RT as distance increases. Close inspection shows this distance effect to be linear.

Table 1: Predicted RT (Arbitrary Units) for Selecting the Greater of Two Digits.

	1	2	3	4	5	6	7	8	9
1	-	-	-	-	-	-	-	-	-
2	50	-	-	-	-	-	-	-	-
3	40	60	-	-	-	-	-	-	-
4	33	50	67	-	-	-	-	-	-
5	29	43	57	71	-	-	-	-	-
6	25	37	50	62	75	-	-	-	-
7	22	33	44	56	67	78	-	-	-
8	20	30	40	50	60	70	80	-	-
9	18	27	36	45	55	64	73	82	-

What is wrong with this preliminary model? It is easy to see from Table 1 and the stated decision rule that the predictions of the model can be completely described by one equation. For greater-than problems,

$$RT = (L+2)/(S+1) \qquad (3)$$

where L is the larger and S the smaller digit. This decision rule could be replaced with a more fitting mathematical model from the literature, such as equations 1 or 2. I consider this option because the ratio decision rule was not routinely used in the model of addition and multiplication.

The fact that the decision rule completely describes the distance effect in this model argues that this model makes no quantitative distance predictions that cannot be changed by changing the decision rule, a weak stand for a model to take. However, the network architecture of the model has supplied a mechanistic framework with which to make other predictions that the psychophysical distance function does not make.

For one thing, this network model assumes that numbers are represented by the activation level of various number nodes. It may be possible to experimentally manipulate these activation values. Perhaps selectively attending to one of two simultaneously presented digits has the effect of increasing the activation of the attended input over the other. This sort of activation would lead to a facilitation of the decision process when the attended input is consistent with the task and a degradation of the decision process when the attended input is incongruent with the task.

For example, if subjects were to choose the greater of two digits presented immediately following an attentional cue indicating the probable location of the greater digit, the cue should facilitate selection RT when it is congruent with the greater digit and retard RT when it is congruent with the lesser digit. A simple pilot experiment has so-far confirmed this hypothesis. In this experiment, the cueing stimulus was an arrow that pointed to the greater of two digits 80% of the time and the lesser digit the other 20%. Using myself and another student as subjects I found that the trials with the congruent cue were indeed completed more quickly than those with the incongruent cue.

Another situation in which selective attention may have an effect on number comparison is in the task of selecting the greater of two digits differing in both size and numerical magnitude. Hinrichs [9] showed that when the physical size discrepancy of the numbers was congruent with their magnitude (i.e. when a large 5 was compared to a small 3), reaction time was facilitated, but incongruence between size and magnitude retarded reaction time. If we assume attention in a choose-greater task is directed toward the digit of greater size, then the network model can account for this effect.

Another prediction of the model is the effect of priming. Priming a number in this model would correspond to partially activating nodes that represent the number. In the model, there are multiple nodes representing the same number; each one of these multiple representations would be activated to some extent. A critical prediction of this scheme is that priming the number 1 would have almost no effect on RT (since that number occurs in the table only once). However, the results from another of my pilot experiments contradicted this prediction. In this experiment, one "priming" number was presented before the comparison and then selection was to occur. The results showed that when the digit 1 was presented first, reaction time was improved considerably. These results make sense given that 1 is almost never the greater of any two single digit comparison. However, the model will need to be changed to account for this adjustment.

Improvements to the Current Model

There are two obvious options for improving the current version of this model. For one thing, the connections that spread activation within the network are currently unweighted. The missing connection weights may account for the model's inability to predict a nonlinear distance effect. Therefore it would be a good idea to define them. As in Ashcraft's arithmetic model, these strengths could be derived from the frequency with which children make errors in the comparison task. Alternatively, these weights could be estimated using an optimization scheme such as gradient descent. Although both of these cases reduce the distance effect prediction to a black box model with many free parameters, having them available would make the other predictions of the model explicit.

Secondly, it would be very advantagous to add a stochastic decision process to the model. In number comparison, random walk decision models have shown enormous power for predicting both RTs and errors [3],[15],[11]. Further evidence in favor of stochasticity comes from arithmetic models. Dallaway [4] successfully used a multi-layer perceptron with cascaded activation functions to model adult error types in multiplication tasks.

85

Similarly, McClosky & Lindeman [12] demonstrated that a model of arithmetic using mean field theory is able to account for reaction time and error data in arithmetic as well as simulating some of the effects of brain lesions.

In conclusion, it does seem possible to use the modeling assumptions of arithmetic theorists in the study of number comparison, though the translation is far from complete. Future models of number comparison should attempt to produce detailed quantitative predictions of the distance effect, and furthermore, empirical research will be needed to rigorously test qualitative predictions suggested by the modeling assumptions.

Acknowledgements

I'm indebted to Gregg Oden, Jim Hinrichs, and John Kruschke for helping me review and edit this chapter, to Peter Meyers for being such a good test subject, and to Gregg Oden and Brad McDowell for production assistance. I'd especially like to thank Mary Zielinski for her moral and aesthetic support.

References

[1] M. Ashcraft, "Childrens' knowledge of simple arithmetic: a developmental model and simulation," in J. Bisanz, C. Brainerd & R. Kail (Eds.), *Formal Methods in Developmental Psychology*, New York:Springer-Verlag, 1987, ch. 9, pp. 302-338.

[2] M. Ashcraft & E. Stazyk, "Mental addition: A test of three verification models," *Memory and Cognition*, vol 9, pp. 185-196, 1981.

[3] B. Buckley. and C. Gillman, "Comparisons of digits and dot patterns," *Journal of Experimental Psychology*, vol. 103, pp. 1131-1136, 1974.

[4] R. Dallaway, "Memory for multiplication facts," in J. Kruschke (Ed.) Proceedings of the Fourteenth Annual Conference of the Cognitive Science Society, Bloomington, IN, 1992, pp. 558-563.

[5] J. Campbell, "Production, verification, and priming of multiplication facts," *Memory and Cognition*, vol 15, pp. 349-364, 1987.

[6] A. Collins and E. Loftus, "A spreading-activation theory of semantic processing," *Psychological Review*, vol. 82, pp. 407-428, 1975.

[7] S. Dehaene, "The psychophysics of numerical comparison: A reexamination of apparently incompatible data," *Perception and Psychophysics*, vol. 46, 557-566, 1989.

[8] J. Hinrichs, "Physical and numerical size in number comparisons," presented at the ? Annual Meeting of the Psychonomic Society, St. Louis, MO, Nov 11-13, 1987.

[9] J. Hinrichs, Yurko, D. and Hu, J., "Two-digit number comparison: Use of place information," *Journal of Experimental Psychology: Human Perception & Performance*, vol. 7, pp. 890-901, 1981.

[10] J. LeFevre, J. Bisanz, and L. Mrkonjic, "Cognitive arithmetic: evidence for obligatory activation of arithmetic facts," *Memory and Cognition*, vol. 16, pp. 45-53, 1988.

[11] S. Link, "Modeling imageless thought: the relative judgment theory of numerical comparisons," *Journal of Mathematical Psychology*, vol. 34, pp. 2-41, 1990.

[12] M. McCloskey, and M. Lindemann, "MATHNET: preliminary results from a distributed model of arithmetic fact retrieval," in J. Campbell (Ed.) *The nature and origins of mathematical skills*, North-Holland:Elsevier Science Publishers B.V., 1992, ch. 10, pp. 365-410.

[13] K. Miller., M. Perlmutter, and D. Keating, "Cognitive arithmetic: comparison of operations," *Journal of Experimental Psychology: Learning, Memory, and Cognition*, vol. 10, pp. 46-60, 1984.

[14] R. Moyer and T. Landauer, "Time required for judgements of numerical inequality," *Nature*, vol. 215, pp. 1519-1520, 1967.

[15] S. Poltrock, "A random walk model of digit comparison," *Journal of Mathematical Psychology*, vol. 33, pp. 131-162, 1989.

[16] R. Seigler and J. Shrager, "Strategy choices in addition and subtraction: How do children know what to do?" in C. Sophian (Ed.), *Origins of cognitive skills*, Hillsdale, NJ:Erlbaum, 1984.

[17] E. Stazyk, M. Ashcraft and M. Hamann, "A network approach to mental multiplication," *Journal of Experimental Psychology: Learning, Memory, and Cognition*, vol. 8, pp. 320-335, 1982.

[18] H. Winkelman and J. Schmidt, "Associative confusions in mental arithmetic. *Journal of Experimental Psychology*, vol 102, pp. 734-736, 1974.

Neural Network Models as Tools for Understanding High-Level Cognition: Developing Paradigms for Cognitive Interpretation of Neural Network Models

Itiel E. Dror
Harvard University
33 Kirkland St.
Cambridge, MA 02138

A framework for using neural network models to study high-level cognition needs to be established. This framework should encompass different paradigms for linking neural networks to cognition. In this paper I suggest four paradigms that should be included in such a framework: 1- Decomposing complex cognitive abilities into their component subsystems; 2- Examining cognitive deficits and normal cognition by exploring lesioned neural networks; 3- Exploring cognitive processing by manipulating the availability of information; and 4- Investigating which principles and properties of information processing give rise to certain cognitive phenomena.

INTRODUCTION

Since the re-introduction of neural networks in the 1980's, numerous models have been proposed for different aspects of high-level cognition. These neural networks vary not only in their technical qualifications, but also in how they are utilized as tools for drawing conclusions about the nature of cognition. Using computer models to draw inferences about cognitive processing is a complicated and delicate task. Although neural network models can potentially serve as tools for making such inferences, neural networks *per se* are not necessarily related to cognitive processing. Their operation may say nothing about the nature of cognition. Indeed, history teaches us that new technologies have been the source for drawing hasty and unsubstantiated conclusions about the nature and mechanisms of cognition. Already several questions and reservations have been raised about the use of neural network models as tools for understanding high-level cognition (e.g., [1]).

With the rapid growth of neural network research, it is important to begin a systematic discussion and overview of the different paradigms for using neural networks as tools for understanding high-level cognition. Establishing a framework that lays out the paradigms for using neural networks to study cognition would guide research within the neural network community. It would constrain neural network researchers in making inferences from a network model to cognition. They would either rely and use this framework or they would try to expand it by carefully justifying a new paradigm for making such inferences. This framework would also enable the neural network community to present a clear research program for studying cognition to the larger scientific community. The discussions on the legitimacy of neural networks as tools for studying high-level cognition would no longer be based on ad-hoc issues and models, but would concentrate on the foundations of its research logic. Furthermore, the process of establishing this framework will provoke important, and hopefully stimulating, discussions on the use of neural networks for studying cognition. This paper is the first step in forming such a framework. It will distinguish between models that encompass different paradigms on how computer neural network models can offer insights into cognition. The paradigms differ in the way they apply cognitive interpretation to the neural network models. This paper only addresses psychologically-motivated models which presume to offer insight into the mechanisms of high-level cognition.

Validation of the neural network model

Before using a neural network model as a tool for learning about cognition, one must first show that the model does simulate the cognitive processes in question. A neural network model needs, first of all, to replicate the experimental data. Usually this is achieved by training the neural network to produce input-output mappings that are similar to those exhibited by human (or animal) subjects. To further validate the performance of the model it is important that the model generalizes and can produce correct output for novel input. Without such validation, there is only a weak indication that the neural network did indeed learn the mechanism to produce the experimental data. The fact that a neural network has learned the training set correctly does not constitute sufficient evidence that it has acquired the mechanism for producing the experimental data. The neural network may have memorized the input-output mapping pairs in the training set. If the neural network is able to produce correct output for novel input, then there is good reason to believe that it produces the experimental data by acquiring the underlying mechanisms. These criteria are minimal requirements that are needed to validate a neural network model.

Beyond the neural network's ability to produce the experimental data that has already been collected, the neural network model may be further validated by examining its predications. Obviously, if the neural network correctly predicts experimental data, further evidence is provided that the neural network does indeed model the underlying cognitive mechanisms. While the above tests examine the performance of the neural network model, additional support for a model may be obtained from its architecture. The model may rely on the neural underpinning for generating guidelines and constraints for constructing the model. However, when dealing with high-level cognition, such links are usually very difficulty to make. The nodes in the neural network do not represent single neurons (plausible neural modeling usually requires an entire neural network to model a single neuron). Linking a neural network model that uses single nodes to represent large population of neurons to its neural underpinnings in the brain is a difficult challenge and must be carefully justified. Nevertheless, making such links is important and it further validates the neural network model.

Making the connection

Once a model has been validated, one can address the following questions: Can a cognitive interpretation be applied to the model, and if so, how? What, if anything, does this model teach us about high-level cognition? What inferences can one make from the model about the nature of cognition?

The above questions are critical for models that strive to understand high-level cognition. These questions, however, may be irrelevant to neural modeling networks (which strive to model mechanisms at the physiological / anatomical level) and to neural network applications (which strive to build computer programs that can perform certain tasks). Although it is beyond the scope of this paper to cover all paradigms for using computer neural network models as tools for understanding cognition, I will try to present four paradigms that seem to have face validity, to be potentially powerful, and are especially interesting. First, the paradigms that will be presented have been used to gain insight to what can clearly be defined as "high-level cognition." Second, although the paradigms have been applied to specific cognitive processes, they seem to capture a basic way of thinking which can be applied to a wide variety of cognitive processes. Third, they seem to rely on solid logical foundations and present valid ways of connecting neural network research to cognition. Fourth, the paradigms that will be presented show how relatively simple networks can be very powerful tools for understanding cognition. The four paradigms that will be presented are:

1. Decomposing complex cognitive abilities into their component subsystems.
2. Examining cognitive deficits and normal cognition by exploring lesioned neural networks.
3. Exploring cognitive processing by manipulating the availability of information.
4. Investigating which principles and properties of information processing give rise to certain cognitive phenomena.

1. TASK DECOMPOSITION

We are always faced with the question of what it means to understand cognition, what counts as an explanation. One of the predominant ways of explaining cognition is to show how a complex ability breaks down into component subsystems. Each component subsystem carries out simple processes of mapping between input and output. Complex cognitive abilities arise when different sets of component subsystems work and interact together. Computer neural network models may be used as an important tool to investigate computationally how complex abilities are decomposed into simpler component subsystems. This decomposition may be achieved by a "split network" technique or by using modular architecture of expert networks, which are discussed below.

Split networks

The "split network" technique examines the effects of decomposing a task by limiting cross-talk in a network. This technique enables researchers to examine whether certain decompositions make sense from a computational viewpoint. Examples of using this technique can be illustrated in the domain of vision. Neuropsychological and neuroanatomical data suggest that the processing of visual images in the brain decomposes into separate processing pathways; one for object properties (e.g., shape and color) and one for spatial properties (e.g., location and size). Rueckl, Cave, and Kosslyn [2] used a neural network to investigate this division computationally.

A neural network was trained to recognize the shape and the location of an image. The network consisted of an input layer of 25 units (representing a 5x5 input matrix), a hidden layer of 18 units, and an output layer of 18 units (9 of the output units indicated the different input shapes, and 9 indicated the different locations). In one version of the model, all of the hidden units were connected to all of the output units; in another version, the neural network was 'split' so some of the hidden units were connected only to the output units that indicated shapes, and the other hidden units were connected only to the output units that indicated locations. Although splitting processing into two distinct streams reduces the overall computational power of the network (eliminating connections by nulling weights), the split network performed much better than the unsplit network. The explanation for this seemingly conflicting finding is that the "what" and "where" functions are computationally distinct. When both functions are computed by the single, undifferentiated system, cross-talk (i.e., interference between two distinct functions) arises and the performance of the network decreases. Thus, a split network technique can be used as a tool for examining whether or not certain processes are computationally distinct.

The split network technique has also been applied to investigate the division of spatial processing into distinct types of spatial judgments [3]. In this case, the neural network model provided evidence that metric spatial judgments (i.e., specific distances, such as 3 inches) are computationally distinct from categorical spatial judgments (i.e., general spatial relations, such as left/right, above/below, and on/off). Additional research (e.g., [4]) suggests that although both processes are carried out in the dorsal visual pathway, the former type of spatial processing is carried out in the right hemisphere, and the latter in the left hemisphere.

The split network technique provides a constructive application of neural networks for understanding how complex abilities are decomposed into component subsystems. However, one needs to further validate the actual performance of the model (as explained in the validation of model section). The performance of the above networks was observed only during training. Thus, there is no indication that the networks did indeed learn the underlying computation for the "what" and "where" functions; the networks may have memorized the mapping pairs in the training set. This weakness can be easily addressed by examining the network's ability to make "what" and "where" judgments on novel input.

Another concern has to do with the logic of the technique; the improved performance of the split network does not necessarily suggests that the "what" and "where" functions are distinct. The observed improvement in the "split network" may stem from numerous factors that are unrelated to the "what" and "where" functions. In order to strengthen the claim that the improvement in performance is due to the distinct properties of the "what" and "where" functions, one needs to use a control network. The construction of the control network is achieved by randomizing the mapping of the original training set. The same input and output vectors are used, however, in the control network, the input-output paired mapping is random (i.e., the input image of a certain shape in a certain location will be mapped randomly to an arbitrary shape in an arbitrary location). If splitting the control network does not enhance performance, then one has demonstrated that splitting the network *per se* does not improve performance. Thus, the specific splitting of the "what" and "where" functions in the non-control network would be the direct cause for the enhanced performance. If, however, splitting the control network, improves performance too, then one cannot claim anything about the "what" and "where" functions. An alternative to using a control network is discussed below.

Expert neural networks

Another technique for decomposing complex cognitive abilities into component subsystems is to use modular architecture of expert networks. Whereas the split network technique examines the computational validity of an assumed decomposition, the modular architecture technique lets the neural network itself perform the actual decomposition.

The modular architecture is achieved through a gating network that modulates expert networks. During training, expert networks compete for learning, in a winner-learn-all fashion. A training pair is given to all the expert networks, and their performance is compared. The expert network which best performs the mapping (has the smallest error term) is allowed to learn (adjust weights). All other expert networks are not allowed to learn this training pair, and they remain unchanged. As training proceeds, the training set is divided among the various expert networks. The division among the different expert networks depends on the underlying functions of the training pairs. If all the training pairs are computed by only one function, then only one expert network will be assigned all the training pairs (this network will learn the function, and will always outperform the rest of the expert networks). If, however, the training pairs are computed by different functions, then each function will be learned by a different expert network. The gating network learns to assign input vectors to the appropriate expert network. Thus, the modular architecture decomposes a task according to the underlying functions of the mapping pairs in the training set.

Jacobs, Jordan, and Barto [5] used a modular architecture to investigate the "what" and "where" tasks used by Rueckl et al. [2]. The modular network decomposed the tasks; it assigned one expert network to compute the "what" task and another network to compute the "where" task. This finding is very elegant because no assumptions on how to decompose the task, and if it should be decomposed at all, were imposed on the network. The network itself, through competitive learning, found that it was computationally efficient to decompose the task into the two functions of "what" and "where".

2. LESIONING NEURAL NETWORK MODELS

Cognitive deficits following brain damage are often used in cognitive psychology as means of exploring normal cognitive processing. Performance deficits of a neural network following controlled lesioning can be an important tool in this line of research.

Lexical processing, as are other cognitive abilities, is comprised of different component subsystems, each of which is dedicated to a particular computation. Reading a word aloud entails the use of the orthographic, semantic, and phonological component subsystems. A visual image of a word is first processed by the orthographic component. Then the semantic and phonological components are invoked, and all components interact together to decode the visual image at all three component subsystems. Hinton and Shallice [6] used this framework to model the process of producing the semantic association to a visually presented word. Then they used this model to investigate the nature of deep dyslexia.

The neural network was first trained to produce correct semantic associations for orthographic input. Then the network was lesioned (adding noise to weights, or deleting weights and nodes). The deficits in the neural network performance following this lesion were similar to those exhibited by patients with deep dyslexia. The network made semantic errors (e.g., dog for cat), and visual errors (e.g., can for cat), as well as mixed errors (e.g., rat for cat). The traditional "Box-and-arrow" models for deep dyslexia require that two different modules be lesioned in order to obtain semantic and visual errors. The lesioning of the neural network model demonstrated that damaging one component can result in both types of errors (for a review of connectionist models for visual word identification, see Rueckl & Dror [7]). Such an approach can be a powerful tool for analyzing and understanding brain deficits. Such insights provide a glimpse into the normal mechanisms of cognition.

A similar approach for using neural network models to account for neurological syndromes, and then applying the results to normal cognitive processes has been used by Mozer and Behrmann [8]. Specifically, they used the MORSEL model (Multiple Object Recognition and Attentional Selection) [9] to investigate the nature of neglect dyslexia, and then applied their findings to processes of selective attention in visuospatial tasks. Patients with visual neglect and neglect dyslexia ignore the left side of space. The experimental data reveals a wide range of behaviors which are puzzling and appear inconsistent. For example, in some cases visual neglect is based on a viewer-centered image (i.e., whether a word is presented in its normal orientation or whether it is rotated 180°, the left side of the retinal frame is neglected [10]). This suggests that neglect occurs at an early stage of processing. However, neglect is more severe in non-words than in words [11], suggesting that neglect occurs at a later stage of processing. Thus, although neglect dyslexia is caused by an impairment to some part of the selective attention system, it is not clear which component subsystems are damaged and how they produce such a wide range of behavioral data.

The MORSEL model seems to provide the appropriate framework to investigate such a disorder because it captures the interaction between different component subsystems. Specifically, the interaction between the attention and associative memory component subsystems enables the use of stored information to guide attention in processing stimuli. The system is comprised of a letter and word recognition component subsystem (the BLIRNET), a selection component subsystem (the Pull-out Network), and an attention component subsystem. The lesioning of MORSEL revealed that damaging the bottom-up connections to the attention component, produces comparable deficits in behavior that are found in patients with neglect dyslexia. Thus, the neural network model suggests how a single deficit can give rise to a wide variety of behavioral impairments. Understanding such deficits reveals the normal mechanisms used in cognitive processing, and hence the strength of the paradigm of lesioning a neural network model as a tool for understanding high-level cognition.

3. AVAILABILITY OF INFORMATION

Understanding an information processing system requires that we know its component subsystems and what they compute. The computations carried out in a component subsystem depend critically on the availability of information to that component subsystem. Because different representations convey different information, the availability of information is determined by the representation of the incoming information. Indeed, the representations used in any model contain implicit assumptions about what information is most relevant for a particular task. Neural networks can be used to examine the importance of specific information and its processing. By systematically manipulating the representations, one can unravel the underlying cognitive processes. Dror, Zagaeski, and Moss [12] used such a technique to examine the cognitive processing involved in sonar shape recognition by bats.

A neural network was trained to recognize three-dimensional shapes, independent of orientation. The network was first trained on a limited set of examples. Then the network's ability to generalize (i.e., correctly identify novel input) was examined. Dror et al. used several networks which only varied in the input representations that they used. Thus, the different networks were required to perform the task based on different input representations. The representations were chosen according to different theories on how bats use sonar. The following representations were used: 1- A time waveform (instantaneous amplitude as a function of time), in accordance with the theory that the bat uses the amplitude envelope of the returning echo for shape recognition (e.g., [13]); 2- A cross-correlation between the emitted sound and returning echoes, in accordance with the theory that the bat operates as an ideal receiver, i.e. that it performs the neural equivalent of cross-correlation of the emitted sounds and the returning echoes (e.g., [14,15]); and 3- A spectrogram generated from the echoes (instantaneous energy within a set of frequency bins as a function of time), in accordance with the theory that the bat uses the time-frequency structure of the echoes to recognize shapes (e.g., [16,17]). Thus, manipulating the input representations enables one to investigate the feasibility of various theories on the nature of cognitive processing of sonar sounds by bats.

The above neural network was not able to recognize shapes in novel orientations when the time waveform and the cross-correlation representations were used. It was able, however, to recognize 90% of the novel echoes when the spectrogram representation was used. Thus, the technique of manipulating the availability of information suggests that the cognitive processing involved in three-dimensional object recognition in sonar is most easily carried out when it is based on spectrogram processing.

One can apply this technique to a wide variety of cognitive phenomena. For example, this technique can be used to better understand the conflicting behavioral evidence on hemispherical differences in visual mental rotation. Several studies on visual mental rotation in the cerebral hemispheres have found a right hemisphere advantage (e.g., [18,19]), but others have found a left hemisphere advantage (e.g., [20]), and still other studies have found no hemispherical differences (e.g., [21,22]). I believe that these conflicting findings are an artifact of the stimuli used, which interacts with general hemispherical differences. There are well established differences in how the two hemispheres process visual images (e.g., the superior temporal gyrus in the right hemisphere processes global features, whereas in the left hemisphere it processes local features [23]). Brown and Kosslyn [24] suggest that the hemispheres differ in attention biases which may be alerted by task demands. Thus, it is possible that both hemispheres perform visual mental rotation equally well, but that the type of stimuli and how it is represented are artifacts that may give advantage to one hemisphere. The technique of manipulating the input representation can be used to explore such a possibility. A neural network model can show that rotation performance critically depends on such factors. The performance of identical neural networks will be examined when different types of stimuli are used and represented in different formats (by right or left hemisphere representation formats). Thus, a neural network model may show that for certain types of stimuli the left hemisphere representation format is more efficient for mental rotation, that for other types of stimuli the right hemisphere representation format is more efficient, and that for some other types of stimuli both representation formats are equally efficient. In the case illustrated above, we can see how this paradigm for using neural networks provides a way for examining cognitive processing and explaining behavioral data which seems inconsistent.

4. PROPERTIES AND PRINCIPLES

Neural network models can be used in order to understand better principles of cognitive processing, as well as specific processing characteristics that give rise to certain cognitive phenomena. McClelland and Rumelhart [25,26] used a neural network model to examine the "phonemic restoration effect" and "word superiority effect." In the phonemic restoration effect a subject can correctly identify a word that has a missing (masked) phoneme [27]. The word superiority effect shows that a letter within a context of a word can be identified faster than a letter that is presented by itself [28].

The model is constructed from three layers of units -- each dealing with a different level of abstraction. The visual input triggers units in the first level. These units represent lower structures, i.e., visual features that make up letters. Each visual feature unit in the first layer is connected to all units in the second layer. The second layer units represent letters. The connections between the two layers are excitatory if the visual feature is part of the letter, and inhibitory if the visual feature is not part of the letter. In addition, there is a within-layer-inhibition. The units in the letter layer are connected to each other by inhibitory connections in a winner-take-all fashion. The model deals only with four-letter words, and therefore each of the first two layers includes four clusters of units. The first cluster deals with the first letter in the word, the second cluster with the second letter, and so on. The units of the third layer represent higher structures, i.e., words. Each letter unit in the first cluster has excitatory connections to all the word units that start with the same letter and inhibitory connections to all the word units that do not start with the same letter. Similarly, the connections of the second, third, and fourth clusters in the letter layer are connected to word units in the third layer. The word units are connected to each other by inhibitory connections. An important feature of the model is that all the connections in the network are reciprocal, and so the activations are interactive.

The interactive nature of this model enables the neural network to correctly identify words, and their constituting letters, even if the presented input is obscured (as in the restoration effect). Similarly, the network identifies a letter in the context of a word faster than a letter that is presented by itself (as in the word superiority effect). In both cases, the activation of visual features in the first layer activates letters in the second layer, which in turn activates words in the third layer. The word that best matches the input has the highest activation. This activation will send inhibitory signals to all the other word units, and excitatory activations back to the letters that form the word (as mentioned earlier, all connections are reciprocal). In the case of an ambiguous letter that was not initially activated by the visual features, the activation of the higher structures will now activate it. In a similar fashion, a letter within a context of a word will receive stronger activation than a letter that is presented by itself because it receives additional activation from the higher structures.

The interactive activation model of context effects in letter perception shows that psychological phenomena arise from interaction and feedback between different component subsystems. Specifically, higher structures are not only facilitated by lower structures, but lower structures are also facilitated by higher structures. These are important general principles of cognitive processing which can be understood better by neural network simulations. The above network also illustrates how a neural network can reveal the processing principles that govern specific cognitive phenomena; in this case the phonemic restoration effect and the word superiority effect. However, in contrast to the three paradigms that were presented earlier, it seems that this paradigm is not sufficiently defined. One needs to define a general class of processing principles that can be examined by this paradigm (feedback and interactivation, and top-down processes are just specific examples of such processing principles). It seems that we want the paradigm to encompass processing characteristics that have a clear cognitive interpretation, i.e., that we understand at a cognitive level what such a processing characteristic means.

CONCLUSIONS

Neural network models have the potential of allowing researchers to make real and valid inferences about the nature of cognition. However, such inferences are hard to make and need to be justified. In many cases neural networks have nothing to do with cognition and should not be linked to cognitive processing. In this paper I suggest that neural networks models can be used as tools for understanding high-level cognition by decomposing tasks into their component subsystems, by observing the deficits of lesioned networks, by examining information processing through manipulating the availability of information, and by studying principles and properties that give rise to certain cognitive phenomena. Establishing such paradigms enables researchers to carefully examine and define the ways neural networks can and ought to (and should not and ought not to) be used as tools for understanding cognition. Such a framework is essential and very needed. The four paradigms suggested in the paper are a first step in this direction. They are not intended to limit the ways neural networks can be linked to cognition. Rather, this is an initial effort in offering a well defined and thought-out framework for making such connections. Additional paradigms are feasible and needed.

Acknowledgments:

This paper was written during my stay at the Neural Information Processing Laboratory, Frontier Research Program, RIKEN, Japan; and supported by NSF Grant INT-9304158 awarded to Itiel E. Dror. I would like to thank Cynthia F. Moss and Catherine Harris for comments on an earlier version of the paper, and Judith M. Dror for proof reading the paper.

References

[1] Massaro, D. W. (1988). Some criticisms of connectionist models of human performance. *Journal of Memory and Language, 27,* 213-234.

[2] Rueckl, J. G., Cave, K. R., & Kosslyn, S. M. (1989). Why are 'what' and 'where' processed by separate cortical visual systems? A computational investigation. *Journal of Cognitive Neuroscience, 2,* 171-186.

[3] Kosslyn, S. M., Chabris, C. F., Marsolek, C. J., & Koenig, O. (1992). Categorical versus coordinate spatial relations: Computational analyses and computer simulations. *Journal of Experimental Psychology: Human Perception and Performance, 18,* 562-577.

[4] Hellige, J. B. & Michimata, C. (1989). Categorization versus distance: Hemispheric differences for processing spatial information. *Memory and Cognition, 17,* 770-776.

[5] Jacobs, R. A., Jordan, M. I., & Barto, A. G. (1991). Task decomposition through competition in a modular connectionist architecture: The what and where vision tasks. *Cognitive Science, 15,* 219-250.

[6] Hinton, G. & Shallice, T. (1991). Lesioning an attractor network: Investigations of acquired dyslexia. *Psychological Review, 98,* 74-95.

[7] Rueckl, J. G. & Dror, I. E. (in press). The effect of orthographic-semantic systematicity on the acquisition of new words. In C. Umilta and M. Moscovitch (Eds.) *Attention and Performance, XV.* Hillsdale, NJ: Erlbaum.

[8] Mozer, M. C. & Behrmann, M. (1990). On the interaction of selective attention and lexical knowledge: A connectionist account of neglect dyslexia. *Journal of Cognitive Neuroscience, 2,* 96-123.

[9] Mozer, M. C. (1991). *The Perception of Multiple Objects: A Connectionist Approach.* Cambridge, MA: MIT Press.

[10] Ellis, A. W., Flude, B., & Young, A. W. (1987). Neglect dyslexia and the early visual processing of letters in words and non-words. *Cognitive Neuropsychology, 4,* 439-464.

[11] Sieroff, E., Pollatsek, A., & Posner, M. I. (1988). Recognition of visual letter strings following injury to the posterior visual spatial attention system. *Cognitive Neuropsychology, 5,* 451-472.

[12] Dror, I. E., Zagaeski, M., & Moss, C. F. (1993). Three-dimensional target recognition via sonar: A neural network model. Harvard University manuscript.

[13] Miller, L. A. & Pedersen, S. B. (1988). Echoes from insects processed using time delayed spectrometry (TDS). In P. E. Nachtigall & P. W. B. Moore (Eds.) *Animal Sonar, Processes and Performance.* New York: Plenum Press.

[14] Simmons, J. A. (1979). Perception of echo phase information in bat sonar. *Science, 204,* 1336-1338.

[15] Simmons, J. A. & Stein, R. A. (1980). Acoustic imaging in bat sonar: Echolocation signals and the evolution of echolocation. *Journal of Comparative Physiology, 135,* 61-84.

[16] Habersetzer, J. & Vogler, B. (1983). Discrimination of surface structured targets by the echolocating bat *Myotis myotis* during flight. *Journal of Comparative Physiology, 152,* 275-282.

[17] Schmidt, S. (1992). Perception of structured phantom targets in the echolocating bat, *Megaderma lyra. Journal of Acoustical Society of America, 91,* 2203-2223.

[18] Corballis, M. C. & Sergent, J. (1989). Mental rotation in a commissurotomized subject. *Neuropsychologia, 27,* 585-597.

[19] Ditunno, P. L. & Mann, V. A. (1990). Right hemisphere specialization for mental rotation in normals and brain damaged subjects. *Cortex, 26,* 177-188.

[20] Fischer, S. C. & Pellegrino, J. W. (1988). Hemisphere differences for components of mental rotation. *Brain and Cognition, 7,* 1-15.

[21] Jones, B. & Anuza, T. (1982). Effects of sex, handedness, stimulus and visual field on "mental rotation". *Cortex, 18,* 501-514.

[22] Van Strien, J. W. & Bouma, A. (1990). Mental rotation of laterally presented random shapes in males and females. *Brain and Cognition, 12,* 297-303.

[23] Robertson, L. & Lamb, M. (1991). Neuropsychological contributions to theories of part / whole organization. *Cognitive Psychology, 23,* 299-330.

[24] Brown, H. D. & Kosslyn, S. M. (1993). Cerebral lateralization. *Current Opinion in Neurobiology, 3,* 183-186.

[25] McClelland, J. L. & Rumelhart, D. E. (1981). An interactive activation model of context effects in letter perception: Part 1. An account of basic findings. *Psychological Review, 88,* 375-407.

[26] Rumelhart, D. E. & McClelland, J. L. (1982). An interactive activation model of context effects in letter perception: Part 2. The contextual enhancement effect and some tests and extensions of the model. *Psychological Review, 89,* 60-94.

[27] Warren, R. M. (1970). Perceptual restoration of missing speech sounds. *Science, 167*, 393-395.

[28] Reicher, G. M. (1969). Perceptual recognition as a function of meaningfulness of stimulus material. *Journal of Experimental Psychology, 81*, 275-280.

LANGUAGE

Modeling Language as Sensorimotor Coordination

F. James Eisenhart
Artificial Intelligence Programs
The University of Georgia
jeisen@ai.uga.edu

Some theorists claim that language is produced by a special rule-processing module located in the association areas of the human neocortex. However, anthropological, neural, and comparative evidence suggest that language is produced by general sensory and motor mechanisms that are common to all mammals. On this view, the prior evolution of advanced cognition preadapted general sensory and motor mechanisms for language. This paper presents a connectionist language model that is consistent with this hypothesis. The model uses general sensory and motor mechanisms to understand and produce English sentences. By doing so, it supports the idea that it is not necessary to postulate an unprecedented new brain adaptation like a special rule-processing module in order to explain language.

1. INTRODUCTION

How does the human brain produce language? There are at least two views on this subject. The first comes from linguistics, rationalist philosophy, and artificial intelligence. It asserts that the brain produces language by processing the same sort of grammatical rules that linguists use to describe syntax. This is done by what Chomsky [1] calls a "language organ". He claims that just as the heart is a separate blood-pumping module that operates on different principles from the lungs, the language organ is a separate cognitive module that operates on different principles from the rest of the brain. Thus, the way to understand how language works is not to compare it to other brain systems; it is to look at its observable behavior. The observable behavior of language is rule-processing, so it is reasonable to hypothesize that the language organ works by rule-processing as well.

A second, opposing view of language comes from biology, neuroscience, and anthropology. It stresses that hypothesized neural mechanisms for language should be consistent with what we already know about brain function and cognitive evolution. One of the things we know is that full-blown language is a recent phenomenon, not more than 200,000 years old [2]. Advanced cognition is much older because *Homo erectus* was already making stone tools, hunting in groups, using fire, and building shelters 1.5 million years ago [3]. This implies that the evolution of language may have depended on the prior existence of a rich cognitive structure. One way that this might have happened is if cognition made it possible for evolution to co-opt existing neural mechanisms to produce language. This sort of co-opting is called *preadaptation*: a structure or function that originally served one purpose is recruited for a new one. For example, the lungs evolved from the swim bladders of fish through a process of preadaptation. In the case of language, the likely preadapted neural mechanisms are those for sensory perception and motor action [4,2]. These are the most basic functions of any nervous system because an organism must be able to sense relevant changes in its environment and make appropriate motor responses in order to survive. They are related to language in that language includes both a sensory component (speech comprehension) and a motor

97

component (speech production). This suggests that general sensory and motor mechanisms may have been preadapted for language by the evolution of advanced cognition. I will call this idea the *sensorimotor preadaptation hypothesis*.

In this paper, I present a connectionist language model that is consistent with the sensorimotor preadaptation hypothesis. My purpose is to show that basic connectionist principles of association can explain, at least in part, how general sensory and motor mechanisms could have evolved into language. The idea underlying the model is that language has two parts: a cognitive part and a sensorimotor part (see figure 1). The cognitive part is descended from the advanced cognitive apparatus that existed before language. It is assumed to be heavily dependent on vision, since visual areas occupy over half of the primate neocortex [5]. The model assumes that the cognitive part exists, but it does not try to explain how it works. Instead, the model represents cognition abstractly by using thematic role/filler pairs [6] like Agent=*cat* and Action=*meow* as stand-ins for the actual high-level representations used by the brain. The idea is that Agent=*cat* corresponds to the brain having a neural picture of a cat, real or imagined, in some higher-order visual area.

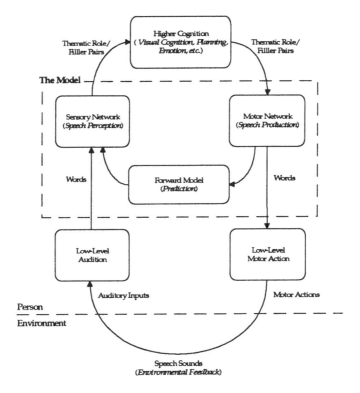

Figure 1: A schematic diagram of the model. The model includes three components (in dashed box): a sensory network, a motor network, and a forward model. The function of each is indicated in italics. Other components are hypothesized brain structures not explicitly modeled.

The model uses these cognitive role/filler pairs to explain the sensorimotor part of language. The purpose of this part is to link cognition to a set of prelinguistic sensory and motor mechanisms. This linking function is performed by three neural networks. The first is a sensory network that translates language inputs into a high-level cognitive representation. Its takes a sequence of words as its input, and it produces a set of thematic role/filler pairs and surface features as its output. The second is a motor network that translates a high-level cognitive representation into language outputs. It takes a set of thematic role/filler pairs and surface features as its input, and it produces a sequence of motor actions representing words as its output. Finally, the third network is what Jordan and Rumelhart [7] call a forward model. Its purpose is to predict the sensory consequences of motor actions. The input to the forward model is a set of motor actions from the output of the motor network, and its output is a prediction of the sensory consequences of those actions. As will be discussed below, these predictions are used in motor learning.

98

2. EMPIRICAL EVIDENCE

The model presented here depends on the idea that language is produced by general sensory and motor mechanisms rather than a special-purpose language module. What evidence is there that this is correct? First, we know that sensory and motor processing are the primary functions of the neocortex, even in humans. At one time, it was thought that humans and other advanced mammals have larger neocortices because they have larger polymodal association areas between their primary sensory and motor areas. It is now known that this is false. Carnivores and primates do have more cortex between their primary and sensory motor areas than primitive mammals like hedgehogs and rodents, but it now appears that this extra cortex is taken up by larger and more numerous unimodal sensory and motor areas rather than larger association areas [5,8]. Phylogenic trends, anatomical comparisons using fixed tissue, and PET studies suggest that this is true for humans as well [5]. Accordingly, it seems that human cognitive evolution did not proceed primarily through the introduction of new cognitive modules located in the association areas, as Chomsky [1] suggests. Instead, human cognitive advances seem to have been driven by elaborations of existing sensory and motor mechanisms.

Second, the neocortex has a relatively constant local organization, which suggests that all areas share a common mode of processing. The six layers of the neocortex vary in thickness between sensory and motor areas, and each area has its own pattern of connections to other areas. However, the basic circuit, in terms of cell types and the pattern of connections between layers, is similar throughout all neocortical areas [9]. This is probably because new areas evolved through the duplication of genes for existing ones [10]. Subsequent functional modifications have no doubt changed the computational properties of local circuits, but it is unlikely that the new areas have developed a novel style of computation like grammatical rule-processing. Instead, all areas of the neocortex probably share a common mode of processing, which evolution has fine-tuned to perform particular functions. Consequently, information processing in specialized language areas is probably a lot like that in known unimodal sensory and motor areas.

Third, the rules of language seem too flexible to be accounted for by a special-purpose language module. Selective pressures limit the scope of any new evolutionary adaptation because as adaptations become more complex they are increasingly likely to fail. This suggests that a special-purpose language module would have a limited, fixed set of rules. However, not only do different languages have different sets of rules, the study of American Sign Language (ASL) has shown that these rules are not even confined to the usual auditory-vocal modality combination. ASL has all of the complexity of spoken language, structured in a way that reflects its visuospatial orientation [11]. For example, the syntax of ASL is spatial rather than temporal. Signs are related to each other by their location in space rather than the order in which they are presented. Nominals can be associated with a particular spatial location, and modifiers applied to that location. This evidence is incompatible with theories like Chomsky's which postulate a special rule-based language processing center in the brain. Such a center would surely be specialized for temporal auditory-vocal rules, so it would be unable to handle the non-temporal syntax of ASL. On the other hand, if language is based on general sensory and motor mechanisms, then ASL's visuospatial orientation would naturally produce non-temporal rules.

3. ARCHITECTURE

In the model presented here, the sensory and motor mechanisms presumed to be responsible for language are represented by three connectionist networks. The sensory network uses a modified version of Jordan's recurrent architecture [12], shown in figure 2. Each unit in the input layer represents a word, and each unit in the output layer represents either a thematic role/filler pair or a surface feature/value pair. The network architecture differs from Jordan's in two ways. First, it uses separate state layers for the hidden and output units. This keeps the contextual information in the hidden layer separate from the semantic information in the output layer, helping the network learn more efficiently. Second, it adds a set of direct connections between the input and output layers. These help the network learn simple relationships between words and meanings quickly. For example, the word *cat* might mean Agent=*cat* or Theme=*cat*, but it cannot mean Action=*meow*. Using direct connections between the input unit for word *cat* and the output units for Agent=*cat* and Theme=*cat* cuts down on the number of word interpretations that the network has to consider. This frees up the hidden units to process contextual information.

The sensory network has 29 input units and 45 output units. The input units represent all of the possible words in a sentence (see table 1). There is one input unit for each possible word. The output units represent all of the

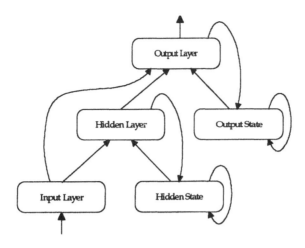

Figure 2: The sensory and motor networks use a modified version of Jordan's [12] recurrent network architecture.

legal thematic role/filler and surface feature/value combinations (see table 2). There is one output unit for each thematic role/filler pair or surface feature/value pair shown in the table. The thematic roles have their usual meanings, after Parsons [13]. There are only three surface features because those are enough to distinguish between the alternative surface forms for any semantic event. The Voice surface feature refers to whether a sentence is active or passive voice (e.g. *the cat chased the dog* or *the dog was chased by the cat*). The Prep1 and Prep2 features identify the first and second prepositions in a sentence. For example, the sentence *the thief was hit by the waitress with the purse* would have Prep1=*by* and Prep2=*with*. In a sentence with only one prepositional phrase, Prep2 is not instantiated, and in a sentence with no prepositional phrases, neither Prep1 nor Prep2 is instantiated.

Table 1: Words used in the model.

Nouns			Verbs			Prepositions	Miscellaneous
billy club	fist	mouse	barked	hit	seen	by	the
bone	mouse	thief	chased	kissed	taken	from	was
cat	policeman	waitress	gave	meowed	took	to	
dog	purse		given	saw	talked	with	

The motor network uses the same recurrent network architecture as the sensory network, but the roles of the input and output layers are reversed. In the motor network, the 45 input units represent the possible thematic role/filler and surface feature/value pairs, and the 29 output units represent the possible words in a sentence. The role/filler and surface feature/value pairs and the words are the same as those for the sensory network.

The forward model predicts the sensory consequences (the input to the sensory network) of a speech action (the output of the motor network). Since the sensory inputs and motor outputs use the same word representation, the forward model only has to learn an identity mapping, so a two-layer feedforward network will suffice. Each layer has 29 units. The input layer is just the output layer from the motor network. This means that every time the motor network produces a command to 'say' some word, the forward model uses the same command to predict the sensory consequences. The output layer of the forward model has the same unit layout as the input layer of the sensory network, but the two are physically separate. Consequently, the output of the forward model can be compared to the input of the sensory network to see if the forward model is making the right prediction.

Table 2: Thematic role/filler and surface feature/value pairs used in the model.

Thematic Roles								Surface Features		
Action		Agent	Theme		Source	Goal	Instrument	Voice	Prep1	Prep2
bark	meow	cat	bone	policeman	cat	cat	billy club	active	by	by
chase	see	dog	cat	ring	dog	dog	fist	passive	from	from
give	take	policeman	dog	thief	policeman	policeman	purse		to	to
hit	talk	thief	mouse	waitress	thief	thief			with	with

100

4. PROCESSING

Processing in both the sensory and motor networks involves a transformation between a temporal representation and a spatial one. The temporal representation is of the sequence of words in a sentence. In both the input layer of the sensory network and the output layer of the motor network, units represent individual words. A sentence is represented by a sequence of single word activations. For example, the sentence *the cat meowed* is represented by the sequence of unit activations shown in table 3. Each row shows the unit activations for one time-step. On each time-step, only one word is active—the word whose position in the sentence matches the time-step number. For instance, the third word of the example sentence (*meowed*) is active at time 3. In both the sensory and motor networks, processing continues for as many time-steps as there are words in the sentence.

Table 3: The temporal representation of the sentence *the cat meowed*. (Not all units are shown.)

Time	Word Unit										
	the	*cat*	*dog*	*thief*	*purse*	*ring*	*chased*	*hit*	*meowed*	*by*	*was*
1	1	0	0	0	0	0	0	0	0	0	0
2	0	1	0	0	0	0	0	0	0	0	0
3	0	0	0	0	0	0	0	0	1	0	0

The spatial representation used by the sensory and motor networks is of the semantic event and surface features for a sentence. In both the output layer of the sensory network and the input layer of the motor network, units represent individual thematic role/filler and surface feature/value pairs. A semantic event and a surface form for a sentence are represented by activating all of the appropriate units at the same time. For example, the semantic event and surface features for the sentence *the thief was kissed by the dog* are represented by the pattern of activations shown in table 4. The sensory network has to produce this spatial pattern from the temporal representation of the corresponding sentence, and the motor network has to use this spatial pattern to produce the temporal representation for the same sentence.

Table 4: The spatial representation of the thematic role/filler and surface feature/value pairs for the sentence *the thief was kissed by the dog*. (Not all units are shown.)

Agent			Action			Theme			Voice		Prep1	
cat	*dog*	*thief*	*bark*	*kiss*	*give*	*cat*	*dog*	*thief*	*active*	*passive*	*by*	*to*
0	1	0	0	1	0	0	0	1	0	1	1	0

Processing in the sensory network simulates what happens when a person hears a sentence. The input to the sensory network is a time-varying pattern of activations representing a sentence, like the one in table 3. In response, the sensory network turns on each thematic role/filler and surface feature/value pair as its key word appears in the sentence. A key word is one that identifies a particular filler or value. The key word for the Action role is always the verb. For example, in the sentence *the thief was kissed the by the dog*, Action=*kiss* is activated at time 4, when *kissed* appears in the sentence. The key word for the other thematic roles is always the noun from the corresponding noun phrase. In the proceeding example, the key word for the Theme is *thief*, so the network should activate Theme=*thief* at time 2. Processing continues for as many time-steps as there are words in the input sentence. On each time-step, activation flows through the layers of the recurrent network as shown by the arrows in figure 2. The hidden and output units are activated according to the standard logistic function. At time $t+1$, each state unit is activated according to the function $activation(t+1) = activation(t) \cdot decay + reccurrent\_input(t)$ where *decay* is a parameter between 0 and 1 that determines the rate at which the memory trace dies out, and *recurrent_input* is the activation of the state unit's hidden or output unit. The *decay* is 0.0 for the hidden state units and 0.6 for the output state units.

Processing in the motor network simulates what happens when a person has an idea and produces a sentence that expresses it. The input to the motor network is a semantic event, representing the idea, and a set of surface features, representing the surface form that the person wants to use, as in table 4. Each thematic role/filler pair in

101

the semantic event and each surface feature/value pair in the surface form is clamped on at time 1. The network then runs for as many time-steps as it takes to complete the sentence. The output of the motor network is a sequence of motor actions that produces the sentence, as in table 3. Processing follows the same rules as in the sensory network, but *decay* is 0.0 for both the hidden and output state units.

Processing in the forward model uses the motor actions from the speech production system to predict the sensory consequences heard by the speech comprehension system. The input to the forward model is a word produced by the motor network . The forward model then activates its own output unit for the same word. This unit should have the same position in the output layer of the forward model as the corresponding word unit does in the input layer of the sensory network. For example, on time-step 5 of the sentence *the waitress gave the cat the mouse* the motor network produces the word *cat*. This might be, leaving out some units, represented by the motor output vector <1,0,0,0,0>. If this motor command is executed and the person says the word, the sensory network will hear the word *cat* through feedback from the environment. This might be represented by the sensory input vector <0,1,0,0,0>. The forward model takes the motor output vector <1,0,0,0,0> as its input, and it produces the vector <0,1,0,0,0> as its output. In this way, it predicts the sensory consequences of a motor action. Because this function is so simple, the forward model uses linear output units.

5. LEARNING

The computer model learns in two stages: a babbling stage and an imitation stage. The babbling stage is like the period that children go through when they talk a lot but do not actually produce any words. The computer model uses this stage to train its sensory network and forward model. The sensory network is trained when the computer model hears a sentence. It learns by forming an association between this sentence and the semantic context in which it occurs. The forward model is trained when the computer model babbles. It learns by associating the motor actions that produced the babble with the sensory consequences that the babble generates.

The imitation stage begins once the sensory network and the forward model are trained. This stage is like the ones that children go through once they are able to form actual words. The motor network learns during this stage by imitating sentences that the computer model hears. The computer model does not actually say a sentence when the motor network imitates it; instead, the computer model feeds the motor output for the sentence through the forward model to predict what it would have sounded like. This prediction is then compared to the sentence that the sensory network actually heard, and the difference between the two is used to correct any mistakes made by the motor network.

The sensory network uses standard backpropagation to learn to translate sentences into semantic events and surface features. During training, each word in a sentence is presented to the network sequentially. On each time-step, the target vector includes those role/filler pairs and surface features whose key words have already appeared in the sentence. For example, the target vector for *the policeman talked to the waitress* would include Agent=*policeman* beginning at time 2 and Action=*talk* and Voice=*active* beginning at time 3.

The forward model uses backpropagation to learn to associate motor actions with their sensory consequences. On each learning trial, a babble is generated by assigning a random value between 0 and 1 to each motor output unit. This babble is then converted into a set of sensory consequences. Since the motor output units and sensory input units use the same word representation, the sensory consequences are identical to the motor babble. The forward model is then trained using these sensory consequences as the target vector. Each weight is restricted to the range from -1.0 to +1.0 to keep the weights from growing unreasonably large, as weights into linear units are prone to do.

The motor network is trained during the imitation stage, after the sensory network and forward model have been trained. The learning situation is that a child hears a sentence that refers to the current semantic event, and he silently imitates that sentence. The input to the motor network comes from two sources. First, the child gets the semantic event from the current visual scene. This is a non-temporal signal because all of the elements of the visual scene are present at the same time. Second, the child gets the surface features for the sentence from the output of the sensory network. This should be a temporal signal because the sensory network activates each surface feature/value pair as its key word appears in the sentence; however, all of the correct surface features were clamped on beginning at time 1 to improve learning. This was necessary because current methods for training connectionist networks to produce sequential output turned out to be inadequate for this task.

Using this non-sequential input, the motor network is trained to produce the appropriate word of the sentence on each time-step. Its target is the pattern of activations across the input units of the sensory network. This pattern represents the sensory impression formed by hearing the current word of the sentence. This target is used to train the motor network by a process called distal supervised learning [7]. First, the motor network tries to produce the current word of the sentence. Then, rather than being executed, the motor actions for this word are fed through the forward model. The output of the forward model is its prediction of what the word would actually sound like if it were said. This prediction is then compared to the actual sensory impression (the target) to compute the error. Finally, this error is backpropagated through the forward model, without changing its weights, to calculate the error for each motor output unit, and the weights in the motor network are modified using standard backpropagation. The equations for distal supervised learning are the same as those for standard backpropagation, except that the motor output units are treated like hidden units because they feed into the forward model.

6. RESULTS AND DISCUSSION

The model was trained on a corpus of English sentences generated by a unification-based grammar from semantic events in a script. The corpus included both active and passive voice sentences and sentences with variable prepositional phrase order (e.g., *the thief was hit by the waitress with the purse* and *the thief was hit with the purse by the waitress*). The grammar generated 395 sentences from a script containing 167 events. Of the 395 sentences, 20 were selected randomly and set aside in a test corpus that was not used for training. The remaining 375 sentences constituted the training corpus. The model was then trained in two stages, as described in section 5.

The sensory network was trained for 150 epochs. Longer training runs were tried, but they did not improve its performance. Each epoch consisted of a single pass through the entire training corpus in a random order. Duplicate presentations were allowed, so a sentence might be presented twice on one epoch and not at all on another. The network's performance was evaluated by counting the number of output errors that it made on each corpus. An output error was defined to be an output unit activation of either less than 0.7 for a unit that should be on or greater than 0.3 for a unit that should be off. This corresponds to a mistake in instantiating either a thematic role/filler unit or a surface feature/value unit. Errors were measured after the last time-step in each sentence, and the total number of errors was counted for each training epoch. Then the total number of errors for each corpus was normalized by dividing by the total number of instantiations in all of the sentences in the corpus. For example, the sentence *the waitress kissed the cat* has four instantiations: Agent=*waitress*, Action=*kiss*, Theme=*cat*, and Voice=*active*, so it would contribute four instantiations to the total for its corpus. This normalized score is referred to as the error ratio.

On the training epoch with the lowest RMS error (0.0214 on epoch 60) the sensory network had an error ratio of 0.4% for the training corpus and 1.9% for the test corpus. This means that it is instantiating over 99% of the thematic role/filler and surface feature/value pairs correctly on the training corpus and over 98% on the test corpus. This is very good performance, although probably not as good as that achieved by human listeners. The primary reason that the sensory network performs so well is that it is able to correct its mistakes as a sentence progresses. For example, when it hears *the cat chased the dog* it cannot say what role the cat will fill at time 2, when it has only heard *the cat*. The cat might be the Agent, as in this example, or it might be the Theme, as in *the cat was chased by the dog*. What the sensory network does, however, is activate both Agent=*cat* and Theme=*cat* weakly at time 2, then correct itself at time 3 when the word *chased* tells it that *cat* should be the Agent.

The forward model was trained until it produced an RMS error of less than 1.0×10^{-6}, which is essentially perfect performance. This took 670 epochs, where an epoch is a single presentation of a one-word babble. The forward model was able to achieve such a high level of performance because the task that it had to learn (an identity mapping) was so simple.

The motor network was trained in the same way as the sensory network, and output errors were recorded for each corpus using the same cutoffs. Here an output error corresponds to a mistake in producing a word. For example, if the motor network produced the sentence *the thief talked to the cat* when the target was *the thief talked to the waitress*, that would be one output error. Output errors were counted after each time-step in a sentence. Then the total number of errors for each corpus was normalized by dividing by the total number of words in all of the sentences in the corpus.

On the training epoch with the lowest RMS error (0.0398 on epoch 60) the motor network had an error ratio of 4.7% for the training corpus and 6.4% for the test corpus. This is not particularly good performance. It means that the network was producing an incorrect word almost 5% of the time on the training corpus and over 6% of the time on the test corpus. The primary difficulty is that the network has trouble activating the appropriate noun for each noun phrase. For example, when the network should produce *the thief hit the dog with the purse*, it fails to activate any word strongly on time 5, when it should produce *dog*. Sometimes the network also activates a second noun weakly when it activates the correct one. These errors may occur because the *decay* parameter values used (0.0 for both the hidden and output state layers) do not give the network a long enough memory. Such problems may be resolved in the future by adopting a more powerful recurrent network architecture that allows a variable-length memory, for instance de Vries and Principe's gamma model [14].

7. CONCLUSION

This paper has shown how a neurally-inspired model based on sensory and motor processing can perform some basic aspects of language processing. By doing so, it attempts to bridge the formidable gap between top-down theories of cognition based on biologically implausible mechanisms like rule-processing and bottom-up theories of neural computation that do not address cognitive issues at all. Obviously this model is only a start. As more detailed information about cognitive processing in the brain becomes available from new techniques like functional MRI, it should be possible to make better models that relate language processing to specific brain areas. Such models should lead to both high-level theories of language processing that are more compatible with the biology of cognition and low-level theories of neural computation that yield information about the likely nature of cognitive processing.

Bibliography

[1] N. Chomsky, "Rules and representations," *Behavioral and Brain Sciences,* vol. 3, pp. 1-61, 1980.

[2] P. Lieberman, *The Biology and Evolution of Language*, Cambridge: Harvard University Press, 1984.

[3] M. Donald, *Origins of the Modern Mind: Three Stages in the Evolution of Culture and Cognition,* Cambridge: Harvard University Press, 1991.

[4] D. Kimura, "Neuromotor mechanisms in the evolution of human communication," in *Neurobiology of Social Communication in Primates*, eds. H. D. Steklis and M. J. Raleigh, New York: Academic Press, 1979.

[5] M. I. Sereno, "Language and the primate brain," in *Proceedings of the Thirteenth Annual Conference of the Cognitive Science Society*, Hillsdale, NJ: Erlbaum, 1991, pp. 79-84.

[6] C. J. Fillmore, "The case for case," in *Universals in Linguistic Theory*, eds. E. Bach and R. T. Harms, New York: Rinehart and Winston, 1968, pp. 1-88.

[7] M. I. Jordan and D. E. Rumelhart, "Forward models: Supervised learning with a distal teacher," *Cognitive Science,* vol. 16, pp. 307-354, 1992.

[8] J. H. Kaas, "The organization of neocortex in mammals: Implications for theories of brain function," *Annual Review of Neuroscience* vol. 38, pp. 129-151, 1987.

[9] G. M. Shepherd, "A basic circuit of cortical organization," in *Perspectives in Memory Research*, ed. M. S. Gazzaniga. Cambridge, MA: Bradford, 1988, pp. 93-134.

[10] J. Allman, "Evolution of neocortex," in *Cerebral Cortex*, Vol. 8A, *Comparative Structure and Evolution of Cerebral Cortex: Part I*, eds. E. G. Jones and A. Peters, New York: Plenum, 1990, pp. 269-283.

[11] U. Bellugi, H. Poizner, and E. S. Klima, "Language, modality and the brain," *Trends in Neurosciences,* vol. 12, pp. 380-388, 1989.

[12] M. I. Jordan, "Attractor dynamics and parallelism in a connectionist sequential machine," in *Proceedings of the Eighth Annual Conference of the Cognitive Science Society*, Amherst, MA, 1986, pp. 531-546.

[13] T. Parsons, *Events in the Semantics of English: A Study in Subatomic Semantics,* Cambridge: MIT Press, 1990.

[14] B. de Vries and J. C. Principe, "The gamma model—A new neural net model for temporal processing," *Neural Networks,* vol. 5, pp. 565-576, 1992.

Structure and Content in Word Production:
Why It's Hard to Say *dlorm*

Anita Govindjee
Dept of Computer Science
Beckman Institute
University of Illinois
Urbana, Illinois 61801 USA
anita@sprach.cogsci.uiuc.edu

Gary Dell
Dept of Psychology
Beckman Institute
University of Illinois
Urbana, Illinois 61801 USA
gdell@s.psych.uiuc.edu

A standard assumption of linguistic theory is that words and sentences are properly described as a merger of structure and content. A sentence description contains both a string of words (its content) and a syntactic tree specifying the hierarchical relations among the words (its structure). An individual word, itself, is viewed as a merger of phonological structure and content. The word's content consists of a string of phonological or phonetic features or segments and its structure describes an arrangement of these features into feet, syllables, syllabic constituents and other levels of organization (*e.g.*, [2, 23]).

Language production models embody this structure/content distinction by using a frame-and-slot mechanism for planning sentences and words. In the case of sentences, words are retrieved from the mental lexicon and then are inserted into syntactically labeled slots. In the case of words, speech sounds are inserted into slots in a phonological frame (see Figure 1).

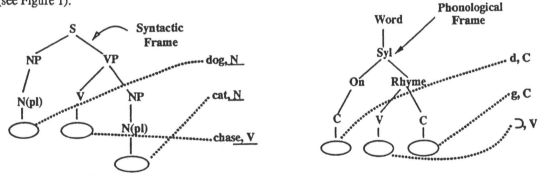

Figure 1 — Syntactic and phonological representations in the standard model.

This paper suggests that much of the psychological data that is thought to support the phonological structure/content distinction in language production can be explained by a mechanism in which no such distinction is explicitly present. Specifically, we show that a parallel distributed processing (PDP) model that maps between lexical representations and sequences of phonological features produces a number of speech-error phenomena — phenomena whose existence has been taken as strong support for the distinction between phonological frames and phonological segments. This occurs even though the model lacks explicit frames. More generally, we suggest that the role of the structure/content distinction in theories of language production needs to be re-examined in the light of PDP accounts of systematicity in language (*e.g.*, [9, 30]).

FRAME CONSTRAINTS IN LANGUAGE PRODUCTION

Four speech error phenomena, referred to as *frame constraints*, support the distinction between phonological frames and segments:

- *Phonotactic Regularity Effect.* Phonological speech errors almost always create sound sequences that occur in the language being spoken. Saying *dlorm* for *dorm* is one of the rare counterexamples [36, 37]. Theories of production locate much of the phonotactic regularity effect in the phonological frame. Frames are specified in such a manner that impossible sound sequences are proscribed.

- *Consonant-Vowel Category Effect.* Consonants slip with consonants and vowels slip with vowels. This effect is considered to be a frame constraint because the categories C and V are assumed to be part of the slot labels in the frame (*e.g.*, [6, 25, 33, 38, 39]). These labels cause the slots to accept only segments of the correct category.

- *Syllabic Constituent Effect.* When an adjacent vowel and consonant are both replaced in a slip, the sequence is more likely a VC than CV. So, for example *dog→tig* would be less likely than *dog→dit*. The syllabic constituent effect supports a role for the phonological frame because the closeness of the V and C in a VC sequence is derivable from the onset-rhyme hierarchical structure of the syllable unit within the frame (See Fig 1).

- *Initialness Effect.* Initial or onset consonants are more likely to slip than noninitial ones. The standard explanation has been that initial consonants of words and syllables are structurally distinct in the phonological frame. They often correspond to a hypothesized phonological constituent, either the word-onset [35] or the syllable-onset (*e.g.*, [24]) and hence are more detachable than the other sounds, which are more buried in the hierarchical structure of the word.

Accounting for these four frame constraints is a central concern of a theory of language production. All current theories of phonological encoding in language production have accounted for the frame constraints by separating phonological structure (frames and rules) from content (segments and features) and assigning the mechanism responsible for each constraint to the structural component [7, 26, 29, 39, 33]. The PDP approach outlined in the next section provides an alternative.

PDP MODELS AND LANGUAGE STRUCTURE

The Models

We develop PDP models that learn to produce the phonological forms of single words. These models lack an explicit structure/content distinction. Our purpose is to determine whether the models' error patterns show effects of phonological structure by evaluating the extent to which the errors obey the four frame constraints. Structural effects may emerge from the massed influence of these words in the absence of a separate set of frames or rules.

The models were *simple recurrent nets* of the type pioneered by Jordan and Elman [18, 9]. Both hidden and output units were copied back to state units. The input was a lexical representation of a word to be spoken. The output was a featural representation (18 features total, *e.g.*, labial, voiced, nasal, back, high) of each phoneme spoken serially in order. For example, a lexical representation of CAT was inputted and then /k/, /æ/, /t/ were outputted one at a time in order.

STUDY 1: FACTORIAL MANIPULATION OF MODEL CHARACTERISTICS

In order to gain some insight into the model's mechanisms, we tested eight versions of it derived from manipulating three factors of two levels each. These factors were (1) the training vocabulary, (2) the nature of the input representation, and (3) the nature of the state representation.

Training vocabulary. Two vocabularies, each comprised of 50 English words, were prepared. Both were samples from the set of all three-segment three-letter words appearing in Kucera and Francis [20]. The *frequent vocabulary* consisted of a sample that was heavily biased toward the most frequent words from the original set. The goal was to create a sample of word types whose tokens comprised around 90% of the word tokens from the set. Thus, the frequent vocabulary represents, in terms of word tokens, the lion's share of English-speakers' experience with short words. The second *infrequent vocabulary* was sampled with a bias toward the middle frequencies and a goal of representing around 10% of the tokens.

Our purpose in comparing the two vocabularies was to examine the dependence of error patterns on the training set. Given that our hypothesis is that the frame constraints on errors reflect nothing more than the mass action of the stored vocabulary, the vocabulary is important. The frequent vocabulary not only contains common words, but it also conforms to the statistics of English sound distribution better than the infrequent vocabulary in two specific respects. First, each existing VC tends to recur in the frequent vocabulary to a greater extent than does each existing CV; the ratio of VC tokens/VC types is 1.62 times larger than the corresponding ratio for CV's. This asymmetry is less pronounced in the infrequent vocabulary (1.37). In general, English has the property that its VC's are more redundant than its CV's. Secondly, the frequent vocabulary has some diversity with regard to word shapes and consonant clusters. 18% of the words in this vocabulary are not CVC's, which is close to the actual percentage of non-CVC's in English word types of this length, 17.3%. (The percentage of non-CVC's for the infrequent vocabulary is 12%.) Moreover, the vocabulary contains a variety of consonant cluster types: nasal-stop, /s/-stop, stop-/s/, stop-liquid, and liquid-stop. The infrequent vocabulary has fewer non-CVC's. Its clusters include only liquid-nasal combinations.

Input representations. The lexical units represented the word to be spoken in one of two ways, a *random* coding or a *correlated* coding. In the random coding, each word was a random 30-bit vector. This encoding can be thought of as a distributed semantic representation of the word in the sense that it is uncorrelated with the word's form. The essence of the correlated coding is that words with similar output feature sequences should have similar input representations and so we used a coding scheme based on the word's spelling.

Nature of the state representation. The state units in simple recurrent nets enable the model to keep track of where it is in the sequence. We compared two kinds of state representations, one in which both the output and hidden units' activation values are copied onto state units (the *internal-external* architecture), and one in which only the hidden units' activation is copied onto state units (the *internal-only* architecture). Both of these architectures are, in principle, capable of supporting sequential output. The internal-only architecture has been explored in detail by Elman [9]. The internal-external architecture has not previously been studied.

Simulation Training

Twenty-four models were created, comprising three replications of the eight conditions (2 vocabularies x 2 input codings x 2 architectures). Each replication was trained from a different set of starting weights. Every 50 epochs, the models were tested by assessing the correctness of the four output vectors associated with each word (the three segments and a concluding null segment). An output vector was deemed correct if it was closer in Euclidian distance to the desired segment than to any other segment. When the model achieved greater than 90% correct segments, training stopped and errors were examined.

Mean Performance of the Models

First, we examined the performance of the models with respect to the frame constraints, and then looked at the results of the factor manipulations.

Phonotactic Regularity Effect. Across the 24 models, 92.6% of the 376 errors created phonotactically legal strings of American English. This compares to a standard of 99% in a natural error collection [36, 37]. Clearly, the average model's behavior is very good, but not quite up to the human error standard.

Consonant-Vowel Category Effect. The average model's errors involved the substitution of consonants for consonants and vowels for vowels 97.6% of the time. In human speech errors, the constraint is upheld 99–100% of the time.

Syllabic-Constituent Effect. Although the vast majority of the models' errors were substitutions, additions, or deletions of single sounds, there were some errors in which more than one sound is replaced. In accord with speech-error data, the models produced more VC than CV substitutions. 5.6% of the total number of errors constituted a VC sequence and 2.1% were CV sequences. This difference is in very close agreement with the 6% VC and 2% CV rates cited in Shattuck-Hufnagel [34].

Initialness Effect. Single consonant substitution errors from the models corresponded to syllable-onset consonants 61.6% of the time. Hence the models exhibit a bias for onset errors. Compared to a standard chosen from Shattuck-Hufnagel [35] of 62% onset errors, the average models' behavior is very good.

Our conclusion is that the average model does fairly well at adhering to the four frame constraints. But why does it work? There are two related forces that determine the models' error pattern, **similarity** and **sequential** bias. When a model errs, the erroneous sound is very likely to be similar to the correct sound. Thus, *car* might slip to *gar*, but not to *uar*, simply because the model's output representation is based on linguistic features. When the model is trained to produce /k/, an output pattern that corresponds to /g/ is much closer to its training than one corresponding to /u/. Sequential bias refers to the fact that the context units bias the models' output toward common sequences of sounds.

Each of the frame constraints results from similarity and/or sequential bias. The phonotactic regularity effect is produced by both of these forces. The substitution of a similar sound usually will not create a phonotactically illegal sequence. This is because the phonotactic patterns of the language are sensitive to similarity; if the sequence Vk is acceptable, the sequence Vg is likely as well. Sequential bias also plays a role in keeping the models' errors phonotactically legal. The previous sounds in a word bias the model to produce a subsequent sound if that combination of sounds (or a similar combination) occurs in the vocabulary.

The consonant-vowel effect arises primarily from similarity. Vowels and consonants are very different from one another in the models' output representations and, hence, there is little tendency for cross-category substitutions. The syllabic constituent and initialness effects arise from sequential bias. In the models' vocabularies, VC units tend to occur with more than one word to a greater extent than CV units. Hence there is a stronger redundancy within the VC than the CV. The initialness effect reflects the fact that there is more uncertainty about sounds in the beginning of a word than elsewhere. At the beginning, the context units have null values and, therefore, are less effective at pointing to the desired sound. Later on in the word, the context units have activation values that are specific for that word and thus are very effective cues for subsequent sounds.

We also examined differences due to the factor manipulations among the eight versions of the model:

Training Vocabulary. As expected, the most representative (frequent) vocabulary generated better error effects than the infrequent vocabulary. For example, the frequent vocabulary produced a strong syllabic constituent effect while the infrequent one did not. This seems to be related to the fact that the frequent vocabulary has, like the vocabulary of English as a whole, greater redundancy among its VC's than its CV's; the infrequent vocabulary has less of a difference.

Effect of input representation. The models with the random input representations performed just about as well as those with the correlated input representations. At least in these models, the input representation is not critical in producing adherence to the frame constraints.

Effect of architecture. As anticipated, the more complex architecture, the one with both external and internal feedback, was superior to the internal-only architecture. Both the phonotactic regularity effect and the consonant-vowel effects were better with the internal-external models, giving some evidence that the extra context supplied by the internal-external model is helpful for producing structural effects on errors.

Discussion

The analyses performed thus far suggest that not all models are equal, but that it is possible to achieve very human-like performance on the frame constraints. In order to have good performance with regard to the phonotactic regularity effect, one needs a solid encoding of the surrounding context (better in the internal-external architecture than the internal-only) and a representative vocabulary. Good performance on the consonant-vowel effect is easier to achieve. As long as consonants and vowels are very different in their output features, the model's slips obey this constraint. The syllabic constituent effect is heavily dependent on the training vocabulary. If there is a large difference in the patterning of VC's and CV's, then the desired effect emerges.

These considerations suggest that the six models created with the internal-external architecture and trained on the frequent vocabulary should be very good. Their errors were phonotactically regular 96.3% of the time and obeyed the consonant-vowel constraint, 100% of the time. VC slips outnumbered CV slips, 9% to 3%, and the initialness effect was 60%. These numbers are very close to the standards.

One of the most important findings from the simulations is that the errors are sensitive to the phonological patterns of English. The fact that this is true of people's errors had prompted some researchers to suggest that phonological rules are actively consulted during production (*e.g.*, [11]). Others [36, 37, 4], however, have been more skeptical and argued that error adherence to phonotactics does not necessarily implicate rule consultation. Our simulations justify this skepticism. They suggest that the phonotactic regularity effect may reflect more simple mechanisms, mechanisms based on the principles of similarity and sequential bias.

Despite the promising results of all of our simulations, there is something a little odd about treating the model's errors as analogous to speech errors. The model's errors reflect a lack of knowledge, rather than a transient inability to use knowledge. Adult speech-errors are clearly the latter rather than the former. We address this in the following section by generating errors through transient degradation.

STUDY 2: ERROR GENERATION BY DEGRADATION

We trained two new models, each using the frequent 50-word vocabulary, the correlated representation, and the internal-external architecture, until they correctly produced all their words. To create errors, random normal deviations to some of the weights were then introduced. For each word tested, different sets of weight changes were made and these were maintained only through the production of that word. The deviations represent the natural variations in lexical knowledge resulting from recent experience, environmental contamination, and other putative causes of error.

When normally distributed noise was added to the connections between hidden and output units, the errors nicely followed the frame constraints. Two models were repeatedly lesioned with varying amounts of noise creating 291 errors. The errors were phonotactically regular 97.9% of the time and followed the consonant-vowel category constraint 97.6% of the time. 3.8% of the errors were VC's and 2.1% were CV's. Finally, 78% of the consonant errors involved onsets. In addition, the tendency for errors to be phonotactically regular increased as error likelihood decreased. This result is encouraging because it suggests that the model's adherence to the frame constraints, if anything, gets better as its error rate decreases. Thus, if we were to extrapolate the model to a level of correctness found in normal adult speech (one error per 300 words, [17]), we might well find the exceptionally high adherence to the phonotactic regularity and consonant-vowel rules seen in speech-error collections. At least we can expect that such adherence would not get worse as correctness increased.

STUDY 3: LARGER VOCABULARY

Although the frequent 50-word vocabulary represents most of the tokens of three-letter three-segments English words, it makes up only about one-sixth of these word types. We therefore examined models trained on all one-syllable words from Kucera and Francis [20] that were three segments and three phonemes in length (298 words). The internal-external feedback architecture with the correlated input representation was used, and also external-context units were given a memory based on 20% of their activation level from the previous time step. All of the words were presented in a random order for each epoch. Thus, we did not weight the presentation frequency of each word by their observed frequencies. Additionally, the strictness of the teacher was varied over time. For the first 50 epochs, an output of greater than .6 or less than .4 was acceptable for units whose targets were 1 and 0, respectively. This was increased to .7 and .3 for the next 50 epochs, and so on until the teacher was as strict as possible (1.0 and 0).

The level of correctness was quite good and so we trained three separate models, resulting in an average of 99.1% correct segments. The few errors obtained (32) exhibited the frame constraints. There were only two phonotactic violations, ask→/ætk/ and out→/aət/. The latter error was the only violation of the consonant-vowel rule because we coded out as /awt/ and, hence, the substitution of /ə/ for /w/ is a vowel for a consonant. So, the phonotactic regularity effect was upheld 93.8% of the time, and the consonant-vowel rule, 96.9% of the time. Furthermore, the initialness effect was a good 66.7%. The syllabic constituent effect, however, could not be examined as there were no errors involving more than a single phoneme. Equivalent results were obtained for the larger vocabulary by the weight degradation method described above.

HIDDEN UNIT ANALYSIS

To better understand the performance of the models, we analyzed the hidden units to determine exactly what regularities the network had found in the input set. We did a principal components analysis (PCA) [9] on the hidden unit activation vectors for both the models with the frequent 50-word and larger 298-word vocabularies. We plotted 9 principal components of which only the first 3 had any noticeable patterns. The first principal component for the frequent 50-word vocabulary model correlated best with initial word position, i.e., it marked the beginning of each word. The second principal component in this model coded for the end of the word. So, position within a word was important. The third principal component appeared to describe something more interesting. The vowels and consonants were separated in a graded fashion, approximating a sonority hierarchy: ϵ, ϑ, a, o, u, I, w, y, m, n, f, p, s, z, g, d, b, t [15]. To some degree, the model was distinguishing vowels from consonants.

The 298-word vocabulary model had similar results. The first principal component also marked the beginning of each word, and the third principal component coded for the end of the word. The second principal component appeared to again differentiate between vowels and consonants. It did this in a graded manner like the second principal component of the smaller, frequent vocabulary model where more vowel-like consonants (*e.g.*, w, y) were in between the vowels and consonants (see Figure 2). Note, though, that since we looked only at monosyllabic words and that the majority of the words were of the form CVC, it is difficult to tell if the principal component is marking position or some other more interesting linguistic regularity. Since the vowel usually occurs in the second position, it may be that this particular principal component in the two models is simply encoding position and not making a vowel-consonant distinction. The graded differentiation between the vowels and consonants with semi-vowels (r, l, w, h, y) falling between the vowels and consonants does seem to support finding a V-C distinction. Further studies with multisyllabic input should bear this out. In fact, we claim that the information that the models have extracted, *i.e.*, position within a word and the V-C distinction, is exactly what is needed to account for much of the speech-error data. The positional information differentiates initial consonants from final ones, accounting for the syllabic constituent effect and the initialness effect; and vowels and consonants are distinguished from one another, accounting for the CV category effect.

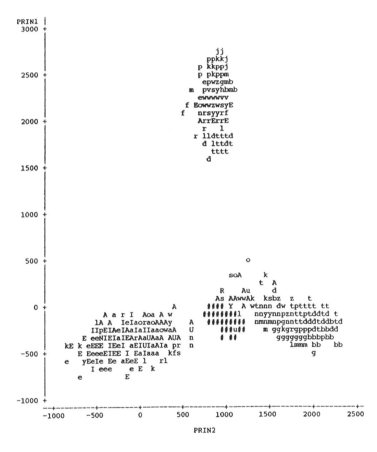

Figure 2 — Principal Component 1 *vs* Principal Component 2 for Larger Vocabulary Model.[1] Principal component 1 codes for initial position within the word. Principal component 2 approximates a sonority hierarchy, with second phonemes of each word mostly clustering to the left in the graph, and third phonemes mostly clustering to the right.

---

[1]The ASCII characters in the figure have the following correspondence: e→ϵ, a→ϑ, N→ŋ, E→æ, A→a, U→ɔ, Y→i, R→syllabic r.

GENERAL DISCUSSION

On average, the models do a reasonable job of simulating four speech error effects: the phonotactic regularity effect, the consonant-vowel category effect, the syllabic constituent effect, and the initialness effect. Earlier, we claimed that these effects are important because they have previously been associated with the action of phonological rules or frames, data structures that are assumed to be separate from the set of phonological segments associated with a word. Our success in simulation using a sequential PDP architecture suggests that the four effects do not necessarily reflect separate rules or frames, rather they can be produced by a mechanism that does not separate linguistic structure and content in an explicit *a priori* fashion.

Issues in Connectionist Models of Language

The model is an example of a simple recurrent network. Much of the interest in these networks has centered on their applications to language and specifically with the hypothesis that the network's treatment of sequencing allows it to represent linguistic structure [1, 8, 9, 12, 13, 14, 18, 21, 28, 32, 40].

In the domain of phonology, other recurrent networks have been applied to coarticulation [18], vowel harmony [13], and other feature-persistence effects [12]. This work has largely been linguistic in nature. It tries to account for facts about the distribution of sounds in words — facts about linguistic competence. In contrast, our approach is psychological. We are attempting to give an account of performance data, findings that result from people actually trying to produce language. This is the main sense in which our research differs from the previous work in phonology using recurrent nets. In fact, we find it unusual that much of the PDP phonology work has had more of a linguistic than a psycholinguistic flavor, given that early applications of connectionist models to language emphasized performance data over competence (*e.g.*, [3, 5, 10, 16, 19, 27, 30, 31, 41]).

CONCLUSIONS: RULES AND FRAMES IN PSYCHOLINGUISTIC MODELS

It is important to distinguish between what our model shows — that certain speech error effects attributed to separate rules and frames can be accounted for otherwise — and the general claim that separate rules and frames are not required in accounts of language performance. We have not addressed any of the data that motivate rules and frames in morphology and syntax. Nor have we addressed phonological facts associated with stress, cliticization, and resyllabification — facts which are standardly accounted for by restructuring phonological frames for single words and which, it can be argued, suggest the need for such frames in production [22]. Consequently, we must be content with making a more limited claim: The PDP model can be taken as a demonstration that sequential biases, similarity, and the structure of the vocabulary are powerful principles in explaining error patterns. In fact, we take the model a bit further and argue that the frame constraints may simply reflect similarity and sequential effects and not phonological frames, at least not directly. Moreover, we interpret the model's success in its domain as evidence that there is something right about it, that the "correct" model would make use of learning and distributed representations in such a way that phonological speech errors result from the simultaneous influence of all the words stored in the system, in addition to the set of words in the intended utterance. At the same time, there may be other effects best explained by structural knowledge that has been separated out from linguistic content. A worthy goal of psycholinguistic research is to determine which is which.

Acknowledgments

This research was supported by NSF BNS-8910546, NIH NS25502, and NIH DC-00191. The authors wish to thank Linda May for work on the manuscript. For further information please refer to: Dell, Juliano, Govindjee, "Structure and Content in Language Production: A Theory of Frame Constraints in Phonological Speech Errors", *Cognitive Science*, **17**, pp. 149-195, 1993.

References

[1] R. B. Allen (1990). Connectionist language users. *Connection Science*, **4**, 279–311.
[2] G. N. Clements & S. J. Keyser (1983). *CV-Phonology: A generative theory of the syllable*. Cambridge, MA: MIT Press.
[3] G. W. Cottrell (1989). *A connectionist approach to word-sense disambiguation*. London: Pittman.

[4] A. Crompton (1981). Syllables and segments in speech production. *Linguistics*, **19**, 663–716.
[5] G. S. Dell (1985). Positive feedback in hierarchical connectionist models: Applications to language production. *Cognitive Science*, **9**, 3–24.
[6] G. S. Dell (1986). A spreading-activation theory of retrieval in language production. *Psychological Review*, **93**, 283–321.
[7] G. S. Dell (1988). The retrieval of phonological forms in production: Tests of predictions from a connectionist model. *Journal of Memory and Language*, **27**, 124–142.
[8] J. L. Elman (1989). Structured representations and connectionist models. *Proceedings of the 11th Annual Conference of the Cognitive Science Society*, Ann Arbor, MI.
[9] J. L. Elman (1990). Finding structure in time. *Cognitive Science*, **14**, 213–252.
[10] J. L. Elman & J. L. McClelland (1984). The interactive activation model of speech perception. In N. Lass (Ed.), *Speech and language*. New York: Academic Press.
[11] V. A. Fromkin (1971). The nonanomalous nature of anomalous utterances. *Language*, **47**, 27–52.
[12] M. Gasser & C-D. Lee (1990). Networks that learn about phonological feature persistence. *Connection Science*, **2**, 265–278.
[13] M. Hare (1990). The role of similarity in Hungarian vowel harmony: A connectionist account. *Connection Science*, **2**, 125–152.

[14] M. Hare, D. Corina, & G. Cottrell (1990). A connectionist perspective on prosodic structure. *Proceedings of the Annual Meeting of the Berkeley Linguistic Society*, **15**.
[15] C. L. Harris (1989). "Connectionist Explorations in Cognitive Linguistics." *Unpublished ms*, UCSD.
[16] G. Hirst (1987). *Semantic interpretation and the resolution of ambiguity*. Cambridge: Cambridge University Press.
[17] W. H. N. Hotopf (1983). Lexical slips of the pen and tongue. In B. Butterworth (Ed.), *Language production, Volume 2*. San Diego, CA: Academic Press.
[18] M. I. Jordan (1986). Attractor dynamics and parallelism in a connectionist sequential machine. In *Proceedings of the Eighth Annual Conference of the Cognitive Science Society*, (pp. 531–546). Hillsdale, NJ: Erlbaum.
[19] A. H. Kawamoto (1988). Distributed representations of ambiguous words and their resolution in a connectionist network. In S. Small, G. Cottrell, & M. Tanenhaus (Eds.), *Lexical ambiguity resolution* (pp. 195–228). San Mateo, CA: Morgan Kaufmann.
[20] H. Kucera & W. N. Francis (1967). *Computational analysis of present-day American English*. Providence, RI: Brown University Press.
[21] A. Lathroum (1989). Feature encoding by neural nets. *Phonology*, **6**, 305–316.
[22] W. J. M. Levelt (1989). *Speaking: From intention to articulation*. Cambridge, MA: MIT Press.
[23] M. Liberman & A. Prince (1977). On stress and linguistic rhythm. *Linguistic Inquiry*, **8**, 249–336.
[24] D. G. MacKay (1972). The structure of words and syllables: Evidence from errors in speech. *Cognitive Psychology*, **3**, 210–227.
[25] D. G. MacKay (1982). The problems of flexibility, fluency, and speed-accuracy trade-off in skilled behavior. *Psychological Review*, **89**, 483–506.
[26] D. G. (1987). *The organization of perception and action: A theory for language and other cognitive skills*. New York: Springer.

[27] J. L. McClelland & A. H. Kawamoto (1986). Mechanisms of sentence processing: Assigning roles to constituents. In J. L. McClelland & D. E. Rumelhart (Eds.), *Parallel distributed processing: Explorations in the microstructure of cognition, Volume II*. Cambridge, MA: Bradford Books.
[28] J. L. McClelland, M. St. John & R. Taraban (1989). Sentence comprehension: A parallel distributed processing approach. *Language and Cognitive Processes*, **4**, 287–335.
[29] A. S. Meyer (1990). The phonological encoding of successive syllables. *Journal of Memory and Language*.
[30] D. E. Rumelhart & J. L. McClelland (1986a). On learning the past tenses of English verbs. In J. L. McClelland & D. E. Rumelhart (Eds.), *Parallel distributed processing: Explorations in the microstructure of cognition, Volume 2* (pp. 216–271). Cambridge, MA: Bradford Books.
[31] M. Seidenberg & J. L. McClelland (1989). A distributed developmental model of visual word recognition and naming. *Psychological Review*, **96**, 523–568.
[32] D. Servan-Schreiber, A. Cleeremans, & J. L. McClelland (1989). Learning and sequential structure in simple recurrent networks. In D. Touretzky (Ed.), *Advances in neural information processing systems 2* (pp. 643–652). San Mateo, CA: Morgan Kaufmann.
[33] S. Shattuck-Hufnagel (1979). Speech errors as evidence for a serial-order mechanism in sentence production. In W. E. Cooper & E. C. T. Walker (Eds.), *Sentence processing: Psycholinguistic studies presented to Merrill Garrett*. Hillsdale, NJ: Erlbaum.
[34] S. Shattuck-Hufnagel (1983). Sublexical units and suprasegmental structure in speech production planning. In P. F. MacNeilage (Ed.), *The production of speech* (pp. 109–136). New York: Springer-Verlag.
[35] S. Shattuck-Hufnagel (1987). The role of word-onset consonants in speech production planning: New evidence from speech error patterns. In E. Keller & M. Gopnik, (Eds.), *Motor and sensory processes of language*. Hillsdale, NJ: Erlbaum.
[36] J. P. Stemberger (1983a). *Speech errors and theoretical phonology: A review*. Bloomington, IN: Indiana University Linguistics Club.
[37] J. P. Stemberger (1983b). The nature of /r/ and /l/ in English: Evidence from speech errors. *Journal of Phonetics*, **11**, 139–147.

[38] J. P. Stemberger (1985). An interactive activation model of language production. In A. Ellis, (Ed.), *Progress in the psychology of language, Vol I* (pp. 143–186). London: Erlbaum.
[39] J. P. Stemberger (1990). Wordshape errors in language production. *Cognition*, **35**, 123–157.
[40] M. F. St. John & J. L. McClelland (1990). Learning and applying contextual constraints in sentence comprehension. *Artificial Intelligence*, **46**, 217–257.
[41] D. L. Waltz & J. B. Pollack (1985). Massively parallel parsing: A strongly interactive model of natural language interpretation. *Cognitive Science*, **9**, 51–74.

Investigating Phonological Representations: A Modeling Agenda

Prahlad Gupta
Department of Psychology
Carnegie Mellon University
Pittsburgh, PA 15217
prahlad@cs.cmu.edu

This paper outlines a bottom-up research approach to studying lexical representation, emphasizing the development of infant phonological perception as a source of data that can illuminate the nature of phonological representations. It is proposed that neural network formalisms can provide a useful framework for thinking about these issues. We identify a key set of empirical results, understanding of which would yield considerable insight; this defines a modeling agenda for investigation of phonological representations. We report preliminary simulations that explore this agenda, exemplifying how network modeling techniques can contribute to understanding of these phenomena.

MOTIVATION

What is the nature of words? How are they represented mentally? What are the properties of these representations? How are these representations evoked in processing speech?

These issues clearly have importance for thinking about language. For example, conceptions of lexical access in sentence processing will differ considerably depending on whether lexical representations are conceived of as being "static" or "dynamic", or whether they are viewed as being "distributed" or "localist". Investigating the mental representation of lexical form can therefore be viewed as part of a "bottom-up" strategy to studying language. Such investigation is also bottom-up in the sense that the development of representations of words necessarily must precede the development of more complex language abilities in the human child.

It seems uncontroversial to suppose that the formation of representations is a major part of what goes on in the early stages of language acquisition, especially over the first two years of life. As Aslin [1] has noted, it seems unlikely that infants actually hear speech as meaningful units until sometime in later infancy when they begin to associate sounds with meanings. It is therefore reasonable to think of these earliest representations as denoting the infant's perception of speech sounds, relatively independent of their meaning.

Consequently, it seems valuable to enquire into the nature of such *phonological* representations, and into the processes by which they might develop: these enquiries would reach into the very heart of early language development. What, then, is the nature of phonological representations? How do they develop? And how are they involved in the processing of spoken words? Important as these issues are, little is known about them, as Lahiri & Marslen-Wilson [13] have pointed out.

The hypothesis advanced in this paper is that neural network formalisms can provide a framework for thinking about phonological perception and its development, and thus can contribute to understanding the nature of phonological representation and processing[1]. The first section of the paper outlines a specific set of developmental phonological perception phenomena, proposing these as a test-bed for the above hypothesis. The second section of the paper reports on some preliminary neural net simulations that explore a subset of these phenomena; the results support the hypothesis that network formalisms may be an illuminating framework for thinking about these issues.

TOUCHSTONE PHENOMENA FOR PHONOLOGICAL PERCEPTION

This section presents and discusses selected empirical results in infant phonological perception, obtained over approximately the first one year of life. It will be argued that these results provide a testbed for the hypothesis that network formalisms can provide a framework for thinking about phonological perception and its development, and thus constitute an agenda for modeling.

Categorical perception. The discrimination functions of human adults listening to phonetic segments varying along an acoustic continuum (such as voice-onset time, or place of articulation) show peaks of discriminability corresponding to the locations of phonemic category boundaries as determined by absolute identification experiments [11]. This phenomenon, viz., the occurrence of steep crossovers for both identification and discrimination, has been termed *categorical perception*. It occurs only for consonants; vowels appear to be perceived continuously [1]. In adults, categorical perception occurs only for sounds in the adult's native language [11]. In human infants, categorical discrimination has been demonstrated as early as 1 month of age: the infants reacted as if they perceived a sudden shift in the series of phonetic (consonantal) segments along an acoustic continuum, at the same point as the adult-defined boundary between two phonemic categories. These effects have been obtained along various acoustic continuua, and it appears that infants can discriminate virtually every speech contrast used in one of the world's languages; it also seeems likely that prior to 6 months of age, infants are performing their analysis of speech sounds solely on the basis of acoustic differences, which are sufficient to permit categorical discrimination [1].

The perceptual magnet effect. Kuhl's work [10] indicates that adult listeners' ratings of the goodness of exemplars of a vowel vary, even while all exemplars are categorized as being the same vowel. Different exemplars of /i/ were rated by adults, and received different ratings of "goodness" (which were very consistent across raters), although always being categorized as /i/. This suggests that there are "prototypically good" vowels.

Adults also show an asymmetry in *discrimination* of "prototypical" vs. "nonprototypical" stimuli. When adults are presented with the "best" exemplar of a vowel repeatedly and then a "peripheral" exemplar of that same vowel, they often fail to discriminate the difference. However, when presented with peripheral exemplars and then tested with the "best" exemplar, discrimination is better. This is what Kuhl [10] has called the *perceptual magnet effect*. According to her, the central member of the category seems to "capture" the other instances, rendering them less discriminable.

Kuhl has also shown that infants' responses to protoypical vs. nonprototypical vowel stimuli correspond with adults' goodness ratings. Stimuli were synthesized to form four concentric rings around each of two central stimuli: an adult-rated prototypical, and an adult-rated non-protoypical /i/. Infants heard one or other of the central stimuli as the reference stimulus, and were tested on discrimination of the surrounding stimuli. Results from infants responding to these stimuli were as follows:

---

[1]There are, of course, existing accounts of phonological perceptual development [8, 21], and the present approach draws importantly on many of their ideas. However, these previous approaches have not focussed on computational instantiation of the frameworks they propose. Other recent work does examine phonological development from a computational standpoint [14], but is not primarily concerned with the nature of representations or with accounting for specific perceptual phenomena.

(1) Stimulus generalization for both groups, i.e., generalization of the head-turn response from the center stimulus to the surrounding stimuli. (2) A group effect, with generalization at a given distance from the central stimulus being higher for the prototype-based group than for the non-prototype-based group. This is consistent with the "perceptual magnet" effect, since greater generalization from the prototype is the same thing as poorer discrimination from the prototype (demonstrated with adults). (3) One vector of stimuli was actually shared between the two concentric rings of stimuli. The two groups of infants were therefore both tested on this set of stimuli, but in opposite "directions". Infants exposed to the prototype as the reference stimulus discriminated only the most distant stimulus along this vector, whereas infants exposed to the non-prototype as reference discriminated stimuli from the second nearest on. This is a direct replication of the adult perceptual magnet effect. (4) There was a .95 correlation of adults' goodness ratings and infants' generalization scores around the prototype.

Language-specificity of the perceptual magnet effect. In further work by Kuhl [12], one set of vowels was synthesized around a prototypic exemplar of English /i/ and another set was synthesized around a prototypic exemplar of Swedish /y/. For English adults /y/ is not perceived as a prototype of any English vowel, and for Swedish adults /i/ is not perceived as prototypical of any Swedish vowel.

6-month old English- and Swedish-learning infants were tested for discrimination from both the central stimuli. English infants showed a stronger generalization from the English /i/ stimulus to its variant stimuli, than from the /y/ stimulus to its surrounding stimuli. The converse was true for the Swedish infants. This suggests that the prototype structure for vowels has begun to be tuned by the ambient linguistic environment at least by 6 months of age.

Discriminability of nonnative contrasts and its development: consonants. Cross-language studies of consonant discrimination have revealed that, up to about 6 months of age, infants can discriminate nearly every phonetic contrast on which they have been tested, including contrasts comprised of phonetic segments that are not phonemically contrastive in their language-learning environment (but that are contrastive in some other human language).

Werker [21] and others have shown, however, that between 8 and 12 months of age, infants seem to lose the ability to discriminate between the same nonnative contrasts that they could earlier discriminate. This loss of nonnative contrasts only appears to take place for phonetic segments that are assimilable to a native language category. Infants retain the ability, however, to discriminate native language contrasts.

Adult speakers are unable to discriminate many nonnative contrasts that infants can discriminate at earlier ages, but lose by 12 months. They are able to discriminate the contrasts that infants continue to be able to discriminate. This is consistent with the notion that nonnative segments are being assimilated to a native language category (if a sufficiently close one exists), in both the older infants, and the adults. Adult discrimination performance can, however, improve with training or practice.

Discriminability of nonnative contrasts and its development: vowels. In further work by Werker and colleagues [16], English-learning infants were tested on their ability to discriminate two pairs of high front-rounded vs. high back-rounded German vowels. All vowels were presented in the context [dVt]. One contrast involved tense high front vs. high back (/u/ vs. /y/) and the other involved lax high front vs. high back (/U/ vs. /Y/). Both contrasts are phonemic in German, but not in English.

Adult English speakers were as good as German speakers at discriminating between members of both contrastive German vowel pairs. However, each back German vowel was perceived to be more like an English vowel than was the front German vowel; in this sense, each German back vowel was designated by the experimenters as the more "prototypical" member (for English adults) of each contrasting German pair.

4-month-old English-learning infants were able to discriminate between members of both contrastive German vowel pairs, irrespective of whether the more or less prototypical member served as the background category. 6- to 8-month-old English-learning infants were able to discriminate the German contrasts when the background stimulus was the non-prototypical member, but not when it was the prototypical member. By 10-12 months, English infants no longer discriminated the German contrasts, irrespective of the "direction" of testing.

The above results can be summarized as follows. (1) First, the perceptual magnet effect seems to exist for vowels, but not for consonants. (2) There is also another basic difference in adult perception of vowels vs. consonants. For phonemically contrastive consonant sounds in the listener's native language, there are steep crossovers for both labeling and discrimination. For nonnative listeners, category labeling boundaries are absent, less sharp, or do not coincide with those of native listeners. Adults have considerable difficulty discriminating certain nonnative contrasts. The situation is slightly different for vowels: as with consonants, there are steep crossovers for labeling of phonemically contrastive vowels in the listener's native language. Discrimination, however, is more continuous, for both native and nonnative listeners, and in fact the discrimination abilities of nonnative listeners are typically quite good compared with those of native listeners. However, these discrimination abilities appear subject to the "perceptual magnet" effect. (3) Infants are initially sensitive to virtually any native or nonnative phonemic contrast, whether between vowels or consonants, up to about 4 months of age. (4) Beyond this age, their sensitivities seem to get attuned to environmental (native) language sounds, leading to loss of sensitivity to nonnative contrasts by 6-8 months for vowels, and by 10-12 months for consonants. (5) For vowels, there seems to be an intermediate point (around 6-8 months) in this loss of sensitivity. At this intermediate point, discriminatory ability is preserved only if the nonnative sound serving as reference stimulus is *not* prototypical, i.e., similar to a native language sound.

These data represent some of the central findings in infant speech perception over the last four decades, and constitute a key and inter-related set of phenomena. An important aspect of the phenomena is their developmental nature, as well as the developmental progression in which they occur. Providing a computational account of these data would yield considerable insight into fundamental questions regarding the nature of phonological representation. This set of phenomena is therefore proposed here as a testbed for investigation of the nature and development of phonological representations via network modeling techniques, in much the same way that a miniature language acquisition problem has been proposed by Feldman and colleagues [2] as a touchstone for cognitive science.

The next section describes simulations that begin to explore this modeling agenda; the results demonstrate the role that neural network techniques can play in thinking about phonological representation and processing.

SIMULATIONS: LOSS OF NONNATIVE CONTRASTS

As discussed above, infants lose sensitivity to nonnative contrasts towards the end of the first year of life. In particular, it has been found by Werker and colleagues [21] that English-learning infants aged 6-8 months are able to discriminate Hindi and certain other nonnative contrasts, while infants aged 10-12 months are mostly unable to do so, as are adult native speakers of English. However, English-learning infants at all ages, as well as adults, retain the ability to discriminate certain other nonnative contrasts, such as that between two Zulu clicks.

Part of Werker's account of these phenomena is that both sounds in the Hindi contrast (involving a dental vs. a retroflex [ta]) may by the later age have become assimilated to the native English alveolar /ta/, and thus ceased to be discriminable. The Zulu clicks, on the other hand, may not be easily assimilable to any known category, and hence remain discriminable. The intuition is that the infant's mental perceptual landscape initially has a topology that allows for discrimination between virtually any speech stimuli; however, this topology is altered by exposure to the native language environment in such a way that nonnative distinctions become blurred and no longer discriminable.

In neural network terms, such properties might be expected to follow naturally from the development of *attractor states*. The idea here is that the energy landscape in the network initially has low-energy basins (i.e., attractors) corresponding to essentially each possible phonetic segment. However, learning through exposure to the native language re-sculpts this energy surface, and the attractor states that continue to exist are those that correspond to the phonemes of the native language.

To examine the ability of neural networks to flesh out these intuitions, we constructed simulations in which

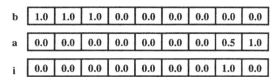 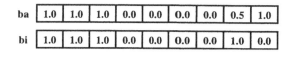

b	1.0	1.0	1.0	0.0	0.0	0.0	0.0	0.0	0.0
a	0.0	0.0	0.0	0.0	0.0	0.0	0.0	0.5	1.0
i	0.0	0.0	0.0	0.0	0.0	0.0	0.0	1.0	0.0

| ba | 1.0 | 1.0 | 1.0 | 0.0 | 0.0 | 0.0 | 0.0 | 0.5 | 1.0 |
| bi | 1.0 | 1.0 | 1.0 | 0.0 | 0.0 | 0.0 | 0.0 | 1.0 | 0.0 |

Figure 1: Input representation for phones and demisyllables.

networks' responses to "nonnative" stimuli were examined both before and after training on a set of "native" stimuli.

Input Representation and Data

The actual input set comprised a set of demisyllables, representing the "native language" sounds to which an infant might be exposed. Of course, a human infant is in reality not exposed to streams of syllables, but rather, to actual linguistic utterances. Gupta & Mozer [3] have shown how demisyllables can be extracted from words, using a simple mechanism based on autopredictive error and stress level, while Gupta & Touretzky [6, 4, 5] have examined the ability of a perceptron to assign stress to syllables. The details of this processing are not important for present purposes; we simply assume some such prior processing that extracts demisyllables from actual words, as a result of which the infant's phonological perceptions are structured in terms of demisyllables. There appears to be considerable agreement that this is the case with human infants [8]. Thus the input corpus we used comprised the syllables *ba be bi d@ di do g@ ga ge go k@ ka ki ko la ma mi mo pa pe pi po t@ ta ti to.*

To represent these syllables, we used a phonetic feature representation scheme proposed by Shillcock et al. [20], in which each possible phone is encoded in terms of a set of 9 feature values, which are intended to have physical correlates in the speech signal. These features are: (1) oral cavity openness, (2) palatality, (3) labiality, (4) occlusion, (5) aperiodic energy, (6) nasality, (7) apicality/coronality, (8) velarity/centrality, and (9) voicelessness [20]. Figure 1 shows the encoding of the phones [b], [a], and [i] in terms of these 9 features. Each bit of the 9-element vector shown in the figure represents the value for that phone on one feature dimension. To encode a syllable such as *ba*, we simply superimposed the 9-element vectors representing the two segments *b* and *a*, as also shown in Figure 1.

To examine the model's responses to unknown sounds, a "dental" and "retroflex" *t* were simulated by modifying the value of the "coronality" feature, from 1.0 for the alveolar *t*, to 0.7 and 0.3 for the dental and retroflex versions respectively. These were used to create "nonnative" stimuli: a dental *ta*, which will be denoted by *t(d)a*, and a retroflex *ta*, denoted by *t(r)a*. The syllables *na* and *nga* were treated as a second nonnative contrast, since neither of them was included in the input corpus.

Network Architecture and Processing

Three alternative architectures were investigated (Figure 2). These were (1) a Deterministic Boltzmann Machine (DBM) [15, 7], (2) a Competitive Learning network (CL) [19], and (3) a Multi-Layer Perceptron (MLP) [17]. In each case, the input to the network was the nine-element vector representing a demisyllable. For the DBM and MLP, the task of the network was to reproduce the input layer vector at the output layer (see Figure 2). For the CL architecture, the task was to categorize the input layer vector, by turning on exactly one of the output layer units.

For the DBM, the output activation is obtained by applying the input vector, and then performing synchronous updates of unit activations in repeated cycles until the magnitude of changes in unit activations falls below a specified criterion, i.e., until the network settles. The output unit activations at this time constitute the network's response. For the MLP, the output layer activation is produced by propagating the input vector forward in one pass. For the CL architecture, the "winner" is chosen to be the unit with weights closest to those of the input vector, as in the standard

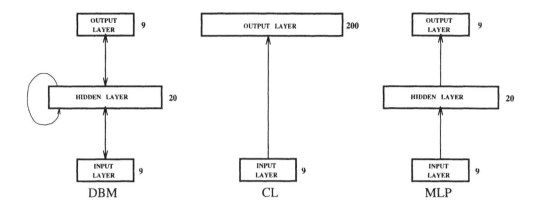

Figure 2: Classification network architectures. Deterministic Boltzmann Machine (DBM); Competitive Learning Network (CL); Multi-Layer Perceptron (MLP). Numbers indicate number of units in a layer. Arrows indicate connectivity.

Table 1: Responses of CL classification network to nonnative stimuli.

Before training				After training			
ta	153	ma	92	ta	153	ma	92
t(d)a	153	na	149	t(d)a	153	na	100
t(r)a	50	nga	204	t(r)a	153	nga	39

Note: The numbers identify the unit responding to a particular stimulus.

algorithm [9], but with the additional requirement that the error for the winner be below a specified criterion; if it is not, an "uncommitted" unit is chosen to be the winner. During training, this error criterion was progressively relaxed.

Weight adjustment for the autopredictive network and MLP classification network was via the back-propagation algorithm [17]. Weights in the DBM classification network were adjusted via contrastive Hebbian learning [7]. In the CL classification network, the winner's weights were adjusted via the standard competitive learning equation [9].

Simulation of Loss of Sensitivity to Nonnative Contrasts

The networks were tested on the nonnative stimuli prior to any training on the input corpus. They were then trained on the input corpus for 20 to 100 epochs, and then tested again on the nonnative stimuli.

For nonnative stimuli *before* training, results from the CL classification network are shown in the left-hand part of Table 1. The numbers are merely identifying labels for the unit responding to a particular stimulus. As shown, the nonnative stimuli are responded to by different units, indicating their discriminability[2]. Results from the CL classification network *after* training are shown in the right-hand part of Table 1. The same unit now responds to *ta*, *t(d)a*, and *t(r)a*, indicating that the nonnative stimuli have been assimilated to the known *ta* category. The *na* and *nga* stimuli are still responded to by different units, however, indicating that they are not assimilable to known categories.

Equivalent results were obtained with the DBM, but not the MLP architecture. Output responses of the DBM classification network are shown projected onto the first two principal components, before training (Figure 3a). The

---

[2]Both *ta* and *t(d)a* are responded to by the same unit, suggesting that these stimuli are already "perceived" as similar. More importantly, however, the two nonnative stimuli *t(d)a* and *t(r)a* are perceived as distinct.

118

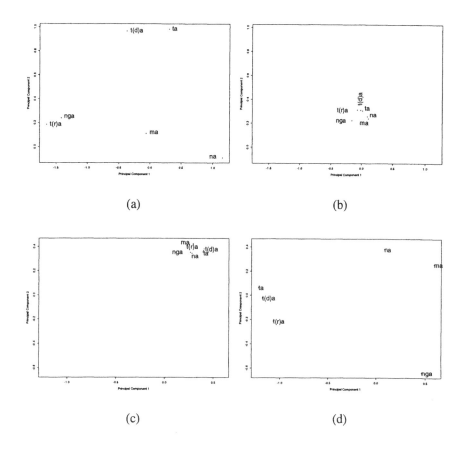

Figure 3: Responses of DBM and MLP classification networks to nonnative stimuli before and after training, projected onto the first two principal components. (a) DBM before training. (b) DBM after training. (c) MLP before training. (d) MLP after training.

network's responses are quite widely separated in state space, indicating discriminability of all the stimuli. After training, however (Figure 3b), responses to the stimuli are much less dispersed in state space. Note, however, that *na* and *nga* are considerably further dispersed than are *t(d)a* and *t(r)a*. These results are analogous to those obtained with the CL architecture. With the MLP architecture, however, the opposite trend appears: responses to the stimuli are more widely dispersed after training (Figure 3d) than before training (Figure 3c).

These results can also be examined in terms of the average pairwise distance between members of the *ta–t(d)a–t(r)a* and *ma–na–nga* triples. With the DBM, the ratio of this average distance *after* training to the average distance *before* training was 0.42 for the stops, and 0.57 for the nasals, illustrating that discriminability had decreased for both groups, but more so for the stops. With the MLP architecture, however, the after-before ratio was 2.77 for the stops and 15.01 for the nasals, indicating that the members of each group had become *more* discriminable after training.

The results obtained with the CL and DBM architectures demonstrate lost sensitivity to certain nonnative contrasts as well as retained sensitivity to certain other nonnative contrasts. This models the observed developmental phenomena, and also provides a computational account of such a process, and thereby a basis for understanding why the observed selective loss of nonnative contrasts in infants might arise. As the perceptual ("classification") system develops, it becomes attuned to, and begins to categorize, sounds occurring in the environment. Other (nonnative) sounds now tend to be interpreted in terms of the categories developed for known, occurring sounds.

We began by hypothesizing that the computational notion of *attractor states* might aid in understanding the phenomena of interest. Pursuing this idea, we now consider the properties of the various classification network architectures examined. First of all, attractor states *necessarily* develop in the DBM, by virtue of its network dynamics. Its learned states thus represent basins of attraction; and this means that inputs similar to those that have been learned will tend to result in one of these attractor states. Second, the CL classification network approximates this property of the DBM, in that an input is mapped to the output unit with most closely similar weights, that is, in virtue of the output rule by which a winner is selected. Third, in a purely feedforward MLP, something like attractor states can develop under certain training regimes. For example, if an MLP is trained to categorize its inputs by turning on particular output units, then the weights developed in this task, together with an output interpretation procedure, will yield input-output mappings that have some of the properties of a system with attractor dynamics, in that many inputs will map onto a particular output state, and in that a given input will be classified by the most activated output unit. However, the MLP in the present case was trained to reproduce its input; such a training regime would not be expected to induce attractor-like properties.

The fact that the loss of nonnative contrasts is simulated with the CL and DBM architectures, but not the MLP architecture is therefore interesting, suggesting that the formation of attractor states is necessary to simulate this developmental trend. In the present simulations, the MLP does not form attractors, and is therefore unable to capture this phenomenon. Although these results need further investigation, they provide preliminary support for the hypothesis that attractor states may be a valuable notion in understanding phonological perception.

This simulation thus yields an interesting new way of thinking about phonological representations: as attractor states that are sculpted in perceptual space by exposure to language-specific input. This not only provides computational specification to the intuition we began with, it also provides a demonstration of how application of network modeling techniques to the set of "touchstone" phenomena proposed in this paper may begin to provide greater understanding of the nature and development of phonological representations.

Acknowledgements

I would like to thank Mike Mozer for collaboration on the simulation work reported in this paper, Janet Werker for bringing the perceptual magnet effect to my attention, Mike Mozer and Dave Plaut for detailed discussion of the ideas outlined here, and Jeff Elman, Brian MacWhinney, Jay McClelland, and Dave Touretzky for helpful comments at various points. Any inaccuracies or inconsistencies are, of course, solely my responsibility.

References

[1] R. N. Aslin, "Visual and auditory development in infancy," in *Handbook of Infant Development* (J. D. Osofsky, ed.), New York: Wiley, 1987.

[2] J. A. Feldman, G. Lakoff, A. Stolcke, and S. H. Weber, "Miniature language acquisition: A touchstone for cognitive science," Report TR-90-009, International Computaer Science Institute, Berkeley, CA, April 1990.

[3] P. Gupta and M. C. Mozer, "Exploring the nature and development of phonological representations," in *Proceedings of the Fifteenth Annual Conference of the Cognitive Science Society*, (Hillsdale, NJ), Lawrence Erlbaum, 1993.

[4] P. Gupta and D. S. Touretzky, "A connectionist learning approach to analyzing linguistic stress," in *Advances in Neural Information Processing Systems 4* (J. Moody, S. Hanson, and R. Lippmann, eds.), (San Mateo, CA), pp. 225–232, Morgan Kaufmann, 1992.

[5] P. Gupta and D. S. Touretzky, "Connectionist models and linguistic theory: Investigations of stress systems in language," *Cognitive Science*, in press.

120

[6] P. Gupta and D. S. Touretzky, "What a perceptron reveals about metrical phonology," in *Proceedings of the Thirteenth Annual Conference of the Cognitive Science Society*, (Hillsdale, NJ), pp. 334–339, Lawrence Erlbaum, 1991.

[7] G. E. Hinton, "Deterministic Boltzmann learning performs steepest gradient descent in weight-space," *Neural Computation*, vol. 1, pp. 143–150, 1989.

[8] P. W. Jusczyk, "From general to language-specific capacities: The WRAPSA model of how speech perception develops," Manuscript, 1992.

[9] T. Kohonen, *Self-Organization and Associative Memory*. Berlin: Springer-Verlag, 1984.

[10] P. K. Kuhl, "Human adults and human infants show a perceptual magnet effect for the prototypes of speech categories, monkeys do not," *Perception and Psychophysics*, vol. 50, pp. 93–107, 1991.

[11] P. K. Kuhl, "Perception, cognition, and the ontogenetic and phylogenetic emergence of human speech," in *Plasticity of Development* (S. E. Brauth, W. S. Hall, and R. J. Dooling, eds.), Cambridge, MA: MIT Press, 1991.

[12] P. K. Kuhl, K. A. Williams, F. Lacerda, K. N. Stevens, and B. Lindblom, "Linguistic experience alters phonetic perception in infants by 6 months of age," *Science*, vol. 255, pp. 606–608, 1992.

[13] A. Lahiri and W. Marslen-Wilson, "The mental representation of lexical form: A phonological approach to the recogniion lexicon," *Cognition*, vol. 38, pp. 245–294, 1991.

[14] L. Menn, K. Markey, M. Mozer, and C. Lewis, "Connectionist modeling and the microstructure of phonological development: A progress report," in *Changes in Speech and Face Processing in Infancy: A Glimpse at Developmental Mechanisms of Cognition* (B. de Boyssons-Bardies, P. Jusczyk, P. MacNeilage, J. Morton, and S. de Schonen, eds.), Dordrecht, The Netherlands: Kluwer, in press.

[15] C. Peterson and J. R. Anderson, "A mean field theory learning algorithm for neural nets," *Complex Systems*, vol. 1, pp. 995–1019, 1987.

[16] L. Polka and J. F. Werker, "Developmental changes in perception of non-native vowel contrasts," Manuscript, 1993.

[17] D. Rumelhart, G. Hinton, and R. Williams, "Learning internal representations by error propagation," in Rumelhart *et al.* [18].

[18] D. E. Rumelhart, J. L. McClelland, and the PDP Research Group, *Parallel Distributed Processing*, vol. 1: Foundations. Cambridge, MA: MIT Press, 1986.

[19] D. E. Rumelhart and D. Zipser, "Feature discovery by competitive learning," in Rumelhart *et al.* [18].

[20] R. Shillcock, G. Lindsey, J. Levy, and N. Chater, "A phonologically motivated input representation for the modeling of auditory word perception in continuous speech," in *Proceedings of the Fourteenth Annual Conference of the Cognitive Science Society*, (Hillsdale, NJ), pp. 408–413, Lawrence Erlbaum, 1992.

[21] J. F. Werker and J. E. Pegg, "Infant speech perception and phonological acquisition," in *Phonological Development: Models, Research and Implications* (C. Ferguson, L. Menn, and C. Stoel-Gammon, eds.), Parkton, MD: York Press, 1992.

Part-of-Speech Tagging
Using A Variable Context Markov Model

Hinrich Schütze
Center for the Study of
Language and Information
Stanford University
USA

Yoram Singer
Institute of Computer Science and
Center for Neural Computation
Hebrew University
Israel

We present a new approach to disambiguating syntactically ambiguous words in context, based on *Variable Context Markov Models*. In contrast to fixed-length Markov models, which predict based on fixed-length histories, Variable Context Markov models dynamically adapt their history length based on the training data, and hence may use fewer parameters. In a test of a VMM based tagger on the Brown corpus, 95.71% of tokens are correctly classified.

INTRODUCTION

Many words in English have several parts of speech (*POS*). For example "book" is used as a noun in "She read a book." and as a verb in "She didn't book a trip." Part-of-speech tagging is the problem of determining the syntactic part of speech of an occurrence of a word in context. In any given English text, most tokens are syntactically ambiguous since most of the high-frequency English words have several parts of speech. Therefore, a correct syntactic classification of words in context is important for most syntactic and other higher-level processing of natural language text.

The two methods that have been mainly used for part-of-speech tagging are fixed order Markov models and Hidden Markov models. Fixed order Markov models are used in [3] and [2]. Since the order of the model is assumed to be fixed, a short memory (small order) is used, since the number of possible combinations grows exponentially. For example, assuming there were 184 different tags, as in our case, there would be $184^3 = 6,229,504$ different order 3 combinations of tags. Because of the large number of parameters higher-order fixed length models are hard to estimate. An alternative is to use *Hidden Markov Models* (HMM) [9, 7]. In an HMM, a different state is defined for each POS tag and the transition probabilities and the output probabilities are estimated using the EM [4] algorithm, which guarantees convergence to a **local** minimum [16]. The advantage of HMMs is that they can be trained using untagged text. On the other hand, the training procedure is time consuming, and a fixed model (topology) is assumed. Another disadvantage, is due to the local convergence properties of the EM algorithm. The solution obtained depends on the initial setting of the model's parameters, and different solutions are obtained for different parameter initialization schemes. This phenomenon discourages linguistic analysis based on the output of the model.

We present a new method, based on *Variable Context Markov Models* (VMM) [13, 14]. The VMM is an **optimal** approximation of an unlimited order Markov source. It can incorporate both the static (order 0) and dynamic (higher-order) information systematically, while keeping the ability to change the model due to future observations. This approach is easy to implement, and the results achieved, using simplified assumptions for the 'static' tag probabilities, are very encouraging.

VARIABLE CONTEXT MARKOV MODELS

Markov models have been a natural candidate for language modeling and temporal pattern recognition, mostly due to their mathematical simplicity. It is nevertheless obvious that finite memory Markov models cannot capture the recursive nature of language, nor can they be trained effectively with long memories. The notion of variable context length also appears naturally in the context of universal coding [10, 12]. This information theoretic notion is now known to be closely related to efficient modeling [11]. The natural measure that appears in information theory is the description length, as measured by the statistical predictability via the Kullback- Liebler (KL) divergence.

The VMM learning algorithm is based on optimizing the statistical prediction power of a Markov model, measured by the instantaneous KL divergence of the following symbols, the current *statistical surprise* of the model. The memory is extended precisely when such a surprise is significant, until the overall statistical prediction of the stochastic model is sufficiently good. For the sake of simplicity, a POS tag is termed a symbol and a sequence of tags is called a string.

Definitions and Notations

Let Σ be a finite alphabet. Denote by $\Sigma^\star$ the set of all strings over Σ. A string s, over $\Sigma^\star$ is denoted by $(\omega_1, \omega_2, \ldots, \omega_n)$. Each string can be identified as a node in a tree that represents $\Sigma^\star$. Each node in the tree has an out degree $|\Sigma|$. Let,

$$Prefix(s) = Prefix(\omega_1, \omega_2, \ldots, \omega_n) = (\omega_1, \omega_2, \ldots, \omega_{n-1}),$$

be the longest prefix of a string s, and denote by,

$$Prefix^\star(s) = Prefix^\star(\omega_1, \omega_2, \ldots, \omega_n) = \{(\omega_1, \ldots, \omega_i) : i < n\},$$

the set of all prefixes of s. Let, $Sufmax^S(s)$, be the longest suffix of s that belongs to a set S.

A *prefix free set* (PFS), is a set $S \subset \Sigma^\star$ such that $\forall s \in S : Prefix^\star(s) \cap S = \phi$. A *prefix free set* S can be represented by a tree whose leaves are the set S. A *full prefix free set* (FPFS) is a prefix free set, where if $s \circ \sigma \in S$ then $\forall \omega \in \Sigma : s \circ \omega \in S$. A prediction pair, $\langle S, P \rangle$, is a combination of a full prefix free set S, and a probability measure over S. We call the set S the prediction set.

A *simple* probabilistic automata PA is a five tuple $\langle S_{PA}, \Sigma_{PA}, \Pi_{PA}, M_{PA}, T_{PA} \rangle$ where S_{PA} is a finite set of states, Σ_{PA} is a finite alphabet, Π_{PA} is the initial probability distribution over S_{PA}, $\Pi_{PA} : S_{PA} \to [0, 1]$, M_{PA} is the output probability, $M_{PA} : S_{PA} \times \Sigma_{PA} \to [0, 1]$, and T_{PA} is the transition function, $T_{PA} : S_{PA} \times \Sigma_{PA} \to S_{PA}$.

Learning Variable Context Markov Sources

A Markov process of order L can be described as a probabilistic automaton where the states are the strings of length L over Σ and the transition function satisfies, $T((\omega_1, \ldots, \omega_L), \omega_{L+1}) = (\omega_2, \ldots, \omega_{L+1})$. A Markov process of order L has $|\Sigma|^L$ states. Suppose that a Markov process is degenerate in the sense that in some cases less than L symbols define a state, i.e. for some sequences of length $K < L$, after observing such a sequence we always get the same probability distribution on the following symbols, independent of the $L - K$ symbols prior to that sequence. In this case the number of states might be much smaller than $|\Sigma|^L$ and we shall call it a Variable Context Markov process.

Given a prediction pair: $\langle S, P \rangle$, we can extend it to induce probabilities, $P^\star$ on every string $s \in \Sigma^\star$ by the following recursion:

If $s \in S$ then $P^\star(s) = P(s)$, else,

$$P^\star(s) = P^\star(Prefix(s)) \times \frac{P^\star(Sufmax^S(s))}{P^\star(Prefix(Sufmax^S(s)))} \quad .$$

This recursion induces probabilities on every string based on the prediction set. At each position in the string the probability of the next symbol is defined by the probability of observing the maximal suffix that belongs to the prediction set ($P^\star(Sufmax^S(s))$) given the fact that we have already observed the prefix of that maximal string ($Prefix(Sufmax^S(s))$). These induced probabilities can be implemented by a simple probabilistic automaton whose states are the words in S, and its next state and transition probabilities are defined by,

$$\forall \omega \in \Sigma : T_{PA}(t, \omega) = Sufmax^T(t \circ \omega) ; \quad M_{PA}(t, \omega) = P^\star(t \circ \omega)/P^\star(t).$$

123

Since a Markov process can be represented by a simple probabilistic automaton, a Variable Context Markov process can be viewed as a prediction pair that contains strings of different lengths. An observation sequence can be produced by a recursive call to $P^\star$ which is equivalent to a biased random walk over the corresponding probabilistic automaton.

Given one sequence of length l or m sequences of lengths $l_1, l_2, \ldots, l_m$ generated by a Markov process we would like to learn its structure and estimate transition probabilities. The key idea is to iteratively build a prediction set whose probability measure will be equal to the empirical probability measure calculated from the observation sequences. During learning, the prefix closure of the prediction set is kept, i.e. the whole tree corresponding to the prediction set is stored, together with the corresponding automaton. At each stage, we look for words whose empirical probabilities are significantly different from the probabilities induced by the current prediction pair (or equivalently by the corresponding automaton). If such differences exist, the prediction set is enlarged and the corresponding automaton is updated. Denote the empirical probability by $\tilde{P}$, and the probability induced by the current prediction set by $\hat{P}$. The current prediction set is denoted by S, and its prefix closure by $S^\star$. The automaton states, transitions, and output probabilities are denoted by, S_{PA}, T_{PA}, and M_{PA} respectively. The prediction error given a string $s = (\omega_1, \ldots, \omega_k)$, is the **KL** distance (also known as the relative entropy) [8] between the empirical probabilities and the automaton induced probabilities on the set of words with one more symbol, denoted by $Pred(s)$,

$$Perr(s) = D^s_{KL}(\tilde{P} \parallel \hat{P}) = \sum_{t \in Pred(s)} \tilde{P}(t) \log \frac{\tilde{P}(t)}{\hat{P}(t)} \;\; , \;\; Pred(s) = \{s \circ \omega \mid \omega \in \Sigma\} \, .$$

Along the run of the algorithm we choose a word s in the prediction set whose prediction error, $Perr(s)$, is the largest and replace the word with its successors. The algorithm halts when all the words in the prediction set have prediction error less than a predetermined accuracy ϵ. See [13, 14] for a more detailed description of the algorithm.

USING A VMM FOR POS TAGGING

We used a tagged corpus to train a VMM. The syntactic information, i.e. the probability of a specific word belonging to a tag class, was estimated using *Maximum Likelihood* estimation from the individual word counts. The states and the transition probabilities of the Markov model were determined by the learning algorithm and tag output probabilities were estimated from word counts (the static information present in the training corpus). The whole structure, for two states, is depicted in Fig. 1. S_i and S_{i+1} are strings of tags corresponding to states of the automaton. $P(t_i|S_i)$ is the probability that tag t_i will be output by state S_i and $P(t_{i+1}|S_{i+1})$ is the probability that the next tag t_{i+1} is the output of state S_{i+1}.

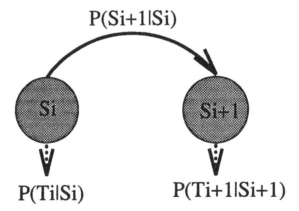

Figure 1: The structure of the VMM based POS tagger

When tagging a sequence of words $w_{1,n}$, we want to find the tag sequence $t_{1,n}$ that is most likely for $w_{1,n}$. We can maximize the joint probability of $w_{1,n}$ and $t_{1,n}$ to find this sequence:[1]

$$T(w_{1,n}) = \arg\max_{t_{1,n}} P(t_{1,n}|w_{1,n}) = \arg\max_{t_{1,n}} \frac{P(t_{1,n}, w_{1,n})}{P(w_{1,n})} = \arg\max_{t_{1,n}} P(t_{1,n}, w_{1,n})$$

$P(t_{1,n}, w_{1,n})$ can be expressed as a product of conditional probabilities as follows:

$$P(t_{1,n}, w_{1,n}) = P(t_1)P(w_1|t_1)P(t_2|t_1, w_1)P(w_2|t_{1,2}, w_1) \ldots P(t_n|t_{1,n-1}, w_{1,n-1})P(w_n|t_{1,n}, w_{1,n-1})$$

$$P(t_{1,n}, w_{1,n}) = \prod_{i=1}^{n} P(t_i|t_{1,i-1}, w_{1,i-1})P(w_i|t_{1,i}, w_{1,i-1})$$

With the simplifying assumption that the probability of a tag only depends on previous tags and that the probability of a word only depends on its tags, we get:

$$P(t_{1,n}, w_{1,n}) = \prod_{i=1}^{n} P(t_i|t_{1,i-1})P(w_i|t_i)$$

Given a Variable Context Markov model M, $P(t_i|t_{1,i-1})$ is estimated by $P(t_i|S_{i-1}, \mathbf{M})$ where $S_i = T_{PA}(\epsilon, t_{1,i})$, since the dynamics of the sequence are represented by the transition probabilities of the corresponding automaton. The tags $t_{1,n}$ for a sequence of words $w_{1,n}$ are therefore chosen according to the following equation using the Viterbi algorithm:

$$T_{\mathbf{M}}(w_{1,n}) = \arg\max_{t_{1,n}} \prod_{i=1}^{n} P(t_i|S_{i-1}, \mathbf{M})P(w_i|t_i)$$

We estimate $P(w_i|t_i)$ indirectly from $P(t_i|w_i)$ using Bayes' Theorem:

$$P(w_i|t_i) = \frac{P(w_i)P(t_i|w_i)}{P(t_i)}$$

The estimation of the static parameters $P(t_i|w_i)$ is described in the next section.

We trained the Variable Context Markov model on the Brown corpus [5], with every tenth sentence removed (a total of 1,022,462 tags). The four stylistic tag modifiers "FW" (foreign word), "TL" (title), "NC" (cited word), and "HL" (headline) were ignored reducing the complete set of 471 tags to 184 different tags.

The resulting automaton has 49 states: the epsilon state, 43 one-symbol states and 5 two-symbol states. This means that 184-43=141 symbols did not have enough "predictive power" to be included as separate states in the automaton. An analysis reveals two possible reasons. Frequent symbols such as "ABN" ("half", "all", "many" used as pre-quantifiers, e.g. in "many a younger man") and "DTI" (determiners that can be singular or plural, "any" and "some") were not included because they occur in a variety of diverse contexts or often precede unambiguous words. For example, when tagged as "ABN" "half", "all", and "many" tend to occur before the unambiguous determiners "a", "an" and "the".

Some rare tags were not included because they did not improve the optimization criterion, minimum description length. For example, "HVZ*" ("hasn't") is not a state although a following "-ed" form is always disambiguated as belonging to class "VBN" (past participle). But since this is a rare event, describing all "HVZ* VBN" sequences separately is cheaper than the added complexity of an automaton with state "HVZ*". We in fact lost some accuracy in tagging because of this property of MDL optimization: Several "-ed" forms after forms of "have" were mistagged as "VBD".

The two-symbol states were "AT JJ", "AT NN", "AT VBN", "JJ CC", and "MD RB" (article adjective, article noun, article past participle, adjective conjunction, modal adverb). Table 1 lists two of the largest differences in transition probabilities for each state. The varying transition probabilities are based on differences between the syntactic constructions in which the two competing states occur. For example, adjectives after articles ("AT JJ")

---

[1]Part of the following derivation is adapted from [2].

125

transition to	one-symbol state	two-symbol state
NN	JJ: 0.45	AT JJ: 0.69
IN	JJ: 0.06	AT JJ: 0.004
IN	NN: 0.27	AT NN: 0.35
.	NN: 0.14	AT NN: 0.10
NN	VBN: 0.08	AT VBN: 0.48
IN	VBN: 0.35	AT VBN: 0.003
NN	CC: 0.12	JJ CC: 0.04
JJ	CC: 0.09	JJ CC: 0.58
VB	RB: 0.05	MD RB: 0.48
VBN	RB: 0.08	MD RB: 0.0009

Table 1: Predictive power gained by two-symbol states

are almost always used attributively which makes a following preposition impossible and a following noun highly probable, whereas a predicative use favors modifying prepositional phrases. Similarly, an adverb preceded by a modal ("MD RB") is followed by an infinitive ("VB") half the time, whereas other adverbs occur less often in pre-infinitival position. On the other hand, a past participle is virtually impossible after "MD RB" whereas adverbs that are not preceded by modals modify past participles quite often.

While it is known that HMM's of order 2 give a slight improvement over HMM's of order 1 [2], the number of parameters in our model is much smaller than in an HMM, even an HMM of order 1 (49*184 = 9016 vs. 184*184 = 33,856).

ESTIMATION OF THE STATIC PARAMETERS

We have to estimate the conditional probabilities $P(t^i|w^j)$, the probability that a given word w^j will appear with tag t^i, in order to compute the static parameters $P(w^j|t^i)$ used in the tagging equations described above. A first approximation would be to use the maximum likelihood estimator:

$$P(t^i|w^j) = \frac{C(t^i, w^j)}{C(w^j)}$$

However, some form of smoothing is necessary, since any new text will contain new words, for which $C(w^j)$ is zero. Also, words that are rare will only occur with some of their possible parts of speech in the training text. One solution to this problem is Good-Turing estimation:

$$P(t^i|w^j) = \frac{C(t^i, w^j) + 1}{C(w^j) + I}$$

where I is the number of tags, 184 in our case. It turns out that Good-Turing is not appropriate for our problem. The reason is the distinction between closed-class and open-class words. Some syntactic classes like verbs and nouns are productive, others like articles are not. As a consequence, the probability that a new word is an article is zero, whereas it is high for verbs and nouns. We need a smoothing scheme that takes this fact into account.

Extending an idea in [2], we estimate the probability of *tag conversion* to find an adequate smoothing scheme. Let $W_l^{i,\neg k}$ be the set of words that have been seen with t^i, but not with t^k in processing all words in the training text up to l. Then we can estimate the probability that a word with tag t^i will later be seen with tag t^k as follows:

$$P_{lm}(i \rightarrow k) = \frac{|\{n|l < n \leq m \wedge w_n \in W_l^{i,\neg k} \cap W_{n-1}^{i,\neg k} \wedge t_n = t^k\}|}{|W_l^{i,\neg k}|}$$

This formula also applies to words we haven't seen so far, if we regard such words as having occurred with a special tag "U" for "unseen". (In this case, $W_l^{U,\neg k}$ is the set of words that haven't occurred up to l.) $P_{lm}(U \rightarrow k)$ then estimates the probability that an unseen word has tag t^k. Table 2 shows the estimates of tag conversion we derived from our training text for $l = 1022462 - 100000$, $m = 1022462$, where 1022462 is the number of words in the training text. To avoid sparse data problems we didn't take cases with less than 100 instances of tag conversion into account.

tag conversion	estimated probability
U → NN	0.29
U → JJ	0.13
U → NNS	0.12
U → NP	0.08
U → VBD	0.07
U → VBG	0.07
U → VBN	0.06
U → VB	0.05
U → RB	0.05
U → VBZ	0.01
U → NP$	0.01
VBD → VBN	0.09
VBN → VBD	0.05
VB → NN	0.05
NN → VB	0.01

Table 2: Estimates for tag conversion

Our smoothing scheme is then the following heuristic modification of Good-Turing:

$$P(t^i|w^j) = \frac{C(t^i, w^j) + \sum_{k_1 \in T_j} P_{lm}(k_1 \to i)}{C(w^j) + \sum_{k_1 \in T_j, k_2 \in T} P_{lm}(k_1 \to k_2)}$$

where T_j is the set of tags that w^j has in the training set and T is the set of all tags. This scheme has the following desirable properties:

- As with Good-Turing, smoothing has a small effect on estimates that are based on large counts.

- The difference between closed-class and open-class words is respected: The probability for conversion to a closed class is zero and is not affected by smoothing.

- Prior knowledge about the probabilities of conversion to different tag classes is incorporated. For example, an unseen word w^j is five times as likely to be a noun than an adverb. Our estimate for $P(t^i|w^j)$ is correspondingly five times higher for "NN", compared to "RB".

ANALYSIS OF RESULTS

Our result on the test set of 114392 words (the tenth of the Brown corpus not used for training) was 95.81%. Table 3 shows the 20 most frequent errors.

Three typical examples for the most common error (tagging nouns as adjectives) are "Communist", "public" and "homerun" in the following sentences.

- the Cuban fiasco and the Communist military victories in Laos

- to increase public awareness of the movement

- the best homerun hitter

127

VMM: correct:	JJ	VBN	NN	VBD	IN	CS	NP	RP	QL	RB	VB	VBG
NN	259						102	100			69	66
VBD		228										
NNS			227									
VBN				219								
JJ			165							71		
VB			142									
CS					112							
NP	110		194									
IN						103						
VBG			94									
RB	63				63				76			
QL										64		

Table 3: Most common errors.

The words "public" and "communist" can be used as adjectives or nouns. Since in the above sentences an adjective is syntactically more likely, this was the tagging chosen by the VMM. The noun "homerun" didn't occur in the training set, therefore the priors for unknown words biased the tagging towards adjectives, again because the position is more typical of an adjective than of a noun.

Two examples of the second most common error (tagging past tense forms ("VBD") as past participles ("VBN")) are "called" and "elected" in the following sentences:

- the party called for government operation of all utilities

- When I come back here after the November election you'll think, you're my man – elected.

Most of the VBD/VBN errors were caused by words that have a higher prior for "VBN" so that in a situation in which both forms are possible according to local syntactic context, "VBN" is chosen. More global syntactic context is necessary to find the right tag "VBD" in the first sentence. The second sentence is an example for one of the tagging mistakes in the Brown corpus, "elected" is clearly used as a past participle, not as a past tense form.

Comparison with other Results

Charniak et al.'s result of 95.97% [2] is slightly better than ours. This difference is probably due to the omission of rare tags with high predictive power in the automaton (the case of "HVZ*").

Kupiec achieves up to 96.36% correctness [9]. However, his results are not comparable with ours since he uses a hidden Markov model. Only the words of the training set are input to the HMM during learning, so that less information is used than in training a VMM. Another difference is that a dictionary is used that lists possible tags that do not occur in the Brown corpus (possibly increasing the error rate), but also covers unseen words. Our error rate on words that do not occur in the training text is 57%, since only the general priors are used for these words in decoding. This error rate could probably be reduced substantially by incorporating ouside lexical information.

FUTURE RESEARCH

Due to the encouraging results, we intend to build a better static model. One of the possible approaches is to use the Dirichlet distribution [1] (or any other discrete probability distribution) and perform Bayesian a-posteriori probability estimation of the individual words, from the word counts and the priors. The priors could then be computed from a mixture of Dirichlet distributions, where each mixture component would correspond to a different tag class.

Modeling using VMMs assumes ergodicity of the source, which is a very crude assumption for natural language. A non-ergodic model might capture the short term statistical dependencies better. Non-ergodic models are hard to learn; in fact, some of the learning problems are computationally intractable [6]. We currently pursue research on sub-optimal estimation schemes, based on similar MDL ideas. We hope that these schemes will better capture the dynamical properties of POS tagging.

Finally, we are planning to use distributionally derived tags [15] as the input to the Markov model, instead of the manually assigned ones in the Brown corpus. This would be completely unsupervised part-of-speech tagging: the static classification as well as the local dynamics would be learned without supervision. We are currently investigating how much of syntactic categorization can be derived from general principles like MDL and how much is rooted in properties specific to language and cognition.

ACKNOWLEDGMENT

Part of this work was done while the second author was visiting the Department of Computer and Information Sciences, University of California, Santa-Cruz, supported by NSF grant IRI-9123692.

We would like to thank Jan Pedersen and Naftali Tishby for helpful suggestions and discussions of this material. Yoram Singer would like to thank the Charles Clore foundation for supporting this research.

References

[1] J. Berger, *Statistical decision theory and Bayesian analysis*. New-York: Springer-Verlag, 1985.

[2] E. Charniak, C. Hendrickson, N. Jacobson, and M. Perkowitz, "Equations for part-of-speech tagging," in *Proceedings of the Eleventh National Conference on Artificial Intelligence*, pp. 784–789, 1993.

[3] K. W. Church, "A stochastic parts program and noun phrase parser for unrestricted text," in *Proceedings of ICASSP-89*, (Glasgow, Scotland), 1989.

[4] A. Dempster, N. Laird, and D. Rubin, "Maximum likelihood estimation from incomplete data via the EM algorithm," *J. Roy. Statist. Soc.*, vol. 39, no. B, pp. 1–38, 1977.

[5] W. N. Francis and F. Kucera, *Frequency Analysis of English Usage*. Boston MA: Houghton Mifflin, 1982.

[6] D. Haussler and Y. Singer, "On the limitations of hidden Markov models," Unpublished manuscript, 1993.

[7] F. Jelinek, "Robust part-of-speech tagging using a hidden markov model," tech. rep., IBM T.J. Watson Research Center, 1985.

[8] S. Kullback, *Information Theory and Statistics*. New-York: Wiley, 1959.

[9] J. Kupiec, "Robust part-of-speech tagging using a hidden markov model," *Computer Speech and Language*, vol. 6, pp. 225–242, 1992.

[10] J. Rissanen, "Modeling by shortest data discription," *Automatica*, vol. 14, pp. 465–471, 1978.

[11] J. Rissanen, "Stochastic complexity and modeling," *The Annals of Statistics*, vol. 14, no. 3, pp. 1080–1100, 1986.

[12] J. Rissanen and G. G. Langdon, "Universal modeling and coding," *IEEE Transaction on Information Theory*, vol. IT-27, no. 3, pp. 12–23, 1981.

[13] D. Ron, Y. Singer, and N. Tishby, "Learning variable memory length Markov sources," In preparation.

[14] D. Ron, Y. Singer, and N. Tishby, "The power of amnesia," in *Advances in Neural Information Processing Systems 6*, 1993. To appear.

[15] H. Schütze, "Part-of-speech induction from scratch," in *Proceedings of ACL 31*, (Columbus OH), pp. 251–258, 1993.

[16] J. Wu, "On the convergence properties of the EM algorithm," *Annals of Statistics*, vol. 11, pp. 95–103, 1983.

Quantitative Predictions From a Constraint-Based Theory of Syntactic Ambiguity Resolution

Michael Spivey-Knowlton
Department of Psychology
University of Rochester, Rochester, NY 14627
e-mail: spivey@psych.rochester.edu

1.0 INTRODUCTION

A great deal of experimental evidence supports the intuition that language comprehension takes place immediately and incrementally. For example, listeners can shadow speech (repeat auditory language input) with a latency of about 250 milliseconds [14]. Unambiguous words are often recognized before the spoken input is even complete [15]. Given this immediacy of comprehension combined with the many local indeterminacies in natural language, it is clear that at least partial commitments are being made to certain interpretations before completely disambiguating information is available.

(1)   a. The actress selected by flipping a coin.
      b. The actress selected by the director quit.

For example, sentences 1a & 1b are temporarily ambiguous at "selected by". "The actress selected by" could continue as an active main clause (1a, where "the actress" is the Agent of the selecting event) or as a passive reduced relative clause (1b, where "the actress" is the Patient of the selecting event). If the reader is understanding the sentence incrementally and "on-line", she must make some form of commitment to an interpretation before completely disambiguating information is available. Since the 1970's, a substantial portion of sentence processing research has addressed the question: What sources of information contribute to this initial parsing commitment?

A few broad categories of approaches have been taken. One type of approach has assumed that syntactic processing is autonomous, and therefore, since nothing else can inform these initial commitments, domain-specific decision principles must be postulated which cause the reader to initially prefer a particular type of syntactic structure over another. Non-syntactic information can then assist in a reinterpretation of the input, should the decision principles lead the reader "down the garden path." A typical example of this approach is the Garden-Path model [5,6,7], in which the syntactically less complex alternative is initially pursued, regardless of the evidence from non-syntactic information sources. Another approach has viewed initial parsing preferences as the result of informational biases set up by the discourse context. The best formulated account in this category is Referential Theory [1,4,27], in which the syntactic alternative which is best supported by the discourse context is initially pursued, regardless of structural complexity or frequency. Recently, a broadly interactive multiple constraints-driven account has been emerging [12,25,26,31,33], in which the available syntactic information strictly defines the possible alternatives but a host of non-syntactic constraints immediately determines which syntactic alternative initially predominates.

There are two critical issues that distinguish these approaches from one another. The first issue is whether initial activation levels of the possible syntactic alternatives are continuous and based largely on contextual information; or whether the alternatives of an ambiguity have categorical (binary) activations, in that an interpretation is either *pursued* or *not pursued*. The second issue of importance is *how* and *when* contextual information modulates resolution of the syntactic ambiguity.

130

The constraint-based approach posits that several contextual influences affect the salience (or activation) of possible syntactic alternatives immediately and in a continuous fashion: for example, 1) frequency of co-occurrence between a sequence of words (or word forms) and its possible syntactic structures, 2) post-ambiguity information that (in reading) may be processed parafoveally, 3) semantic fit between the verb and a noun as its Agent or Patient, and 4) discourse context biasing the reader toward one or the other interpretation. These constraints can interact to produce a wide range of results. For example, if discourse context supports an alternative that is already supported by many of the other constraints, then discourse context will appear to drive the interpretation its way. On the other hand, if discourse context supports one alternative while the other constraints strongly prefer another, then discourse influence will appear weak and/or delayed. In this kind of model, syntax plays an important role. It narrows the search space of possible interpretations to only those that are, at a given point in the input, syntactically well-formed. Syntax cannot, however, choose on its own among a set of alternatives that all meet the syntactic well-formedness constraints of the language. (As far as the syntax is concerned, all the permissible interpretations are acceptable to pursue.) That's the job of various non-syntactic constraints, such as frequency, lexical semantics and discourse context, which immediately influence the activation of the possible alternatives, thus determining on-line syntactic ambiguity resolution.

(2) A hunter was chasing two deer. He put a bullet in one of them and let the other escape.
     The deer shot by the hunter and sprinted away.

For example, the full syntax of the last sentence in passage (2) forces an active main clause interpretation. However, the discourse context (two deer, one being distinguished from the set) AND the lexical semantics ("deer" is a typical Patient of "shot", and "hunter" is a typical Agent of "shot") support a passive reduced relative. Moreover, the lexical ambiguity of the verb "shot" is strongly biased by the context toward the *rifle* sense of "shot" (and away from the *running* sense of "shot"). Thus, before syntactically disambiguating information is encountered (that is, before reaching the end of the sentence), the reader is likely to be pursuing the reduced relative interpretation. Upon encountering the conjoined verb phrase "and sprinted away", however, the strict syntactic constraints rule out the reduced relative interpretation, no matter how strong the discourse and semantic evidence is. This example demonstrates how syntax provides relatively strict and discrete constraints on parsing, while non-syntactic information sources provide more flexible and continuous constraints. One consequence of this is that non-syntactic constraints can execute "gang effects" [24] on one another, but not on syntactic constraints. A gang effect is where two or more numerical (continuous) constraints provide enough combined support for one output alternative to override the support provided by other numerical constraints for a different output alternative. If an output alternative (an interpretation) has been ruled out by a strict constraint, however, no amount of numerical support from continuous constraints will revive that excluded alternative.

This kind of distinction between the powers of syntax and the powers of context has led many theorists to postulate autonomy and primacy in the processing of syntax, relative to other information sources that may be relevant to parsing. This, however, is not a necessary consequence of the discrete/continuous constraint distinction. The strict constraints can be seen simply as highly reliable regularities, and the continuous constraints as relatively informative regularities. Clearly, syntactic constraints do not *always* win out. For example, in everyday speech, syntactic constraints may occasionally, in the right context, be violated with little or no hindrance to successful communication. Thus, labeling (and implementing) the syntactic constraints as "strict", is largely an idealization used to make description, and modeling, of the phenomena simpler. (Is any constraint ever 100% strict?)

In the rest of this paper, I will discuss a few very recent approaches taken toward how to represent strict constraints and continuous constraints. I will also propose a kind of architecture for modeling sentence processing based on a competition between alternatives that incorporates both types of constraints, and describe some preliminary computations that make a first step toward implementing such an architecture. The results of these simple computations are then compared to psycholinguistic data. Finally, I will argue that this type of architecture, when compared to others, is better suited to accounting for the existing data in sentence processing.

2.0 TYPES OF CONSTRAINTS

2.1 Symbolic and Numerical Integrated

Smolensky and colleagues [11,21,24] have proposed an approach to *cognition in general* that incorporates both symbolic (discrete) constraints as well as numerical (continuous) constraints. They point out that symbolic and sub-symbolic representations are simply different levels of analysis, not mutually exclusive forms of description. Thus, their view "integrates" symbolic and sub-symbolic approaches to representation [24], without actually

131

developing a "hybrid" system that *attributes* one form of representation to one process and another form to another process [8]. For example, if a fundamentally probabilistic phenomenon is 99% predictable from a set of strict rules, modeling it with discrete symbolic relations may produce equal accuracy and lower computational cost, as compared to modeling it with continuous values. Phenomena with greater uncertainties will, of course, be better modeled with continuous values.

Computational work on binding fillers to roles (or values to variables) has successfully used both *distributed numerical constraints* [23] and *strict dominance constraints* [11,21]. Smolensky's [23] *tensor product representation* combines one vector of inputs (for the roles) with another (for the fillers) to get a matrix of binding unit activations. This form of encoding is amenable to both localist *and* distributed input representations, binary *and* continuous input activations. Legendre et al.'s [11] and Prince & Smolensky's [21] *strict dominance constraints* are a collection of simple and violable discrete constraints hierarchically ordered to result in an input producing the output which violates the lowest ranked constraint(s) (regardless of quantity). For example, if an output violates four of the lowest ranked constraints, it will be preferred over an output which violates a single higher ranked constraint. This could also be implemented in the form of weighted and unordered (rather than explicitly hierarchical) constraints by simply weighting each constraint by twice as much as its immediately lower-ranked neighbor. Thus, violating the four lowest-ranked constraints would incur 15 (1+2+4+8) "points" of constraint violation, whereas violating only the next highest-ranked constraint would incur 16 "points" of constraint violation.

For representing the temporary syntactic ambiguities that occur in language, however, <u>hierarchical</u> strict constraints may be inappropriate. In its current implementations [11,21], this mapping from input to output always results in a *single* most preferred output. If the constraint-based approach to sentence processing is to represent syntactic information in the form of strict constraints, these strict constraints will sometimes need to be able to provide equal support (or lack of violation) for more than one output alternative at a time.

2.2 Symbolic and Numerical Hybridized

A number of cognitive scientists have explored hybrid architectures that use both discrete rules *and* numerical strengths [8,9,20]. A common interpretation of such work is that the separate components, with their different forms of representation, imply that the cognitive phenomena is governed by separate components using those very forms of representation. The "integrative" viewpoint espoused by Smolensky and colleagues, however, does not require this interpretation. A discrete rule representation is used for one component of a system because it's what works best. A numerical strength representation is used for the other component because that's what works best. A molar analysis of the phenomena may cause it to look like it follows discrete rules most of the time, but the underlying (albeit in some cases more confusing) level of analysis is certainly based on continuous biases. To artificially split these *levels of analysis* into *separate components* of one system, allows the rule-based component to account for the fraction of data that behaves like rule-governed data, and the continuum-based component to account for the data that behaves like continuum-based data. Not a parsimonious solution, but often an effective one.

As an example of a hybrid system that addresses sentence processing, Stevenson [28] has recently developed a parsing model, implemented in LISP, which postulates multiple possible attachment sites in parallel at syntactically ambiguous regions of the input according to standard syntactic rules [3]. After parallel proposal of syntactic attachments, numerical activations for these attachment sites then compete with one another for limited activation resources. While her model is, in spirit, similar to what I will be proposing in this paper, she does not impose *contextual influences* upon those numerical activations. Such contextual influences are crucial to the constraint-based approach to sentence processing. Moreover, the existing psycholinguistic data show such influences rather commonly [1,9,12,19,25,26,31-33].

2.3 Numerical Alone

Sentence processing has also been modeled with systems using only numerical constraints [16,30], with no strict constraints. The Sentence Gestalt (SG) model described by St. John & McClelland [30] receives input in the form of sentence constituents plus the "sentence gestalt" output from the previous iteration. This recurrence of the network allows it to interpret each constituent within the contextual (syntax counts as context in this model) constraints provided by the recent input. St. John & McClelland argue that connectionist modeling of sentence processing has been held back because it is difficult to determine *what* and *how strong* those contextual constraints are. They suggest that using a connectionist learning algorithm is a useful method of obtaining such information while at the same time implementing it in a working model. The solutions arrived at by the connectionist model, however, may depend crucially upon its architecture. For example, since the SG model does not provide separate components (regardless of the degree of interaction one might impose) for the processing of syntax and of semantics, its solutions to the problem of how to weight different constraints assumes that syntax and semantics are not fundamentally different forms of information. (However, the hidden layer of units could conceivably be separating themselves into pseudo-components and using syntactic principles independently of semantic regularities; but even if this were the case, it is important to note that this need not be hard-wired into the system [29].) Without a very careful analysis of the hidden units, it is impossible to know how they are encoding the input/output relationships. Thus, while the SG model may "know" what constraints (with what strengths) interact to produce its output, we still don't. This is a common, but not insurmountable, drawback of complex connectionist models. They solve the input/output problem, but it can be extremely difficult to figure out exactly how they did so.

A crucial aspect of St. John & McClelland's approach to modeling sentence processing, is that no constraints are "all-or-none". In this view, if semantic and discourse context biases the reader toward one interpretation, and the syntax of the full sentence does not permit that interpretation, the reader may still end up with the contextually supported interpretation. The example passage in (2) argues against this claim (see accompanying text). Nonetheless, it may be possible that on rare occasions, particularly in spoken language, syntax can be completely overridden by context. (However, many examples of syntax providing what appear to be continuous constraints are actually due to verb argument frames having continuous preferences for particular thematic roles.)

A more recent purely connectionist model, aimed specifically at syntactic ambiguity resolution, has been developed by Pearlmutter, Daugherty, MacDonald & Seidenberg [18]. Their model does not explicitly address the discreteness or continuousness of syntactic constraints. This feed-forward network receives a verb as input along with the animacy of the preceding noun and produces as output the thematic grid preferred for the verb in that context. This corresponds exactly to the example given in (1). "The actress selected" is comprised of 1) an animate noun (thus a viable Agent of the verb), and 2) a verb that generally prefers both an Agent and a Patient. With input such as this, the model produces a thematic grid involving an Agent and a Patient. Assuming the Agent is to be "the actress", this output means that the initial parsing preference for that input is toward a main clause interpretation. On the other hand, if the model receives an inanimate noun with the same verb as input ("The book selected"), it produces as output a thematic grid specifying only a passive Patient. Thus, its initial parsing preference would be toward a reduced relative. Although sentence-by-sentence comparisons of model output to human reading times have not been made, this basic effect of noun animacy influencing initial parsing preferences for the main clause/reduced relative ambiguity has been observed in the sentence processing literature [33]. However, "the book", despite its inanimacy, can still be a viable Agent for *some* verbs: "The book described the legend of King Tut.". Clearly, the likelihood of a main clause vs. a reduced relative is contingent on finer details than simple noun animacy. Future modeling efforts by Pearlmutter and colleagues will no doubt address some of these details.

3.0 A THEORETICAL MODEL

3.1 Discrete Syntactic Constraints

The model presented here incorporates syntactic constraints as discrete restrictions. For example, when the reader has read "The actress selected by", the syntax proposes two possible discrete classes of sentence: the fragment could continue as an active main clause (sentence 1a), or as a passive reduced relative clause (sentence 1b). Finally, upon reaching the end of the sentence, the syntax rules out one of those two alternatives, forcing the remaining alternative to be the ultimate interpretation. However, if there is no discourse or semantic support for this single remaining interpretation, actually understanding it may take a great deal of time. For example, upon first encountering sentence (3), many readers simply conclude that it is ungrammatical. The full syntax allows only a reduced relative structure, but very little contextual information supports this interpretation. For example, the verb "raced" is 11 times more likely to be used in its active past tense form (main clause) than in its passive participial form (relative clause) [10]. Moreover, "horse" is a reasonably typical Patient of "race", but arguably an even more typical Agent of "race". Finally, the post-ambiguity information "past the barn" is highly consistent with a main clause interpretation. Competition between alternatives would likely leave the reduced relative interpretation with zero activation before syntactic disambiguation (the matrix verb "fell") was encountered.

(3) The horse raced past the barn fell.

An important consequence of implementing syntactic constraints as though they were discrete is that they act as a kind of all-or-none filter. Syntax does not *provide support* for an alternative, it only *rules out* other alternatives. One result of this is that if the contextual constraints (that were encountered before syntactic disambiguation) provide support predominantly for an interpretation that then gets ruled out by syntax, then there is little or no support (or activation) for any interpretation at all. Readers' initial failure to understand sentence (3) is a good example this.

133

3.2 Continuous Contextual Constraints

Although contextual constraints cannot "gang up" on syntax and cause the reader to settle on an interpretation that has been disallowed by syntax, *they can "gang up" on one another* and cause the reader to pursue a different syntactic alternative than the one which some contextual constraint(s) happen to support. Under this version, the model incorporates syntax as providing constraints that *strictly prohibit* certain interpretations, and context as providing constraints that *numerically support* a particular alternative. One example of continuous contextual constraints producing continuous effects in syntactic ambiguity resolution comes from work by Trueswell, Tanenhaus & Garnsey [33]. They demonstrated that peoples' ratings of how typically the subject noun phrase is the Patient of the given verb (i.e., "How typical is it for an actress to be selected by someone?") inversely correlated with the degree of initial processing difficulty in reading the corresponding reduced relative clause. If the subject noun phrase was a highly typical Patient of the verb, then the reader had strong evidence for the passive relative clause interpretation, and this interpretation was pursued with little or no processing difficulty. If, on the other hand, the subject noun phrase was a very *atypical* Patient of the verb (and at least a *reasonable* Agent of the verb), then the noun phrase's Agenthood supported the active main clause alternative and the presence of "by" after the verb supported the reduced relative alternative. Competition between these two comparably supported alternatives caused slowed processing at the syntactically ambiguous regions of the sentence.

3.3 Syntactic Ambiguity Resolution

The psycholinguistic data to be modeled in this paper is the amount of processing difficulty human subjects encounter while reading a syntactically ambiguous region of a reduced relative clause, such as the verb+"by" of sentence (1b). Subjects read sentences in various contexts by pressing a button to reveal two-word segments of the target sentence. Reading times were collected for particular regions of the sentence by recording time between button presses. By comparing reading times of the verb+"by" region when preceded by "who was" and when not (see 4a & 4b), the amount of processing difficulty caused by the syntactic ambiguity (absent in 4a, but present in 4b) can be assessed [26]. The model I will describe allows syntax to filter out only the syntactically possible alternatives and simultaneously computes the amount of numerical support provided by the contextual constraints for those possible alternatives. This numerical support determines the initial activation level of each possible alternative. Competition between these syntactically well-formed alternatives then commences with mild autofacilitation and strong mutual inhibition until a criterion amount of supremacy (a steady state) is reached. The number of cycles, or iterations, of this competition represents the amount of processing difficulty for a given stimulus item. An important aspect of this model is that difficulty in processing a syntactic ambiguity is due to *competition between alternatives*, not to a conscious misinterpretation followed by strategic reinterpretation [6,7].

(4) a. The woman who was watched by the guard realized that she was no longer inconspicuous.
   b. The woman watched by the guard realized that she was no longer inconspicuous.

4.0 A COMPUTATIONAL MODEL

4.1 Choice of Constraints

The inputs to this model are based on the parameters of the individual stimuli used in a study by Spivey-Knowlton, Trueswell & Tanenhaus [26]. Norming studies and corpus analyses provide the continuous values for the contextual constraints. For example, a sentence completion task on the stimuli in different contexts revealed that in the main clause supporting context, the sentence fragments (i.e., "The actress selected") were completed as main clauses 75% of the time, and as reduced relatives 25% of the time. In the relative clause supporting context, they were completed as main clauses only 57% of the time, and as reduced relatives 43% of the time [26]. A typicality rating task [25] provided values for the Agenthood and Patienthood for each subject noun phrase and its corresponding verb (i.e., on a 1-7 scale, "actress" received an Agenthood of 2.1 and a Patienthood of 6.1 for the verb "selected", whereas "woman" received an Agenthood of 5.3 and a Patienthood of 4.0 for the verb "watched".). Also, frequency of the verb being used as a simple past tense versus a past participial was collected from the Brown corpus of English usage [10]. For example, the "-ed" form of "kill" was used as a simple past tense 45% of the time and as a past participial 55% of the time. Finally, because the presence of "by" immediately following the verb provides probabilistic evidence for the reduced relative interpretation [31], it was given a small constant amount of strength to support that alternative. All stimulus items to be modeled had "by" immediately following the verb.

Returning to St. John & McClelland's [30] point of *what* and *how strong* the contextual constraints should be, I have assumed in this computational model that discourse context [1,4,26] (Main clause- and relative clause-supporting contexts), semantic fit [19,25,31-33] (Agenthood and Patienthood), verb form frequency [13] (Simple past vs. Past participial), and post-ambiguity evidence [2,12,26] ("by" following the verb) are all relevant sources of contextual constraint and are used in immediate syntactic ambiguity resolution. Determining the *strength* of each of these constraints is more complicated. There are two types of constraint strength that one can measure, and both are important. An individual stimulus input may have a very strong bias in one of its sources of constraint. For example, "punished" is much more commonly used as a passive participial (89%) than an active past tense (11%). However, if that source of constraint (verb-form frequency) is not a highly valid cue, in general, it will have a small weight in the model, and therefore show a relatively small influence on performance. Nonetheless, if a heavily weighted constraint (e.g., Agenthood) happens to provide very weak support in an individual stimulus for an alternative ("family" has 1.7 Agenthood for the verb "robbed"), then it may show *even less* influence on the model's performance. Thus, the *strength* of a bias in an individual stimulus and the *weight* of that general constraint in the model together determine the input activation to a syntactically-permitted interpretation.

4.2 Weight of Constraints

For each stimulus item tested on the model, the strengths of these biases were collected from sentence completion tasks, rating tasks, and corpus analyses. Then these bias strengths were matched with the processing difficulty (reduced relative reading time minus full relative reading time) at the verb+"by" region of the corresponding sentence in a multiple linear regression. While this linear regression accounted for only 6% of the variance in processing difficulty (r^2=.057), it did provide ball-park figures of how to weight each of the relevant constraints in the model. These parameters went into equations (1) and (2).

At the verb+"by" region, the only syntactically possible alternatives are the passive reduced relative clause and the active main clause. Therefore, the present small-scale implementation of the model computes only the activations of those two alternatives via equations (1) and (2):

$$a_r = .3D_r + .2P + .15B + .05F_r \qquad (1)$$

$$a_m = .3D_m + .3A + .05F_m \qquad (2)$$

In these equations, a is the activation of the passive reduced relative alternative (a_r) or the active main clause alternative (a_m). D is the discourse context support for the reduced relative (D_r) or the main clause (D_m). P is the Patienthood rating divided by its maximum (7) to produce a value between .16 and 1. It provides support only for the reduced relative. A is the Agenthood rating divided by its maximum (7); and provides support only for the main clause. B is the support for the reduced relative from "by" following the verb, and is given a constant strength of .3 because all the items in the input have "by" following the verb. Finally, F is the verb-form frequency percentage of passive participial usage (F_r) and active past tense usage (F_m).

4.3 Competition

After these initial activations are computed for the two alternatives, the architecture of the model forces the higher activated alternative to inevitably be the winning interpretation for that region of the sentence (verb+"by"). The crucial performance feature of the model is how long the iterative competition goes on before one alternative reaches criterion for "winning". This criterion is that the winning alternative must be .3 higher in activation than its competitor. The criterion is eventually met by each alternative sending inhibition (proportional to its own activation) to the other alternative and feeding itself facilitation (again, proportional to its own activation). Equations (3) and (4) are computed simultaneously and successively until one alternative reaches a criterion of supremacy.

$$a_{r,t} = a_{r,t-1} + .018a_{r,t-1} - .04a_{m,t-1} \qquad (3)$$

$$a_{m,t} = a_{m,t-1} + .018a_{m,t-1} - .04a_{r,t-1} \qquad (4)$$

Activation of the passive reduced relative alternative at time t ($a_{r,t}$) equals its activation at the previous cycle, t-1, plus autofacilitation from its previous activation level ($a_{r,t-1}$), and minus inhibition from the previous activation level of the competing alternative ($a_{m,t-1}$). The opposite takes place for the active main clause alternative.

Negative activation values are truncated at zero, and the maximum number of cycles to criterion is truncated at 150.[1] Number of cycles to criterion was collected for each of the 16 stimulus items in each of their two contexts. These values for each item were compared to the amount of processing difficulty for each corresponding item in a simple linear regression. The output of this competition-based model accounted for 50% of the variance in the processing difficulty exhibited by readers across the various stimulus items. See Figure 1. Sentences that elicited great processing difficulty at the verb+"by" likewise took many cycles of the model to reach criterion. Sentences that elicited little processing difficulty at that region took fewer cycles to reach criterion. This model puts to shame the multiple linear regression described earlier not because of its dynamic nature, but because of its *competition*.

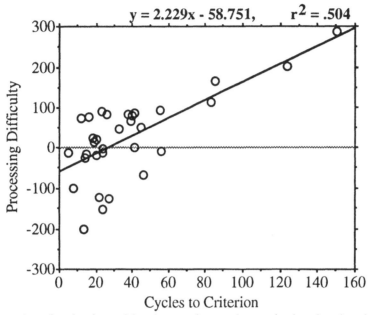

$$y = 2.229x - 58.751, \qquad r^2 = .504$$

Figure 1. The number of cycles the model took to reach a steady state is plotted against the amount of processing difficulty (in milliseconds) readers exhibited at the verb + "by" of the reduced relative clause for each of the 16 stimulus items in each of their two contexts. Processing difficulty is determined by subtracting reading times for the unambiguous *full* relative clause (4a) from reading times for the ambiguous *reduced* relative clause (4b). The r^2 value above shows that the output of the model accounts for 50% of the variance across the 32 stimuli.

5.0 CONCLUSION

With very simple computations, a competition-based model of syntactic ambiguity resolution integrates various contextual constraints immediately and simultaneously. In this model, the number of cycles to reach a steady state correlates well with the degree of processing difficulty exhibited by readers on a number of syntactically ambiguous sentences. The weights given to discourse and semantic influences in this model suggest that theories which incorporate such influences as fundamentally weak and/or delayed [5,17,22] are incorrect. Moreover, models which implement syntactic constraints as continuous (and therefore flexible) [16,30] allow context to completely override syntax, which involves great computational cost to account for a very small portion of the data. Syntactic constraints are "strict" in this evidential approach to sentence processing and contextual constraints are "numerical". Future computational implementations of the constraint-based theory of syntactic ambiguity resolution will expand the present work and explore possible contingency relationships between individual contextual constraints [2,25,26].

Acknowledgments
This work was supported by an NSF Graduate Research Fellowship and by NIH grant #HD27206. The design of the computational model presented herein benefited from discussions with Ken McRae and with Paul Smolensky. I am grateful to Jay McClelland and Mike Tanenhaus for comments on the manuscript.

---

[1] Only one stimulus input had to have its number of cycles truncated at this ceiling value. This was because its contextual constraints caused the initial activations of the two alternatives to be almost exactly equal, and competition lasted over 1000 cycles. Interestingly, reading times of the next region of this item showed uniquely high processing difficulty.

References

[1] G. Altmann, & M. Steedman, "Interaction with context during human sentence processing," *Cognition*, vol. 30, pp. 191-238, 1988.

[2] C. Burgess, "The interaction of syntactic, semantic and visual factors in syntactic ambiguity resolution," Unpublished Ph.D. Dissertation, University of Rochester, 1991.

[3] N. Chomsky, *Lectures on Government and Binding: The Pisa Lectures*, Dordrecht: Foris Publications, 1981.

[4] S. Crain & M. Steedman, "On not being led up the garden path: The use of context by the psychological parser," in Dowty, Kartunnen & Zwicky (Eds.), Natural Language Parsing. Cambridge: Cambridge U. Press, 1985.

[5] L. Frazier, "Sentence processing: A tutorial review," In Coltheart (Ed.), *Attention & Performance XII: The Psychology of Reading*. Hillsdale, NJ: Erlbaum, 1987.

[6] L. Frazier & J. D. Fodor, "The sausage machine: A two-stage parsing model," *Cognition*, vol. 6, pp. 291-325, 1978.

[7] L. Frazier & K. Rayner, "Making and correcting errors during sentence comprehension: Eye movements in the analysis of structurally ambiguous sentences," *Cognitive Psychology*, vol. 14, pp. 178-210, 1982.

[8] J. Hendler, "Special Issue: Hybrid systems (symbolic/connectionist)," *Connection Science*, vol. 1, pp. 227-342, 1989.

[9] M. Just & P. Carpenter, "A capacity theory of comprehension: Individual differences in working memory," *Psychological Review*, vol. 99, pp. 122-149, 1992.

[10] H. Kucera & W. Francis, *Computational analysis of present-day American English*. Providence, RI: Brown University Press, 1967.

[11] G. Legendre, W. Raymond & P. Smolensky, "Analytic typology of case marking and grammatical voice," in *Proceedings of the 19th Conference of the Berkeley Linguistic Society*, in press.

[12] M. MacDonald, "Probabilistic constraints and syntactic ambiguity resolution," Manuscript submitted for publication, 1993.

[13] M. MacDonald, N. Pearlmutter, & M. Seidenberg, "Syntactic ambiguity resolution as lexical ambiguity resolution," in Rayner, Clifton & Frazier (Eds.), *Current Research in Sentence Processing*, in press.

[14] W. Marslen-Wilson, "Linguistic structure and speech shadowing," *Nature*, vol. 244, pp. 522-523, 1973.

[15] W. Marslen-Wilson & A. Welsh, "Processing interactions and lexical access during word recognition in continuous speech," *Cognitive Psychology*, vol. 10, pp. 29-63, 1978.

[16] J. McClelland, M. St. John, R. Taraban, "Sentence comprehension: A parallel distributed processing approach," *Language and Cognitive Processes*, vol. 4, pp. 287-336, 1989.

[17] D. Mitchell, M. Corley & A. Garnham, "Effects of context in human sentence parsing: Evidence against a discourse-based proposal mechanism," *Journal of Experimental Psychology: Learning, Memory and Cognition*, vol. 18, pp. 69-88, 1992.

[18] N. Pearlmutter, K. Daugherty, M. MacDonald & M. Seidenberg, "Constraint satisfaction in main verb/reduced relative ambiguities," presented at the 6th annual CUNY Sentence Processing Conference, Amherst, MA, 1993.

[19] N. Pearlmutter & M. MacDonald, "Plausibility effects in syntactic ambiguity resolution," in *Proceedings of the 14th Annual Conference of the Cognitive Science Society*, 1992, pp. 498-503.

[20] S. Pinker, "Rules of language," *Science*, vol. 253, pp. 530-535, 1991.

[21] A. Prince & P. Smolensky, *Optimality Theory*, in press.

[22] K. Rayner, S. Garrod, & C. Perfetti, "Discourse influences during parsing are delayed," *Cognition*, vol. 45, pp. 109-139, 1992.

[23] P. Smolensky, "Tensor product variable binding and the representation of symbolic structures in connectionist systems," *Artificial Intelligence*, vol. 46, pp. 159-216, 1990.

[24] P. Smolensky, G. Legendre & Y. Miyata, "Principles for an integrated connectionist/symbolic theory of higher cognition," Tech. Report CU-CS-600-92, University of Colorado at Boulder, 1992.

[25] M. Spivey-Knowlton & M. Tanenhaus, "Referential context and syntactic ambiguity resolution," in Rayner, Clifton & Frazier (Eds.), *Current Research in Sentence Processing*, in press.

[26] M. Spivey-Knowlton, J. Trueswell & M. Tanenhaus, "Context effects and syntactic ambiguity resolution: Parsing relative clauses," *Canadian Journal of Experimental Psychology*: Special Issue, vol. 47, pp. 276-309, 1993.

[27] M. Steedman & G. Altmann, "Ambiguity in Context: A reply", *Language and Cognitive Processes*, vol. 4, pp. 105-122, 1989.

[28] S. Stevenson, "A competition-based explanation of syntactic attachment preferences and garden-path phenomena," in *Proceedings of the Association for Computational Linguistics*, 1993, pp. 266-273.

[29] M. St. John, "Language learning in the service of a task," presented at the 14th Annual Conference of the Cognitive Science Society, Bloomington, IN, 1992.

[30] M. St. John & J. McClelland, "Learning and applying contextual constraints in sentence comprehension," *Artificial Intelligence*, vol. 46, pp. 217-257, 1990.

[31] P. Tabossi, M. Spivey-Knowlton, K. McRae & M. Tanenhaus, "Semantic effects on syntactic ambiguity resolution: Evidence for a constraint-based resolution process," *Attention and Performance XV*, in press.

[32] R. Taraban & J. McClelland, "Constituent attachment and thematic role assignment: Influences of content-based expectations," *Journal of Memory and Language*, vol. 27, pp. 597-632, 1988.

[33] J. Trueswell, M. Tanenhaus & S. Garnsey, "Semantic influences on parsing: Use of thematic role information in syntactic disambiguation," *Journal of Memory and Language*, in press.

Optimality Semantics

Bruce B. Tesar
University of Colorado
Campus Box 430
Boulder, CO USA 80309-0430
`tesar@cs.colorado.edu`

This paper outlines a general proposal for a theory of semantic structuring. The proposal focuses on a set of semantic structuring notions proposed by Talmy, and on relations between closed class elements of a sentence and the semantic structural interpretation carried by the sentence. The theory is cast within the connectionist-based formal framework of Optimality Theory, and makes predictions about the semantic structural interpretations of sentences.

INTRODUCTION

Several research efforts in linguistic semantics have been particularly concerned with semantic structure. Recent examples include Lakoff's image schemas [4], Jackendoff's conceptual semantics [3], and Langacker's cognitive semantics [5]. In particular, Talmy [8] has written on the distinction between semantic structure and semantic 'content', or 'filler' material, and on the ways in which languages express structural notions.

This paper makes a very general proposal for a theory of semantic structuring, cast in a constraint satisfaction-style formal framework. The proposal actually considers a restricted subset of semantic structuring notions, Talmy's Disposition of Quantity. The formal framework chosen is Optimality Theory, a connectionist-based framework. A theory of the type proposed here demonstrates how semantic structure is determined in language, and explains data on what semantic structure interpretations are made of particular sentences.

SEMANTIC STRUCTURE AND CLOSED CLASS FORMS

Leonard Talmy has proposed that closed-class linguistic forms play a crucial role in semantic structuring [8]. The claim is that closed-class forms play an abstract structuring role in contributing to meaning; they form the conceptual "skeleton" of the meaning, while open-class forms provide the filler material, or the "flesh hanging on the skeleton."

Open and Closed Classes

An open class is one that has many members, and to which new members are easily added. Examples of open classes are nouns, adjectives, and verbs. A closed class, by contrast, typically has relatively few members, and new members cannot easily be added. Examples of closed classes are prepositions, determiners, and affixes.

Talmy's claim is that, while open classes can include forms that contain nearly any sort of meaning, members of closed classes (Talmy sometimes refers to them as 'grammatical forms') are largely restricted to structural kinds of meaning. Many languages have a closed-class form designating plurality (e.g., the "-s" suffix in English). Virtually no language has a closed-class form designating color. Further, when an open class form clashes with a closed class form, the closed class form usually wins.

According to Talmy, a general property of the semantic structuring notions expressed by closed class forms is that they are "relativistic or topology-like, and exclude the absolute or the metrically Euclidean" [8]. The English closed class deictic terms *this* and *that* can be used to distinguish 'this chair I am sitting in' from 'that chair across the room', or to distinguish 'this country I am living in' from 'that country across the ocean.' The terms are insensitive to the absolute distances involved (a few meters vs. thousands of miles). The English pluralizing morpheme "-s" can be applied to any kind of entity that can be expressed as a noun in language, including physical objects, actions, and emotions.

Along with this is the property of productivity. Because they are insensitive to 'filler' types of semantic stuff (like 'objectness' or 'emotionness'), closed class forms can be highly productive. Because of these properties, Talmy has further conjectured that the structuring notions expressed by closed class forms reflect general human conceptual structure.

Disposition of Quantity

Although Talmy has suggested several different kinds of semantic structure, he has most extensively explored what he calls "configurational structure."[8] This is the way that entities contained (or referred to) in the meaning of the sentence are structured. The most crucial categories are *plexity, boundedness*, and *state of dividedness*.

Plexity is the state of a quantity's articulation into equivalent elements. The category has two values: uniplex and multiplex. A quantity has uniplex plexity if it is conceptualized as a single unit. A quantity has multiplex plexity if it is conceptualized as a group of units.

Boundedness concerns the sense of containedness of a conceived entity. The two values of this category are bounded and unbounded. A bounded entity is conceptualized as an individuated entity with intrinsic bounds (in space, time, or other dimension). An unbounded entity is not conceptualized as having any intrinsic bounds.

State of dividedness concerns an entity's internal segmentation. The two values of this category are discrete and continuous.

These three categories, taken together, form a system which Talmy calls Disposition of Quantity (which will be abbreviated QD). The following examples can briefly illustrate this system. A single *jellybean* would typically be conceptualized as uniplex/bounded/discrete, a single point entity. *Water*, on the other hand, would typically be conceptualized as multiplex/unbounded/continuous, a continuous mass of substance. As a plural, *jellybeans* is multiplex/unbounded/discrete, an unbounded collection of units, while *a glass of jellybeans* is multiplex/bounded/discrete, a bounded collection of units. By contrast, *a glass of water* is multiplex/bounded/continuous, a bounded mass of substance. Notice that an entity that, overall, is conceptualized as uniplex must necessarily be bounded/discrete.

The preceding examples all involve structure in space. But the same system applies to structure in other dimensions, such as time. An action such as *(to) blink* is normally conceptualized as a point event in time, and thus uniplex/bounded/discrete. An instance of the action *(to) sleep* is normally conceptualized as an ongoing event, and would be multiplex/unbounded/continuous.

Figure, Ground, and Path

In separate work [9], Talmy has described a kind of semantic case structure. The structure applies to what Talmy calls a 'motion situation', where one entity, called the figure, is either located or moving with respect to another entity, called the ground. The figure may be thought of as the 'conceptually movable object', while the ground may be thought of as the reference object. The choice between location (denoted BE) and motion (denoted MOVE) is called the 'fact of motion', and the specific relationship between the figure and ground is called the 'path'. Talmy's concepts of figure and ground are similar in many respects to Langacker's trajector and landmark [5], and to the argument slots of Jackendoff's conceptual semantic functions [3].

These concepts are most easily exemplified in sentences describing everyday motion and location in space. In *the pen is on the table*, *the pen* is the figure, *the table* is the ground, *is* contains the fact of motion BE, and *on* is the path. With *the pen rolled across the table*, *the pen* is the figure, *the table* is the ground, *rolled* contains the fact of motion as MOVE, and *across* is the path. The same concepts apply in other dimensions as well: *the clock chimed at three o'clock* has the event 'the clock chimed' being located in time at three o'clock: *the clock chimed* is the figure, *three o'clock* is the ground, *at* is the path, and the fact of motion (BE) is not explicitly expressed in the sentence.

The figure/ground/path structure fits with the structure/filler view of semantic notions discussed earlier. The figure and ground usually include filler material, while the path is a structural semantic notion. It should not be too surprising, given Talmy's observations about open class and closed class, that path is often expressed by closed class forms, while figure and ground are more commonly expressed via open class forms.

139

A Brief Example

The following example (taken from [8]) illustrates how closed class forms can win out over open class forms. Consider the sentence *the beacon flashed*. *Flash* by itself is normally conceptualized as a point event in time. The sentence would have the QD values uniplex/bounded/discrete in time. Now consider the sentence *the beacon flashed until dawn*. The closed class form *until* implies an event that has an extent (duration) in time, which ends at *dawn*. This conflicts with the point event structure implied by the open class item *flash*. The result is that the QD values of the *flash* event are shifted from uniplex/bounded/discrete to multiplex/bounded/discrete, with the light flashing repeatedly over a duration of time. This example is more carefully examined below, as Example 2.

OPTIMALITY THEORY

The Theory

Optimality theory [7] is a framework for generative grammar. In [7] it is applied to phonology. The framework can be applied to domains other than phonology, however, and in fact has recently been applied to syntax [6][1]. This section will very briefly describe the framework.

Optimality theory concerns mappings between input spaces and output spaces. A particular model within this framework will consist of an input space, an output space, and an evaluation function, or Harmony function, which applies to particular input/output pairs (a pair consisting of one member of the input space and one member of the output space). For a given input, the appropriate output is selected by determining which member of the output space, when paired with the given input, is determined to be the best, or optimal, output by the Harmony function. The actual output determined by the model is the optimal one with respect to the Harmony function. The actual output is sometimes called the "optimal parse" of the input.

The theory further requires that the Harmony function be embodied as a ranked set of constraints. Specifically, the constraints must be in a 'strict dominance hierarchy'. This means that the highest ranked constraint 'counts' for more than all of the lower ranked constraints put together, the second-highest ranked constraint counts for more than all the constraints below it, and so forth. For any given input/output pair, a particular constraint may or may not be violated. (Note: it is possible to violate a constraint more than once). When the highest-ranked constraint is said to 'count' for more than those ranked below it, what is meant is that any output that does not violate that constraint will automatically be judged as better than any output that does violate that constraint, no matter how many violations of lower ranked constraints occur.

It is important to note that optimality-theoretic models do not make absolute well-formedness judgements of the inputs. For every member of the input space, a member of the output space is selected, the output which is optimal with respect to the ranked set of constraints.

Opportunities for Formal Results

Optimality theory provides opportunities for mathematically proving results about the structures in the output space. It is possible, under the right conditions, to prove that certain members of the output space will never be chosen. Such a proof can be accomplished by demonstrating that, for a given structure in the output space, some other structure will better satisfy the constraints, no matter what the input is. It need not be the case that the provably better structure is overall the best for many (or even any) inputs. But if output X is better than output Y for all inputs, then clearly Y will never be the optimal output for any input. Such a proof would demonstrate that structure Y, while a member of the output space, is blocked by the constraints, and is in this sense ill-formed. For examples and discussion of these types of proofs, see [6] and [7].

The ability to use the constraints to prove that some members of the output space are ill-formed is another appealing feature of optimality theory. The space of outputs itself may be defined somewhat more simply and generally, because it need not reflect all the complex details of what structures are and aren't well-formed. The real work is done by the constraints, which together with the inputs determines what subset of the output space is well-formed.

The Connection with Connectionism

By now it should be apparent that optimality theory is a kind of connectionist theory. One of the fundamental theoretical concepts contributed by connectionism is that of 'soft' constraints, that is, constraints that may on occasion be violated. Optimality theory uses soft constraints, with the restriction that the constraints be in a 'strict dominance hierarchy.' Implementational issues, such as units and weighted connections, are not of concern here; the ranked set of soft constraints is the focus.

SEMANTIC STRUCTURING IN AN OPTIMALITY THEORY FRAMEWORK

This section proposes a way of placing Talmy's semantic structuring ideas within an Optimality Theory framework. The descriptions are in terms of the figure/ground/path semantic case role system, and the QD structure categories. It is important to stress that this proposal is at a general level; many details are not given here, and several potential difficulties exist.

The examples referred to throughout this section will be found at the end of this section.

The Input and Output Spaces

Each member of an input space corresponds to a pre-processed version of a sentence. The sentence is analyzed into a figure/ground/path structure. Some recursive phrase structure is permitted. For example, the main figure of the sentence may itself be composed of a figure/ground/path structure. The default QD values (plexity, boundedness, and dividedness) of the open class constituents of the sentence are inserted into the input in place of the open class words themselves, while the closed class elements appear directly in the input. The QD values may be applied to more than one dimension, so a dimension indication (e.g., space, time) accompanies each set of values. Because sets of open class words can be found such that each word in the set has the same default QD values (e.g., both *water* and *wood* are multiplex/unbounded/continuous in space by default), numerous sentences may correspond to the same point in the input space, so long as they have the same closed-class elements, and the corresponding open class elements have the same default QD values.

The output space also consists of recursive figure/ground/path structures. However, for the figure and ground semantic roles, the collection of open class elements (represented by the default QD values) and closed class elements in the input is replaced with a simple specification of QD values. The path role in the output is occupied by a one of a set of path primitives, as well as a set of QD values. The path primitives can be thought of as 'structural schemas', built-in to the system. The output space represents possible interpretations of the sentences given by the input.

Consider Example 1 below. The figure input has two closed class items and one set of semantic structure values. The closed class items are the article *the* and the plural morpheme *-s*. The set of QD values are for the space dimension, and are the default values for the open class word *pen* in the sentence. The input entries for the ground and verb roles may be understood similarly (note that for the open class verb *roll*, the default QD values are for the time dimension; the MOVE is also brought in by *roll*). The output's figure and ground, however, have only QD values. And they don't always match the input.

The label "OC:" followed by a word in an input and output constituent may be thought of as showing the open class or "filler" semantic material. The word following the label shouldn't be thought of as representing the entire word, but only the structureless filler part. These entries are included in the representations here primarily to help show which parts of the structures correspond to which parts of the original sentence. No constraints make reference to the OC values, and they don't affect the input/output correspondences.

It should be acknowledged here that the figure/ground/path formal structure, along with the QD categories, are not sufficient to represent all of semantic structure; a richer collection of formal structures will be necessary. For example, there is no clear way to distinguish between the sentence *the cup is on the table* and the noun phrase *the cup on the table*, where *cup* is the head of the phrase. Jackendoff in particular has proposed quite a variety of formal structures [3]. The challenge, when working within an optimality theory framework, is to keep the collection of possible formal structures strictly specified and under control, so that the output space remains well-defined. The examples in this paper are restricted to recursive compositions of the figure/ground/path formal structure.

The Nature of the Constraints

The examples given below each have a list of 'relevant' constraints. These are listed in order of their ranking, from highest-ranked to lowest ranked. Each list should be thought of as a subset of a much larger set of constraints covering the entire structuring system.

There are two general kinds of constraints. One kind specifies correspondence requirements between the input and the output. In Example 1, the constraint "-s in an input requires the output entity to be multiplex" is of this first kind. The other kind of constraint places restrictions on what kinds of output entities may co-occur. These may be thought of as "well-formedness constraints" on the output. The constraint "an output entity that is uniplex must be bounded and discrete" in Example 1 is of this kind.

In Example 1, the preposition *across* communicates that the output should have the semantic path primitive ACROSS. The path ACROSS implies that the ground has some extension to it, such that it may be crossed. An interpretation that had a path of ACROSS and a ground that was conceptualized as a point (uniplex/bounded/discrete) would violate the constraint "ACROSS requires the ground to be continuous", which captures this intuition. The preservation of the default QD values for open class items is reflected in the much lower ranked constraint "QD values in the input should be left unchanged in the output". This latter constraint is violated in Example 1 several times. For example, the ground is uniplex in the input, but multiplex and continuous in the output. The ranking of the constraints reflects Talmy's claim that closed class specifications of semantic structure generally win when they conflict with open class specifications.

It must be emphasized that the examples listed below are intended to illustrate the general nature of the theory. The listed constraints are at best incomplete, and quite likely flawed. Future work will focus on developing a more complete set of constraints, and testing its empirical adequacy.

The Mapping

As dictated by Optimality Theory, each input sentence representation is mapped to the point in the output space that best satisfies the ranked constraints. This output point represents the structural interpretation of the sentence.[1]

In Example 2, the given output violates the constraint "TO requires the figure to be uniplex". This constraint is in the system intentionally; it is respected in instances of an object moving through space *to* a goal, like in *Bob went to the store*, where *Bob* is conceptualized as a point moving along a path. However, in Example 2, the figure is not being conceptualized as moving, but as being located, and distributed across multiple points in time. This is reflected by the verb primitive BE in the input and the output. The presence of BE in the output invokes the highly ranked constraint "BE requires that the figure QD values match the path QD values". Relevant to the path QD values are the next three constraints in the ranking, including "*until* in the input path requires TO as the output path", and "TO requires the path to be multiplex". So, *until* requires the output path primitive be TO, TO requires that the path to be multiplex, and the BE verb primitive requires the figure plexity to match the path plexity. The constraint directly relating TO and the figure ends up being violated, because to satisfy it would require the violation of at least one of these higher ranked constraints.

If there were never any clashes in structural specifications between different sentence elements, and there were never any structural elements of standard interpretations that went unexpressed at the surface level, then constructing the structural interpretations of sentences would be a simple compositional matter. Under those conditions, the construction of the input representation (as described above) would effectively do all the work, and the optimality theory model would simply map each surface syntactic element to its pre-defined underlying primitive (not a particularly exciting function). However, those conditions are far from true for natural language. Structural specifications often clash (as in the clash between *flash* and *until* in Example 2) and structural elements of an interpretation are often not directly expressed at the surface level in a sentence.

---

1. It is possible that more than one structural interpretation will 'tie' as the best; such a case would be an example of 'semantic structural synonymy'.

Examples

Example 1: *the pens rolled across the table.*
INPUT
    Figure: {*the*, *-s*, [dim:space, uniplex, bounded, discrete]} OC:*pen*
    Ground: {*the*, [dim:space, uniplex, bounded, discrete]} OC:*table*
    Path: {*across*}
    Verb: {MOVE, *-ed*, [dim:time, multiplex, unbounded, continuous]} OC:*roll*
OUTPUT
    Figure: [dim: space, multiplex, bounded, discrete] OC:*pen*
    Ground: [dim: space, multiplex, bounded, continuous] OC:*table*
    Path: ACROSS [dim: space, multiplex, bounded, continuous]
    Verb: MOVE [dim: time, multiplex, bounded, continuous] OC:*roll*
RELEVANT CONSTRAINTS
    An output entity that is uniplex must be bounded and discrete.
    across in the input path requires ACROSS as the output path.
    ACROSS requires the path to be continuous.
    ACROSS requires the ground to be continuous.
    -s in an input requires the output entity to be multiplex.
    -s in an input requires the output entity to be discrete.
    the in an input requires the output entity to be bounded.
*   *-s* in an input requires the output to be unbounded. {violated in the figure}
    -ed requires that the VERB aspect be bounded.
*   QD values in the input should be left unchanged in the output. {violated in several places}

Example 2: *the beacon flashed until dawn.*
INPUT
    Figure: Figure: {*the*, [dim:space, uniplex, bounded, discrete]} OC:*beacon*
                Ground: <none>
                Path: <none>
                Verb: {MOVE, *-ed*, [dim:time, uniplex, bounded, discrete]} OC:*flash*
    Ground: {[dim:time, uniplex, bounded, discrete]} OC:*dawn*
    Path: {*until*}
    Verb: {BE}
OUTPUT
    Figure: Figure: [dim:space, uniplex, bounded, discrete] OC:*beacon*
                Ground: []
                Path: []
                Verb: MOVE [dim:time, multiplex, bounded, discrete] OC:*flash*
    Ground: [dim:time, uniplex, bounded, discrete] OC:*dawn*
    Path: TO [dim:time, multiplex, bounded, discrete]
    Verb: BE
RELEVANT CONSTRAINTS
    An output entity that is uniplex must be bounded and discrete.
    BE requires that the figure QD values match the path QD values.
    until in the input path requires TO as the output path.
    TO requires the path to be bounded.
    TO requires the path to be multiplex.
*   TO requires the figure to be uniplex.
    TO requires the ground to be uniplex.
    the in an input requires the output entity to be bounded.
    -ed requires that the VERB aspect be bounded.
*   QD values in the input should be left unchanged in the output. {violated in several places}

APPLYING THE THEORY TO LINGUISTIC DATA

As mentioned earlier, optimality theory does not divide inputs into acceptable and unacceptable, but instead finds the best possible interpretation for whatever input it is given. Therefore, the semantic model will not explain judgements of semantic meaningfulness of sentences. What the model will explain are judgements concerning the semantic structure of sentences. It will make predictions about what structural interpretations informants will make of sentences.

The model could make predictions about the inputs in a weaker sense than meaningful/meaningless. Suppose two different sentences had the same structural interpretation: two different inputs both mapped to the same output. This implies that both sentences are attempting to express the same structure. If the parse of the first has higher Harmony (violates only lower ranked constraints) than the parse of the second, then the model could be said to indicate that the first sentence would normally be preferred to the second as a way of expressing that structure. Notice that this is an entirely relative sense of well-formedness.

The 'soft' nature of the judgements made by this model can actually be seen as advantageous. Trying to make absolute meaningful/meaningless judgements about sentences can be quite difficult. The human mind seems to be remarkably adept at imposing some sort of interpretation on whatever is presented to it. In addition, with many 'odd' sentences, the informant will nevertheless often have a strong sense of 'what the speaker meant', even if the informant agrees that the sentence is not what they themself would have said. A model which searches for the best possible interpretation of a sentence captures some of this.

Optimality Theory, as employed in models of phonology and syntax, has sometimes been used to explain typological data. The different language classes of the typologies are explained by different rankings of the constraints. To avoid confusion, it is here emphasized that the semantic model being proposed in this paper is not intended to explain typological data. Much of the recent work in semantic structure has taken inspiration from the work of Gruber [2], who proposed that the structural elements for non-spatial fields are a subset of those used for interpreting spatial motion and location (this is sometimes called the Thematic Relations Hypothesis). The approach presented in this paper further assumes that there is a universal hierarchy of structural constraints, of which the closed class elements of any particular language may represent a subset.

DISCUSSION

Talmy has suggested that the semantic structuring system embodied by closed class forms in language reflects characteristics of general conceptual structure. If this is so, then the model proposed here, in addition to explaining how language expresses conceptual structure, can provide the basis for a theory of conceptual structure. The relationships between the constraints and the output space would provide strong information about what kinds of conceptual structures are 'preferred', that is, better satisfy the constraints. The implied theory of conceptual structure would say that people employ the higher-ranked structures when forming conceptual representations.

Such a theory would be significant for psychological models that involve representations of conceptual structure. A particularly clear example is analogical reasoning, which crucially depends upon representations of structural relations, and the discovery of abstract structural similarities between the representations of examples in different domains. Models of analogical reasoning would benefit from independently motivated restrictions on the kind and nature of the representations to be used.

Acknowledgments

I would like to give special thanks to Leonard Talmy for several helpful discussions of his work, and to my advisor Paul Smolensky for tremendous assistance and support. Thanks are also due to the members of the "University of Colorado Talmy Reading Group" for their hours of valuable discussion: Geraldine Legendre, Jim Martin, Mike Peirce, and Bill Raymond. Further thanks go to Mike Mozer, and many of the other faculty and students of the 1993 Connectionist Models Summer School, for useful discussion and feedback. This work was supported by a National Science Foundation Graduate Research Fellowship to the author.

References

[1] J. Grimshaw, "Minimal Projection, Heads, and Inversion," Ms., Rutgers University, New Brunswick, NJ, 1993.

[2] J. Gruber, *Studies in Lexical Relations*, Doctoral Dissertation, MIT, Cambridge, 1965.

[3] R. Jackendoff, "Parts and Boundaries," *Cognition* 41, pp. 9-45, 1991.

[4] G. Lakoff, "The Invariance Hypothesis: is abstract reason based on image-schemas?," *Cognitive Linguistics* 1-1, pp. 39-74, 1990.

[5] R. Langacker, "An Introduction to Cognitive Grammar," *Cognitive Science* 10, pp. 1-40, 1986.

[6] G. Legendre, W. Raymond, and P. Smolensky, "An Optimality-Theoretic Typology of Case and Grammatical Voice Systems," in *Proceedings of the 19th Meeting of the Berkeley Linguistics Society*, 1993.

[7] A. Prince and P. Smolensky, *Optimality Theory: Constraint Interaction in Generative Grammar*, Linguistic Inquiry Monograph, Cambridge: MIT Press (to appear).

[8] L. Talmy, "The Relation of Grammar to Cognition," in *Topics in Cognitive Linguistics*, Brygida Rudzka-Ostyn, ed., 1988, pp. 165-207.

[9] L. Talmy, "Figure and Ground in Complex Sentences," in *Universals of Human Language*, J. Greenberg, C. Ferguson, E. Moravcsik, eds., 1978, pp. 625-649.

SYMBOLIC COMPUTATION AND RULES

What's in a Rule? The Past Tense by Some Other Name Might be Called a Connectionist Net

Kim G. Daugherty
Hughes Aircraft Company
and
Department of Computer Science
University of Southern California
Los Angeles, CA 90089-2520
kimd@gizmo.usc.edu

Mary Hare
Department of Psychology
Birkbeck College
University of London
hare@crl.ucsd.edu

INTRODUCTION

Linguistic rules have been widely studied as a means of capturing and applying a broad range of language knowledge, from generation of phoneme strings to discourse understanding. Somewhere between these two extremes, considerable effort has been spent on understanding the role of linguistic rules in inflectional morphology, and particularly in the generation of English past tense verbs. Although an impoverished example of a rule-based system, the English past tense has provided the foundation of a debate that can either further support the traditional theory, or provide insight into perhaps a new way of accounting for linguistic knowledge; namely, a connectionist approach.

How will this debate be settled? One tactic has been to account for the mass of behavioral data that has been so painstakingly collected, and show that one approach accounts for the data while the other approach has shortcomings. A different tactic is to show how the data may be accounted for by both approaches, although at different levels of complexity. It is the goal of this paper to apply this approach to the question of low-frequency default inflection, which is the application of a regular marking when the default category does not outnumber the other categories. An account of this phenomenon exists in the traditional approach, and our aim is to show that a connectionist account is possible as well. In this case, the past tense by some other name might be called a connectionist net.

BACKGROUND

The great majority of modern English verbs mark the past tense by adding the regular and productive suffix /d/ to the verb stem, but approximately 160 irregular verbs form the past tense in some other way. Irregular inflection seems to differ from regular in a number of interesting ways. In particular, irregular inflection is highly sensitive both to frequency and to phonological information. Irregulars that are of low frequency and do not belong to a phonologically-defined similarity cluster tend to be regularized over time [1,2,3], and the more strongly a novel verb phonologically resembles a known irregular, the more likely it is to receive irregular inflection in experimental tests [4]. Such sensitivity does not appear to be a mark of the regular verbs, although recent evidence suggests that the production of the regular form is in fact sensitive to phonological similarity with irregular neighbors [5]. Instead, the regular suffix /d/ acts like the *default* inflection: that is, unless it is superseded by a more specific irregular form, it will apply to any verb stem regardless of that verb's phonological shape.

There are a number of proposals on how to account for these facts. The traditional account of the past tense holds that regular forms are generated by rule and irregular past tenses are stored in the mental lexicon. This is an example of a dual-route account: a set of phenomena in a given domain are characterized in terms of a set of rules, and cases where the rules fail to make the correct predictions are listed separately.

A contrasting view, first proposed by Rumelhart and McClelland [6] is that both regular and irregular inflection result from the same mechanism, a single connectionist network. In a series of articles, Pinker and his colleagues [7,8] argue that a rule-governed mechanism is necessary in an inflectional morphology system, and that connectionist accounts of the past tense had little to add to traditional linguistic theory. However, many of their criticisms were leveled again the shortcomings of Rumelhart and McClelland's model of the past tense, and have been addressed by more recent connectionist models (see [9] for a review).

A major criticism of existing connectionist models are their supposed inability to acquire a true default category of past tense inflection. On the dual mechanism approach, the default status of the regular suffix is due to the fact that it is the rule-based form. In early network accounts, the cause of default generalization was less clear. The Rumelhart & McClelland model did generalize appropriately, but this success may have been due to the fact that in their model the regular verbs vastly outnumbered the irregulars. While this is consistent with the English facts, it is not true of all languages, and it would be a mistake to equate default behavior with statistical dominance. In the next section we lay out the problem in more detail.

THE PROBLEM OF THE LOW FREQUENCY DEFAULT

Cross-linguistically it is possible to find languages where, unlike in English, a default class is not significantly larger than its competitors. One frequently cited example is the Arabic plural system, in which the "sound" plural, the default, is of relatively low type and token frequency compared to the many non-default, or "broken" plural classes [10]. In relying on modern English data, network accounts may have given the erroneous impression that in the models a class can become the default only as a consequence of its superior size.

Why might a network need superior class size in order to achieve default behavior? Prasada and Pinker contend that networks can generalize only on the basis of frequency and surface similarity [11]. If this were true, then a novel form could be treated as a member of a default class only if it resembled a previously learned member of that class. To get true default behavior a network would need a default category that was extremely well-populated, for its members would have to span the entire phonological space of the language. Prasada and Pinker show that the original Rumelhart and McClelland model does indeed generalize on the basis of surface similarity, and conclude that the network was able to produce what looked like default behavior only because of the great difference in size between the regular and irregular classes.

Prasada and Pinker take this as evidence that this shortcoming is equally true of all connectionist networks. In the rest of this paper we will argue that this claim is unjustified, since it takes an overly simplistic view of network dynamics, on the one hand, and of the linguistic facts to be accounted for, on the other. We will show instead that under specific circumstances a simple feed-forward network learns a default classification without relying on superior class size or complete coverage of the phonological space. Significantly, the necessary circumstances are also those that are found in the documented real-language examples.

A Connectionist Account

In addressing this issue, there are two crucial point to be made. First, the Rumelhart & McClelland model was a two-layer perceptron, capable only of a linear mapping between input and output. Current models can take advantage of an intermediate processing layer, and this leads to a significant difference in the dependence on input similarity. The second crucial point has to do with the data, specifically with the structure of the non-default classes. Plunkett and Marchman raise this issue in their discussion of the Arabic plural system [10], where they suggest that the solution lies in the fact that "the numerous exceptions to the default mapping . . . tend to be clustered around sets of relatively well-defined features." In other words, while the sound plural encompasses an essentially arbitrary and phonologically disparate group of nouns, the various broken plural classes exhibit clear phonological cues to class membership.

Our operating assumption is that this phonological information is what allows the regular-irregular patterns to be learned in a connectionist net. In learning to produce the non-default classes, the net naturally learns to respond to the phonological characteristics that are cues to each class. If a network is taught a series of such mappings, and generalizes on the basis of the shared regularities, then novel patterns lacking those regularities can not be adopted into the class. If, in addition, the inflectional system includes a class whose membership is not keyed to phonological generalizations, this class can become productive since it is capable of accepting members that do not fit elsewhere.

Hare and Elman (1992)

To test this hypothesis, Hare and Elman [2] taught a network a simple categorization task. The model used a feed-forward, three-layer network, trained with the backpropagation algorithm. Input to the net was a set of 50-element vectors, each representing a word. A subpart of that word was a particular vowel or vowel + consonant pattern defined over distinctive features, while the rest was a unique random pattern. On the output layer there were six nodes, one for each of six categories. The task of the network was to categorize each input by activating the appropriate category label on the output.

The input data were divided into the six categories based on the phonological form of the word. To make the data more realistic, the first five categories were actually based on the phonological characteristics of five Old English verb classes. These were the following:

1. *i* + any one consonant
2. *e* + one stop or fricative
3. *e* + a consonant cluster
4. *i* + a nasal + stop cluster
5. *a* + any one consonant

The sixth class had no class characteristics, but instead could contain any other VC or VCC string.

The goal of the simulation was to show that the net would learn to take the feature combinations in the first five classes as predictive of class membership. As a result, it would generalize novel items displaying those characteristics into the appropriate classes, and treat any novel item *not* displaying those characteristics as a member of the sixth class.

The training set consisted of 32 randomly generated members of each of the six classes. After 20 passes through the data set, performance on the training items was essentially perfect. In the first testing phase, the trained net was shown 32 randomly generated patterns that matched the criteria for each of classes 1-5, and all were categorized correctly. It was then shown 63 novel patterns that did not precisely match any subtype seen in the training phase. In classifying these data the net was clearly influenced by similarity to learned patterns. If a novel item differed from a learned class by only one or two features it was placed in that class. Test patterns that shared features of two classes ambiguously activated both class nodes to an intermediate degree. Similarity cannot explain the entire set of results, however, since the majority of patterns were devised to be dissimilar to any training exemplars. Significantly, these dissimilar patterns were all placed in Class 6.

One possibility is that the network was still relying on similarity in generalizing to Class 6, even though the "most similar" training pattern was very distant from the test item. To eliminate this possibility the authors computed the distance between all test items and all members of the test set. The results show that novel items placed in classes 1-5 always had a learned class member as their closest match, while many of the items placed in Class 6 had a closest match in some other category. Furthermore, for classes 1-5 the network exhibited the sort of graded response shown by English speakers in the Bybee and Modor experiment [4]: a novel item strongly activated the category node for these classes only if it closely matched a training exemplar. As the match became more distant category activation decreased, and as the distance became too great the item was placed in Class 6. For Class 6, on the other hand, there was no such effect of distance: category node activation remained high regardless of the distance between test and training exemplars, or the presence of closer targets from some other class. This suggests, again, that while resemblance to a learned member was crucial for generalization to Classes 1-5, it was irrelevant for generalization to Class 6.

These results are consistent with an account which says that the network normally generalized on the basis of phonological similarity, but treated Class 6 as a default for patterns not fitting one of the learned prototypes. As such, they demonstrate that a network is capable of developing a default category without the benefit of superior frequency.

It is possible, however, that the task facing the Hare and Elman network was overly simple, and this simplicity added to the success of the model. On the input layer, the phonological string that was intended as the basis for generalization was clearly presented to the model in each of the five predictable classes. On the output layer, the model was compelled to accept one of the six categories offered, eliminating the possibility of a no-response or entirely novel response to a test item. By presenting the problem as an overt categorization task, instead of requiring the network to categorize implicitly by producing correctly inflected forms, this model may have achieved a satisfactory result for reasons that would not allow it to be extended to the more detailed data sets required of an actual model of verb production.

A NEW CONNECTIONIST MODEL

In the remainder of this paper we will replicate the earlier results with a more complex task, in order to demonstrate that the simplifying assumptions of the earlier model were not responsible for that model's performance. This second simulation differs from the first in two ways. First, the input is "words" represented as phonological strings, forcing the model to decide what the relevant generalizations are for each class. Second, the task of the model is to produce not a decision about the correct inflectional category, but an inflected version of the input string. The choice of inflection, in this case, can be taken as an indication of how the network categorizes each input.

The underlying assumptions with which we approach the model are the same as for the previous model. As in the first simulation, we expect that the net will extract relevant generalizations about the structure of the phonologically defined classes, and inflect novel items in the same way if they fit those generalizations. As in the earlier set of results, test items that are a close but not exact fit to a certain class can be expected to be placed in that class, and items that equally well match two or more predictable classes should be placed ambiguously between the two. Test items that differ sufficiently from the training exemplars of the defined classes should be placed in the default class, regardless of whether they match any learned member of that class.

The model should be able to learn a training set that is representative of a real language and generalize properly to novel verbs. As in the earlier simulation, the language chosen for the data set is Old English. By Early OE (ca. 870) the equivalent of the modern regular verbs already vastly outnumbered any irregular forms. In earlier stages of the language, however, the suffixed past appears to have been the default despite its small size relative to other classes of past tense inflection. For this reason we will use the earlier stage as an example of a low-frequency default.

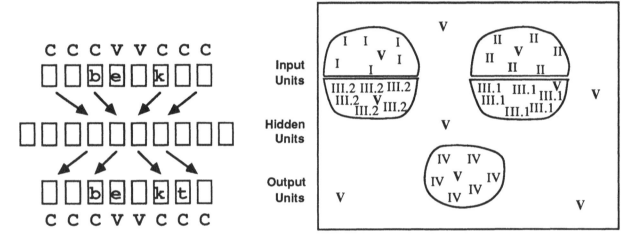

Figure 1: Architecture of the Model

Figure 2: Phonological Space of Rime for Class Items

Architecture of the Model

This work builds on previous connectionist models of the past tense by Daugherty and Seidenberg [12,13]. The architecture of the model is a simple feed-forward network with input, hidden, and output layers. The input layer represents the phonological form of a monosyllabic present tense verb in English, conforming to a CCCVVCCC template, which is the maximum size of a syllable in English. Each segment is represented by 8 articulatory features and a sonority hierarchy. The features are back, tense, labial, coronal, velar, nasal, sibilant, and voiced, which are represented by one unit each. The sonority hierarchy ranges from 1 to 7 and is represented by 7 units. This results in 15 units being dedicated to each segment in the template, or 125 total phonological units. If a feature is active for a segment, its value is set to 1.0; if not, its value is 0.0. Unused segments have all units set to 0.0. The output layer represents the phonological form of a monosyllabic past tense verb and is also comprised of 125 units.

These phonological representations are centered on the stem vowel of the syllables, as shown in Figure 1. Hence identical sounding rimes (i.e. stem vowel + C(C) cluster) in verbs will have identical representations with this encoding (e.g. /stek/ and /mek/). Aligning the representations on the rimes was thought to be desirable because of the perceptual salience of these units as observed in the sub-regular classes of English verbs (see [7]) and in the spelling-to-sound correspondences of English words (see [5]).

There are 175 hidden units in the model. During training, the phonological form of a present tense verb is activated on the input units. The task of the model is to generate the phonological form of the past tense on the output units.

Training

A training set was selected based on Old English strong verb classes as defined in Table 1. 25 items from each class were chosen for the training set. In classes that did not have 25 actual words in Old English, we created additional verbs to extend the set. The strong verbs form their past tense by changing the present tense vowel. In our set the past tense vowel is predictable from the present tense rime. Note that the stem vowel alone does not provide enough information to predict the past tense form. Only the Class IV past tense is predictable based on the stem vowel (/a/ goes to /o/).

Table 1: Training Set Classes

Class	Stem Vowel	Coda	Changed Vowel	Example
I	i	{d, t, g, p, k, b}	a	bid -> bad
II	e	{T, w, s, f, v}	ea	dref -> dreaf
III.1	e	{rst, rS, zd}	æ	kerst -> kærst
III.2	i	(n, m, N} + C	u	SriNk -> SruNk
IV	a	{r, l, k}	o	brak -> brok

In addition to the 125 strong verbs, there were 25 verbs in the training set that take the regular past tense suffix /t/ or /d/, depending on the voicing of the final consonant. We define these verbs as Class V. Verbs in this class can have any stem vowel, including the vowels used by verbs in Classes I to IV. Furthermore, these verbs can have rimes that cause them to fall into one of the strong classes. For example, /kark/ -> /karkt/ is a member of Class V, even though its rime is phonologically identical to members of Class I.

The introduction of Class V items in the training set poses an interesting constraint for the model, since it cannot solely count on the consistency of the strong classes to predict the past tense of any verb. Figure 2 shows the phonological space of the present tense verbs in the data set. Note that verbs from Classes I to IV are phonologically consistent, while Class V verbs can occur anywhere in the space.

When both regularly governed and exception items are learned by a single mechanism, the frequency of occurrence and consistency of mapping of the classes play an important role in the learnability of the training set and in proper generalization to novel items. In the current model we have made the simplifying assumption that all classes are equally frequent, and only the strong Classes I to IV have consistent mappings between their present tense and past tense. Thus, novel verbs that are phonologically similar to one of the strong classes would be expected to naturally generalize and take the predicted past tense for that class. On the other hand, novel verbs that are phonologically distant from any strong class would be expected to generalize to the default or regular past tense. Note that Class V does *not* contain a majority of items from the training set, nor does it cover the phonological space of the language, yet still is expected to behave as the default class.

The model was trained using the standard back-propagation learning algorithm [14], with learning rate of 0.001 and momentum of 0.9. Training progressed for 2000 epochs, at which point performance on the training set reached asymptote. The results below were averaged over three simulation runs with random initial weights.

Results

In scoring the model's performance, we determined for each phonemic segment whether the best fit to the computed output was provided by the correct target. The output pattern was scored as correct only if the correct targets provided the best fit for all segments in a word. The total sum of squared error was also calculated as a measure of goodness of fit.

The model learned 148 of the 150 words (99%) in the training set. Both items that were not learned were Class V verbs /spar/ -> /spor/ instead of /spard/ and /war/ -> /wor/ instead of /ward/. Note that these verbs were generalized into Class IV, since they differ only by a single feature from the Class IV verbs /spal/ and /wal/. Given the consistency of Class IV, the model found it easier to assimilate /spar/ and /war/ into Class IV rather than devote the necessary resources to learn their idiosyncratic past tense mappings.

Three generalization sets were created to test the model's response to new words. The first set contained new verbs that were perfect examples of the strong classes. 5 verbs were created to exactly match the definitions of the five strong classes. The expected past tense was generated for 21 out of 25 (84%) of these. The following verbs generated past tenses that were not expected:

153

Class I:	/lig/ -> /log/ instead of /lag/	Vowel Feature error
Class IV:	/far/ -> /ford/ instead of /for/	Overregularization error
Class II:	/smev/ -> /smev/ instead of /smeav/	No Change error
Class II:	/keT/ -> /keas/ instead of /keaT/	Consonant Feature error

Each of these verbs was then examined in detail. In three cases, the output can be explained by competing pulls from two possible outcomes. /lig/ is equally close to a Class I item in the training set (/clig/ -> /clag/) and a Class V item (/tig/ -> /tag/). Assuming both these items affect generalization, the generated output /log/ is a plausible blend between the two outputs /lag/ and /ligd/. Likewise, /far/ is equally close to a Class IV item (/bar/) and a Class V item (/war/). The generated output is an overregularization, indicating a blend between the two possible outputs of /for/ and /fard/. The no change error of /smev/ is probably due to conflicting constraints between the two strong classes that use /e/ as the stem vowel, Classes II and III.1. /keT/ did generalize properly, except for a single feature error on the coda (/s/ is one feature from /T/).

The second generalization set consisted of 27 new verbs that did not exactly match the definitions of the strong classes. These verbs varied in the number of features of the rime that differed from the closest verbs in the training set. Table 2 describes the performance of the model on this generalization set.

Table 2: Performance on Generalization Set

Closest Class	Num	Correct	Error Types	Dist	Comments
I	6	4	Blend (2): /lif/ -> /lef/ instead of /laf/	1	Equidistant to Classes I, II, V
II	8	3	Blend (1): /slelp/ -> /slol/ instead of /slealpt/	3	Closest to Class V
			No Change (4): /trek/ -> /trek/ instead of /treak/	1	Closest to Class I
III.2	2	2	None		
IV	11	5	No Change (6): /dat/ -> /dat/ instead of /dot/	2 or 3	Closest to Class IV

The network showed interesting performance on these verbs. As in the earlier model, the network extracted information about the phonological definition of the first four classes, and used these when generalizing to novel verbs. In the test set, 14 of the 27 novel verbs are "good" examples of a training class: they differ from training set exemplars by only 1 to 3 features, and do not also resemble members of other classes. As expected, these verbs were given the past tense inflection of the class whose members they most closely resemble[1].

The remaining verbs can all be considered "bad" examples of the classes. Many of the novel verbs matched the characteristics of 2 or more classes equally well. In these cases the conflict was resolved in two different ways. In the first case, the verbs generated past tenses that were blends of the competing class outcomes. For example, /lif/ generated /lef/ instead of /laf/. Note that /lif/ is equally close to members of Classes I, II and V in the training set. On our representation, the /e/ in /lef/ can result from a blend of the vowels /a/, /ea/ and /i/, which would be predicted by generalization to the three competing classes.

In the second case there was no change between the present and past tenses. Two kinds of verbs that demonstrated this behavior. /trek/ represents one of several verbs whose stem vowels match Class II, but that are actually closest to a member of Class I. /dat/ is one of several Class IV verbs that are closest to a member of Class IV, but do not meet the strict coda constraints of that class. In both these conditions, the network has conflicting constraints. In the first, both Classes I and II exert influence on the novel verb, while in the second the novel verb is not a sufficiently good example of the nearest class.

The no-change response has two possible explanations. On the one hand the network could simply be unable to respond due to conflicting constraints. This is not an implausible outcome, since people in similar situations can also find themselves unable to chose an alternative [11]. Since the network does not have the option of refusing to respond, a no change response is perhaps most similar to a non-response.

Alternately, the no change response may actually be an affixing error. A look at the items in question offers a reason why this may occur. The two /a/-stem verbs that undergo no change at all are /dat/ and /stad/, both

---

[1] The one exception to this is /slelp/ -> /slol/ which should have been /slealp/ according to the vowel. However, the closest match in the training set was the word /torf/, a Class V verb, which could explain the choice of output vowel.

ending in consonants identical to the Class V suffix. Experimental evidence shows that children who are aware of the regular past suffix often avoid applying it to verbs that end in /t/ or /d/ [15], and it is conceivable that the network is doing the same. This suggestion is strengthened by the network's response to two other /a/-stem verbs, /glaS/ and /slaz/. In both cases the vowel remains /a/, but the final consonant is changed to /T/ and /D/, respectively. By our code, this final consonant is a combination of the original fricative and the alveolar stop of the Class V affix, suggesting that the output error is due to an incomplete attempt to suffix these items.

The final generalization set consisted of 12 verbs with the novel vowel /^/ in the stem. By our hypothesis these verbs should be placed in Class V, on the crucial assumption that generalization to Class V does not require similarity to trained patterns. And, as Table 3 shows, this was overwhelmingly the case. Only one word, /tr^v/ -> /trav/, takes a vowel change without affixation. All others generated the Class V past tense even though most of these items were closest to training set verbs from some other class. Table 3 organizes the /^/ stem verbs by their closest class, and as it shows, the novel vowel items generalize into Class V with no regard for whether their closest match was also a Class V item. For some of these items, /^/ was changed to /a/ in the past tense. Since /^/ never appears in the training set, it is not unreasonable for the model to assimilate /^/ into another similar vowel (/^/ only differs from /a/ by one feature).

Table 3: Performance on Verbs with the Novel Stem Vowel

Closest Class	Num	Correct	Generated Past Tense	Dist	Comments
II	2	2	/keb/ -> /kebd/	1	Equidistant to Classes I, II
			/gr^S/ -> /gr^Tt/	1	1 feature off
IV	6	6	/gl^g/ -> /glagd/	2	/a/ instead of /^/
			/b^g/ -> /bagd/	2	/a/ instead of /^/
			/st^d/ -> /stadd/	3	/a/ instead of /^/
			/sl^z/ -> /sl^zd/	3	
			/m^d/ -> /m^dd/	3	
			/l^w/ -> /loyt/	3	3 features off
V	4	3	/st^th/ -> /statht/	1	/a/ instead of /^/
			/st^T/ -> /staTt/	2	/a/ instead of /^/
			/tr^v/ -> /trav/ instead of /tr^vd/	2	Error
			/gr^sh/ -> /gr^TTt/	3	4 features off

Finally, one verb that did not use the /^/ stem vowel was regularized, the verb /keb/. This item is equidistant to training set verbs from both Classes I and II, and we believe that regularization is the manner the model chose to resolve the competing attraction to the two classes.

In summary, the model was able to learn the distinct classes of the training set, and generalize properly to novel items. New verbs were adopted into a phonologically-based class if they were good examples of that class. If the verb was an equally good match to two or more classes, either a blended past tense or a no change past tense would be produced. Finally, If the verb was very different from the training set, the Class V past tense would be produced regardless of similarity to other Class V items.

DISCUSSION

Default categorization has generally been considered a hallmark characteristic of a rule-based account of inflectional morphology, and the fact that some languages exhibit default inflectional categories of relatively low frequency has been taken as evidence of the inadequacy of the connectionist approach to morphology. Our results suggest that connectionist networks can indeed model true default behavior, including the low frequency default class. Following Plunkett and Marchman's claims, we show that the crucial aspect of modeling default behavior is the structure of the data. Proper generalization of novel items is not strictly dependent on similarity to known items: if there is sufficient structure to the non-default classes, default generalization can be influenced by the *absence* of similarity to known items.

The account given in this paper relies on certain parameters: an input representation that reflects the phonological information in the data set, a network architecture and learning rule that permit the model to generalize on grounds other than input similarity, and a data set based the systematic structure that real-language examples of the phenomenon appear to require. In combination, these allow us to predict the model's responses to novel items,

155

and gave results that closely matched both the predictions and the observed data in the inflectional systems of real languages. While the traditional rule-based theory is a concise and elegant means of describing the data at a high level, its success does not entail that default behavior cannot also be explained by a connectionist net.

We suggest that the two theories of the past tense can be reconciled by considering that they each address different levels of the phenomena. Looking down on our model and attempting to formulate a high-level description of its performance, one might say that a "rule" to generate the past tense is applied when there are no compelling reasons to choose a strong class inflection. But if one wished to know how the rule-like behavior arises, an understanding of the connectionist account is in order.

Acknowledgements

The authors wish to thank Mark Seidenberg and Jeff Elman for previous collaborative work in connectionist modeling that provided the foundation for these simulations.

References

[1] J.L. Bybee. *Morphology*, Philadelphia: John Benjamins, 1985.

[2] M. Hare and J.L. Elman. "A connectionist account of English inflectional morphology: Evidence from language change," in *Proc. of the Fourteenth Annual Conference of the Cognitive Science Society*, 1992, pp. 265-270.

[3] M. Hare and J.L. Elman. "From weared to wore: A connectionist account of language change," in *Proc. of the Fifteenth Annual Conference of the Cognitive Science Society*, 1993, pp. 528-533.

[4] J.L. Bybee and C. Modor. "Morphological classes as natural categories," *Language*, vol. 59, pp. 251-270, 1983.

[5] M.S. Seidenberg. "Connectionism without tears," in S. Davis (Ed.), *Connectionism: Theory and Practice*. Oxford University Press, 1992.

[6] D. Rumelhart and J. McClelland. "Learning the past tense," in D. Rumelhart and J. McClelland (Eds.), *Parallel Distributed Processing, Vol. 2*. Cambridge: MIT Press, 1986, pp. 216-271.

[7] S. Pinker and A. Prince. "On language and connectionism," *Cognition*, vol. 28:1, pp. 73-194, Feb. 1988.

[8] S. Pinker. "Rules of language," *Science*, vol. 253, pp. 530-534, 1991.

[9] K.G. Daugherty and M.S. Seidenberg. "Beyond rules and exceptions: A connectionist modeling approach to inflectional morphology," in S. Lima (Ed.), *The Reality of Linguistic Rules*. John Benjamins, in press.

[10] K. Plunkett and V. Marchman. "U-shaped learning and frequency effects in a multi-layered perceptron," *Cognition*, vol. 39, pp. 43-102, 1991.

[11] S. Prasada and S. Pinker. "Generalization of regular and irregular morphological patterns," *Language and Cognitive Processes*, vol. 8, pp. 1-56, 1993.

[12] K.G. Daugherty and M.S. Seidenberg. "Rules or connections? The past tense revisited," in *Proc. of the Fourteenth Annual Conference of the Cognitive Science Society*, 1992, pp. 259-264.

[13] K.G. Daugherty and M.S. Seidenberg. "Why no mere mortal has ever flown out to center field but people often say they do," in *Proc. of the Fifteenth Annual Conference of the Cognitive Science Society*, 1993, pp. 383-388.

[14] D. Rumelhart, G. Hinton, and R.J. Williams. "Learning Internal Representations by Error Propagation," in D. Rumelhart and J. McClelland (Eds.), *Parallel Distributed Processing, Vol. 1*. MIT Press, 1986, pp. 318-362.

[15] J.L. Bybee and D. Slobin. "Rules and schemas in the development and use of the English past tense," *Language*, vol. 58, pp. 265-289, 1982.

On the Proper Treatment of Symbolism
A Lesson from Linguistics

Amit Almor
Department of Cognitive and Linguistic Sciences
Box 1978
Brown University
Providence, RI 02912 USA
almor@cog.brown.edu

Michael Rindner
Computational Linguistics Program
135 Baker Hall
Carnegie-Mellon University
Pittsburgh, PA 15213 USA
and
Department of Linguistics
CUNY - Graduate Center
benchaim@cs.cmu.edu

This paper argues for the indispensable value of linguistics for any account of language, symbolic or connectionist. We argue that the kind of data considered by linguists and the theories derived from this data should not be dismissed.

Firstly, linguistic theory can be used as a source of informed bias for connectionist models. This bias can be implemented in the architecture of a model or in the structure of the training set. We suggest that the usefulness of linguistic theory as a source of bias can be quantified by an entropy-based measure. In addition, some previous research using Simple Recurrent Network (SRN) models of language is shown to involve the use of linguistic-theoretic knowledge as means for bias introduction.

Secondly, the design of any model of linguistic phenomena benefits immensely from a working knowledge of contemporary theories of language and the data used to support them. The fact that some interesting results have been achieved with connectionist models of language independent of linguistic consideration, is indicative of the preliminary stage of research rather than of the irrelevance of linguistic data. In fact, these models make use of linguistic theory, although at a very simplistic level.

Thirdly, high-level symbolic accounts of linguistic theory alert the connectionist researcher to the existence of important phenomena and bodies of data relevant to the phenomena. Furthermore, this data and insights provided by high-level accounts constitute a solid starting point for developing low-level models of the phenomena. For example, we argue that consideration of certain syntactic concepts, such as governing category descriptions of the referential domain of nouns (from Government and Binding (GB) theory [1,2]) would lead to enhanced capabilities in SRN models of language.

THE BIAS/VARIANCE DILEMMA, LINGUISTICS, AND CONNECTIONISM

The value of using insights from linguistics in connectionist models of language becomes apparent when that use is recast as an introduction of informed bias. A prominent factor in the general task of discovering an estimator of a function given a possibly noisy set of samples is the bias/variance dilemma. Geman, Bienenstock, and Doursat [3] offer an extensive discussion of the bias/variance dilemma in general, and of its implications for connectionist models of cognition. The following is a short summary of their discussion.

Generally, when given a set of sampled values generated by a function which is to be estimated, the estimation error can be divided into two competing components: the variance component and the bias component. The variance is the component of the error which is due to the idiosyncrasy of the particular sample. The bias is the component of the error which is due to the prior assumptions about the class of possible estimators. As fewer assumptions are made a-priori about the class of possible estimators, more weight is given to the particular points in the sample. The bias/variance dilemma is the trade-off between overfitting the data, that is, letting the particular idiosyncrasies of the sample data take a pronounced effect (high variance), and not giving the sampled data enough weight (high bias).

There are two extreme cases which are worth noting. The first is the maximum bias case where the entire model is hard-wired, and no learning takes place. In this case, the estimator is fully specified by the bias. The other extreme case is where there is no bias at all. There are no a-priori assumptions and the sample data is the only factor which is used to select the estimator. In the context of cognitive modeling, the maximum-bias extreme represents a strong rationalist stance, whereas the no-bias extreme represents a strong empiricist, tabula-rasa stance.

Geman, Bienenstock, and Doursat provide a general review of statistical estimation techniques and arrive at the following conclusions: (1) In asymptotic conditions, many statistical estimation problems are solvable, that is, given a sufficiently large sample, there are methods that are guaranteed to converge to a consistent estimator of the desired function; (2) In practice, however, the data in many cognitive domains is too sparse. Therefore, the only way to arrive at a good estimator is by introducing bias that will narrow the class of candidate functions from which the estimator will be selected, but will still keep the desired regression function in this class; (3) In many cases, a good method is to start with a strongly biased model and gradually progress towards a less biased model.

There are two separate issues to resolve when introducing an informed source of bias. First, how to introduce the bias into the model. Second, what constitutes a source of bias which sufficiently constrains the class of possible estimators while still maintaining the desired estimator within this class.

Bias can be introduced into connectionist models by several means: The topology of a network can reflect some known facts about the domain [4,5]; the input representation can be transformed so as to highlight certain features which are known to be dominant [6]; or, a training set can be carved to reflect some known fact about the domain [7].

As for the second question, we argue that linguistic theory is one of the best sources for informed bias. We believe that many models have linguistically inspired bias, whether explicitly acknowledged or not. This bias may be reflected in the representations or in the structure of the training set. We consider even simple concepts, such as the general notion of phrase structure, as expressing linguistic-theoretic bias.

Elman [7,9] describes a series of experiments which show that an SRN cannot be trained unless the training set is structured such that in the first epochs only short sentences are presented to the network. Alternatively, the whole training corpus can be used starting from the first epoch, but the network's memory has to be initially short and gradually grow as training proceeds. This phenomenon makes perfect sense in light of Geman, Bienenstock, and Doursat's third conclusion. A good method for constructing a consistent estimator is to start with a high bias and gradually decrease it. From this perspective, the shorter sentences, and shorter memory, embody high bias. However, as Elman himself notes, it is not the length of the sentences per se which renders them easier for the network to learn, but the fact that the linguistic dependencies they contain are more local. In other words, the high bias is due to a "linguistic simplicity" assumption that are no dependencies between items that are not adjacent in the input stream. The point is that linguistic simplicity is a linguistic theoretic notion. Even if not stated explicitly, linguistics played a role in introducing the necessary bias into these experiments.

The fact that the linguistic knowledge required for this task is very basic reflects the simplicity of the task. A more complex task, such as the noun reference resolution as described below, might require more complex linguistic knowledge.

EXPLOITATION OF LINGUISTIC THEORY IN CONNECTIONIST MODELS

Elman [9,10] presents a series of connectionist models of language based on the SRN architecture. One of his most intriguing claims is that many prominent linguistic features can be extracted by an SRN from a text corpus without any a-priori linguistic assumptions. In other words, context sensitive distributional analysis can be used to extract the set of important features that linguists have been claiming to be attainable only by using theory. This suggests that all we need to know about language can be extracted automatically from a large enough corpus. Although we question the validity of this view, we do not underestimate the significance of the information extracted by Elman's SRN. Rather, we aim to highlight the indispensability of linguistic theory. Our argument is twofold. First, as argued in the previous section, Elman does use some knowledge of linguistics. Second, linguistic theory is necessary for expanding the coverage of Elman's model to further data. The following discussion illustrates this point by describing the notion of Governing Category, and its importance for interpreting the reference of nouns.

Generally, there are three kinds of nouns: 1) names - which have direct reference; 2) pronouns - which have a pragmatically defined reference - like *him*, *her*, and *they*; and 3) anaphors - which also have a pragmatically defined reference - like reflexives such as *himself* and reciprocals such as *each other*. Pronouns and anaphors require an antecedent in the same sentence or in previous discourse. For the current purpose, we will only consider relations within the same sentence.

One of the most fundamental aspects of comprehending an utterance is determining the referential relations among the nouns in it. Language exhibits strict constraints governing these referential relations. There is substantial evidence that these constraints are highly structure dependent. The theoretical notion of Governing Category (GC) plays a major role in defining the structural domain in which these constraints operate. The structural domain in which referential constraints apply is called "referential domain."

In order to get a preliminary understanding of the notion of referential domain, consider the following sentences: (the reference of the nouns is indicated by subscript indices - an asterisked index means an impossible reference).

(1) Jay_j likes $David_k$
(2) Jay_j likes $Jay_{j,k}$
(3) Jay_j likes $him_{j*,k}$
(4) Jay_j likes $himself_{j,k*}$
(5) Jay_j thinks $David_k$ likes $him_{j,k*}$
(6) Jay_j thinks $David_k$ likes $himself_{j*,k}$

The first two sentences show that two names can refer to different entities, or to the same entity. Sentence (3) shows that pronouns (*him*) cannot have their antecedent within a referential domain, which seems to be the entire sentence. Similarly, sentence (4) shows that anaphors (*himself*) must have their antecedent within a referential domain, which again seems to be the entire sentence. Together, sentences (4) and (5) seem to suggest that the relevant referential domain in which constraints on pronouns and anaphors apply is the entire sentence. However, consider examples (5) and (6). In these sentences the referential domain is not the entire sentence. In both sentences, the domain of reference is only the embedded sentence. The question is how does one define the referential domain?

The answer is not simple. There are many examples indicating that the domain of reference cannot be defined in simple terms of sentences and embedded sentences (e.g., in *John's_j cat_k likes him_j/himself_k* the antecedents of the anaphora and the pronoun are all within the same sentence.) Rather, one must employ notions such as GC, which is the characterization of referential domain offered by Government and Binding theory [1]. While a detailed discussion of GC is beyond the scope of this paper, it is sufficient here to simply recognize that the GC for a particular noun is defined by hierarchical structural notions[1].

It would be a non-trivial task for an SRN to extract the notion of referential domain, and provide a distributional-based analog for the theoretical notion of GC which linguists have used to define referential domain. We do not claim that this is impossible. We do claim that in order to achieve this goal, the problem has to be identified and, moreover, the data exhibiting all the relevant complexities should be considered. This can only be done after studying the relevant linguistic literature.

Thus, high level symbolic theory plays several roles in directing connectionist research. First, symbolic accounts alert the researcher to the existence of a particular phenomenon, including the array of high-level data relevant to that phenomenon. Second, high level notions can be used as means to introduce informed bias into the model, making it more likely to succeed.

QUANTIFYING LINGUISTIC-THEORETIC BIAS

Geman, Bienenstock, and Doursat comment that the introduction of bias into a model, when done in the appropriate way, can be conceived of as a way to decrease some measure of entropy stated in terms which are appropriate to the

---

[1] An example of these sructural notions are the relations of c-command and government, as defined by Government and Binding theory [1]. Analogous mechanisms exist in other generative linguistics theories.

particular model. The notion of entropy as a tool for the evaluation of models of language has also gained recent popularity in computational linguistics. In their recent work, Brown et al. [8] use a model which is devoid of almost any linguistic knowledge to calculate an estimate of an upper bound for the entropy of printed English. Their purpose is to establish a standard against which the performance of more linguistically informed models can be matched.

Generally speaking, cross entropy measures the fitness of an estimator to a probabilistic model. It is therefore a convenient measure to use when comparing two competing estimators of a given probabilistic model. When the true probabilistic model is unknown, as in all natural language models, the cross entropy of an estimator can be approximated by using a test sample which is drawn independently of the training data.

Since the cross entropy can be used to compare any two estimators, it can be used to quantify the contribution of each biasing assumption separately. We suggest adopting the general procedure described in Brown et al. [8] to evaluate the contribution of linguistics-inspired bias. The cross-entropy can be used as a performance measure for the contribution of specific linguistic assumptions to the overall performance of a model. To use our previous example, the particular structural relations which define the notion of GC can be added one by one as bias to an SRN. Since an SRN is a probability model of the corpus it is trained on, the cross entropy is an appropriate measure of its performance. After the introduction of each piece of bias, a test set can be used to approximate the cross-entropy of the model. The difference in cross-entropy between the model with the bias and the model without it constitutes a quantified evaluation of the bias.

CONCLUSION

The bias/variance dilemma is a major concern for all sample-based modeling, and therefore for any connectionist model in a linguistic domain. One way to relax the bias/variance dilemma is to introduce some informed bias. We have argued that linguistic theory should be taken as a primary source for such bias. The value of using linguistic data is evidenced in statistical language models. These models, which are based on large corpora, have been successful in accounting for various linguistic phenomena. For example, consider the problem of PP-attachment resolution as in:

(7) Dave bought a chair with Andreas.

(8) Dave bought a chair with wheels.

In (7), the prepositional phrase "with Andreas" is most likely modifying the verb "bought", while in (8) the prepositional phrase "with wheels" is most likely modifying the noun "a chair". Since syntactically both options are possible, this is a case of syntactic ambiguity. Deciding on the most likely pp-attachment is a very hard problem which has not been completely solved by symbolic natural language parsers. Hindle and Rooth [11] have used a statistical method based on t-test to resolve cases of pp-attachment, attaining performance compatible with those of human subjects. However, this result would have not been possible without using the elaborate linguistic model which underlies the statistical process.

We have argued that connectionist SRN models have already been employing linguistic knowledge as a form of bias. In order to extend these models, further insights derived from linguistic theory would have to be considered. Although the focus of much connectionist effort has been on simple linguistic phenomena, this tendency does not constitute a valid argument for the outright rejection of more sophisticated linguistic concepts. Indeed, in light of the points put forth in the above discussion, it is apparent that linguistic analysis is indispensable.

Fodor and Pylyshyn [12] have posed some provocative challenges to connectionism which have since been addressed in several connectionist models [10,13]. However, the desire to meet these challenges has led connectionist research to overlook a fundamental contribution of the symbolic paradigm, namely the classification of interesting data according to theoretical insights, and the predictive power which results from it. Although accounting for compositionality might be a necessary step, it is not the ultimate goal of connectionist research. The critical challenge facing connectionist models of language is to provide an account which captures the insights of symbolic theories and improves upon those insights [14]. We have made several proposals about the proper treatment of symbolic insights from linguistic theory in connectionist research. The proper treatment of symbolism is definitely not an outright dismissal.

Acknowledgments

We would like to acknowledge an intellectual debt to Paul Smolensky, whose published work and conversation have inspired this work.

References

[1] N. Chomsky, *Lectures on Government and Binding*, Dordect: Foris, 1981.

[2] N. Chomsky, *Some Concepts and Consequences of the Theory of Government and Binding*, Cambridge, Mass: MIT Press, 1982.

[3] S. Geman, E. Bienenstock, and R. Doursat, "Neural Networks, and the Bias/Variance Dilemma," *Neural Computation*, vol. 4. pp. 1-58.

[4] M. Fanty. "Context free parsing in Connectionist Networks," technical report #174, University of Rochester, 1985.

[5] B. Selman, G. Hirst, "Parsing as an Energy Minimization Problem," in *Genetic Algorithms and Simulated Annealing*, L Davis (ed), Los Altos, California: Morgan Caufman, 1987. pp. 141-154.

[6] P. Smolensky, G. Legendre, Y. Miyata, "Principles for an integrated Connectionist/Symbolic Theory of Higher Cognition," report CU-CS-600-92, Computer Science Department, University of Colorado at Boulder, July 1992.

[7] J. L. Elman, "Incremental Learning, or The Importance of Starting Small," CRL technical report 9101, March 1991.

[8] P. L. Brown, S. A. Della Pietra, V. J. Della Pietra, J. C. Lai, and R. L. Mercer, "An Estimate of an Upper Bound for the Entropy of English," *Computational Linguistics,* vol. 18, pp. 31-40, March 1992.

[9] J. L. Elman, Representation and Structure in Connectionist Models, in *Cognitive Models of Speech Processing.* In G. T. M. Altman (ed), Cambridge, Mass: MIT Press, 1990. pp. 345-382.

[10] J. L. Elman, "Finding Structure in Time," *Cognitive Science.* vol. 14, pp. 179-211, 1990.

[11] D. Hindle, and M. Rooth, "Structural Ambiguity and Lexical Relations," in *Proceedings of the ACL*, 1991.

[12] J. Fodor, and Z. Pylyshyn, "Connectionism and Cognitive Architecture: A Critical Analysis," in *Connections and Symbols,* S. Pinker and J. Mehler (eds),Cambridge: MIT Press.

[13] J. B. Pollack, "Recursive Distributed Representations," *Artificial Intelligence.* vol. 46 pp. 77-105. Elsevier Science Publication. 1990.

[14] P. Smolensky, "On the Proper Treatment of Connectionism," *Behavioral and Brain Sciences*, vol. 11, pp. 1-74, 1988.

Structure Sensitivity in Connectionist Models

Lars F. Niklasson[1]

The Connectionist Research Group

University of Skövde, Sweden

lars@his.se

BACKGROUND

Ever since the birth of connectionism, it has had to fight for survival. In 1969 Minsky and Papert [1] argued that connectionist models suffered from a severe limitation in their mathematical foundation, which was not likely to be overcome, even if several layers of network-units were used. As we all know, this limitation was overcome by the introduction of the backpropagation algorithm and connectionism was revitalised. In 1988 a new attack was launched against connectionism (cf. Fodor & Pylyshyn [2]; Fodor & McLaughlin [3]). This time the claim was that connectionist models could not be regarded as models explaining cognition. They could, at best, be implementations of classical models. The connectionist defence has basically taken two forms; theoretical argumentation (cf. Smolensky [4]; Chalmers [5]; van Gelder [6], [21]; van Gelder & Niklasson (forthcoming)) and practical modelling (cf. Pollack [7]; Chalmers [8]; Smolensky [9]; Niklasson & Sharkey [10], [11], [12]; Blank, Meeden and Marshall [13]).

The theoretical approach questions the philosophical foundation of the classical denial of a possible connectionist cognitive model. This foundation is based on the idea that a cognitive architecture must generate representations for complex expressions according to a combinatorial syntax and semantics (often referred to as *concatenative compositionality*). An example of this is the generation of the complex expression "John loves Mary", from the constituents "John", "loves" and "Mary". It is also vital that the architecture uses processes that are sensitive to the constituents (often referred to as *systematicity*). An example of this is that the ability to understand/produce some thoughts (e.g. "John loves Mary") is intrinsically connected to the ability to understand/produce certain others (e.g. "Mary loves John").

In the following, the focus will be on the practical approach. This approach concentrates on showing that connectionist models can utilize the processes that the classicists claim that they can not. It also involves some specific connectionist features, e.g. non-concatenative compositionality, holistic structure sensitive processes and different levels of generalisation. Before discussing these issues, let me give the motivation for the type of connectionist architecture used in this paper.

MOTIVATION

In order to solve the task of structure sensitivity (systematicity) in connectionist architectures, we first have to look at some related problems. Fodor and Pylyshyn [2] pointed out a problem that connectionists had to solve before even attempting to solve the actual problem with systematicity. This was the problem of composing representations for complex expressions/events out of a set of atomic ones, i.e. the compositionality problem. One complication, if connectionists were to avoid the implementation accusation, was that it had to be solved in a functional but non-classical fashion, i.e. it could not be solved by using a combinatorial syntax which (by concatenation) preserves the tokens for the atomic constituents, in the representation for the complex expressions.

A type of connectionist architecture that uses an encoding scheme that differs from the concatenative, is the recurrent network. Here, the representation for a complex expression is formed under the influence of feed-back loops.

---

1. Currently at the University of Exeter, UK.

Elman [14] used a recurrent network for language processing, in which the activation at the hidden layer at time *t* was copied onto a type of input units, called context units, at time *t+1*. The task was to predict the next word in a word sequence. In one simulation, a 27,534-word sequence (containing two- an three-word sentences) was used to train the network. After this the network's weights were frozen and the sequence was presented once again, this time the hidden unit representations for all the words, in their context, were saved for later analysis. Cluster analysis showed that these representations could be categorised in several major categories (e.g. verbs, nouns, etc). This meant that this recurrent network showed the same characteristics as Hinton [22] earlier had found for feed-forward networks. He observed that feed-forward networks, with modifiable representations for the constituents, formed similar distributed representations (also called confluent representations) for constituents used in similar contexts. This was achieved by propagating the error signal to a dynamic representation, for a certain constituent, and modifying it. The same idea for forming distributed representations was also found in the FGREP algorithm, presented by Miikkulainen & Dyer [17].

The question was if this type of representation could form the basis for a new type of processing; one that was not sensitive to certain tokened constituents, but to a representation's position in the high-dimensional representational space. This question was, in part, answered by Pollack [15] when he devised the Recursive Auto-Associative Memory (RAAM), which was an encoding/decoding scheme for connectionist representations. It took the representations for two atomic constituents, represented by $2n$ units in total, and generated a representation for their combination, represented by n units (i.e. a compression 2:1), as shown in fig 1. The representation for this complex expression could then be combined with the representations for other atomic/complex expressions. Since the RAAM was auto-associative, the reverse process was also possible.

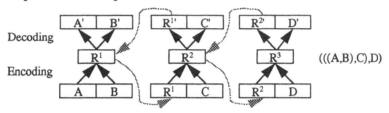

Fig. 1 RAAM

We now had a functional non-classical compositional/decompositional scheme (defined as non-concatenative compositionality by van Gelder [6]), which resulted in, what is sometimes referred to as, superpositional representations. This scheme could help connectionists solve the problem of systematicity, without creating a mere implementation of a classical model.

In one simulation, Pollack [16] trained a 48*16*48 network to encode/decode representations for relations of the type (LOVED X Y), where X and Y where chosen from the set {JOHN, MARY, PAT, MAN}. Distributed representations for the relations were generated at the hidden layer of the network. These representations were then used to train another network to perform a number of inferences, e.g. "If (LOVED X Y) then (LOVED Y X)". The latter network was trained on a subset of the possible inferences, but never the less processed the remaining correctly. This was an indication that the representational space could be used as a basis for structure sensitivity, not only in the sense that the model did place similar expressions close in the representational space, but also that it was possible to define holistic processes that could create mappings between different clusters of points (cf. Blank et al. [13]).

Chalmers [8] continued along Pollack's line of work. He trained a ternary RAAM (i.e. a 3:1 compression) to encode/ decode 125 active sentences (e.g. [JOHN LOVES MICHAEL]) and their passive counterpart (e.g. [MICHAEL [IS LOVED NIL] [BY JOHN NIL]]). The hidden layer representations in the RAAM, for 75 randomly selected active sentences, were then used to train a second network, which he called the Transformation Network (hereafter, TN), to produce their passive counterpart. During testing, a transformed distributed representation was decoded by the RAAM network, in a recursive manner, until the decoded representation was considered to refer to an atomic constituent. He trained two TNs; one associated active with passive sentences, and another associated passive with active sentences. When presented with the remaining 50 sentences, both of these networks showed a generalisation rate of 100%.

Niklasson & Sharkey [10], [11], [12] reported similar results as Chalmers, even if the same TN was trained to do a number of different transformations. They also showed that it was possible to introduce atomic constituents at novel positions in the test set, i.e. a certain constituent does not have to appear in all of its syntactically allowed positions, in the training set. This introduces the question of different levels of generalisation, which we will return to in the following sections.

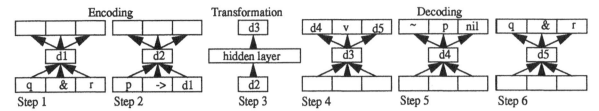

Fig. 2 Holistic transformation of *p -> (q & r)* into *~p v (q & r)*

The architecture used by Niklasson & Sharkey (see fig. 2) was basically the same as Chalmers, but with the difference that the RAAM network had been extended with a facility that made it possible for the decoder to be trained to separate an atomic constituent (indicated by a zero in the last position of its representation) from a complex constituent (indicated by a one in the last position of its representation), rather than being told to look for a certain number of active units in a representation (see fig. 3). Since the decoder was trained to be sensitive to the representations for the individual atomic constituents, their representations could have different numbers of units active, or use real-valued activity vectors instead of discrete ones.

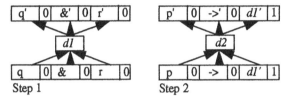

Fig. 3 Encoding/decoding of representation for *p -> (q & r)*

All of the approaches mentioned so far made use of the structure in the distributed representations, generated at the hidden layer of a network for encoding/decoding (hereafter, EN), in order to train a separate TN to achieve structure sensitive transformation tasks. The representation for a complex expression, at the hidden layer of the EN, was formed under the influence of the representations for its constituents. Now, it is also possible to generate distributed representations which are influenced not only by the representation of their constituents but also by the processes they are involved in. Chrisman's architecture [18], see fig 4, used a confluence approach in combination with a composite architecture with two connected RAAMs which, in addition to error propagation within an EN, propagated the error signal for the transformation task back to the EN.

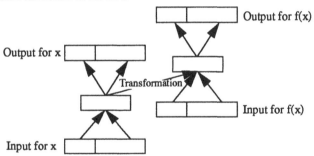

Fig. 4 Chrisman's composite architecture

This meant that the distributed representations were formed under influence of both the encoding/decoding and the transformation processes. His simulations indicated that the use of representations formed under this influence results in even better performance for holistic structure sensitive transformational processes (in his case English-Spanish translation).

The need for an extended model became apparent, after Hadley [19] claimed that the type of systematicity that had been shown by connectionist architectures, was not sufficient. He distinguished different degrees of systematicity ranging from weak to strong, and claimed that connectionists only had managed weak systematicity. The problem he focused on was the degree of novelty in many connectionist test corpora. He defined a system as being weakly systematical when the training corpus is *representative* in the sense that every atomic constituent (that occurs in some expression in the test corpus) occurs in every syntactically allowed position. A system was defined as strongly systematical when the test corpus contained constituents in positions where they did not appear in the training corpus.

164

I do not agree with Hadley that these are problems related to the systematicity issue. I do agree with him that these are problems that connectionist models must solve, in order to be as powerful as symbolic computation is for particular problems, but under the notion of different levels of generalisation. If Hadley wanted to give the connectionists something to chew on, he could have set an even harder task (see point 3, 4 and 5 below). I therefore propose the following different levels of generalisation.

0) No generalisation. The network memorizes the whole training set.

1) Generalisation to novel expressions. The training set is representative in the sense that all the constituents, in the test set, appear in all of their syntactically allowed positions.

2) Generalisation to novel positioning of constituents. All atomic constituents, in the test set, appear in the training set, but some do not occur in all of their syntactically allowed positions.

3) Generalisation to novel constituents. Not all atomic constituents, in the test set, appear in the training set.

4) Generalisation to novel complexity. The test set contains expressions with different complexity, than appears in the training set. This means that the network has to be able to process expressions with a different level of embedding, than appears in the training set.

5) Generalisation to novel constituents at novel complexity. The network has to be able to process a different level of embedding that also contains novel constituents.

A re-specification of Hadley's claim, using the levels defined above, would mean that no connectionist model had reached above level 1. Neither Pollack [16] nor Chalmers [8] explicitly stated which positions the atomic constituents occupied in their training sets. It is therefore hard, with absolute certainty, to classify them. It is, however, likely that their models resided at level 1. Niklasson & Sharkey [12] used a carefully designed training set, which placed their model at level 2. Elman [14] showed that a recurrent network clustered representations for novel constituents close to learned ones. He introduced, in the test set, the word 'zog' in all the places where 'man' had occurred in the training set, with the result that 'zog' was clustered close to where 'man' had been clustered earlier. The question we have to investigate, in order to solve the level 3 generalisation, is if the structure of the formed clusters will be preserved by the transformation process. It must be possible, not only to separate but also, to decode representations containing both novel and learned constituents, which was not possible with the architecture that Elman used. An example of this is the transformation of $p \rightarrow q$ into $\sim p \vee q$. Suppose that the constituent r appears as a novel constituent in the test set. It would not be satisfying if the transformation of $p \rightarrow r$ was decoded as *[~p], [v] and ["something similar to p"]*, when it should have been *[~p], [v] and [r]*. The implication of this is that we need a model that can both encode and decode representations for complex expressions, as well as do the holistic transformation on these superpositional representations, even if the process involves dealing with the novel constituents of level 3. The intention of this paper is to explore such a model.

THE MODEL

An architecture, which is influenced by the ideas of Chrisman [18], was developed. It has a dual RAAM as the EN and a TN directly connected to the hidden layer of the EN (see fig. 5). The EN has three layers of units, the input and output layers consists of $2n$ units (where n is the number of units chosen to represent an atomic expression, in this case 40) and the hidden layer consists of n units. Since the input layer of the TN is the same layer as the hidden layer of the EN, it, and the output layer of the TN, therefore consists of n units. The number of units in the hidden layer of the TN was in these simulations set to $n/2$ units, but the implications regarding efficiency of this decision has not been subjected to investigation.

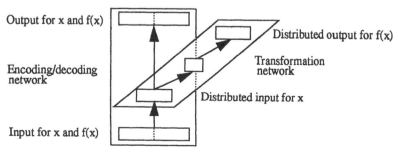

Fig. 5 The architecture

165

The two parts of the architecture are trained in the following way:

> First the EN is trained to compose distributed representations for all the expressions that are to be processed, in the manner explained earlier. The EN is updated with the use of the backpropagation algorithm. In order to make training more efficient, a global dictionary (equivalent to the lexical used my Miikkulainen & Dyer) is used to store the distributed representations for all the complex expressions. An entry in the dictionary contains the actual representation, its label (e.g. *p->*) and the labels for its constituents (e.g. *p* and *->*).

> After one iteration through all the composition/decomposition examples, the transformation task is performed. If the task is to transform *p->q* into *~p v q*, then the distributed representations for them are fetched from the global dictionary and placed at the input and output layer of the TN. Again, the backpropagation algorithm is used but, in addition to propagating the error within the TN, the error is propagated to the input-hidden layer of the EN, and its weights are also updated. In the current implementation the global dictionary is used to find the constituents (i.e. the input to the EN) for the expression that is currently under transformation. This is needed since the input-hidden weights are updated according to $\Delta W_{ji} = \text{error}_j * \textbf{input}_i * $ learning rate. Another possible option could be to use the activation at the hidden layer of the EN, and let the activation flow to the output layer. Since EN is auto associative, that output representation could have been used instead of the input.

The test phase (see fig. 6) is characterised by the presentation of test expressions at the input of TN, which are transformed at the output layer. This transformed representation is then presented to the decoder in the EN, which results in a representation of two constituents at the output layer. If any of these refers to a complex expression, then it is decoded further until all the representations refer to atomic constituents.

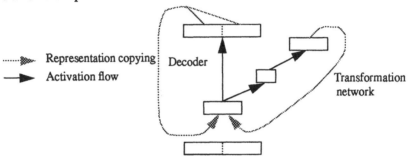

Fig. 6 The test phase

The domain chosen for these simulations is the domain of syntactic transformation in logic, according to the following scheme:

From:

(prop conn prop) implication prop

not(prop conn prop) disjunction prop

prop implication (prop conn prop)

not prop disjunction (prop conn prop)

To:

not(prop conn prop) disjunction prop

(prop conn prop) implication prop

not prop disjunction (prop conn prop)

prop implication (prop conn prop)

The symbols used are:

prop = {p, q, r, s}, *conn* = {*implication, disjunction*}, *implication* = {*->*}, *disjunction* = {v}

This results in a domain consisting of 512 formulae. From this set, all the formulae containing the constituent *s*, in total 296 formulae, were extracted. In principle, what we wanted to do is to train the architecture on the 216 formulae in the training set, and then test it on the remaining 296 formulae.

The choice of representation is important. The underlying idea in this model is that similar constituents (e.g. of the same type) should have similar representations, since that is the only thing that can be used for generalisation. That this idea could form the basis for systematicity was expressed by Barnden & Pollack [20] in the following words:

> Structural similarities between representations should be reflected in similarity of the processing that can be applied to them. This is almost identical to Fodor and Pylyshyn's (1988) notion of "systematicity".... (p 5)

This means, in our case, that the representation for a proposition symbol (i.e. an atomic constituent) is more similar to the other proposition symbols than to the implication symbol. This is the motivation for the representations chosen for the atomic constituents:

```
P     = 1 1 1 0 0 0 0 0 0 0 0 0 0 0 0 0 0 0 0 0 0 0 0 0 0 0 0 0 0 0 0 0 0 0 0 0 0 0 0 0 0 0 0 0 0 0 0 0
Q     = 1 0 0 1 1 0 0 0 0 0 0 0 0 0 0 0 0 0 0 0 0 0 0 0 0 0 0 0 0 0 0 0 0 0 0 0 0 0 0 0 0 0 0 0 0 0 0 0
R     = 1 0 0 0 0 1 1 0 0 0 0 0 0 0 0 0 0 0 0 0 0 0 0 0 0 0 0 0 0 0 0 0 0 0 0 0 0 0 0 0 0 0 0 0 0 0 0 0
v     = 0 0 0 0 0 0 0 0 0 1 1 1 0 0 0 0 0 0 0 0 0 0 0 0 0 0 0 0 0 0 0 0 0 0 0 0 0 0 0 0 0 0 0 0 0 0 0 0
->    = 0 0 0 0 0 0 0 0 0 0 0 0 1 1 1 0 0 0 0 0 0 0 0 0 0 0 0 0 0 0 0 0 0 0 0 0 0 0 0 0 0 0 0 0 0 0 0 0
not   = 0 0 0 0 0 0 0 0 0 0 0 0 0 0 0 1 1 1 0 0 0 0 0 0 0 0 0 0 0 0 0 0 0 0 0 0 0 0 0 0 0 0 0 0 0 0 0 0
nil   = 0 0 0 0 0 0 0 0 0 0 0 0 0 0 0 0 0 0 1 1 1 0 0 0 0 0 0 0 0 0 0 0 0 0 0 0 0 0 0 0 0 0 0 0 0 0 0 0
```

The representations for the complex expressions are formed under the influence of two processes, namely the encoding and the transformation processes. This influence generates similar representations for similar expressions and expressions which are used in similar processes.

When it comes to the representation for the novel constituent we manually simulate the influence of the compositionality process, but not the transformation task. This results in a representation for the novel constituent that is similar to the representations for the other tokens of the proposition type, resulting in:

```
S     = 1 0 0 0 0 0 0 0 0 0 0 0 0 0 0 0 0 0 0 0 0 0 0 0 0 0 0 0 0 0 0 0 0 0 0 0 0 0 0 0 0 0 0 0 0 0 0 0
```

RESULTS

The architecture was trained to encode/decode and transform the 216 formulae not containing the constituent s. It was trained for 10000 epochs with a learning rate of 0.05, for all the weight layers, and a momentum term of 0.1.

When the 296-formulae test set is presented and the output from the TN is analysed, it is obvious that the representations containing the new constituents have settled into distinct clusters, but as stated earlier that is not satisfactory for this task. The transformed representations must be decoded recursively in the EN, where an atomic constituent is separated from a complex one by using a similar approach as Chalmers [8]; if the number of units that are above a certain threshold, here 0.7, is equal (for the known constituents) or less (for the novel constituent) than the number of units active in an atomic expression, in this case 3, then the decoded representation refers to an atomic constituent, otherwise to a complex one. The next problem, when a representation for an atomic constituent has been identified, is to find out which atomic constituent it refers to. The encoding/transformation/decoding process was, in fact, so accurate that a threshold of 0.5 could be used to find "perfect matches", since the error margin for all the units in the training set was less than 0.1.

Despite the fact that the decoder never have been exposed to expressions containing the novel constituent, it still manages to correctly decode about 50% of the transformed expressions. The error in all of the incorrectly decoded expressions is that the decoded constituents, not surprisingly, are closer in Euclidean space to other atomic tokens of the proposition type, than to the novel one.

In order to investigate if this error is caused by the generalisation error in the RAAM, observed by Chalmers, a second training session takes place. This time using the previously trained networks as starting point. The EN is trained on all the 512 formulae and the TN is trained on the same 216 formulae as before. This time the number of iterations through the training set is about 150. When the whole 512-formulae domain is presented as a test set, the model correctly transforms and decodes all of these formulae. The highest activation for a unit that should be 0 was 0.45, and the lowest activation for a unit that should have been 1 was 0.80.

The key idea, in the above simulations, is that the representation for a novel constituent should be more similar to the representations for tokens of its own type, then of other types. Different representations for the novel constituent were tested, in order to evaluate how sensitive the model was to the choice of representation, e.g.:

```
S     = 0 1 0 1 0 1 0 0 0 0 0 0 0 0 0 0 0 0 0 0 0 0 0 0 0 0 0 0 0 0 0 0 0 0 0 0 0 0 0 0 0 0 0 0 0 0 0 0, and
S     = 0 0 1 0 1 0 1 0 0 0 0 0 0 0 0 0 0 0 0 0 0 0 0 0 0 0 0 0 0 0 0 0 0 0 0 0 0 0 0 0 0 0 0 0 0 0 0 0
```

For both of these, the result was the same as reported above.

The architecture described so far only allows modifiable representations for complex expression. A desirable feature would be to use initial representations for the atomic constituents from, for instance, a vision system. These representations should then be gradually changed in the same manner as for the complex expressions above. This could be a model of how we receive a static external stimuli, e.g. on the retina, and from that form a mental representation for it. The model would also avoid the argument against using structured input representations to the networks. A possible extension to the model could be a similar approach as the FGREP [17] algorithm. At the moment this idea is only partially implemented, by using an extra circulation in the EN, for an atomic constituent. The resulting distributed representation (e.g. P^D or Q^D in fig. 7) is the one that is used in the further processing.

Fig. 7 The generation of trainable representations for atomic constituents.

By adopting this approach, it is possible to implement trainable atomic constituents, which are influenced by both the composition and transformation tasks. The extension, used here, is not powerful enough to handle random initial patterns for the atomic constituents, but it allows some investigation of the effects the transformation and encoding processes have on the learned distributed representations for the atomic constituents.

The extended model was re-evaluated from this perspective, using the same initial representations and settings as described above. The performance was the same as without the extension. Investigation of the encoding process indicates that very similar, i.e. short Euclidean distance, distributed representations for the different tokens of a certain *type*, are generated. Now, the problem is if this similarity process is the only one that is allowed to influence the representations for the constituents, that would eventually result in that the representations for all the tokens of a type of constituent, become so similar that a decoder would have problems separating them. Therefore, there is also a need for a process that can make the representations for the tokens of a certain type, different. Investigation of the effects of the transformation process on the representations for the atomic constituents indicates that it, in fact, has this effect. This could be used as further argument for the initial representations used in these simulations.

To fully understand the influence of the encoding/decoding and the transformation processes, the model will be extended to in corporate a more powerful learning procedure for the atomic constituents.

CONCLUSION

This paper set out to examine the claim that connectionist models can not exhibit systematicity, or at least not a sufficiently strong degree of it. After re-defining the degrees of systematicity, in terms of different levels of generalisation, it was argued that some connectionist models have shown high degrees of generalisation, and that it is actually possible to go further than what was demanded by Hadley. The results reported here shows that connectionists can solve, at least, the first three levels of generalisation. So the claim that connectionist models can utilize structure sensitive processes, still stands. We now face the challenge of explaining *why* these models entail systematicity. Maybe the answer to this question can be found in the increasingly popular non-linear dynamical systems approach to cognition. This is the hypothesis for the further development of the model.

The question of level 4 and 5 generalisations brings us to another of the objections that Fodor & Pylyshyn had against connectionism as an approach to explaining cognition, namely the idea of productivity. Under this notion, the compositionality idea could be used, in combination with a finite grammar, to generate infinitely complex expressions. To my knowledge, no connectionist model have fully solved these levels, but several interesting approaches can be identified, e.g. Smolensky's [23] tensor product or Pollack's [24] ideas about the use of the dynamics of the recurrent network. In the light of this, connectionism can definitely not be regarded as a dead-end in the cognition debate - on the contrary, connectionism once again comes strengthened out of the battle.

Acknowledgments

This research was supported by an award from the University of Skövde, Sweden. I am indebted to Noel E. Sharkey, Tim van Gelder and Jordan Pollack for supplying useful comments on and motivation for this paper. I also would like to thank the organisers of the Connectionist Models Summer School, for accepting my application and organising a very interesting summer school.

References

[1] Minsky M. L. & Papert S. A, (1988), *Perceptrons (Expanded Edition)*, MIT Press.

[2] Fodor J. A. & Pylyshyn Z. W., (1988), Connectionism a cognitive architecture: A critical analysis, In *Connections and symbols*, (Eds) Pinker Steven & Mehler Jacques, MIT Press, pp 3 - 71.

[3] Fodor J. A. & McLaughlin B. P., (1990), Connectionism and the problem of systematicity: Why Smolensky's solution did not work, *Cognition*, 35, pp 183 - 204.

[4] Smolensky P., (1988), On the proper treatment of connectionism, *The Behavioural and Brain Sciences*, **11**, pp 1 - 17.

[5] Chalmers D. J., (1990), Why Fodor and Pylyshyn Were Wrong: The Simplest Refutation, *Proceedings of the Twelfth Annual Conference of the Cognitive Science Society*, pp 340 - 347.

[6] van Gelder T., (1990), Compositionality: A Connectionist Variation on a Classical Theme, *Cognitive Science*, **Vol. 14**, pp 355 - 364.

[7] Pollack J. B., (1990), Recursive Distributed Representations, *Artificial Intelligence*, 46, pp 77 - 105.

[8] Chalmers D. J., (1990), Syntactic Transformation on Distributed Representations, *Connection Science*, **Vol. 2**, Nos 1 & 2, pp 53 - 62.

[9] Smolensky P., (1990), Tensor Product Variable Binding and the Representation of Symbolic Structures in Connectionist Systems, *Artificial Intelligence*, 46, pp 159 - 216.

[10] Niklasson L. F. & Sharkey N. E., (1992), Connectionism and the Issues of Compositionality and Systematicity, In *Proceedings of the Cybernetics and Systems Research*, (Ed) Robert Trappl, **Vol 2**, World Scientific, pp 1367 - 1374.

[11] Niklasson L. F. & Sharkey N. E., (1993), The Miracle Mind Model, In *Selected Readings from the Swedish Conference on Connectionism - 1992*, (Eds) Niklasson L. F. & Bodén M. B., Ellis Horwood.

[12] Niklasson L. F. & Sharkey N. E., (1993), Systematicity and Generalisation in Connectionist Compositional Representations, In *Neural Networks and a new 'AI'*, (Ed) Dorffner G., under preparation.

[13] Blank D. S., Meeden L. A. & Marshall J. B., (1992), Exploring the Symbolic/Subsymbolic Continuum: A Case Study of RAAM. In *The Symbolic And Connectionist Paradigms: Closing the Gap*, (Ed) Dinsmore J., Hillsdale.

[14] Elman J. L., (1988), Finding Structure in Time, Technical Report 8801, Center for Research in Language, University of California, San Diego. Published (1990), *Cognitive Science* 14, pp 179 - 211.

[15] Pollack J. B., (1988), Recursive Auto-Associative Memory: Devising Compositional Distributed Representations, *Proceedings of the Tenth Annual Conference of the Cognitive Science Society*, pp 33 - 39.

[16] Pollack J. B., (1989), Implications of Recursive Distributed Representations, In *Advances in Neural Processing Systems I*, Touretzky D. S. (Ed), pp 527 - 536.

[17] Miikkulainen R. & Dyer M. G., (1988), Forming Global Representations with Extended Backpropagation, *Proceedings of the IEEE Second Annual International Conference on Neural Networks*, pp 285 - 292.

[18] Chrisman L., (1991), Learning Recursive Distributed Representation for Holistic Computation, In *Connection Science*, **Vol. 3**, No. 4, pp 345 - 366.

[19] Hadley R. F., (1992), Compositionality and Systematicity in Connectionist Language Learning, *Proceedings of the Fourteenth Annual Conference of the Cognitive Science Society*, pp 659 - 664.

[20] Barnden J. A. & Pollack J. B., (1991), Problems for High-Level Connectionism, In *Advances in Connectionist and Neural Computation Theory*, (Eds) Barnden J. A. & Pollack J. B., Vol 1, pp 1 - 16.

[21] van Gelder T., (1991), A Survey of the Concept of Distribution, *Philosophy and Connectionist Theory*, (Eds) Ramsey W., Stich S. P. & Rumelhart D. E., pp 33 - 59.

[22] Hinton G. E., (1986), Learning Distributed Representation of Concepts, In *Proceedings of the Eighth Annual Conference of the Cognitive Science Society*, pp 48 - 54.

[23] Smolensky P., Legendre G. & Miyata Y., (1992), Principles for an Integrated Connectionist/Symbolic Theory of Higher Cognition, *Tech. Report CU-CS-600-92*, University of Colorado at Boulder.

[24] Pollack J. B., (1992), The Induction of Dynamical Recognizers, *Machine Learning* 7, pp 227 - 252.

Looking for Structured Representations in Recurrent Networks

Mihail Crucianu
LIMSI – CNRS, BP 133
91403 Orsay, France
crucianu@limsi.fr

We make explicit the structure of internal representations developed by learning in recurrent networks. The analysis shows that this structure reflects the structure of the complex external entities being represented, thus providing a basis for systematic connectionist processing. We also find that the networks can represent graded variables, so the representation scheme developed is a general one.

INTRODUCTION

In [7] it was argued that, to provide effective solutions to high-level tasks, AI systems must have *systematic* behavior. Explicitly, they must ensure that the structural similarities between the complex entities they represent have a causal effect on building and processing these representations. The solution offered by symbolic AI is: i) let the representations of elementary entities be context-independent symbols, ii) let the representations of complex entities token the representations of their components and explicitly specify the pattern these components must fill in (*concatenative* compositionality), iii) use processes that are sensitive to this kind of structure representation.

According to [9], this solution is unnecessarily restrictive. All that is needed to account for systematicity is to reliably maintain the similarities between complex entities in their representations, and to ensure that the processing of these representations is sensitive to such similarities. In the connectionist framework it is usually considered that external entities are represented by activation vectors and processing is naturally sensitive to the similarities between these vectors. The corresponding sufficient condition was then expressed as: networks should translate the structural similarities between complex entities into vectorial similarities between the internal representations of these entities. While the requirement for compositional representations is maintained, the mechanism for composition is no longer restricted to concatenation.

It was proven that non-concatenative compositional representations can be formally defined, employing the tensor product in [16] or the circular convolution in [12]. Also, it was experimentally shown, for certain connectionist models, that learning can develop representation schemes that allow both the components of the complex entities represented and the way they are structured to have a causal effect on processing — see [1], [2], [5], [10], [13], [15]. These schemes — which appear to be non-concatenative — are not yet well understood, so it is difficult to evaluate to what extent systematicity is accounted for.

Our main concern in the following is to make explicit the structure of certain connectionist representations developed by learning, and thus better understand how this structure relates to the structure of the entities being represented. This would provide evidence that the condition put forward in [9] is met even by existing connectionist models. One should further notice this condition implies that if the reliable translation of structural into vectorial similarities holds for some entities, it must thereupon hold for all the similar entities. A question is then raised by the presence of learning: can the representation scheme developed be successfully applied not only to the training corpus, but to all the entities having the required similarities? This explains why we are also concerned with studying what underlies generalization in this context.

AN ANALYSIS OF THE REPRESENTATIONS

Defining a Suitable Task

Several researchers (see [3], [6], [10]) studied the state space of recurrent networks having learned to accomplish sequential prediction tasks. They found global vectorial similarities between network states, related to symbolic similarities in the task domain. However, these tasks do not force individual network states to reliably represent all the information specified in the entities being input. Here, we want the networks to build *intra-state* representations that keep as much as possible of this information, so we have to choose the learning task accordingly.

We consider the schema-like structure model employed by Smolensky, when introducing tensor product representations (see [16]), to be relatively general and provide sufficient complexity. A schema is regarded as a set of <role | filler> bindings. This model was already been given some attention in a connectionist framework — see [11], [17] and [18] — and some results on the ability of the networks to represent such structures were obtained. The tasks used in these papers have an important temporal component — a network must learn to translate a sequence of words into a schema-like representation — and the required complexity to force networks to keep as much information as possible in the intra-state representations. They are also well adapted to analysis.

For these reasons, and to allow comparisons, we decided to use the schema model employed by Smolensky, restricted to non-recursive structures, and a task that is similar to those we just referred to. Specifically, the task we chose is as follows: a sentence is input to the network as a sequence of words; after each word is input, the network must instantiate at the output the semantic roles corresponding to the part of the sentence it has already seen.

Network Architecture and Learning

To ease analysis, the recurrent networks (RNs) we use have only three layers, with only one — recurrent — hidden layer (see figure 1). Local coding is employed for the input words. At the output, a different set of units is associated with each of the semantic roles (at most five in the experiments reported here: agent, action, patient, recipient and instrument). The output representation is conjunctive: an active unit represents the binding of a word to a semantic role.

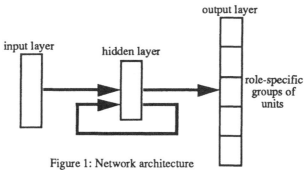

Figure 1: Network architecture

The learning algorithm we use is back-propagation through time [14]. It was shown — see [2] and [10] — to learn long-range dependencies better than usual back-propagation plus copy-back mechanism as in [3] or [5]. Also, we do not have to present a target vector to the network at every time step. In [2] and [10] a fixed-length temporal window is employed for back-propagation through time. We back-propagate error to the beginning of a sequence and do not cross the frontier between sequences. This choice is justified by the specifics of the task: we want the network to develop representations of whole sentences, without any interference between sentences.

The training sequences (a sequence corresponds to a sentence) are randomly arranged in the corpus, but their presentation always respects the same order, so we can speak of training epochs. Error is back-propagated and weights are modified after the presentation of each sequence. The error measure we use is cross-entropy. Learning policy is as follows: learning proceeds until error evolution reaches a plateau; at that moment, the learning rate is decreased and training continues. For the recurrent networks we employed, learning rate when training began was 0.02 and momentum 0.0. To avoid weight destruction when crossing a very steep region of the error landscape, the back-propagated error for each unit is normalized if higher than a fixed limit.

Each of the following experiments was performed on several networks and the results obtained were qualitatively similar to those presented here. However, the number of networks was not big enough and their parameters were not systematically varied, so that no statistical results are given.

Analysis Method

We want to find out how the structural similarities between complex entities relate to the vectorial similarities between their representations in recurrent networks. Hierarchical clustering analysis was employed in [3], [6] and [10] to obtain *global* similarities between hidden unit activation vectors. But many different types of similarity can exist between complex entities. If some network states represent such entities, the global relationships between states only reflect a mixture of the similarities. We must be able to isolate one type of similarity at a time, by selecting relevant dimensions of the hidden unit state space and relating the similarities obtained along them with those between the entities being represented.

In the case of the task we use, each semantic role generates one type of similarity: two sentences are similar if they have the same word bound to this role. For each role, we thus have a different classification of the sentences and, correspondingly, of the set of hidden unit activation vectors (which we shall call "network states") representing them. We should then look for a subspace of the hidden unit state space that reflects as accurately as possible this classification. This is exactly what a discriminant analysis (DA) of the set of network states should do. Given a classification of a set of vectors in some high-dimensional space, DA projects these vectors on a subspace so as to optimize a joint criterion: maximize between-class dispersion while minimizing total dispersion. DA was used in [8] to evaluate the quality of the clustering obtained in the hidden layers of multi-layer perceptrons performing a classification task. In our experiments, given the classification induced by one role on the sentences in the corpus, we make a DA of the set of network states representing them. The pictures show the projections of the set of states on 3-dimensional subspaces obtained by DAs. In the analyses, we only use network states which are supposed to represent entire sentences. Such a state is obtained after the last word of a sentence is input.

Intra-state Structure Made Explicit

This analysis method was employed in a first experiment. Using a vocabulary of 28 words (7 verbs, 17 nouns and 4 auxiliary words) and schema patterns having five semantic roles, 966 sentences were generated, in both active and passive voices. Here are, as an example, two sentences corresponding to a same schema:

The_schoolgirl gave the_coffee to the_player.   ← *active voice sentence*
The_coffee was given to the_player by the_schoolgirl.   ← *passive voice sentence*
((*agent* I schoolgirl) (*action* I give) (*patient* I coffee) (*recipient* I player))   ← *associated schema*

The words *was*, *to*, *by* and *with* are introduced into the recurrent networks as distinct inputs, and have distinct codes, though they are never requested at the output; the word *the* is not represented in the input. To remain compatible with French, we did not use passive voice sentences beginning with the recipient.

A random set of 900 sentences was selected for learning, the other 66 were kept to test generalization. Learning was stopped after 1600 epochs. We used 25 hidden units. Figures 2 and 3 present results of discriminant analysis (DA) performed on the set of hidden unit vectors associated to all the 966 sentences. The figures were obtained by projecting the same vectors on different subspaces, given by DA as corresponding to the different roles.

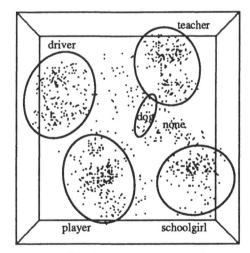

Figure 2: Discrimination between the fillers of the agent role (discriminant components 1, 2 and 3, with 966 points)

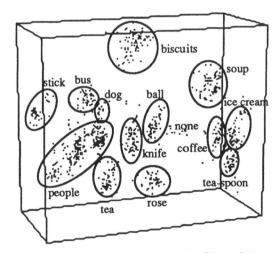

Figure 3: Discrimination between the fillers of the patient role (discriminant components 1, 2 and 3, with 966 points)

Good discrimination is found between the fillers of the *agent* role (figure 2), *action* role and *recipient* role. Due to cross-correlations in the training corpus, (e.g. the patients can be animates or not, depending on the verb), separation is not very good between the fillers of *patient* (figure 3) or *instrument*. However, when a DA was performed only on the set of hidden unit activity vectors corresponding to sentences containing *gave*, perfect discrimination between the possible *patients* was found.

Similar analyses were performed on the sets of hidden unit vectors before learning, when the transformations input → hidden and hidden → hidden are random. Networks discriminate well between words in the last position in the sentences (that is, last words being input), regardless of their semantic role, and any other information is lost.

The results we obtained show that the networks dedicate independent subspaces of the hidden unit state space to the semantic roles. When projected on the subspace associated to a given role, the hidden unit activation vectors which represent sentences having a same word bound to this role form clusters. This is how the elementary structural similarities between sentences are translated into vectorial similarities between their representations. The presence of strong cross-correlations in the training corpus affects the quality of the clusters (or the extent to which the subspaces are dedicated). This problem is further explored in the next paragraph.

What Underlies Generalization

We mentioned that, in order to account for systematicity, if the reliable translation of structural into vectorial similarities holds for some entities, it must thereupon hold for all the similar entities. This implies that the networks should correctly process not only the sentences in the training corpus, but also all the sentences generated by the same set of semantic roles and the same set of fillers. To do so, networks should be able to infer that the different semantic roles are independent variables in the structure of the sentences. But the networks can only have access to this structure using the statistics of the training corpus. We should then find the conditions these statistics must satisfy for network generalization to reflect the presence of the variables. Experiments described in [11], [17] and [18] show that this can be achieved by recurrent networks, in tasks similar to the one we study. They also suggest that such generalization is underlain by a decorrelation between context and the bindings of specific semantic roles. We now develop this idea and present two experiments to support it.

Concerning the ability of a network to represent role | filler bindings, two limit cases can be considered. In one, the bindings of a role to many different fillers can be successfully represented, even if these bindings were not present, in the same contexts, in the examples the network saw during training. The network behaves as if it has associated a perfect variable to this role. In the other case, for a certain context, the binding of a role to a certain filler cannot be represented — the network replaces at the output the actual filler with one it "prefers" in the current context — even if in a different context such a binding is well represented. The network did not infer that this role is to be regarded as an independent variable.

If, for a certain set of sentences, we analyze the set of vectors requested as outputs from a network, we find that it displays an important variability along certain directions in the corresponding space. The adaptation of network parameters — giving the mapping input → hidden vectors and the position and orientation of the output detection hyperplanes — will pay more attention to these directions. Networks will thus have better performance when the important information in the sentences is conveyed by the components of the concatenated input vectors along these high variability directions. For sentences outside the training corpus, they will better accept variability along these directions than along others. We consider "hidden" variables are associated to these privileged directions. If strong cross-correlations between the fillers of different roles are present in the training corpus, these "hidden" variables do not correspond to the semantic roles we use in our external, symbolic representation. So, strong context effects appear. If a role not regarded by the network as a variable is bound to a "wrong" filler, the network will probably replace this filler, at the output, with the filler(s) best correlated with the context. This because in this context the contribution of the filler to the internal representation of the sentence is reduced and the network will map it close to the representation(s) of other sentence(s) it knows better (that is, with the "wrong" filler replaced by the best correlated ones). In this case similarity is almost completely given by the context, so that generalization will make the network "correct" a "wrong" part of the input (note that it may be sometimes desirable).

We performed two experiments to verify these hypotheses and see how the correspondence previously established between the structure of sentences and the structure of the representations developed by the networks is influenced by characteristics of the training corpus.

A first experiment was devised to study, in the absence of strong cross-correlations, what influence the size of the training corpus has on the ability of a network to infer the presence of variables in the structures to be represented.

173

Ten proper names and ten transitive verbs were used to generate all the 2000 active and passive voice sentences having the semantic roles *agent*, *action* and *patient* (this corpus was designed following an experiment in [18]). Some networks were trained on a random subset of 1600 sentences (80% of the corpus), others on a random subset of 1200 sentences (60% of the corpus). All the networks had 25 hidden units and were trained for 1000 epochs. Network performances are given in table 1. Figures 4 and 5 present results of discriminant analysis — corresponding to the *action* role — performed on the set of hidden unit vectors associated to all the 2000 sentences.

Table 1: Number of errors on the training and test corpora

Network	Training corpus	Test corpus
RN 80%	0 (1600 sentences)	0 (400 sentences)
RN 60%	0 (1200 sentences)	17 (800 sentences)

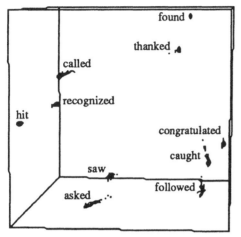

Figure 4: RN 80% — discrimination between the fillers of the action role (discriminant components 2, 3 and 4, with 2000 points)

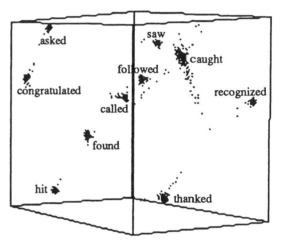

Figure 5: RN 60% — discrimination between the fillers of the action role (discriminant components 1, 2 and 3, with 2000 points)

We see that both generalization for all the three semantic roles and discrimination (presented here for actions) in state space are very good. And this even when the training corpus is 60% of the entire corpus. We can say that important variations in the size of the training corpus have little influence on network ability to infer the presence of variables in the structures to be represented. This result is in agreement with the one obtained in [19] for multi-layer perceptrons trained to perform auto-association on small fragments of highly combinatorial corpora. However, the task seems to be more difficult for recurrent networks.

A second experiment was devised to study what influence the presence of strong cross-correlations in the training corpus has on the ability of a network to infer the right variables in the structures to be represented. From the 1000 active voice sentences of the previous corpus, we selected 300 in which each verb was associated with only three patients but all the possible agents. This introduced a strong correlation between the verbs and the fillers of the *patient* role. Two hundred random sentences were then selected as training corpus. We thus have two test corpora: one of 100 sentences respecting the cross-correlations and another of 700 sentences violating them. The recurrent networks had 15 hidden units and were trained for 6000 epochs. Network performances are given in table 2. Figures 6, 7 and 8 present results of discriminant analysis — corresponding to each of the three semantic roles — performed on the set of hidden unit vectors associated to all the 1000 sentences.

Table 2: Number of errors on the training and test corpora

Training corpus of 200 sentences	Test corpus of 100 sentences	Test corpus of 700 sentences
0 for *agent*	0 for *agent*	2 for *agent*
0 for *action*	0 for *action*	572 for *action*
0 for *patient*	2 for *patient*	323 for *patient*

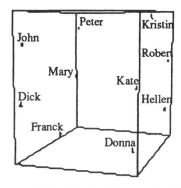

Figure 6: Discrimination between the fillers of the agent role (discriminant components 1, 2 and 3, with 1000 points)

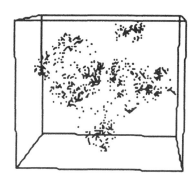

Figure 7: Lack of discrimination between the fillers of the patient role (discriminant components 1, 2 and 3, with 1000 points)

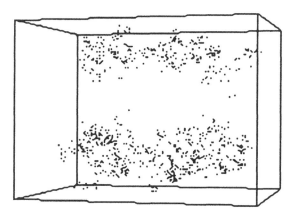

Figure 8: Lack of discrimination between the fillers of the action role (discriminant components 1, 2 and 3, with 1000 points)

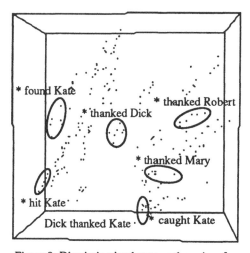

Figure 9: Discrimination between the pairs of fillers of the action and patient roles (principal components 1, 2 and 3, with 210 points)

The results on the 100 sentence test corpus show that generalization is very good for all the semantic roles if the cross-correlations in the training corpus are not violated. On the 700 sentence test corpus, generalization is good only for *agent* and very poor for *action* or *patient*. Good discrimination in state space is found between the fillers of the *agent* role, which thus proves to be regarded as an independent variable. No discrimination is found between the fillers of *action* or *patient*. We mention that training completely changes the behavior of the networks: *untrained* networks discriminate well between words in the last position in the sentences being input — in this experiment these are fillers of the *patient* role. We used cross-validation on both test corpora, but we did not notice any overfitting before training was stopped.

175

A principal components analysis (PCA) was then performed on the set of hidden vectors corresponding only to the training corpus. By PCA, one finds orthogonal directions along which the variance within a given set of vectors is maximal. These directions are obtained in the order of the corresponding variances. PCA was employed, in [6] and [10], as a method for dimension reduction, allowing one to visualize the organization of the state space of the hidden units. Here, we wanted to see which regularities of the sentences have the highest importance for the behavior of the networks. Along the first three principal components we find clusters containing sets of points corresponding to sentences having a same *pair of fillers* for the *action* and *patient* roles — see figure 9. With the "surface" variables *action* and *patient* the network associates only one "hidden" variable — *action & patient*.

Figure 9 also exemplifies the replacement effect. In the training corpus, *thanked* is only associated with *Dick, Mary* and *Robert* as patients, while Kate as patient only with *found, hit* and *caught*. The sentence "Dick thanked Kate" in the test corpus is mapped somewhere near the sentences ended in "caught Kate", and the network replaces *thanked* with *caught* at its output. As seen in table 2, sometimes the filler of *patient* is replaced.

These results show that networks can infer the right variables present in the structures to be represented, provided that the training corpus does not contain strong correlations between the fillers of different variables. If such cross-correlations are present, the networks will infer instead graded variables. We may be interested in using graded variables if we want context to play an important role in processing.

CONCLUSION

In [9] it was argued that, for connectionist networks to have the systematic behavior required by high-level tasks, it is sufficient to reliably translate the structural similarities between complex entities into vectorial similarities between their connectionist representations. We wanted to find to what extent this condition can be satisfied by an existing connectionist model. For this, we studied the representations developed by recurrent networks in learning to solve the task of translating the sequence of words composing a sentence into the corresponding set of <semantic role | word> bindings. We employed discriminant analysis on sets of network states to make explicit the internal structure of these representations. The experiments we presented show that the networks dedicate an independent subspace of the hidden unit state space to each semantic role. When projected on the subspace dedicated to a given role, the vectors representing sentences having a same word bound to this role form tight clusters. This means that the translation process takes place indeed. For further details please refer to [4].

But the condition in [9] implies that if the reliable translation holds for some entities, it must thereupon hold for all the similar entities. The fact that a representation scheme is developed by learning, on a specific training corpus, and not formally defined starting from some model of the complex entities, could raise the following question: can the networks infer the presence of the right variables in the structures they must represent? It was suggested (see [11], [17]) that this is underlain by the decorrelation between the fillers of the different variables, which increases the context independence of the representations. We put forward some more arguments to support this idea and concluded that graded variables can be represented by the networks. Our analysis of network state space provided means to evaluate the "degree" of the learned variables.

Learning links the structure of the representations to the global organization of the hidden unit state space. We could make explicit the intra-state structure by finding clusters of states along specific directions in this space. The link should make these connectionist representations better in using context and more efficient in using resources than the existing formally defined representation schemes. We hold that recurrent networks succeed in finding a compromise between the generality of a representation scheme and its ability to inherently use context.

The results obtained must be more systematically explored and then extended. More effective tools for the analysis of the state space, eventually providing better prediction abilities, must be developed. Means to obtain a better compromise between ability to use context and ability to generalize in connectionist networks must be found. Finally, network capabilities to represent recursive structure — like sentences with embedded clauses — should be further explored.

Acknowledgements

The author is very grateful to Jean-François Jodouin and Daniel Memmi for useful discussions. The comments and suggestions of Paul Smolensky were essential in improving the quality of this presentation. The author is supported by grant 900621 from the French Government.

References

[1] D. J. Chalmers, "Syntactic transformations on distributed representations", *Connection Science*, vol. 2, pp. 53-62, 1990.

[2] N. Chater and P. Conkey, "Finding linguistic structure with recurrent neural networks", in *Proceedings of ICANN'92*, Brighton, UK, 1992.

[3] A. Cleeremans, D. Servan-Schreiber and J. L. McClelland, "Finite state automata and simple recurrent networks", *Neural Computation*, vol. 1, pp. 372-381, 1989.

[4] M. Crucianu, "Finding structured representations in recurrent networks", *Notes et documents du LIMSI*, nr. 93-21, LIMSI - CNRS, Orsay, France, 1993.

[5] J. L. Elman, "Finding structure in time", *Cognitive Science*, vol. 4, pp. 179-211, 1990.

[6] J. L. Elman, "Distributed representations, simple recurrent networks and grammatical structure", *Machine Learning*, vol. 7, pp. 195-224, 1991.

[7] J. A. Fodor and Z. W. Pylyshyn, "Connectionism and cognitive architecture: a critical analysis", *Cognition*, vol. 28, pp. 3-71, 1988.

[8] P. Gallinari, S. Thiria, F. Badran and F. Fogelman-Soulié, "On the relations between discriminant analysis and multilayer perceptrons", *Neural Networks*, vol. 4, pp. 349-360, 1991.

[9] T. van Gelder, "Compositionality : a connectionist variation on a classical theme", *Cognitive Science*, vol. 14, pp. 355-384, 1990.

[10] J.-F. Jodouin, "Réseaux de neurones et traitement du langage naturel: étude des réseaux de neurones récurrents et de leurs représentations", *Thèse de Docteur en Sciences*, Université de Paris-Sud, Orsay, France, 1993.

[11] R. Miikkulainen and M. G. Dyer, "Natural language processing with modular PDP networks and distributed lexicon", *Cognitive Science*, vol. 15, pp. 343-400, 1991.

[12] T. Plate, "Holographic reduced representations", *Technical Report CRG-TR-91-1*, Department of Computer Science, University of Toronto, 1991.

[13] J. B. Pollack, "Recursive distributed representations", *Artificial Intelligence*, vol. 46, pp. 77-105, 1990.

[14] D. E. Rumelhart, G. E. Hinton and R. J. Williams, "Learning internal representations by error propagation", in Rumelhart, D.E., McClelland, J.L.(1986, eds.): *Parallel distributed processing: explorations in the microstructure of cognition*, Vol.2: Psychological and biological models, MIT Press, pp. 7-57, 1986.

[15] N. E. Sharkey, "The ghost in the hybrid: a study of uniquely connectionist representations", *AISB Quarterly*, vol. 79, pp. 10-16, 1992.

[16] P. Smolensky, "Tensor product variable binding and the representation of symbolic structures in connectionist systems", *Artificial Intelligence*, vol. 46, pp. 159-216, 1990.

[17] M. F. St. John, "The story gestalt: a model of knowledge-intensive processes in text comprehension", *Cognitive Science*, vol. 16, pp. 271-306, 1992.

[18] M. F. St. John and J. L. McClelland, "Learning and applying contextual constraints in sentence comprehension", *Artificial Intelligence*, vol. 46, pp. 217-256, 1990.

[19] J. Wiles, "Representation of variables and their values in neural networks", presented at the 15th Annual Meeting of the Cognitive Science Society, Boulder, Colorado, June 1993.

Back Propagation with Understandable Results

Irina Tchoumatchenko
LAFORIA-CNRS
University of Paris-VI
4 Place Jussieu
75252 Paris CEDEX 05 France
irina@laforia.ibp.fr

Abstract

In this paper, we present an approach to understanding trained neural networks. We start with a simple observation that a neural net trained on a classification task and having weights clustered around $-1, 0$ and 1 can be interpreted as a majority-vote rule. A weight penalty technique is used to force the weights to discrete values. This technique requires quite a bit of tuning of control parameters over time. A large number of parameters involved makes our method difficult to replicate and its generality doubtful. To remede such a situation we propose a generalization of this empirical method through a Bayesian framework and Gaussian mixture models. We conduct our experiments on the real-world problem of protein secondary structure prediction. With our approach we have extracted a majority vote rule explaining the neural net's classification of protein secondary structure without losing prediction accuracy.

INTRODUCTION

Understanding of the trained neural nets is a central concern of the current neural network research. We observe two closely related yet distinct ways of tackling this problem. Statistical interpretation of neural nets seems to put the rapid end to the happy old "black-boxing" style of solving problems with neural nets [1] [2] [3]. On the other hand, there is a strong interest in logical understanding of neural networks [4] [5] [6]. Typically, to extract rules a neural network is prestructured before training using initial knowledge expressed as a set of logical rules [5] or as a probabilistic model [6]. Recently, the more challenging problem of extracting logical rules from *arbitrary* neural networks has been addressed [4]. The underlying premise of most rule-extraction methods is that each hidden and output unit in the network can be thought of as implementing a symbolic rule. Our method deals with extracting logical rules from scratch and we do not rely on iterpretation of each unit as a logical rule. We get a decision scheme directly mapping the input features to the output classes without using intermediate concepts corresponding to hidden units. We have adopted the idea of applying constraints to understand a neural network's training results [7]. It turns out that constraining the weights to be contained in the set $\{-1, 0, 1\}$ enable the network's decision to be interpreted as a majority vote rule. We have succeeded in respecting the imposed constraints without losing of the prediction accuracy on the real-world problem of protein secondary structure prediction often addressed with neural network-based approaches [8].

PROTEIN SECONDARY STRUCTURE PREDICTION PROBLEM

The problem of the protein secondary structure prediction consists in finding a mapping between the primary structure, which is a string of characters (each character stands for one of the 20 amino acids), and the secondary structure, which is another string of characters (each character stands for one of the three types of secondary structure, namely, helix, sheet or coil). In most of neural network-based studies of structure prediction, a NetTalk-like network is used [8].

The neural network is a one-hidden layer perceptron that receives the sequence of amino acids as an input (see Fig 1). The secondary structure of a pacticular residue is considered to be a function of the residue and the environement around the residue. In practice, this has meant that the secondary structure of a central residue is determined by all residues within a neighborhood of the center. Such a neighborhood is refered to as a "window". A fixed size window is passed through the input sequences and the network is trained by back propagation to produce at the output the secondary structure corresponding to the central residue. Each amino acid is coded by 21 bits (20 amino acids plus one for the empty position tag). We fix the number of hidden units equal to 10 and the size of the window equal to 13. The data set used in our study is a classical one [8].

CONSTRAINING A NEURAL NETWORK

We impose the constraint on the basic neural network's weights to be in the finite set of values $\{-1, 0, 1\}$. The constrained neural network can be approximately interpreted as the following majority vote rule:

Let I_α, I_β, I_γ be the counters calculating the contribution of each input unit (i.e. the contribution of an amino acid at a given place) into the final decision of the neural network on the type of secondary structure (helix, sheet, coil respectively).

Let path p_{nm}^i be a conjunction of two non-zero weighted connections, where the first comes from n-th input unit to m-th hidden unit and the second comes from m-th hidden unit to i-th output unit ($i \in \{\alpha, \beta, \gamma\}$). We call p_{nm}^i a positive (negative) path if the product of its weights is positive (negative). We denote a positive (negative) path as p_{nm}^{i+} (p_{nm}^{i-}).

The work of the discrete-weighted neural network can be approximated as:

- calculate the counters: $I_i = \sum_{p_{nm}^{i+}} 1 - \sum_{p_{nm}^{i-}} 1$, $i \in \{\alpha, \beta, \gamma\}$

  This means that the presence of each amino acid having a positive (negative) path to i-unit, $i \in \{\alpha, \beta, \gamma\}$ will cause I_i to be incremented (decremented). We say that such an amino acid "votes" for (against) the i-conformation.

- compare counters and make a decision:

  if $I_i = \max\{I_\alpha, I_\beta, I_\gamma\}$ then the center amino acid conformation is predicted as i.

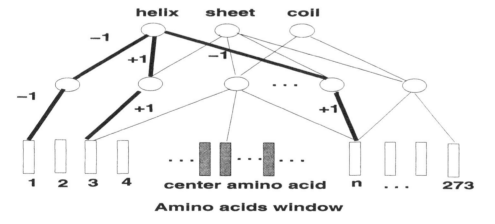

Figure 1: Neural network using to predict the protein secondary structure and its constraining. Thin lines represent non-zero connections after training. Thick lines represent all helix-contributing paths.

A possible state of a constrained neural network after training is shown in Fig 1. The k-th bit codes the presence of an amino acid represented as the $mod(k, 21)$-th bit at the $\lfloor \frac{k}{21} \rfloor$-th place of the input window. The presence of an acid

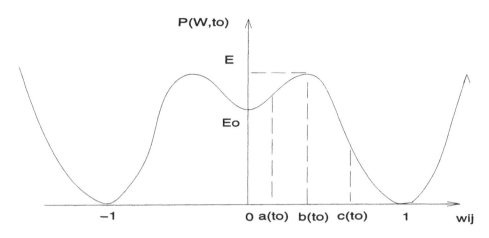

Figure 2: Instantaneous penalty term shape $P(W,t)$, $t = t_0$, where $a(t_0), b(t_0), c(t_0)$ are the transition points between the paraboles.

coded by the first or the third bit at the first place of the input window will lead to vote for the α-conformation, while the presence of the amino acid $mod(n, 21)$ at $\lfloor \frac{n}{21} \rfloor$ (coded by the n-th bit of the input window) will lead to a vote against the α-conformation. In the same manner all bits of the input window connected by a positive (negative) path with a particular output unit are interpreted as the presence of an amino acid AA at place k, voting for (against) the particular conformation. All votes are counted and a final majority vote is made.

TRAINING A CONSTRAINED NEURAL NETWORK

To respect the imposed constraints we add an extra term $P(W)$ to the standard error function $E(W)$. The penalty term $P(W)$ will force weights to approach -1 or 0 or 1 during training. We have used the penalty term $P(W)$ represented as:

$$P(W,t) = P(W_1,t) + k(t)P(W_2,t)$$

where W_1 is the set of weights between the input and the hidden layers, W_2 is a set of weights between the hidden and the output layers, t is an index over the training patterns. Parameter $k(t)$ compensates the lower representation capacity of the hidden-output mapping (10 into 3 units) in comparison with the input-hidden mapping (273 into 10 units). The penalty $P(W_i,t)$, $i = 1, 2$ is a differentiable juxtaposition of paraboles (Fig 2) dynamically parameterized with the set of control experimentally adjusted values $a(t), b(t), c(t), E(t), E_0(t)$ (Table 1). We stop stop training when correct rate reaches 60%. Then the constraints are introduced gradually and are controlled by a half dozen parameters (see Fig 2 and Table 1). Dynamics of constraints introduction consist of the following.

- *gradual constraints introduction:* Without stopping the training we gradually add the penalty to each weight of the network. Slowly we push each weight into a cluster around $-1, 0$ or $+1$. At this time the learning and the constraints are opposed but the weights of particular interest (i.e. connections bringing a discriminating information) are kept far from zero and the other weights (without statistical significance) are gradually reduced to 0. If one weight is significant (useful for the prediction) the learning will keep its value sufficiently important to preserve its significance. First, we put a small penalty error for the weights near 0.3 then we increase its value but move the position of the maximum to 0.1. The weights are pushed towards zero for a while (when their value is under the position of the maximum of the penalty error) but if they can resist to the constraint they will be pushed towards $+1$ or -1 when their value will become over the position of the maximum of the penalty.

Table 1: Linear dynamic of the control parameters

Control parameters	Number of window presentation, t		
	40000	60000	80000
$a(t)$	0.2	0.1	0.01
$b(t)$	0.3	0.15	0.6
$c(t)$	0.4	0.3	0.99
$k(t)$	10	30	40
$E(t)$	0.00005	0.01	0.05
$E_0(t)$	0.000005	0.0001	0.005

- *final transformation:* Keeping on with the back propagation training we increase the constraint penalty and so reduce the size of the clusters. At the end of this short period the values of the weights are as close as wanted to $-1, 0$ or $+1$.

BIOLOGICAL RESULTS

Having applied our method for extracting a majority vote rules from trained neural network to the constrained $273 - 10 - 3$ neural network, we have obtained three majority vote rules (one per secondary structure type). The helix decision scheme summarizing the positive/negative votes of a given amino acid at a given place is presented in Table 2. The extracted schemes for sheet and coil predictions are summarized in Tables 3 and 4 respectively. While the constrained neural network does almost as good as the non-constrained one (62.3% vs. 61.4%), the extracted vote scheme does as good as the constrained neural network (being tested on the Sejnowski's test set they give different predictions only on 126 examples from 3520). The prediction accuracy of the extracted scheme is 61.2%.

Table 2: Amino acids increasing (AA) and decreasing (!AA) the helix counter

Residue position	Amino acids																	
1		!C		E														
2		!C		E														
3	A			E		!G						!P						Y
4	A			E		!G	!H					!P						
5	A			E		!G			L	M		!P			!S			
6	A			E		!G			L	M		!P			!S	!T		
7	A			E	F	!G			L	M	!N	!P			!S	!T		
8	A			E	F	!G		K	L	M		!P	Q	R				
9	A		!D		F		H	K	L	M		!P			!S	!T		
10	A		!D		F	!G	H	K	L	M		!P			!S			
11	A		!D				H	K	L	M		!P						
12	A						H	K	L	M		!P						
13		!C	!D	!E		!G		K				!P			!S	!T		

A PROBABILISTIC MODEL

The experimental technique for extracting logical information from trained neural networks described above suffers from a large number of control parameters. That makes our method difficult to replicate and its generality doutful. In this section we describe how to generalize this empirical method through Bayesian framework. From a Bayesian

Table 3: Amino acids increasing (AA) and decreasing (!AA) the sheet counter

Residue position	A	C	D	E	F	G	H	I	K	L	M	N	P	Q	S	T	V	W	Y
1					!F	G									S				
2		!C				G				!L	!M	N			S			!W	
3						G				!L					S				
4		!C	!D	!E		G				!L									
5	!A		!D	!E			!H	I	!K			!N	!P				V		Y
6	!A		!D	!E	F	!G	!H	I	!K	L		!N	!P			T	V	W	Y
7	!A		!D	!E	F	!G		I	!K	L		!N	!P				V	W	Y
8	!A	C	!D	!E	F			I	!K	L			!P	!Q			V	W	Y
9				!E	F			I	!K				!P	!Q			V		
10									!K					!Q	S				
11						G			!K	!L					S				
12						G		!I	!K	!L					S				
13								!I	!K	!L	!M				S	T			

Table 4: Amino acids increasing (AA) and decreasing (!AA) the coil counter

Residue position	A	C	D	E	F	G	H	I	K	L	M	N	P	Q	S	T	V	W	Y
1																			
2		C																	
3															!S				
4											!M		P						
5			D			G	H	!I	K	!L	!M	N	P				!V		
6			D	!E	!F	G		!I	K	!L	!M	N	P		S		!V		
7			D		!F	G		!I		!L	!M	N	P		S		!V	!W	!Y
8	!A	!C	D		!F	G		!I		!L	!M		P				!V	!W	!Y
9			D		!F			!I		!L			P				!V		
10			D				!H			!L	!M		P						
11	!A												P						
12													P						
13									!K										

perspective, neural nets learning can be described as follows [1] [2]. Let us denote M to be a model representing a neural net and weights $\mathbf{w}$ to be model's parameters. Using Bayes' rule the posterior probability of the parameters $\mathbf{w}$ given the data D is:

$$P(\mathbf{w}|D,M) = \frac{P(D|\mathbf{w},M)P(\mathbf{w}|M)}{P(D|M)}$$

where $P(D|\mathbf{w},M)$ is a likelihood of the data given the network with parameters $\mathbf{w}$ (measure how well the network accounts for the data). $P(\mathbf{w}|M)$ is a prior probability of such a network (our belief in the plausibility of the network before we have seen any data). $P(D|M)$ is the evidence for the network. To find the network which is the most likely explanation of the data we maximize the posterior probability, ignoring the normalising constant $P(D|M)$. If no priors are assumed for the neural net, then to maximize the posterior we should maximize log likelihood, otherwise we should maximize the sum of log likelihood and priors. At this point we can map our constraints on neural network's weights to be in $\{-1, 0, 1\}$ into Bayesian priors, namely, by setting $P(\mathbf{w}|M)$ equal to a three component gaussian mixture clustering weights around values $-1, 0$ and 1 [9]. That makes possible the automatic estimation of model's parameters using conjugate gradient or EM methods. Finally, as we deal with "one-of-n" classification we should assume rather multinomial distribution for neural network's outputs resulting in soft-max error term and normalized exponential output functions.

CONCLUSION

A constrained-based technique for extracting logical information from neural networks trained with standard back propagation is proposed and validated on the real problem of the protein secondary structure prediction. We have succeded in extracting a majority vote rules explaining the neural net's classification of protein secondary structure without losing prediction accuracy.

There are two major drawbacks in our approach. First, our method for logical rule extraction includes a large number of control parameters adjusted experimentally. To overcome the first problem we came up with Bayesian description of extraction process, which makes possible automatic parameter estimation. The second and more serious problem is related to the low prediction accuracy on the chosen testbed, that is due to intrinsic shortcomings in the setting of the secondary structure prediction problem. It is clear that the knowledge representation issues should be approached to handle this situation.

References

[1] MacKay D.J.C. (1991) A practical bayesian framework for backprop networks, Neural Computation.

[2] Rumelhart D.E. (1993) Backpropagation: The Basic Theory, lecture given at theConnectionist Summer School, Univ. of Colorado at Boulder, June, 1993.

[3] Hinton G.E. and Drew van Camp (1993) Keeping neural networks simple by minimizing the description lenghth of the weights, Proc. of COLT-93, Santa Cruz, CA, July 1993.

[4] Craven M. W., Shavlik J.W. (1993) Learning symbolic rules using artificial neural networks, in Proc. of the 10th Intern. Conf. on Machine Learning, Ahmarest, MA.

[5] Towell, G.G., Shavlik J. (1992) Interpretation of artificial neural networks: mapping knowledge-based neural networks into rules, in Neural Information Processing Systems, Vol.4, pp.977-984, Denver, CO, Morgan Kaufmann.

[6] Goodman M.R., Higgins, Miller J.W. (1992) Rule-based neural networks for classification and probability estimation, Neural computation, 4, 781-804.

[7] Kane R., I. Tchoumatchenko, M.Milgram. (1992) Extracting knowledge from data using constrained neural networks, in Proc. of the European Conference on Machine Learning, Austria, Vienne, 5-8 Apr, 1992.

[8] Qian N., Sejnowski T. (1988) Predicting the secondary structure of globular proteins using neural network models, J. Mol. Biol., 202, pp.865-884

[9] Nowlan, S.J., Hinton, G.E. (1991) Symplifying neural networks by soft weight-sharing. In Advances in Neural Information Processing Systems, vol.4, Denver, CO, Morgan Kaufmann.

Understanding Neural Networks via Rule Extraction and Pruning

Mark W. Craven and Jude W. Shavlik
Computer Sciences Department
University of Wisconsin
Madison, Wisconsin 53706 USA
craven@cs.wisc.edu

INTRODUCTION

Artificial neural networks (ANNs) have been successfully applied to real-world problems as varied as steering a motor vehicle [10] and pronouncing English text [13]. In addition to these practical successes, several empirical studies have concluded that neural networks provide performance comparable to, and in some cases, better than common symbolic learning algorithms [1, 3, 6]. A distinct advantage of symbolic learning algorithms, however, is that the concept representations they form are usually more easily understood by humans than the representations formed by neural networks. In this paper we describe and investigate an approach for extracting symbolic rules from trained ANNs. Our approach uses the NOFM algorithm [16] to extract rules from networks that have been trained using Nowlan and Hinton's method of *soft weight-sharing* [7]. Although soft weight-sharing was designed as a technique for improving generalization in neural networks, we explore it here as a means for facilitating rule extraction. We present experiments that demonstrate that our method is able to learn rules that are more accurate than rules induced using a common symbolic learning algorithm – Quinlan's C4.5 system [11]. Furthermore, the rules that are extracted from our trained networks are comparable to rules induced by C4.5 in terms of complexity and understandability. We also present a method that simplifies extracted rules by pruning antecedents from them. Our experiments show that this technique improves both the comprehensibility and the generalization performance of extracted rules.

The experiments reported in this paper use the problem domain of *promoter recognition* to investigate the effectiveness of our approach. Promoters are DNA subsequences that serve as useful "signals" for locating genes. Previously reported work has also described the application of our approach to a scaled-down version of the NETtalk task [2].

RULE EXTRACTION

An important criterion by which a machine learning algorithm should be judged is the comprehensibility of the representations formed by the algorithm. That is, does the algorithm encode the information it learns in such a way that it may be inspected and understood by humans? There are at least five reasons why this is an important criterion.

- *Validation.* If the designers and end-users of a learning system are to be confident in the performance of the system, then they must understand how it arrives at its decisions.

184

- *Discovery.* Learning algorithms may discover salient features in the input data whose importance was not previously recognized. If the representations formed by the learner are comprehensible, then these discoveries can be made accessible to human review.

- *Explanation.* If the representations are understandable, then an explanation of the classification made on a particular case can be garnered.

- *Improving generalization.* The feature representation used for an inductive learning task can have a significant impact on generalization performance. Understanding learned concept representations may facilitate the design of a better feature representation for a given problem.

- *Refinement.* Some researchers use inductive learning systems to refine approximately-correct domain theories [8, 9, 17]. When a learning system is used in this way, it is important to understand the changes to the knowledge base that have been imparted during the training process.

A significant limitation of artificial neural networks is that the concepts they learn are usually impenetrable to human understanding because the concepts are represented by a large number of real-valued parameters: the weights and biases of the network. One approach toward understanding the representations formed by a neural network is to extract symbolic rules from the network [4, 5, 12, 14].

The underlying premise of these rule-extraction methods is that each output unit (and in some cases, each hidden unit) in the network can be thought of as implementing a symbolic rule. The concept associated with each unit is the consequent of the rule, and the antecedents of the rule are either certain subsets of the units that feed into this unit, or certain subsets of the input features. As shown in Figure 1a, the process of rule extraction involves finding the *sufficient* conditions for each consequent. In order to find such sets of sufficient conditions, most rule-extraction methods assume that, after training, units tend to be either maximally active (i.e., have activation near one), or inactive (i.e., have activation near zero). Given this assumption, a rule-extraction algorithm can search for minimal sets of antecedent units that, when maximally active, cause the consequent unit to become maximally active. The process of searching for rules is problematic because of the combinatorics involved. The complexity of searching for rules like those in Figure 1a, is $O(2^n)$ where n is the number of connections impinging on the consequent unit. Moreover, many of these algorithms extract a large number of rules (e.g., [12]), even for networks of moderate complexity.

THE NOFM ALGORITHM

Towell and Shavlik previously described an algorithm [16], called NOFM, that handles the combinatoric problems of searching for rules by clustering weights into equivalence classes. They have demonstrated that their NOFM algorithm is able to extract accurate and concise rules from trained knowledge-based neural networks; that is, networks for which the topology and initial weights have been specified by an approximately-correct domain theory. The algorithm is called NOFM because it explicitly searches for rules of the form:

If (*N* of the *M* antecedents are true) then ...

The NOFM algorithm comprises five steps:

1. **Clustering.** The weights impinging on each hidden and output unit of the trained network are grouped into clusters. The distance metric used for clustering is the difference in the means of the weight magnitudes for two clusters. Additionally, weights with small magnitudes are pruned from the network at this step.

2. **Averaging.** The magnitude of each weight is set to the average value of the weights in its cluster.

3. **Eliminating.** Weight clusters that are not needed in order to correctly activate a unit are eliminated. Two elimination procedures are applied: one algorithmic and one heuristic. The algorithmic elimination

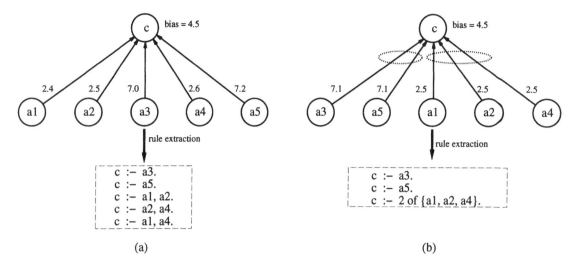

Figure 1: Extracting Rules from a Unit in a Neural Network. The figure on the left illustrates the general process of rule extraction. The extracted rules show the combinations of antecedent units which must be active for the consequent unit's bias to be exceeded. The figure on the right illustrates the NoFM method. The dotted ovals show how the weights have been grouped into clusters. Each weight has been set to the average value of its cluster.

procedure identifies clusters that *cannot* have an effect on whether or not a unit's bias is exceeded. The heuristic elimination step eliminates clusters that do not have such an effect for any of the training examples.

4. **Optimizing.** The unit biases are retrained to adapt the network to the changes that have been imparted by the previous steps.

5. **Extracting.** Each hidden and output unit is translated into a set of *N*-of-*M* rules that describe the conditions under which the unit will be activated.

Figure 1b illustrates the application of the NoFM to the unit shown in Figure 1a. The weights have been grouped into two clusters, and each weight has been set to the average value of its cluster. One of the extracted rules is expressed in the NoFM format; the other two rules are trivial NoFM cases (i.e., 1 of 1). The *eliminating* and *optimizing* steps are not depicted in this example.

EXTENDING NoFM WITH SOFT WEIGHT-SHARING

An underlying assumption of the NoFM method is that the distribution of weights in the network will be conducive to forming a small number of clusters for each hidden and output unit. For knowledge-based neural networks, this is a reasonable assumption since the weights are clustered before training. For example, using the KBANN algorithm [17] to map a set of symbolic rules into a knowledge-based network, the weights that are specified by the domain theory have values of approximately 4 and -4, whereas the rest of the weights have values near 0. Experimental evidence indicates that the weights tend to be fairly well clustered after training as well [15].

The applicability of the NoFM method might seem to be limited to knowledge-based networks, since in conventional neural networks there is usually not a bias that leads weight values to be clustered after training. In fact, Towell [15] reported that NoFM did not extract small sets of accurate rules from conventional networks. However, the approach that we explore in this paper does not rely on the network weights being initially clustered, but instead encourages clustering *during* network training. We use a method developed by Nowlan and Hinton [7], termed *soft weight-sharing*, that encourages weights to form clusters during the training process. Although their method was motivated by the desire for better generalization, we explore it here as a means for facilitating rule extraction.

Soft weight-sharing uses a cost function that penalizes network complexity. The complexity term in soft weight-sharing models the distribution of weights in the network as a mixture of multiple Gaussians. A set of weights is considered to be simple if the weights have a high likelihood under the mixture model. Specifically, the cost function in soft weight-sharing is the following:

$$C = \lambda E - \sum_{i \in wgts} \log \left[\sum_{j \in Gauss} \pi_j \ p_j(w_i) \right]$$

where E is the data-misfit term, λ is a parameter used to balance the tradeoff between data misfit and complexity, w_i is a weight in the network, $p_j(w_i)$ is the density value of w_i under the jth Gaussian, and π_j is the mixing proportion of the jth Gaussian. A mixing proportion is a weight that determines the influence of a particular Gaussian. The mixing proportions are constrained to sum to 1.

The effect of each Gaussian during learning is to pull each weight toward the mean of the Gaussian with a force proportional to the density of the Gaussian at the value of the weight. The parameter settings of each Gaussian – the mean μ_j, standard deviation σ_j, and mixing proportion π_j – are learned simultaneously with the weights during training.

Our approach to rule extraction involves training networks using a variant of soft weight-sharing and then applying the NOFM algorithm to the trained networks. Although the NOFM method was designed for knowledge-based neural networks, we hypothesized that it could be successfully applied to conventional networks, provided that the weights of the networks were grouped into clusters during training.

Whereas the NOFM algorithm works best when the weights impinging on *each unit* form clusters, standard soft weight-sharing tends to *globally* cluster network weights. Our implementation of soft weight-sharing hence assigns a local set of Gaussians to each unit. The complexity cost of a given weight is calculated with respect to only the Gaussians associated with the unit to which the weight connects.

EXPERIMENTAL RESULTS

Our experiments address the hypothesis that soft weight-sharing is able to cluster the network weights during training such that NOFM is able to extract a small set of accurate rules. In order to evaluate the effectiveness of our approach, we use a difficult real-world domain to compare the accuracy and succinctness of our extracted rules against rules induced by Quinlan's C4.5 system [11].

The Promoter Data Set

The domain that we use in our experiments is that of recognizing *promoters* in DNA [17]. Promoters are short nucleotide sequences that occur before genes and serve as binding sites for the protein *RNA polymerase* during gene transcription. Identifying promoters is an important step in locating genes in DNA sequences.

The *promoter* data set comprises 468 examples,[1] half of which are positive examples (i.e., promoters). Each example has 57 features which represent a fixed-length "window" onto the DNA sequence of interest. A single strand of DNA is a linear chain composed from the four nucleotides represented by the letters {A, G, C, T}. Thus all of the features for this problem are nominal features that can take on the values *A*, *G*, *C*, *T*, or *unknown*. Each example is a member of one of two classes: *promoter* or *non-promoter*. The positive examples for this data set are aligned such that the gene following each promoter begins in the seventh position from the right end of the window. Thus the leftmost 50 window positions are labelled -50 to -1, and the rightmost seven are labelled 1 to 7.

---

[1]Note that this data set is larger and more biologically complicated than the one that was used by Towell et al. [17]. The latter data set is available by anonymous ftp from the UC-Irvine Repository of Machine Learning Databases and Domain Theories (ftp.ics.uci.edu).

Table 1: Performance on the *Promoter* Data.

approach		% test set error	# rules	# antecedents
C4.5	decision trees	16.9		
	extracted rules	13.5	23.2 ± 3.9	47.3 ± 9.4
ANNs	networks	7.9		
	extracted rules	11.1	8.2 ± 2.3	119.6 ± 59.1

Rule Extraction

We evaluate our approach to rule extraction by comparing the accuracy and comprehensibility of (1) rules extracted from neural networks, and (2) rules learned using C4.5. The comprehensibility of a set of rules is difficult to measure; we measure the syntactic complexity of the rule sets and use this as a proxy. Specifically, we consider the number of rules and antecedents as measures of syntactic complexity.

We use a ten-fold cross-validation methodology to assess the ability of our approach to extract accurate, comprehensible rules from trained networks. Our reported results represent averaged values for the ten validation sets.

The neural networks have fully-connected hidden units in a single layer. The number of hidden units used in each network is determined by cross-validation *within* the training set. That is, using just the examples allocated to each training set, we perform 10-fold cross-validation runs using networks with 20, 15, 10, 5 and no hidden units. The run that results in the best generalization performance determines the network architecture that is actually used for the given training set. A similar cross-validation procedure is used to determine the λ parameter for soft weight-sharing. We use a conjugate-gradient learning algorithm to train the weights and the Gaussian parameters of the networks. Each hidden and output unit has five local Gaussians which act on the weights feeding into the unit.

The C4.5 system is used to induce decision trees and to extract rules from them. Cross-validation within each training set is used to determine the confidence levels for both tree and rule pruning. The confidence level selected for tree pruning does not affect the rule-extraction results since the C4.5 rule-extraction program operates on unpruned trees and performs its own pruning independently. For each training set, we test confidence levels ranging from 5% to 95% and separately select tree-pruning and rule-pruning levels.

Table 1 shows the test set error rates on the *promoter* data set for the decision trees, rules extracted from the trees, neural networks, and rules extracted from the networks. As can be seen in the table, neural networks perform significantly better on this task than decision trees and the rules extracted from them. Additionally, the performance of the symbolic rules extracted from the neural networks is fairly close to the performance of the networks themselves, and better than the rules extracted from the decision trees. The difference in error rates between the rules extracted from networks and the C4.5 rules is significant at the 0.05 level using a paired, 1-tailed t-test.

Table 1 also shows the average number of rules and antecedents for the extracted rule sets, as well as the standard deviations for these values. The values for antecedents indicate the *total* number in a rule set. The rules extracted by the C4.5 algorithm are purely-conjunctive rules that tend to have few antecedents. Thus, the sets extracted from the decision trees contain more rules but fewer antecedents than those extracted from networks. The additional complexity of the rules extracted from networks, however, results in a significant gain in accuracy. Moreover, the rules extracted from networks have only 14.6 antecedents per rule on average, and these antecedents often refer to localized, contiguous parts of the DNA sequence. We feel, therefore, that their complexity is within the bounds of what biologists can readily understand. The network-extracted rule sets exhibit considerable variance in their size. Most of this variance is due to the different sizes of the networks from which the rules were extracted.

Table 2 shows an especially concise rule set extracted from one of the *promoter* networks. The rule set shown exhibits several interesting characteristics. First, the rules abstract away a significant amount of

Table 2: Rules Extracted from a *Promoter* Network. The notation A@-36 indicates the nucleotide A in the position 36 nucleotides before the start of a putative gene. The notation not(A@-36), indicates a nucleotide other than A in the same position.

```
promoter :- 2 of { hidden-3, hidden-4, hidden-5 }.

hidden-3 :- 7 of { not(A@-36), not(G@-35), not(A@-34), not(G@-33), C@-32,
                   not(C@-31), not(G@-21), not(C@-15), T@-12, T@-8 }.

hidden-4 :- 10 of { not(G@-44), not(C@-36), T@-35, not(G@-33), not(G@-32),
                    not(C@-31), not(G@-13), not(C@-12), A@-11, not(G@-10),
                    not(G@-9), not(G@-8), T@-7, not(G@2) }.

hidden-5 :- 4 of { T@-36, not(A@-35), not(G@-13), A@-10, not(G@-3) }.
```

the complexity of the network from which they are extracted. There are only five rules and a total of 32 antecedents. Two of the hidden units and more than 1100 of the weights that were present in the neural network are not represented in the rules. A second observation is that the rules focus on what are known by biologists to be the most significant regions of the DNA sequence. In particular, a domain theory developed by M. Noordewier [17] identifies the -14 to -7 and the -37 to -31 regions as containing the most important features of a promoter. These are termed the *contact* regions. The rules extracted from all of the hidden units specify antecedents primarily in these areas.

Although we have used the number of rules and antecedents as a basis for comparing the comprehensibility of extracted rule sets, it is important to note that this comparison does not take into account the semantic differences between the two types of rules. Whereas we have employed the *N*-of-*M* construct in the network-extracted rules, C4.5 rules are purely conjunctive. A second difference is that the rules extracted from networks identify intermediate concepts between the input features and the output classes; these are the rules whose consequents correspond to hidden units. Although it is difficult to attach meaningful labels to the concepts represented by hidden units, we believe that in some cases, these intermediate terms might lead to rule sets that are more comprehensible than those which simply include the input and output terms. A third difference is that the network-extracted rules define only the positive (promoter) class, and employ the closed-world assumption to classify examples as negative.

Rule Pruning

Although the results presented in the previous section indicate that our approach to rule extraction can produce rules that generalize better than rules learned using a purely symbolic method, our extracted rules are not as concise as the rules learned by C4.5. The C4.5 system, however, incorporates algorithms that prune rules and antecedents during its extraction process. In this section we describe and evaluate a method that we have recently developed for simplifying our network-extracted rules. In addition to producing simplified rules, this method aims to increase the fidelity of the rules to the network.

Our approach to rule pruning employs a greedy algorithm that deletes antecedents from NofM rules. This algorithm involves two primary steps: a blame-assignment process and a hill-climbing search. The blame-assignment process seeks to identify rules that are responsible for misclassifying members of the training set. The search process incrementally deletes antecedents and rules when doing so improves both correctness on the training set and fidelity to the network.

The goal of the blame-assignment process is to identify individual rules that might be responsible for misclassifications on the training set. This algorithm associates two counters with each rule: a *specialize* counter and a *generalize* counter. The *specialize* counter for a rule is incremented whenever it is likely that the rule incorrectly fired. Similarly, the *generalize* counter is incremented whenever a rule did not fire, but possibly should have. The blame-assignment process involves propagating blame backward through rule

Table 3: The Effect of Rule Pruning

rule set	% test set error	# rules	# antecedents
before pruning	11.1	8.2	119.6
after pruning	10.2	8.1	97.2

firings. Blame propagation begins whenever the rule set misclassifies a training example that the network itself correctly classified. In the case of a false-positive prediction, a rule that generates the false-positive by incorrectly firing has its *specialize* counter updated. In the case of a false-negative prediction, the *generalize* counters are updated for all of the rules that have the target class as their consequent. After a rule is assigned blame, it then propagates blame backward to those rules whose consequents match its antecedents.

The purpose of the blame-assignment process is merely to establish an ordering on the rules that can be employed by the hill-climbing search procedure. The search process itself involves two phases: specialization and generalization. In the generalization phase, rules with non-zero *generalize* counters are considered in descending order. Thus, the rule that took the most blame for being too specialized is considered first. The generalization operator involves deleting an antecedent from an NoFM rule and decrementing the N counter. For example, the following rule can be generalized as shown:

$$\text{a :- 2 of } \{x, y, z\}. \quad \Longrightarrow \quad \text{a :- 1 of } \{y, z\}.$$

The generalization operator is applied when doing so results in increased correctness on the training set and increased fidelity to the network. Note that the entire training set does not need to be evaluated in order to make this determination; only those examples on which the rule previously did not fire need to be considered.

The specialization step considers, in descending order, rules that have non-zero *specialize* counters. The specialization operator deletes an antecedent from an NoFM rule without changing the N counter. The specialization step can also delete an entire rule; this effectively happens when the number of antecedents is less than the N value for a NoFM rule.

Table 3 shows the results of running this pruning algorithm on rules that were extracted using the NoFM approach. The first row in the table shows the results that were presented in the previous section. The second line shows the generalization performance and the complexity measures for the same rule sets *after pruning*. These results show that our rule pruning method significantly reduces the complexity of extracted rules, and additionally, improves their generalization ability. All differences in the table are significant at the 0.05 level using a paired, 1-tailed, t-test.

CONCLUSIONS

Extracting accurate, comprehensible rules from neural networks is an important problem in machine learning. We have demonstrated that small sets of accurate, reasonably concise symbolic rules can be extracted from ordinary artificial neural networks. Our approach to this problem involves exploiting the effectiveness of the NoFM algorithm by encouraging weight clustering during training. For a difficult problem domain, recognizing promoters in DNA, our approach was able to induce rules that resulted in better generalization than rules learned using a popular symbolic learning algorithm. Additionally, we have presented a method for simplifying network-extracted rules. Our experiments indicate that this method not only improves the concision of extracted rules, but also their accuracy. These promising results indicate that the problem of understanding representations learned by artificial neural networks may be tractable.

Acknowledgements

This work was supported by DOE Grant DE-FG02-91ER61129 and NSF Grant IRI-9002413. Thanks to Dave Touretzky and Rich Maclin for providing insightful comments on an earlier draft of this paper.

References

[1] L. Atlas, R. Cole, J. Connor, M. El-Sharkawi, R. J. Marks II, Y. Muthusamy, and E. Barnard, "Performance comparisons between backpropagation networks and classification trees on three real-world applications," in *Advances in Neural Information Processing Systems* (D. Touretzky, ed.), vol. 2, pp. 622–629, San Mateo, CA: Morgan Kaufmann, 1989.

[2] M. W. Craven and J. W. Shavlik, "Learning symbolic rules using artificial neural networks," in *Proc. of the 10th International Machine Learning Conference*, (Amherst, MA), Morgan Kaufmann, 1993.

[3] D. H. Fisher and K. B. McKusick, "An empirical comparison of ID3 and back-propagation," in *Proc. of the 11th International Joint Conference on Artificial Intelligence*, (Detroit, MI), pp. 788–793, August 1989.

[4] L. M. Fu, "Rule learning by searching on adapted nets," in *Proc. of the 9th National Conference on Artificial Intelligence*, (Anaheim, CA), pp. 590–595, 1991.

[5] C. McMillan, M. Mozer, and P. Smolensky, "The connectionist scientist game: Rule extraction and refinement in a neural network," in *Proc. of the 13th Conference of the Cognitive Science Society*, (Chicago, IL), Erlbaum, 1991.

[6] R. Mooney, J. Shavlik, G. Towell, and A. Gove, "An experimental comparison of symbolic and connectionist learning algorithms," in *Proc. of the 11th International Joint Conference on Artificial Intelligence*, (Detroit, MI), pp. 775–780, 1989. (A longer version appears in *Machine Learning*, vol. 6, 1991).

[7] S. J. Nowlan and G. E. Hinton, "Simplifying neural networks by soft weight-sharing," *Neural Computation*, vol. 4, pp. 473–493, 1992.

[8] D. Ourston and R. J. Mooney, "Changing the rules: A comprehensive approach to theory refinement," in *Proc. of the 8th National Conference on Artificial Intelligence*, (Boston, MA), pp. 815–820, Aug 1990.

[9] M. Pazzani and D. Kibler, "The utility of knowledge in inductive learning," *Machine Learning*, vol. 9, pp. 57–94, 1992.

[10] D. A. Pomerleau, "Efficient training of artificial neural networks for autonomous navigation," *Neural Computation*, vol. 3, pp. 88–97, 1991.

[11] J. R. Quinlan, *C4.5: Programs for Machine Learning.* San Mateo, CA: Morgan Kaufmann, 1993.

[12] K. Saito and R. Nakano, "Medical diagnostic expert system based on PDP model," in *Proc. of the IEEE International Conference on Neural Networks*, (San Diego, CA), pp. 255–262, IEEE, 1988.

[13] T. Sejnowski and C. Rosenberg, "Parallel networks that learn to pronounce English text," *Complex Systems*, vol. 1, pp. 145–168, 1987.

[14] S. B. Thrun, "Extracting provably correct rules from artificial neural networks," tech. rep., Department of Computer Science, University of Bonn, 1993.

[15] G. G. Towell, *Symbolic Knowledge and Neural Networks: Insertion, Refinement and Extraction.* PhD thesis, University of Wisconsin – Madison, 1991.

[16] G. G. Towell and J. W. Shavlik, "The extraction of refined rules from knowledge-based neural networks," *Machine Learning*, vol. 13, no. 1, pp. 71–101, 1993.

[17] G. G. Towell, J. W. Shavlik, and M. O. Noordewier, "Refinement of approximately correct domain theories by knowledge-based neural networks," in *Proc. of the 8th National Conference on Artificial Intelligence*, (Boston, MA), pp. 861–866, MIT Press, 1990.

RULE LEARNING AND EXTRACTION
WITH SELF-ORGANIZING NEURAL NETWORKS

Ah-Hwee Tan
Department of Cognitive and Neural Systems
Boston University, Boston, MA 02215, USA
atan@park.bu.edu

This paper describes an algorithm for extracting knowledge, in the form of fuzzy rules, from a self-organizing supervised learning neural network called fuzzy ARTMAP. Rule extraction proceeds in two stages: pruning removes those recognition nodes whose confidence index falls below a selected threshold; and quantization of continuous learned weights allows the final system state to be translated into a usable set of rules. Using a molecular biology problem of recognizing DNA subsequences, comparisons are drawn between fuzzy matching rules of ARTMAP networks and Craven and Shavlik's NofM rules extracted from backpropagation networks. Preliminary results indicate that while the predictive performance of both systems is comparable, there are tradeoffs to be made between learning speed and system size.

Fuzzy ARTMAP developed by Carpenter, Grossberg, Markuzon, Reynolds and Rosen [1, 3] is a neural network architecture that performs incremental supervised learning of recognition categories (pattern classes) and multidimensional maps of both binary and analog patterns. When performing classification tasks, fuzzy ARTMAP formulates recognition categories of input patterns, and associates each category with its respective prediction. The knowledge that ARTMAP discovers during learning, is compatible with if-then rules which link sets of antecedents to their consequences. At any point during the incremental learning process, the system architecture can be translated into a compact set of rules analyzable by human experts. This paper describes such a procedure for extracting knowledge from fuzzy ARTMAP systems.

Rules can be derived more readily from an ARTMAP network than from a backpropagation network, in which the roles of hidden units are usually not explicit. In a fuzzy ARTMAP network, each recognition node in the F_2^a field (Figure 1) roughly corresponds to a rule. Each node has an associated weight vector that can be directly translated into a verbal description of the corresponding rule. However, large databases typically cause ARTMAP to generate too many rules to be of practical use. The goal of the rule extraction task is thus to select a small set of highly predictive recognition nodes and to describe them in a comprehensible form. To evaluate a recognition node, a *confidence factor* that measures both *usage* and *accuracy* is computed. Removal of low confidence recognition categories created by atypical examples produces smaller networks. In fact, this network pruning procedure can even improve test set performance by removing misleading special cases. In order to describe the knowledge in simplified rule form, real-valued weights are quantized into a small set of values.

The rule extraction methods have been previously evaluated using a Pima Indians Diabetes (PID) data set in which the predicting index is whether or not a patient shows signs of diabetes [4]. Simulation results showed that pruning produced rule sets that were consistently 1/3 the size of the original networks, and also produced superior test set performance. Quantization produced more comprehensible rules at only a slight cost in terms of performance. This paper reports a preliminary study of applying fuzzy ARTMAP and its rule extraction algorithm to a molecular biology problem. The task is to recognize a specific type of DNA subsequence – *promoters*. This data set has been used by Craven and Shavlik [5, 6] in evaluating their NofM algorithm for extracting rules from backpropagation networks. The predictive performance and system complexity of ARTMAP rules are compared to Craven and Shavlik's results. While the predictive performance of both systems is comparable, tradeoffs are observed between learning speed and system size.

Fuzzy ARTMAP for Rule Learning

Fuzzy ARTMAP consists of two fuzzy ART modules [2] connected by a map field (Figure 1). The ART_a and ART_b modules create recognition categories of input patterns in their respective modules. The map field forms predictive associations between ART_a and ART_b categories. Internal control mechanisms realize the match tracking rule whereby the vigilance parameter of ART_a increases in response to a predictive mismatch at ART_b. This on-line error-correction procedure allows the system to function in a fast-learning mode. For completeness, a brief functional outline of fuzzy ARTMAP dynamics is provided below. Please refer to [3] for a detailed description of the system.

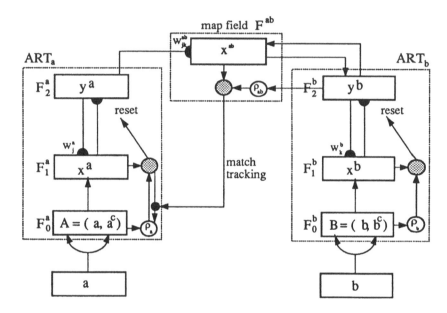

Figure 1: Fuzzy ARTMAP architecture: A and B are input vectors in complement coding form. x^a and x^b are activity vectors for matching and learning. y^a and y^b represent compressed recognition codes, associated by the inter-ART map field F^{ab}.

Complement Coding: Complement coding is a normalization rule which represents both on-response and off-response of an input feature. It solves the category proliferation problem described by Moore [7] by ensuring all patterns are of the same norm. Using complement coding, an input pattern **a** is concatenated with its complement vector: $\mathbf{A} = (\mathbf{a}, \mathbf{a}^c)$.

Bottom-up Activation: Given an input pattern, **A**, the activity of each ART_a F_2^a node is computed based on a fuzzy subset match function, as follows:

$$y_j^a = \frac{|\mathbf{A} \wedge \mathbf{W}_j^a|}{\alpha + |\mathbf{W}_j^a|} \tag{1}$$

where α is a choice parameter, the fuzzy AND operator $\wedge$ is defined by $(\mathbf{p} \wedge \mathbf{q})_i \equiv min(p_i, q_i)$ and the norm $|.|$ of a vector **p** is defined by $|\mathbf{p}| \equiv \sum_i |p_i|$. The system is said to make a *category choice* when at most one

F_2 node can become active at a given time:

$$y_j^a = \begin{cases} 1 & \text{if } y_j^a = max\{y_j^a : \text{for all nodes } j \text{ in the } F_2^a \text{ field}\} \\ 0 & \text{otherwise} \end{cases} \quad (2)$$

Resonance or reset: Resonance occurs if the match between the input pattern and the chosen category node J meets the vigilance criterion:

$$\frac{|\mathbf{A} \wedge \mathbf{W}_J^a|}{|\mathbf{A}|} \geq \rho_a. \quad (3)$$

Otherwise, ART_a mismatch resets the selected F_2^a node J and chooses a winning recognition node again.

Template learning: Once resonance occurs, the weight template $\mathbf{W}_J^a$ of node J is updated as follows:

$$\mathbf{W}_J^a(t+1) = \beta(\mathbf{A} \wedge \mathbf{W}_J^a(t)) + (1-\beta)\mathbf{W}_J^a(t), \quad (4)$$

where β is the learning rate. Using the fast learning and slow recoding option, we set $\beta = 1$ when J is an uncommitted node and take $\beta < 1$ after the category is committed.

Prediction: If the selected F_2^a node has an associated prediction, the output vector $\mathbf{x}^{ab}$ is predicted in the map field: $\mathbf{x}^{ab} = \mathbf{W}_J^{ab}$. In general, instead of selecting just one winner in the ART_a module, a set of highly activated recognition categories can be combined to yield a probabilistic prediction:

$$\mathbf{x}^{ab} = \sum_{j \in C} \mathbf{W}_j^{ab} * y_j^a, \quad (5)$$

where C is the set of F_2^a recognition categories for combined prediction. Multiple category prediction provides a more robust predictive performance in problem domains with sparse training sets, such as the promoter recognition problem to be discussed later.

Map field Learning: If the selected F_2^a node J is not associated with any prediction, it is associated to the output category K of the output pattern $\mathbf{B}$ in ART_b as follows: $W_{JK}^{ab} = 1$.

Match Tracking: At the beginning of each input presentation, the ART_a vigilance ρ_a is set to a baseline vigilance $\bar{\rho}_a$. If the output prediction matches the recognition category of the output pattern $\mathbf{B}$, resonance in the map field is achieved. Otherwise, match tracking occurs which raises the system ART_a vigilance ρ_a by just the amount needed to cause a mismatch and reset in the ART_a module. The system then goes through another round of memory search to look for the next best recognition node with the higher vigilance until resonance is achieved. During learning, the weights of the eventually selected node are changed so that the node is more likely to win the competition with the previously selected but rejected nodes, when the same input is presented. The on-line tuning of the vigilance parameter allows the system to function in a fast-learning mode, and to learn both fine and coarse rules.

EXTRACTING RULES FROM FUZZY ARTMAP

In an ARTMAP network, each node in the F_2^a field learns to form a recognition category of ART_a input patterns. Through the inter-ART map field, each such node is associated to an ART_b category in the F_2^b field, which in turn encodes a prediction. Learned weight vectors, one for each F_2^a node, thereby constitute a set of rules that link antecedents to consequences (Figure 2).

Pruning

To reduce the complexity of fuzzy ARTMAP, a pruning procedure aims to select a small set of good rules from a trained network. The algorithm evaluates each F_2^a recognition node in terms of its coding statistics in the training set and its predictive performance on a test set, resulting in a confidence factor. With confidence factors, good rules can be identified as cognitive codes that are frequently used and reinforced. This allows

194

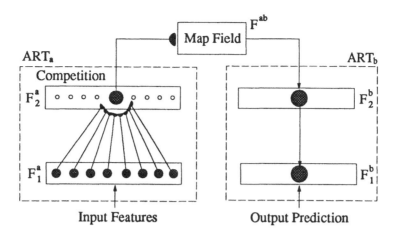

Figure 2: Schematic diagram of a rule in fuzzy ARTMAP. Each F_2^a node maps a prototype feature vector to a prediction.

pruning of ARTMAP by removing less useful rules. In fact, the generalization of the system can be improved by removing rules which were created to handle misleading special cases.

The pruning algorithm evaluates a F_2^a recognition category j in terms of a confidence factor CF_j:

$$CF_j = \gamma U_j + (1 - \gamma)A_j, \qquad (6)$$

where U_j is the usage of node j, A_j is its accuracy and γ is a real number between 0 and 1.
For an ART_a category j that predicts outcome k, its usage U_j equals the fraction of training set patterns with outcome k coded by node j (F_j), divided by the maximum fraction of training patterns coded by any node J (F_J):

$$U_j = F_j/max\{F_J\}. \qquad (7)$$

For an ART_a category j that predicts outcome k, its accuracy A_j equals the percent of test set patterns predicted correctly by node j (P_j), divided by the maximum percent of test patterns predicted correctly by any node J (P_J) predicting outcome k:

$$A_j = P_j/max\{P_J : \text{node } J \text{ predicts outcome } k\}. \qquad (8)$$

Those F_2^a nodes with confidence factors below a given threshold τ are removed from the network. By doing so, a more compact set of important rules can be obtained, which can then be analyzed by human experts.

Quantizing Weight Values

When learning analog patterns, ARTMAP often creates weight vectors composed of real numbers. In order to describe the rules in words rather than real numbers, the feature values represented by weights $\mathbf{W}_j^a$ are quantized. A *quantization level* Q is defined as the number of feature values used in the extracted fuzzy rules. For example, with $Q = 3$, feature values are described as Low, Medium, or High in the fuzzy rules. Two quantization algorithms are studied as follows:
Quantization by Truncation - Divide the range of [0,1] into Q intervals. Assign a quantization point to the lower bound of each interval; i.e., for $q = 1 \ldots Q$, let $V_q = (q - 1)/Q$. When a weight w falls in interval q, reduce the value of w to V_q.
Quantization by Round-off - Distribute Q quantization points evenly in the range of [0,1], with one at each end point; i.e., for $q = 1 \ldots Q$, let $V_q = (q - 1)/(Q - 1)$. Round off a weight w to the nearest V_q value.

Experiments

The Promoter Data Set

The test bed for evaluating the ARTMAP rule extraction algorithm, and for comparison to the NofM algorithm, is that of recognizing *promoters* in DNA sequences [5, 6, 8]. Promoters are short nucleotide sequences that occur before genes and serve as binding sites for the enzyme *RNA polymerase* during gene transcription. The promoter data set consists of 468 patterns, half of which are positive instances (promoters). Each input pattern represents a 57-position window, with the leftmost 50 window positions labeled -50 to -1 and the rightmost seven labeled 1 to 7. Each position is a nominal feature which takes one of the four nucleotide values {A, G, T, C}. Missing features values, which are indicated as "?" in the data set, comprise 1% of the total feature population.

Simulation Results

In our experiments, the nominal features {A,G,T,C} of each position were represented locally. Each 57-position pattern was expanded into a 228 (57*4) nucleotide-position string. For features with missing values, zeroes were assigned to all four of the corresponding nucleotide positions. As complement information already existed in the input patterns, complement coding was not applied.

The promoter data set has very few (468) examples considering the size of its input dimension (228). For such problems with sparse data points, the multiple category prediction method proves to be more effective. During learning, ARTMAPs are trained as usual using the category choice rule in the ART_a F_a^2 field. During prediction, probabilistic prediction scores are computed by averaging over predictions of a set of highly activated recognition nodes. In ARTMAP simulations reported below, prediction scores were thresholded at 0.55 to yield the final binary predictions. A ten-fold cross-validation methodology was used to evaluate the system performance. The data set was divided into ten partitions. ARTMAPs were trained on nine partitions and tested on the partition left out, using the following set of parameter values: $\alpha = 10$, $\beta = 1$, and $\bar{\rho}_a = 0$. As shown in Table 1, the multiple category prediction method significantly reduced the error rate from 17.8% with 1 predictive category to 8.1% with 20 predictive categories.

Table 1: Average predictive error of ARTMAP over 10 runs using different number of predictive recognition categories.

# Predicting Recognition Categories	% Predictive Error
1	17.8
10	10.1
20	8.1

In the rule extraction simulations, seven partitions were used for training ARTMAPs and evaluating *usage* of each rule; two partitions were used for evaluating *accuracy* of each rule; and the remaining one for final testing of the extracted rules. The weighting factor γ was set to 0.4 and the pruning threshold τ was set to 0.6. No quantization was needed as the input patterns were in binary form. During testing, 10 predictive categories were used to compute the predictive scores which were thresholded at 0.60. Table 2 summarizes ARTMAP performance on the promoter data set, with comparison to those of backpropagation networks and the NofM rules obtained by Craven and Shavlik [5, 6]. Their best results were obtained with a rule antecedent pruning procedure after the NofM algorithm.

Note that the performance of both the neural networks and the extracted rules was roughly comparable. While the fuzzy ARTMAP networks performed slightly worse than the backpropagation networks, the ARTMAP rules were slightly more accurate than the NofM rules. The difference in performance between networks and rules was smaller for fuzzy ARTMAP than for backpropagation networks. In fact, nearly

Table 2: Comparison of ARTMAP predictive performance to Craven and Shavlik's results using backpropagation networks and the NofM algorithm.

Systems		% Predictive Error
Backpropagation	Networks	7.9
NofM rules	Before Pruning	11.1
	After Pruning	10.2
Fuzzy ARTMAP	Networks	8.1
	Rules	9.8
Voting ARTMAP	Networks	3.9
	Rules	6.1

two thirds of original ARTMAP rules (average of 117.8 rules) were dropped with only 1.7% degradation in accuracy. Also reported are the results obtained with 10 voting ARTMAPs. Under the voting strategy, an ARTMAP system is trained repeatedly using different ordering of input patterns. The output predictions of ARTMAP across runs are averaged to form a final prediction for each test case [1]. When extracting rules, the predictions of rule sets extracted across runs are averaged to form a final prediction. As shown below, voting gave ARTMAP a two fold improvement in performance. Even after pruning, the rules still performed significantly better than the original neural networks. In fact, voting has been generally found to be a useful technique for ARTMAP systems in which fast learning leads to different sets of recognition categories and hence different predictive errors across simulations.

Table 3 shows a sample set of rules extracted from a fuzzy ARTMAP system. For each rule, the antecedents, the rule statistics (including confidence factor, usage and accuracy), and the test performance are listed. Reasonably good correlation between a rule's confidence factor and its performance supports the validity of the rule extraction approach. Note that the rules for identifying positive instances (promoters) are quite simple, while the rules for identifying non-promoters are slightly more complicated. This is perhaps due to the randomness of non-promoters. Certain interesting regularities in the rules can also be observed. For example, features like T@-36 and T@-35 consistently appear across positive rules and none of them appears in negative rules. This suggests that they are good indicators for promoters.

ARTMAP rules are different from NofM rules in several ways. First, ARTMAP creates rules for both promoters and nonpromoters, while NofM rules only focus on positive instances (promoters) and use the closed world assumption to identify non-promoters. Second, ARTMAP rules only involve input and output variables whereas NofM rules use internally created intermediate variables (corresponding to hidden units). Third, the negative weights in backpropagation networks allow NofM rules to include negative terms; in ARTMAP rules, the effect of negative terms is obtained through complement coding of input patterns.

Neither system requires an exact match to fire a rule. The NofM rules are fired based on the satisfaction of individual condition (NofM) stated within each rule, whereas ARTMAP rule firing is based on competition among all rules, on top of the global vigilance criterion. Considering each rule independently, an ARTMAP rule is roughly equivalent to a $(M \times \rho_a)$-of-M rule. However, when functioning as a whole, each ARTMAP rule has a different threshold which depends on the input pattern and the other rules. Another feature of ARTMAP rules is that each of them can be assigned a confidence factor which reflects its usefulness and reliability. This information can be very useful to human experts when assigning priorities to rules.

Comparing the system complexity, the ARTMAP rule sets are syntactically more complex than the NofM rule sets in terms of the number of rules and antecedents (Table 4). One possible explanation for this is that ARTMAP learns both the positive and negative promoter patterns, whereas the NofM rules

---
[1]This technique was used by Towell, Shavlik and Noordewier in their promoter simulations [8] to obtain a slight improvement in performance. The rule extraction simulations of Craven and Shavlik [5, 6] however did not utilize this technique.

Table 3: A sample set of 24 ARTMAP rules. They consists of a total of 140 antecedents. The antecedent notation T@-36 indicates the nucleotide T in the position 36 nucleotides before the start of a putative gene.

Promo-	Feature Template/	Rule Statistics			Testing	
ters	Conditions	CF	Usage	Acc	Fired	Acc
+	T@-36 T@-35 T@-13 A@-12 T@-8	0.99	1.00	0.98	4	1.00
+	A@-45 T@-36 T@-35 T@-14 A@-11 A@5	0.93	0.82	1.00	2	1.00
+	T@-38 T@-13 T@-11 A@-10 T@-8	0.82	0.55	1.00	3	1.00
+	T@-36 T@-35 A@-20 T@-14 T@-9	0.81	0.55	0.98	3	1.00
+	T@-35 G@-34 T@-19 A@-11 T@-7	0.79	0.55	0.95	3	0.67
+	G@-34 A@-31 A@-30 G@-15 A@-9 A@6	0.79	0.55	0.95	2	1.00
+	A@-33 C@-29 T@-19 A@-12 T@-8 T@-1	0.78	0.64	0.88	0	-
+	T@-36 T@-35 C@-32 T@-29 T@-7 A@-6	0.75	0.45	0.95	3	1.00
+	A@-38 G@-34 A@-31 T@-13 A@-12	0.75	0.45	0.95	5	0.80
+	T@-36 T@-35 G@-34 A@-28 G@-24 A@-10	0.74	0.55	0.88	1	1.00
+	T@-35 T@-30 T@-28 A@-12 T@-8	0.71	0.45	0.88	2	1.00
+	T@-35 A@-31 T@-28 G@-16 A@-13	0.67	0.36	0.88	0	-
-	G@-47 C@-35 C@-22 A@-9 G@-6 C@-4 G@-2	0.73	0.36	0.97	4	1.00
-	C@-49 A@-39 G@-37 C@-26 C@-23 G@-4 G@-3	0.73	0.36	0.97	1	1.00
-	T@-49 C@-37 G@-35 C@-34 G@-24	0.73	0.36	0.97	0	-
-	C@-47 C@-36 T@-29 G@-26 A@-24 A@-21 G@-4 C@6	0.71	0.27	1.00	2	1.00
-	G@-50 A@-36 G@-34 G@-31 C@-14 A@-12 A@-6 C@-3	0.69	0.27	0.97	1	0.00
-	G@-47 C@-24 G@-18 G@-3	0.69	0.27	0.97	0	-
-	G@-23 C@-19 G@-17 G@1 C@2	0.69	0.27	0.97	2	0.50
-	C@-49 G@-48 G@-12 T@-8 G@-3 T@7	0.68	0.36	0.89	1	1.00
-	G@-37 C@-8 G@-5 G@-1 T@3	0.68	0.36	0.89	1	1.00
-	A@-46 T@-28 G@-24 C@-19 G@-8 T@-6	0.68	0.36	0.89	2	1.00
-	G@-45 G@-25 A@-12 A@-11 G@-7 C@-6	0.67	0.18	1.00	3	1.00
-	C@-48 G@-43 A@-36 G@-35 G@-33 C@-29 A@-5 G@1	0.64	0.27	0.89	2	1.00

employ the closed world assumption to classify negative instances; this eliminates the need for the more complex negative rules. The use of intermediate variables (hidden units) and the NofM construct may have also helped in code compression. While losing ground in term of system size, ARTMAP has virtues that are lacking in backpropagation networks. With fast learning, ARTMAP usually achieves 100% accuracy on the entire training set within 5-10 iterations. A complete ten-fold cross-validation simulation on the promoter problem, including learning, rule extraction and testing, typically finishes within 20 minutes. The fast learning capability makes voting strategy remain feasible with large problem size. Moreover, ARTMAP learns incrementally. At any point during learning, meaningful rules can be extracted and new rules can be added without having to re-train the whole system. These learning properties enable ARTMAP to function in an on-line real-time environment and scale up readily to larger problems.

Table 4: Comparison of system size. # rules is the average number of rules, and # antecedent is the total number of antecedents in a rule set.

Systems		# Rules	# Antecedents
NofM rule set	Before Pruning	8.2	119.6
	After Pruning	8.1	97.2
ARTMAP rule set		39.4	225.4

CONCLUDING REMARKS

By using the promoter recognition task as a common ground, we are able to compare the rule extraction algorithms for two different classes of supervised learning neural networks. While the predictive accuracy of the rules extracted from both systems is roughly comparable, gradient descent learning and ARTMAP learning lead to different knowledge structures, and hence different extracted rules. Gradient descent learning performs iterative optimization of an error function and thus results in better code compression. Fast learning as in ARTMAP has the advantage of real-time, on-line learning and prediction, but could result in a larger network size.

The current paper however only reports a preliminary study of applying ARTMAP to the promoter recognition problem. With more careful tuning, improvement in ARTMAP performance can be obtained. Moreover, the current rule extraction algorithm only performs pruning at the rule level. Algorithms similar to Craven and Shavlik's rule pruning procedure can be developed for pruning antecedents from rules. On the other hand, since voting ARTMAP provides significantly better predictive accuracy, it may be worthwhile to carry good rules identified in a simulation over to the next simulation. By accumulating good rules across simulations, a single compact rule set with voting performance might be obtained.

Acknowledgements

The author is on leave from the Institute of Systems Science, National University of Singapore. The ARTMAP rule extraction algorithm was jointly developed with Gail Carpenter. The author wishes to thank Mark Craven for sharing the promoter data set and his simulation details. The author is very grateful to Dave Touretzky for suggesting the writing of this paper, and for providing many useful comments and suggestions.

References

[1] G.A. Carpenter, S. Grossberg, and J.H. Reynolds, "ARTMAP: Supervised real-time learning and classification of nonstationary data by a self-organizing neural network," *Neural Networks*, vol. 4, p. 565–588, 1991.

[2] G.A. Carpenter, S. Grossberg, and D.B. Rosen, "Fuzzy ART: Fast stable learning and categorization of analog patterns by an adaptive resonance system," *Neural Networks*, vol. 4, p. 759–771, 1991.

[3] G.A. Carpenter, S. Grossberg, N. Markuzon, J.H. Reynolds, and D.B. Rosen, "Fuzzy ARTMAP: A neural network architecture for incremental supervised learning of analog multidimensional maps," *IEEE Transactions in Neural Networks*, vol. 3, p. 698–713, 1992.

[4] G.A. Carpenter, and A.H. Tan, "Fuzzy ARTMAP, Rule Extraction and Medical Databases," in *Proceedings, World Congress on Neural Networks, Portland, OR*, vol. I, p. 501–506, 1993.

[5] M.W. Craven, and J.W. Shavlik, "Learning symbolic rules using artificial neural networks," in *Proceedings, Tenth International Machine Learning Conference*, Amherst, MA, Morgan Kaufmann, 1993.

[6] M.W. Craven, and J.W. Shavlik, "Understanding Neural Networks via Rule Extraction and Pruning," this volume.

[7] B. Moore, "ART 1 and Pattern Clustering," in *Proceedings, 1988 Connectionist Models Summer School*, p. 174–185, 1989.

[8] G.G. Towell, J.W. Shavlik, and M.O. Noordewier, "Refinement of approximately correct domain theories by knowledge-based neural networks," in *Proceedings, Eighth Conference on Artificial Intelligence*, Boston, MA, p. 861–866, MIT Press, 1990.

RECURRENT NETWORKS AND TEMPORAL PATTERN PROCESSING

RECURRENT NETWORKS:
STATE MACHINES OR ITERATED FUNCTION SYSTEMS?

John F. Kolen

Laboratory for AI Research
Department of Computer and Information Science
The Ohio State University
Columbus, OH 43210
kolen-j@cis.ohio-state.edu

Introduction

Feedforward neural networks process information by performing fixed transformations from one representation space to another. Recurrent networks, on the other hand, process information quite differently. To understand recurrent networks one must confront the notion of state as recurrent networks perform iterated transformations on *state representations*. Many researchers have recognized this difference and have suggested parallels between recurrent networks and various automata[1, 2, 3]. First, I will demonstrate how the common notion of deterministic information processing does not necessarily hold for deterministic recurrent neural networks whose dynamics are sensitive to initial conditions. Second, I will link the mathematics of recurrent neural network models with that of iterated function systems [4]. This link points to model independent constraints on the recurrent network state dynamics that explain universal behaviors of recurrent networks like internal state clustering.

Recurrent Networks as State Machines

Current models of human intellectual competence demand the potential to store and act upon any one of an infinite collection of internal representations (e.g., [5, 6]). Inspired by the pioneering work of McCulloch and Pitts [7], several simulation proofs of universal computation in recurrent networks have appeared over the last few years [8, 9, 10, 11]. Each of these projects clearly supports the claim of representational adequacy for recurrent networks by showing that recursive computation can arise by *design*. These projects, however, provide little insight in the *detection* of computation occurring in a system. In other words, they don't tell us how to recognize computation when it is happening before our eyes.

The attribution of computational behavior to a system traditionally rests on the discovery of an isomorphism between states of the physical (or dynamical) system to the information processing states of the computational model [12]. Certain voltage levels of particular wires in a CPU, for instance, are isomorphic to the bits processed by the machine. A modeler must measure the current state of a process with sufficient resolution to justify the isomorphism. In models capable of recursive computation, the information processing state can demand unbounded accuracy from the modeler's measurements.

Many researchers studying the computational power of recurrent networks have followed this tradition. These researchers clustered internal state vectors and drew correspondences between these clusters and the deterministic state machine generating the training data [13]. This work was extended and can be summarized as variants of dynamic state partitioning [1]. While Giles and his collaborators use arbitrary partitions of state space to build clusters, others employ statistical clustering techniques to extract their state clusters[2]. Each of these methods shares the same problem of multiple inductions; a single recurrent network can produce many state machine interpretations.

The work of Crutchfield and Young [14] suggests that information processing states can be assigned without highly precise examination of the internal dynamics. Rather than assuming a stream of noisy numerical measurements, they construct models from periodic samplings with a single decision boundary. The binary sequence they collect requires a computational description (i.e. what kind of automaton could have generated the sequence), unlike numerical measurements that are often described mathematically. The minimal finite state automaton induced from this sequence of discrete measurements provides a realistic assessment of the intrinsic computational complexity of the physical system under observation.

An important distinction can be drawn between the methods of Crutchfield and Young with those used by the multitude of researchers studying recurrent networks. Dynamical systems theory, particularly the study of systems producing chaotic behavior, demonstrates that significant "state" information can be buried deep within the system's initial conditions. This sensitivity to initial conditions implies that often best way to "measure" a system's state is to simply observe its behavior over long periods of time and retroactively determine the state. Other methods of system identification employ this an approach. For instance, Takens' [15] method of embedding a single dimensional measurement into a higher dimensional space can provide a judgment of the underlying system's dimensionality. Crutchfield and Young extended this method to the computational understanding of systems by reconstructing the computational dynamics of the system from the sequence of boolean measurements.

The Counterexample

Two methods of assessing the computational ability of a system were described above. One relies on the identification of an isomorphism between the information processing (IP) states of a computational model and the observables of a system. The other method induces a computational model from a sequence of behaviors. The following example demonstrates how clustering of observable states can lead to the extraction of nonexistent deterministic states from recurrent networks. Recall the conditions under which two deterministic IP states are the same. Two states are the same if and only if they generate the same output responses for all possible future inputs. Clustering methods, as we shall see, cannot establish the existence of IP states when dealing with systems whose dynamics are sensitive to initial conditions. Consider a recurrent network with three state units in vector $S(t)$ and its dynamics specified by Equation 1 (with $a = 2$)[1]. The output of this network is a zero-thresholding of the first state unit. That is, when the current state is to the right of the boundary then the output is positive. The output is negative when it's to the left.

$$S(t+1) = \tanh(\begin{bmatrix} 0 & 0 & a & 0.5a \\ 0 & 0 & a & -0.5a \\ a & -a & 0 & -a \end{bmatrix} \cdot \begin{bmatrix} S(t) \\ 1 \end{bmatrix}) \tag{1}$$

Figure 1 illustrates what happens when the network iterates from a large set of initial conditions selected from within a small ball of radius 0.01. In one iteration these points migrate down to the lower corner of the state space, elongating along one dimension. After ten iterations the original ball shape is no longer visible. After twenty, the points are spread along a two dimensional sheet within state space. By fifty iterations we see the set of network states reaching their extent in state space. This behavior is ubiquitous in systems sensitive to initial conditions [16]. The assumption that the initial neighborhood defined an information processing state of a deterministic system is clearly invalidated by the vast set of unique output sequences that follow from this "state" without any assistance from inputs.

Iterated Function Systems

This section provides a brief overview of a new branch of mathematics known as iterated function theory [4]. While the limit behavior of single affine transformations (like $Ax + b$) can be determined analytically by examining eigenvalues of the transformations, iterated function theory can account for the limit behavior of systems of affine transformations.

---

1. $A \cdot \begin{bmatrix} B \\ 1 \end{bmatrix}$ indicates the inner product between A and the vector B with a 1 appended to that vector.

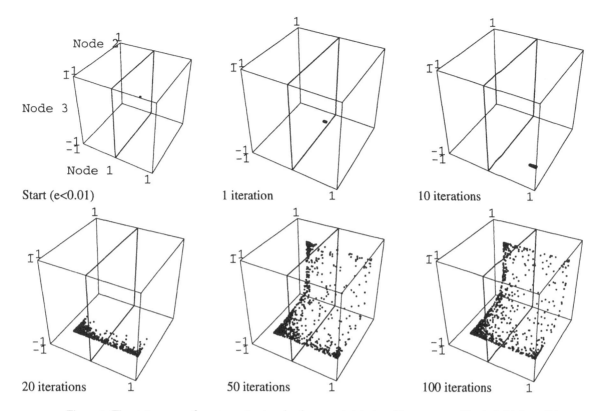

Figure 1: The state space of a recurrent network whose next state transitions are sensitive to initial conditions.

Basic Iterated Function Systems Theory

Formally, an iterated function system (IFS) is a metric space (X, d) and finite collection of affine transformations, $\{\omega_i | i \leq n, \omega_i: X \to X\}$. The attractor of an IFS is the set of points $A \subset X$ such that $\bigcup_{i=1}^{n} \omega_i(A) = A$. What makes IFSs so fascinating is that the limit behavior of a single transformation is just a point, yet the limit set over the union of the transformations can be extremely complex with recursive structure. IFSs are responsible for the structure seen in the Sierpinski triangle (Figure 2) and other fractals.

A metric space (X, d) is the combination of a set X and distance metric $d: X \times X \to \Re$. Consider the unit square and Euclidean distance function as our metric space. The three functions in Equation 2 map the unit square into three of the four quadrants of the unit square.

$$\omega_1((x, y)) = (0.5x, 0.5y + 0.5) \qquad \omega_2((x, y)) = (0.5x, 0.5y) \qquad \omega_3((x, y)) = (0.5x + 0.5, 0.5y) \qquad (2)$$

If we focus on a single transform, we find that there exists a limit of iterating this function starting with any point in the unit square. For instance, the fixed point of transform ω_1 of $(0,1)$. This is an attracting fixed point since iteration draws other points closer to it over time.

A system of three transformation does not collapse into a single point. Rather, it has an attracting set with infinite recursive structure. A single transformation shrinks the entire limit set into a one-fourth sized copy of the original, while the union operation pastes the different copies together to form the original image again. This process is illustrated in Figure 3.

The attractor structure depends upon the transients of the transformation. In other words, the limit behavior of the individual transformations contributes little to the emergent shape of the attracting set. A simple example will demonstrate this fact. Each of the three transformations comprising the Sierpinski triangle IFS has an attracting limit point. These points, $(0,1)$, $(0,0)$, and $(1,0)$, are also the limits of the transformations in Equation 3. The attractor of this set of transformations is the finite set $\{(0,1),(0,0),(1,0)\}$, which looks nothing like the Sierpinski triangle.

$$\omega_1((x, y)) = (0, 1) \qquad \omega_2((x, y)) = (0, 0) \qquad \omega_3((x, y)) = (1, 0) \qquad (3)$$

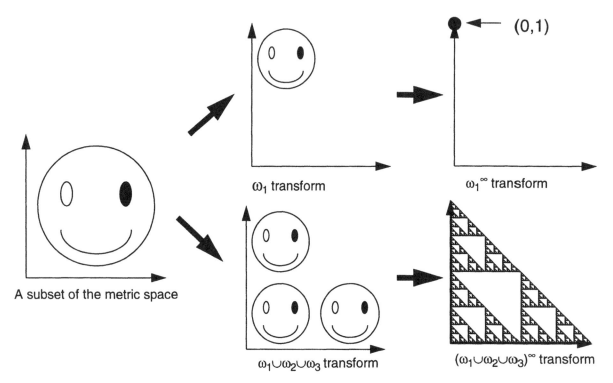

Figure 2: The difference between the limit of a single transformation (a point) and the limit of a collection of transformations (a Sierpinski triangle). The actual affine transformations are defined in Equation 2. The infinity superscript denotes the limit of an infinite sequence of function compositions.

An important concept for the understanding of iterated function systems is the Hausdorf space. The Hausdorf space of a complete metric space (X, d) is the set of all compact subsets of X, excluding the empty set. A compact set is a set that is both closed and totally bounded. The distance between two points in Hausdorf space is given by Equation 4. This metric measures the distance between two sets as the maximal distance between a point in A and the nearest point in B. Hausdorf space allows us to consider subsets of (X, d) as single points. It also lets us view the set of iterated transformations over the metric space as a single transformation in Hausdorf space. The theory laid out by Barnsley shows that IFSs composed of transformations which go to fixed points also produce fixed-point dynamics in Hausdorf space. For instance, it can be shown that the Sierpinski triangle is a point in $H(X)$ and that the Sierpinski IFS reduces the distance between any starting subset of X and the Sierpinski triangle.

$$h(d)(A, B) = \sup \{ \inf \{ d(x, y) | \ x \in A \} | \ y \in B \} \tag{4}$$

Random Iteration

An interesting side effect of the unique attractor for Barnsley's IFSs is that approximations to the attractor are easy to construct. Random iteration, also known as the chaos game, produces attractor approximations very rapidly. Take an initial point in the metric space and create a sequence of points by randomly selecting *one* IFS transformation at each iteration. The initial portion of the sequence is ignored as transients and the resulting union of the sequence remainder is a finite approximation to the attractor. It is easy to show that after each iteration the distance between the current point and the attractor geometrically decreases and approaches zero. The random transformation enforces coverage of the attractor, i.e. an infinite sequence of points generated this way will be dense in the attractor. The random iteration algorithm is sensitive to the method of selecting the transformations for each iteration. First, the probability of selecting a particular transformation can lead to an abnormal distribution of points approximating the attractor. Second, the selection generator must be ergodic, i. e. the selection must be independent of previous selections.

Language theory provides an alternative way of describing the random iteration algorithm. The sequence of transformations produced during random iteration can be compactly described with a stochastic finite state generator. The generator has probabilities associated with its transitions which produce variations in the sequence necessary for the production of the approximation. Without the probabilities, the generators produce a uniform distribution of sequences

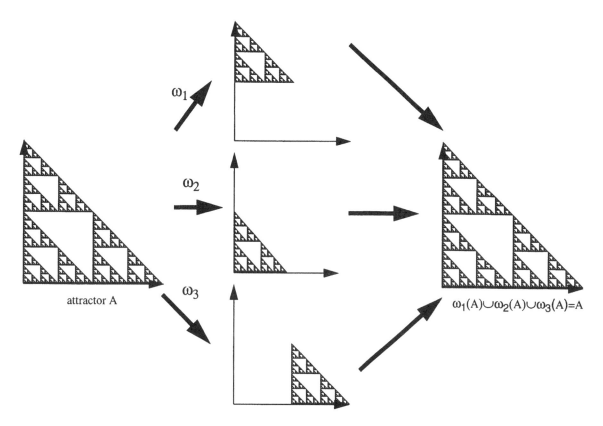

Figure 3: The individual transformations make three reduced copies of the attractor. Taking the union of the individual copies pastes together a the original attractor.

in Σ^∞, the set of all possible infinite sequences. Other "attractors" are possible by defining generators that produce subsets of Σ^∞.

Recurrent Networks as Iterated Function Systems

The behavior of recurrent networks in symbolic processing applications can be explained in terms of iterated function systems. This section provides a demonstration of the emergence of a complex recurrent network state space from the interaction of two simple state spaces. The recurrent network selected for this demonstration is a second order recurrent network know as the sequential cascaded network (SCN)[17]. An SCN can be described by two dynamic equations show in Equation 5.

$$O(t) \;=\; g\!\left(\left[W \cdot \begin{bmatrix} S(t) \\ 1 \end{bmatrix}\right] \cdot \begin{bmatrix} I(t) \\ 1 \end{bmatrix}\right) \qquad S(t+1) \;=\; g\!\left(\left[V \cdot \begin{bmatrix} S(t) \\ 1 \end{bmatrix}\right] \cdot \begin{bmatrix} I(t) \\ 1 \end{bmatrix}\right) \tag{5}$$

Where $O(t)$ is the output vector at time t, $S(t)$ is the state vector, $I(t)$ is the input vector, and W and V are three dimensional weight matrices describing state-to-state and state-to-output transformations performed by the SCN. The function g is the sigmoid function. Learning takes place in the SCN by adjusting the weight matrices W and V according to a modified form of back propagation. Training continues when the network successfully generates the desired outputs since overtraining forces the network through a qualitative change from a fixed point attractor to a limit cycle.

Pollack initially applied SCNs to the task of formal language recognition where the networks apparently induced regular languages. The internal states of these dynamical recognizers, however, were *not* finite. Dimensional analysis revealed a fractal dimension of 1.4 for the set of all possible internal states indicating an infinitely structured set [18].

In symbolic applications the set of predefined input vectors, Φ, is finite and we may write the dynamic in the

207

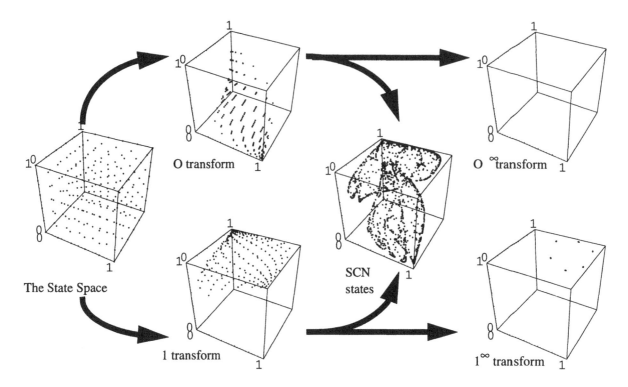

Figure 4: Dissection of the sequential cascaded network trained to accept 0*1*0*1*.

form shown in Equation 6.

$$O(t) = g(W_I \cdot \begin{bmatrix} S(t) \\ 1 \end{bmatrix}) \qquad S(t+1) = g(V_I \cdot \begin{bmatrix} S(t) \\ 1 \end{bmatrix}) \qquad (6)$$

The parameters W_I and V_I are two dimensional matrices selected by input pattern $I \in \Phi$. If the transfer function g is linear and the set of inputs is finite, the SCN is mathematically equivalent to the set of affine transformations of an IFS. The SCN adds a sigmoid to "squash" the internal state into a small subregion, preventing activations from growing toward infinity and allowing non-fixed point attractors, such as limit cycles and chaos, in the individual transformations. To display an attractor formed by the selection of transformations, one can play the "chaos game" [4] by plotting a sequence of state points transformed by all sequences of transformations up to length ten. Pollack trained an SCN to recognize regular languages from a set of positive and negative examples. Figure 4 shows a state space dissection of the SCN trained on examples from the language 0*1*0*1*. While the network never learned the target language, it did exhibit the state space marked as "SCN states" in Figure 4. By breaking the SCN into two transformations, one for each input symbol, we can examine the individual transformations that produced the "magic mushroom." The first iteration of the 0 transformation maps the state space onto a thin sheet along the diagonal while the first iteration of the 1 transformation pushes the state space to the ceiling with a one-sixth twist. In the limit, the 0 transformation produces a fixed point, while the 1 transformation gets closer and closer to this period 6 attractor.

The mushroom example demonstrates the existence of both fixed point and limit cycle attractors for individual inputs. Chaotic, or aperiodic, attractors are also possible in SCN state space. Figure 5 illustrates the effects of increasing parameter a on the asymptotic trajectories of the function f_a as shown in Equation 7.

$$f_a(x) = \tanh(a\tanh(ax + 0.5a) - a\tanh(ax - 0.5a) - a) \qquad (7)$$

The resulting plot, known as a bifurcation diagram, captures the underlying structure of the period doubling phenomena. At the limits of period doubling (such as $a \approx 1.7$), the systems attractor is chaotic, thus implying infinite state behavior. The function f_a can be expressed as a SCN-like input selected transformation by spreading the iterated computation of over two time steps, as in Equation 1 where the third element of $S(t+1)$ is $f_a(x(t))$ and the first and second elements of $S(t)$ are $\tanh(ax + 0.5a)$ and $\tanh(ax - 0.5a)$.

208

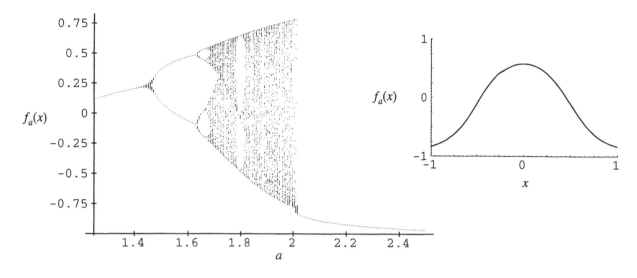

Figure 5: Sample mapping function and the bifurcation diagram that results from changes in control parameter a.

Discussion

Learning systems relying on recurrent networks carry a difficult burden; it is still unclear what these networks are processing, let alone what they learning. Many have assumed that the networks are learning to simulate finite state machines in their state dynamics and have begun to extract finite state machines from the networks' state transition dynamics [1, 2, 13]. The extraction methods employ various clustering techniques to partition the internal state space of the recurrent network into a finite number of regions corresponding to the states of a finite state automaton. As demonstrated in the first part of this paper, clustering of hidden unit activations, or recurrent network state space, provides incomplete information regarding the IP state of the network. IP states determine future behavior as well as encapsulate input history. The network's state transformations can exhibit sensitivity to initial conditions and generate disparate futures for state clusters of all sizes.

The second part of the paper presents IFS theory and shows how it can explain recurrent network state dynamics. By linking IFSs and recurrent networks, existing constraints on network dynamics independent of network models are now evident. By assuming a finite set of inputs, which is often the case in symbolic domains, one can describe recurrent network models as a finite collection of nonlinear state transformations. The interaction of several transforms produces complex state spaces with recursive structure. The limit behavior of the collection of transformations, and recurrent networks in symbolic applications, is more complex than the union of the individual transformations. An input driven recurrent network behaves like the random iteration algorithm. Infinite input sequence generates sequences of points dense in the state space attractor when the transformations are contractive. While the demonstration in this paper used the SCN, other models produce similar IFS-like behaviors as long as the network's input selects transformations [19].

The IFS approach also explains the phenomena of state clustering in recurrent networks. In [20], Serven-Schreiber *et al* report significant clustering in simple recurrent networks [21] both before and after training from the Reber grammar prediction task. A set of random transformations will normally reduce the volume of the recurrent networks state space, and place an upper bound on the distance between two transformed points. The upper bound has a significant effect on the clustering, especially when the transformations map to very small regions of state space. The task required that the clusters arranged themselves in a particular structure constrained by the single layer network generating predictions.

The utility of network states, however, is directly related to the complexity of the mechanism measuring the state. A computational system has three requirements. First, it should be input driven. Second, a computational system needs to dynamically change state. Third, it must generate output. While much has been written about the importance of state dynamics, the other two requirements are capable of elevating the behavioral complexity of the other two. Some systems produce perform transductions of periodic oscillations into complex signals. Different measurement devices can produce increases in both the number of apparent IP states and the observed complexity class of the system [22]. In other words, the recurrent network states are not IP states in of themselves; they require an appropriate context which can elevate them to IP-hood. This context consists of a set of input sequences and an observation method for generating outputs. While the recurrent network's state dynamics may be described as an IFS, any IP interpretation will involve a holistic combination of the set of possible inputs, the state dynamics, and the output generation mechanism of a network.

Acknowledgments

This work was supported by Office of Naval Research grant N00014-92-J-1195. The inspiration for this paper came from endless discussions with Jordan Pollack.

References

[1] C. L. Giles, C. B. Miller, D. Chen, G. Z. Sun, H. H. Chen and Y. C.Lee, "Extracting and Learning an Unknown Grammar with Recurrent Neural Networks," in *Advances in Neural Information Processing Systems 4*, 1992, pp. 317-324.

[2] R. L. Watrous and G. M. Kuhn, Induction of Finite-State Automata Using Second-Order Recurrent Networks, in *Advances in Neural Information Processing Systems 4*, 1992, pp. 309-316.

[3] C. L. Giles, S. Das and G. Sun, Learning context-free grammars: Capabilities and limitations of a recurrent neural network with an external stack memory, in *The Proceedings of the Fourteenth Annual Conference of the Cognitive Science Conference*, 1992, pp. 317-324.

[4] M. Barnsley, *Fractals Everywhere*, Academic Press, San Diego, CA, 1988.

[5] N. Chomsky, *Syntactic Structures*, Mounton & Co., The Hague, 1957.

[6] A. Newell and H. A. Simon, "Computer science as empirical inquiry: symbols and search," *Communications of the Association for Computing Machinery*, vol. 19, pp. 113-126, 1976.

[7] W. P. McCulloch and W. Pitts, "A logical calculus of the ideas immanent in nervous activity," *Bulletin of Mathematical Biophysics*, vol. 5, pp. 115-133, 1943.

[8] S. Franklin and M. Garzon, "Neural network implementation of Turing machines," in *The Proceedings of the Second Institute of Electrical and Electronics Engineers International Conference on Neural Networks*, 1988.

[9] J. B. Pollack, *On Connectionist Models of Natural Language Processing*, University of Illinois at Urbana-Champaign, Ph.D. thesis, 1987.

[10] H. T. Siegelmann and E. D. Sontag, "On the Computational Power of Neural Networks," Report SYCON-91-11, Rutgers Center for Systems and Control, 1991.

[11] B. MacLennan, "Field Computation in the Brain," Technical Report CS-92-174, University of Tennessee, 1992.

[12] W. R. Ashby, *An Introduction to Cybernetics*, Chapman and Hall, London, 1956.

[13] A. Cleeremans, D. Servan-Schreiber and J. L. McClelland, "Finite state automata and simple recurrent networks," *Neural Computation*, vol. 1, pp. 372-381, 1989.

[14] J. Crutchfield and K. Young, "Computation at the Onset of Chaos," in *Entropy, Complexity, and the Physics of Information*, W. Zurek (ed.), Addison-Wesely, Reading, 1989.

[15] F. Takens, "Detecting strange attractors in turbulence", in *Lecture Notes in Mathematics 898*, Springer-Verlag, Berlin, 1981.

[16] J. Crutchfield, J. D. Farmer and N. Packard, "Chaos," *Scientific American*, vol. 255, pp. 46-57, 1987.

[17] J. B. Pollack, "The Induction of Dynamical Recognizers," *Machine Learning*, vol. 7, pp. 227-252, 1991.

[18] B. Mandelbrot, *The Fractal Geometry of Nature*, Freeman, San Francisco, CA, 1983.

[19] J. F. Kolen, Ph.D. thesis in progress, The Ohio State University.

[20] D. Servan-Schreiber, A. Cleeremans and J. L. McClelland, "Encoding Sequential Structure in Simple Recurrent Networks," Technical Report CMU-CS-183, 1988.

[21] J. Elman, "Finding structure in time," *Cognitive Science*, vol. 14, pp. 179-211, 1992.

[22] J. F. Kolen and J. B. Pollack, "The apparent computational complexity of physical systems," in *Proceedings of the Fifteenth Annual Conference of the Cognitive Science Society*, Laurence Erlbaum, 1993.

On the treatment of time in recurrent neural networks

Fred Cummins† and Robert F. Port‡
Department of Linguistics
and Cognitive Science Program
Indiana University
port@cs.indiana.edu
fcummins@cs.indiana.edu
† To whom correspondence should be addressed
‡ Also of Dept of Computer Science

Temporal patterns such as those presented to perceptual systems typically have the property of invariance across wide variation in the rate of presentation. Recurrent neural network models which exhibit global point attractor dynamics recognize temporal patterns in spite of this variation. While this is a significant improvement on many existing models such as feed forward networks, much remains to be done in developing representations of the full temporal structure of a signal. In particular, although recurrent neural networks can be constructed which are sensitive to the relative durations of sequence components, such a network may rely for its solution on an artifact of the discretization brought about by sampling a continuous signal.

What's in a temporal pattern

Many kinds of information can be carried in the temporal dimension of a signal. Within connectionist modelling most attention has been paid to the learning of *sequences of discrete elements* [25, 22]. The individual sequence elements do not typically have any intrinsic durations, and all the information lies in the ordinal position of the elements, i.e. what comes before what.

The sort of signals with which perceptual systems are faced, however, are usually continuously varying in nature. There are many more ways in which information can then be coded in time. If the signal can be easily segmented, then sequence information is available. So too are the relative and absolute durations of segments and local and global rates of change, together with higher derivatives. Periodicities may yield information about rhythmic structure. As yet, no good taxonomy of the forms of temporal structure which encode information is available. We may look at a highly structured temporal signal such as speech to see some of the variety and complexity involved:

• Overall speaking rate conveys salient information about a speaker's affect and the relative urgency of an utterance. Detecting the rate of a signal which has yet to be identified is a notoriously hard problem [14, 2] yet one which seems to be relatively easy for human perceptual systems.

• Relative duration often carries linguistically significant information. Port and Dalby [19] identified the ratio of consonant to vowel duration as being a cue for determining whether a syllable final consonant is voiced (e.g *fuzz* vs. *fuss*). Likewise, altering only the duration of a vowel within a constant consonantal environment can induce a shift in percept from a short vowel to a long one (e.g. from *bid* to *bead*).

• The local rate of spectral change has been implicated in the identification of both consonants and vowels. It is known that it is formant transitions rather than steady states which are primarily responsible for vowel perception

211

[24, 10], while Furui [8] found "perceptual critical points" in Japanese syllables to be related to positions of maximum spectral transition. Thus, speech carries information, at least, in the sequential order of linguistic units, in rhythmic structure and in local and global rates of spectral change.

One defining characteristic of a temporal pattern is that it is invariant across some range of variation in its rate of presentation. E.g. the word "armadillo" is interpreted in the same way whether it is spoken slowly or rapidly. This is perfectly analogous to the problem of size invariance in the analysis of static images. Any perceptual model of temporal pattern processing must address the problem of developing representations for patterns which are independent of rate. It must treat tokens of a pattern which arrive at different rates in a similar manner, at least within some non-trivial range of variation. In later sections, we will examine a connectionist model which has this quality and investigate its advantages and shortcomings.

Models for temporal pattern processing

In order to justify the use of recurrent neural networks for temporal pattern processing, it will be to our advantage to show why some other candidate models do not adequately address the above problem of rate invariance.

One common engineering approach is to sample a continuous signal at regular intervals, and to put the current sample together with the previous n samples into a buffer, essentially converting a temporal pattern into a static spatial pattern. Such an approach has a long history in conventional AI approaches to speech recognition (e.g., HEARSAY-II [16]), where spectral segments were given integer labels, (e.g., $t_0, t_{-1}, t_{-2}....$), and were stored in a long 'blackboard' buffer. When networks are used, however, the serial time labels are lost and replaced with a nominal level scale for time. For example, Elman and Zipser [7] fed a network an entire window of acoustic spectra simultaneously. In such a model different points in time are theoretically equivalent.[1] Since a change in rate of presentation will change the spatial layout in ways that are arbitrary with respect to time, this approach has serious intrinsic limitations. Changes in the rate of presentation of a pattern in ways that are not explicitly trained will greatly reduce its ability to recognize familiar patterns. This limitation makes it implausible as a model for recognition of many kinds of auditory patterns, where patterns, such as words, melodies etc., that are the 'same' occur at a wide range of different rates [21]. Other techniques employed in the speech-recognition literature like dynamic time-warping [12] and hidden Markov-models (e.g. [15]) cause the model to filter out absolute durations in very unconstrained ways, while retaining sequence information. Although many of the temporal patterns of English can be captured by HMMs, much is missed at many different time scales [14, 20].

One way of doing without the fixed-size buffer while still giving the network a memory is through the provision of recurrent connections among units, so that the network state is a function not only of present external input, but also of past states. Many such architectures have been proposed [18, 6, 13]. Much work has addressed its concern primarily to the issue of the complexity (in terms of the generating string grammar) of the symbolic sequence that can be predicted or recognized by a network [25, 5, 9]. Less work with recurrent networks has examined the ways in which other kinds of temporal information than just sequence might be encoded. In the next section we present a recurrent connectionist model that is capable of recognizing patterns irrespective of a large degree of variation in the rate of presentation.

A model which provides rate invariance

We designed a network consisting of a small number of input nodes, one for each of the orthogonal input vectors, with complete feed-forward connection to a fully recurrently connected layer of 7 sigmoidal nodes. One or two of these recurrent units were designated output nodes, i.e. training values were provided for these and only these nodes. In the first task, the network was trained to identify two target sequences from a set of targets and distractors. One output node was associated with each target. These nodes were trained to remain off (activation = 0) at all times except upon presentation of the final sequence element in the respective target, at which time they were to go on (activation = 1) and remain on during presentation of said final element. In order to provide input similar to a sampled continuous

---

[1]This is because temporal order itself is not directly coded into the representation. Different points in time are nominally rather than ordinally distinct [23] as far as this backpropagation model is concerned.

Function	Sequence
Target	FFFAAABBBEEECCCDDD
Target	BBBAAAEEEFFFDDDCCC
Distractor	EEEBBBFFFAAACCCDDD
Distractor	EEEBBBCCCDDDFFFAAA
Distractor	BBBEEEFFFAAADDDCCC
Distractor	DDDCCCFFFAAAEEEBBB

Table 1: Example set of sequences used in the simulations. Input vectors are given a simple localist encoding on the input layer. The output node associated with Target 1 (2) is trained to remain off until presentation of the final element, **DDD (CCC)**, for which time it must come on.

signal, each sequence element (e.g. **A**) was presented for a number of network timesteps. This allowed us to model the duration of a sequence element directly by increasing (decreasing) the number of "samples". Table 1 gives an example set of targets and distractors, each element being presented for three time steps. The network was trained using real time recurrent learning, including teacher forcing [26]. For testing purposes, the same sequences were presented at rates different from those on which training was done (e.g. FFFFFAAAAA...instead of FFFAAA...). A correct "on" response was allowed if the output unit activation exceeded 0.75, while a correct "off" required the activation to be below 0.25. Full details of the simulations and resultant dynamics are given in [4].

The network learned this task and made no mistakes on the training set whatever. Furthermore, this performance was maintained during testing at presentation rates varying from one sample per element up to 10 and more per element, despite having been trained on only one fixed presentation rate (the precise ranges varied depending on the complexity of the sequences being learned, see [4]). An analysis of the dynamics of the trained network shows why this is so.

Analysing the dynamics of the trained network

Because the state of a recurrent neural network evolves over time, it is possible to study the dynamics of the trained network in order to understand how it has solved a given task. The state space of a trained network is defined by the activations of its units. As the state changes, the network traces out a trajectory in state space, shaped by the attractor states for each of the input vectors. The most common dynamics which result are global point attractors for each input vector, and the trajectories are completely determined by the approach towards first one and then the next point attractor. In the following analyses we will investigate the dynamics of the networks by looking at the attractor states for each possible input vector. This should provided an understanding of why the state trajectories are as they are, and thus how the network has solved the given task.

Because of the task construction, the state space of the network contains a well-defined sub-space associated with recognition of each of the targets. This space is defined by the hyperplane $N_{out} = 1$ where N_{out} is the activation of an output node. This region is bounded, as unit activations are constrained to be between zero and one. We call this the *recognition region* for a target.

The network develops simple global point attractors for each of the input vectors (**A, B**...), i.e. if we present **AAAAAAA**..., the network will eventually settle to a stable equilibrium.

The manner in which generalization across rates is achieved can most easily be illustrated with the use of a schematic diagram. In Fig 1 we present a much simplified version of the above sequence identification task to show how rate invariance is achieved with point attractor dynamics. In Fig 1.A we can see how the trajectories for the sequences **ABC** (target) and **BAC** (distractor), presented at a rate of two samples per sequence element, are shaped by approach to one point attractor after the other. In this manner the network can ensure that only the target trajectory passes through the recognition region. In Fig 1.B we compare the trajectory on presentation of the target at the rate at which the network was trained (dashed line) with presentation at a much slower rate (5 samples per sequence element, solid line). It can be easily seen that the trajectory is qualitatively unaltered as it is still shaped by piecewise approach to the same point attractors. This allows the network to recognize targets at rates other than that at which it was trained.

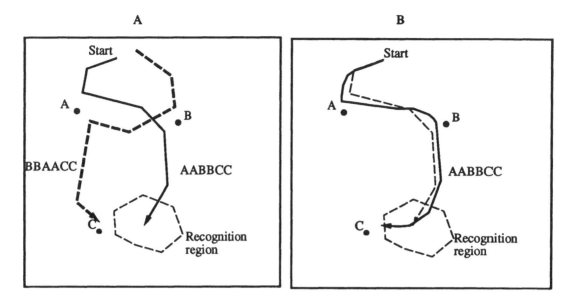

Figure 1: A. Telling a target, **ABC**, from a distractor, **BAC**. The trajectories are shaped by sequential approach to the point attractors. Only the target trajectory passes through the bounded recognition region. B. Trajectories for presentation of **ABC** at 2 (dashed line) and 5 (solid) time steps per sequence element.

Class	Sequence
I	AAB
	AAAB
II	AB
	AAAAB

Table 2: Training set used to sensitize the network to relative duration. Presentation of a medium number of As constitutes membership of one class, less or more As places the sequence in the second class.

Sensitivity to relative durations

Although the model does the right thing for patterns whose overall rate may change, this method of achieving rate invariance is not completely satisfactory. While maintaining invariance across uniform global rate variation, the network is similarly insensitive to local changes in rate. That is, the model is insensitive to the relative durations of sequence elements. We therefore designed a series of experiments to investigate whether the same network could develop dynamics which allowed it to recognize the relative duration of an element in a sequence. Table 2 gives one such training set. The task of the network is to classify sequences of the form **AB** into two classes, those in which the **A** lasts for two or three network time steps, and those in which the **A** is *either* shorter (one **A**) or longer (four As). The network has a single output node trained to remain off except upon presentation of the final sequence element **B** in sequences of the first class. Clearly, the dynamics of the above type of solution will not suffice for this task.

Again using real time recurrent learning and teacher forcing, the network solves this task. An understanding of how the solution is achieved and how the network will generalize to novel sequences of the form **AAA...B** can be achieved by looking at the attractor dynamics for each possible input vector. Fig 2 shows a view of the arrangement of the attractors in state space as seen in cross section through the space.[2] Before presentation of each sequence, a

---

[2]The cross section is obtained by performing a principal components analysis of movement in state space for one of the target sequences and looking at the plane defined by the first two components.

214

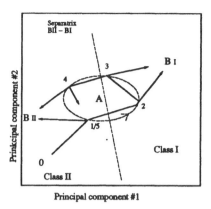

Figure 2: View of the first two principal components of state space showing two point attractors for **B** and a discrete periodic attractor for **A**.

number of zero vectors are presented to the network. This ensures that we are always starting from the same region of state space, as the network has a global point attractor for zero input, marked **0** in the figure. The classification decision is made upon presentation of the final sequence element, a **B**. Accordingly, two separate point attractors develop for **B**, one associated with Class I (in the recognition region) and one with Class II. These are labelled B_I and B_{II}. The basins of attraction for the two point attractors meet along a watershed called a separatrix. The sequences are being classified based on the duration of the element **A**, and this element has developed a discrete periodic attractor, which is walked around in four steps. The separatrix for the two **B** attractors bisects this periodic attractor. After starting at the point labelled **0**, successive time steps at which **A** is presented march it around the periodic attractor, from one basin of attraction to the other. In this manner, when **B** is presented, the attractor to which the system goes (and hence the classification) is based on which side of the $B_I - B_{II}$ separatrix the system finds itself on, which is itself a simple function of the number of time steps for which **A** has been presented. It can be seen that the network's generalization of the given task is to classify 0,1,4,5,8,9...As into one class and 2,3,6,7,10,11...into the other. (In fact, the fifth step does not coincide exactly with the first. A small amount of phase shifting is found, which causes the solution to degenerate on presentation of a very long sequence of **A**s. This phase shifting can be almost completely eliminated by a small amount of further training on a few such long sequences).

In further simulations with tasks similarly designed to force the network to attend to the relative duration of sequence elements, comparable solutions were obtained, all predicated on the bisection of a discrete periodic attractor for the sequence element whose length was being measured [3].

A problem with the solution

When dealing with a continuous signal, the use of digital computers forces us to use discrete samples, obtained at a rate which, hopefully, captures the salient information in the signal. Typically, the (difference) unit equations of the network are also derived from continuous (differential) equations. The hope in each case is, of course, that the discrete system is a good model of the underlying continuous system. There is an easy way to test this assumption in the case of network dynamics. It is possible to more closely approach a continuous mode of operation of the networks by calculating a more exact approximation to the derivative in updating unit activations, i.e. by reducing Δt in the approximation $\frac{dy}{dt} = \frac{y(t+\Delta t)-y(t)}{\Delta t}$. Although somewhat more computationally expensive, this should smooth out any artifacts introduced into a continuous system by the process of discretization. In the present case, however, an interesting result is obtained. As shown in Fig 3, as we near the continuous dynamic system, the radius of the periodic orbit shrinks. We infer that in the limit, the apparently periodic attractor is in fact a global point attractor. This means that the solution, which is predicated on the bisection of a periodic attractor, does not exist in the continuous case. The same problem is illustrated by the two functions shown in Fig 4. Although the discrete approximation $f(x)$ is everywhere close to the continuous function $g(x)$, it exhibits qualitatively different behavior: oscillation between

215

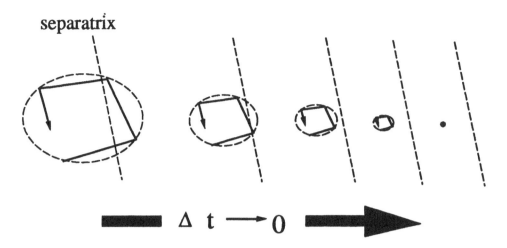

separatrix

$\Delta t \longrightarrow 0$

Figure 3: As Δt approaches zero, the radius of the discrete periodic orbit shrinks and approaches zero in the limit.

two fixed values rather than asymptotic approach to a fixed point. The finite number of steps taken in traversing the periodic orbit provide the network with a simple measure of time.

Discussion

We posed above the goal of building a processor for temporal patterns which will handle changes in rate of presentation with facility. Through the use of a fully recurrent network with global point attractor dynamics we showed how this might be achieved. We also showed that different qualitative dynamics induced in the same network architecture may enable the network to be sensitive to relative durations. We do not as yet know of a way to marry these two solutions.

The first solution with the simpler dynamics achieves rate invariance at the cost of ignoring all information about relative durations and local rates of change. This does not seem to be a sufficiently powerful model to handle the rich temporal structure of a signal such as speech. Simple point attractor dynamics are, however, common to numerous recurrent models [11, 1], and the rate insensitivity associated therewith could conceivable be exploited by recurrent architectures with separate mechanisms for treating of relative durations, rates of change etc. For example, McAuley [17] has developed adaptive oscillator models which might be used within a recurrent network. Adaptive oscillation allows the detection of information in discrete pulse codes and may be used to detect temporal information to which our model is oblivious. The fact that pattern identity across rate variation can be achieved using very simple dynamics might conceivably be exploited by a range of different architectures.

The second problem led to reliance on an artifact of the discretization procedure required by a digital computer model, and does not work in the continuous case. It is therefore probably not the right approach to take in making the network sensitive to relative durations.

We see the study of the dynamics of the trained networks as providing insight into the manner in which subsequent models might achieve the goal of perceptual invariance across global change in rate. Additional mechanisms will be necessary to extract much of the richer temporal structure.

In our treatment of time, we have made many simplifying assumptions. In order to fully understand the dynamics of the networks, we used a minimal set of orthogonal input vectors, thereby avoiding the problem of the segmentation of a continuous temporal signal. We also used a very crude sampling rate. We used 1 - 4 samples per sequence element, which, if applied to a signal such as speech, would mean that our patterns were very short indeed. Our current attention is on the investigation of networks which extract temporal structure at a variety of different time scales, from that of a few samples, such as above, to much longer periods of time.

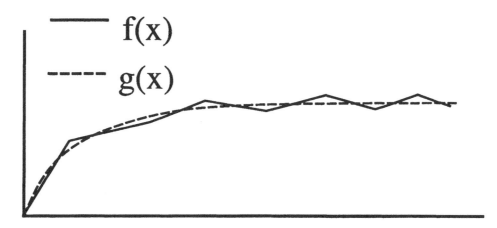

Figure 4: Example of qualitatively different behavior of a discrete approximation to a continuous function. The function $g(x)$ approaches a fixed point while $f(x)$ oscillates.

In conclusion, recurrent networks do offer certain improvements over previous models in dealing with many problems of time. Simple dynamics lend attractive possibilities in overcoming the problem of percpetual invariance despite variation in the rate of presentation of a signal.

Acknowledgements

The authors are grateful to Devin McAuley, Sven Anderson and Mike Mozer for many helpful discussions. The shortcomings however we claim for ourselves. This research was supported by ONR grant N00014-91-J1261.

References

[1] M. Cohen, "The construction of arbitrary stable dynamics in nonlinear neural networks," *Neural Networks*, vol. 5, pp. 83–103, 1992.

[2] G. W. Cottrell, M. Nguyen, and F.-S. Tsung, "Tau net: The way to do is to be," in *Proceedings of the Fifteenth Annual Conference of the Cognitive Science Society*, pp. 365–370, 1993.

[3] F. Cummins, "Representation of temporal patterns in recurrent neural networks," in *Proceedings of the Fifteenth Annual Conference of the Cognitive Science Society*, pp. 377–382, 1993.

[4] F. Cummins, S. Anderson, R. Port, and J. D. McAuley, "A dynamic systems model for temporal pattern recognition," Tech. Rep. 93, Cognitive Science Program, Indiana University, 1993.

[5] S. Dehaene, J.-P. Changeux, and J.-P. Nadal, "Neural networks that learn temporal sequences by selection," in *Proceedings of the National Academy of Science*, vol. 84, p. 2727, National Academy of Science, May 1987.

[6] J. Elman, "Finding structure in time," *Cognitive Science*, vol. 14, pp. 179–211, 1990.

[7] J. Elman and D. Zipser, "Learning the hidden structure of speech," *Journal of the Acoustical Society of America*, vol. 83, pp. 1615–26, 1988.

[8] S. Furui, "On the role of spectral transition for speech perception," *Journal of the Acoustical Society of America*, vol. 80, no. 4, pp. 1016–1025, October 1986.

[9] C. L. Giles, G. Z. Sun, H. H. Chen, Y. C. Lee, and D. Chen, "Higher order recurrent networks and grammatical inference," in *Advances in Neural Information Processing Systems 2* (D. S. Touretzky, ed.), San Mateo, California: Morgan Kaufmann, 1990.

[10] J. Hillenbrand and R. T. Gayvert, "Identification of steady-state vowels synthesized from the Peterson and Barney measurements," *Journal of the Acoustical Society of America*, vol. 94, no. 2 (Part 1), pp. 668–674, 1993.

[11] M. Hirsch, "Convergent activation dynamics in continuous time networks," *Neural Networks*, vol. 2, pp. 331–349, 1989.

[12] F. Itakura, "Minimum prediction residual principle applied to speech recognition," *IEEE Transactions on Acoustics, Speech, and Signal Processing*, vol. 23, pp. 67–72, 1975.

[13] M. Jordan, "Serial order," Tech. Rep. 8604, Institute for Cognitive Science, U. of California at SanDiego, La Jolla, CA, 1986.

[14] D. Klatt, "Linguistic uses of segmental duration in English: Acoustic and perceptual evidence," *Journal of the Acoustical Society of America*, vol. 59, pp. 1208–21, 1976.

[15] K.-F. Lee, *Automatic Speech Recognition: The Development of the SPHINX System*. Boston: Kluwer Academic Publishers, 1989.

[16] V. R. Lesser, R. D. Fennel, L. D. Erman, and D. R. Reddy, "Organization of the Hearsay-II speech understanding system," *International Conference on Acoustics, Speech, and Signal Processing*, vol. 23, pp. 11–23, 1975.

[17] J. D. McAuley, "Finding metrical structure in time," in *Proceedings of the 1993 Connectionist Models Summer School* (M. C. Mozer, P. Smolensky, D. S. Touretzky, J. L. Elman, and A. S. Weigend, eds.), (Hillsdale, NJ), L. Erlbaum Assoc, 1993. This volume.

[18] M. C. Mozer, "Neural net architectures for temporal sequence processing," in *Predicting the Future and Understanding the Past* (A. Weigend and N. Gershenfeld, eds.), Addison- Wesley Publishing, 1993.

[19] R. Port and J. Dalby, "C/V ratio as a cue for voicing in English," *Journal of the Acoustical Society of America*, vol. 69, pp. 262–74, 1982.

[20] R. F. Port, "Linguistic timing factors in combination," *Journal of the Acoustical Society of America*, vol. 69, pp. 262–274, 1981.

[21] R. F. Port, "Representation and recognition of temporal patterns," *Connection Science*, vol. 2, pp. 151–176, 1990.

[22] M. Reiss and J. G. Taylor, "Storing temporal sequences," *Neural Networks*, vol. 4, pp. 773–787, 1991.

[23] S. S. Stevens, "Mathematics, measurement and psychophysics," in *Handbook of Experimental Psychology* (S. S. Stevens, ed.), pp. 1–49, Wiley, New York, 1951.

[24] W. Strange, J. J. Jenkins, and T. Johnson, "Dynamic specification of coarticulated vowels," *Journal of the Acoustical Society of America*, vol. 74, pp. 695–705, 1983.

[25] D. Wang and M. A. Arbib, "Complex temporal sequence learning based on short-term memory," *Proceedings of the IEEE*, vol. 78, no. 9, pp. 1536–1542, 1990.

[26] R. Williams and D. Zipser, "A learning algorithm for continually running fully recurrent neural networks," *Neural Computation*, vol. 1, no. 2, pp. 270–280, 1989.

Finding Metrical Structure in Time

J. Devin McAuley
Department of Computer Science
Cognitive Science Program
Indiana University
Bloomington, Indiana 47405
mcauley@cs.indiana.edu

The problem of how neural systems represent and process temporal patterns such as language and music is central to cognition (Port 1990; Elman 1990; Jones 1976). Although a number of solutions have been proposed, this problem is far from being solved. The most common approach is to represent time by transforming it into a spatial dimension (Elman and Zipser, 1988). In this approach, temporal patterns are processed in chunks by collecting input for a fixed number of time steps and placing this information in a 'buffer', the size of which is fixed *a priori*. Time is represented explicitly by the input's serial position within the buffer; i.e., the input at time t is adjacent to the input at time $t + 1$. There are a number of problems with this approach which have been elaborated on by Port (1990) and Elman (1990). A system using a spatial representation requires an interface with the world which is able to correctly guess the appropriate buffer size for each input pattern. An incorrect guess may result in relevant information dropping off the end of the buffer. Another problem with this approach is that it is inflexible to changes in pattern presentation rate. Patterns that are faster or slower than the 'training' rate have different input representations and hence have different effects on processing. This does not seem to be the case with language as we are capable of adapting our perceptual systems to different language production rates.

Another way to process temporal patterns is to represent time only implicitly by the effect it has on processing. The most common implementation of this approach is to use a recurrent neural network model. In a recurrent neural network, temporal events remain 'in-time' by presenting input sequentially. Earlier items are retained in a 'processing' short-term memory in which the context-dependent state of the network enables the prediction of the next event. These models have been applied to a number of temporal pattern processing problems such as sequence recognition, language induction, time series prediction, and motor control (Jordan, 1986; Dehaene, Changeux, & Nadal, 1987; Elman, 1990; Anderson & Port, 1990; Wang & Arbib, 1990; Mozer, 1993). Although these models have been able to maintain sequential information, their ability to code relative duration, an important aspect of speech and music, is limited (Cummins and Port, 1993).

Our lab has examined this issue in a couple of studies (Anderson & Port, 1990; Cummins, Port, McAuley, & Anderson, 1993). We proposed that the representations for well-learned auditory patterns might take the form of trajectories shaped by a chain of stable states in a dynamical system. In these studies, a fully-recurrent neural network was trained to identify multiple productions of two familiar 'target' melodies among a set of distractors. This model generalizes recognition to target melodies at unfamiliar rates very nicely by maintaining the same trajectory shape independent of tempo. However, trajectory shape is also maintained for non-uniform/non-metrical rate changes (e.g., by lengthening or shortening each note in a melody by an arbitrary amount). A better characterization of this model is that it only measures ordinal time. It is sensitive to almost nothing about the relative durations of pattern elements.

The problem of rate generalization with recurrent neural networks brings up a useful distinction between patterns *in* time and patterns *of* time (Jones, 1990). Patterns in time, such as sequences, require coding the order of events. Patterns of time, such as rhythms, require coding the relative durations of events within the sequence; that is, the *metrical structure* of the pattern.

The main concern of this paper is processing patterns *of* time such as musical rhythms. I present an approach to this

219

problem which I have termed *adaptive oscillation.* An initial goal is to develop a system of oscillators which develops sensitivity to metrical structure in ways that are similar to humans. Each oscillator is able to continuously adapt its intrinsic (resting) oscillation period to match periodic components of an input pattern. This mechanism was initially introduced by Torras (1985). Her interests were not in modeling cognitive phenomena, but in modeling single neuron response to periodic electrical stimulation. However, her basic ideas seem very applicable to the problem of high-level rhythm perception and may offer a way of developing a theory which binds the psychophysics of meter perception to the underlying neural dynamics of audition. So far in the connectionist community, this approach has received very little attention, although in the last few years, several researchers have proposed that a network of interacting oscillators might be used to extract the metrical structure of musical patterns (Gasser, 1989; Scarborough, Miller, & Jones, 1990; McAuley, 1992, 1993; Large & Kolen, 1993).

Rhythm and Meter

In order to explain the purposes of this approach, the terms rhythm and meter, as they are applied in music, need clarification. A *rhythm* is a temporal pattern in which each element (note or rest) has a duration. The pattern of durations is constrained by a meter, where *meter* involves at least a two-level hierarchy of temporal intervals: the beat and the measure. The beat period defines the fundamental duration for constructing pattern elements. That is, all pattern elements have durations which are integer multiples or fractions of the beat period. The beat period also determines the tempo or pace of the pattern. A change to the beat period affects all of the pattern element durations. An increase or decrease to the beat period slows down or speeds up the tempo respectively, but maintains the relative durations between pattern elements. The measure is a larger period which serves to group pattern elements. Its duration is also defined relative to the beat period. For example, in a triple meter, the ratio between beat and measure is one to three. Given a meter, there are arbitrarily many rhythms which can be constructed from it. Given a rhythm, there are arbitrarily many meters which could have generated it. That is, the mapping from meter to rhythm is many-to-many.

Rhythm production and perception can be thought of as a process of communication. A musician performing a piece of music is likely to know what the underlying meter is. It is the performers job to communicate this meter to the listener. It is the listeners job to extract a plausible meter from the expressive cues provided by the performer and from structural cues in the sound pattern of the music (Jones, 1987). When we tap along with tunes on the radio, at least a beat-level description of the meter has been communicated successfully. If the measure-level description of the meter is communicated as well, then we have a richer 'sense of meter' that includes the perception of strong and weak beats.

An obvious question is whether meter is still perceived when there are no cues provided to the listener? To answer this question, Bolton (1894) investigated the perception of isochronous patterns. All pattern elements had the same pitch and duration and were separated by equal intervals. Even without physical cues, listeners still perceive meter. Perception of duple, triple, and quadruple meters is common. These subjective rhythms reveal the importance of top-down context and rhythmic experience in segmenting a temporal pattern.

Many researchers have explored the effects of variation in intensity, duration, intervals, pitch, and timbre on metrical structure and grouping (Handel 1989; Povel & Essens 1985; Povel & Okkerman 1981; Fraisse 1978). Subtle changes in all of these factors have been shown to affect the underlying perception of meter. For example, if every second element of an isochronous sequence is accented by increasing its intensity, then the sequence is perceived to have a duple meter and the accented element tends to begin each group. Changes in element duration have been shown to have similar effects, except that the longer element tends to end each group. The context of a local change can bring about global temporal reorganization of the entire sequence percept. To paraphrase Handel (1989), there is a lack of direct correspondence between the characteristics of the physical events and the perceived meter and accentuation. The perception of meter is an emergent phenomenon.

Jones (1976) argues that meter perception is an important and overlooked aspect of attention. That is, attention is most often thought of as a static process, but, it can be shown to be mediated by the temporal structure of the attended pattern. In one experiment, four rhythms were constructed from a nine-tone melody by manipulating the temporal context surrounding the middle three tones. The context change was intended to induce a perceived accent in either the 4th or 6th serial position. Listeners were asked to judge the equivalence of standard-comparison pairs. For each trial, the comparison pattern was either the same as the standard or differed only in the pitch of the 4th or 6th tone. The pitch change was found to be more noticeable to subjects if occurred on an accented position (Jones, Boltz, & Kidd, 1982). A conclusion to draw from this work is that attention is not a temporally continuous process. Instead, metrical structure influences our attentional focus, creating 'pulses of attention' and an expectancy for *when* events will occur (Jones, 1982). Rhythmic stimulation 'entrains' the listener. [1]

Adaptive Oscillators

In this section, I define a general framework for investigating adaptive oscillator models for meter perception. These models are amplitude-sensitive mechanisms which entrain to periodic components of an input pattern using a gradient-descent procedure. All of the models that fit into this framework exhibit entrainment patterns which are synchronized with the input. Unlike a forced oscillator, the period of the adaptive oscillator is incrementally modified so that after stimulation stops, the oscillator continues to pulse at a rate that is entrained to a frequency component of the input. Thus, adaptive oscillators embody a temporal expectation for a continuing pattern of input pulses.

Currently, I am investigating very simple input patterns. These patterns are roughly similar to the output of a drum machine with hard and soft beats (see Figure 1). For simplicity, each drum pulse has a duration of 1 / sampling-rate.

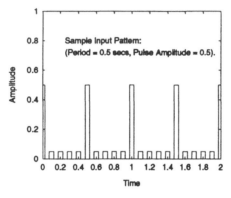

Figure 1: Discrete construction of a sample input pattern. Values for each pulse vary between [0, 1] and provide a rough intensity measure. All other time slices are zero.

This is of course a discrete construction for input, which has its disadvantages. As Δt goes to zero, the pulse duration also approaches zero. Continuous patterns of input pulses can be constructed by narrowing the peaks and widening the troughs of a cosine function (see the description of the extended harmonic oscillator in Figure 2D).

The main components of an adaptive oscillator are an activation function $\phi(t)$ and a threshold $\theta > 0$. The dynamics of the activation function do not depend upon any external variables such as input. When the state of the activation function reaches or exceeds threshold, the oscillator 'spikes' by generating an output signal for that time-slice. At this time, the state of the activation function is reset to its initial value. Spikes occur at a regular rate. This is the preferred spike rate. The duration between intrinsic spikes is the *resting period* of the oscillator. Figure 2 shows the activation function dynamics for four adaptive oscillators, each with a threshold of 1.0 and a preferred spike rate of 1.0 Hertz. The graphs show the activation function trajectories for two resting periods. The equations for each oscillator are described in the following table.

Oscillator	Activation	Threshold	Resting Period
Ramp	Ωt	1	$1/\Omega$
Integrate-and-Fire	$(\Omega + 1)(1 - e^{-\tau t})$	1	$\ln(\frac{\Omega}{\Omega+1})/ - \tau$
Harmonic	$(1 + \cos(\frac{2\pi t}{\Omega}))/2$	1	Ω
Extended Harmonic	$(1 + \tanh(\gamma(\cos(\frac{2\pi t}{\Omega}) + \beta)))/2$	1	Ω

---

[1]More formally, entrainment is the phase-locked response of a system to periodic patterns. For example, a system that is 2 : 1 entrained 'oscillates' once every two periods of the input pattern.

221

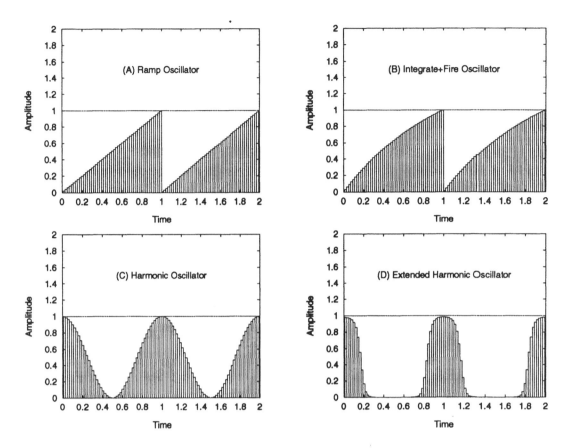

Figure 2: The activation function dynamics are shown for the the ramp, integrate+fire, harmonic, and extended harmonic oscillators. Each oscillator has a spiking threshold of approximately 1.0 and a preferred spike rate of 1 Hz.

For each oscillator there is a parameter Ω which controls, implicitly or explicitly, the resting period of each oscillator. These models can be divided into two classes. Both the ramp and integrate+fire oscillator have monotonically increasing activation functions with a discontinuity at threshold; i.e., $\phi(t)$ at reset changes from 1.0 to 0.0. On the other hand, the harmonic and extended harmonic oscillators have continuous activation functions; i.e., their activation at reset does not change. The differences between these two classes of models are profound with respect to adaptation.

So far, we have not discussed the effect of input on an adaptive oscillator, or the adaptation process itself. There are a number of ways to handle input. In this paper, we will only discuss the processing of a single input channel which is added to the activation function, and the effects this has on the oscillator dynamics. Total activation is defined as the sum of the 'spontaneous' activation $\phi(t)$ and the input $i(t)$. The effect of an input is to possibly force the oscillator to spike before or after a spontaneous spike. One way to adapt the oscillator so that it becomes entrained to a periodic component of the input pattern is to define an error term which measures the 'temporal distance' between input-forced spikes and spontaneous spikes, and then perform gradient descent on Ω at the time of a spike. At the time of a spike, the difference between the threshold and the spontaneous activation function can be used to define a sum-squared error measure:

$$E(t) = 1/2(\theta - \phi(t))^2.$$

This error term is zero for all input-forced spikes that coincide with spontaneous spikes. If the input forces the oscillator to spike before or after the spontaneous spike, then the error term is greater than zero, with the magnitude of the error being proportional to the distance the spontaneous activation function is from threshold. At times other than a spike, the error term is not useful. At each training step, the change in Ω is (negatively) proportional to the partial derivative of the error function with respect to Ω, which by the chain rule is

$$\Delta\Omega = -\eta\frac{\delta E}{\delta\Omega} = -\eta\frac{\delta E}{\delta\phi}\frac{\delta\phi}{\delta\Omega} = \eta(\theta - \phi(t))\frac{\delta\phi}{\delta\Omega}.$$

Simulations have evaluated the success of this learning rule when it is applied to the four adaptive oscillators described in this section. These results are discussed in the remained of this paper.

The Dynamics of Adaptive Oscillation

The first simulation explored how well each oscillator entrained to input patterns with a constant drum-pulse amplitude (see Figure 1). To be able to compare across models, all shared parameters were fixed at the same values. Each oscillator's period was initialized to 0.5 seconds and the input pulse amplitude was fixed at 0.5. The responses of each oscillator to input patterns with periods ranging from 0.01 to 0.99 seconds in steps of 0.01 were recorded after the learning algorithm converged or after it was clear that the algorithm would not converge. Convergence time varied over a wide range (two to one hundred 'model' seconds). Within a particular model, the main variable was the learning rate, with the largest learning rates yielding the fastest convergence times. Not surprisingly, large learning rates also tended to produce very erratic behavior by jumping the oscillator spikes back and forth over the entraining input pulses. If a small learning rate still produced non-convergent behavior, then the data point was thrown out, so as to only show the input periods for which each oscillator entrained its response.

The results for a learning rate of 0.05 are shown in Figure 3. These graphs share a couple of very noticeable properties. The response of the oscillators to clusters of input periods often falls along a straight line. These line segments correspond to entrainment regions, with the entrainment ratio $m : n$ (number of input pulses per oscillator pulse) specified by the slope of the segment. 'Breaks' between line segments are bifurcations in the oscillators response. The oscillators activation function is the main variable in determining the different entrainment regions and where the bifurcation points are located.

In developing a model for human meter perception, the obvious question is what should these curves look like. Unfortunately, this does not afford an easy answer, but the desired form of the oscillators adaptive response should have certain features. In the context of a larger system responding to the underlying meter of a rhythmic pattern, it is desirable for the oscillators to have entrainment ratios other than $1 : 1$ (corresponding to multiple line segments in the Figure 3); e.g., a bank of oscillators responding to a 'strong-weak' pattern should adopt $1 : 1$ and $2 : 1$ entrainment ratios, at the beat and measure level respectively. Since our perception of meter is not affected by modest variations in tempo, a viable oscillator model should also be able to track tempo changes by being able to speed up and slow down over a modest range without encountering a bifurcation. In the graphs, this corresponds to 'medium' length line segments which extend above and below the resting period of 0.5 seconds.

The ramp and integrate+fire oscillators are unsuitable models because they can only adapt to an input pattern by speeding up. The derivative of their activation functions is always positive resulting in a $\Delta\Omega$ that always has the same sign. If the input pattern slows down, these models have to find a different entrainment ratio. Notice also that the integrate+fire oscillator shows fewer bifurcations. This occurs because its activation function increases at a faster rate than the constant slope ramp oscillator. The net result is an 'effective' increase in input amplitude. Although it is not shown in these graphs, an actual increase in input amplitude will decrease the number of bifurcations. A simulation was run in which the input amplitude was increased to 0.8. The entrainment ratios of the ramp oscillator for this condition matched the entrainment ratios for the integrate+fire oscillator depicted in Figure 3B.

Unlike the ramp and integrate+fire oscillators, but more like human listeners, the harmonic and extended harmonic oscillators can adapt to tempo changes by speeding up and slowing down their responses. For these models, this implies that $\Delta\Omega$ can be both positive and negative. Notice however, that a large portion of the extended harmonic's activation function is flat (see Figure 2D). Since the error gradient for flat curves is almost zero, this oscillator does not adapt to input-forced spikes which occur during the flat segment. If instead, an input-forced spike occurs during the steep portion of the activation function, the system adapts very quickly. The main consequence of having very flat and steep activation function segments is to implement a form of *temporal receptive field*. That is, the adapted period of the extended harmonic oscillator tends to remain within a small 'window' of its initial resting period (see Figure 3D). As a

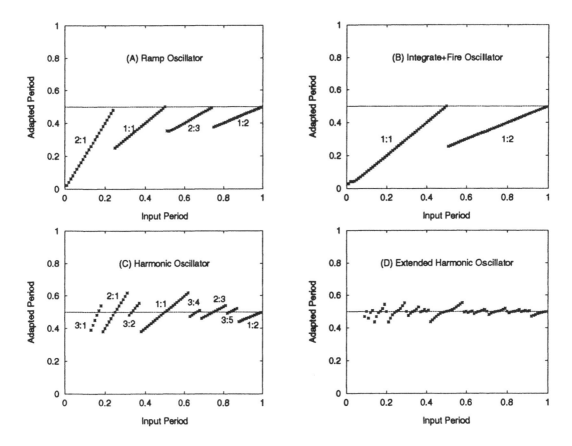

Figure 3: These graphs compare the entrainment ratios and bifurcation points of the ramp, integrate+fire, harmonic, and extended harmonic oscillators for 0.5 amplitude input patterns. Along each x-axis is a 'sweep' of input periods ranging from 0.01 to 0.99 in steps of 0.01. Along each y-axis is the adapted period of the oscillator. The resting period of each oscillator is initially 0.5 seconds and the learning rate is fixed 0.05.

result, it must find more exotic entrainment ratios to minimize error. This greatly increases the number of bifurcation points and makes tracking a pattern which changes tempo very difficult.

On the other hand, the activation function for the harmonic oscillator is not as flat. For the most part, its slope is roughly a constant positive or negative non-zero value. Consequently, the harmonic adaptive oscillator has fewer bifurcations, is more stable, and converges fairly quickly. It is a more plausible model for tracking tempo changes. In the next section, we explore the ability of this model to track tempo changes and maintain sensitivity to metrical structure in a way that is similar to humans.

Structure Sensitivity and Rate Change

It is the purpose of this simulation to show that a cluster of four adaptive harmonic oscillators with a range of initial periods can adapt to the beat and measure level components of two simple rhythmic patterns and that the entrainment ratios that these oscillators adopt is sensitive to the meter of the stimulating rhythm. Furthermore, when the tempo of the rhythm drifts, the oscillators are able to track the change without losing their 'sense of meter'.

The oscillators received only unweighted bottom-up input; lateral connections between oscillators were not included. In a more complete system, oscillators would have lateral connectivity and would develop sensitivity to metrical structure as the result of two interactive learning procedures: a gradient descent entrainment process (as discussed in the previous section) and a Hebbian learning process for adjusting lateral connection strengths (Hebb, 1949). By definition, Hebbian learning will reinforce the connections between the oscillators entrained to the beat-level pattern and the measure-level pattern each time the ensemble 'fires' in-phase (once every two beats for a duple pattern). Note that by virtue of their initial resting periods, some oscillators in the group will not entrain to either the beat or measure level, but may in fact discover a more exotic entrainment ratio. This is problematic if these oscillations conflict with a description of the meter. There are at least two potential ways of suppressing the unwanted oscillations. Connections to oscillators not responding the beat or measure level could be weakened by virtue of the fact that their entrainment patterns do not correlate well with the input amplitude pattern. A second approach would be to use the effect of a substantial number of oscillators responding to the beat and measure level to 'swamp' the extraneous oscillations. The design and implementation of lateral connections is in progress.

The two rhythms in this simulation were a strong-weak 'duple' pattern with amplitudes alternating between 0.5 and 0.2 and a strong-weak-weak 'triple' pattern described by the repeating amplitude sequence 0.5,0.2, and 0.2. The initial tempo for these patterns was 143 beats per minute which corresponds to a beat period of approximately 0.42 seconds. To change the tempo of the rhythms, a random number of zero amplitude time-slices were added to the beat period of each measure. This procedure was cumulative so that the new tempo of each measure varied from the previous measure's tempo by at most 10%. The net result is a gradual drift in tempo. The tempo changes were the same for both rhythms so as to compare the responses of the oscillators. For the simulation, the tempo varied for 150 measures. This pattern of tempos is shown in Figure 4A and B as a solid line by plotting the beat period of the input as a function of the measure number.

The periods of the four oscillators were initialized to 0.25, 0.5, 1.0, and 2.0 seconds; in terms of musical tempo, this corresponds to 30, 60, 120, and 240 beats per minute respectively, ranging from very slow to very fast. These choices were somewhat arbitrary and were not selected so as to model specific psychophysical data. However, when enough is known about the dynamics of adaptive oscillation, this is an important goal. So that the oscillators would adapt quickly, the learning rate was set to 0.4. The dotted lines in Figure 4A and B, labelled Unit 1, Unit 2, and Unit 3, show the tracking histories for the first three oscillators in response to the 'duple' and 'triple' rhythms respectively. For both rhythms, all of the oscillators (including Unit 4 which is not shown) converged to stable entrainment ratios after only a few measures, and were able to track subsequent shifts in tempo. This is manifest by the similar shape of these tracking histories to the drift pattern of the tempo.

With respect to the entrainment ratios, it is important to make two observations which are reflected in Figure 4C and D. These bar-graphs compare the entrainment 'profiles' of the bank of oscillators in response to the duple and triple rhythms. Each oscillator is labelled as a unit number along the x-axis. Bar height indicates the corresponding entrainment ratio. Associated with each ratio is an error-bar indicating the variance in the entrainment ratio as the unit adapted to changes in tempo.

The first observation is that a unit by unit comparison between the profiles reveals some important similarities and differences. Unit 1 entrained 1 : 1 in response to both rhythms, providing a beat-level description of the underlying meter. The responses to the rhythms for units 2, 3, and 4 were different and consistent with a description of a duple or triple meter respectively. In particular, Unit 3 entrained 2 : 1 to the strong-weak pattern and entrained 3 : 1 to the strong-weak-weak pattern, providing a measure-level description of the underlying meter. The second observation is that the small error-bar variances reveal that the description of meter is invariant across tempo.

Conclusions

In this paper, I have described a general class of *adaptive oscillator* models for meter perception and temporal pattern processing. All models in this class have the same basic building blocks and use gradient-descent to entrain to periodic input patterns. Of the four models investigated in the simulations, the adaptive harmonic oscillator is best suited for modeling human meter perception. This model is capable of maintaining sensitivity to the meter of simple rhythmic patterns, despite modest changes to the pattern tempo. It is likely that such 'hardware' designed specifically to encode timing relationships is likely to be more useful for metrical structure processing than generic recurrent neural networks.

At present, the adaptive oscillator approach to temporal pattern processing is very early on in its development.

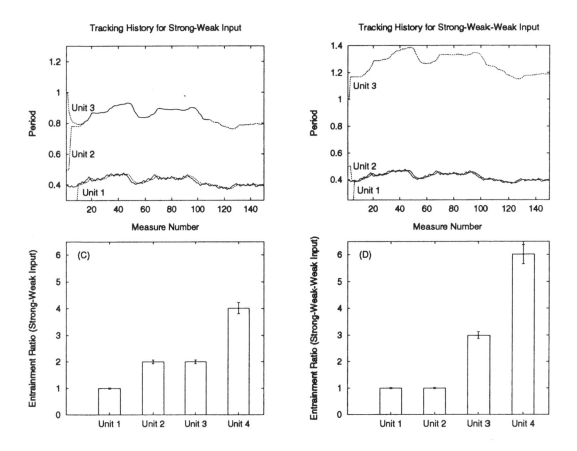

Figure 4: (A) and (B) show the ability of a bank of four harmonic oscillator units to track tempo changes to two simple rhythmic patterns. (C) and (D) show that the entrainment ratio profiles in response to these rhythms is sensitive to the underlying meter. This property is independent of tempo.

There is a clear need for formalizing the mathematical properties of these models. The description of a general class of adaptive oscillators is a step in this direction. As a next step, a careful comparison needs to be made between the adaptive oscillator paradigm and earlier work which investigated the dynamics of forced oscillation (Keener et al, 1981; Stiber, 1992). This would establish a better foundation for designing models with specific constraints on entrainment ratios and bifurcations. Current research is directed towards achieving this goal.

Acknowledgments

The author is grateful to Mike Mozer, Joe Stampfli, Bob Port, Mike Gasser, Cathy Rogers, Fred Cummins, Sven Anderson, and Louis Merlin for their comments and criticism during the development of this manuscript. This research was supported by ONR grant N00014-91-J1261.

References

[1] S. Anderson and R. Port, "A network model of auditory pattern recognition," Tech. Rep. 1, Indiana University, Institute for the Study of Human Capabilities, 1990.

[2] T. L. Bolton, "Rhythm," *American Journal of Psychology*, vol. 6, no. 2, pp. 145–238, 1894.

[3] F. Cummins and R. Port, "On the treatment of time in recurrent neural networks," in *Proceedings of the 1993 Connectionist*

Models Summer School (M. C. Mozer, P. Smolensky, D. S. Touretzky, J. L. Elman, and A. S. Weigend, eds.), L. Erlbaum, 1993. This Volume.

[4] F. Cummins, R. F. Port, J. D. McAuley, and S. Anderson, "Temporal pattern recognition with fully-recurrent networks," Tech. Rep. 93, Cognitive Science Program, Indiana University, 1993.

[5] S. Dehaene, J.-P. Changeux, and J.-P. Nadal, "Neural networks that learn temporal sequences by selection," in *Proceedings of the National Academy of Science*, vol. 84, p. 2727, National Academy of Science, May 1987.

[6] J. Elman, "Finding structure in time," *Cognitive Science*, vol. 14, pp. 179–211, 1990.

[7] J. Elman and D. Zipser, "Learning the hidden structure of speech," *Journal of the Acoustical Society of America*, vol. 83, pp. 1615–26, 1988.

[8] P. Fraisse, "Time and rhythm perception," in *Handbook of Perception VIII: Perceptual Coding* (E. C. Carterette and M. P. Friedman, eds.), pp. 203–254, New York: Academic Press, 1978.

[9] M. Gasser, "Towards a connectionist model of the perception and production of rhythmic patterns," Presented at the International Joint Conference on Artificial Intelligence, 1989.

[10] S. Handel, *Listening: An introduction to the perception of auditory events*. Cambridge, Mass.: Bradford Books/MIT Press, 1989.

[11] D. O. Hebb, *The Organization of Behaviour*. New York: John Wiley and Sons, 1949.

[12] M. R. Jones, "Musical events and models of musical time.," in *Cognitive Models of Psychological Time*. (R. Block, ed.), Hillsdale, NJ: Lawrence Erlbaum Associates, 1990.

[13] M. R. Jones, "Dynamic pattern structure in music: Recent theory and reseach," *Perception and Psychophysics*, vol. 41, no. 6, pp. 621–634, 1987.

[14] M. R. Jones, "Music as a stimulus for psychological motion: Part II. an expectency model.," *Psychomusicology*, vol. 2, pp. 1–13, 1982.

[15] M. R. Jones, "Time, our lost dimension: Toward a new theory of perception, attention, and memory," *Psychological Review*, vol. 83, pp. 323–355, 1976.

[16] M. R. Jones, M. Boltz, and G. Kidd, "Controlled attending as a function of melodic and temporal context," *Perception and Psychophysics*, vol. 32, no. 3, pp. 211–218, 1982.

[17] M. Jordan, "Serial order," Tech. Rep. 8604, Institute for Cognitive Science, U. of California at SanDiego, La Jolla, CA, 1986.

[18] J. P. Keener, F. C. Hoppensteadt, and J. Rinzel, "Integrate-and-fire models of nerve membrane response to oscillatory input," *SIAM Journal of Applied Math*, vol. 41, no. 3, pp. 503–517, 1981.

[19] E. Large and J. Kolen, "A dynamical model of the perception of metrical structure," Presented at the Society for Music Perception and Cognition, 1993.

[20] J. D. McAuley, "Learning to perceive and produce rhythmic patterns in an artificial neural network," Tech. Rep. 371, Computer Science Department, Indiana University, 1993.

[21] J. D. McAuley, "A model for the perception of temporal patterns," in *Proceedings of the International Joint Conference on Neural Networks*, vol. 3, pp. 798–803, IEEE, 1992.

[22] M. C. Mozer, "Neural net architectures for temporal sequence processing," in *Predicting the Future and Understanding the Past* (A. Weigend and N. Gershenfeld, eds.), Addison-Wesley, 1993.

[23] R. F. Port, "Representation and recognition of temporal patterns," *Connection Science*, vol. 2, pp. 151–176, 1990.

[24] D. Povel and P. Essens, "Perception of temporal patterns," *Music Perception*, vol. 2, 1985.

[25] D. Povel and H. Okkerman, "Accents in equitone sequences," *Perception and Psychophysics*, vol. 30, no. 6, pp. 565–572, 1981.

[26] D. L. Scarborough, B. O. Miller, and J. A. Jones, "PDP models for meter perception," in *Proceedings of the Twelfth Annual Meeting of the Cognitive Science Society*, (Hillsdale, NJ), pp. 892–899, L. Erlbaum Assoc, 1990.

[27] M. Stiber, *The Dynamics of Synaptic Integration*. PhD thesis, UCLA, 1992.

[28] N. P. M. Todd, "Recovery of rhythmic structure for expressive signals," Presented at the 124th Meeting of the Acoustical Society of America, 1992.

[29] C. Torras, *Temporal-Pattern Learning in Neural Models*. Berlin: Springer Verlag, 1985.

[30] D. Wang and M. Arbib, "Complex temporal sequence learning based on short-term memory," *Proceedings of the IEEE*, vol. 78, no. 9, pp. 1536–1542, 1990.

227

Representations of Tonal Music:
A Case Study in the Development of Temporal Relationships

Catherine Stevens[†] & Janet Wiles[‡]
[†]Department of Psychology
[‡]Departments of Psychology & Computer Science
University of Queensland
Brisbane Australia 4072
kates@psych.psy.uq.oz.au

INTRODUCTION

Connectionist models of musical ability such as tonal composition [11,31,41], performance [1,37] and perception [3,10,23] entail representation of properties of music including tonal expectancies and note-chord-key hierarchies [2,18]. Many of the models *assume*, rather than investigate, the representation of tonal music. Given that neural networks comprise a dual mechanism capable of *learning* representations and of applying the *processes* which act upon them, networks can, in principle, be used to explore the construction of representations which may mediate cognition. Thus, it is now possible to ask: how are representations of music constructed during learning, and what form do they take? The question is addressed in the present study using a recurrent network to simulate the first stage of music cognition, namely the construction of a representation of the temporal contiguities implicit in a Western tonal composition. We begin with a discussion of the nature of input to the network, followed by a description of the model, and, finally, we examine the time course of learning. The development of representations is traced through an analysis of the prediction performance of the network at various stages of training. The network was exposed to a single composition to explore the *veridical* expectancies or "instance-based expectations for events that follow in a particular familiar sequence" [3]. The simulation results indicate that learning involves representation of interactions and interdependencies between components of music such as tone, octave, duration, and accent. As the single composition embodied melodic, harmonic, and rhythmic conventions of a particular style of tonal music, the representations constructed by the network also approximated *schematic* expectancies "for events that typically follow familiar contexts" [3]. More specifically, the distribution of mean activations across the output vector approximated the tonal hierarchy for the key of C major [19,22], in that the notes of the tonic C chord (C, E, G) were most active and highly stable.

NETWORK DESIGN

Input Representations of Tonal Music

The dynamic, temporal flow of music presents a problem for connectionist models which, by design, process information in parallel. Models which were designed to process sequential patterns, such as speech

[8,16,24], have been adapted for use with musical patterns. For example, the temporal order of musical tones can be translated into an ordered spatial dimension over which a sliding window passes, activating tone units for time periods of a fixed size [40,41]. However, the varying note durations and tempos of musical compositions make it difficult to divide the musical pattern into fixed time periods, whether measured in real time (e.g. one second) or musical time (e.g. a quarter note). The problems associated with segmentation of the acoustic signal and pre-specification of a fixed time period can be circumvented if a musical event or note is regarded as the basic input to the network. In the present study, a musical event is coded in terms of pitch- and time-based components, and the musical composition is input to a simple recurrent network [7] one note or event at a time. Inclusion of a bottleneck of hidden units forces the network to construct representations of the transitions and relations between musical events as they unfold in time.

A review of music cognition literature reveals that the majority of distinctive features or attributes of Western tonal compositions, such as melodic contour, rhythmic pattern, and inter-note intervals, can be described in terms of two systems - pitch and timing [6,29,38]. The two systems are often disjoined and modeled independently of one another [e.g. 3,23,25,35]. However, psychological research has emphasized the importance of inter-dependencies between tonal and metric information in music cognition [5,13,30]. For example, [12,14] showed that rhythmic structure influences judgments of pitch information, and [5] demonstrated that memory for pitch sequences was influenced by the temporal dimension: temporal sequences that coincided with pitch structures enhanced recall whereas conflicts between temporal and pitch structures induced poorer performance. Similarly, [30] reported that rhythmic consonance facilitated musicians' performance on a discrimination task. Input to the present model, therefore, includes both pitch- and time-based components.

The components of music selected as input to the network derive from frequency, time, and amplitude dimensions of the physical signal. Musical information is input as a sequence of events using unary representation of values of four components: pitch, octave, duration and accent/loudness. Pitch information is coded as the particular value of the twelve tones of the Western chromatic scale: A, A#, B, and so on. The input of pitch values assumes pre-processing in the form of a frequency-to-pitch classifier [36]. Rests are also coded by the activation of a single input unit, and the octave from which a particular tone derives is coded by one of three octave input units. Although it is possible to code all frequencies of the Western tonal scale without reference to the octave, the separation of tone and octave information is a psychologically valid distinction [27], and permits the translation of musical segments into higher or lower octaves while retaining information about key and segment similarity. The separate coding of tone and octave on both the input and output layers also facilitates interpretation of note predictions made by the network.

Information derivable from the temporal dimension of music is coded by two sets of input units, namely duration and accent. Ideally, a neural network designed to process a musical composition would receive pitch information in real time and, in so doing, capture the duration or onset to offset interval of each note. However, real-time processing assumes complex signal segmentation and requires a perceptual level of analysis which is beyond the scope of the proposed cognitive model. In the present model, the segmentation of the musical stream has already occurred and the duration of each musical event (tone or rest) is coded by one of six input units. The units range from an eighth note (quaver) to a dotted half note tied to a quarter note (dotted minim tied to a crotchet). Duration information is represented on the output layer using six output units, one for each note value present in the composition. As recent psychological research has emphasized the role of accent structure in cognition of musical compositions [15,34], three input units are used to code event accent according to the location of the note in a bar (strong, weak, or very weak). Although disjoined at the input layer level, it was expected that duration and accent information would interact and combine in the network to represent the meter of the composition.

Network Architecture and Training

The network was a simple recurrent network (SRN) [7] consisting of 25 input and output units, and 20 hidden and context units. The recurrent connections, which linked the hidden units to the input units, gave the network memory inasmuch as they allowed the hidden units to be influenced by their previous activations. The model was trained using online learning and Backprop Through Time for one time step. The network was required to predict the next event in the musical sequence; the patterns of activation on the 25-unit output layer were mappings of activation patterns on the 25-unit input layer, one time step later. The network was simulated using a modification of the *bp* program in the *pdp* software package [26], and learning and momentum rates were set at 0.05 and 0.2, respectively. The training set comprised the 153-note melody of *The Blue Danube* by Johann Strauss. The composition was in the key of C major and in

3/4 time. A record of the developmental performance of the network was made at log steps from Epoch 0 through to Epoch 4096, where an epoch referred to one pass through the melody or 153 training steps. The aim in training the network was to study the way in which effects of temporal transitions between events were incorporated into the representation constructed gradually by the network.

RESULTS AND DISCUSSION OF NETWORK PERFORMANCE

Musical Prediction by the SRN

Output from the SRN at each time step consisted of a distribution of activations across tone, octave, duration and accent units of the output vector. The distribution reflected the likelihood of a component being active given the preceding musical context. During the early stages of training, the network learned to predict the base probabilities of events, and, as expected, it gave evidence of being sensitive to the statistical regularities in the training set (*veridical* information) by responding initially with the average combination of tone, octave, duration and accent components. Figure 1 shows the comparison of the target activations of the output vector averaged across all 153 events in the piece, and the obtained activations for a single note – Event 1 – at Epoch 4. With further training, the network learned context-sensitive variations from the mean component activations for each time step.

The distributions of activity across the output vector of the network in the early stages of training demonstrate the statistical learning properties of the network. The statistical regularities extracted and learned by the network are of psychological interest for a number of reasons. First, the mean activations of the tone units across the entire composition are reminiscent of the tonal hierarchy which has been described by both music theorists and psychologists. [19,22]. During the initial epochs of training, the network responds with the most stable and frequently occurring tones, namely tones C, E, and G which comprise the tonic chord. This kind of hierarchical ordering of tones characterises the relative importance of tones in particular keys and has been shown to influence performance on a range of experimental tasks including judged relatedness of tones, judged key membership, judgments of phrase endings, and patterns of memory confusions [20]. The network, therefore, provides a mechanistic account of the way in which statistical properties of music are learned and represented; for example, frequently occurring tones are weighted heavily. The statistical probabilities extracted by the network can also be used for predictive purposes: is it the case that listeners, when exposed initially to a novel musical composition and asked to predict the next tone in a sequence, predict the most frequent or probable tone? Given the distribution of activity across the time-based components, duration and accent, it is also possible to use the network to produce a time-based analogue of the tonal hierarchy. For example, the activation of the duration units during the initial training epochs imply that a quarter note is the most frequent and stable note length in the composition and could be compared with predictions of note length made by musically trained and untrained listeners when assigned a prediction task. Finally, based on the assumption that the composition used to train the network shares tonal properties with a large set of compositions, the mean activation of tone units is analogous to a probability distribution of tones in *any* C major composition (*schematic* information).

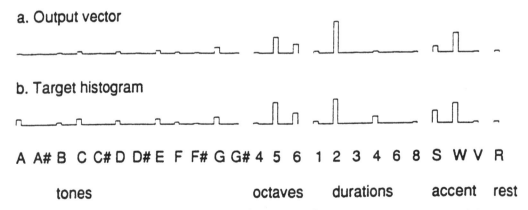

a. Output vector

b. Target histogram

A A# B C C# D D# E F F# G G# 4 5 6   1 2 3   4 6 8   S W V   R

tones   octaves   durations   accent   rest

Figure 1: Comparison of output vector for the first event at Epoch 4 (a) and a histogram of the target vector averaged over all events (b). The upper graph is the predicted output of Event 1 at Epoch 4 (from Figure 2, Block 3). The lower graph is a histogram of all the events in the piece, created by averaging all the target vectors. The comparison shows that the net learns initially to predict the mean target before learning the variations specific to each event.

The gradual development of the network's ability to predict accurately was gauged by i) applying a winner-take-all algorithm which converted the obtained output values to a "best guess"; and ii) playing the predicted musical events. Two different performances were produced. First, the *predicted melody* was recorded as the target component values were fed back into the network and second, the *generated melody* was produced as the activations output by the SRN were fed back to the net.

i)   **Predicted melody.**   In the initial training stages, Epochs 0 to 2, the net selected one or two notes at random and played them for the duration of a half-note or quarter-note. By Epoch 4, three different pitches sounded and were played with alternating strong and weak accents. By Epoch 8, the different note durations began to emerge so that a closer approximation to the correct rhythm was achieved. By Epoch 16, appropriate intervals, octaves and durations sounded although the pitches were incorrect. The 3/4 meter of the waltz was apparent in the produced accent pattern. Octave, duration and accent selections were accurate by Epoch 32, and by Epoch 64, the opening C-E-G interval and durational pattern had been correctly learned. The two opening phrases were learned and predicted correctly from Epoch 128 onwards although rests, rather than tones, were predicted erroneously at the end of the second phrase. The second section of the waltz was established by Epoch 128, and the first eight events of the melody, as predicted by the network at three different stages of training, are shown in Figure 2. The increasing similarity of the target vector and the activations predicted by the network illustrates the attunement of the network to the specific context of the musical event at each time step. In addition to noting those units which received the highest activation per time step (the "best guess"), the concomitant component activations can be regarded as tonal and metric expectancies [2,28,32]. Consider the prediction paradigm: the output of a musical event *y*, is the product of the input of the preceding musical event, *x*. Based on the statistical properties of the training set, certain events, such as tonalities, are induced or elicited by prior pitch and metric contexts. It would be informative to compare the output distributions of a network trained on a range of musical compositions with confidence ratings obtained from human subjects who had been asked to rate the appropriateness of particular "probe" tones or durations given a prior musical context [17,21]. Subjects' ratings could be obtained as a function of varying amounts of their exposure to the musical composition and compared with the distributions produced by the network at similar stages of training. If subjects are sensitive and responsive to the statistical regularities of the musical composition, a positive correlation between subjects' ratings and the output vectors of the network should be obtained.

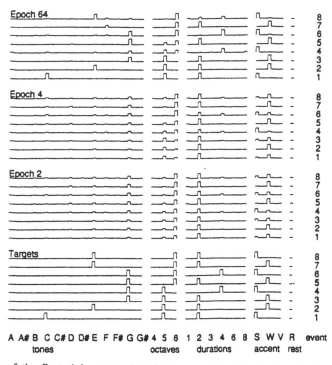

Figure 2: Evolution of the first eight events (predicted melody). The bottom block (targets) shows the correct sequence of events for the four components. In the next block (Epoch 2), the net is beginning to predict activation of strong and weak accents. In the next block (Epoch 4), the transition from one octave to another is evident. By the last block (Epoch 64), all four components are substantially correct.

231

In addition to expectancies induced within a single component such as tone, the sequence of output vectors also show evidence of interactions within and between pitch and timing components. For example, in the evolution of the first eight events illustrated in Figure 2, a long duration becomes locked with a strong accent by Epoch 64. The long duration and associated accent was elicited by three relatively short durations of strong, weak, weak accents. Here, prediction accuracy is maximised by combining information from components; particular tones, coupled with particular durations and accents invoke subsequent tones, durations and accents. This process is an example of *analysis-by-synthesis* [33], and constitutes one of the strengths of the network in that isolated component predictions are not required. Rather the network responds to implicit relations between and within components in the temporal unfolding of the composition.

ii)   **Generated melody.** In the generate condition, after one epoch of training, a note of a constant pitch was produced with an unchanging accent for the duration of a half-note. By Epoch 2, strong and weak accents alternated. While the opening interval sounded at Epoch 4, correct durations and pitches began to sound at Epoch 16. By Epoch 32, the C-E-G opening interval was detected and the duration and correct strong-weak-weak accent pattern began to emerge. By Epoch 128, the generated melody contained the correct durations, intervals and accents but, in place of the second phrase, contained a phrase which belonged to a later section of the composition.

Analysis of Network Errors

Network performance was also measured by calculating the total sum of squared error (TSS) at various stages of training, and the mean contribution of the four components to the TSS error are depicted in Figure 3. In the latter stages of training, the tone, duration and accent TSS errors were close to zero, and the small TSS values recorded at Epoch 128 corroborate the above description of the overall accuracy of the predicted melody.

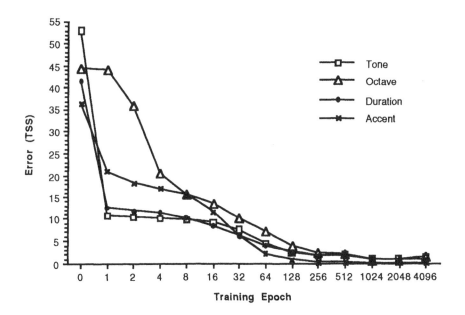

Figure 3:   Mean sum of squares error shown for each of the four music components as a function of amount of training. The mean was calculated by dividing the raw TSS value for each component by the number of associated output units.

The graph in Figure 4, depicts the number of unique patterns generated and predicted by the SRN. The unique patterns were calculated by counting the number of unique tone-octave-duration-accent combinations. The small number of unique patterns recorded during the initial stages of training reflects the initial redundancy and repetition of a single tone, duration, octave and accent, and suggests that, over time, the network response became attuned to the context of each musical event. Figure 4 also shows that,

232

although the maximum number of unique patterns relevant to each network differed, there was a comparable increase in the prediction and generation of unique patterns.

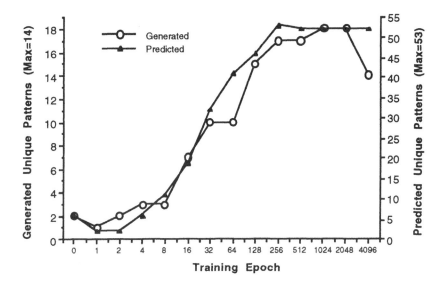

Figure 4: Number of unique patterns generated by the SRN where the obtained output was fed back, and predicted by the SRN where the target output was fed back. Predicted values were collated over the entire composition (maximum unique patterns = 53), whereas generated values were collated over 18 generated events (maximum unique patterns = 14).

CONCLUSIONS

The focus of the present study has been the extraction of information from the environment – the temporal stream of events representing *The Blue Danube* – and its incorporation into the atemporal parameters of the weights and biases in the network. The pitch and timing components of Western tonal music have been further divided into tone, octave, duration, and accent which can be regarded as a quasi-componential code. The distinguishing feature of a componential code is that each component can be viewed as systematic in its own right [9], and such codes are of benefit to learning systems in that they increase productivity: a small number of training examples can generalise to an exponential test set [4]. The way in which the present network learned transitions and relations between and within pitch and timing components suggests the possible existence of a componential code in Western tonal music. The course of learning in the network shows an increasing specificity of predicted events to the changing context: during the early stages of training, the default output or bias of the network is towards the average pattern of activation across the entire composition but, over time, predictions are refined and become attuned to the pattern of activation in particular contexts. The network responds according to the statistical regularities of the composition to which it has been exposed (*veridical* information) and, as these regularities characterise the larger set of tonal compositions, the mean activation of tone units can be regarded as a distribution of the relative frequency of tones in any C major composition (*schematic* information). Thus, the representation created by the network is reminiscent of the tonal hierarchy which reflects regularities of tonal music and has been shown to be responsible for a number of performance and memory effects observed in both musically trained and untrained listeners [19].

Based on the assumption that differing kinds of information in musical components give rise to different musical styles, the present results imply that the accent and duration components of a waltz take complementary roles in regulating rhythm. From the durations of events alone, the position of a note in a bar could be predicted without error. However, if the performer or the listener made a single error of duration, a rhythm system based on durations alone could not recover. By contrast, accent is not a completely reliable predictor of the bar structure, but is effective for recovery from rhythmic errors. The interaction between these two timing components provides an efficient error-correcting representation for the rhythmic aspect of the system, and it is likely that other musical styles have similar regulatory functions performed by different components. Consider the use of ornaments, such as trills and mordents, in Baroque harpsichord music which, in the absence of variations in dynamics, help to signify the beat and metric structure. Alternatively, [13] has emphasized the interaction of pitch and timing components evident in the placement of harmonically-important tones at accented positions in a bar.

Directions for Further Research

The predictive musical network is the first stage in the development of an integrated model of music cognition. Currently, the efficacy of the acquired representation is being explored. The framework within which the study is couched assumes that higher-order mechanisms of music cognition may involve memory processes which utilize the kinds of representations constructed in the present network [39]. As mentioned, a probe-tone study is planned to measure subjects' ratings of the appropriateness or expectancy associated with tones and durations in specific contexts, after varying amounts of exposure to a novel composition. It is hypothesized that if the subjects are sensitive to the statistical regularities of the musical sequence, then their ratings and the output vector distributions of the network will be positively correlated. Tests of the generalization of the present results also await completion. Validation of the present findings will consist of the training and analysis of a schematic rather than instance-based network, wherein the network has been exposed to a large set of tonal compositions.

Acknowledgments

This research was supported by an Australian Research Council Postdoctoral Fellowship granted to the first author and equipment and travel funds to both authors from the Departments of Psychology and Computer Science, University of Queensland. The authors wish to thank Michael Mozer for comments on an earlier draft of the paper and for providing the musical database which was adapted and used in the present simulation. The modification to McClelland & Rumelhart's [26] *bp* program, *bp.extra*, was developed by Paul Bakker, Departments of Computer Science and Psychology, University of Queensland. The suggestions made by members of the Connectionist Research Group at the University of Queensland and Cyril Latimer at the University of Sydney are also gratefully acknowledged.

References

[1]   R. Alpaydin, "Connectionist approach to improvisation using fingering pattern association," presented at the Second International Conference on Music Perception and Cognition, University of California, Los Angeles, February 22-26, 1992.

[2]   J. J. Bharucha, "Tonality and learnability," in M. R. Jones & S. Holleran (Eds.), *Cognitive Bases of Musical Communication*, Washington: American Psychological Association, 1992, pp. 213-223.

[3]   J. J. Bharucha and P. M. Todd, "Modeling the perception of tonal structure with neural nets," *Computer Music Journal*, vol. 13, pp. 44-53, 1989.

[4]   O. Brousse and P. Smolensky, "Virtual memories and massive generalization in connectionist combinatorial learning," in *Proceedings of the 11th Annual Conference of the Cognitive Science Society*, Hillsdale, NJ: Lawrence Erlbaum, 1989, pp. 380-387.

[5]   D. Deutsch, "The processing of structured and unstructured tonal sequences," *Perception & Psychophysics*, vol. 28, pp. 381-389, 1980.

[6]   W. J. Dowling, "Scale and contour: Two components of a theory of memory for melodies," *Psychological Review*, vol. 85, pp. 341-354, 1978.

[7]   J. L. Elman, *Structured Representations and Connectionist Models* (CRL Tech. Rep. No. 8901), San Diego: University of California, Center for Research in Language, 1989.

[8]   J. L. Elman and D. Zipser, "Discovering the hidden structure of speech," *Journal of the Acoustical Society of America*, vol. 83, pp. 1615-1626, 1988.

[9]   J. A. Fodor and Z. W. Pylyshyn, "Connectionism and cognitive architecture: A critical analysis," *Cognition*, vol. 28, pp. 3-71, 1988.

[10]   R. O. Gjerdingen, "Categorization of musical patterns by self-organizing neuronlike networks," *Music Perception*, vol. 7, pp. 339-370, 1990.

[11]   H. Hild, J. Feulner and W. Menzel, "HARMONET: A neural net for harmonizing chorales in the style of J. S. Bach," in J. E. Moody, S. J. Hanson & R. Lippmann (Eds.), *Advances in Neural Information Processing Systems 4*, San Mateo, CA.: Morgan Kaufmann, 1992, pp. 267-274.

[12]   M. R. Jones, "Time, our lost dimension: Toward a new theory of perception, attention, and memory," *Psychological Review*, vol. 83, pp. 323-355, 1976.

[13]   M. R. Jones, "Attending to musical events, " in M. R. Jones & S. Holleran (Eds.), *Cognitive Bases of Musical Communication,* Washington: American Psychological Association, 1992, pp. 91-110.

[14]   M. R. Jones, M. Boltz, and G. Kidd, "Controlled attending as a function of melodic and temporal context," *Perception & Psychophysics,* vol. 32, pp. 211-218, 1982.

[15]   M. R. Jones and J. T. Ralston, "Some influences of accent structure on melody recognition," *Memory & Cognition,* vol. 19, pp. 8-20, 1991.

[16]   M. I. Jordan, *Serial Order: A Parallel Distributed Processing Approach* (Tech. Rep. No. 8604), San Diego: University of California, Institute for Cognitive Science, 1986.

[17]   C. L. Krumhansl, "The psychological representation of musical pitch in a tonal context," *Cognitive Psychology,* vol. 11, pp. 346-374, 1979.

[18]   C. L. Krumhansl, "Perceptual structures for tonal music," *Music Perception,* vol. 1, pp. 28-62, 1983.

[19]   C. L. Krumhansl, *Cognitive Foundations of Musical Pitch,* Oxford: Oxford University Press, 1990.

[20]   C. L. Krumhansl, "Music psychology: Tonal structures in perception and memory," *Annual Review of Psychology,* vol. 42, pp. 277-303, 1991.

[21]   C. L. Krumhansl and M. A. Castellano, "Dynamic processes in music perception," *Memory & Cognition,* vol. 11, pp. 325-334, 1983.

[22]   C. Krumhansl and R. N. Shepard, "Quantification of the hierarchy of tonal functions within a diatonic context," *Journal of Experimental Psychology: Human Perception & Performance,* vol. 5, pp. 579-594, 1979.

[23]   B. Laden, B. and D. H. Keefe, "The representation of pitch in a neural net model of chord classification," *Computer Music Journal,* vol. 13, pp. 12-26, 1989.

[24]   K. J. Lang, A. H. Waibel and G. E. Hinton, "A time-delay neural network architecture for isolated word recognition," *Neural Networks,* vol. 3, pp. 23-43, 1990.

[25]   C. Linster, "Rhythm analysis with back-propagation," in R. Pfeifer, Z. Schreter, F. Fogelman-Soulie, L. Steels (Eds.), *Connectionism in Perspective,* North-Holland: Elsevier Science, 1989, pp. 385-393.

[26]   J. L. McClelland and R. E. Rumelhart, *Explorations in Parallel Distributed Processing: A Handbook of Models, Programs and Exercises,* Cambridge, Mass.: MIT Press, 1989.

[27]   D. W. Massaro, H. J. Kallman and J. L. Kelly, "The role of tone height, melodic contour, and tone chroma in melody recognition," *Journal of Experimental Psychology: Human Learning & Memory,* vol. 6, pp. 77-90, 1980.

[28]   L. B. Meyer, *Emotion and Meaning in Music,* Chicago: University of Chicago Press, 1956.

[29]   C. B. Monahan and E. C. Carterette, "Pitch and duration as determinants of musical space," *Music Perception,* vol. 3, pp. 1-32, 1985.

[30]   C. B. Monahan, R. A. Kendall and E. C. Carterette, "The effect of melodic and temporal contour on recognition memory for pitch change," *Perception & Psychophysics,* vol. 41, pp. 576-600, 1987.

[31]   M. C. Mozer and T. Soukup, "Connectionist music composition based on melodic and stylistic constraints," in R. P. Lippmann, J. E. Moody, & D. S. Touretzky (Eds.), *Advances in Neural Information Processing Systems 3,* San Mateo, CA.: Morgan Kaufmann, 1991, pp. 789-796.

[32]   E. Narmour, *The Analysis and Cognition of Basic Melodic Structures,* Chicago: University of Chicago Press, 1990.

[33]   U. Neisser, *Cognitive Psychology,* New York: Appleton-Century-Crofts, 1967.

[34]   C. Palmer and C. L. Krumhansl, "Mental representations for musical meter," *Journal of Experimental Psychology: Human Perception and Performance,* vol. 16, pp. 728-741, 1990.

[35]   D. Rosenthal, "Emulation of human rhythm perception," *Computer Music Journal,* vol. 16, pp. 64-76, 1992.

[36]   H. Sano and B. K. Jenkins, "A neural net model for pitch perception," *Computer Music Journal,* vol. 13, pp. 41-48, 1989.

[37]   S. Sayegh, "Fingering for string instruments with the optimum path paradigm," *Computer Music Journal,* vol. 13, pp. 76-84, 1989.

[38]   M. J. Steedman, "The perception of musical rhythm and metre," *Perception,* vol. 6, pp. 555-569, 1977.

[39]   C. Stevens, *Derivation and Investigation of Features Mediating Musical Pattern Recognition,* Unpublished doctoral dissertation, University of Sydney, 1992.

[40]   C. Stevens and C. Latimer, "A comparison of connectionist models of music recognition and human performance," *Minds and Machines,* vol. 2, pp. 379-400, 1992.

[41]   P. M. Todd, "A connectionist approach to algorithmic composition," *Computer Music Journal,* vol. 13, pp. 27-43, 1989.

235

Applications of Radial Basis Function fitting to the analysis of dynamical systems

Michael A. S. Potts

Aston University

Aston Triangle, Birmingham B4 7ET, UK.

pottsmas@cs.aston.ac.uk

D. S. Broomhead and J. P. Huke

DRA at RSRE Malvern

St. Andrews Road, Malvern, Worcestershire WR14 3PS, UK.

dsb@hermes.mod.uk

We review some preliminary results in fitting maps between dynamical systems constructed by embedding experimental time series. We describe two applications of the Radial Basis Function (RBF) network trained with Least Squares error minimisation: in iteratively predicting a time series by modelling its generating dynamics; and, combined with a linear filter, in separating nonlinear noise from a corrupted signal. We then discuss a symmetrical modification of the RBF network trained with Total Least Squares error minimisation, and its application in testing for differentiable equivalence between embedded systems.

1 Introduction

An increasing number of important and interesting phenomena in the physical sciences are turning out to be highly nonlinear. Recent advances in the theory of nonlinear dynamics have led to the development of embedding techniques for the analysis of time series obtained from such systems (section 2). These techniques reconstruct experimental systems up to a diffeomorphism. This paper presents some preliminary results in fitting nonlinear maps between embedded systems. Such maps may be used to recover dynamical information about the system, or to investigate the differentiable equivalence between systems. To construct these maps we concentrate on the Radial Basis Function (RBF) network, viewed as the composition of an adaptive linear map with a fixed nonlinear transformation. In its traditional form the RBF network is trained by Least Squares error minimisation (section 3) to produce a good forward fit without regard to the existence of its inverse. We apply this map to the problem of iteratively predicting a chaotic time series in section 4. In section 5 we use a linear filter, together with the RBF network, to perform a nonlinear filtering operation on a time series corrupted by chaotic noise. A modification of the adaptive part of the RBF network to Total Least Squares error minimisation (section 6) allows us to construct maps which we use to test for differentiable equivalence between embeddings (section 7). Finally, we present out conclusions in section 8.

236

2 Embedding Dynamical Systems

We are concerned with discrete time dynamical systems defined in a phase space $\mathcal{S}$ by a diffeomorphism (a smooth map with a smooth inverse) $\vartheta\colon \mathcal{S} \to \mathcal{S}$. The state ξ_i is determined, for some starting point $\xi_0 \in \mathcal{S}$, by $\xi_i = \vartheta^i(\xi_0)$. In particular we consider only dissipative systems where trajectories evolve asymptotically towards an attractor contained in an m-dimensional manifold $\mathcal{M} \subset \mathcal{S}$. In practice we often cannot measure ξ_i directly, and are restricted to sampling a (nonlinear) measurement function $v\colon \mathcal{M} \to \mathbb{R}$ whose values $v_i = v(\xi_i)$ form the time series $\{v_0, v_1, \ldots\}$.

We can make use of the dynamical information contained in the time series by constructing 'Takens' vectors $x_i \in \mathbb{R}^n$ by the method of delays so that $x_i = (v_i, v_{i-1}, \ldots, v_{i-(n-1)})^\mathsf{T}$. Takens [8] has shown that, in the absence of noise, this action generically defines an embedding $\Omega\colon \mathcal{M} \to \mathbb{R}^n$ if $n \geq 2m + 1$, although in practice there may be problems with under- or over-sampling. This map provides us with a diffeomorphic copy of $\mathcal{M}$ in $\mathbb{R}^n$, on which is induced a dynamical system $\psi = \Omega \circ \vartheta \circ \Omega^{-1}$. We can also work with noisy time series: following Broomhead and King [1] we define a matrix $X \in \mathbb{R}^{N \times n}$ with N row vectors x_i^T. We can then define the rank-r ($r \leq n$) truncated Singular Value Decomposition (SVD) of X by

$$XV_r = U_r \Sigma_r \tag{2.1}$$

where the columns of $V_r \in \mathbb{R}^{n \times r}$ and $U_r \in \mathbb{R}^{N \times r}$ are the first r principal components of the rows and columns, respectively, of X, and $\Sigma_r = \mathrm{diag}(\sigma_1, \ldots, \sigma_r)$ is a matrix of corresponding singular values. We determine the rank r by an estimate of the noise level in $\mathbb{R}^n$, and then work with the projection of the x_i onto the columns of V_r.

3 The Least Squares RBF Map

A key element of this work is the ability to fit a nonlinear transformation $y = f(x)$ between embedding spaces or time series with an adaptive map $\hat{y} = s(x)$. We concentrate on the Radial Basis Function (RBF) network [2][10] $s\colon \mathbb{R}^n \to \mathbb{R}^d$ defined as

$$s(x) = W^\mathsf{T} \varphi(x) \tag{3.1}$$

where $W \in \mathbb{R}^{p \times d}$ is an adaptive weight matrix and $\varphi\colon \mathbb{R}^n \to \mathbb{R}^p$ is a fixed nonlinear function of the distances from a given vector $x \in \mathbb{R}^n$ to a set of p 'centers' $\tilde{x}_j \in \mathbb{R}^n$, defined by $\varphi_j(x) = \phi(\|x - \tilde{x}_j\|_2)$. The nonlinearity $\phi\colon \mathbb{R}^+ \to \mathbb{R}$ we shall take to be monotonic; for a smooth fit the derivative of ϕ must vanish at the origin. We find that the cubic $\phi(x) = x^3$ to be useful: it does not require the choice of any additional parameters, and avoids the artifacts which can arise with rapidly decaying functions. The last word on choosing the centers for RBF approximation has yet to be said; here, we position the centers on an n-dimensional grid contained in a box which bounds the data. The reasons for this are twofold: firstly, if the centers are allowed to cluster, the data matrix Φ (see below) may become ill-conditioned; and secondly, it reduces so-called edge effects, where the quality of the fit degrades towards the boundaries of the data. Such grids, however, become less useful as n increases.

The Least Squares (LS) training procedure consists of fitting a hyperplane $\mathcal{H}_{\mathrm{LS}}$ to a collection of N points $z_i^\mathsf{T} = (\varphi_i^\mathsf{T}, y_i^\mathsf{T})$, where $\varphi_i = \varphi(x_i)$, in the product space $\mathbb{R}^{M=p+d}$ by minimising the error

$$\epsilon_{\mathrm{LS}}^2 = \sum_{i=1}^{N} \|z_i - \pi_{\mathrm{LS}}(z_i)\|_2^2$$

where $\pi_{\mathrm{LS}} \colon \mathbb{R}^M \to \mathcal{H}_{\mathrm{LS}} \subset \mathbb{R}^M$ projects the z_i into $\mathcal{H}_{\mathrm{LS}}$. The LS projection is defined by $\pi_{\mathrm{LS}}(z_i) = (\varphi_i^{\mathrm{T}}, \hat{y}_i^{\mathrm{T}})^{\mathrm{T}}$, and the error reduces to

$$\epsilon_{\mathrm{LS}}^2 = \sum_{i=1}^{N} \|y_i - \hat{y}_i\|_2^2 = \|Y - \hat{Y}\|_{\mathrm{F}}^2$$

where we have defined matrices $Y, \hat{Y} \in \mathbb{R}^{N \times d}$ with rows y_i^{T} and $\hat{y}_i^{\mathrm{T}}$, respectively, and similarly $\Phi \in \mathbb{R}^{N \times p}$ with rows φ_i^{T}, and can therefore write $\hat{Y} = \Phi W$. This error is a minimum for $\hat{Y} = U_r U_r^{\mathrm{T}} Y$, where $U_r \in \mathbb{R}^{N \times r}$ is the matrix of left singular vectors obtained from the rank-r SVD of Φ, by analogy with (2.1). The LS solution is then $W = V_r \Sigma_r^{-1} U_r^{\mathrm{T}} Y = \Phi_r^{\dagger} Y$, where $\Phi_r^{\dagger}$ is the rank-r pseudo-inverse of Φ. The rank can be varied to prevent over-fitting by reducing the number of degrees of freedom embodied by the network in a systematic manner. If Φ is rank deficient, the solution is not unique – matrices whose column vectors are in the kernel of Φ can be added to W without changing the error – but the pseudo-inverse selects the W with smallest Frobenius norm. The LS solution can be shown to be optimal when each component of the y_i is corrupted by independent, identically distributed (IID) gaussian noise but the x_i and hence φ_i are noise-free.

4 Iterative Prediction of Time Series

Having created an embedded dynamical system from an experimental time series, we might wish to build a model with which to predict that time series – indeed, there has been considerable recent interest in this problem. The dynamical systems approach to prediction is based on the fact that if we can embed the system in $\mathbb{R}^n$ then clearly we must also be able to embed it in $\mathbb{R}^{n+1}$, in which case $v_{i+1} = f(x_i)$ must be a smooth function. We can therefore approximate f with the LS RBF map $s \colon \mathbb{R}^n \to \mathbb{R}$, where $s(x_i) = \hat{v}_{i+1}$. This map is a one-step predictor for the time series, which we can iterate to give a predicted trajectory $\{\hat{x}_1, \hat{x}_2, \ldots\}$, and hence an approximator $\hat{\psi}$ for the embedded dynamics [9].

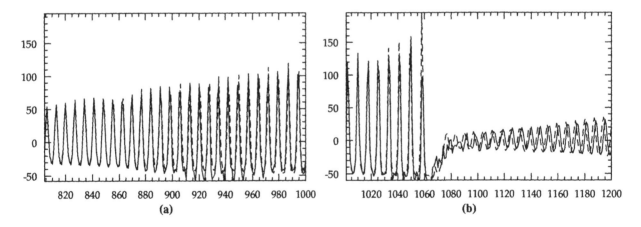

Figure 4.1 Time series v_i (dashed) and predictions $\hat{v}_i$ (solid): **(a)** between collapses; **(b)** during a collapse.

Figure 4.1 shows the application of this technique to a chaotic time series – 'a.dat' – released for the Santa Fe time series prediction competition. These results are to illustrate the general approach – no real attempt has been made to fine-tune the network parameters – for a more detailed description of the time series, and an RBF approach to fitting

238

it, see [11]. We reconstructed the system in a four dimensional principal component subspace of $\mathbb{R}^{50}$ and the network used a lattice of 144 centers, although the pseudo-inverse was restricted to a rank of 128 to avoid over-fitting. The time series exhibits two distinct time scales: a high frequency oscillation within an envelope of gradually increasing amplitude with occasional collapses. The figures show iterative predictions for out-of-sample portions of the data. In figure 4.1(a) the data v_i and predictions $\hat{v}_i$ are shown for a portion between collapses, and in figure 4.1(b) they are shown during a collapse which was the subject of the prediction competition for this data set.

5 Extracting Signals from Chaos

An interesting application of the embedding technique arises in the separation of signals from noise which has a chaotic component [4]. Existing work (see for example [5] or [12]) relies directly on nonlinear predictors, as in section 4. However, since these models do not depend linearly on their inputs, the predicted values of the chaotic component depend sensitively on the signal. The usual approach has therefore been to consider only small signals, and to proceed through Taylor expansion. We have developed an alternative approach which does not require the small signal assumption, instead assuming some prior knowledge about the spectrum of the signal to be extracted.

We write $v_i = v_i^{(s)} + v_i^{(c)}$, for the composite time series of signal and chaos, respectively, assuming any stochastic noise to be incorporated into the signal component for convenience. Given some limited knowledge of the signal's spectral characteristics we can construct a Finite Impulse Response (FIR) filter which will pass as little of the signal as possible. Chaotic processes are generally observed to have broadband power spectra, so by applying this filter to the composite time series we expect to largely eliminate the frequencies present in the signal, leaving just filtered chaos.

The FIR filtered time series is written

$$u_i = \sum_{j=1}^{L} a_j v_{i-(j-1)}$$

for L finite, which has the form of a scalar product of Takens vectors in $\mathbb{R}^L$ with a fixed vector $a \in \mathbb{R}^L$. It follows [3] that Takens vectors $x_i \in \mathbb{R}^n$ constructed from the *filtered* time series u_i generically constitute an embedding of the original system for large enough n. As in section 4 the map $v_{i+\delta}^{(c)} = f(x_i)$ is therefore a smooth function (written more generally with offset $\delta \in \mathbb{Z}$) so we can fit it with a LS RBF map $s : \mathbb{R}^n \to \mathbb{R}$. In constructing this map there are two cases to consider: (1) if we can obtain a portion of time series with zero signal component, ie. $v_i = v_i^{(c)}$, then we can fit it directly; (2) if not, then we simply fit to the composite time series, and rely on the lack of correlation between chaos and signal to average out the latter in the limit of a large training set. Either way, we obtain the reconstructed chaotic component as $\hat{v}_{i+\delta}^{(c)} = s(x_i)$. The signal component is obtained as $\hat{v}_{i+\delta}^{(s)} = v_{i+\delta} - \hat{v}_{i+\delta}^{(c)}$. As we are no longer relying on s to predict the time series directly, we are free to choose δ so as to provide the 'easiest' fit. In the absence of stochastic noise this will typically be $\delta = 0$, but if noise is present, we may have to increase δ in order to avoid correlation due to the effect of FIR filtering on the noise itself.

To illustrate this technique we created a composite time series comprising a signal part in the form of a sparsely sampled sine wave, $\{\ldots, 0.4, 0.4, -0.4, -0.4, \ldots\}$, of period 4 and amplitude 0.4, and a chaotic part generated by the x-component of the Ikeda map [7], defined by

$$x_{i+1} = 1 - \mu(x_i \cos\theta - y_i \sin\theta)$$
$$y_{i+1} = \mu(x_i \sin\theta + y_i \cos\theta)$$

239

with $\theta = 0.4 - 6/(1 + x_i^2 + y_i^2)$ and $\mu = 0.7$, which has a standard deviation of approximately 0.2. In this somewhat idealised instance the FIR filter $u_i = (3v_i + v_{i-1} + 3v_{i-2} + v_{i-3})/8$ is able to completely remove the single frequency of the signal component, although in general this would clearly not be the case. With the filtered time series providing an embedding of the system in $\mathbb{R}^3$ we used a lattice of 125 centers to fit the LS RBF map $\hat{v}_i^{(c)} = s(x_i)$ with zero offset.

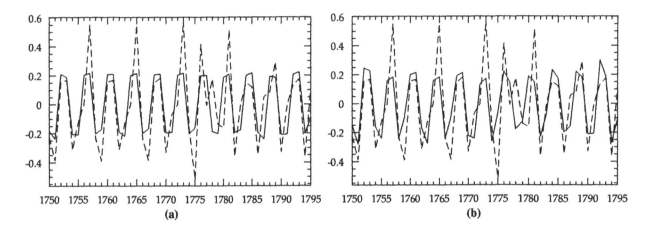

Figure 5.1 Composite time series v_i (dashed) plotted with reconstructed signal $\hat{v}_i^{(s)}$ obtained by fitting with: **(a)** zero signal component (case 1); **(b)** non-zero signal component (case 2).

Figures 5.1(a) and (b) show the composite time series v_i overlayed on the reconstructed signal component $\hat{v}_i^{(s)}$ for cases (1) and (2), respectively. We see from these figures that the signal component has been successfully extracted from a chaotic background of comparable magnitude – that is, in a regime where the Taylor expansion method would not be applicable – although the more challenging fit in figure 5.1(b) clearly suffers from a lack of training data. We are currently applying this techinque to the extraction of more complicated signals.

6 The Total Least Squares RBF Map

As it specifically minimises a fitting error in the codomain, the LS RBF is suited to problems in which a good fit is required without regard to the existence of its inverse: in sections 4 and 5, for example. However, we may also be interested in capturing a linear relationship in $\mathbb{R}^M$ without preferring one direction of fit over the other. In this case, we modify the RBF network by adopting a simplified form of the Total Least Squares (TLS) error minimisation method [13]. Defining the matrix $Z \in \mathbb{R}^{M \times N}$ with rows z_i^T, we find the matrix of principal components $V_r \in \mathbb{R}^{M \times r}$ from its rank-r SVD, by analogy with (2.1). Then the approximating hyperplane $\mathcal{H}_{TLS}$ is defined by $\pi_{TLS} = V_r V_r^T$, which projects the z_i orthogonally onto $\mathcal{H}_{TLS}$. The training error is thus

$$\epsilon_{TLS}^2 = \sum_{i=1}^N \|z_i - \pi_{TLS}(z_i)\|_2^2 = \sum_{i=1}^N \|z_i - V_r V_r^T z_i\|_2^2 = \sum_{i=1}^N \|\bar{V}_r \bar{V}_r^T z_i\|_2^2$$

where $\bar{V}_r \in \mathbb{R}^{M \times r'}$ is the matrix of $r' = M - r$ prinipal components spanning the orthogonal complement of $\mathcal{H}_{TLS}$ in $\mathbb{R}^M$. Since $\bar{V}^T z = 0$ for $z \in \mathcal{H}_{TLS}$ we make the partition $\bar{V}_r^T = (P_x^T, P_y^T)$, where $P_x \in \mathbb{R}^{p \times r'}$ and $P_y \in \mathbb{R}^{d \times r'}$, and write

$$P_y^T y = -P_x^T \varphi(x) \qquad (6.1)$$

Then the forward fit exists, and is given by $W = -P_x P_y^{-1}$, if $r = p$ and P_y^{-1} exists. Similarly, but not so usefully in this context, the inverse exists, and is given by $W^{-1} = -P_y P_x^{-1}$, if $r = d$ and P_x^{-1} exists. The existence of a fit in a particular direction is thus driven by the data itself, rather than by an in-built preference for that direction as in the LS model. The TLS RBF is a natural solution for problems in which both the x_i and y_i are corrupted by IID noise, although we note that the isotropy of the noise in an embedding space is broken under the action of φ.

7 Testing for Equivalence

We are currently investigating the use of the TLS RBF network to look for differentiable equivalence [6] between embedded systems. A linear relationship is a diffeomorphism if it is invertible, so a TLS fit between x and y,

$$P_y^T y = -P_x^T x$$

is a diffeomorphism if both P_x and P_y are invertible matrices.

We have already described RBF models as a composition of a fixed nonlinear map with an adaptive linear map, and demonstrated the usefulness of this simple arrangement. It can be shown that under rather weak assumptions the nonlinear map is an embedding of compact manifolds (the proof, however, is beyond the scope of this brief note). We therefore have extended the RBF model by incorporating a second nonlinear transformation $\varphi_y \colon \mathbb{R}^d \to \mathbb{R}^p$. With this class of 'symmetric' models we fit a linear relationship between data in the form $(\varphi_x(x), \varphi_y(y))$. TLS is a natural choice of fitting procedure, and results in a model of the form $P_y^T \varphi_y(y) = -P_x^T \varphi_x(x)$. By construction, P_x and P_y are square ($p \times p$) matrices. Thus, the forward map

$$s(x) = -\varphi_y^{-1} \circ \left(P_y^{-1} \right)^T \circ P_x^T \circ \varphi_x(x) \qquad (7.1)$$

now exists if P_y is invertible, and its inverse

$$s^{-1}(y) = -\varphi_x^{-1} \circ \left(P_x^{-1} \right)^T \circ P_y^T \circ \varphi_y(y) \qquad (7.2)$$

exists if P_x is invertible. A convenient way to test for differentiable equivalence is to examine the condition numbers (ratio of the highest to lowest singular values) of P_x and P_y.

We illustrate this approach with the following problem. Consider a non-planar circle $\mathcal{C}$ embedded in $\mathbb{R}^3$. The projections of $\mathcal{C}$ into $\mathbb{R}^2$ have three possible forms: (1) the projection may be an embedding of $\mathcal{C}$, (2) the image of $\mathcal{C}$ may have one or more self-intersections and (3) the image of $\mathcal{C}$ may have a cusp. In cases (2) and (3) the projection is not a diffeomorphism – case (3) is rather special, and may be thought of as transitional between cases (1) and (2). We looked at a family of projections, parameterised by an angle α, spanning these three cases. For convenience we shall call the resulting projected circles $\mathcal{C}_\alpha$, and note that $\mathcal{C}_0$ is a perfect circle, $\mathcal{C}_{25}$ has a cusp, and $\mathcal{C}_{\alpha > 25}$ all resemble a 'figure-of-eight'.

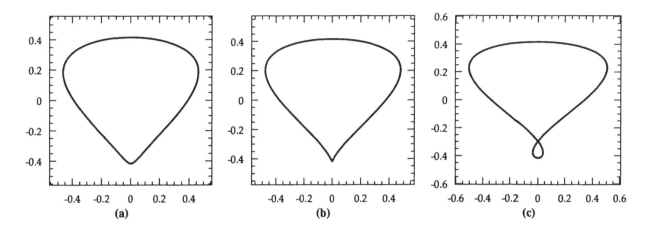

Figure 7.1 Fitting the map $s: \mathcal{C}_0 \rightarrow \mathcal{C}_\alpha$ for the three cases. Image $s(\mathcal{C}_0)$ (dots) plotted with (solid):
(a) $\mathcal{C}_{20}$; (b) $\mathcal{C}_{25}$; (c) $\mathcal{C}_{35}$.

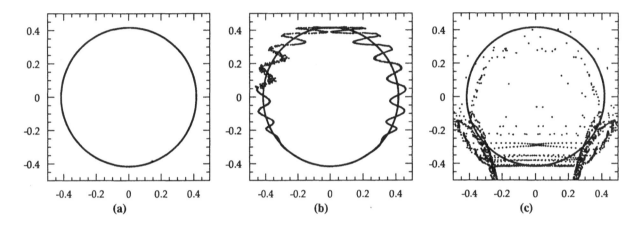

Figure 7.2 Fitting the inverse $s^{-1}: \mathcal{C}_\alpha \rightarrow \mathcal{C}_0$ for the three cases. $\mathcal{C}_0$ (solid) plotted with image
(dots): (a) $s^{-1}(\mathcal{C}_{20})$; (b) $s^{-1}(\mathcal{C}_{25})$; (c) $s^{-1}(\mathcal{C}_{35})$.

Figures 7.1 and 7.2 show the result of fitting symmetric TLS RBF maps $s: \mathcal{C}_0 \leftrightarrow \mathcal{C}_\alpha$ between $\mathcal{C}_0$ and a selection of other projections, using a lattice of 36 centers in each space. Each plot in figure 7.1 shows $\mathcal{C}_\alpha$ and $s(\mathcal{C}_0)$, while the corresponding plots in figure 7.2 show $\mathcal{C}_0$ and $s^{-1}(\mathcal{C}_\alpha)$. In all three cases shown in figure 7.1, $s(\mathcal{C}_0)$ is indistinguishable from $\mathcal{C}_\alpha$. This is clearly not the case for the corresponding plots in figure 7.2. In figure 7.2(a) the image $s^{-1}(\mathcal{C}_{20})$ is indistinguishable from $\mathcal{C}_0$. It is clear, therefore, that the symmetric TLS RBF map has found a diffeomorphism between $\mathcal{C}_0$ and $\mathcal{C}_{20}$. In the opposite extreme, figure 7.2(c) shows a poor correspondence between $s^{-1}(\mathcal{C}_{35})$ and $\mathcal{C}_0$. In this case, the symmetric TLS RBF network produces an accurate representation of the many-to-one map $\mathcal{C}_0 \rightarrow \mathcal{C}_{35}$. The relationship $\mathcal{C}_{35} \rightarrow \mathcal{C}_0$, however, is one-to-many and this is reflected in the scatter of points shown in figure 7.2(c). We observe in figure 7.2(b) an interesting transition between these two cases.

A summary of these results for a larger number of examples is given in figures 7.3(a) and (b), which show the out-of-sample error (labelled with triangles) plotted against $\sin \alpha$, for s and s^{-1}, respectively. The onset of self-intersection in $\mathcal{C}_\alpha$ is marked by a sharp increase in the error in figure 7.3(b).

The error plotted in these figures is not the error minimised by the TLS algorithm, since it is calculated in the image

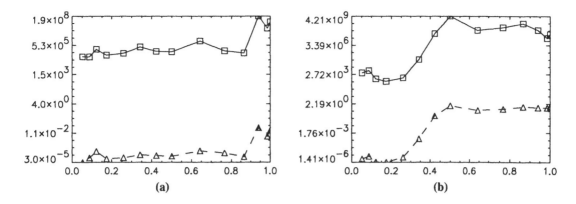

Figure 7.3 Out-of-sample test error calculated in image space (dashed/triangles) and condition number (solid/squares) for: (a) forward fit; (b) inverse fit.

space and uses one of the explicit forms in (7.1) and (7.2). Also shown in figures 7.3(a) and (b) (labelled with squares) are plots of the condition number of the weight matrices P_y and P_x, respectively. The close resemblance between the error and condition number plots indicates that the large increase in errors is connected with the ill-conditioned inverse of P_x, and hence that the explicit inverse given by (7.2) is meaningless in these cases. The practical implication of this is that the condition numbers of P_x and P_y obtained from a symmetric TLS RBF fit of data can be used to test whether or not the data is related by a diffeomorphism. In particular, since we know by construction that C_0 is embedded in $\mathbb{R}^2$, we can deduce from the condition number of P_x whether or not a given C_α is also embedded.

We hope to apply this technique to the comparison of time series. Do two time series of measurements made on a spatially extended system, for example, contain different dynamical information? Or given two different ways of observing the same system, for example two probes which respond on different time scales, does one convey information not present in the other? A specific example, which we are currently examining, is the determination of a minimum embedding dimension for time series.

8 Conclusions

We have examined the problem of fitting relationships between embedded systems. The traditional LS RBF map has been found to be appropriate for producing a fit in a particular direction, without regard to the condition of its inverse. As it explicitly minimises an error in its image space, such a map has been used to construct an iterative predictor for chaotic time series. It has also been applied, in conjunction with a linear filter, to the problem of separating a signal from nonlinear noise. The TLS RBF map, in symmetric form, is naturally suited to fitting diffeomorphisms, and has been applied to a series of curves to determine whether or not they are embedded in the plane.

Acknowledgments

We would like to thank Geoff de Villiers and Ian Proudler for many useful discussions.

References

[1] D. S. Broomhead and G. P. King, "Extracting qualitative dynamics from experimental data", *Physica D* **20** (1986) 217–236.

[2] D. S. Broomhead and D. Lowe, "Multivariable functional interpolation and adaptive networks", *Complex Systems* **2** (1988) 321–355.

[3] D. S. Broomhead, J. P. Huke and M. R. Muldoon, "Linear filters and non-linear systems", *J. R. Statist. Soc. B* **54** 2 (1992) 373–382.

[4] D. S. Broomhead, J. P. Huke and M. A. S. Potts, "Nonlinear noise removal", *in preparation*.

[5] J. D. Farmer and J. J. Sidorowich, "Exploiting chaos to predict the future and reduce noise", in *Evolution, Learning and Cognition, Y. C. Lee, Editor*, World Scientific, Singapore (1988).

[6] J. Guckenheimer and P. Holmes, "Nonlinear oscillations, dynamical systems, and bifurcations of vector fields", *Applied Mathematical Sciences* **42**, Springer-Verlag, New York (1983).

[7] K. Ikeda, "Multiple-valued stationary state and its instability of the transmitted light by a ring cavity system", *Opt. Commun.* **30** (1979) 257.

[8] F. Takens, "Detecting strange attractors in turbulence", Dynamical Systems and Turbulence, *Lecture Notes in Mathematics* **898**, Springer, Berlin (1981) 366–381.

[9] M. A. S. Potts and D. S. Broomhead, "Time series prediction with a Radial Basis Function neural network", in *Adaptive Signal Processing, Simon Haykin, Editor, Proc. SPIE* **1565** (1991) 255–266.

[10] M. J. D. Powell, "The theory of Radial Basis Function approximation in 1990", *DAMTP 1990/NA11* (1990)

[11] L. Smith, "Forced chaos", in *Time Series Prediction: Forecasting the Future and Understanding the Past, A. S. Weigend and N. A. Gershenfeld, Editors*, Addison-Wesley (1993).

[12] J. Stark and B. V. Arumugam, "Extracting slowly varying signals from a chaotic background", *Int. J. Bif. Chaos* **2** (1992) 413–419.

[13] S. Van Huffel and J. Vandewalle, "The Total Least Squares Problem: Computational Aspects and Analysis", *Frontiers in Applied Mathematics* **9**, SIAM (1991).

Event Prediction: Faster Learning in a Layered Hebbian Network with Memory

Michael E. Young
Dept. of Psychology
University of Minnesota
317 Elliott Hall
Minneapolis, MN 55455
young@turtle.psych.umn.edu

Todd M. Bailey
Dept. of Linguistics
University of Minnesota
142 Klaeber Court
Minneapolis, MN 55455
todd@turtle.psych.umn.edu

This paper describes a connectionist architecture designed to learn temporal relationships between input events in a relatively small number of training trials, and presents results of simulations applying the network to an A→B+ vs. B- serial conditioning task. The proposed architecture employs a cascade of hidden layers with memory which feed into a single output layer. The hidden layers were trained using unsupervised Hebbian learning while the output layer was trained using supervised gradient descent. The network was given the task of learning that the sequence A→B was a predictor of C, while B alone predicted C's absence. After as few as 20 training trials, 4 of 7 randomly initialized networks were making the required distinction. This represents a significant improvement in learning rate over networks trained on similar tasks using a recurrent backpropagation algorithm, and more closely models results obtained in animal conditioning experiments.

INTRODUCTION

Event prediction is central to human and animal thought processes. Conditioning and causal attribution have both been described as essentially an encoding of the temporal relationships among important environmental events [7, 12]. During conditioning a subject must determine a) which events (Conditioned Stimuli or CSs) are the best predictors of other important events (Unconditioned Stimuli or USs), and b) the temporal relation among the events, i.e. the delay in time between onset or offset of one event and the onset of another. The former provides subjects information about which cues are best and the latter allows them to time their responses to these cues. Causal attribution may follow a similar process: the task of an observer is to determine the relative predictive relations among environmental stimuli [16, 20]. People *know* that turning on a light switch will turn on the light because the second event consistently and quickly follows the first. The causal relation between smoking and lung cancer is more tenuous but is derived from similar principles. Difficulties arise because a) not all smokers get lung cancer while some non-smokers do and b) the temporal relation between the smoking and cancer is far from immediate. Others have argued (e.g. [17, 21]) that the primary variable which affects causal attribution is our prior knowledge of possible causal mechanisms in operation. One of us [23] has suggested that while knowledge of mechanism does affect attributions, data-based cues like covariation and temporal contiguity are central to the *development* of our mechanism knowledge. A model which encodes the temporal relations among environmental events and which predicts future events might demonstrate the behaviors observed in conditioning and causal attribution. In recent years a number of connectionist models have been developed for encoding such temporal relations, but it remains to be seen how appropriate these are for modeling behavior observed experimentally.

In earlier work we investigated the suitability of a partially recurrent backpropagation network [1] to the modeling of conditioning and causal attribution [22, 23]. The results were promising, but some important limitations of the model were evident: learning was quite slow and the system's performance fell off dramatically as the length of time between cues and predicted events increased. Increasing the learning rate (by increasing the rate or momentum parameters) resulted in unstable and maladaptive results (unpublished data). While the model is suitable for conditioning paradigms where learning is slow and long inter-stimulus intervals (ISIs) are not well tolerated (e.g. rabbit nictitating membrane response (NMR) [8]), its predictions are not as well suited to paradigms like aversive conditioning where significant learning can take place in less than ten trials. Although it is always possible to suggest that some number of our model's trials correspond to one "real" trial and that many model time steps are equal to shorter time durations in the real world, this approach seems to beg the question. In search of a more principled solution, we investigated methods for increasing the rate of learning in recurrent models in an attempt to develop a network architecture which exhibits the more rapid learning observed in paradigms like aversive conditioning.

Hybrid learning networks (e.g. counterpropagation networks and radial basis function networks) achieve faster learning by using an unsupervised system to preprocess inputs for a simple supervised system. This approach results in much faster learning than conventional backpropagation since learning in the unsupervised part of the network proceeds quickly and without the propagation of errors from the output layer back to earlier layers (this is not to suggest that hybrid learning is a panacea, however; see [4]). We analyzed the behavior of a hybrid system which used a series of Hebbian layers to perform principal components analysis (PCA) of their inputs. Each unit in these layers had a memory or capacitance so that its output value changed slowly in response to changes in its input. We hoped that the unsupervised network would develop a representation of temporal relations among environmental events that could be used in the service of any number of supervised or unsupervised tasks that a system must perform. Higher levels in the hierarchy should extract higher order temporal information (a backpropagation analog is presented in [15]). For our purposes, the utility of the unsupervised representation was judged by its usefulness in a one-time-step prediction task performed by a single layer Widrow-Hoff supervised network.

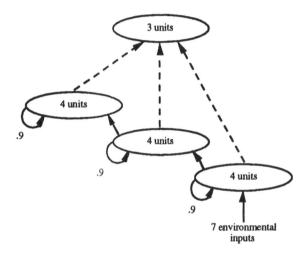

Figure 1: Architecture of the system. Solid arrows represent weights that change according to Oja's rule; dashed arrows use Widrow-Hoff learning. Recurrent connections are 1-1 with non-modifiable weights of .9.

THE MODEL

We integrated a number of current modeling techniques, with minor modifications to improve performance. The unsupervised portion of the system consisted of three layers of units, the output of each providing the input to the next layer. Each layer performed distributed PCA using Oja's M-unit rule ([11]; this is a non-local learning rule, but performance should be similar with local rules, e.g. [2, 13]). To encode the temporal dimension, each unit had a memory of its previous value so that the activation of a unit was not solely dependent on current input:

$$\bar{y}_i^t = \sigma\left(\frac{y_i + ck\bar{y}_i^{t-1}}{1+c}\right) \tag{1}$$

$$y_i = \sum_{j=1}^{N} w_{ij} x_j$$

246

where k was the memory parameter, c provided for a weighted average of input and memory, and σ was a sigmoidal squashing function. The y_i was the activation of a unit, $\bar{y}_i$ was its output, and x_j the output from a lower layer. The unsupervised representations were fed into an output layer of *linear* nodes as represented in Figure 1.

The number of hidden units in the first Hebbian layer should be sufficient to capture the significant principal components in the environmental input. However, there is no a priori method for knowing independent of a task how many units will be necessary in successive layers nor how many layers would be optimal. In earlier simulations we found that for our task four units at each Hebbian level were sufficient (seven units provided no advantage) and that layering was required, even when as many as seven units were used for the first PCA.

Learning in the unsupervised and supervised portions of the system took place concurrently. For the weights between the unsupervised representations and the output units, Widrow-Hoff learning was used. This is a relatively strong test of the utility of the input representations since the single layer of Widrow-Hoff units is limited to linearly separable classifications (in contrast to backpropagation with hidden layers). The unsupervised layers used a slight modification of Oja's M-unit rule:

$$\Delta w_{ij} = \eta y_i \left(2x_j - \sum_{k=1}^{N} y_k w_{kj} \right)$$

The inputs to each unit (the x_js) were doubled in value for all layers but the first to offset attenuation of activation values resulting from the squashing of outputs at each layer. Doubling was chosen for pragmatic reasons but methods of gain modification could presumably be adopted to allow the network to arrive at its own gain values. Note that the gain only had an effect in weight modification and did not reflect any direct change in the actual output or activation of a unit in Equation 1.

TRAINING

The task chosen for testing this approach is based upon animal learning research on occasion setting [5, 6]. When a subject is exposed to an AB+ vs. B- conditioning schedule (A&B represent concurrent events/CSs, + represents reinforcement/US following, and - is no reinforcement), it will quickly learn that A is the relevant predictor of reinforcement and B is irrelevant. However, when A is temporally distant and B contiguous with the US, it is frequently observed that A will function as an "occasion setter" for determining whether B will be followed by reinforcement. Figure 2 illustrates the pattern of events on which a set of 7 networks (7 different initial weight settings) were trained. On one trial, A was followed by B (after a brief gap to avoid A's offset being contiguous with B's onset - see [5]), which was subsequently followed by C (the reinforcer in animal experiments). On alternate trials, B occurred alone.

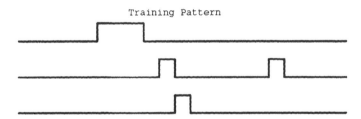

Figure 2: The training stimuli used as input in the reported simulations. The top line represents event A, the second event B and the third event C. Range of values is [-1,1].

The A event was twelve discrete time steps in duration, and B and C were each four time steps long. These durations were chosen to make the task suitably challenging for the system and in no way represent the maximum temporal capacity of the network. Each "trial" in our analyses consisted of one exposure to the *two* trials indicated in Figure 2, each of which was separated by a relatively long inter-trial interval (ITI) of 40 time steps. Long ITIs are necessary to minimize the effect of one trial on the next by allowing the network to return to baseline between trials.

For all simulations, we used Widrow-Hoff and Hebbian learning rates of .1, no bias on the Widrow-Hoff units and no momentum. In Equation 1, k was .9 and c was 5. Setting c to 5 emphasized the prior state of a unit relative to exterior input. Initial weights were uniformly distributed at random in the range [-.4,.4]. The seven environmental input units (see Figure 1) encoded the occurrence of an event by having a pair of inputs change value from -1 to 1 for the duration of the event. The first two units represented A, the second two B and the third two C; the seventh input was always -1. Two units were used for each stimulus to allow for future tests of generalization to similar events and to give the PCA a representation to reduce. To verify the utility of the hidden unit representations for a temporal task, the Widrow-Hoff outputs were predictive. Each of the three Widrow-Hoff outputs was trained to predict the occurrence of A, B or C one time step in the future. For these outputs, a 1 signaled the expected occurrence of the event and a 0 signaled its expected non-occurrence.

RESULTS AND DISCUSSION

If A is properly functioning as an occasion setter for B, a subject should expect C after an A→B sequence, but not after B alone, resulting in a positive AB-B difference. As Figure 3 shows, after 50 trials four of the seven networks (referred to as "subjects" in the figures) were clearly making a distinction between B alone and B following A. Subject 6's expectation of C is representative of a network which learned to use A as an occasion setter (Figure 4a). Importantly, the response to A→B is greater than the sum of the responses to A and B alone. This indicates that the subject is using A as an occasion setter for B, and not merely predicting C based on the occurrence of A. Predicting C based on A alone is frequently observed in animals when the time between A and C is relatively short and there is little advantage to having A modulate a response to the more contiguous B.

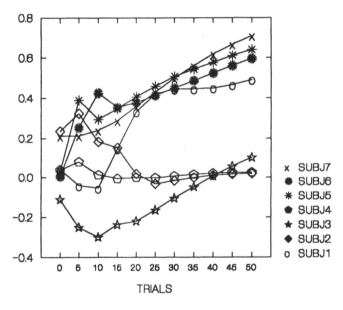

Figure 3: Difference in C expectancy following A→B
sequence vs. B alone. C expectancy is measured at the end of
the interval during which C would have occurred.

In contrast, Subject 4 made no progress toward using A as an occasion setter, relying solely upon the temporally contiguous B event, treating B as a predictor which did not highly covary with C. Subject 3 treated A as a negative signal early on in training, possibly because the unsupervised representations were changing faster than the supervised layer could accommodate, but subsequently got on the right track. One of the nets that apparently did not learn the task (Subject 2 - Figure 4b) opted for a rather unique prediction strategy. After observing A, B or A→B, its expectation of C increased and did not subsequently decrease until C actually did occur. This likely accounts for nullifying its good performance early in training by providing a higher overall baseline for comparison of A→B vs.

B (Figure 3). In fact, most networks had an expectation of C that "lingered" for a period of time following A→B if C did not occur (Subject 6 is a good example, Figure 4a).

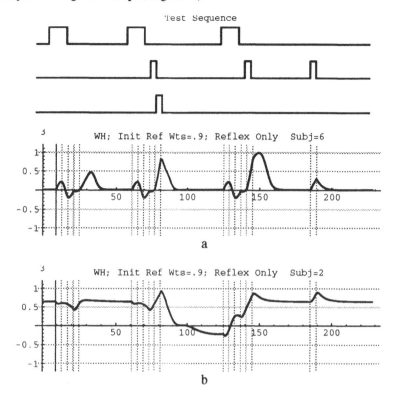

Figure 4: Expectation of C during testing for two of the networks. Figure 4a is a prototypical network/subject. Figure 4b is a network which adopted an unusual solution strategy - see text for discussion. Vertical bars mark four-time-step intervals. The test sequence is included for interpretability of the graphs (top line is A, second B, and third C).

In general, the use of unsupervised hidden layers succeeded in increasing the rate of acquisition of our task. The Hebbian units generally converged after 5-15 trials, thus leaving most of the later learning to the Widrow-Hoff units. We have not explored the use of higher Widrow-Hoff learning rates within the current context; it is possible that stable performance could be achieved with higher rates. We tried to ensure that the rate of change of the unsupervised portion of the network remained lower than that in the supervised portion. Otherwise, the supervised representation would be built on an unstable foundation. The rate of acquisition in our task is similar in magnitude to that obtained by Schmajuk & DiCarlo's model of classical conditioning [14], which relied upon a "biologically plausible version of backpropagation" and a STM memory trace with gradual onsets and offsets as input to their system.

In Figure 4 it is clear that the predictions of C's occurrence are not particularly accurate. There is a gradual increase to a peak and a gradual decay. This is largely the result of the exponential memory trace we adopted - accuracy is traded off against duration [10]. The smoothing of stimuli in memory inevitably results in a loss of accuracy in determining exactly when an event occurred. This is likely to be further exacerbated with higher order temporal information which will consist of traces of traces of traces in our three layer system. As cognitive scientists we are less concerned with a system's accuracy per se and more concerned with its ability to capture the essence of human and/or animal behavior. At times, animals seem remarkably accurate in their timing of responses, but their response profile smooths as the distance between the CS and US increases (rabbit nictitating membrane response is a good example of this [8]). Modelers interested in greater accuracy of response may wish to use backpropagation as a backend to a layered Hebbian network. Backpropagation should be better at amplifying small differences observed in the unsupervised representations while its nonlinear activation functions would prevent it from overexpecting C.

GENERAL DISCUSSION

In previous work using Elman nets [1], learning tasks similar to the one used here generally took hundreds of trials to reach asymptote and demonstrated no significant performance improvement during the first fifty trials of learning [22, 23]. In contrast, the present networks demonstrate significant learning in a much shorter period of time. This clearly satisfied our desire for faster learning of these tasks for the purpose of modeling conditioning data (cf. [14]).

Memory or capacitance in a neural unit has been used on many occasions to encode time in connectionist networks (e.g. the temporal-difference and time-derivative models of Sutton & Barto [18, 19]). Our approach is different in that we use unit memory within a PCA framework. The networks also consist of layers so that subsequent layers can develop representations that are sensitive to successively higher orders of temporal information. This contrasts with approaches like that adopted by Grossberg & Schmajuk [3] where a set of synapses are posited for each input, each responsive to different time characteristics of the input (cf. [9]). In these approaches, a modeler must both predetermine the range and choice of synaptic or unit responsiveness and, in the case of Grossberg & Schmajuk, multiplicatively increase the number of weights for a single input to adequately cover the temporal range of interest.

Occasion setting represents a set of important tasks that a network model of event prediction should be capable of capturing. In future research we plan to investigate a broader scope of conditioning data and to test predictions of the model in human or animal domains. We also hope to explore the ability of this model to encode more complex temporal information (e.g. in a domain like word acquisition). In conclusion, we are pleased with the results obtained to date and will continue to broaden our understanding of the strengths and weaknesses of this approach.

Acknowledgments

This research supported in part by the University of Minnesota Center for Research in Learning, Perception and Cognition and the National Institute of Child Health and Human Development (HD-07151).

References

[1] J.L. Elman, "Finding structure in time", *Cognitive Science*, vol. 14, pp. 179-211, 1990.

[2] P. Földiák, "Adaptive network for optimal linear feature extraction", in *International Joint Conference on Neural Networks*, IEEE: New York, 1989. pp. 401-405.

[3] S. Grossberg and N.A. Schmajuk, "Neural dynamics of adaptive timing and temporal discrimination during associative learning", *Neural Networks*, vol. 2, pp. 79-102, 1989.

[4] J. Hertz, A. Krogh, and R.G. Palmer, *Introduction to the Theory of Neural Computation*. 1991, Redwood City, CA: Addison-Wesley.

[5] P.C. Holland, "Temporal determinants of occasion setting in feature-positive discriminations", *Animal Learning & Behavior*, vol. 14, pp. 111-120, 1986.

[6] P.C. Holland, "Occasion setting with simultaneous compounds in rats", *Journal of Experimental Psychology: Animal Behavior Processes*, vol. 15, pp. 183-193, 1989.

[7] D. Hume, *A Treatise of Human Nature*. ed. L.A. Selby-Bigge. 1739/1978, New York: Oxford University Press.

[8] E.J. Kehoe, *et al.*, "Real-time processing of serial stimuli in trace conditioning of the rabbit's nictitating membrane response", *Journal of Experimental Psychology: Animal Behavior Processes*, vol. 19, pp. 265-283, 1993.

[9] M.C. Mozer, "Induction of multiscale temporal structure", in *Advances in Neural Information Processing Systems IV*, J.E. Moody, S.J. Hanson, and R.P. Lippman, Editor, Morgan Kaufmann: San Mateo, CA, 1992.

[10] M.C. Mozer, "Neural net architectures for temporal sequence processing", in *Predicting the Future and Understanding the Past*, A. Weigend and N. Gershenfeld, Editor, Addison-Wesley Publishing: Redwood City, CA, in press.

[11] E. Oja, "Neural networks, principal components and subspaces", *International Journal of Neural Systems*, vol. 1, pp. 61-68, 1989.

[12] R.A. Rescorla, "Pavlovian conditioning: It's not what you think it is", *American Psychologist*, vol. 43(3), pp. 151-160, 1988.

[13] T.D. Sanger, "Optimal unsupervised learning in a single-layer linear feedforward neural network", *Neural Networks*, vol. 2, pp. 459-473, 1989.

[14] N.A. Schmajuk and J.J. DiCarlo, "Stimulus configuration, classical conditioning, and hippocampal function", *Psychological Review*, vol. 99, pp. 268-305, 1992.

[15] J. Schmidhuber, "Learning complex, extended sequences using the principle of history compression", *Neural computation*, vol. 4, pp. 234-242, 1992.

[16] D.R. Shanks and A. Dickinson, "Associative accounts of causality judgment", in *The Psychology of Learning and Motivation*, G.H. Bower, Editor, Academic Press: San Diego, 1987.

[17] T.R. Shultz, "Rules of causal attribution", *Monographs of the Society for Research in Child Development*, vol. 47(1, Serial No. 194), 1982.

[18] R.S. Sutton and A.G. Barto, "Toward a modern theory of adaptive networks: Expectation and prediction", *Psychological Review*, vol. 88, pp. 135-170, 1981.

[19] R.S. Sutton and A.G. Barto, "Time-derivative models of Pavlovian reinforcement", in *Learning and Computational Neuroscience*, M. Gabriel and J.W. Moore, Editor, MIT Press: Cambridge, MA, 1991.

[20] E. Wasserman, "Detecting response-outcome relations: Toward an understanding of the causal structure of the environment", in *The Psychology of Learning and Motivation*, G.H. Bower, Editor, Academic Press: San Diego, 1990.

[21] P.A. White, "Causal processing: Origins and development", *Psychological Bulletin*, vol. 104, pp. 36-52, 1988.

[22] M.E. Young, "A Simple recurrent network model of serial conditioning: Implications for temporal event representation.", in *Proceedings of the Fourteenth Annual Conference of the Cognitive Science Society.*, Lawrence Erlbaum: Hillsdale, NJ, 1992.

[23] M.E. Young and B. DeBauche, "Causal mechanisms as temporal bridges in a connectionist model of causal attribution", in *Proceedings of the Fifteenth Annual Conference of the Cognitive Science Society.*, Lawrence Erlbaum: Hillsdale, NJ, 1993.

CONTROL

Issues in Using Function Approximation for Reinforcement Learning

Sebastian Thrun
Institut für Informatik III
Universität Bonn
Römerstr. 164, D–53225 Bonn, Germany
thrun@cs.uni-bonn.de

Anton Schwartz
Dept. of Computer Science
Stanford University
Stanford, CA 94305
schwartz@cs.stanford.edu

Reinforcement learning techniques address the problem of learning to select actions in unknown, dynamic environments. It is widely acknowledged that to be of use in complex domains, reinforcement learning techniques must be combined with generalizing function approximation methods such as artificial neural networks. Little, however, is understood about the theoretical properties of such combinations, and many researchers have encountered failures in practice. In this paper we identify a prime source of such failures—namely, a systematic overestimation of utility values. Using Watkins' Q-Learning [18] as an example, we give a theoretical account of the phenomenon, deriving conditions under which one may expected it to cause learning to fail. Employing some of the most popular function approximators, we present experimental results which support the theoretical findings.

1 Introduction

Reinforcement learning methods [1, 16, 18] address the problem of learning, through experimentation, to choose actions so as to maximize one's productivity in unknown, dynamic environments. Unlike most learning algorithms that have been studied in the field of Machine Learning, reinforcement learning techniques allow for finding optimal action sequences in temporal decision tasks where the external evaluation is sparse, and neither the effects of actions, nor the temporal delay between actions and its effects on the learner's performance is known to the learner beforehand. The designated goal of learning is to find an *optimal policy*, which is a policy for action selection that maximizes future payoff (reward). In order to do so, most current reinforcement learning techniques estimate the *value* of actions, *i.e.*, the future payoff one can expect as a result of executing an action, using recursive estimation techniques.

In recent years, various theoretical results have been obtained that characterize the convergence properties of reinforcement learning algorithms. Strong stochastic convergence has been shown for a class of learning algorithms including Q-Learning, the most frequently used reinforcement learning technique [1, 6, 18, 19]. Others [7, 20] have characterized the convergence speed in terms of the size and other key characteristics of the domain at hand. While all these results apply exclusively to non-generalizing look-up table representations, it has often been argued, and seems to be generally accepted, that reinforcement learning techniques must be combined with powerful function approximators in order to scale to more complex tasks. This is because most domains studied in AI are too large to be searched exhaustively, hence demanding some kind of generalization. Generalization replaces costly training experience. Indeed, generalizing approximation techniques such as artificial neural networks and instance-based methods have been used in practice with some remarkable success in domains such as game playing [17, 2] and robotics [5, 8, 10]. For example, Tesauro [17] reports a backgammon computer program that reaches grand-master level of play, which has been constructed using a combination of reinforcement learning techniques and artificial neural networks.

Despite these encouraging empirical results, little is known about the general implications of using function approximation in reinforcement learning. Recently, Bradtke [3] has shown the convergence of a particular policy iteration algorithm when combined with a quadratic function approximator.[1] To our knowledge this is the only convergence proof for a reinforcement learning method using a generalizing function approximator to date. Singh and Yee [14] proposed a theoretical justification for using certain error-bounded classes of function approximators in the context of reinforcement learning.[2] Others, however, report failure in applying function approximators such as the Backpropagation algorithm [4, 8, 9]. In some cases learning failed since the function approximator at hand was not capable of representing reasonable value functions at all [13]. In other cases, however, failure was observed even though the function approximator at hand was able to represent a suitable value function, and thus a near-optimal policy could have been learned [3, 9]. In this paper we will focus our attention primarily on the latter cases. Obviously, there are inherent difficulties in combining function approximation and reinforcement learning techniques that do not exist for each component in isolation.

In the current paper we point out some significant pitfalls and limitations that arise from this combination. First, we present a theoretical analysis that elucidates effects that may occur when reinforcement learning is combined with a generalizing function approximator. Generally speaking, function approximators induce some noise (generalization error) on the output predictions. The key observation here is that such noise can lead to a *systematic overestimation effect* of values. As a consequence of this overestimation, as well as of the discounting typically used in reinforcement learning, the learner is *expected* to fail to learn an optimal policy in certain situations. We use this observation to derive practical bounds on (a) the necessary accuracy of the function approximator, and (b) the temporal discount factor used in learning. The theoretical analysis is followed by empirical results in a simple robot navigation domain using a variety of non-linear function approximators.

The goal of the papers is twofold. For one, we wish to contribute to the understanding of the effects that function approximation has in the context of reinforcement learning. In addition, we aim to elucidate practical pitfalls and to provide guidelines that might be helpful for actual implementations. This research has been driven by empirical difficulties that were encountered when combining various function approximators in a variety of domains, ranging from robot learning domains to learning in chess. The effects described in this paper match our personal experimental experience to a high degree, hence provide reasonable explanations for a multitude of previously unexplained findings.

2 The Overestimation Phenomenon

In this and the following section we present a theoretical analysis of systematic overestimation effects in reinforcement learning. Throughout this analysis we use Watkins' Q-Learning as an example [18]. Q-Learning is a technique for learning optimal policies in Markovian sequential decision tasks. It does this by incrementally learning a function $Q(s, a)$ which it uses to evaluate the utility of performing action a in state s. More specifically, assume the agent observes during learning that action a executed at state s resulted in the state s' and some immediate reward r_s^a. This observation is employed to update Q:

$$Q(s, a) \quad \longleftarrow \quad r_s^a \; + \; \gamma \; \max_{\hat{a} \text{ action}} Q(s', \hat{a}) \tag{1}$$

Here γ is a *discount factor*[3] ($0 < \gamma < 1$), used to give a preference for rewards reaped sooner in time. At any time, the Q-values suggest a policy for choosing actions—namely the one which, in any state, chooses action a which maximizes $Q(s, a)$. It has been shown that repeated application of this update equation eventually yields Q-values that give rise to a policy which maximizes the expected cumulative discounted reward [18]. However, such results only apply when the Q-values are stored precisely, *e.g.*, by a look-up table.

Assume, instead, that Q is represented by a *function approximator* that induces some noise on the estimates of Q. More specifically, let us assume that the currently stored Q-values, denoted by Q^{approx}, represent some implicit target

---

[1] This proof addresses control problems solvable by *linear quadratic regulation*, a specific set of control tasks with linear dynamics and linear optimal policies.

[2] They derive worst-case bounds on the loss in performance in cases where, after learning, function approximation noise disturbs the optimal value function by some small amount.

[3] We ignore the degenerate case of $\gamma = 0$ to simplify the statement of the theorems.

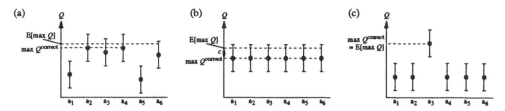

Figure 1: Overestimation: (a) Q-values for six actions $a_1, \ldots, a_6$ are shown. If these Q-values are noise-free, the "max" will return the correct value Q^{target}. If there is noise, some overestimation of the maximum value is likely, as the expected return is $E[\max Q]$. (b) The expected overestimation is maximal if all Q-values are the same, and (c) minimal if the error interval of the best and the second best Q-value do not overlap (*cf.* the Corollary).

values Q^{target}, corrupted by a noise term $Y_{s'}^{\hat{a}}$ which is due to the function approximator.

$$Q^{\text{approx}}(s', \hat{a}) \;=\; Q^{\text{target}}(s', \hat{a}) \;+\; Y_{s'}^{\hat{a}}$$

Here the noise is modeled by the family of random variables $Y_{s'}^{\hat{a}}$ with zero mean. Clearly, this noise causes some error on the left-hand side of Eq. (1), denoted by the random variable Z_s:

$$
\begin{aligned}
Z_s \;&\stackrel{\text{def}}{=}\; r_s^a + \gamma \max_{\hat{a}\ \text{action}} Q^{\text{approx}}(s', \hat{a}) \;-\; \left(r_s^a + \gamma \max_{\hat{a}\ \text{action}} Q^{\text{target}}(s', \hat{a}) \right) \\
&=\; \gamma \left(\max_{\hat{a}\ \text{action}} Q^{\text{approx}}(s', \hat{a}) - \max_{\hat{a}\ \text{action}} Q^{\text{target}}(s', \hat{a}) \right)
\end{aligned}
\tag{2}
$$

The key observation underlying our analysis is that *zero-mean noise* $Y_{s'}^{\hat{a}}$ may easily result in Z_s with *positive mean*, i.e.,

$$E[Y_{s'}^{\hat{a}}] = 0 \ \forall \hat{a} \;\stackrel{\text{often}}{\Longrightarrow}\; E[Z_s] > 0$$

To see this, consider the situation depicted in Fig. 1a, which illustrates a single update step according to Eq. (1). In this example, as well as in our theoretical analysis, the noise variables $Y_{s'}^{\hat{a}}$ are modeled by independent, uniformly distributed random variables in the interval $[-\varepsilon, \varepsilon]$ (for some $\varepsilon > 0$), as indicated by the error bars. Now consider the calculation of the maximum in Eq. (1), assuming that there is more than one action to choose from. Due to the function approximation noise, some of the Q-values might be too small, while others might be too large. The max operator, however, always picks the largest value, making it particularly sensitive to overestimations. If several Q-values are alike and their error intervals overlap, one is likely to overestimate the correct Q-value for some action, which will make the max operator overestimate as well. In short, max causes overestimation because it does not preserve the zero-mean property of the errors of its operands.

We now address the question of how large the expected overestimation $E[Z_s]$ may be.

Lemma. *Let n denote the number of actions applicable at state s'. If all n actions share the same target Q-value, i.e., $\exists q : \forall \hat{a} : q = Q^{\text{target}}(s', \hat{a})$, then the average overestimation $E[Z_s]$ is γc with $c \stackrel{\text{def}}{=} \varepsilon \frac{n-1}{n+1}$.*

The proof of this Lemma, as well as those of the theorems below, can be found in the Appendix. This Lemma demonstrates that each time the update rule (1) is applied, the expected overestimation can be as large as γc, depending on the Q-values at the state s'. Hence:

Corollary. $0 \le E[Z_s] \le \gamma c$ with $c = \varepsilon \frac{n-1}{n+1}$.

The particular expected overestimation $E[Z_s]$ depends on the environment at hand. In many fine-grained navigation domains a variety of movement actions may result in transition to locations of approximately equal merit—in such cases the actions will have roughly equal Q-values, and we may expect $E[Z_s]$ to be close to γc (*cf.* Fig.1b). In game playing domains we expect $E[Z_s]$ to be closer to 0 (*cf.* Fig.1c), since often the number of good moves is small.

3 Bounds for Expected Failure of Q-Learning

Thus far, we have looked at the error induced by *single* applications of the update rule. In what follows, we will explore the effects of systematic overestimation on Q-Learning, in which the update rule is applied iteratively.

For the sake of simplicity, let us assume (a) that there is a set of goal states, (b) positive reward r_{goal} is only received upon entering a goal state, (c) $r_{\text{goal}} = 1$, and (d) the state-transition function is deterministic.[4] Consider an optimal state-action sequence $\langle s_i, a_i \rangle$ ($i \in \{0, \ldots, L\}$) from some initial state, denoted by s_0, to the nearest goal state. One necessary condition for the the success of Q-Learning (except for some degenerate cases) is that the sequence of Q-values $Q(s_i, a_i)$ is monotonically increasing in i:

$$Q(s_i, a_i) \leq Q(s_{i+1}, a_{i+1}) \quad \text{for all } i \in \{0, \ldots, L-1\} \tag{3}$$

It is easy to see that a violation of the monotonicity condition may result in a wrong ordering of utilities, which generally precludes optimal action choice. We will now consider two more concrete "worst-case" scenarios.

<u>Case 1.</u> Assume that the learner *always* overestimates Q-values by γc. In order to ensure the monotonicity, the discount factor γ must compensate for this. This observation leads to the first theorem:

Theorem 1. *If there is maximal, repeated overestimation of magnitude γc along an optimal path, Q-Learning is expected to fail to learn an optimal policy if $\gamma > \frac{1}{1+c}$.*

<u>Case 2.</u> Now assume that Q-Learning managed to learn the last $L-1$ Q-vales of this optimal path *correctly*—Depending on the task at hand, this might nor might not be what one would expect (*cf.* the Corollary), but this is the designated goal of learning[5]. Then these Q-values are given by iteratively discounting the final reward with the distance to the goal state, *i.e.*, $Q(s_{L-i}, a_{L-i}) = \gamma^i$ for $i \in \{1, \ldots, L-1\}$. Consequently, the *correct* Q-value $Q^{\text{correct}}(s_0, a_0)$ is γ^L. What happens if noise in function approximation results in an expected overestimation γc when updating this value? In order to ensure the monotonicity of Q, we have to make sure that the difference between $Q(s_1, a_1)$ and $Q(s_0, a_0)$ is at least γc, *i.e.*,

$$\gamma^{L-1} - \gamma^L \geq \gamma c. \tag{4}$$

This leads to the following theorems, which represent average-case analyses for learning paths of length L in such "worst-case" environments.

Theorem 2. *Under the conditions stated above, Q-Learning is expected to fail if $\varepsilon > \frac{n+1}{n-1} \cdot \frac{(L-2)^{L-2}}{(L-1)^{L-1}} \left(\approx \frac{1}{L} \right)$.*

Table 1 shows upper bounds on ε for some choices of L and n. It can be seen that for reasonably large L and n the function approximator must be extremely accurate, if Q-Learning is to successfully identify optimal policies.

The bound in Theorem 2 does not depend on γ. Given that ε is small enough to fulfill the condition in Theorem 2, condition (4) also establishes bounds on the choice of the discount factor γ.

Theorem 3. *Under the conditions stated above, Q-Learning is expected to fail if $\gamma^{L-1} - \gamma^L < \gamma c$.*

Table 2 shows some bounds on γ as a function of ε and L. Note that Theorem 1 is a special case of Theorem 3 for $L = 1$. For larger values of L the bounds are tighter. For example, if $L \geq 2$, Theorem 3 implies that γ must be smaller than $1 - c = 1 - \varepsilon\frac{n-1}{n+1}$. If $L \geq 3$, γ must be between $.5 - \sqrt{.25 - c}$ and $.5 + \sqrt{.25 - c}$.

---

[4] Assumption (c) is made without loss of generality, if we assume that the error ϵ scales linearly with the range of values to be represented. Assumption (d) is inessential to the analysis but is adopted to simplify the presentation here. (a) and (b) are restrictive, but describe a large number of the tasks addressed in the literature.

[5] Surprisingly, this turns out to be a worst case scenario for this analysis.

Table 1: Upper bound on the error ε of the function approximator, according to Theorem 2. These bounds are significant. For example, if episodes of length $L = 60$ with $n = 5$ actions shall be learned, ε must be smaller than .00943 (bold number).

	$L=10$	$L=20$	$L=30$	$L=40$	$L=50$	$L=60$	$L=70$	$L=80$	$L=90$	$L=100$	$L=1000$
$n = 2$	.12991	.05966	.03872	.02866	.02275	.01886	.01611	.01405	.01247	.01120	.00110
$n = 3$	.08660	.03977	.02581	.01911	.01517	.01257	.01074	.00937	.00831	.00746	.00073
$n = 4$	.07217	.03314	.02151	.01592	.01264	.01048	.00895	.00781	.00692	.00622	.00061
$n = 5$	.06495	.02983	.01936	.01433	.01137	**.00943**	.00805	.00702	.00623	.00560	.00055
$n = 6$	.06062	.02784	.01807	.01337	.01061	.00880	.00751	.00656	.00581	.00522	.00051
$n = 8$	.05567	.02557	.01659	.01228	.00975	.00808	.00690	.00602	.00534	.00480	.00047
$n = 10$	.05292	.02430	.01577	.01167	.00927	.00768	.00656	.00572	.00508	.00456	.00045
$n = 20$	.04786	.02198	.01426	.01056	.00838	.00695	.00593	.00517	.00459	.00412	.00040
$n = \infty$	.04330	.01988	.01290	.00955	.00758	.00628	.00537	.00468	.00415	.00373	.00036

Table 2: Upper and lower bounds for the choice of γ due to Theorem 3 for the fixed number of actions $n = 5$. Open slots indicate that no γ is expected to work at all (*cf.* Theorem 2). For example, function approximators with $\varepsilon = .05$ are unlikely to learn optimal action sequences longer than $L = 11$. $\gamma = .7$ diminishes the maximum length L to 8.

	$\varepsilon = .3$	$\varepsilon = .2$	$\varepsilon = .15$	$\varepsilon = .125$	$\varepsilon = .1$	$\varepsilon = .075$	$\varepsilon = .05$	$\varepsilon = .025$
$L = 1$	.0000/.8333	.0000/.8823	.0000/.9090	.0000/.9230	.0000/.9375	.0000/.9523	.0000/.9677	.0000/.9836
$L = 2$	.0000/.8000	.0000/.8666	.0000/.9000	.0000/.9166	.0000/.9333	.0000/.9500	.0000/.9666	.0000/.9833
$L = 3$	.2763/.7236	.1584/.8415	.1127/.8872	.0917/.9082	.0718/.9281	.0527/.9472	.0345/.9654	.0169/.9830
$L = 4$	—	.5361/.7819	.4126/.8669	.3611/.8962	.3110/.9214	.2599/.9438	.2047/.9641	.1391/.9827
$L = 5$	—	—	.6753/.8158	.5861/.8760	.5166/.9121	.4495/.9397	.3767/.9626	.2857/.9824
$L = 6$	—	—	—	—	.6708/.8970	.5914/.9344	.5109/.9609	.4099/.9820
$L = 7$	—	—	—	—	.8182/.8477	.6978/.9269	.6121/.9588	.5081/.9817
$L = 8$	—	—	—	—	—	.7829/.9145	**.6893/.9564**	.5852/.9813
$L = 9$	—	—	—	—	—	—	.7497/.9534	.6463/.9809
$L = 10$	—	—	—	—	—	—	.7986/.9495	.6954/.9804
$L = 11$	—	—	—	—	—	—	.8401/.9440	.7355/.9800
$L = 12$	—	—	—	—	—	—	**.8791/.9340**	.7687/.9794
$L = 13$	—	—	—	—	—	—	—	.7965/.9789
$L = 14$	—	—	—	—	—	—	—	.8202/.9783
$L = 15$	—	—	—	—	—	—	—	.8405/.9776
$\vdots$	$\vdots$							$\vdots$
$L = 23$	—	—	—	—	—	—	—	.9436/.9640
$L \geq 24$	—	—	—	—	—	—	—	—

Figure 2: (a) The simulated robot domain. (b) Action space. (c) Learning curves as a function of γ. Each diagram shows the performance (probability of reaching the goal state) as a function of the number of training episodes. The performance is evaluated on an independent testing set of twenty initial robot positions. All curves are averaged over eight runs. Note that learning fails completely if $\gamma \geq .98$.

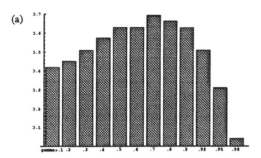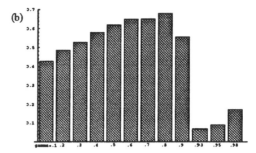

Figure 3: Performance as a function of γ, averaged over the first 300 episodes of learning (eight runs each). (a) Instance-based learning and (b) plain Backpropagation (sigmoidal transfer functions).

4 Empirical Results

The theoretical results were empirically validated using the simulated robot environment depicted in Fig. 2a (*cf.* [9]). The task is to learn a policy that carries the robot agent from arbitrary starting positions to the goal. The robot can sense the state it is in using sensors which measure the distance and orientation of both the goal and the obstacle. It has five actions to chose from, as depicted in Fig. 2b. Positive reward $+1$ is received upon entering the goal region, while collisions are penalized by a reward of -1.

Six series of simulations were performed using (a) instance-based learning with local polynomial approximation, as described in [9, 11], and Backpropagation learning [12] with (b) standard sigmoidal, (c) sinusoidal and (d) radial basis transfer functions. In two further experiments we used radial basis functions for the hidden units only, together with (e) sigmoidal and (f) linear output units. In all experiments the Q-functions for the different actions were represented by separate function approximators. In order to exploit the training information maximally, we used an off-line replay technique similar to that reported in [8]. Parameters were optimized individually for the different approximation techniques.

In a systematic comparison, (a) was empirically found to work best for the task at hand, followed closely by (b) and (e). (f) managed to archive a mediocre level of performance in the given time for a small range of discount factors, and (c) and (d) failed completely to learn a policy that resulted in a better-than-random performance. Figure 2c shows learning curves for the instance-based function approximator (a). Summaries for the techniques (a) and (b) are depicted in Figure 3. These results illustrate the existence of practical bounds on γ as predicted by Theorems 1 and 3. In the less successful cases, visual inspection of the Q-values during learning showed that overestimation prevented these techniques from learning a reasonable policy. For example, in (f) we frequently observed that the learned values exceeded the corresponding target values by a difference of 10 or more, even though the maximum final reward 1 establishes an upper bound on the values. Theorem 2 gives a reasonable explanation for these findings.

5 Discussion

In this paper we have pointed out pitfalls of combining reinforcement learning with function approximators. In particular, we described a *systematic overestimation effect* of values which is due to function approximation when used in recursive value estimation schemes. We analyzed this effect to derive bounds on (a) the necessary accuracy of the function approximator ε, and (b) the discount factor γ. An empirical comparison of different function approximators illustrated the phenomena presented in the theoretical analysis.

Both the analysis and the experimental results give rise to the following potential strategies for diminishing the catastrophic effects of overestimation.

- The results can be interpreted as an argument in favor of approximators with *unbounded memory*. The error of instance-based approximation techniques, such as the one we used in the experiments, may approach zero as the number of training examples goes to infinity. Therefore, we would expect that the overestimation gradually vanishes over time. This seems implausible to assume for approximators with bounded memory, such as the

Backpropagation algorithm. Approximators with bounded memory are often likely to have some minimum residual error, unless specific information about the environment is available that ensures that the error can go to zero.

- Reinforcement learning techniques based on $TD(\lambda)$ [15] update values according to a multitude of values and observed rewards. Using a $TD(\lambda)$ scheme with $\lambda > 0$ should reduce the effects of overestimation, since incorporating actual sample rewards rather than (over)estimated values in the update equation will give rise to less overestimation.

- The analysis suggests a move from discounted to undiscounted frameworks, in which additive rather than multiplicative costs are applied at every step. Recall that temporal discounting, which imposes a cost term that is applied multiplicatively, makes differences in neighboring values exponentially decrease, as the distance to the goal state increases. This observation played a crucial role in Sect. 3, where we derived bounds on ε and γ. With additive costs, the differences in neighboring values do not go to zero as distance to the goal increases, but remain constant, preserving the results of Sect. 2 but not of Sect. 3. It remains to be seen in practice, though, to what extent the expected failure discussed in the paper can be reduced by using costs instead of discounting.

- The effects of overestimation can also be diminished by introducing pseudo-costs to offset overestimation. Given that one knows enough about the domain and the function approximator at hand to estimate the overestimation which occurs, one could impose that estimate as an additional cost on actions to compensate for the effect. Pseudo-costs may be used in either discounted or undiscounted scenarios.

- Another strategy to diminish the effects of overestimation is to introduce function approximators that are biased toward making low predictions. For example, in instance-based learning techniques one could bias the learner to predict low values whenever the data points are sparse. Similar effects can be achieved for Backpropagation-type algorithms, if one trains on additional, synthetic training points that have a low target value. Both techniques will encourage approximators to generate low predictions on regions with sparsely distributed training points. In general, such modifications decrease the likelihood of overestimation by increasing the likelihood of underestimation, which reduces the amount of systematic overestimation.

When drawing conclusions from the theoretical analysis, one must be aware of the limiting assumptions made therein. In particular, we assumed uniform distributed, independent generalization error, and addressed a restricted class of deterministic domains. We based our analysis on the Q-Learning algorithm with zero costs and temporal discounting. However, many of these assumptions were violated in the experimental setting. Although the theoretical analysis addresses exclusively the learning of optimal policies, the results seem to carry over to learning good approximations as well. We suspect that the effects described in this paper carry over to other dynamic programming-related reinforcement learning techniques, to other models of function approximators, to mutually dependent errors[6], and to stochastic domains. These effects, however, address only one facet of using function approximation in the context of reinforcement learning; clearly, the full consequences of this combination are far more complex, and are the subject of ongoing research.

Acknowledgment

We thank Peter Dayan for his thoughtful comments on an earlier version of this paper. We also thank Matthew McDonald for making us aware of two typos in the proof section of this paper.

---

[6]It should be noted that errors in function approximation are generally not independent. Dependencies are likely to affect the amount of overestimation, but prove difficult to quantify and analyze.

References

[1] A. G. Barto, S. J. Bradtke, and S. P. Singh, "Learning to act using real-time dynamic programming," *Artificial Intelligence*, 1993. (to appear).

[2] J. A. Boyan, "Modular neural networks for learning context-dependent game strategies," Master's thesis, University of Cambridge, UK, August 1992.

[3] S. J. Bradtke, "Reinforcement learning applied to linear quadratic regulation," in *Advances in Neural Information Processing Systems 5* S. J. Hanson, J. Cowan, and C. L. Giles, eds., San Mateo, CA, pp. 295–302, Morgan Kaufmann, 1993.

[4] D. Chapman and L. P. Kaelbling, "Input generalization in delayed reinforcement learning: an algorithm and performance comparisons," in *Proceedings of IJCAI-91*, Darling Habour, Sydney, Australia, IJCAI, Inc., 1991.

[5] V. Gullapalli, *Reinforcement Learning and its Application to Control*. PhD thesis, Department of Computer and Information Science, University of Massachusetts, 1992.

[6] T. Jaakkola, M. I. Jordan, and S. P. Singh, "On the convergence of stochastic iterative dynamic programming algorithms," Tech. Rep. 9307, Department of Brain and Cognitive Sciences, Massachusetts Institut of Technology, July 1993.

[7] S. Koenig and R. G. Simmons, "Complexity analysis of real-time reinforcement learning applied to finding shortest paths in deterministic domains," Tech. Rep. CMU-CS-93-106, Carnegie Mellon University, December 1992.

[8] L.-J. Lin, *Self-supervised Learning by Reinforcement and Artificial Neural Networks*. PhD thesis, Carnegie Mellon University, School of Computer Science, Pittsburgh, PA, 1992.

[9] T. M. Mitchell and S. B. Thrun, "Explanation-based neural network learning for robot control," in *Advances in Neural Information Processing Systems 5* S. J. Hanson, J. Cowan, and C. L. Giles, eds., San Mateo, CA, pp. 287–294, Morgan Kaufmann, 1993.

[10] A. W. Moore, *Efficient Memory-based Learning for Robot Control*. PhD thesis, Trinity Hall, University of Cambridge, England, 1990.

[11] A. W. Moore and C. G. Atkeson, "Memory-based function approximators for learning control," MIT AI-Lab Memo, July 1992.

[12] D. E. Rumelhart, G. E. Hinton, and R. J. Williams, "Learning internal representations by error propagation," in *Parallel Distributed Processing. Vol. I + II* D. E. Rumelhart and J. L. McClelland, eds., MIT Press, 1986.

[13] P. Sabes, "Q-learning with a basis function representation for the Q-values," same volume.

[14] S. P. Singh and R. C. Yee, "An upper bound on the loss from approximate optimal-value functions," (submitted for publication), 1993.

[15] R. S. Sutton, "Learning to predict by the methods of temporal differences," *Machine Learning*, vol. 3, 1988.

[16] R. S. Sutton, *Temporal Credit Assignment in Reinforcement Learning*. PhD thesis, Department of Computer and Information Science, University of Massachusetts, 1984.

[17] G. J. Tesauro, "Practical issues in temporal difference learning," *Machine Learning Journal*, vol. 8, 1992.

[18] C. J. C. H. Watkins, *Learning from Delayed Rewards*. PhD thesis, King's College, Cambridge, England, 1989.

[19] C. J. Watkins and P. Dayan, "Q-learning," *Machine Learning Journal*, vol. 8, pp. 279–292, 1992.

[20] S. D. Whitehead, "A study of cooperative mechanisms for faster reinforcement learning," Tech. Rep. 365, University of Rochester, Computer Science Department, Rochester, NY, March 1991.

262

Appendix: Proofs

Lemma. Let $f(x)$ denote the density of the noise variables $Y_{s'}^{\hat{a}}$, i.e., $f(x) \overset{def}{=} Prob[Y_{s'}^{\hat{a}} = x] = \frac{1}{2\varepsilon}$. Then

$$
E[Z_s] \overset{(2)}{=} E\left[\gamma \left(\max_{\hat{a} \text{ action}} Q^{\text{approx}}(s', \hat{a}) - \max_{\hat{a} \text{ action}} Q^{\text{target}}(s', \hat{a}) \right) \right] = \gamma E\left[\max_{\hat{a} \text{ action}} Y_{s'}^{\hat{a}} \right]
$$

$$
= \gamma \int_{-\infty}^{\infty} x \, n \, \underbrace{f(x)}_{Prob[Y=x]} \left(\underbrace{\int_{-\infty}^{x} f(z) \, dz}_{Prob[Y \le x]} \right)^{n-1} dx = \gamma \, n \int_{-\varepsilon}^{\varepsilon} x \, \frac{1}{2\varepsilon} \left(\frac{1}{2} + \frac{x}{2\varepsilon} \right)^{n-1} dx
$$

$$
= \gamma \, n \int_0^1 (2\varepsilon y - \varepsilon) y^{n-1} \, dy \qquad \text{(by substituting } y = \frac{1}{2} + \frac{x}{2\varepsilon})
$$

$$
= \gamma \, n \, \varepsilon \int_0^1 2y^n - y^{n-1} \, dy = \gamma \, n \, \varepsilon \left(\frac{2}{n+1} - \frac{1}{n} \right) = \gamma \underbrace{\varepsilon \frac{n-1}{n+1}}_{=: \, c} = \gamma \, c \qquad \square
$$

Theorem 1. Let $q_i \overset{def}{=} E[\mathcal{Q}(s_i, a_i)]$ (for $i \in \{0, \ldots, L\}$) under the conditions stated in Theorem 1. Then $q_L = 1$ and $q_i = \gamma(q_{i+1} + c)$. It is easy to show by induction that

$$
q_i = \gamma^{L-i} + \sum_{k=1}^{L-i} \gamma^k c
$$

Using this closed-form expression, condition (3) can be re-written as

$$
0 \overset{(3)}{\ge} q_i - q_{i+1} = \gamma^{L-i} + \sum_{k=1}^{L-i} \gamma^k c - \gamma^{L-i-1} - \sum_{k=1}^{L-i-1} \gamma^k c = \gamma^{L-i-1}(\gamma - 1) + \gamma^{L-i} c
$$

$$
\overset{\gamma \ge 0}{\Longleftrightarrow} \quad 0 \ge \gamma - 1 + \gamma c = \gamma(1 + c) - 1 \iff \gamma \le \frac{1}{1+c} \qquad \square
$$

Theorem 2. Condition (4) can be re-written as

$$
\gamma^{L-1} - \gamma^L \overset{(4)}{\ge} \gamma c \iff \gamma^{L-1} - \gamma^L - \gamma c \ge 0 \overset{\gamma \ge 0}{\Longleftrightarrow} \underbrace{\gamma^{L-2} - \gamma^{L-1} - c}_{(*)} \ge 0 \qquad (5)
$$

The left-hand expression $(*)$ takes its maximum at $\gamma^* = \frac{L-2}{L-1}$, since the first derivative of $(*)$

$$
\frac{\partial}{\partial \gamma} \gamma^{L-2} - \gamma^{L-1} - c = (L-2)\gamma^{L-3} - (L-1)\gamma^{L-2} = -(L-1)\gamma^{L-3}\left(\gamma - \frac{L-2}{L-1} \right) \qquad (6)
$$

is 0 and $(*)$ is concave at $\gamma = \gamma^*$. Hence

$$
0 \overset{(5)}{\le} \gamma^{L-2} - \gamma^{L-1} - c < \gamma^{*\,L-2} - \gamma^{*\,L-1} - c \overset{(6)}{=} \left(\frac{L-2}{L-1} \right)^{L-2} - \left(\frac{L-2}{L-1} \right)^{L-1} - c
$$

$$
= \frac{(L-2)^{L-2}[(L-2)+1] - (L-2)^{L-1}}{(L-1)^{L-1}} - c = \frac{(L-2)^{L-2}}{(L-1)^{L-1}} - c
$$

$$
\iff c \le \frac{(L-2)^{L-2}}{(L-1)^{L-1}} \overset{c=\varepsilon \frac{n-1}{n+1}}{\Longleftrightarrow} \varepsilon \le \frac{n+1}{n-1} \cdot \frac{(L-2)^{L-2}}{(L-1)^{L-1}} \approx \frac{n+1}{(n-1)L} \approx \frac{1}{L} \qquad \square
$$

Approximating Q-values with Basis Function Representations

Philip Sabes
Department of Brain and Cognitive Sciences
Massachusetts Institute of Technology
Cambridge, MA 02139
sabes@psyche.mit.edu

The consequences of approximating Q-Values with function approximators are investigated. Two criteria of optimality are introduced, a global and local criterion, and the viability of each is investigated for the case of a linear combination of prechosen basis functions. It is found that optimizing the global cost function is unlikely to result in nearly optimal policies when the set of bases is not complete. The local cost function is found to be plagued by local minima.

Introduction

Recently, the subject of learning from delayed rewards has attracted a good deal of interest. This interest is due in part to the development of algorithms such as Q-Learning [6], which are stochastic extensions of Dynamic Programming techniques. While Q-Learning is capable of learning to interact optimally with its environment without any *a priori* knowledge, it has some limitations. Q-Learning requires the storage of a Q-Value for every state-action pair, a daunting memory requirement for large dimensional real-world problems. For example, a 3-D Pole Balancing problem has a 10-D state space and a 3-D action space, requiring 10^{13} Q-Values for a crude 10 bins/dimension discretization. Additionally, the standard look-up table version of Q-Learning allows for no generalization over the state×action space, which seems unreasonably conservative for most real-world problems. Finally, it is usually the case that only a small number of the total state-action pairs are ever really visited. Thus it could be possible, using an alternative representation for the Q-Values, to concentrate computational power in the part of the domain that is relevant for the agent, thereby greatly reducing the number of free parameters needed.

For these reasons, a Q-Learner that employs an approximating representation for the estimated Q-Value function could extend the range of applications for which the algorithm is suited. While Q-Learning with lookup table Q-Value estimates provably converges to an optimal solution given some reasonable conditions [3, 7], these proofs do not extend in a straightforward manner to the case where general function approximators are used for the estimated Q-Values. Although there have been a number of successes combining reinforcement learning with function approximation, e.g. [4], there is evidence that approximating the value function can, in general, lead to problems when that value function is used for control. Thrun and Schwartz show, in this volume, that approximation can lead to systematic overestimation of the Q-Values during training [5]. Here, the effects on policy of estimating Q-Values with function approximators is investigated.

The next section provides a brief introduction to Q-Learning. Then two different error functions for Q-Learning with approximated Q-value estimates are presented, and, in the two sections which follow, each is evaluated.

Q-Learning

Q-Learning is an on-line, interactive, algorithm for learning an optimal policy in a markov state environment [6]. At each time step the agent is in a state, $x \in S$, and must take an action, $a \in A$. The agent then incurs a random cost, $C(x, a)$, with expected value $\bar{C}(x, a)$, and moves to a new state with transition probabilities $P(y|x, a), \forall y \in S$.

The goal of the learner is to find the policy which minimizes the total discounted cost-to-go, $\sum_{t=0}^{\infty} \gamma^t C(x_t, a_t)$, where $\gamma \leq 1$ is the discount rate. Q-Learning achieves this goal by learning, for each $(x, a) \in S \times A$, an estimate of the expected optimal discounted cost-to-go after executing action a in state x. In other words, it estimates the expected cost-to-go given that the current state is x, the current action is a, and for all future time steps it will execute the (unknown) optimal policy. These estimates are called Q-Values. Formally, the true Q-Values are define as,

$$Q^*(x_t, a_t) \equiv \bar{C}(x_t, a_t) + E_{\{x_t, x_{t+1}, \ldots\}}[\sum_{s=t+1}^{\infty} \gamma^{(s-t)} \bar{C}(x_s, a_s^*)], \tag{1}$$

where a_s^* is the optimal action for state x_s. It can easily be shown that the Q-Values satisfy a version of the Bellman Equations:

$$Q^*(x, a) = \bar{C}(x, a) + \gamma[\sum_{y \in S} P(y|x, a) \min_{b \in A} Q^*(y, b)], \qquad \forall (x, a) \in S \times A. \tag{2}$$

Dynamic Programming uses an iterative application of the Bellman Equations, with the current estimate plugged into the right hand side, to find the true value function. Here, since the learner does not know the transition probabilities or the $\bar{C}(x, a)$'s, it must use a Monte-Carlo sample of the new D.P. style estimate, giving the Q-Learning update rule:

$$Q_{t+1}(x_t, a_t) = (1 - \alpha_t)Q_t(x_t, a_t) + \alpha_t[C(x_t, a_t) + \gamma \min_b Q(x_{t+1}, b)], \tag{3}$$

where $\alpha_t < 1$ is the learning rate at time t.

Basis Function Representations of the Q-Values

The estimated Q-Value function will be approximated by a linear combination of a prechosen set of basis functions,

$$\hat{Q}(x, a) = \sum_i w_i g_i(x, a) = \mathbf{w}^T \mathbf{g}(x, a). \tag{4}$$

The bases could, for example, be gaussians randomly placed in the $S \times A$ space. The goal of the learner is to find the optimal set of weight vectors, $\mathbf{w}^*$. However, it is not clear what the criterion of optimality should be in this case. There are two immediate candidates for an error function, a global criterion, based on the distance from the estimate to the true Q-Values, and a local criterion, which measures the discrepancy between the left and right hand sides of Equation (2).

The global error function is defined as the L_2 distance from the true Q-Values, .

$$E_1(\mathbf{w}) \equiv \frac{1}{2} \sum_{x,a} [\hat{Q}(x, a) - Q^*(x, a)]^2 = \frac{1}{2} \sum_{x,a} [\mathbf{w}^T \mathbf{g}(x, a) - Q^*(x, a)]^2$$

which has the gradient,

$$\partial E_1(\mathbf{w})/\partial \mathbf{w} = \sum_{x,a} [\mathbf{w}^T \mathbf{g}(x, a) - Q^*(x, a)] \mathbf{g}(x, a). \tag{5}$$

To develop a learning rule from this gradient, one might proceed in a manner similar to stochastic gradient descent, with $\Delta \mathbf{w}$ at time t proportional to the (x_t, a_t) term in the above sum, except that the $Q^*(x, a)$'s

265

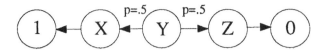

Figure 1: An example where the sampled gradient of the local error function points to the wrong minimum.

are unknown. However, at time t, the learner has a new Monte-Carlo estimate of the right hand side of Equation (2) (with the Q^*'s replaced by the $\hat{Q}_t$'s) available, which it can use as a new (biased) estimate of $Q^*(x_t, a_t)$. This gives an update rule for the w's:

$$\mathbf{w}_{t+1} = \mathbf{w}_t - \alpha_t \ [\mathbf{w}_t^T \mathbf{g}(x_t, a_t) - C(x_t, a_t) - \gamma \min_b \mathbf{w}_t^T \mathbf{g}(x_{t+1}, b)] \ \mathbf{g}(x_t, a_t). \tag{6}$$

Note that this rule is exactly Q-Learning for the case where there is basis function for each state-action pair which is unity for that pair and zero elsewhere. The weights then become the Q-Value estimates, and there is clearly a unique global minimum of $E_1(\mathbf{w})$, and a stationary point of Equation (6), when the $\mathbf{w}$ are the true Q-Values. However, in the general case it is not true that the update rule has a stationary point at the minimum of $E_1(\mathbf{w})$. This is due both to the fact that the current Q-Value estimate is biased with respect to the true Q-Values and to the fact that the probability of visiting a given state-action pair depends on the current Q-Values estimates. In the sequel, the issue of convergence of Equation (6) will be set aside, and the the Q-Values which would result if the optimum of the global criterion could be achieved will be examined.

A second error function, more locally defined, is the squared difference between the two sides of Equation (2), again with the Q^*'s replaced by the $\hat{Q}$'s.

$$\begin{aligned} E_2(\mathbf{w}) & \equiv \frac{1}{2} \sum_{x,a} [\hat{Q}(x, a) - \bar{C}(x, a) - \gamma \sum_{y \in S} P(y|x, a) \min_b \hat{Q}(y, b)]^2 \\ & = \frac{1}{2} \sum_{x,a} [\mathbf{w}^T \mathbf{g}(x, a) - \bar{C}(x, a) - \gamma \sum_{y \in S} P(y|x, a) \min_b \mathbf{w}^T \mathbf{g}(y, b)]^2 \end{aligned} \tag{7}$$

which has the gradient,

$$\begin{aligned} \partial E_2(\mathbf{w})/\partial \mathbf{w} = \sum_{x,a} [\mathbf{w}_t^T \mathbf{g}(x, a) - \bar{C}(x, a) \quad - \quad \gamma \sum_{y \in S} P(y|x, a) \mathbf{w}_t^T \mathbf{g}(y, b^*(y, w))] \\ [\mathbf{g}(x, a) - \gamma \sum_{y \in S} P(y|x, a) \mathbf{g}(y, b^*(y, \mathbf{w}))], \end{aligned} \tag{8}$$

where $b^*(y, \mathbf{w}) \equiv \arg\min_b \mathbf{w}^T \mathbf{g}(y, b)$. In this case, we can derive the weight update rule,

$$\begin{aligned} \mathbf{w}_{t+1} = \mathbf{w}_t - \alpha_t [\mathbf{w}_t^T \mathbf{g}(x_t, a_t) - C(x_t, a_t) \quad - \quad \gamma \mathbf{w}_t^T \mathbf{g}(x_{t+1}, b^*(x_{t+1}, w))] \\ [\mathbf{g}(x_t, a_t) - \gamma \mathbf{g}(x_{t+1}, b^*(x_{t+1}, w))]. \end{aligned} \tag{9}$$

Consider again the case where there is basis function for each state-action pair and the weights become the Q-Value estimates. One sees that the difference between the two update rules is that the second learning rule, Equation (9), has the learning proceeding in both a forward and backward direction, temporally. It would seem that in many cases this is not desirable. For example, when there is an absorbing state where the true Q-Values are known after the first visit, knowledge of cost-to-go until reaching that state should percolate backwards only, as it does with the global rule. The local rule will, however, allow the incorrect estimates from states that immediately proceed the absorbing state to affect the correct absorbing state Q-Value estimate.

To be more concrete, consider the example in Figure 1, where each state has only one action, and the end states are absorbing with costs 1 and 0, respectively. The true Q-Values are $[Q_x^*, Q_y^*, Q_z^*] = [1, .5, 0]$. With a lookup table representation of the Q-Values, these values also minimize E_2, and hence are a zero point of its gradient. However, if the learner is started in state Y on every trial, and moves down the gradient by stochastic sampling with the rule Equation (9), the surface that the learner is really moving down is

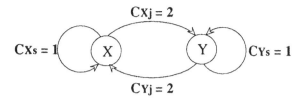

Figure 2: A simple environment.

$1/2[(Q_x^* - 1)^2 + (Q_y^* - Q_x^*)^2 + (Q_y^* - Q_z^*)^2 + (Q_z^* - 0)^2]$, which has a minimum at $[.75, .5, 25]$. Stochastic gradient descent of E_2 does not find the true minimum. In [8], Werbos finds the same problem with a similar error function defined for Dynamic Programming value function estimates. He evaluates the case where the dynamic equations are linear with additive zero-mean noise, and the cost function and value function estimates are linear functions of the current state. For his version of the local error function, he finds that the sampled gradient has an extra term which depends on the variance of the state transition noise, a term which is averaged over in the case of the global error function. In both his case and the one considered here, the source of the error is due to averaging over sampled transitions in a noisy environment. The global error function, which implements what Werbos called Heuristic Dynamic Programming, is able to converge despite this noise, due to the contraction properties of the D.P. Iteration (see, for example, [2]).

THE GLOBAL ERROR FUNCTION

The global criterion will not, in general, have an optimal Q-Value function which leads to a nearly optimal policy in the case where the bases do not span the space of functions from $S \times A$ to $\Re$. To see why this should be the case, consider the simple environment shown in Figure 2, with $S = \{X, Y\}$ and $A = \{stay, jump\}$. If the true Q-Value function is represented as a four dimensional vector, and $\gamma = .5$, then the true Q-Value vector is $\mathbf{Q}^* \equiv [Q_{X_s}^*, Q_{X_j}^*, Q_{Y_s}^*, Q_{Y_j}^*]^T = [2, 3, 2, 3]^T$. The optimal policy is to always *stay*.

Assume that there is only one basis function, $\mathbf{g} = [1, 0, 1, 0]^T$, say. Then the estimate of the Q-Values is just a single parameter multiplying the basis, $\hat{\mathbf{Q}} = w\mathbf{g} = [w, 0, w, 0]^T$. It can easily be seen that the weight which minimizes $E_1(w)$ is $w^* = 2$. However, this results in an estimate $\mathbf{Q}$ which leads to exactly the wrong policy, always *jump*.

In fact, considering the four basis functions below, which span $\Re^4$,

$$
\begin{pmatrix} 1 \\ 0 \\ 1 \\ 0 \end{pmatrix} \begin{pmatrix} 1 \\ 1 \\ -1 \\ -1 \end{pmatrix} \begin{pmatrix} 1 \\ -1 \\ -1 \\ 1 \end{pmatrix} \begin{pmatrix} 0 \\ 1 \\ 0 \\ 1 \end{pmatrix}
\tag{10}
$$

it can be seen that any combination of the first three bases will lead to the wrong policy. Only the fourth of the bases above captures the component of the true Q-Value vector needed to produce the optimal policy. In order to be able to learn the correct policy with one basis vector, that vector must lie sufficiently close to the fourth basis above. If the bases are chosen randomly from a spherically symmetrical distribution, the probability of being able to learn the correct policy is approximately .29, .36, or .53, for 1, 2 or 3 bases, respectively.

In general, the effect of minimizing $E_1(\mathbf{w})$ is to project the true Q-Values onto the space spanned by the available bases. Upon such projection, the relative ordering of two elements in the vector can switch. For example, in the case above, $Q_{X_s}^* > Q_{X_j}^*$, but after projecting $\mathbf{Q}^*$ onto $\mathbf{g} = [1, 0, 1, 0]^T$, the inequality is reversed, $\hat{Q}_{X_j} < \hat{Q}_{X_s}$. If the two elements in question represent Q-Values for two different actions starting from the same state, and if the larger of the two, in $\mathbf{Q}^*$, represents the optimal action from that state, then such a flipping of order upon projection would result in the wrong policy for that state.

In order to determine the probability of order flipping due to projection, a Monte Carlo simulation was performed with random Q-Vectors and bases. N-dimensional Q-vectors were chosen with uniform probability in $[0, 1]^N$, and basis vectors were chosen uniformly from a zero mean spherical gaussian with unit variance.

267

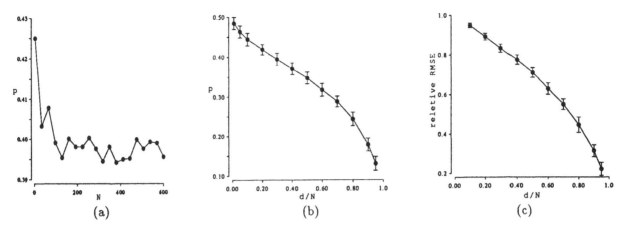

Figure 3: Percentage of N-dimensional vector element pairs that flipped their relative order upon projection onto a random d-dimensional subspace: (a) as a function of N, for $d/N = .30$; and (b) as a function of d/N. (c) Relative RMSE as a function of d/N.

A run consisted of selecting one Q-Vector and d bases, projecting $\mathbf{Q}^*$ onto the d-dimensional space spanned by the bases, and comparing the $.5N(N-1)$ pairs of elements in the original and projected Q-vectors to see if the relative order of the pair switched.

When the ratio of d/N was fixed, and the dimension of the space, N, was varied, a surprising result was observed. The percentage, p, of element pairs that flipped order started out high and decreased with increasing N until about $N = 100$, at which point it leveled off. A typical plot of p vs.N, for $d/N = .30$, is shown in Figure 3(a).

Next, the dependence of the large N value of p on the number of bases was investigated. For a given value of d/N, 50 runs were performed for each of 6 equally spaced values of $300 \leq N \leq 600$, and p was calculated for each run. The overall means and standard deviations of p as a function of d/N are shown in Figure 3(b). Note that the flipping probabilities are significant, even in the case when the number of independent bases is a large fraction of the dimension of the space of functions from $S \times A$ to $\Re$. For comparison, Figure 3(c) also shows the relative root mean square error, $\|\hat{\mathbf{Q}} - \mathbf{Q}^*\|^2/\|\mathbf{Q}^*\|^2$, as a function of d/N. Not surprisingly, the curve of p and relative RMSE have a qualitatively similar shape.

For a given state, it might be the case that one action has a much larger Q-Value than any other action. If the flipping probabilities depend heavily on the magnitude of the ratio of the two Q-Values, then in such a case, the probability of finding the correct policy might still be high. Thus, the dependence of $p = P(\hat{Q}_i > \hat{Q}_j | Q_i^* <= Q_j^*)$ on the the ratio Q_i^*/Q_j^* was investigated. Simulations were conducted as above, with $N = 400$ and $d/N = .3$ and $.8$. For each d/N, 75 runs were performed and flipping percentage was tallied in a histogram of bin-width .001. The results are shown in Figure 4, with each point representing 10 bins. Note that although p does depend on the ratio of the Q-Values, the flipping percentage is still significant even for very small ratios. Even in the case when one Q-Value is more than 1000 times the magnitude of another, the average flipping probability, $p_{.001}$, is approximately .30, for $d/N = .3$, or .070, for $d/N = .8$.

These results have strong implications for the likelihood of finding a nearly optimal policy. Consider the case of an environment where n actions are available at each state and the largest ratio between Q-Values for a given state is 100. Then, assuming independence of the behavior of different pairs, the probability of the optimal action, $\arg\min_b Q^*(x, b)$, still being optimal with respect to $\hat{\mathbf{Q}}$ is bounded above by $(1 - p_{.01})^{(n-1)}$. Then, even if the learner is using $.80 * N$ bases (in which case $p_{.01} = .09$), the expected fraction of states with the correct policy will only be about .68 if there are 5 actions per state, and .43 if there are 10 actions per state. Since a major motivation of using function approximators was to reduce memory requirements, it is likely that values of d/N used in practice will be much smaller, and as the d/N gets smaller and the number of actions per state grows, these probabilities fall off quickly.

To see how these results held up when the Q-Values were taken from a real problem and more typical basis functions were chosen, the global criterion was applied to the race track problem with gaussian basis functions. Details of the race-track follow [1]. The state space was discrete, with a 2-D position and a 2-D

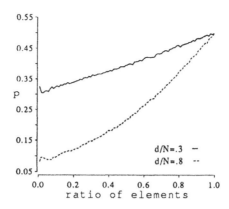

Figure 4: Percentage of N-dimensional vector element pairs that flipped their relative order upon projection onto a random d-dimensional subspace as a function of the ratio of the smaller element to the larger.

velocity. The actions consisted of forces (accelerations) applied to the car: +1,0,or -1 in each direction, giving 9 possible actions. The dynamics were stochastic, in that 10 percent of the time the action chosen was ignored and the car continued on with the same velocity as before, i.e.

with probability .9: $\quad \mathbf{x}_{t+1} = \mathbf{x}_t + \mathbf{v}_t + \mathbf{a}_t \qquad$ with probability .1: $\quad \mathbf{x}_{t+1} = \mathbf{x}_t + \mathbf{v}_t$
$$\mathbf{v}_{t+1} = \mathbf{v}_t + \mathbf{a}_t \qquad\qquad\qquad\qquad \mathbf{v}_{t+1} = \mathbf{v}_t + \mathbf{a}_t$$

A trial consisted of the car starting at one of the randomly chosen starting positions with zero velocity and being charged a cost of one for each time step until it crossed over the finish line. There was no explicit cost for running off the track, but the car was then sent back to (randomly) one of the start states and the velocity was reset to zero. Finally, there was no discount factor used, since in any case the optimal solution is simply the shortest path to cross the finish line.

Lookup table Q-Learning can can be used to find nearly optimal solutions to these problems. Given these Q-Values, the weight vector, $\mathbf{w}^*$, which minimizes the $E_1(\mathbf{w})$ can be computed directly by setting the gradient in Equation (5) to zero:

$$\mathbf{w}^* = [\sum_{x,a} \mathbf{g}(x,a)\mathbf{g}^T(x,a)]^{-1} [\sum_{x,a} \mathbf{g}(x,a)Q^*(x,a)]. \tag{11}$$

Weights were actually computed with a weighted least-squared version of Equation (11), where each (x,a) was weighted by the number of times the lookup table Q-Learner visited the state, x. The weights found by this method were optimal in the $E_1(\mathbf{w})$ sense (modulo the weighting factors), but they often lead to policies which never made it to the finish line.

In the case of a very simple race-track with 40 positions and over 29,000 state-action pairs, lookup table Q-Learning converged to within 10 percent of the optimal average trial length (approximately 5 steps/trial) after 15,000 trials, and performed optimally by 30,000 trials. After convergence, only about 15 state-action pairs were visited with probability greater than .01 (about 1 visit per 20 runs), meaning that the effective number of dimensions in the weighted problem was on the order of $100 - 150$. 100 guassians with preset covariance matrices (a variety of diagonal covariances were tried) and centers chosen uniformly over the $S \times A$ space were used, and the optimal weights were found for 10 different bases sets. The average weighted relative RMSE was .29, a value comparable to the values found in the previous section for similar d/N. For all 10 cases, the Q-Values led to policies that never reached the finish line.

The Q-Values for each state were compared pairwise (i.e. only Q-Values for different actions in the same state compared), and the average fraction (weighted as above) that flipped their relative order after projection onto the gaussian bases was .43. This value is somewhat larger than what was seen above for similar d/N and relative RMSE, but a difference is not unexpected given the radically different distribution of the bases. The average, weighted, percentage of the states for which the optimal action, according to the lookup table Q-Values, was no longer optimal with respect to the approximated values was .81. This number is smaller than the value we would expect if the flipping probabilities were independent, but it is still quite

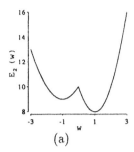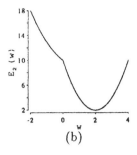

Figure 5: $E_2(w)$ vs. w. (a) for the basis $[1, 0, 1, 0]^T$, (b) for the basis $[0, 1, 0, 1]^T$.

large. It must be noted, however, that in cases when the true Q-Values are almost equal, relative flipping of their order upon projection does not matter. In this example, most states had more than one optimal action, and the Q-Values for those actions were often nearly equal. Thus, one should consider the average, weighted, fraction of states for which the action chosen had a lookup table Q-Value more than .30 below the optimal lookup table Q-Value. (True Q-Values were all integers, as they represented steps-to-go until the finish line. Thus a difference of .3 meant that the action really was non-optimal.) This fraction was computed to be .45. Again, this is lower than would be expected if the flipping probabilities were independent, but it is still high enough to prevent the policy from reaching the finish line.

In summary, when the Q-vector is projected onto a subspace of reduced dimension, the probability of the relative order of two Q-values flipping is high, resulting in an even higher probability of choosing a suboptimal action in any given state. The basic problem is that function approximation, which minimizes $E_1(\mathbf{w})$, is an indirect route to the ultimate goal of minimizing the expected cost-to-go. The relatively small errors introduced in the intermediate step can, as seen in the race track example, cause very large deviations from optimal performance.

The Local Error Function

One reason for being suspicious of the local error function has already been seen: the zero of the sampled gradient does not lie at the minimum of the error function itself. Here a second reason will be discussed. Even if unbiased estimates of the gradient were available, it is unlikely that a good policy would result, due to a proliferation of local minima on the the surface of the local error function.

Consider again the simple example from the previous section, illustrated in Figure 2. Again, assume the single basis vector, $g = [1, 0, 1, 0]^T$, so that our estimated Q-Values depend only on the scalar parameter, w, i.e. $\hat{\mathbf{Q}} = [w, 0, w, 0]^T$. Note that the error function $E_2(\mathbf{w})$ (see Equation (7)) depends on terms which include $b^*(y, \mathbf{w})$, and is otherwise quadratic in w. Thus, $E_2(\mathbf{w})$ must be evaluated separately for the case where $w < 0$, so the $b^*(y, w) = stay$, $\forall y$, and the case where $w > 0$, so the $b^*(y, w) = jump$, $\forall y$.

$$E_2(w) = \begin{cases} (w+1)^2 + 9 & \text{if } w < 0 \\ 2(w-1)^2 + 8 & \text{if } w > 0 \end{cases} \tag{12}$$

As can be seen in Figure 5(a), $E_2(w)$ has two local minima, one on each side of the origin. The deeper minimum, at $w = 1$, leads to the incorrect policy, always *jump*. However, the minimum at $w = -1$ gives the desired policy, always *stay*. The existence of these two local minima means that convergence to the optimal policy using the local learning rule will depend heavily on the initial conditions. In general, the minimum of the parabola corresponding to one side of the origin may or may not lie on that side. If, for example, the analysis is redone for the basis $[0, 1, 0, 1]^T$, one sees that there is only one local minimum, at the value $w = 2$, which will lead to the optimal policy (see Figure 5(b)). Although, in these two examples there was a local minimum in the optimal policy's half-plane, this is not always true; it is a simple exercise to construct a cost schedule that results in no local minima or a local minimum only on the side of the origin corresponding to the incorrect policy.

The piecewise quadratic nature of $E_2(\mathbf{w})$ is completely general. The quadratic pieces lie in conical regions, "policy cones", which are separated by hyperplanes with O^{th} or 1st order discontinuities, corresponding to

270

the values of $\mathbf{w}$ where $\mathbf{w}^T g(x,a) = \mathbf{w}^T g(x,b)$, for some $x \in S$, and some $a,b \in A, a \neq b$. A general rule has yet to be found for predicting whether a policy cone's quadratic surface will have a local minimum inside the cone, generating a policy stable with respect to the local learning rule. In any case, it is likely that there will be more than one stable solution, and thus even if unbiased gradient information were available, the final policy would depend heavily on the initial weights of the bases.

CONCLUSION

The implications of using function approximators to represent Q-Values has been investigated. Two criteria of optimality were considered. The main result concerning the global criterion is that optimality in the sense of least-squares distance of the Q-Value estimates to their true values does not translate into nearly optimal policies. When the global criterion is used in conjunction with a linear combination of bases functions, it will, with high probability, lead to extremely suboptimal policies in the case where the bases do not span the state×action space.

The local learning criterion, on the other hand, may have local minima in the conical regions of weight space corresponding to any of the possible policies. Thus, while there may be minima near the optimal policy, the policy the learner finds will depend heavily on the initial conditions of the weight vector.

These results suggest that a linear combination of basis functions will often not be a feasible representation for estimating the Q-Values. Although a crafty choice of bases could result in a good policy with a relatively small number of bases, this could require knowing the Q-Values in advance. Although that assumption was made here, the goal of this work is to point out potential difficulties with using function approximators in more general reinforcement learning settings. In any case, success of combining function approximators with Q-Learning will require careful selection of the approximators being used. More complicated or more specialized representation schemes will have to be employed, making analysis of convergence and performance even more difficult.

Acknowledgments

This research was supported by an ONR Graduate Fellowship. I would like to thank my advisor, Michael Jordan, for his guidance, and Peter Dayan for his insightful comments and helpful criticism.

References

[1] Barto, A. G., Bradtke, S. J., and Singh, S. P. (1993). Learning to Act Using Real-Time Dynamic Programming. (COINS technical report 91-57). Amherst: University of Massachusetts.

[2] Bertsekas, D.P. (1987). *Dynamic Programming* Englewood Cliffs, NJ: Prentice Hall, Inc.

[3] Jaakkola, T., Jordan, M. I., and Singh, S. P. (1993). On the Convergence of Stochastic Iterative Dynamic Programming Algorithms. Submitted for Publication.

[4] Tesauro, G. J. (1992). Practical Issues in Temporal Difference Learning *Machine Learning*, **8**, pp.257–277.

[5] Thrun, S. B. and Schwartz, A. (1993). Issues in Using Function Approximation for Reinforcement Learning. Same volume.

[6] Watkins, C. J. C. H. (1989). Learning from Delayed Rewards. PhD Thesis, University of Cambridge, England.

[7] Watkins, C. J. C. H. and Dayan, P. (1992). Q-Learning. *Machine Learning*, **8**, pp.279–292.

[8] Werbos, P. J. (1990). Consistency of HDP Applied to a Simple Reinforcement Learning Problem. *Neural Networks*, **3**, pp.179–189.

Efficient Learning of Multiple Degree-of-Freedom Control Problems with Quasi-independent Q-agents

Kevin L. Markey

Department of Computer Science and Institute of Cognitive Science
University of Colorado
Boulder, Colorado 80309-0430
markey@cs.colorado.edu

We propose a new architecture in which autonomous or quasi-independent agents cooperate to solve control problems in large action spaces. Action space is decomposed according to its degrees of freedom, and each agent uses the Q-learning algorithm to control actions along a single action space dimension. The technique outperforms a single agent in the control of a small, abstract speech articulation model. It also learns to perform some simple articulatory tasks in controlling a realistic vocal tract model with 10 degrees of freedom.

Introduction

With few exceptions (e.g., [10]), reinforcement learning algorithms have been applied to relatively small problems with very simple action spaces: simple mazes and maze games, the inverted pendulum on a cart, abstract robotic tasks, and the like. Larger scale problems of realistic robotic or industrial control or even speech production will require more complex action spaces. It would be helpful if learning complexity need not keep pace with the increased complexity of the tasks, or at least not grow exponentially with the dimensionality of the problem.

One popular strategy is to decompose a complex task into smaller, less complex tasks. Dayan & Hinton's "feudal reinforcement learning" [3] and Moore & Atkeson's kd-tree tessellation [6] offer territorial or *state space* decomposition strategies. Singh [8] splits up the *goal space* of a complex sequential task using an adaptive mixture of experts [4]. Whitehead [14] shows that a committee of agents can decrease learning time by observing each other's experience. Tan [11] pioneers the use of cooperating agents on a joint task. Our contribution also uses several agents in a joint task, but we propose to decompose the *action space* according to its degrees of freedom.

We employ a collection of cooperating autonomous or semi-autonomous agents. They operate in parallel. Each controls only a single dimension in action space: one joint angle of a multi-joint arm, one vocal tract articulator, one parameter of an industrial process. Their collective behavior replaces the behavior of a single agent. Agents share state information. Each agent employs the Q-learning algorithm [12] to estimate the long-term expected value of each action given the state, but for only those actions within a single dimension.

If this technique is successful, Q-learning could be applied to much larger scale problems. Standard Q-learning requires a unique utility estimate for each state-action pair. Consider the Q-table needed to control a vocal tract model which has 10 control parameters, each having between 2 and 10 possible values. That amounts to upwards of 10 million utility estimates for each state. Certainly, many vocal tract configurations overlap anatomically or acoustically and many are anatomically impossible, but what if such constraints are not known in advance? Traditional Q-learning can have difficulty sampling the entire action space. Independent agents can sample actions along a single degree of freedom exhaustively and quickly, even if collectively they still have difficulty covering the entire space.

We test the technique to control the phonetic output of a small, abstract speech articulation model involving only 4 binary phonological features. We then apply it to a realistic vocal tract model with 10 degrees of freedom. We have not tested the method in other domains, and vocal tract control results are still preliminary, but our results are encouraging. We explore the possibilities and limitations of the technique in discussion, below.

Reinforcement Learning and Q-learning Architectures

Reinforcement learning — and the Q-learning algorithm in particular — is a method for learning an extended plan of action which maximizes the net long-term discounted reward received by an agent as result of its actions. Q-learning has been shown to converge to an optimal plan for a finite Markov decision process [13] under a number of specific conditions. Despite evidence that convergence is not guaranteed for Q-values estimated by function approximation [12], approximation by neural networks and other means is widespread in order to take advantage of their generalization properties, especially for large state spaces.

Single-agent Q-learning with function approximation by a single multi-layer network

Our method of approximating a Q-value table for a *single agent* with a single multi-layer feedforward network is adapted from Lin [5]. The network takes state x as input. It has one output for each possible action in the agent's action space. The action space A from which an action a is chosen has n degrees of freedom, each defining a separate subspace, A^j, $j=1..n$, where $A = A^1 \times ... \times A^n$. Each action a is represented as an n-tuple in A. If the number of possible actions in each dimension is d^j, $j=1..n$, then the number of actions and the number of network outputs is $\prod d^j$.

At time t, a single agent observes state x. The i-th output of the network is the currently estimated utility $Q(x, a_i)$ of action a_i given the current state x as its input. Action a is chosen according to a Boltzmann distribution $p(a_i|x)$ across all possible actions A, where temperature T determines the randomness of the action selection and is varied during learning according to some annealing schedule.

$$p(a_i|x) = e^{Q(x, a_i)/T} \Big/ \sum_{a_k \in A}^{n} e^{Q(x, a_k)/T} \tag{1}$$

Action a is performed, thence new state y and a scalar reinforcement signal r are sensed at time $t+1$. The newly predicted utility is the sum of the current reinforcement r and the maximum estimated utility in state y discounted by rate γ: $r + \gamma \cdot \max_{a_k \in A} \{Q(y, a_k)\}$. The network is adjusted by back propagating the square of the utility function's temporal difference error E [9] only for that output unit corresponding to the action a chosen at time t.

$$E = r + \gamma \cdot \max_{a_k \in A} \{Q(y, a_k)\} - Q(x, a) \tag{2}$$

No error is back propagated through the other output units. The calculation uses activations stored at time t.

Q-learning with cooperating autonomous subagents

We employ one autonomous agent (henceforth "subagent") for each degree of freedom in the action space A. Each is implemented as a separate network. The method for each subagent is similar to that used by the single agent; however, instead of learning a complete Q-value table, each subagent explores only those actions in its own subspace and learns only the corresponding portion of the Q-table. There is no explicit representation of the entire Q-table; together the agents must cooperatively explore the entire action space.

1. There are n networks, one for each degree of freedom j, each computing the estimated value $Q^j(x, a^j)$ of some action $a^j \in A^j$, the subspace of actions in dimension j. All networks receive the same global state x.

2. Network j has only d^j outputs, one for each action in dimension j, its action a^j chosen only from A^j. The Boltzmann distribution is computed as in (1) but only over actions in A^j. The action seen by the environment is the n-tuple $a = (a^1, ..., a^n)$ constructed of the actions chosen independently by each network. Action selection by each subagent is independent of the selections by other subagents.

3. The temporal difference error E^j is computed for each network j similar to the single-agent case, except that actions range over the subspace A^j, not A. The square of this error is back propagated through the output unit corresponding to the action a^j selected at time t.

$$E^j = r + \gamma \cdot \max_{a^j_k \in A^j} \{Q^j(y, a^j_k)\} - Q(x, a^j) \tag{3}$$

273

Q-learning with quasi-independent subagents

Quasi-independent subagents are similar to autonomous subagents insofar as they compute the Q-values and select actions independently for each degree of freedom in the action space. They resemble single-agent approximators in that they are implemented by a single network in order to share internal hidden unit features.

1. There is one network. The number of outputs is $\sum d^j$, not $\prod d^j$. The outputs are organized into n groups, each group representing a subagent, one for each degree of freedom j. Subagent group j has only d^j outputs; each computes the estimated value $Q^j(x, a^j)$ of some action $a^j \in A^j$. The Boltzmann distribution is computed only over actions in A^j and only over outputs in group j. Like autonomous subagents, the action seen by the environment is constructed of actions chosen independently by each group.

2. The temporal difference error E^j is computed *for each subagent group j* per equation (3). *In each subagent group j the square of this error is back propagated through the output unit corresponding to the action a^j* selected by group j at time t. The quasi-independent subagent network receives n error signals, one for each dimension; the n autonomous subagent networks together receive n error signals; but the single-agent network receives only *one* error signal among all its output units.

Class of candidate problems

The domains for which this technique is intended are those whose complex actions may be naturally decomposed along multiple degrees of freedom. The requirements of Q-learning must not be violated by the task decomposition. Together all subagents must jointly visit all states and test all possible joint actions. The natural class of candidate problems are those involving the control of multiple articulators. Motor control, including control of the vocal tract, are candidates. The technique should be attractive for control problems with especially high dimension action spaces.

Demonstration 1: Control of a simple, abstract speech articulation model

We compare each technique's ability to learn the "pronunciation" of a target consonant-vowel syllable using a small, abstract, greatly simplified articulatory model. There are four articulators — voice, jaw, tongue body, and lips — each capable of two actions. The voice is "on" or "off", and the jaw, tongue body, and lips each move to jointly open or close the vocal tract to various degrees and at various locations. There are 16 possible actions, the cross product of the action spaces of each articulator.

$$A = A_{\text{voice}} \times A_{\text{jaw}} \times A_{\text{tongue}} \times A_{\text{lips}} \qquad (4)$$

Each sequence of actions is interpreted for its "phonetic" results, which is encoded as a set of phonetic features for vowel quality, place of contact, voicing, and the change in each such phonetic feature since the prior time step. Interpreting the sound of each articulatory configuration depends on surrounding context. Hence, the sound which results from actions at time t is not determined until time $t+1$.

The target sound pattern used in the simulations reported here is /ki/ ("key"). For this simple phonological model, the target sound initially requires simultaneous closure of the jaw and tongue body with silent vocal cords and open lips, a configuration interpreted as a posterior stop consonant when adjacent to a vowel. This must be followed by simultaneous voicing and lowering of the tongue body while the jaw remains partially closed and the lips remain open, a configuration interpreted as a high vowel.

Each trial starts at some random articulatory configuration with voicing set "off". Reinforcement of 1.0 is received and the trial ends after the target sound is detected. A trial may also end after some maximum number of steps without hitting the target. State consists of the current and previous articulatory configurations. There are 256 possible states. All articulatory configurations are possible, but not all configurations and sequences are "audible".

Interpretation as a maze task

Despite this articulatory and phonetic interpretation, the task may be viewed more simply and more abstractly as traversing a 4-dimension maze (one dimension for each articulator.) Each action moves the player from one vertex to another (or keeps it at the same vertex). The goal of the task is to traverse the maze along a particular route (see Figure 1). Reinforcement is received one step after having traversed the target route. For this reason, state must consist of

274

the current *and* previous vertices in the maze. Otherwise, the Q-function is ill-defined. All phonetic interpretation "adds" to this simple maze interpretation is a method to detect whether the target route is traversed.

Figure 1: Abstract vocal tract control problem viewed as an *n*-dimensional maze.

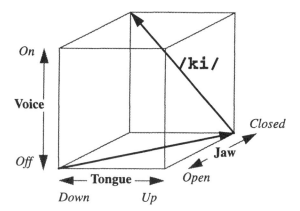

The articulatory trajectory for the target utterance /**ki**/. In this instance, we start with voice *off*, tongue *down*, and jaw *open*. To form the target syllable we first nearly *close* the jaw, move the tongue *up*, and keep the voice *off* to start the /k/. Next we turn the voice *on* and *lower* the tongue while keeping the jaw nearly *closed* to form the high vowel /i/. The lip dimension is not shown.

Details, parameters, procedures

The input representation for each network is a 16-unit localist representation of state. The single agent has 16 output units. It implements a complete table of Q-values for all state/action pairs. There are 4 autonomous subagent networks, each with 2 outputs. The quasi-independent subagent network has 8 outputs, organized into four 2-output groups, one for each subagent. Each subagent network or subagent group implements a separate Q-value table; each table stores Q-values only for that subagent's 2 possible actions paired with all possible states.

The single-agent network has 9 hidden units, the quasi-independent-subagent network has 12 hidden units, and each autonomous-subagent network has 4 hidden units to ensure that each architecture has 288 free parameters. The discount rate γ is 0.9; learning rate η is varied from 0.1 to 1.5. Temperature T starts at 1.0. After every 1000 steps we increase the reciprocal of T by θ, 0.5. Temporal difference recency parameter λ is zero.

Reinforcement of 1.0 is received after the target sound is detected, but only for honest work. The vocal tract may sometimes start randomly from the /k/ configuration, but the agent(s) are not rewarded for simply generating the next segment /i/ until they generate the full sequence /ki/ independently of initial configuration. A network is judged to converge to the solution if it "pronounces" the target "sound" and receives reward in at least 90% of its trials (tallied over bins of about 320 trials each), and remains above 90% performance until the temperature reaches 0.01. Results are averaged over 50 to 100 simulations for each set of experimental conditions.

Results

Quasi-independent and autonomous subagent architectures learn this task and significantly outperform the single-agent architecture. Assuming that each method operates at its optimal learning rate, the single agent method still takes 56% longer to converge than either independent subagent method. Moreover, we have never found a set of learning parameters for which the single agent converges reliably. Success rates exceeding 90% occur only within narrow windows of learning and annealing rates. We have been able to tweak the success rate up to 94% but only at the expense of training speed — with a learning rate of 0.9 and an annealing rate of 0.25, convergence requires more than 120,000 steps. On the other hand, the independent subagent methods prove reliable over wide ranges of learning parameters.

Table 1: Performance of Three Designs for Optimal Learning Rates

Design	Learning Rate	% Success	Steps before convergence	Standard deviation
Single agent	1.3	92%	50,700	8,810
Autonomous subagents	0.9	100%	32,300	2,620
Quasi-independent agents	0.5	100%	32,500	2,640

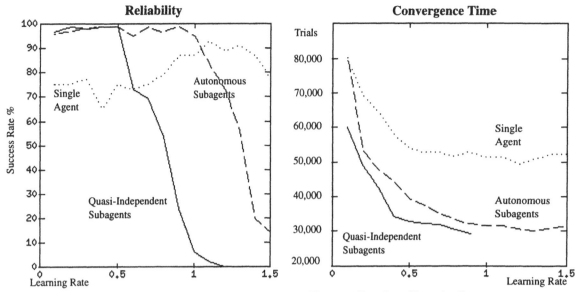

Figure 2: Reliability and Convergence Time as a Function of Learning Rate

This task is unable to distinguish the performance of quasi-independent and autonomous subagents, despite practical advantages of the former. For any given learning rate, the quasi-independent method outperforms the others. However, when comparing performances given each method's optimal learning rate, there is little difference between the two autonomous subagent architectures.

These results assume a constant number of free parameters (288 weights) across all architectures. Nearly identical results are obtained when the number of hidden units is kept constant (4 hidden units for each network). The quasi-independent method requires fewer free parameters for a given number of hidden units: for this task 25% fewer weights than the single agent and only one-third of the weights needed by the four autonomous subagents.

Demonstration 2: Controlling a realistic vocal tract model.

We use the quasi-independent architecture to control a realistic vocal tract model. The vocal tract model is based in part on Haskins Laboratories' ASY articulatory synthesizer [7]. Six articulators which vary along 10 degrees of freedom specify the vocal tract's configuration: jaw (joint angle), tongue body (distance and angle relative to the jaw hinge), tongue tip (length and angle relative to a point on the tongue body), lips (protrusion and height), hyoid (anterior and superior distance relative to a fixed point), and voicing amplitude (decibels).

Following [2], each articulator's trajectory conforms to the motion of a critically damped spring from its current position to the chosen target position, its speed specified as a spring constant set such that the motion approximates the speed of the human vocal tract. We shall refer to each such motion as a "gesture." The controller does not choose each point through which an articulator will pass during a gesture, only the location of the terminating point. A lower level model of spring dynamics controls the actual motion until interrupted by a new gesture. Successful completion of any task requires the proper timing and sequence of gestures in all articulatory dimensions.

The controller is a quasi-independent Q-approximator with one subagent for each articulatory degree of freedom. We define a set of gestural targets corresponding to values spaced roughly evenly along each articulator's range of possible configurations plus a "null" gesture which has no effect on the current trajectory. At each discrete time step (corresponding to 8 msec of real world time), trajectories are updated and each subagent chooses the next gesture. A gesture which matches the previously chosen gesture has no effect. If a new gesture is chosen during a refractory period immediately following the start of the previous gesture, it replaces the old gesture with a probability quadratically proportional to the progress of the old gesture.

The controller's input is the state of the vocal tract: its present configuration and trajectory plus tactile and other proprioceptive feedback. Vocal tract configuration is a real vector of articulator positions, each scaled between 0 and 1. Trajectory is a similarly scaled real vector representing the target vocal tract configuration plus a measure of the progress of each current gesture along its trajectory which roughly corresponds to its "phase" in state space. Six units represent "phase" for each of the 10 active articulatory parameters, 13 inputs represent vocal tract configuration and another 13 units represent target positions of the active gestures (including 3 inactive articulators). An extra 3 units measure other proprioceptive signals for a total of 89 inputs.

We test the architecture's performance on two tasks. Task 1 corresponds to the motion of a stop consonant without regard to place-of-articulation. Starting in some neutral position, the tongue must lift and make contact with some region of the roof of the mouth and then release contact, or the lips must close, touch, then release. This must occur in minimal time without encountering physically impossible configurations. Task 2 requires contact to be made at a particular place-of-articulation. In order to accomplish these tasks, the controller must learn the right combination, sequence, and timing of gestures. Successful completion of the task within a time-out period garners a reward of 1.0 and ends the trial. An impossible physical configuration receives a penalty of –1.0 and ends the trial. Otherwise, a trial ends without reward or penalty after timing out. There is a secondary reinforcement signal whose purpose is to discourage new gestures during the refractory period. Learning rates and annealing schedules are task-dependent.

For task 1 we test two output/action representations. The more constrained representation divides action space into 6 degrees of freedom, one for each major vocal tract articulator. A range of gestures is defined for each articulator — 7 jaw, 7 lip, 3 tongue tip, 10 tongue body, 7 hyoid, and 5 voicing gestures — for a total of 51,450 possible action combinations. In the less constrained representation, we let each of 9 articulatory dimensions vary over a greater range of actions. There are 9 jaw angle, 5 lip height, 7 lip protrusion, 7 tongue tip angle, 6 tip length, 12 tongue body angle, 10 tongue body displacement, 7 hyoid, and 5 voicing targets for a total of 55.6 million possible action combinations. Implementing such an action space would be unthinkable with a single Q-value table or with one network output per action. However, the quasi-independent architecture needs only 68 outputs.

Results

We measure the success of these tasks by the average time per trial necessary to complete the target trajectory and reach the final desired configuration. Worst case is to time out after 2.0 seconds. Based on the time required for a hand-crafted solution to accomplish each task, best case for tasks 1 or 2 is about 65 to 75 msec per trial. "Time" here is as simulated by the vocal tract model's dynamics.

Task 1 easily discovers stop-consonant motion regardless of action/output representation. During the first 500 trials, simulations can generate stop-consonant motion by random or near-random flailing in 263 to 370 msec per trial (33 to 46 time steps). Within 6,400 to 9,800 trials, performance improves to less than 100 msec per trial. The less constrained action/output representation is more likely to experience success by random flailing, but it takes longer to converge and is less likely to find the optimal solution. Indeed, neither representation is guaranteed to be optimal. Given the huge action space, each learns to "satisfice" the task's requirements given the learning rate and annealing schedule. Agents learn to choose the place-of-articulation (alveolar ridge or lips) which they can contact and release in the least time, but they waffle between different nearly equivalent solutions.

Table 2: Stop-consonant Motion Comparing Action/Output Representations (Task 1)

Action/Output Representation	Time/trial at start of simulation	Time/trial after 10,000 trials	Trials to converge to <100 msec
6 degrees of freedom, 39 outputs	370 msec	78 msec	6,420
9 degrees of freedom, 68 outputs	263 msec	86 msec	9,800

The second, more difficult task takes longer to learn, but after 20,000 trials the quasi-independent subagent architecture has achieved near-optimal alveolar and labial stop-consonant motions. The velar stop-consonant motion is attained by a narrower range of gesture combinations than the alveolar motion. This greater difficulty is reflected in initial near-random performance and time until convergence, as summarized in Table 3.

Table 3: Stop-consonant Motion to Specific Place-of-Articulation with Less-Constrained Representation (Task 2)

Place-of-Articulation	Time/trial at start of simulation	Time/trial after 20,000 trials	Trials to converge to <200 msec
Labial	830 msec	77 msec	8,450
Velar	1,267msec	95 msec	13,550

Discussion

Each autonomous or quasi-independent agent implements a Q-value table only for its own actions. Why does the technique succeed without an explicit representation of the utility of all possible action combinations and without any explicit communication or planning among subagents?

Consider the problem from the point of view of one subagent exploring one degree of freedom. It attempts to maximize its future return without explicit regard for the behavior of others. It is probable, given some experience, that one action maximizes future return in any one particular state and is thus more likely to occur per the Boltzmann distribution (1). This will be the case for each subagent. But, the subagent's estimate of its *own* action's value is not a simple function of its own isolated behavior; rather it is a function of the joint behavior of all subagents. Since the subagent is not privy to other subagents' "planned" behavior for the current time step, it can only estimate it. Thus, its value estimate for its own actions in the current state is a function of the *expected behavior of the other subagents, conditioned on the current state*. A complete expression of subagent j's Q-value for action a^j in state x is thus:

$$Q^j(x, a^j) = Q^j(x, a^j | \{\mathbf{E}\{a^k | x\}, k \neq j\}), \quad j = 1 \ldots n \tag{5}$$

All agents are linked through a common shared state. Hence, current state — together with the distribution of other subagents' actions as conditioned on current state — is the implicit mechanism to "transmit" information about what agents are likely to do.[1]

The method succeeds *not* because subagents make mutually independent decisions. As we have argued, the decision along one dimension is based on the expected subagent behavior in other dimensions. Nor does the method succeed because each subagent's Q-value estimate somehow contributes additively to a joint estimate of state-action values. Instead, each subagent's estimate of the value of its own action must ultimately approximate the value of the joint action a of all subagents in state x.

$$\max_{a^j \in A^j} [Q^j(x, a^j | \{\mathbf{E}\{a^k | x\}, k \neq j\})] \to \max_{a \in A} [Q(x, a)], \quad j = 1 \ldots n \tag{6}$$

The subagents' cooperative, self-interested behavior [1] should ensure that this occurs, and independence of action space dimensions should prevent one subagent's hedonistic behavior from blocking another's optimal behavior.

In some applications it may be necessary to use singular value decomposition or measure mutual information to determine whether action space dimensions are truly independent. This may be more crucial for the autonomous than the quasi-independent architecture. The latter's shared features may be able to resolve dependencies among action space dimensions, whereas autonomous subagents have no such mechanism. The abstract articulatory "maze" task is unable to distinguish performance between the two methods. We have not yet compared their performance in controlling the realistic vocal tract model.

Relative Performance

Why are the independent subagents faster and more robust? They automatically generalize among points in action space which agree in one or more dimensions. This occurs by virtue of the subagent architecture. State transition and reinforcement is a function of joint action, but joint action is sparsely represented, distributed among d subagents. Error correction is likewise distributed among d subagent actions. In contrast, the single agent has a local representation of joint action and learns about only one action at a time. Subagent generalization results in a speed and reliability advantage for tasks in which similar input states demand similar subagent actions. Our demonstration problems are rich with such examples. For tasks in which similar input states lead to dissimilar actions, the single agent might perform better.

Also contributing to independent subagent speed and reliability are sample effects. Since the subagent action space over which Q-values are estimated is much smaller than the joint action space, estimates should converge faster with a lower variance. The greater the joint action space dimension, the greater is the advantage.

Why is the performance gain not more dramatic? Each subagent depends in part on the existence of a well-defined action distribution for each other subagent. Yet, action distributions are not stationary, since each subagent is

---

1. I am indebted to Steve Nowlan for suggesting this interpretation.

still learning the task. Furthermore, they must still jointly explore the entire action space. For huge spaces this may be impossible for all but the slowest annealing schedules. To the extent that a task is aided by generalization among actions which agree in one or more dimensions, independent subagents may avoid the need for exhaustive search. Single agents are not so fortunate. Still, it is clear from our results that such generalization is not a panacea, as independent subagents do not always find the optimal solution, and most of the instability in our simulations occurs as subagents abandon a suboptimal solution in search of a better one.

Future Research

We plan to extend our results to more complex tasks using the gestural vocal tract model. First on the agenda is to learn primitive consonant-vowel syllables — a simple extension of the stop-consonant motion tasks, but one which involves considerable delay between required actions and final reinforcement upon recognition of the target syllable. Also, application of the technique to new problems and domains is needed to better characterize its generality and limitations.

Acknowledgments

This research is supported by NSF Presidential Young Investigator award IRI-9058450 and grant 90-12 from the James S. McDonnell Foundation to Michael Mozer. We thank Philip Rubin and Haskins Laboratories for making the ASY articulatory synthesizer software available and Troy Sandblom for rewriting it for C and Unix. I acknowledge the guidance of Mike Mozer and Lise Menn, editorial assistance and insights by Steve Nowlan, and assistance by Chuck Anderson, Brian Bonnlander, Franco Callari, Peter Dayan, Satinder Singh, Andreas Weigend and Richard Yee.

References

[1] A.G. Barto, "Learning by statistical cooperation of self-interested neuron-like computing elements," *Human Neurobiology,* vol 4, pp. 229-256, 1985.

[2] C.P. Browman and L. Goldstein, "Articulatory gestures as phonological units," *Phonology,* vol. 6, pp. 102-151, 1989.

[3] P. Dayan and G.E. Hinton, "Feudal reinforcement learning," in *Neural Information Processing Systems 5,* 1993, pp. 271-278.

[4] R.A. Jacobs, M.I. Jordan, S.J. Nowlan and G.E. Hinton, "Adaptive mixtures of local experts," *Neural Computation,* vol. 3, pp. 79-87, 1991.

[5] L-J. Lin, "Self-improving reactive agents based on reinforcement learning, planning and teaching," *Machine Learning,* vol 8, pp. 293-321, 1992.

[6] A.W. Moore and C.G. Atkeson, "Memory-based reinforcement learning: efficient computation with prioritized sweeping," in *Neural Information Processing Systems 5,* 1993, pp. 263-270.

[7] P. Rubin, T. Baer, and P. Mermelstein, "An articulatory synthesizer for perceptual research," *Journal of Acoustic Society of America,* vol. 70, pp. 321-328, August 1981.

[8] S.P. Singh, "Transfer of learning by composing solutions of elemental sequential tasks," *Machine Learning,* vol. 8, pp. 323-339, 1992.

[9] R.S. Sutton, "Learning to predict by the methods of temporal differences," *Machine Learning,* vol. 3, pp. 9-44, 1988.

[10] G. Tesauro, "Practical issues in temporal difference learning," *Machine Learning,* vol. 8, pp. 257-277, 1992.

[11] M. Tan, "Multi-Agent Reinforcement Learning: Independent vs. Cooperative Agents." in *Machine Learning: Proceedings of the Tenth International Conference,* 1993.

[12] C.J.C.H. Watkins, *Learning from delayed rewards,* Ph.D. Thesis, University of Cambridge, England, 1989.

[13] C.J.C.H. Watkins and P. Dayan, "Technical note: Q-Learning," *Machine Learning,* vol. 8, pp. 279-292, 1992.

[14] S.D. Whitehead, "A complexity analysis of cooperative mechanisms in reinforcement learning," In *Proceedings of AAAI-91,* pp. 607-613, 1991.

NEURAL ADAPTIVE CONTROL OF SYSTEMS WITH DRIFTING PARAMETERS

A. Tascillo and V. Skormin
T.J. Watson School of Engineering and Applied Science
Binghamton University
Binghamton, NY 13902
BB05244@BINGVAXA.CC.BINGHAMTON.EDU

A neural network controller is designed to effectively control a plant with drifting parameters. In response to parameter drift the *parent* network transitions to a specifically trained *child* control network exhibiting increased accuracy in the new parameter space if such accuracy is necessary and attainable. The controlling neural network itself possesses efficiently trained outputs to diagnose the drift of crucial plant parameters. Results are demonstrated for two plants, one linear, the other nonlinear.

INTRODUCTION

Although recent literature indicates a proliferation of neural network applications, significant challenges remain in the area of control engineering. The typical parallel algorithm [1] can effectively execute one repetitive, short term robotic task involving parameter estimation, command of motor joints, trajectory planning, and simple object grasping. In an increasing number of applications, however, product runs change and interchange rapidly requiring frequent adjustment, retooling, and maintenance. It would be desirable to implement an algorithm that could adapt to mechanical wear and product variation, greater required MTBF (Mean Time Between Failures).

The most common assumption of conventional parameter estimation techniques is that initial conditions be close to their target values. One alternative to this requirement is to employ a robust control scheme performing acceptably throughout the entire expected parameter space. However, even in this case it is required that the system be linear time invariant (LTI) and at least partially known [2]. The above approach becomes difficult to implement when the control task is extended from simple planar demonstrator models to redundantly jointed robots required to precisely manipulate unstable, variable loads at high speed in a cluttered workspace.

When faced with a highly complex and nonlinear control task, a human will split the problem up into manageable tasks. With this approach in mind, some neural network based controllers [3,4] have broken up the dynamic equations for a specific robot into small functional blocks, and then developed optimal linear combinations of these blocks via training. Unfortunately, robot configuration flexibility and some nonlinear effects cannot be properly addressed.

Can a control network be developed that is both sensitive and adaptive to the parameter variations of an arbitrary robot such that prespecified performance and robustness criteria shall be met? Inverse kinematics and dynamics can be estimated for a given robot in many ways, but the effect of parameter variation is most noticeable at individual joints. The function of a robot joint is theoretically simple: at any given moment, it must rotate clockwise or counterclockwise a specified distance. The movement control problem can be complicated, however, by variable parameters such as initial position with respect to gravity, load and environmental disturbances, sensor noise, friction, and beam stiffness. Any combination of the above can compound errors across many joints and result in excessive overshoot and/or settling time.

It was observed in [5] that a standard feedforward backpropagation neural network had little trouble learning the three dimensional inverse kinematics relationship for a five axis robot, but fine tuning of the position and orientation across the entire workspace was a more difficult task. In [6] a solution to the accuracy problem was attempted by training networks to operate within a sequence of small windows spanning the workspace. However, sudden transitions between window dedicated networks can result in unacceptable joint motor performance.

Various researchers have attempted to add intelligent decision making to alleviate performance degradation caused by these transitions. In [7], for instance, a supervisory gating network is utilized to determine the control signal based upon the weighted contributions of specialized expert controllers. Pomerleau's ALVINN [8], which interprets camera images to guide an automobile, employs a supervisory algorithm to choose a steering command by prioritizing the suggestions of individual expert networks, each specializing in highway driving, off road driving, obstacle avoidance, and the like. Upon implementation, data input interpretation difficulties have persisted, periodically confusing the networks. It is difficult to teach an algorithm a continuous sense of the driving experience when the task is interrupted by turns, obstacles, traffic patterns, road surface irregularities, scenery, and weather conditions. Whether multilayer perceptrons [8] or ART2 networks with edge detection preprocessing [9] are employed, these chaotically cyclic environmental factors must be incorporated into the training set and accounted for by the neural network.

It is known that the accuracy of a neural net based controller is affected by the way a training set is generated. In [5] it was suggested that a training set accumulated along a spiral shaped trajectory of points within a small three dimensional volume can considerably increase the accuracy of full size test trajectories spanning the workspace. Once the network extracts the inverse kinematics relationship, the relationship is valid everywhere.

PROBLEM APPROACH

The goal of the proposed neural network based controller is to generate a control effort for the system (or plant) of interest by minimizing some performance criterion. This problem can become complex due to non-stationary effects such as drifting plant parameters. This issue is addressed by system adaptation, traditionally requiring an additional control loop responsible for maintaining optimal controller characteristics. A neural network based approach has the potential for incorporating both the control and adaptation tasks in the same procedure, providing that a rational training set has been generated. Assuming no direct state or other parameter feedback, only integral and derivative variations of system output error and control effort are used as inputs for the networks.

While the control problem is the major emphasis of this effort, some valuable diagnostic information may be generated by the neural network controller. The advantage of adaptation emerges when additional diagnostic outputs can recognize the beginning of a parameter shift, revert to a network capable of handling all anticipated cases to an acceptable degree, then execute a smooth transition to a chosen specialized, more accurate network.

In order to accomplish these goals for a given system, a *parent* network is trained to thoroughly learn the desired control functional relationship across all anticipated operating conditions. This stable control can then be enhanced by initializing specialized *child* networks with the parent's weight values and then exposing each network to a new training set devoted to a system with a varied parameter. Having achieved an already similar relationship, the child will not need to radically alter its weights, thus offering a more continuously stable transition from the parent system. A separate diagnostic unit for each variable parameter is added to the parent network by freezing all of its existing weights and training a new set of linear connections leading directly to the diagnostic unit.

To demonstrate the approach, two types of systems are considered. The first evaluates the efficiency of the adaptive control procedure. A simple linear controlled plant, $1/(s+p)$, is designed with a constant gain feedback controller, $10-p$, that guarantees a first order response with a 0.4 second settling time. A neural network was trained to both imitate this adaptive controller and identify any drift of the time dependent parameter p (potentially a value between 1 and 5). It was found that linear connections from the network inputs to the diagnostic output were sufficient to accurately diagnose p, and that a linear transition between the two sets of weights resulted in a smooth control.

The simulation diagram used to train a neural controller for the second system, a DC motor, is shown in Figure 1. A pole placement state feedback controller is first found for each set of variable plant parameters, in this example load inertia J_{load}, friction b_{load}, and joint arm stiffness, k_{load}. Secondly, the network is trained with an enhanced backprop-based algorithm that has been designed to repeatably converge within a minimal number of epochs (Figure 2) and provide a stable and somewhat accurate control command, u_{new}, for all example parameter variations. A weighted error evaluation function is also used for training this output, varying the emphasis on initial transient control efforts versus those exerted near steady state. For the DC motor, linear connections from both the network inputs and the second layer of sigmoidal units are necessary for proper identification of drifted parameters. Pole placement creates a controller which assumes full access to all system states and generates unrealistically high feedback gains in order to achieve an ideal response (i.e., minimal settling time).

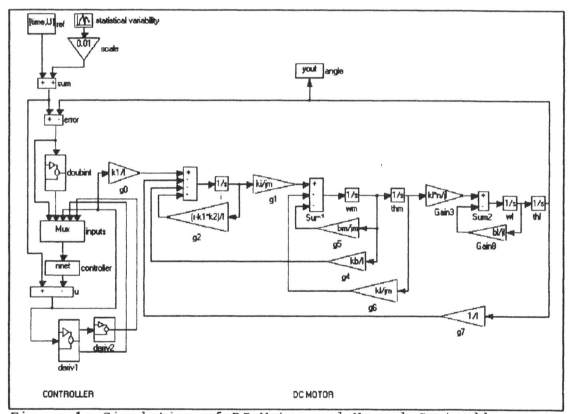

Figure 1: Simulation of DC Motor and Neural Controller.

The architecture of the neural controller network is shown in Figure 3, in which the hidden layer units are hyperbolic tangent sigmoidal activation functions and the output layer is linear.

Both neural network inputs and second hidden unit layer neurons contribute weighted connections to the output nodes. The inputs to the motor network are the error between the reference and the plant output, the error doubly integrated, the previous control input to the plant, and its derivative and second derivative values.

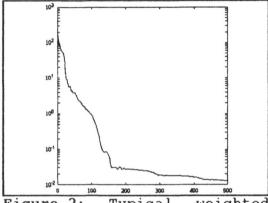

Figure 2: Typical weighted sum squared error curve.

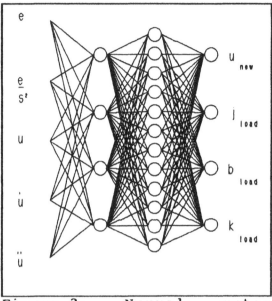

Figure 3: Neural motor controller.

RESULTS

Figure 4 shows the first order pole placement target response superimposed with both the slower, highly overshooting, uncontrolled plant and the improved, realistically implementable neural response. Figures 5 and 6 illustrate a series of linear system and motor neural controller responses to commands for a given set of parameters superimposed with the reference. Figures 7 and 8 are filtered responses to drifting parameters, closely fitting the actual values, some of which vary considerably from the initial system parameter. The actual output of the node follows a shape similar to the control output u_{new}, but the magnitude information can be easily and accurately extracted. Noise was then added to all inputs, resulting in the parameter diagnoses of Figures 9 and 10. Finally, parameter shifts were imposed upon the neural controlled system during implementation, an example of which is shown in Figure 11. Exhibiting a slightly different transient response, the new system picks up smoothly at a reference of two where the parent left off at the reference of one.

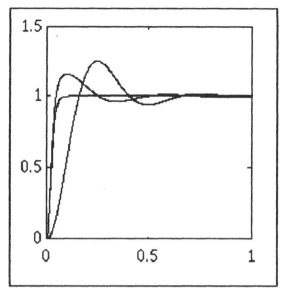

Figure 4: First order pole placement, high overshoot uncontrolled plant, and neural controller responses.

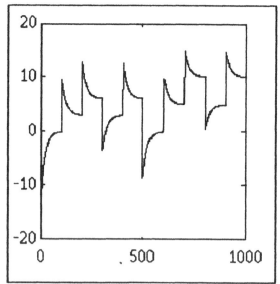

Figure 5: Trained linear system neural control efforts for small (1st 500 pts) and large (2nd 500 pts) parameter p.

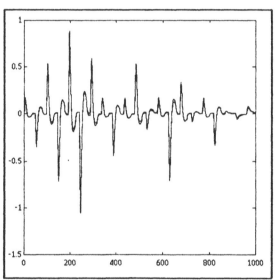

Figure 7: Trained neural motor control effort compared to pole placement effort for large and small inertia values.

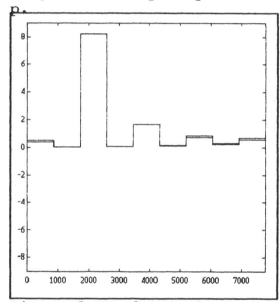

Figure 6: Load inertia output unit diagnosis, target versus actual for various values, determined as an average across 1000 sampled points.

INSIGHTS

Instantaneous disturbances affect the short term behavior of a system, potentially confusing local estimation schemes. A network of this type searches for a recognizable trend before

285

adjusting the controller, thus avoiding a cyclic oscillation of controller shifts. An additional supervisory layer could also be added to intelligently interpret multiple diagnostic outputs for the recognition of parameter interdependencies and rejection of noise.

Monitoring of limited local child network weight variations could provide insight regarding the network representation of a system's dynamics. By observing the changes in distinct features of a signal, a diagnostic network might be applied to the characterization of signals which are locally chaotic but globally structured such as music, speech, or power line resonance.

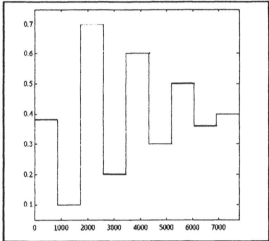

Figure 8: Load friction output unit diagnosis target versus actual for various values.

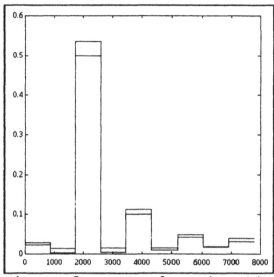

Figure 9: Load inertia diagnosis with sensor noise.

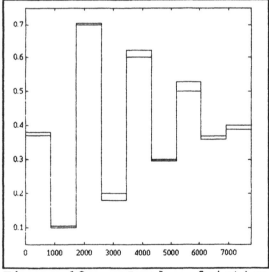

Figure 10: Load friction diagnosis with sensor noise.

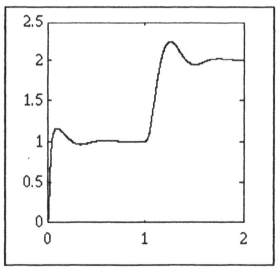

Figure 11: Neural controlled DC motor system response to a reference and parameter change.

286

REFERENCES

[1] Fijany, A., and A.K. Bejczy, "A Class of Parallel Algorithms for Computation of the Manipulator Inertia Matrix," **IEEE Transactions on Robotics and Automation**, vol. 5, pp. 600-615, 1989.

[2] Miller, D. and E. Davison, "Adaptive Control of a Family of Plants," **Control of Uncertain Systems**, ed. by D. Hinrichsen and B. Martensson. Boston: Birkhauser, 1990. pp. 197-219.

[3] Miyamoto, H., M. Kawato, T. Setoyama, and R. Suzuki, "Feedback-Error-Learning Neural Network for Trajectory Control of a Robotic Manipulator," **Neural Networks**, Vol. 1, pp. 251-265, 1988, pp. 251-265.

[4] Bassi, D., and G. Bekey, "Decomposition of Neural Network Models of Robot Dynamics: A Feasibility Study," in **Simulation and AI**, ed. by W. Webster. Society for Computer Simulation, 1989.

[5] Simons, A., **Robotic Trajectory Control Employing Anyanet Neural Architecture**, Master's Thesis, Rensselaer Polytechnic Institute, 1992.

[6] Goldberg, K., and B. Perlmutter, **Using a neural network to learn the Dynamics of the CMU Direct-Drive Arm II**, Report CMU-CS-88-160, Department of Computer Science, Carnegie Mellon University, 1988.

[7] Jordan, M., and R. Jacobs, "Hierarchical Mixtures of Experts and the EM Algorithm," in press, **Neural Computation**.

[8] Pomerleau, D. A., "Input Reconstruction Reliability Estimation," **Advances in Neural Information Processing Systems 5**, ed. by C. Giles, S. Hanson, and J. Cowan. San Mateo, Ca.: Morgan Kaufmann, 1993.

[9] Kornhauser, A. L., and E. C. Huber, "Lateral Control of Highway Vehicles Using Image Processing and Neural Networks," **Proceedings of the 2nd Regional Conference on Control Systems NJIT**, New Jersey, August 1993.

LEARNING ALGORITHMS
AND ARCHITECTURES

TEMPORALLY LOCAL UNSUPERVISED LEARNING: THE MAXIN ALGORITHM FOR MAXIMIZING INPUT INFORMATION

Randall C. O'Reilly
Department of Psychology
Carnegie Mellon University
Pittsburgh, PA 15213 USA
oreilly@cmu.edu

There are many appealing aspects of self-organizing learning rules, among them the notion that they are more "biologically plausible" than supervised learning algorithms. This plausibility usually derives from the ability to compute the algorithm with variables available locally to the unit or "neuron", typically using some variant of a Hebbian learning rule. Ironically, however, the locality *in time* of the variables that determine the learning is often ignored. This temporal non-locality presents a problem both from a biological and a psychological standpoint. In this paper, I present an alternative objective function for self-organizing algorithms that is local in both space and time, and results in a simple learning rule that can be implemented with properties of neuronal synaptic modification.

The issue of temporal non-locality takes several forms, some of which can be subtle. However, the central problem that lies behind the use of variables that are non-local in time is that they depend upon seeing a uniform random sample of the environment over the time period during which learning is to take place. While it is almost always possible to engineer the training set for a simulation so that the uniformity condition holds, the real world might not be so obliging. To instantiate the problem more fully, imagine the task of classifying different types of trees. In the real world, the kinds of trees one sees across different climates are not very uniformly distributed. Each climate zone tends to have associated with it a different set of trees, from palm trees to pine trees. Thus, if one were to spend several month's vacation in the tropics, where palm trees abound, the units representing these kinds of trees would be firing quite often, and those for the coniferous trees would be silent. Then, upon traveling to the Rocky Mountains for the remainder of the year, the reverse would occur. If one imagines that the entire space of trees is to be represented, then the appropriate time period to sample variables over is an entire year. However, this is clearly too long to wait to learn something new. With shorter time samples, the clustering of category instances over time will bias estimates of the mean and variance of unit firing rates, which might compromise the learning algorithm.

In its most obvious form, temporal non-locality is evident in the variables appearing directly in the learning rule. For example, the most general (and optimal with respect to the signal-to-noise ratio under certain conditions (Gaussian signal and noise, etc.) [16]) formulation of the Hebb rule is in terms of the covariance between pre and postsynaptic unit activities x_i and y_j:

$$\Delta w_{ij} \propto (x_i - \bar{x}_i)(y_j - \bar{y}_j) \tag{1}$$

This rule requires the average unit activities $(\bar{x}_i, \bar{y}_j)$, which in general must be estimated by measuring the activities of the units over time. This is clearly a violation of temporal locality, and it would suffer from the kind of temporal clustering described in the tree-classification example. A common solution to this problem is to assume that the means are constant and known in advance. This simply replaces the problem of temporal non-locality with that of introducing *a priori* assumptions about the environment and unit activities.

A more subtle example of temporal non-locality is that of Oja's learning rule [11], which extracts the first principle component of the input distribution:

$$\Delta w_{ij} \propto y_j (x_i - y_j w_{ij}) \qquad (2)$$

This appears to be completely local in both space and time. However, Linsker's analysis [8] of this learning rule in terms of the Infomax principle of this learning rule shows that it is approximately maximizing the output variance. Thus, the objective function that this algorithm is optimizing is non-local in time, since the variance of the output signal can only be defined over time. I would like to argue that even this kind of temporal non-locality presents a problem from a psychological, if not biological, perspective.

The problem is that the stochastic estimate of unit variance implicit in the Oja algorithm would be distorted by the clustering of categories in time. In the tree-classification example, all of the units in the network would end up representing subspecies of palm trees in the tropics and subspecies of pine trees in the Rockies, in order to maintain high levels of output variance over time spans shorter than half a year. Clearly, people are capable of maintaining representations even after years without using them, and extended exposure to a particular environment does not automatically lead to the kind of fine representation of the categories or features of that environment that one would expect if all of one's neurons were maintaining a high variance of activity. However, some movement in these directions is to be expected, so that there should be some sensitivity to the relevance of a category over time.

One implication of this argument is that any reliance on the information content of a unit's output signal constitutes a temporal non-locality. Under this definition, a wide range of unsupervised algorithms suffer from the problem, including the BCM rule and its derivatives [3, 6], decorrelation algorithms [4], and algorithms that maximize mutual information between units [2]. In Linsker's [8] proposal of the Infomax principle, which clearly depends on the information content of the output signal, he acknowledges the assumption of a uniformly distributed input environment, but claims that Infomax is more general than variance maximization because it is really about maximum information *preservation*, which can be defined even for non-uniform input environments. Instead of attempting to conditionalize something like the Infomax principle on various non-uniform assumptions about the input environment, the approach presented in this paper is to formulate the objective of an unsupervised algorithm in a way that avoids the use of the output signal information entirely.

The principle that I would like to suggest is called "MaxIn" for MAXimizing INput INformation. The objective of MaxIn is to develop units in a network which maximize the quality of information they receive from input patterns, as opposed to the amount of information they transmit over time. The central idea behind MaxIn is that the units can be viewed as something like matched filters [5, 15] which are optimally tuned to respond to a signal in the presence of noise. When matched filters are used in signal processing, they typically respond to a temporal signal like a pulse of light in a fiber-optic channel. In applying the concept to neural networks, the signal is instead the instantaneous pattern of activity over the input units, and the filter is parameterized by the weights of the unit from these input units. The objective of MaxIn is to adapt these weights so as to maximize the signal-to-noise ratio (SNR) of a given input. More precisely, it seeks to maximize the divergence between the probability of a unit becoming active when the signal is present and the probability when the signal is not present.

DERIVATION OF THE MAXIN ALGORITHM

To formalize this notion, consider a network having input units $\vec{x}$ whose activity is governed by an environment which contains regularities that are to be abstracted. A particular state of the input vector is denoted by the subscript k. For a given input vector, the output unit activations reflect the similarity between the input vector and the weight matrix (i.e. filter) for the output unit. For the sake of analytical simplicity, we model the activation of the output unit states y_j in probabilistic terms. Adopting a *generative model* with spherical Gaussian basis functions [10], it is useful to consider the activation as reflecting the probability that the input vector is generated by a given output unit whose mean is given by the weight vector $\vec{w}_j$. This probability is:

$$P_j(\vec{x}_k) = \frac{1}{K\sigma_j} e^{-\frac{\|\vec{x}_k - \vec{w}_j\|}{2\sigma_j^2}} \quad (3)$$

For the moment, we consider a single output unit, and compute the MaxIn function for it. In this case, the activation state of the output unit y_j is just $P_j(\vec{x}_k)$. The MaxIn objective function can be specified as the divergence between the probability of the unit having generated the input vector and the probability of the same unit (with the same mean $\vec{w}_j$) having generated an input vector of random noise:

$$M_s = P_j(\vec{x}_k) ln \frac{P_j(\vec{x}_k)}{P_j(\vec{n}_k)} \quad (4)$$

where the noise vector $\vec{n}_k$ is a vector of normally distributed random numbers with variance σ_k^2 and mean μ_k.

This function is maximized when the probability of generating the input vector is large relative to the probability of generating the random noise vector. Put another way, the unit will respond maximally to the input vector signal relative to its response to the noise. This is the same underlying principle as the G-Max algorithm proposed by Pearlmutter & Hinton [13], which maximizes the information gain of a unit from structured input patterns relative to the case where the input units are statistically independent (i.e. "unstructured"). Recently, Linsker [7] proposed a formulation that includes an idea similar to G-Max, which also makes use of the difference between structured and unstructured input "phases".

The critical difference between MaxIn and these G-Max style algorithms is the way in which the noise is estimated and used in the weight update. In G-Max, the network is run in two different phases, one with structured input and another with unstructured input, in order to sample both the actual environment and the case of independent input units. This makes the learning rule non-local in time, since two phases must be run to update the weights. In MaxIn, the unstructured input or "noise vector" is estimated using variables which are local to the unit both in space and time. Instead of sampling many different noise vectors to obtain the necessary estimate, the expected value of the noise vector is used. Thus, assuming normally distributed noise, this is just a vector having each element equal to the mean μ_k. Further, the value of μ_k for the noise is estimated based on the mean input activity level for the current input vector:

$$\mu_k = \frac{1}{N_i} \sum_i x_{ik} \quad (5)$$

providing the necessary locality of information. Thus, the noise is assumed to be of the same overall strength as the signal, only it is uniformly distributed across the input lines. MaxIn causes the weights to accentuate any deviation from this uniform distribution present in the signal.

The derivative of the MaxIn objective function with respect to the weights provides the gradient which can be used for learning. The complete derivative is somewhat complicated, and it is difficult to imagine a biological neuron computing it:

$$\frac{\partial M_s}{\partial w_{ij}} = \frac{1}{\sigma_j^2} P_j(\vec{x}_k) \left[(x_{ik} - \mu_k) + (x_{ik} - w_{ij}) ln \frac{P_j(\vec{x}_k)}{P_j(\vec{n}_k)} \right] \quad (6)$$

We label this the "Single-unit Full Derivative" or SFD MaxIn. However, there is a simplification which results in a very simple and biologically plausible weight update rule. This simplification is derived by assuming that the weight update is only supposed to optimize the log SNR term, and not the overall probability of generating the input vector. Under this assumption, the first $P_j(\vec{x}_k)$ term is treated as a constant with respect to the weights, resulting in the following approximation of the full derivative:

$$\frac{\partial M_s}{\partial w_{ij}} \approx \frac{1}{\sigma_j^2} P_j(\vec{x}_k)(x_{ik} - \mu_k) \quad (7)$$

The weight update rule that results from the simplified derivative is just:

$$\Delta w_{ij} = \frac{\epsilon}{\sigma_j^2} y_j (x_{ik} - \mu_k) \tag{8}$$

which we label "Single-unit Simplified Derivative" or SSD MaxIn.

SFD MaxIn can be thought of as the combination of the simpler SSD MaxIn learning rule with a learning rule that closely resembles standard competitive learning (CL) [14]. In our notation, CL can be written as:

$$\Delta w_{ij} = \epsilon y_j (x_{ik} - w_{ij}) \tag{9}$$

while a learning rule based on the full derivative contains equation 8 plus:

$$y_j (x_{ik} - w_{ij}) ln \frac{y_j}{y_j'} \tag{10}$$

where y_j' denotes the response of the unit to the noise input vector. Interestingly, if the unit is responding the same to the signal and the noise, this term goes to zero, and only the SSD equation is effective. However, as the SNR improves, this term gets stronger. The relevance of this additional term is explored in simulations reported below. Further, a hybrid algorithm that is a simple combination of SSD MaxIn and CL (without the log SNR weighting term of SFD) is tested as well.

One consequence of the SSD equation is that individual weights can increase or decrease without bound. Thus, in order for a MaxIn algorithm to be used in simulations, a weight bounding procedure must be used. While it is possible to simply clip the weights at 0 and 1, a more natural form of weight bounding multiplies weight increases by $(1 - w_{ij})$ and weight decreases by w_{ij}, resulting in an exponential approach to the limits of 0 and 1. This was used in all MaxIn simulations reported below.

EXTENSION TO MULTIPLE OUTPUT UNITS

The algorithm described above was derived for a single unit functioning in isolation. Such a unit would have a tendency to respond to all the input patterns. Usually it is desirable to have a layer of units which specialize on different clusters of the input patterns. One way this can be done is by making the activation of the unit reflect the likelihood that it generated the input vector as compared to all the other units. This could be thought of as the probability of the output unit having generated the given input vector [10]:

$$y_j = P(j|\vec{x}_k) = \frac{P_j(\vec{x}_k)}{\sum_l P_l(\vec{x}_k)} \tag{11}$$

where the index l goes over all the output units. Thus, the total probability of generating the input vector, summed over all units, is one.

Given the network just described, the MaxIn objective becomes:

$$M_m = P(j|\vec{x}_k) ln \frac{P(j|\vec{x}_k)}{P(j|\vec{n}_k)} \tag{12}$$

This can be expanded into a form that more easily shows the relationship between this multi-unit version and the previous single-unit version:

$$M_m = P(j|\vec{x}_k) \left(ln \frac{P_j(\vec{x}_k)}{P_j(\vec{n}_k)} - ln \frac{\sum_l P_l(\vec{x}_k)}{\sum_l P_l(\vec{n}_k)} \right) \tag{13}$$

Taking the derivative of this function is simplified by noting that $\frac{\partial (ln \sum_l P_l(\vec{x}_k))}{\partial w_{ij}} = P(j|\vec{x}_k)(x_i - w_{ij})$. This results in the "Multi-unit Full Derivative" (MFD):

$$\frac{\partial M_m}{\partial w_{ij}} = \frac{1}{\sigma_j^2} P(j|\vec{x}_k) ([(x_{ik} - \mu_k) - (P(j|\vec{x}_k)(x_{ik} - w_{ij}) - P(j|\vec{n}_k)(\mu_k - w_{ij}))] +$$

294

$$\left[(x_{ik} - w_{ij})(1 - P(j|\vec{x}_k)ln\frac{P(j|\vec{x}_k)}{P(j|\vec{n}_k)}\right]\right) \tag{14}$$

Obviously, this is a rather more complicated function than the simple single-unit MaxIn functions derived above. However, a simplification can be made by ignoring the effect of weight changes on the sum terms from equation 13 under the assumption that the effect of a single weight change on a sum over all the output units will likely be small. This results in the "Multi-unit Constant-sum Full Derivative" (MCFD):

$$\frac{\partial M_m}{\partial w_{ij}} \approx \frac{1}{\sigma_j^2} P(j|\vec{x}_k) \left[(x_{ik} - \mu_k) + (x_{ik} - w_{ij})(1 - P(j|\vec{x}_k)ln\frac{P(j|\vec{x}_k)}{P(j|\vec{n}_k)} \right] \tag{15}$$

which resembles the SFD equation (6).

In addition, the same arguments made for simplifying the SFD into the SSD equation can be made here (i.e. maximizing only the SNR term, while treating the $P(j|\vec{x}_k)$ as a constant with respect to the weights), resulting in a MSD (Multi-unit Simplified Derivative) equation:

$$\frac{\partial M_m}{\partial w_{ij}} \approx \frac{1}{\sigma_j^2} P(j|\vec{x}_k)(x_{ik} - \mu_k) \tag{16}$$

which produces the same weight update function as SSD (see equation 8) when $y_j = P(j|\vec{x}_k)$. This simple learning rule has the form of a noise differentiation term $(x_{ik} - \mu_k)$ which is gated by a kind of "competitive success" term $(P(j|\vec{x}_k))$, so that only those units which are likely to generate a given input vector have their weights updated. This allows the representational space to be partitioned off by the different units.

BIOLOGICAL COMPUTABILITY

The critical feature of the simplest MaxIn algorithm (equation 8) in terms of biological computability is that the weight change is driven by a simple difference between the input from one unit and the average of all other inputs to the unit. It is well known that the passive dendrite on a neuron acts like a diffusion process, so that discrete synaptic inputs in different spatial locations will result in a moderate elevation of the membrane potential over a wide region of the dendrite. Thus, the potential at any given synapse will be a sum of both the local input from the synapse and a more global potential elevation due to other synaptic inputs. The μ_k parameter in the MaxIn algorithm plays the role of this diffuse, global potential elevation. Thus, we can write the local synaptic potential as $V_{ij} = x_{ik} + \mu_k$.

Recent findings in long-term potentiation (LTP) and depression (LTD) [1] suggest that whether a weight experiences potentiation or depression depends upon two thresholds. If the cell is not potentiated at all, no weight change occurs. If the cell is somewhat potentiated (e.g. above a low threshold) weight decrease occurs. However, if the cell is potentiated above a higher threshold, weight increase occurs. In the context of the synaptic potential V_{ij} given above, the low threshold might be right around μ_k, so that a synapse receiving no additional input while the cell is being excited by other inputs will experience LTD. If the high threshold were around $2\mu_k$, then inputs around the average would fall between LTD and LTP, and would not experience synaptic modification. However, inputs stronger than μ_k would be above the LTP threshold, and would result in potentiation.

EVALUATION OF THE MAXIN ALGORITHM

There are a multitude of other algorithms which MaxIn can be compared to, but the simplest is probably the competitive learning (CL) algorithm [14]. In particular, the "Soft" version of this algorithm (SCL) as presented by Nowlan [10] shares the same probabilistic assumptions as those used in the derivation of the MaxIn algorithm. SCL uses the following weight update rule:

$$\Delta w_{ij} = \frac{1}{k_j(t-1) + y_j} y_j(x_{ik} - w_{ij})$$

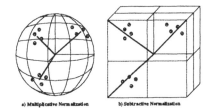

Figure 1: **a)** Multiplicative weight normalization yields (n-dimensional) spherical weight vectors pointed at the center of cluster of input patterns. **b)** Subtractive weight normalization yields weight vectors pointing at the corner of a (n-dimensional) hypercube closest to the input cluster.

$$k_j(t) \quad = \quad k_j(t-1) + y_j \tag{17}$$

where the parameters y_j, w_{ij} and x_{ik} are defined as in the multi-unit MaxIn derivation. This learning rule is the same as CL (equation 9) using a learning rate that decreases over time. This is the "statistically correct" way to perform iterative (on-line) weight updates, but in practice k_j is initialized to $.5N/M$ and bounded by N/M, where N is the number of input patterns and M is the number of output units. Thus, it is a reasonable simplification to replace this adaptive learning rate with a constant, which is what we do in our simulations for reasons that are explained below.

In comparing MaxIn with SCL, the issue of multiplicative *vs* subtractive normalization is relevant. This is explored first, followed by simulations which show what happens to these algorithms when the input patterns are clustered in time.

Subtractive *vs* Multiplicative Normalization

Competitive Learning is closely related to the Oja rule (equation 2), which, with linear output units, normalizes the weight vector to unit length. This causes each weight to reflect the weighted average (over all input units and input patterns) of each input's tendency to be active. This can be seen in a simple way by replacing y_j with the linear activation function: $\sum_i x_{ik}w_{ij}$, and computing the equilibrium weight value for a single input vector. When $\Delta w_{ij} = 0$, $x_{ik} = y_j w_{ij}$, and:

$$\breve{w}_{ij} = \frac{x_{ik}}{\sum_l x_{lk}w_{lj}} \tag{18}$$

where (˘) denotes equilibrium, and l is an index over all the input units. The pattern-wise equilibrium is just a similar weighted sum over all input patterns. This makes it clear that the Oja rule is performing what Miller & MacKay [9] term "multiplicative" (i.e. dividing by the sum) normalization.

In contrast, the MaxIn learning rule (in the simplified form) performs a kind of subtractive normalization. Indeed, the MaxIn rule of equation 8 is identical to the Zero-Sum Hebbian learning rule (ZSH) [12], which causes the total weight increase to a unit to be balanced by an equal amount of weight decrease, yielding a net change of zero. This should be evident from equation 8 since μ_k is the mean of the elements in the vector $\vec{x}_k$ (see equation 5). While Miller & MacKay [9] discuss the differences between multiplicative and subtractive normalization at length, a simple figure captures the essence. The multiplicative normalization in the Oja rule causes the weight vector to move to the *center* of the clusters in the data as can be seen in the hypersphere representation in figure 1. In contrast, the subtractive normalization in MaxIn causes the weights to go towards the *nearest corner* of the hypercube to the data cluster. Note that this effect is independent of the activation function.

While SCL does not have the normalization properties of the Oja rule, it does result in a weight vector pointing at the center of the cluster of input patterns the unit represents. The importance of the corner *vs* the center distinction is that since the weights under MaxIn have a pressure to end up in a corner of weight space, they have an intrinsic preferred direction for distinguishing between input clusters. As is shown in figure 2

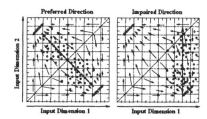

Figure 2: Subtractive normalization like that present in MaxIn results in a preferred direction (indicated by the vector field lines) for the weight changes, enhancing distinctions along this direction and impairing them otherwise. The second panel shows an example of an impaired dimension.

for the two-dimensional case, this direction lies perpendicular to the diagonal between input dimensions. Interestingly, this direction corresponds to the case of the input clusters having their centers at points where the coordinates sum to the same value (i.e. they have the same mean in the sense in which μ_j is computed for the MaxIn algorithm).

One would expect that the subtractive normalization in MaxIn would enhance its ability to distinguish categories along the preferred direction and impair distinctions along other directions. Algorithms that put the weight vectors at the center of the clusters, like SCL, on the other hand, should not have a preferred direction. These predictions were tested by constructing two-dimensional input patterns drawn from two Gaussian generators located at different points in the input space, but with a common σ of .2. In one case, the centers of the Gaussians were located along the preferred direction for MaxIn. As noted above, the coordinates of these centers have the same mean for the two Gaussians, so this is called the Same Mean (SM) condition. The coordinates used were [(.1,.9) (.9,.1)], [(.2,.8) (.8,.2)], [(.3,.7) (.7,.3)], [(.4,.6) (.6,.4)], and [(.45,.55) (.55,.45)]. In contrast, the Different Mean (DM) Gaussians were located at a fixed coordinate for the first dimension (either .8 or .2) with the coordinate for the second dimension varied as in the SM case. For example, DM8 is [(.8,.1) (.8,.9)], [(.8,.2) (.8,.8)], [(.8,.3) (.8,.7)], [(.8,.4) (.8,.6)].

Temporal Clustering of Input Patterns

A distribution of input patterns from the same category clustered over time presents a problem for algorithms which assume a uniform distribution in time. The relationship between SCL and Oja's algorithm, which approximately maximizes the variance of a unit's output signal under the assumption that input samples are distributed uniformly in time, indicates that temporal clustering should affect SCL. However, since MaxIn requires no such assumptions, it should be relatively less affected by clustering. These predictions were tested using the input clusters described above by either presenting all instances of a given cluster together, followed by all of those from the other cluster, or by permuting the presentation order so that the instances were uniformly distributed in time. Any differences between these two conditions should indicate a sensitivity to temporal clustering. Obviously, the learning rate parameter and the number of patterns from each cluster presented in a row will affect the sensitivity observed. If the learning rate is low relative to the number of patterns, then the stochastic estimate of output variance will not be dramatically affected by temporal clustering.

Methods and Results

The networks for the MaxIn and SCL algorithms were the same except for the learning rule used. There were 2 input units and 2 output units receiving connections from both input units. The output units computed their activations based on the multi-unit equations described above, with a fixed σ_j parameter of .2. The learning rate ϵ for the MaxIn simulations was either .1 or .02, and .05 or .01 for SCL. The difference is due to the use of weight bounding for MaxIn that can result in smaller weight changes (if the weight was at .5, the weight change would be half as strong in either direction compared with no weight

Model	SM		PSM		DM8		PDM8		DM2		PDM2	
	$\Delta\mu$	%	$\Delta\mu$	%	$\Delta\mu$	%	$\Delta\mu$	%	$\Delta\mu$	%	$\Delta\mu$	%
SFD MaxIn	.1	100	.1	100	.2	76	.2	68	.2	96	.2	44
lrate=.02	.1	100	.1	100	.2	80	.2	72	.2	88	.2	52
MCFD MaxIn	.1	100	.1	100	.2	52	.2	68	.2	88	.2	20
lrate=.02	.1	100	.1	100	.2	64	.2	20	.2	12	.2	12
HYB MaxIn	.1	100	.1	100	.2	100	.2	52	.8	0	.2	40
lrate=.02	.1	100	.1	100	.2	100	.2	36	.8	100	.2	28
SSD MaxIn	.1	100	.1	100	.6	100	.8	24	.8	36	.8	0
lrate=.02	.1	100	.1	100	.8	16	.8	28	.8	0	.8	0
Soft CL	.6	100	.1	72	.8	100	.2	100	.8	100	.2	100
lrate=.01	.1	84	.1	100	.2	100	.2	100	.2	100	.2	100

Table 1: Results of simulations comparing several versions of the MaxIn algorithm (see text for a description) with the Soft Competitve Learning (Soft CL) algorithm. The centers of two clusters in the 2-dimensional input data were separated by $\Delta\mu$ in each dimension. The means of these clusters were either the same distance away from the origin (SM) or different distances from the origin (DM, with X=.8 or X=.2). The results show the % of networks (sample N of 25) that successfully discriminated these clusters at the lowest $\Delta\mu$ for which they had a non-zero %. For SM, the minimum $\Delta\mu$ was .1 and the maximum .8, while DM had a min of .2 and the same max. The input patterns were presented sequentially by cluster, except in the Permuted (P) cases. See text for a description of SM vs. DM.

bounding). However, since strong weights decrease faster than weak ones (and weak weights increase faster) with the weight bounding than without, this would tend to impair the ability to maintain extreme weights under pressure to move to the other corner of weight space. Thus, the robustness of MaxIn under temporal clustering of input patterns cannot be attributed to the weight bounding procedure.

Simulation results are shown in table 1. The manner in which the centers of the input Gaussians were selected is denoted across the top (see description above), with 200 points per cluster used in training. The learning algorithms tested are listed in order of performance. In addition to the flavors of MaxIn described previously, a hybrid algorithm consisting of SSD plus the SCL algorithm was tested. For each cell in the table, the $\Delta\mu$ indicates the distance between the means of the input Gaussians along each dimension, and the % indicates the percent of trained networks having each unit's weight vector closest to the center of a different cluster (i.e., each unit represents one of the clusters).

DISCUSSION

Using just the SM results, it is clear that SCL was quite impaired with the .05 learning rate in the temporally clustered condition, as it failed to distinguish Gaussian categories centered closer than .6 on each dimension. However, when the patterns were presented in permuted order (PSM), or when the learning rate was lowered to .01, the performance improved significantly, so that it was able to distinguish clusters only .1 apart on each dimension. In comparison, all of the MaxIn algorithms achieved this level of performance even in the temporally clustered, high learning rate condition. Also, even in the PSM condition, MaxIn exhibited better performance at the .1 distance than SCL for the high learning rate, indicating that MaxIn is better able to distinguish clusters along its preferred direction.

The DM conditions reveal that the SSD MaxIn rule is quite impaired at distinguishing clusters along directions other than its preferred one, even with permuting and low learning rate. However, the more complete derivative formulations of MaxIn, including a simple hybrid of SSD MaxIn and SCL, retain the insensitivity to temporal clustering but also enable the representation of clusters that are along impaired directions for SSD. The best overall performance appears to come from SFD MaxIn, but the difference between it and MCFD are probably not significant. However, both of these algorithms require the computation of $P(j|\vec{n}_k)$, which complicates the algorithm and makes it less biologically plausible. Thus, the hybrid probably represents the best balance between simplicity and overall performance.

References

[1] A. Artola, S. Brocher, and W. Singer, "Different voltage-dependent thresholds for inducing long-term depression and long-term potentiation in slices of rat visual cortex," *Nature*, vol. 347, pp. 69–72, 1990.

[2] S. Becker and G. E. Hinton, "Learning mixture models of spatial coherence," *Neural Computation*, vol. 5, pp. 267–277, 1993.

[3] E. L. Bienenstock, L. N. Cooper, and P. W. Munro, "Theory for the development of neuron selectivity: Orientation specificity and binocular interaction in visual cortex," *The Journal of Neuroscience*, vol. 2, no. 2, pp. 32–48, 1982.

[4] P. Földiák, "Forming sparse representations by local anti-Hebbian learning," *Biological Cybernetics*, vol. 64, no. 2, pp. 165–170, 1990.

[5] R. Hecht-Nielsen, *Neurocomputing*. Redwood City, CA: Addison-Wesley, 1990.

[6] N. Intrator, "Feature extraction using an unsupervised neural network," *Neural Computation*, vol. 4, pp. 98–107, 1992.

[7] R. Linsker, "Local synaptic learning rules suffice to maximize mutual information in a linear network," *Neural Computation*, vol. 4, pp. 691–702, 1992.

[8] R. Linsker, "Self-organization in a perceptual network," *Computer*, pp. 105–117, March 1988.

[9] K. D. Miller and D. J. MacKay, "The role of constraints in hebbian learning," CNS Memo 19, Caltech, 1992.

[10] S. J. Nowlan, "Maximum likelihood competitive learning," in *Advances in Neural Information Processing Systems 2* (D. S. Touretzky, ed.), San Mateo, CA: Morgan Kaufmann, 1990.

[11] E. Oja, "A simplified neuron model as a principal component analyzer," *Journal of Mathematical Biology*, vol. 15, pp. 267–273, 1982.

[12] R. C. O'Reilly and J. L. McClelland, "The self-organization of spatially invariant representations," Parallel Distributed Processing and Cognitive Neuroscience PDP.CNS.92.5, Carnegie Mellon University, Department of Psychology, 1992.

[13] B. A. Pearlmutter and G. E. Hinton, "G-maximization: An unsupervised learning procedure for discovering regularities," in *Neural Networks for Computing* (J. Denker, ed.), pp. 333–338, New York: American Institute of Physics, 1986.

[14] D. E. Rumelhart and D. Zipser, "Feature discovery by competitive learning," in *Parallel Distributed Processing. Volume 1: Foundations* (D. E. Rumelhart, J. L. McClelland, and PDP Research Group, eds.), ch. 5, pp. 151–193, Cambridge, MA: MIT Press, 1986.

[15] M. Schwartz, *Information Transmission, Modulation, and Noise*. New York: McGraw-Hill, 4 ed., 1990.

[16] D. Willshaw and P. Dayan, "Optimal plasticity from matrix memories: What goes up must come down," *Neural Computation*, vol. 2, pp. 85–93, 1990.

MINIMIZING DISAGREEMENT FOR SELF-SUPERVISED CLASSIFICATION

Virginia R. de Sa
Department of Computer Science
University of Rochester
Rochester, NY 14627
desa@cs.rochester.edu

In natural environments, the sensations arriving at two or more sensory modalities are often correlated. We derive an algorithm for a piecewise linear classifier which uses the relationship between patterns presented simultaneously to two or more networks as a supervisory signal. The algorithm is based on the idea of minimizing the disagreement error — the proportion of patterns disagreed upon — between two or more networks receiving correlated patterns. We test the algorithm on a ten class vowel classification problem and find that it performs better than a hybrid unsupervised/supervised algorithm and, with two iterations, almost as well as a related supervised algorithm (Kohonen's LVQ2.1).

One of the most ubiquitous tasks for both animals and machine recognition systems is to classify novel patterns based on prior experience with other similar patterns. For machine applications, a supervised approach (in which prior patterns are presented together with their classification label or target output) is often used and these systems have produced many successful pattern recognition systems.

Humans and other animals learn to form complicated categories seemingly without this kind of supervision. However, while no explicit labeling signal is present, there is more information available than is modeled with conventional unsupervised approaches. Natural environments are structured such that sensations to different sensory modalities (and sub-modalities) are correlated. For example, "hearing mooing" and "seeing cows" tend to occur together.

We develop a model in which two "modalities" provide the labeling signal for each other. The algorithm is derived by minimizing the disagreement error —the proportion of patterns on which the modalities disagree— between the outputs of the two networks that receive correlated input patterns from a world consisting of a number of discrete classes. Each class has a particular probability distribution for the sensation received by each modality. Figure 1 represents a simple 2-Class world, with two 1-D modalities. Experience with the world does not consist of the usual input sensation and pattern label (as for regular supervised learning), but instead appropriate sensations to two or more modalities. If modality 1 experiences a sensation from its pattern A distribution, modality 2 experiences a sensation from its own pattern A distribution. That is, the world presents patterns from the appropriate corresponding distributions.

MINIMIZING DISAGREEMENT

Consider the task of iteratively learning to discover the optimal class boundary for distinguishing whether Class A or Class B occurred in the one-dimensional problem of two classes in Figure 1. Let the current boundary for modality i be represented with b_i (see Figure 1). The ideal goal is to minimize the probability of misclassified patterns for each modality. That is, to minimize

$$E = \int_{b_1}^{\infty} P(C_A)p(x_j|C_A)dx_j + \int_{-\infty}^{b_1} P(C_B)p(x_j|C_B)dx_j \tag{1}$$

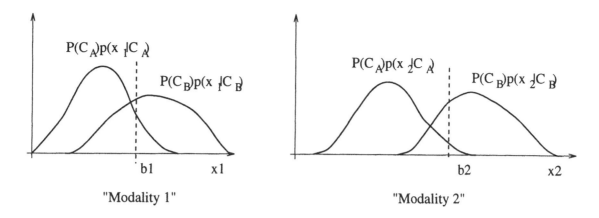

"Modality 1"　　　　　　　"Modality 2"

Figure 1: This figure shows an example world as sensed by two different modalities. If modality A receives a pattern from its Class A distribution, modality 2 receives a pattern from its own class A distribution (and the same for Class B). Without receiving information about which class the patterns came from, they must try to determine appropriate placement of the boundaries b_1 and b_2.

for both modalities ($j = 1, 2$) where $P(C_i)$ is the a priori probability of Class i and $p(x_j|C_i)$ is the conditional density of Class i for modality j.

The problem with this formulation is that the estimation of the conditional probabilities depends explicitly on class information. Instead consider minimizing the Disagreement Error between the networks [1]

$$E(b_1, b_2) = Pr\{x_1 < b_1 \ \& \ x_2 > b_1\} + Pr\{x_1 > b_1 \ \& \ x_2 < b_2\} \tag{2}$$

That is,

$$\begin{aligned}
E(b_1, b_2) &= P(C_A)\left[\int_{-\infty}^{b_1} p(x_1|C_A)dx_1 \int_{b_2}^{\infty} p(x_2|C_A)dx_2 + \int_{b_1}^{\infty} p(x_1|C_A)dx_1 \int_{-\infty}^{b_2} p(x_2|C_A)dx_2\right] \\
&+ P(C_B)\left[\int_{-\infty}^{b_1} p(x_1|C_B)dx_1 \int_{b_2}^{\infty} p(x_2|C_B)dx_2 + \int_{b_1}^{\infty} p(x_1|C_B)dx_1 \int_{-\infty}^{b_2} p(x_2|C_B)dx_2\right]
\end{aligned} \tag{3}$$

This heuristic measure is motivated by the fact that in the case where both modalities have distributions in which the Bayes optimal border is such that the fraction of misclassification is equal for both classes (as for example in identical symmetric distributions), if (3) has a single non-trivial local minimum it is the same as the minimum of (1). But the key point is that (3) does not depend on the class information as can be seen by letting

$$f(x_1, x_2) = P(C_A)p(x_1|C_A)p(x_2|C_A) + P(C_B)p(x_1|C_B)p(x_2|C_B) \tag{4}$$

and rewriting (3) as

$$E(b_1, b_2) = \int_{-\infty}^{b_1} \int_{b_2}^{\infty} f(x_1, x_2)dx_1 dx_2 + \int_{b_1}^{\infty} \int_{-\infty}^{b_2} f(x_1, x_2)dx_1 dx_2 \tag{5}$$

---

[1] Actually we are interested in finding a non-trivial local minimum of the Disagreement Error. Such a local minimum exists when there exists a pair (b_1^*, b_2^*) such that $\int_{-\infty}^{b_2^*} f(b_1^*, x_2)dx_2 = \int_{b_2^*}^{\infty} f(b_1^*, x_2)dx_2$ and $\int_{-\infty}^{b_1^*} f(x_1, b_2^*)dx_1 = \int_{b_1^*}^{\infty} f(x_1, b_2^*)dx_1$ and $\partial^2 E(b_1^*, b_2^*)/\partial b_1^2 \times \partial^2 E(b_1^*, b_2^*)/\partial b_2^2 - (\partial^2 E(b_1^*, b_2^*)/\partial b_1 \partial b_2)^2 > 0$ and $\partial^2 E(b_1^*, b_2^*)/\partial b_1^2 > 0$. A local minimum is not guaranteed to exist even for distributions for which the optimal boundary could be found with a supervised algorithm.

It is not necessary to know the class labels as $f(x_1, x_2)$ is the joint density for the inputs of the two modalities.

The derivative of (3) with respect to b_1 is

$$\partial E/\partial b_1 = \int_{b_2}^{\infty} f(b_1, x_2)dx_2 - \int_{-\infty}^{b_2} f(b_1, x_2)dx_2 \qquad (6)$$

and similarly with respect to b_2

$$\partial E/\partial b_2 = \int_{b_1}^{\infty} f(x_1, b_2)dx_1 - \int_{-\infty}^{b_1} f(x_1, b_2)dx_1 \qquad (7)$$

Using an extension by Wassel and Sklansky [1972], to the stochastic approximation method [10] gives the following iterative calculation for b_1 (see the Appendix for the derivation) where the hypothesized output class from the other modality network replaces the correct label.

$$b_1(n+1) = b_1(n) + \alpha(n)Z_n(X_1(n), X_2(n), b_1(n), b_2(n), c(n)) \qquad (8)$$

with

$$Z_n = \begin{cases} 1 & \text{for } X_2(n) < b_2(n), |X_1(n) - b_1(n)| < c(n) \\ -1 & \text{for } X_2(n) > b_2(n), |X_1(n) - b_1(n)| < c(n) \end{cases}$$

In analogy with Competitive Learning[5, 7, 12] and LVQ2.1 [6] consider moving the borders indirectly through the motion of codebook vectors. The borders arise from the Voronoi tessellations of the codebook vectors. In the 1-D case the borders b_j can be defined by $b_j = (w_{j,1} + w_{j,2})/2$, where $w_{j,k}$ is a codebook vector for modality j. Thus the codebook vectors move according to

$$\partial E/\partial w_{j,1} = \partial E/\partial w_{j,2} = .5\partial E/\partial b_j.$$

Rewriting (8) in terms of the codebook vector motion gives

$$w_{1,i}(n+1) = w_{1,i}(n) + \alpha_2(n)\frac{(X_1(n) - w_{1,i}(n-1))}{|X_1(n) - w_{1,i}(n)|}$$

$$w_{1,j}(n+1) = w_{1,j}(n) - \alpha_2(n)\frac{(X_1(n) - w_{1,j}(n-1))}{|X_1(n) - w_{1,j}(n)|}$$

if $X_1(n)$ lies in a window of width $2c(n)$ centred at $b_1(n)$; $w_{1,i}$ and $w_{1,j}$ are the two closest codebook vectors to $X_1(n)$; $w_{1,i}$ is a codebook vector belonging to the same class as the closest codebook vector to $X_2(n)$ in Modality 2; and $w_{1,j}$ belongs to a different class [2]. Otherwise no updates are made. Note that here we have removed the restriction that Class A lies to the left of Class B.

Expanding the problem to more dimensions, and more classes with more codebook vectors per class, complicates the analysis as a change in two codebook vectors to better adjust their border affects more than just the border between the two codebook vectors. However ignoring these effects, a first order approximation suggests the algorithm shown in Figure 2. Note that this algorithm is identical to the modified LVQ2.1 [6] algorithm in [3] except that the labeling signal is not the actual class but the class hypothesized by the other modality (and the unsupervised initialization).

The label initialization algorithm mentioned in the second step above, can best be described by considering the network shown in Figure 3. Each output class has associated with it a vector in the space of codebook vector activations. These vectors can be represented as weights from hidden neurons (whose weights are the

---

[2]How the unsupervised labeling initialization of the codebook vectors is accomplished, is discussed at the end of this section.

- Generate initial codebook vectors (currently randomly chosen data vectors)

- Initialize labels of codebook vectors using the network shown in Figure 3 with the algorithm described below

- Repeat for each presentation of input patterns $X_1(n)$ and $X_2(n)$ to their respective modalities

    - find the two nearest codebook vectors $w_{1,i_1^*}, w_{1,i_2^*}, w_{2,k_1^*}, w_{2,k_2^*}$ to the respective input patterns

    - Find the hypothesized ouput class (C_A, C_B) in each modality (as given by the label of the closest codebook vector)

    - For each modality update the weights according to the following rules (Only the rules for modality 1 are given)
    If neither or both w_{1,i_1^*}, w_{1,i_2^*} have the same label as w_{2,k_1^*} or $X_1(n)$ does not lie within c(n) of the border between them no updates are done, otherwise

$$w_{1,i^*}(n) = w_{1,i}^*(n-1) + \alpha(n)\frac{(X_1(n) - w_{1,i^*}(n-1))}{\|X_1(n) - w_{1,i^*}(n-1)\|}$$

$$w_{1,j^*}(n) = w_{1,j}^*(n-1) - \alpha(n)\frac{(X_1(n) - w_{1,j^*}(n-1))}{\|X_1(n) - w_{1,j}^*(n-1)\|}$$

    where w_{1,i^*} is the codebook vector with the same label, and w_{1,j^*} is the codebook vector with another label.

    - update the labeling weights as described below

Figure 2: Minimizing Disagreement (M-D) Algorithm

codebook vectors) to output neurons—one for each class as shown in the figure. The weights are trained with a Competitive learning [5, 7, 12] rule which tends to connect co-active neurons (representing closest codebook vectors in each modality) to the same output class. During this stage the codebook vectors themselves are not modified.

During the main part of the algorithm described in the third step of Figure 2, the connections to the output neurons are also adjusted in the same way by increasing the weight to the output class hypothesized by the other modality, from the neuron with the closest codebook vector. Experiments show that this makes the algorithm more robust because codebook vectors that are not able to find one particular boundary (due perhaps to no local minimum in the Disagreement Error) may be reassigned.

SIMULATIONS

The algorithm was tested using a version of the Peterson and Barney vowel formant data [3]. The dataset consists of the first and second formants for ten vowels in a /hVd/ context from 75 speakers (32 males, 28 females, 15 children) who repeated each vowel twice [4]. For comparison with other algorithms, the training set and test set were the same. In order to facilitate evaluation, the algorithm was tested by giving the same distributions to each modality. That is $p(x_1|C_j) = p(x_2|C_j)$ for all j. A pattern presentation consisted of randomly choosing one of the data patterns for the first modality and randomly choosing a pattern from the same class for the second modality.

The algorithm obtained an average performance of 74% with 30 codebook vectors and 40000 pattern

---

[3]obtained from Steven Nowlan

[4]3 speakers were missing one vowel and the raw data was linearly transformed to have zero mean and fall within the range $[-3, 3]$ in both components

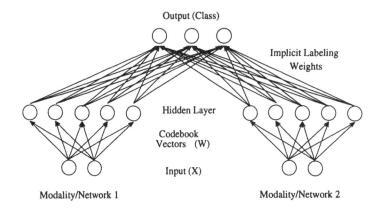

Figure 3: This figure shows a network for learning the labels of the codebook vectors. The weight vectors of the hidden layer neurons represent the codebook vectors while the weight vectors of the connections from the hidden layer neurons to the output neurons represent the output class that each codebook vector currently represents. In this example there are 3 output classes and two modalities each of which has 2-D input patterns and 5 codebook vectors.

presentations. Performance was averaged between modalities [5] and over 30 runs from different initial codebook vector positions. This was a big improvement over the initial accuracy after the label initialization step (where the positions of the codebook vectors are still random but the output weights have been trained) which had an average performance of 59%. The final performance figures were positively correlated with the performance after the label initialization step, which in turn was correlated with (in fact bounded by) the best performance possible with the initial codebook vectors (as measured independently with optimal labels). Improved methods of choosing the initial codebook vectors and algorithms for label initialization result in improved performance. For example, using the final codebook vectors from a run of the M-D algorithm as the initial codebook vectors for another run (replacing the first step in Figure 2) results in a final performance of 76%. This can be seen in Figure 4 which shows performance after the initial labeling, first application of the M-D algorithm, and second application of the M-D algorithm.

The algorithm's performance compares favourably with the 72% resulting from a hybrid unsupervised-supervised algorithm — Kohonen feature mapping algorithm (with 30 codebook vectors) followed by optimal labeling of the codebook vectors. (In fact if the same optimal labeling algorithm is applied to the codebook vectors resulting from the M-D algorithm, an average performance of 76% and 78% (for applying after one or two iterations respectively) results.) Performance is not as good as that of the related fully supervised algorithm, LVQ 2.1 which achieved an average performance of 80%, but is comparable to the performance of (supervised) back-propagation (with 25-200 hidden layer neurons) which obtained average performances of 73.4-78.5% [8]. Nowlan's mixture model (supervised) achieved an average performance of 86.1%.

DISCUSSION

In summary, we have shown that classification borders can be learnt without an explicit labeling or supervisory signal. For the particular vowel recognition problem, the performance of this "self-supervised" algorithm is almost as good as that achieved with supervised algorithms. This algorithm would be ideal for tasks in which signals for two or more modalities are available, but labels are either not available or expensive to obtain. One specific task is learning to classify speech sounds from images of the lips and the acoustic

---

[5] Each modality was tested separately for its ability to output the same label for all occurrences of the same vowel.

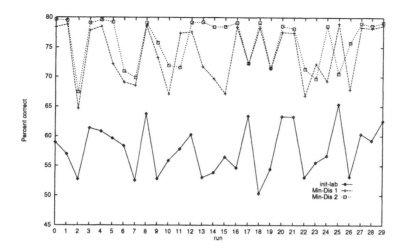

Figure 4: The performance (for 30 different initial configurations) after: initial labeling (init-lab), one application of the M-D algorithm (Min-Dis 1), and two applications of the M-D algorithm (Min-Dis 2)

signal. Stork et. al. [1992] performed this task with a supervised algorithm but one of the main limitations for data collection was the manual labeling of the patterns [David Stork, personal communication, 1993].

The algorithm could also be used for learning to classify signals to a single modality where the signal to the other "modality" is a temporally close sample. As the world changes slowly over time, signals close in time are likely from the same class. This approach should be more powerful than that of [4] as signals close in time need not be mapped to the same codebook vector but the closest codebook vector of the same class.

This work is similar in general motivation to that of [1, 2], but differs significantly in the derivation and resulting algorithm. Both algorithms are able to self-supervise from spatial/temporal/multi-modality relationships between their sub networks. This algorithm, however is restricted to classification tasks but requires less computation, memory storage and communication complexity. The different advantages and disadvantages with both algorithms are analogous to those between their related supervised algorithms, LVQ [6] and back-propagation [11].

APPENDIX: DERIVATION OF THE MINIMIZING DISAGREEMENT ALGORITHM

The algorithm we derive for minimizing (3) is patterned after [14] and uses their extension to the stochastic approximation method [10]. In stochastic approximation, iterative approximations are made by adding to the current estimate an appropriately scaled random variable (which is a function of the received input) whose expected value is the gradient, at the current estimate, of the function to be minimized. In this case the function to be minimized is a regression function. Wassel and Sklansky [1972] extended this method to work for functions that are the limit of a sequence of regression functions. Thus the solution to the minimization of (3) involves finding a sequence of functions whose limit is given by (6)(and similarly for (7)).

Consider the function

$$\hat{g}(b_1, b_2, c) = \int_{-\infty}^{\infty} \Psi(x_1 - b_1, c) \left[\int_{b_2}^{\infty} f(x_1, x_2) dx_2 - \int_{-\infty}^{b_2} f(x_1, x_2) dx_2 \right] \qquad (9)$$

where $\Psi(x - z, c)$ is a Parzen window function [9] centred at z with width parameter c that satisfies the following conditions

$$\Psi(x - z, c) \geq 0 \quad \forall x, z \quad c > 0$$

305

$$\int_{-\infty}^{\infty} \Psi(x - z, c) dx = 1 \quad \forall z \quad c > 0$$

$$c \int_{-\infty}^{\infty} \Psi^2(x - z, c) dx < \infty \quad \forall z \quad c > 0$$

$$\lim_{c \to 0} \Psi(x - z, c) = \delta(x - z) \quad \forall x, z \quad c > 0$$

then

$$
\begin{aligned}
\lim_{c \to 0} \hat{g}(b_1, b_2, c) &= \int_{b_2}^{\infty} f(b_1, x_2) dx_2 - \int_{-\infty}^{b_2} f(b_1, x_2) dx_2 \\
&= \partial E / \partial b_1
\end{aligned}
\tag{10}
$$

We now show that $\hat{g}$ is a regression function by showing that there is a random variable Z such that $\frac{1}{2c} E(Z|B_1 = b_1) = -\hat{g}(b_1, b_2, c)$

Let

$$Z_i = 2c S(X_2(i)) \Psi(X_1(i) - B_1, c)) \tag{11}$$

Then,

$$\frac{1}{2c} E(Z|B_1 = b_1) = E(S(X_2) \Psi(X_1 - b_1, c)) = \lim_{n \to \infty} \frac{1}{n} \sum_{i=1}^{n} S(X_2(i)) \Psi(X_1(i) - b_1, c)$$

where $X_j(i)$ is the sample data point at time i presented to modality j, and $S(X_2(i))$ is $+1$ if $X_2(i) < b_2$ and -1 if $X_2(i) > b_2$.

But,

$$
\begin{aligned}
E(S(X_2) \Psi(X_1 - b_1, c)) &= \int_{-\infty}^{\infty} \int_{-\infty}^{\infty} f(x_1, x_2) S(x_2) \Psi(x_1 - b_1, c) dx_1 dx_2 \\
&= \int_{-\infty}^{\infty} \int_{-\infty}^{b_2} f(x_1, x_2) \Psi(x_1 - b_1, c) dx_1 - \int_{-\infty}^{\infty} \int_{b_2}^{\infty} f(x_1, x_2) \Psi(x_1 - b_1, c) dx_1 \\
&= -\hat{g}(b_1, b_2, c)
\end{aligned}
$$

Thus (6) is the limit of a sequence of regression functions and the position of b_1 can be iteratively calculated according to[6]

$$b_1(n + 1) = b_1(n) + \alpha(n) Z_n(X_1(n), X_2(n), b_1(n), b_2(n), c(n)) \tag{12}$$

where

$$Z_n = \begin{cases} 2c(n) \Psi(X_1(n) - b_1(n), c(n)) & \text{for } X_2(n) < b_2(n) \\ -2c(n) \Psi(X_1(n) - b_1(n), c(n)) & \text{for } X_2(n) > b_2(n) \end{cases}$$

Using rectangular Parzen window functions, the above simplifies to

$$Z_n = \begin{cases} 1 & \text{for } X_2(n) < b_2(n), |X_1(n) - b_1(n)| < c(n) \\ -1 & \text{for } X_2(n) > b_2(n), |X_1(n) - b_1(n)| < c(n) \end{cases}$$

---

[6]The theorem in [14] guarantees convergence under the condition that the function to be minimized has a single, minimum; as we are searching for a local minimum, convergence is only guaranteed if (b_1, b_2) stay within the area in which (b_1^*, b_2^*) is a local minimum and the only local extremum. . The following conditions are also required : $\alpha(n), c(n) > 0$; $\lim_{n \to \infty} \alpha(n) = 0$; $\lim_{n \to \infty} c(n) = 0$; $\Sigma_{n=1}^{\infty} \alpha(n) c(n) = \infty$; $\Sigma_{n=1}^{\infty} \alpha(n)^2 c(n) < \infty$; and $p(x_i|C_j) < \infty$, $i, j = A, B$

Acknowledgements

I would like to thank Steve Nowlan for making the vowel formant data available to me. Many thanks also to Dana Ballard and Geoff Hinton for their helpful conversations and suggestions.

References

[1] S. Becker and G. E. Hinton, "A self-organizing neural network that discovers surfaces in random-dot stereograms," *Nature*, vol. 355, pp. 161–163, Jan. 1992.

[2] S. Becker, "Learning to categorize objects using temporal coherence," in *Advances in Neural Information Processing Systems 5* (C. Giles, S.J.Hanson, and J. Cowan, eds.), pp. 361—368, Morgan Kaufmann, 1993.

[3] V. R. de Sa and D. H. Ballard, "a note on learning vector quantization," in *Advances in Neural Information Processing Systems 5* (C. Giles, S.J.Hanson, and J. Cowan, eds.), pp. 220—227, Morgan Kaufmann, 1993.

[4] P. Földiák, "Learning invariance from transformation sequences," *Neural Computation*, vol. 3, no. 2, pp. 194–200, 1991.

[5] S. Grossberg, "Adaptive pattern classification and universal recoding: I. parallel development and coding of neural feature detectors," *Biological Cybernetics*, vol. 23, pp. 121–134, 1976.

[6] T. Kohonen, "Improved versions of learning vector quantization," in *IJCNN International Joint Conference on Neural Networks*, vol. 1, pp. I-545-I-550, 1990.

[7] T. Kohonen, "Self-organized formation of topologically correct feature maps," *Biological Cybernetics*, vol. 43, pp. 59–69, 1982.

[8] S. J. Nowlan, *Soft Competitive Adaptation: Neural Network Learning Algorithms based on Fitting Statistical Mixtures*. PhD thesis, School of Computer Science, Carnegie Mellon University, 1991.

[9] E. Parzen, "On estimation of a probability density function and mode," *Annals of Math. Stat.*, vol. 33, pp. 1065—1076, 1962.

[10] H. Robbins and S. Monro, "A stochastic approximation method," *Annals of Math. Stat.*, vol. 22, pp. 400—407, 1951.

[11] D. E. Rumelhart, G. E. Hinton, and R. J. Williams, "Learning internal representations by error propagation," in *Parallel Distributed Processing: Explorations in the Microstructure of Cognition* (D. E. Rumelhart, J. L. McClelland, and the PDP Research Group, eds.), vol. 1, pp. 318–364, MIT Press, 1986.

[12] D. E. Rumelhart and D. Zipser, "Feature discovery by competitive learning," in *Parallel Distributed Processing: Explorations in the Microstructure of Cognition* (D. E. Rumelhart, J. L. McClelland, and the PDP Research Group, eds.), vol. 2, pp. 151–193, MIT Press, 1986.

[13] D. G. Stork, G. Wolff, and E. Levine, "Neural network lipreading system for improved speech recognition," in *IJCNN International Joint Conference on Neural Networks*, vol. 2, pp. II–286—II-295, 1992.

[14] G. N. Wassel and J. Sklansky, "Training a one-dimensional classifier to minimize the probability of error," *IEEE Transactions on Systems, Man, and Cybernetics*, vol. SMC-2, no. 4, pp. 533—541, 1972.

Comparison of two Unsupervised Neural Network Models for Redundancy Reduction

Stefanie Natascha Lindstaedt

University of Colorado at Boulder

Boulder, CO 80309-0430

stefanie@cs.colorado.edu

We compare two unsupervised neural network models that perform redundancy reduction on static input data. One was introduced by Peter Földiàk, and the other by Jürgen Schmidhuber. We also extend their functionality in order to deal with dynamic time varying pattern sequences and perform comparisons of the models. The results we obtain are consistent across both static and dynamic input data. Though the two models discover very different types of codes, they perform in a similar fashion. With increasing code size and bit probability, the entropy of the codes increases, and at the same time the redundancy and dependency between code symbols increase. In general, trade-off decisions have to be made between information preservation, redundancy/dependency, generalization/comprehensibility, density, distribution and sparseness of the code. The outcome of this analysis determines which of the versions of which model is most suitable.

FACTORIAL REPRESENTATION

Researchers in symbolic as well as nonsymbolic AI identify the need for good, useful representations of the data to be processed. This representation or coding of the input stimuli is extremely important because the quality of the representation determines how easy the task can be solved, or if it can be solved at all. We focus here on two artificial neural network (ANN) models which can be seen as a first step in a data refining hierarchy. They are designed with respect to usability of their output representations (codes) as input to standard statistical analysis methods and higher level ANN models. These preprocessing modules should be able to adapt themselves to the changing input environment by just looking at the raw data but without requiring labeled training examples (in other words by using the unsupervised learning paradigm). This is crucial for further applicability and generality. For a complete description of this research please refer to [4].

What kind of representations do we consider "useful" for successive processing? We claim and motivate in the next paragraph that a representation consisting of binary vectors with independent components (bits) can be useful for a number of applications. In such a representation scheme the probability of one symbol to be active is independent from the probabilities of all other symbols to be active. We call this a binary factorial code (compare to minimum entropy codes [1]). Reducing linear as well as higher dimensional correlations between the code symbols results in reducing the redundancy of the representation. A factorial code does not transmit redundant information.

Usability of Factorial Representations for Statistical Methods and for Supervised Learning

Factorial codes prove useful for a number of statistical applications. In statistics, many practical methods like linear models, least squares estimation, non-linear models, variants of Bayesian analysis, the Cheeseman algorithm, etc. are based on the assumption of independent input symbols. But in most real world problems variables are substantially correlated in a complicated manner. Because a detailed analysis of these dependencies is infeasible in practice, this independence is often simply assumed and can cause substantial errors [2].

Factorial codes can help to speed up learning in supervised ANNs and reduce the number of labeled training examples needed. Our goal is to condition the error surface for a supervised ANN while preserving maximal information about the input. We consider the amount of information preservation as crucial because each informational aspect in the input might provide a succeeding layer with additional hints for solving a given task. To ensure fast and good convergence in a supervised ANN with no hidden units performing gradient descent on the error surface, the Hessian matrix of the error function should be diagonal. This can be achieved when the input data is represented by a code with uncorrelated components. In this case, the change of one variable (weight) does not influence other variables and so each can be adjusted separately without crosstalk.

Outline

We compare two unsupervised ANN architectures which aim at finding factorial representations for the input data while preserving as much information as possible. In the following we briefly introduce each of the ANNs and then describe one simulation with static input data. In addition we modify and extend the two basic models in order to enable them to encode time varying pattern sequences. We present one simulation to illustrate this additional ability. The purpose of this study is first, to point out the conceptual differences and theoretical limitations of the two models, and second, to compare their performance along different perspectives in order to find their practical differences, drawbacks, and to distinguish their applications.

DESCRIPTION OF THE ANN MODELS

Földiàk's Model

We focus on Földiàk's most elaborate model, which he refers to as model number 6 in his dissertation [3]. The motivation of this model is its biological relevant mechanism which uses only local information for learning. The network is organized in two layers. The input layer consists of m input units x_j, j=1, 2, ..., m and the output layer is composed of n representational units y_i, i=1, 2, ..., n. These two layers are fully connected with connection strengths q_{ij} from input unit x_j to output unit y_i and thus are equivalent to n parallel PCA modules [6], except for the difference that the output units y_i are binary threshold units. In order to achieve sparse coding each output unit tries to keep its probability of firing close to a fixed value (bit probability p) by adjusting its own threshold: $\Delta t_i = \gamma (y_i - p)$. By changing the bit probability p, one has control over the degree to which sparse coding occurs. For a detailed description of the advantages of sparse coding please refer to [3]. During training, the weights q_{ij} are modified according to Oja's learning rule: $\Delta q_{ij} = \beta y_i (x_j - q_{ij})$. Without an additional mechanism, all the n PCA modules would find the same eigenvector of the input's covariance matrix, which belongs to the largest eigenvalue. Several proposals have been made to combine PCA modules to extract the n maximal components. Most of them suffer from the necessity of sequential learning [5]. Using symmetrically combined PCA modules, and an anti-Hebbian decorrelation mechanism, Földiàk ensures that all principal components can be concurrently computed. Each representational unit y_j (output) has inhibitory connections w_{ij} to all other representational units y_i, where $i \neq j$. These inhibitory connections have to be symmetric ($w_{ij} = w_{ji}$ for $i \neq j$, and $w_{ij} = 0$ for $i = j$) in order to ensure that the network is able to find an equilibrium state after each input presentation. These inhibitory connections are modified according to an anti-Hebb rule: $\Delta w_{ij} = -\alpha (y_i y_j - p^2)$, if (i = j or $w_{ij} > 0$) then $w_{ij} = 0$. Through the use of binary threshold units, the network is able to not only detect linear, but also higher-order correlation between the output units which eventually can lead to independence. This method does not implement a systematic search through the code-space to reduce higher order correlation. The representational units are updated asynchronously (on-line) according to the following rule where f(x) is a sigmoidal function:

$$ y_i^* = f \left(\sum_{j=1}^{m} q_{ij} x_j + \sum_{j=1}^{n} w_{ij} y_j^* - t_i \right). $$

The outputs are calculated by rounding the values of y_i^* in the stable state to 0 or 1 ($y_i = 1$ if $y_i^* > 0.5$, $y_i = 0$ otherwise). The feed-forward weights are initially randomly selected from a uniform distribution of [0, 1] and then normalized to unit length; the inhibitory weights w_{ij} are initially set to zero. The thresholds of the output units are initially set to zero but get preadjusted in a 100 cycle prerun before the real training begins.

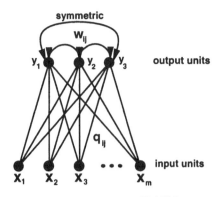

Figure 1: Architecture of Földiàk's model

Predictability Minimization (PredMin)

Based on the principle of predictability minimization [8], the architecture of Schmidhuber's model is rather different from Földiàk's network. It is composed of several simple fully connected feed-forward modules which all see the same input at a time. Throughout this paper, we focus on the simplest case: one representational output unit per module, uniform module structure of two layers, and direct connections between all input and all representational units. For each output unit of the representational modules, there exists one corresponding predictor module. These predictor modules are the same kind of feed-forward architectures as the representation modules. They each only have one output unit (predictor) P_i and their input units (# input units = # representational units - 1) are clamped to the representational units y_j, where $j \neq i$; i.e. to all representational units except the one P_i is associated with. Here we focus on predictor modules with one hidden layer (3 layer modules).

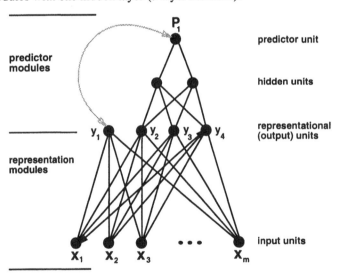

Figure 2: Architecture of the PredMin model

The purpose of the predictor modules is to predict the output activation of the associated representational unit given the activities of all the other representational units as input. In this way, the predictors learn the conditioned mean activations (probabilities) of the representational units. With simple back propagation, the predictors are trained to minimize the following error function:

$$\sum_p (P_i^{(p)} - y_i^{(p)})^2.$$

The representational modules, on the other hand, are supposed to find independent features in the input stimuli; that is, they try to be not predictable through the other representational units. They try to escape their associated predictors by maximizing the same error function (see above) which the predictors try to minimize. This creates two

310

symmetrical forces that oppose each other. The goal is to find a binary factorial representation of the input stimuli. To achieve near-binary values while applying the back-propagation algorithm, we use a sigmoidal function to compute the activations of the representational units:

$$y_i = \frac{1}{1 + e^{-\text{net}_i}}, \text{ where net}_i = \sum_{j=1}^{\#\text{input}} w_{ij} x_j .$$

The network is trained on-line in two passes using the same input pattern. *Pass 1:* The input is propagated forward through the representational modules, and their output is fed into the predictor modules. There, the difference between the actual output of the representational unit and its predictor $(y_i - P_i)$ is computed and back-propagated through the predictor modules. Only the weights in the predictor modules are modified in this pass. *Pass 2:* Again the input is fed forward through the representational modules. This time the weights of the predictor modules are fixed, while the weights of the representational modules are modified by back-propagating the error of the predictor units $(P_i - y_i)$ and the error of the representational units $(y_i - P_i)$ through the net.

This network implements a novelty or negative filter [1]. Though in general it does not minimize entropy directly, it systematically aims for a factorial code. Schmidhuber's network prefers shorter, more compact codes over more extensive, local codes with less entropy (Occam's razor). Representational units that are not needed to code the input, emit a constant value but stay available for use when a change in the environment's statistical structure suggests another independent feature. Note that this model performs unsupervised learning even though it uses the standard back-propagation algorithm for training.

STATIC EXPERIMENTS: IMAGE SEGMENTATION

To ensure that our work is comparable with the work of Földiàk [3], Barlow [1], and Rumelhart & Zipser [7], we replicate the two static experiments that Földiàk describes in his dissertation. Static here means, that the network is learning one pattern at a time, rather than a time varying sequence of input data. In this paper, we describe only the more interesting and complex experiment. The input to the networks are images of fixed size. Each input value corresponds to one pixel in the image which can be either on or off (1 or 0). Thus the input is a binary string of fixed length, and it does not contain spatial information. The goal is to explore the ability of the networks to extract, code, store, and generalize spatial features in these unstructured input events. To ensure comparability between the results of the different network models, we keep all experimental conditions the same. Network parameters were chosen individually to optimize the quality of the results, not to optimize training time. To ensure the correctness and reliability of the results, we ran 10 trials of each simulation with its individual parameter settings.

Letter Experiment

The input to the networks are 10x15 images of 82 different letters, numbers, and symbols. The shapes of the symbols are taken from the DEC courier font. Each pattern is presented to the networks with the probability of its symbol's appearance in a standard English text [1]. We use standard measures like entropy, summed bit-entropy, and redundancy (redundancy = (summed bit-entropy - entropy) / entropy) to compare the different codes. In addition, we introduce a means to measure to what degree the individual symbols of each code word are dependent upon each other. If the bits of the code words are independent, then the conditional probability of one bit to be active is equal to its unconditioned probability to be active. Using this, we can define:

$$\text{Dependency(Code)} = \sum_{l=1}^{82} \sum_{i=1}^{n} (p(b_i | \text{rest}_i) - p(b_i))^2 p(\text{symbol}) .$$

Here b_i stands for the ith bit of a n bit code word and rest_i determines the n-1 bits b_j, $j \neq i$ of the code word. That is, we compute the squared difference between the conditional and unconditional probability of the bits weighted by the probability of the appearance of the associated input symbol. The smaller this dependency measure, the less dependent the code symbols are.

The input data has an entropy of about 4.34 bits and the summed bit-entropy of the input representation (10x15 matrix) is about 62.56 bits. Therefore, the input "code" has a redundancy of 13.41; that is, 1341% of the carried information is redundant. Our goal is to minimize the summed bit-entropies (thereby minimizing redundancy) and the dependency between code symbols, while at the same time making the entropy to as close to the input entropy as possible. Theoretically the 82 patterns can be coded in 7 bits. To determine the influence of the code size on the values of those measures we vary it from 8 to 16 bits and in Földiàk's model we also vary the bit probability stepwise from 0.1 to 0.5.

The PredMin model performs comparably to Földiàk's model with low bit probability. For very sparse (local) codes (bit probability around p = 0.1), Földiàk's model outperforms PredMin with respect to all three measures (entropy, redundancy, and dependency). But as soon as we want to create slightly more distributed codes, Pred-Min offers a real alternative to Földiàk's model. Especially for applications in which the probability distribution of the input data should not be mirrored in the encoding or in which similar input should not result in similar output (no generalization) the PredMin model has advantages. The entropies of the created codes vary less for the PredMin model; thus, it performs more reliably. In both models, we discover that with increasing code size and bit probability, the entropy increases while at the same time, the redundancy and the dependency increase as well.

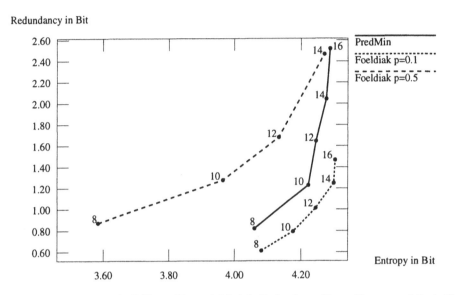

Figure 3: Overview over the Different Network Models: Redundancy Versus Entropy and Code Size

The codes produced by both models are very noise sensitive. It is interesting to note, that in both models, the codes created by a network trained with no noise, show a more graceful degradation when tested with polluted patterns than the codes created by a network trained with some noise. Codes of the PredMin model are slightly more noise resistant than the ones of Földiàk's model. An interesting quality of the PredMin model is that training with slight input noise speeds up learning, and the code entropies increase slightly. This seems to be due to the fact that small noise in the input can help the back propagation algorithm to escape local minima.

The connection strengths in Földiàk's model develop into positive receptive fields (positive weights) for the most frequent shapes of the letters and symbols. Frequent letters like "a", "e", etc. can be recognized easily and are coded by a code word with a few active bits, while infrequent symbols are produced by combining basic shapes and are represented by codes with a number of active bits. The PredMin model forms positive as well as negative receptive fields (positive and negative weights) which seem to model microfeatures of the symbols. The codes are very distributed (the number of active and inactive bits is approximately the same) and do not mirror the input distribution.

REDUNDANCY REDUCTION IN TIME VARYING SEQUENCES

As mentioned in the outline, we do not want to focus solely on feature extraction in static input data, but we also want to explore feature extraction in time varying pattern sequences. The goal is to code each sequence and subsequence unambiguously while again minimizing redundancy of the code and dependencies between code symbols. That is, we want to find a reversible, non-redundant, factorial, reduced sequence description. Note that this is a different goal from the one Földiàk expresses in his thesis. He focuses on extracting time and space invariant features out of image sequences. To stress this distinction, in this section we refer to Földiàk's extended model as the Anti-Hebb sequence model.

To encode sequences in time, a network must have some mechanism to build upon its input history; i.e. it must be able to interpret a new input in the context of previously received information. In the preceding paragraphs, each pattern had its meaning independent of when and where it occurred, isolated from position and time. The activation levels of the representational units are an encoding of the internal state of the network, which can now be used as the basis for the coding of subsequent patterns. This can be achieved by providing the network with a concatenation of its own internal state (activations of representational units at time t-1) and the actual input pattern at time t as input. We extend the described models by introducing special input units in addition to the conventional input units. There are always the same number of special input units as there are representational (output) units. Otherwise, the models stay the same and the learning algorithms do not change. This method tends to throw away redundant temporal information and is able to bridge long time lags by learning unique representations of extended sequences.

DYNAMIC EXPERIMENTS: SEQUENCE SEGMENTATION

This is a description of one of the experiments we did with the extended models [4]. The input are images of a line sweeping over a matrix. The experimental conditions are kept the same for both network models. The network parameters are chosen individually in order to optimize the quality of the results, not to optimize training time. Each sequence occurs with the same frequency. At the beginning of a sequence the activations of the special input units (internal state) are set to zero, i.e. the context is cleared. Then the sequence patterns are presented one at a time, and after each pattern the internal state (activations of output units) is copied to the special input units. Thus the network receives a concatenation of internal state and actual new input pattern as input data. In this way the network can build upon its input history and can encode sequences of arbitrary patterns and (at least in theory) of arbitrary length. Each simulation with its individual parameter settings is run 5 times to ensure reliability of the reported results.

Line Sequence Experiment

The inputs to the networks are the sequences of line images sweeping over an array of 8x8 pixels. The line has one of four possible orientations (horizontal, vertical, and the two diagonals) and is swept over the image in one of two possible directions (see figure 4).

Figure 4: A sample of input sequences presented to the network during the line sequence experiment.

Whenever a pixel is part of the line, the corresponding unit in the pattern string has the value 1, otherwise 0. No information about the spatial relation between pixels is provided. Each of the 8 possible sequences consists of 8 snapshots of the line sweeping over the image. Our goal is to find a code for all 64 possible (sub)sequences of the sweeping line. Note that this task is not trivial because a pattern always appears in two different sequences and has to be coded differently depending on its context. That is, the network has to find a reversible coding for each position, orientation, and direction a line has at a certain point in time. The input entropy is 6.0 bits. With the minimum possible code size of 6 bits, we vary the number of representational units from 6 to 16 bits and the bit probability in the Anti-Hebb sequence model from 0.1 to 0.5.

In general, the models modified in order to deal with time varying sequences exhibit the same properties as their originals. Both perform significant redundancy and dependency reduction while preserving most of the input information. Again, we have to deal with the trade-off that increasing entropy always implies increasing redundancy as well as dependency. Differences are that learning is slower compared to the static experiment, i.e. we need significantly more training epochs, and with higher code sizes the trade-off between entropy and redundancy/dependency reaches a saturation point. From this point on, the quality of the codes can not be increased by simply increasing the code size, because redundancy and dependency increase exponentially while the entropy stays the same or even decreases. Also, unlike in the static case, the PredMin model exhibits a close to linear dependence between redundancy in the code and dependency between code symbols. In respect to our main code measures, the PredMin model performs superior to the Anti-Hebb sequence model. Even with a bit probability of p = 0.1 the codes of the Anti-Hebb model carry more redundancy and dependency, but at the same time they preserve less information about the input.

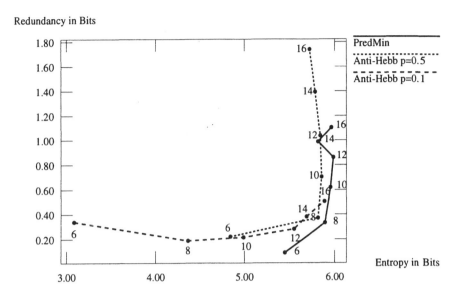

Figure 5: Overview over the Different Network Models: Redundancy Versus Entropy and Code Size.

The Anti-Hebb model forms line shaped positive receptive fields of different orientations and positions which suggests that the network is able to extract the main independent features of the input. In the PredMin model we observe negative and positive receptive fields which are only remotely relatable to lines of different orientations.

CONCLUSION

We compare two basic unsupervised artificial neural network models which perform redundancy reduction on static input data. One is from Peter Földiàk, and the other one was introduced by Jürgen Schmidhuber. We also extend their functionality in order to deal with dynamic time varying pattern sequences and compare them as well. Note that the motivation behind these two models are different. Földiàk's model is intended as a biological relevant mechanism (local learning) while Schmidhuber's concept of predictability minimization uses the back-propagation algorithm. The results we obtain are consistent for both static as well as dynamic input data. Though the two models discover very different types of codes, they perform in a similar fashion. With increasing code size and bit probability, the entropy of the codes increases, but at the same time the redundancy and dependency between code symbols increase as well.

Földiàk's model performs best for low bit probabilities and large code sizes. The codes found are very sparse and have a good ability to generalize between similar inputs. The receptive fields clearly mirror interesting, independent features of the input; thus, the code is well comprehensible for humans. The model accounts for the probability distribution of the input by coding frequent patterns unambiguously while infrequent ones are stored together. With increasing bit probability the codes loose their smoothness and comprehensibility because now several of the observed features are coded in one unit. The PredMin model has its strength in building compact, highly distributed codes which preserve most of the input information. Providing no means for adjusting the bit probabilities, most of the units are active 40% to 60% of the time. The positive and negative receptive fields capture more subtle, hidden microfeatures. Thus, the codes do not support human understanding nor generalization. The codes are nearly invertible especially the ones of larger size.

The noise resistance of both models is poor. While the PredMin model performs slightly better, adding even small noise (< 0.1) to the test patterns cuts performance in half (only 50% of the invertible pattern-code mappings can still be recognized).

314

One goal of the research presented here is to point out which of the models discussed would be more suitable for which type of application. We suggest using Földiàk's model for applications that require a sparse code with good generalization abilities (smoothness) and where it is crucial for humans to understand the encoding. The code size should be chosen large enough and the bit probability should not exceed 0.2. The redundancy will be reduced significantly, and the code symbols will be highly decorrelated. For example, in order to count the number of lines in an image, a sparse representation obtained from Földiàk's model [4] will simplify the task significantly by reducing it to the counting of active units. Using a representation, as produced by the PredMin model [4], would complicate this task.

On the other hand, the codes produced by PredMin prove useful when it is crucial that the code is indeed invertible or when the code should be as dense and distributed as possible. In addition to this, some applications require that the code does not perform destructive interference; that is, that the code does not generalize between similar inputs. For example consider, the physical experiment of particles colliding in a test tube. Each collision results in one special event but we are especially interested in one which happens very infrequently. The resulting events might have very similar properties but should be classified in totally different categories. A code similar to the ones produced by PredMin seems applicable here.

These criteria only can serve as coarse classification hints. Each application has to be analyzed carefully in order to determine which kind of input representation would be helpful and on which properties of the code the focus lies. In general, trade-off decisions between information preservation, redundancy/dependency, generalization/comprehensibility, density, as well as distribution and sparseness of the code, have to be made. The outcome of this analysis determines which of the versions of which model is most suitable.

Acknowledgments

I would like to thank Dr. Jürgen Schmidhuber, Prof. Mike Mozer, and Prof. Paul Smolensky. Their advice, comments, and discussions provided an inspiring environment for the research reported here.

References

[1] H. B. Barlow, T. P. Kaushal, and G. J. Mitchison, "Finding Minimum Entropy Codes," Neural Computation, vol. 1, pp. 412-423, 1989, MIT.

[2] R. Farber, A. Lapedes, and K. Sirotkin, "Determination of Eukaryotic Protein Coding Regions using Neural Networks and Information Theory," Journal of Molecular Biology, vol. 226, pp. 471-479, 1992.

[3] P. Földiàk, "Models of Sensory Coding," Ph.D Dissertation, University of Cambridge/England, 1992, Technical Report CUED/F-INFENG/TR 91, January 1992.

[4] S. N. Lindstaedt, "Comparison of Two Unsupervised Neural Network Models for Redundancy Reduction," M. S. Thesis, University of Colorado at Boulder, 1993.

[5] R. Linsker, "An Application of the Principle of Maximum Information Preservation to Linear Systems," Advances in Neural Information Processing Systems, vol. 1, Nov.-Dec., 1988, Ed.: D.S. Touretzky (Morgan Kaufman, San Mateo, Ca., 1989, in press).

[6] E. Oja, "Neural Networks, Principal Components, and Subspaces," International Journal of Neural Systems, vol. 1, no. 1, pp. 61-68, 1989, World Scientific Publishing Company.

[7] D. E. Rumelhart and D. Zipser, "Feature Discovery by Competitive Learning," Cognitive Science, vol. 9, pp. 75-112, 1985.

[8] J. H. Schmidhuber, "Netzwerkarchitekturen, Zielfunktionen und Kettenregel," Habilitationsschrift, Institut für Informatik, Technische Universität München, 1993.

[9] J. H. Schmidhuber, "Learning Unambiguous Reduced Sequence Descriptions," Advances in Neural Information Processing Systems, vol. 4, pp. 291-298, 1992, Ed.: Moody, Hanson, and Lippman, Morgan Kaufmann, CA.

Solving inverse problems using an EM approach to density estimation

Zoubin Ghahramani[1]
Department of Brain & Cognitive Sciences
Massachusetts Institute of Technology
Cambridge, MA 02139
zoubin@psyche.mit.edu

This paper proposes density estimation as a feasible approach to the wide class of learning problems where traditional function approximation methods fail. These problems generally involve learning the inverse of causal systems, specifically when the inverse is a non-convex mapping. We demonstrate the approach through three case studies: the inverse kinematics of a three-joint planar arm, the acoustics of a four-tube articulatory model, and the localization of multiple objects from sensor data.

The learning algorithm presented differs from regression-based algorithms in that no distinction is made between input and output variables; the joint density is estimated via the EM algorithm and can be used to represent any input/output map by forming the conditional density of the output given the input.

Causality in physical systems induces directionality in the relations between variables measured from them. Thus, one can generally define a forward and an inverse direction of mapping. The forward direction is the causal direction, for example, from the forces applied to an object to the motion outcome, from the joint angles of an arm to the Cartesian coordinate of the finger, or from the configuration of a vocal tract to the sound frequencies produced. Similarly, the inverse direction is the non-causal direction. If the goal is to control the physical system the the inverse direction of mapping is particularly relevant. Returning to the above examples, this is the mapping from desired motion of an object to the forces required, from desired Cartesian finger coordinates to required joint angles, or from desired sound frequencies to required vocal tract configuration. In general the forward direction will be a function, whereas the inverse direction may be one-to-many and therefore not a function.

One-to-many relations are often difficult to learn with function approximation methods. This difficulty arises from the fact that if the image of an input is a non-convex region in the output, then the least-squares solution may fall outside this region (for further discussion of non-convexity see [12]).

This paper proposes density estimation as a feasible approach to the wide class of non-convex learning problems where function approximation and non-linear regression methods fail. The learning algorithm presented here differs from regression-based algorithms in that no distinction is made between input and output variables; the joint density is estimated and this estimate can then be used to form any input/output map. Thus, to estimate the vector function $\mathbf{y} = f(\mathbf{x})$ the joint density $P(\mathbf{x}, \mathbf{y})$ is estimated and, given a particular input $\mathbf{x}$, the conditional density $P(\mathbf{y}|\mathbf{x})$ is formed. If a single estimate of $\mathbf{y}$ is desired rather than the full conditional density, several methods can be applied. For example, the estimate can be set to $\hat{\mathbf{y}} = E(\mathbf{y}|\mathbf{x})$, the expectation of $\mathbf{y}$ given $\mathbf{x}$.

In particular, the density estimation algorithm presented is based on maximizing the likelihood of a parametric mixture model using the EM algorithm [3]. This approach provides a single framework for real, discrete, or mixed data, and generalizes naturally to data sets with arbitrary missing data patterns. In

[1]This research was supported by a grant from the McDonnell-Pew Foundation. This paper would not have been possible without the support and helpful comments of Michael I. Jordan and his research group. Thanks to Geoff Hinton for his insightful comments and review and to John F. Houde for the data from the four-tube model of the vocal tract.

principle any density estimation algorithm (e.g. [16, 17]) could be used within this framework for solving inverse problems. However, the parametric mixture models presented here benefit from the simple form of their conditional densities, the convergence speed of the EM algorithm, and a principled way for dealing with missing data.

DENSITY ESTIMATION USING EM

General Theory

This section outlines the learning algorithm for mixture models [3, 4, 15]. We assume that the data $\mathcal{X} = \{\mathbf{x}_1, \ldots, \mathbf{x}_N\}$ were generated independently by a mixture density:

$$P(\mathbf{x}_i) = \sum_{j=1}^{M} P(\mathbf{x}_i|\omega_j; \theta_j) P(\omega_j), \tag{1}$$

where each component of the mixture is denoted ω_j and parametrized by θ_j. Thus the log of the likelihood of the parameters given the data set is

$$l(\theta|\mathcal{X}) = \log \prod_{i=1}^{N} \sum_{j=1}^{M} P(\mathbf{x}_i|\omega_j; \theta_j) P(\omega_j) = \sum_{i=1}^{N} \log \sum_{j=1}^{M} P(\mathbf{x}_i|\omega_j; \theta_j) P(\omega_j). \tag{2}$$

We seek to find the parameter vector that maximizes $l(\theta|\mathcal{X})$. However, this function is not easily maximized numerically because it involves the log of a sum. Intuitively it is not easily maximized because for each data point there is a "credit-assignment" problem, i.e. it is not clear which component of the mixture generated that data point and thus which parameters to adjust to fit that data point.

The EM algorithm applied to mixtures is an iterative method for overcoming this credit-assignment problem. The intuition behind it is that if one had access to a "hidden" random variable $\mathbf{z}$ that indicated which data point was generated by which component, then the maximization problem would decouple into a set of simple maximizations. Mathematically, given $\mathcal{Z} = \{\mathbf{z}_1, \ldots, \mathbf{z}_N\}$ a "complete-data" log likelihood function could be written,

$$l_c(\theta|\mathcal{X}, \mathcal{Z}) = \sum_{i=1}^{N} \sum_{j=1}^{M} z_{ij} \log P(\mathbf{x}_i|\mathbf{z}_i; \theta) P(\mathbf{z}_i; \theta), \tag{3}$$

such that it does not involve a log of a summation.

As proven in [3], $l(\theta|\mathcal{X})$ can be maximized by iterating the following two steps,

$$
\begin{array}{lrcl}
\text{E step:} & Q(\theta|\theta_k) & = & E[l_c(\theta|\mathcal{X}, \mathcal{Z})|\mathcal{X}, \theta_k] \\
\text{M step:} & \theta_{k+1} & = & \arg\max_\theta Q(\theta|\theta_k).
\end{array} \tag{4}
$$

The E (Expectation) step computes the expected complete data log likelihood and the M (Maximization) step finds the parameters that maximize this likelihood.

Real case: mixture of Gaussians

Real valued data will be modeled as generated by a mixture of Gaussians. For this model the E-step simplifies to computing $h_{ij} \equiv E[z_{ij}|\mathbf{x}_i, \theta_k]$, the probability that Gaussian j, as defined by the mean $\hat{\mu}_j$ and covariance matrix $\hat{\Sigma}_j$ estimated at time step k, generated data point i:

$$h_{ij} = \frac{|\hat{\Sigma}_j|^{-1/2} \exp\{-\frac{1}{2}(\mathbf{x}_i - \hat{\mu}_j)^T \hat{\Sigma}_j^{-1}(\mathbf{x}_i - \hat{\mu}_j)\}}{\sum_{l=1}^{M} |\hat{\Sigma}_l|^{-1/2} \exp\{-\frac{1}{2}(\mathbf{x}_i - \hat{\mu}_l)^T \hat{\Sigma}_l^{-1}(\mathbf{x}_i - \hat{\mu}_l)\}}. \tag{5}$$

The M-step then involves re-estimating the means and covariances of the Gaussians using the data set weighted by the h_{ij}:

$$\hat{\mu}_j^{k+1} = \frac{\sum_{i=1}^{N} h_{ij}\mathbf{x}_i}{\sum_{i=1}^{N} h_{ij}}, \qquad \hat{\Sigma}_j^{k+1} = \frac{\sum_{i=1}^{N} h_{ij}(\mathbf{x}_i - \hat{\mu}_j^k)(\mathbf{x}_i - \hat{\mu}_j^k)^T}{\sum_{i=1}^{N} h_{ij}}. \tag{6}$$

Discrete case: mixture of Bernoullis

D-dimensional binary data $\mathbf{x} = (x_1, \ldots, x_d \ldots x_D)$, $x_d \in \{0, 1\}$, will be modeled as generated by a mixture of m Bernoulli densities. That is,

$$P(\mathbf{x}|\theta) = \sum_{j=1}^{M} P(\omega_j) \prod_{d=1}^{D} \mu_{jd}^{x_d} (1 - \mu_{jd})^{(1-x_d)}. \tag{7}$$

For this model the E-step and M-step are:

$$\text{E step:} \quad h_{ij} = \frac{\prod_{d=1}^{D} \hat{\mu}_{jd}^{x_{id}} (1 - \hat{\mu}_{jd})^{(1-x_{id})}}{\sum_{l=1}^{M} \prod_{d=1}^{D} \hat{\mu}_{ld}^{x_{id}} (1 - \hat{\mu}_{ld})^{(1-x_{id})}}, \qquad \text{M step:} \quad \hat{\boldsymbol{\mu}}_j^{k+1} = \frac{\sum_{i=1}^{N} h_{ij} \mathbf{x}_i}{\sum_{i=1}^{N} h_{ij}}. \tag{8}$$

More generally, discrete or categorical data can be modeled as generated by a mixture of multinomial densities and similar derivations for the learning algorithm can be applied. Moreover, the extension to data with mixed real, binary, and categorical dimensions can also be readily derived.

The EM algorithm has traditionally been used in statistics for two distinct applications: to estimate the parameters of mixture models, as shown here, and to deal with arbitrary patterns of missing values in the data. A combination of both these applications of the EM algorithm, resulting in a general learning algorithm for incomplete data, is presented in [7].

SUPERVISED LEARNING

The above sections have outlined the learning algorithms for estimating a mixture density from a data set. When viewed as supervised learning each vector $\mathbf{x}_i$ in the training set is composed of an "input" subvector $\mathbf{x}_i^i$ and a "target" or output subvector $\mathbf{x}_i^o$. Applying the learning algorithm we obtain an estimate of the density of the data in this input/output space. For the Gaussian mixture case this estimate can be used to approximate a function in the following way:

Given the input vector $\mathbf{x}_i^i$ we extract all the relevant information from the joint p.d.f. $P(\mathbf{x}^i, \mathbf{x}^o)$ by conditionalizing to $P(\mathbf{x}^o|\mathbf{x}^i)$. For a single Gaussian this conditional density is normal, and by linearity, since $P(\mathbf{x}^i, \mathbf{x}^o)$ is a mixture of Gaussians so is $P(\mathbf{x}^o|\mathbf{x}^i)$. In principle, this conditional density is the final output of the density estimator. That is, given a particular input the network returns the complete conditional density of the output. However, for the purposes of comparison to function approximation methods and since many applications require a single estimate of the output, we will outline three possible ways to obtain such an estimate $\hat{\mathbf{x}}$ of $\mathbf{x}^o = f(\mathbf{x}_i^i)$:

- Least squares estimate (LSE) takes $\hat{\mathbf{x}}^o(\mathbf{x}_i^i) = E(\mathbf{x}^o|\mathbf{x}_i^i)$;
- Stochastic Sampling (STOCH) samples according to the distribution $\hat{\mathbf{x}}^o(\mathbf{x}_i^i) \sim P(\mathbf{x}^o|\mathbf{x}_i^i)$;
- Single component LSE (SLSE) takes $\hat{\mathbf{x}}^o(\mathbf{x}_i^i) = E(\mathbf{x}^o|\mathbf{x}_i^i, \omega_j)$ where $j = \arg\max_k P(z_k|\mathbf{x}_i^i)$. That is, for a given input, SLSE picks the Gaussian with highest posterior, and for that Gaussian approximates the output with the LSE estimator given by that Gaussian alone.

Looking more closely at the LSE estimator we note that we can write it as

$$\hat{\mathbf{x}}^o(\mathbf{x}_i^i) = \frac{\sum_{j=1}^{M} h_{ij} [\boldsymbol{\mu}_j^o + \Sigma_j^{oi} \Sigma_j^{oo^{-1}} (\mathbf{x}_i^i - \boldsymbol{\mu}_j^i)]}{\sum_{j=1}^{M} h_{ij}}, \tag{9}$$

from which we see that the LSE function estimate is a weighted sum of linear approximations, where the weights h_{ij} vary nonlinearly over the input space. In fact, the LSE estimator on a Gaussian mixture has interesting relations to algorithms such as CART [2], MARS [6], and competitive modular networks [11], as the mixture of Gaussians competitively partitions the input space, and learns a linear regression surface on each partition (details are given in [7]). In the limit, as the covariance matrices go to zero the approximation becomes a nearest-neighbour map.

318

For the discrete case, if we wish to obtain the posterior probability of the output given the input and the model of the data, we would use the LSE estimator. On the other hand, if we wish to obtain output estimates that fall in our discrete output space we would use the STOCH estimator. [2]

Returning to the Gaussian mixture case, the STOCH and the SLSE estimators are more appropriate for learning non-convex inverse maps, where the mean of several solutions to an inverse might not be a solution. Both STOCH and SLSE take advantage of the explicit representation of the input/output density by selecting one of the several solutions to the inverse.

In the next three sections we illustrate, through case studies, the general phenomenon of non-convex inverses in learning. We also provide empirical evidence for the claim that density estimation using the STOCH or SLSE estimators, but not the LSE estimator, is a feasible approach to learning in these contexts.

INVERSE KINEMATICS

As a first example of a non-convex inverse problem we present the inverse kinematics of a three-joint planar arm. This problem involves learning the mapping between end-point Cartesian positions $\mathbf{x} = (x, y)$ and joint angles $\boldsymbol{\theta} = (\theta_1, \theta_2, \theta_3)$ of a robotic arm. Whereas the forward kinematic map from joint angles to end-point positions is always well-posed, it has been noted that redundancy of of the arm allows for many solutions to the inverse, causing a form of ill-posedness known as the "degrees-of-freedom problem" [1]. Approaches to learning the inverse kinematic map by sampling the $(\mathbf{x}, \boldsymbol{\theta})$ space and directly estimating a function $\boldsymbol{\theta} = \hat{f}(\mathbf{x})$ have met with some success [13]. However, as Jordan and Rumelhart (1992) have pointed out, the non-convexity of the map places a lower bound on the achievable error of any direct least-squares algorithm. Jordan and Rumelhart propose an indirect approach to this non-convexity problem based on forming an internal model of the arm and using this model to transform errors in Cartesian space to errors in joint-angle space.

Here we propose an alternative direct method where we will use our density estimation technique to form a model of the arm. Conditionalizing this density at values along the joint-angle space gives us a forward kinematic model of the arm. Conditionalizing at values along the end-point space gives us the inverse kinematic map. Since non-convexity implies that this latter conditional density is multimodal, we expect the LSE estimator to be inferior to the STOCH or SLSE estimators.

Figure 1 shows the results of learning the kinematics of an unconstrained three-joint planar arm with relative link lengths 1.0, 1.0, and 0.5. In Figure 1 (a) we see large reaching errors obtained on a feedforward backpropagation network using a least-squares error criterion to learn the inverse kinematics. Figure 1 (b) shows that first performing density estimation and then taking the conditional expectation (LSE) of the density yields qualitatively similar results to the last-squares backprop network. On the other hand, it can be seen in Figures 1 (c & d) that the density estimate actually contains enough information so that, if sampled properly with STOCH or SLSE, satisfactory solutions to the inverse can be obtained.

ACOUSTICS OF THE VOCAL TRACT

The motor theory of speech perception proposes that knowledge of speech production is used in the perception of speech [14]. One form of the motor theory proposes that speech perception is the process of inverting an internal model of speech production. Thus, speech is perceived by taking a model of how phonemes arise from the vocal tract and predicting from the acoustic signal what the speaker's intended vocal tract configuration was—i.e. speech perception is an inverse acoustics problem.

---

[2]Here an analogy can be made to Boltzmann machine learning [9]. Boltzmann machines minimize the relative entropy between their state distribution and the target state distribution. This corresponds to maximum likelihood density estimation, taking the target distribution to be the empirical distribution of the data. Analogously, the EM approach to Bernoulli mixtures estimates the target density by placing the component means in parts of the space with high data density. Using the approximation $\hat{\mathbf{x}}^o(\mathbf{x}^i) = \mu_j^o$ where $j = \arg\max_k P(z_k|\mathbf{x}_i^i)$ emulates basins of attraction by completing patterns with the probabilistically nearest mean, with the number of such "basins" equal to the number of components in the mixture. Finally, it is worth noting that Boltzmann machine learning is also an instance of generalized EM [9].

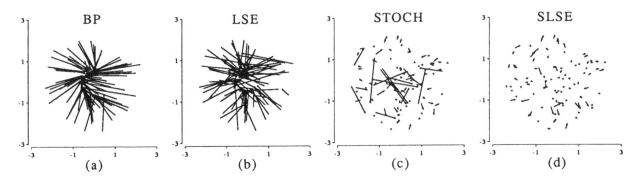

Figure 1. Learning direct inverse kinematics: Vector fields of reaching errors of a three-joint planar arm. Each of the above was trained on 1000 pairs of Cartesian (x, y) inputs and $(\theta_1, \theta_2, \theta_3)$ joint angle targets. The vectors are calculated on a test set of 200 points as the difference between an (x^*, y^*) command given to the network and the forward kinematic transformation of the output of the network $(x, y) = \text{KIN}(\theta_1, \theta_2, \theta_3)$. (a) Backpropagation (RMS error = 1.211; a coarse search over the learning rate, momentum, and number of hidden units did not yield qualitatively different solutions from this). (b) EM Mixture of 60 Gaussians using the LSE estimator, (RMS error = 1.128). (c) Same mixture using the STOCH estimator (RMS error = 0.247). (d) Using the SLSE estimator (RMS error = 0.134).

In this section of the paper we observe that the non-convexity issue also arises in the context of this inverse acoustics problem. We limit our analysis to vowel production in a simplified four-tube model of the vocal tract [5] (see Figure 2 (a)). Tongue position and constriction of the model are varied as the tract resonances corresponding to the first three formants F_1, F_2 and F_3, are measured. These three formants are perceptually salient features of vowels in human speech. The learner is presumed to randomly sample the configuration space of the vocal tract, observe the vowels produced, and attempt to learn the mapping between vowels formants and tract configuration – essentially a static inverse acoustics problem. More sophisticated schemes involve a learner that uses a dynamic model of the articulators to recursively estimate the vocal tract configuration [10]. We will focus on the simpler static case.

One thousand data points were generated by randomly varying the tongue position between −6.5cm and 6.5cm and the tongue constriction between −1.0cm and 1.0cm about their resting states, and measuring the first three vowel formants (in Hertz). The learner estimated this 5 dimensional density using 60 full covariance Gaussians and 20 iterations of the EM algorithm, enough for approximate convergence. The density was then used to estimate tongue position and constriction $(\hat{x}_1, \hat{x}_2)$ from the formants. The acoustic outcome of this estimate was then compared to the actual input formants to obtain an error measure. Figures 2 (b& c) show that the least-squares estimates of tongue position and constriction obtained by taking the conditional expectation of the density do not correspond to the actual formants. On the other hand we see in Figure 2 (d & e) that the estimates obtained from the SLSE estimator can accurately reproduce the formants. The mean euclidean errors were 169.9 ± 5.6 Hz for the LSE estimator and 15.6 ± 1.5 Hz for the SLSE estimator (n=5 runs).

Thus, as with the inverse kinematics problem, non-convexity is of high relevance in predicting articulator configuration from formants, even though strictly speaking the problem in this case is not due to excess degrees of freedom but to symmetries in the vocal tract.

LOCALIZATION OF MULTIPLE OBJECTS FROM SENSOR DATA

As a final example of a non-convex learning problem we present the localization of multiple objects from sensor readings. The framework for this problem is one in which the learner is presented sensor readings from a room and the location of a *single* object in that room. The goal is to learn to determine from a sensor reading the locations of all the objects in the room. Given that there may be more than one object in the room contributing to the sensor readings at any time, we view this problem as one in which there are hidden sources and the learner is given incomplete data. The non-convexity in the problem arises from the hidden

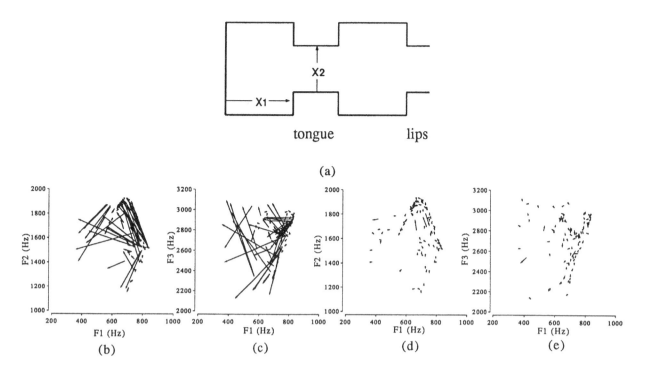

Figure 2. Four-tube model of the vocal tract. (a) Two parameters of the model, the tongue position x_1 and the tongue constriction x_2, are varied and the acoustic resonances of the four-tube model are computed. (b & c) Projections of the error vector field in formant space for the LSE estimator. (d & e) Projections of the error vector field for the SLSE estimator.

source: one object at the average location of two objects in the environment does not give the same sensor readings as the two objects combined.

For this particular example we assume that the contribution of each object in the room to the sensor readings is additive, and that a reading is inversely proportional to the square distance between the object and the sensor – a situation roughly analogous to point light sources being detected by light meters in a non-reflecting room. 1225 data points were generated by independently placing two objects, (x_1, y_1) and (x_2, y_2), on a grid in the room and calculating the sensor readings (s_1, s_2, s_3, s_4). The learner was trained using only the first object (i.e. on data points $(x_1, y_1, s_1, s_2, s_3, s_4)$) with a mixture of 60 Gaussians for 20 iterations of the EM algorithm.

Figure 3 shows four examples of the learner's estimated conditional density of object location given sensor readings calculated over the room, $\hat{P}(x, y | s_1, s_2, s_3, s_4)$. Four pairs of object locations were randomly generated and their corresponding sensor representations were computed as the input to the network. The density estimated by the learner is multimodal and tends to agree with the actual object locations; whereas a learner which simply attempts to predict (x, y) location by non-linear regression on the same data set would always falsely detect a single object intermediate between the two objects.

Two things should be noted about this example. First, even this simple multiple object localization problem suffers from exponential growth in number of data points as the number of objects increases. That is, for n objects each represented at a resolution of $1/k$ in each dimension, there are k^{2n} configurations of the room and sensor readings. This makes training the density estimator infeasible as the number of objects increases.

Second, it should be noted that for this example the generative model assumed by the mixture density does not reflect the way the data were actually generated. That is, even though the sensor data are the result of several simultaneous objects in the room, the mixture model assumes that each data point was generated by exactly one Gaussian. Thus, if the network output is a bimodal conditional density it should

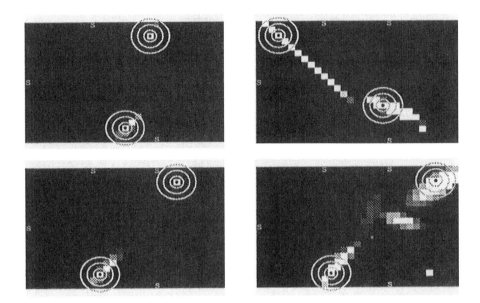

Figure 3. Localizing multiple objects from sensor data; four examples. The shading of the background represents the estimated probability density over object location given the sensor readings. (Shade at (x, y) is proportional to $\log(1 + \hat{P}(x, y | s_1, s_2, s_3, s_4))$, with brighter representing higher estimated probability). The concentric circles mark at their center the actual locations of the two objects that generated the sensor data. The letter "s" marks sensor position. Note that the learner always estimated the actual locations to have relatively high probability (white squares).

be interpreted as a single object whose location is uncertain, not as two objects. However, from the data vectors alone there is no way of distinguishing between one object which gives the same sensor readings at two locations, and two objects, only one of which is present in the data vector.

An idea which may overcome the exponential growth of samples by explicitly representing the multiple causes in this data is the cooperative vector quantizer (CVQ) based on Minimum Description Length principles [8]. The CVQ extracts a compact code for the data by assuming that several independent sources collaborate to generate the data vector. In this example, the CVQ would extract such a code for the sensor readings, and the mapping from this code to sets of (x, y) positions could simultaneously be learned in a supervised fashion.

DISCUSSION

Many learning problems do not fall under the rubric of traditional function approximation or classification. In this paper we have outlined one such class of problems, those involving non-convex learning, and an approach to solving them through parametric density estimation.

The three examples presented are instances of different sources of non-convexity. In the inverse kinematics problem the non-convexity arises from the excess degrees of freedom in a three-joint planar arm. In the vocal tract configuration problem the non-convexity arises from symmetries in the vocal tract. In the object localization problem it arises from the fact that the learner is presented with incomplete information about the environment—that is, it learns with one target object location at a time when there are in fact multiple objects in the room.

The particular density estimation procedure, applying maximum likelihood to a parametric mixture model using the EM algorithm, has the attractive properties that it generalizes to real and discrete data, can handle arbitrary patterns of incompleteness, and takes advantage of the convergence speed of EM. For

322

applicability to large problems full data-parallel implementations of this algorithm have also been coded on a Connection Machine CM5.

Further directions of research include extending the implementations, running on high dimensional real-world data sets, and testing an on-line weighted recursive least squares update rule.

References

[1] N. Bernstein, *The coordination and regulation of movements*. London: Pergamon, 1967.

[2] L. Breiman, J. H. Friedman, R. A. Olshen, and C. J. Stone, *Classification and Regression Trees*. Belmont, CA: Wadsworth International Group, 1984.

[3] A. P. Dempster, N. M. Laird, and D. B. Rubin, "Maximum likelihood from incomplete data via the EM algorithm," *J. Royal Statistical Society Series B*, vol. 39, pp. 1–38, 1977.

[4] R. O. Duda and P. E. Hart, *Pattern Classification and Scene Analysis*. New York: Wiley, 1973.

[5] G. Fant, *Acoustic Theory of Speech Production*. Mouton and Co., 1960.

[6] J. H. Friedman, "Multivariate adaptive regression splines," *The Annals of Statistics*, vol. 19, pp. 1–141, 1991.

[7] Z. Ghahramani and M. I. Jordan, "Function approximation via density estimation using the EM approach," Computational Cognitive Science TR 9304, MIT, 1993.

[8] G. E. Hinton, "Using the minimum description length principle to discover factorial codes." Lecture given at the 1993 Connectionist Models Summer School, 1993.

[9] G. E. Hinton and T. J. Sejnowski, "Learning and relearning in Boltzmann machines," in *Parallel Distributed Processing: Explorations in the Microstructure of Cognition. Volume 1: Foundations* (D. E. Rumelhart and J. L. McClelland, eds.), Cambridge, MA: MIT Press, 1986.

[10] J. F. Houde, "Recursive estimation of articulatory control," Computational Cognitive Science TR, MIT, Cambridge, MA, 1991.

[11] M. I. Jordan and R. A. Jacobs, "Hierarchical mixtures of experts and the EM algorithm," tech. rep., MIT, 1993.

[12] M. I. Jordan and D. E. Rumelhart, "Forward models: Supervised learning with a distal teacher," *Cognitive Science*, vol. 16, pp. 307–354, 1992.

[13] M. Kuperstein, "Neural model of adaptive hand-eye coordination for single postures," *Science*, vol. 239, pp. 1308–1311, 1988.

[14] A. M. Liberman, F. S. Cooper, D. P. Shankweiler, and M. Studdert-Kennedy, "Perception of the speech code," *Psychological Review*, vol. 74, pp. 431–461, 1967.

[15] S. J. Nowlan, *Soft Competitive Adaptation: Neural Network Learning Algorithms based on Fitting Statistical Mixtures*. CMU-CS-91-126, School of Computer Science, Carnegie Mellon University, Pittsburgh, PA, April 14 1991.

[16] D. W. Scott, *Multivariate Density Estimation: Theory, Practice, and Visualization*. New York: Wiley, 1992.

[17] D. F. Specht, "A general regression neural network," *IEEE Trans. Neural Networks*, vol. 2, no. 6, pp. 568–576, November 1991.

Estimating A-Posteriori Probabilities
using Stochastic Network Models

Michael Finke
Institut für Logik, Komplexität und
Deduktionssysteme, University of Karlsruhe
D-76128 Karlsruhe, Germany.
`finkem@ira.uka.de`

Klaus-Robert Müller
GMD-FIRST
Rudower Chaussee 5
D-12489 Berlin, Germany.
`klaus@first.gmd.de`

In this paper we present a systematic approach to constructing neural network classifiers based on stochastic model theory. A two step process is described where the first problem is to model the stochastic relationship between sample patterns and their classes using a stochastic neural network. Then we convert the stochastic network to a deterministic one, which calculates the a-posteriori probabilities of the stochastic counterpart. That is, the outputs of the final network estimate a-posteriori probabilities by construction. The well-known method of normalizing network outputs by applying the *softmax* function in order to allow a probabilistic interpretation is shown to be more than a heuristic, since it is well-founded in the context of stochastic networks. Simulation results show a performance of our networks superior to standard multilayer networks in the case of few training samples and a large number of classes.

INTRODUCTION

During the last few years there has been a growing interest in deriving a sound interpretation of neural network outputs in terms of probabilities. This happened due to the fact that a number of *new* techniques in this field like automatic model selection and the construction of soft-classifiers depend on the knowledge of the *a-posteriori* probabilities $p(\vec{y}|\vec{x}, \vec{w})$ of a network. These are the probabilities with which a network generates an output $\vec{y} \in \mathcal{Y} \subset \mathbf{R}^M$ given input $\vec{x} \in \mathcal{X} \subset \mathbf{R}^N$ and parameter vector $\vec{w}$. In this paper we refer to the M-class classification task and present a framework for deriving the *a-posteriori* probabilities involved. There are two basic approaches to derive a probabilistic interpretation of the neural network outputs, which we will call the **deductive** and the **constructive** approach in the following.

In the **deductive approach** the basic components of the network are defined in advance: the network, the training set and the training error which is to be minimized. Then, assuming a network $\vec{w}^*$ with minimal training error, it is proved that the outputs have a certain probabilistic interpretation. For example, for infinite sets of statistically independent training samples it has been proved recently that outputs of multilayer perceptron classifiers estimate *a-posteriori* probabilities of classes [7, 6, 10]. This fact is a late justification for commonly employed methods of training networks using 1-of-M coded classes and mean-squared error or cross entropy as objective functions.

In this paper we present a **systematic construction** of neural classifiers based on stochastic model theory. We refer to one basic idea in statistical pattern recognition which consists in treating the data $\mathcal{D}$ as if it were the output of a stochastic system governed by a fixed but unknown probabilistic law q. That means, we assume that each pattern-class pair $(\vec{x}, C_m)$ consisting of a vector $\vec{x}$ and the class C_m has a certain joint probability of $q(\vec{x}, C_m) = q(\vec{x}|C_m)\, Q(C_m)$, where $Q(C_m)$ is the a-*priori* probability of class C_m and $q(\vec{x}|C_m)$ is the probability that class C_m generates a vector $\vec{x}$. In the classification task a given vector $\vec{x}$ is to be assigned to the most probable class C_m, i.e., the class with maximum a-*posteriori* probability $q(C_m|\vec{x})$. In order to build a perfect pattern classifier we need an accurate approximation of the a-*posteriori* probabilities $q(C_m|\vec{x})$ [3].

The first step towards a neural classifier with a sound statistical background is the so-called stochastic network model. This is a network whose binary output vector is not a deterministic function of the input but subject to a conditional probability distribution π completely defined by the parameters of the network. By coding the classes C_m as binary vectors it is possible to interpret the network as a system that emits different class labels with probabilities depending on the input vector. The idea is to *model* the stochastic relationship between input vectors and the class they belong to by using a stochastic network. The network training task is to approximate the a-*posteriori* probabilities of the stochastic system by the conditional probabilities represented by the network. Therefore, a trained network should emit class C_m given input $\vec{x}$ with a probability $p(C_m|\vec{x}, \vec{w})$ nearly equal to the unknown probability $q(C_m|\vec{x})$.

Going a step beyond this network, which models the stochastic relationship between a vector and its class, we convert the stochastic network to a deterministic one which calculates the conditional output probabilities of the original network **directly**. This deterministic network is the final neural classifier. The advantage of this two stage process (see figure 1) is that the resulting network has a sound statistical background and there is no question of how to interpret the network outputs, since they estimate a-*posteriori* probabilities by construction.

In the following section we refer to the modelling aspect of the classifier construction. We outline the classification problem and how it can be solved using a neural network. In the next section we define a stochastic network that models a given probability distribution and derive a deterministic classifier that calculates the probabilities of its stochastic counterpart. The result for a special class of stochastic models is a network which has a softmax normalized output. The network normalization trick has already been proposed in the literature [1] as a heuristic to make network outputs look like probabilities. Our derivation of the network based on statistical theory shows that they are a-posteriori probabilities by construction and clarifies the probabilistic assumptions inherent in the softmax approach. In the simulation section we present a number of results that show a performance of our ansatz superior to the standard multilayer perceptron classifiers justified by the deductive approach.

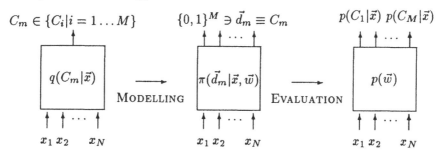

Figure 1: Construction of a stochastic pattern classifier. The stochastic system which has the probability distribution $q(C_m|\vec{x})$ is modelled by a stochastic network, i.e. the probability $\pi(\vec{d}_m|\vec{x}, \vec{w})$ of the stochastic network to emit the 1-of-M vector $\vec{d}_m$ representing class C_m is nearly equal $q(C_m|\vec{x})$. The stochastic network is then converted to a deterministic one, which calculates the a-posteriori probabilities of the stochastic network directly.

MODELLING

In a number of classification applications we are not only interested in detecting the class having maximum a-posteriori probability (cf. classification figures of merit [7]) but also in approximating the actual probabilities $q(C_m|\vec{x})$ (**soft-classification, regression problem**). Therefore, the extended classification task deals with the problem of estimating the a-posteriori probabilities such that the difference between the actual probabilities $q(C_m|\vec{x})$ and the estimated probabilities $p(C_m|\vec{x},\vec{w})$ is reduced to a minimum. The goal is to minimize the **Kullback-Leibler** difference (KL-difference)

$$D(q,p(\vec{w})) = \int d\vec{x}\, q(\vec{x}) \sum_{m=1}^{M} q(C_m|\vec{x}) \ln \frac{q(C_m|\vec{x})}{p(C_m|\vec{x},\vec{w})}, \tag{1}$$

which is a natural distance measure between the two probability distributions.

However, the joint probability $q(\vec{x}, C_m)$ is typically unknown. The only information we have on q is a set $\mathcal{D}_P = \{(\vec{x}^p, c^p)|p = 1\ldots P\}$ of P samples distributed subject to the joint distributions $q(\vec{x}, C_m)$ for $m = 1\ldots M$. Therefore, the empirical joint distribution according to this training set is given by

$$q^*(\vec{x}, C_m) = \frac{1}{P} \sum_{p=1}^{P} \left\{ \begin{array}{lll} 1 & : & \vec{x} = \vec{x}^p \text{ and } C_m = c^p \\ 0 & : & \text{otherwise} \end{array} \right. \tag{2}$$

and the KL-difference we have to minimize is

$$D(q^*, p(\vec{w})) = \sum_{p=1}^{P} \sum_{m=1}^{M} q^*(\vec{x}^p, C_m) \ln \frac{q^*(C_m|\vec{x}^p)}{p(C_m|\vec{x}^p,\vec{w})} = -\frac{1}{P} \sum_{p=1}^{P} \ln p(c^p|\vec{x}^p,\vec{w}). \tag{3}$$

It can be shown that, in a certain sense, minimizing the empirical KL-difference (3) is equal to a maximum likelihood estimation of the synaptic weight vector [6, 4]. For the minimization of $D(q^*, p(\vec{w}))$ a stochastic gradient descent is used [8].

Stochastic Networks

There is a straightforward way of using neural networks in order to solve the regression problem. Consider a network which receives a real-valued input vector $\vec{x} \in \mathbf{R}^N$ and emits an M-dimensional binary output vector $\vec{y} \in \{0,1\}^M$. We call a network **stochastic** when $\vec{y}$ is not a function of $\vec{x}$ but subject to a known probability distribution $\pi(\vec{y}|\vec{x},\vec{w})$ specified by $\vec{x}$ and the vector $\vec{w}$ of all weights and bias values of the network.

For each class C_m a unique binary vector $\vec{d}_m \in \{0,1\}^M$ is defined to be the class representative. The standard choice of coding $\vec{d}_m$ is the 1-of-M code, where $\vec{d}_m = (0,\ldots 0,1,0,\ldots 0)$ with only the m-th coefficient being 1. The network output $\vec{d}_m$ will then be identified with the output of class C_m and the training set $\mathcal{D}_P$ is translated according to $\{(\vec{x}^p, c^p) \mid p = 1\ldots P\} \rightsquigarrow \{(\vec{x}^p, \vec{y}^p = \vec{d}_{c^p}) \mid p = 1\ldots P\}$. The network itself can be interpreted as a classifier that depending on the probabilities $\pi(\vec{y}|\vec{x},\vec{w})$ either assigns an input vector $\vec{x}$ to one of the classes C_m or emits an invalid class label $\vec{y} \neq \vec{d}_k \forall k$. To solve the classification problem means in this context to approximate $q(C_m|\vec{x})$ by the network probability $p(C_m|\vec{x},\vec{w})$, where $p(C_m|\vec{x},\vec{w})$ depends on the probabilities $\pi(\vec{d}_k|\vec{x},\vec{w})$ of observing valid class representatives.

We now follow the notion of step one of our construction process described in figure 1, i.e., we define a stochastic network that mimics the stochastic relationship $\pi(\vec{d}_m|\vec{x},\vec{w})$ between a pattern vector $\vec{x}$ and the expected class representative $\vec{d}_m$. At this point we are free to select an **arbitrary** stochastic network model, e.g. Boltzmann machine, Mean Field Approximation or stochastic feed-forward networks, whose probabilities $\pi(\vec{y}|\vec{x},\vec{w})$ can be calculated explicitly [4]. But note that the selection of a specific network model is equivalent to making a distribution assumption regarding the binary class vectors $\vec{d}_m$ [5].

Stochastic Feed-Forward Network

In order to present one application of our framework which leads to a better understanding of a normalization technique defined earlier [1] we consider in this paper a special kind of stochastic network: the **stochastic feed-forward network**. The basic components of such a network are a number of deterministic layers with sigmoid squashing functions, which implement a deterministic function $f : \mathcal{X} \rightarrow \mathcal{Z} \subset \mathbf{R}^H$, and an output layer, which consists of stochastic binary output units. Let $h_m(\vec{x}) = v_{m0} + \sum_{h=1}^{H} v_{mh} f_h(\vec{x}, \vec{w})$ be the post-synaptic potential of output unit m, where $\mathbf{v}_m$ is the weight vector to this unit and $\mathbf{v}_{m0}$ is the respective bias. The binary state $y_m \in \{0,1\}$ of an output unit will then be randomly determined according to the probability

$$\pi_m(y_m|h_m(\vec{x})) = \frac{1}{1 + \exp(-\beta(2y_m - 1) \, h_m(\vec{x}))}. \tag{4}$$

So the probability that the state of output unit m is 1 given a post-synaptic potential $h_m(\vec{x})$ is specified by $\pi_m(1|h_m(\vec{x}))$. This indeterminism in the output layer induces the stochastic behaviour of the network, i.e. given an input vector $\vec{x}$ the network generates the output $\vec{y}$ with a certain probability. Since the different output units are **stochastically independent** we can calculate this conditional probability by

$$\pi(\vec{y}|\vec{x}) = \prod_{i=1}^{M} \pi_i(y_i|h_i(\vec{x})) = \frac{\exp(\beta \sum_{i=1}^{M} y_i \, h_i(\vec{x}))}{\prod_{i=1}^{M} 2 \exp(h_i(\vec{x})/2) \, \cosh(\beta \, h_i(\vec{x})/2)}. \tag{5}$$

Using (5) the empirical KL-difference $D(q^*, \pi(\vec{w}))$ reduces to the **cross entropy** [8, 1, 6] function

$$D(q^*, \pi(\vec{w})) = -\frac{1}{P} \sum_{p=1}^{P} \ln \pi(\vec{y}^p|\vec{x}^p, \vec{w}) = -\frac{1}{P} \sum_{p=1}^{P} \sum_{i=1}^{M} \ln \pi_i(y_i^p|h_i(\vec{x}^p)) \tag{6}$$

where y_i^p denotes the i-th component of the output vector $\vec{y}^p$.

EVALUATION

Until this point we have considered only the probabilities $\pi(\vec{d}_m|\vec{x}, \vec{w})$ of emitting vectors and **not** classes. In order to specify a neural classifier we define three possible methods to calculate the **class** conditional probability $p(C_m|\vec{x}, \vec{w})$.

Stochastic Network Classifiers

The first idea is to identify the class conditional probability with the relative frequencies of observing its class representative (i.e. $p(C_m|\vec{x}, \vec{w}) \equiv \pi(\vec{d}_m|\vec{x}, \vec{w})$). The training algorithm tries to minimize (3) by maximizing the probabilities $\pi(\vec{y}^p|\vec{x}^p, \vec{w})$. The problem with this interpretation is that the training algorithm increases the probability of one class without considering the effects on the probabilities of the other classes. As shown in [4], it is possible that an increase of the intended probability yields an unwanted increase of other probabilities, too. In addition, the a-posteriori probabilities $p(C_m|\vec{x}, \vec{w})$ do not sum to one, which is a necessary condition for a proper set of class conditionals.

Another idea is to assume that the output units of a network are statistically independent from each other, i.e. $\pi(\vec{y}|\vec{x}, \vec{w}) = \prod_{i=1}^{M} \pi_i(y_i|\vec{x}, \vec{w})$. Then the conditional probability of class C_m can be defined as the probability that the state of output neuron m (i.e. y_m, the m-th component of $\vec{y}$) is 1

$$p(C_m|\vec{x}, \vec{w}) \equiv \pi_m(y_m = 1|\vec{x}, \vec{w}). \tag{7}$$

Since a training pattern $(\vec{x}, C_m)$ is an argument that $\vec{x}$ belongs to class C_m and not to any other class and $\pi(\vec{d}_m|\vec{x}, \vec{w})$ is exactly the probability of this situation, it makes sense to minimize the KL-difference (6) instead of (3). Increasing $\pi(\vec{d}_m|\vec{x}, \vec{w})$ in this interpretation is guaranteed to increase the probability of class C_m and to decrease the probability of the alternative classes. But because of the statistical independency assumption, which is not fulfilled in general, the conditional probabilities do not sum to one again.

In the first two approaches we have completely neglected one constraint on the output vectors of the classifier. This constraint, which is also inherent in the training set, is that only 1-of-M vectors are valid class representatives. The idea is that at each time step the stochastic net assigns the input vector to exactly one class. All outputs different from 1-of-M vectors are ignored. But, since only M vectors of the 2^M possible output vectors are valid class representatives, the sum of the probabilities of the class representatives will be less than one in general. Therefore, instead of interpreting $\pi(\vec{d}_m|\vec{x}, \vec{w})$ as the probability of class C_m, the relative probability of observing $\vec{d}_m$ given by

$$p(C_m|\vec{x}, \vec{w}) \equiv \frac{\pi(\vec{d}_m|\vec{x}, \vec{w})}{\sum_{k=1}^{M} \pi(\vec{d}_k|\vec{x}, \vec{w})} \tag{8}$$

must be considered as the true class conditional probability of the network. Since for a fixed weight vector $\vec{w}$ the probabilities $\pi(\vec{d}_k|\vec{x}, \vec{w})$ are well-defined and can be calculated explicitly, we have with (8) a formula to calculate the **exact** probability of a specific class C_m. The training procedure used to minimize (3) is the gradient descent algorithm with respect to this KL-difference $D(q^*, p(\vec{w}))$. We find the following learning rule [4]: In learning step k, a new example $(\vec{x}^p, c^p) \in \mathcal{D}_P$ is chosen and $\vec{w}$ is modified according to

$$\vec{w}_{k+1} = \vec{w}_k + \varepsilon_k \sum_{m=1}^{M} \left[q^*(C_m|\vec{x}^p) - p(C_m|\vec{x}^p, \vec{w}) \right] \frac{\partial \ln \pi(\vec{d}_m|\vec{x}^p, \vec{w})}{\partial \vec{w}}, \tag{9}$$

where ε_k denotes a positive learning rate.

Feed-Forward Classifier

For the construction of a feed-forward classifier based on a stochastic feed-forward network the two methods (7) and (8) might be considered as possible output interpretations.

A classifier based on the independency assumption and thus the interpretation (7) will be called **FF-I(ndependent)** classifier in the following. The replacement of the stochastic output layer by a deterministic layer consisting of units having transfer function $\pi_m(1|h_m(\vec{x}))$ leads to a network whose individual output units calculate the probability of the different classes in the sense of (7). The constructed deterministic feed-forward network is just the classifier commonly used in literature [1, 6, 8]. The training algorithm is a gradient descent method with respect to the cross entropy (6). It can be implemented in backpropagation fashion by using the error signal $\delta_m = 1 - \pi_m(1|h_m(\vec{x}))$ for the output unit of the target class and $\delta_k = -\pi_k(1|h_k(\vec{x}))$ for all other output units. It has been proved recently that a multilayer perceptron of this kind really estimates a-posteriori probabilities in the limit of infinitely many training samples [7, 6, 10].

By inserting the conditional probabilities (5) of the class representatives in a stochastic feed-forward network into (8) and using 1-of-M coded class representatives we find the following formula

$$p(C_m|\vec{x}, \vec{w}) = \frac{\exp(\beta\, h_m(\vec{x}))}{\sum_{i=1}^{M} \exp(\beta\, h_i(\vec{x}))} \tag{10}$$

expressing the **exact** a-posteriori probability of class C_m as modelled by a stochastic feed-forward network.

Note that we can always obtain distribution (10) for all factorising conditional probabilities $\pi(\vec{y}|\vec{x})$ from (5), where no explicit dependency on the output $\vec{y}$ is found in the denominator of eq.(5). Implicitly this means that the distribution of the binary vector $\vec{y}$ in eq.(5) has to be member of a rather general class of distributions: the exponential family [9]. Furthermore, it can be shown in this scenario [5, 12] that eq. (10) is nothing but a Bayes formulation of the a-posteriori probabilities $p(C_m|\vec{x}) = p(C_m|f(\vec{x}, \vec{w}))$ over the output vectors of the deterministic network component, if we assume that the distribution $p(f(\vec{x}, \vec{w})|C_m)$ is a member of the exponential family. More details on these rather general statistical insights go beyond the scope of this paper and will be published elsewhere [5].

From the stochastic network we can derive a deterministic feed-forward classifier based on the relative probability interpretation called **FF-R(elative)** classifier. Instead of the stochastic output units we use deterministic units with the non-local activation function (10). Thus, the activation of the new deterministic output unit m is equal to the probability that the underlying stochastic network emits class C_m. The training algorithm for the deterministic network is a gradient descent with respect to the KL-difference (3). As shown in [4] this procedure can be implemented as backpropagation algorithm using the error signals $\delta_m = 1 - p(C_m|\vec{x}, \vec{w})$ for the target class C_m and $\delta_k = -p(C_k|\vec{x}, \vec{w})$ for the other classes (resp. output units).

A network of sigmoid hidden units and output units having the activation function (10) has already been proposed by Bridle in 1989 [1]. His idea was to enforce the summing to one condition of the class conditionals, which is ignored in a FF-I classifier, by normalizing the outputs of a deterministic network. He proposed the heuristic of the exponential normalization (10) which he calls **softmax** function to make the outputs look like probabilities. Obviously, this is not the only possible method of normalizing the output (see for example Gish [6]). Our derivation of the FF-R network and thus the softmax function offers some new insight in the distribution assumption inherent in the exponential normalization technique. The basic assumption of neural network training in general is that the stochastic system which generated the training data can be modelled using a specific network. Our derivation shows that: *using a feed-forward network with softmax output assumes that the training data can be modelled by a stochastic feed-forward network which emits binary output vectors subject to a distribution in the exponential family* [5].

RESULTS

In this section we compare the performance of FF-I and FF-R networks on two different problems. The first one – defined in [10] – consists of approximating the univariate probability distributions of three classes. Each class has a unit variance, gaussian distribution which differ only in their means ($\mu_1 = -3, \mu_2 = 0$ and $\mu_3 = 3$). We use a small, fully connected network consisting of four hidden units and three output units. The input unit is also directly connected to the output layer (short-cut connection). The standard backpropagation plus momentum ($\mu = 0.4$) method is used to train the networks for 5000 epochs (1 epoch $\equiv$ parallel presentation of 16 patterns). Figure 2 shows the estimated a-posteriori probabilities of the FF-I and FF-R classifiers after training with a set of 300 patterns. The FF-I network produces probabilities which do not sum to one (see dotted line in figure 2(a)) and shows an inaccurate approximation of the a-posteriori probability function of class 2. In figure 2(c) we compare the approximation accuracy of the two classifiers depending on the number P of training patterns. Here, percentage of KL-difference (i.e. KL-difference divided by the entropy of distribution q) serves as a distribution-independent measure to evaluate the performance of the networks. We had 4096 simulations on this problem for both classifiers and figure 2(c) presents the mean and median trial results versus P. The results show that the performance of the FF-R network is by far superior to that of the conventional FF-I ansatz.

In order to investigate the generalization capabilities of the two types of classifiers, we performed experiments on a vowel recognition problem defined in [11]. The data used were collected by Deterding [2] who recorded examples of the eleven steady state vowels in the English words *heed, hid, head, had, hard, hud, hod, hoard, hood, who'd, heard*. There are 90 examples for each vowel derived from 15 speakers, each consisting of a ten dimensional input vector. For our simulations we use a fully connected (short-cut connections included) network with one hidden layer and eleven output units – one for each vowel. We treat the first 48 utterances of different speakers of each vowel as training set. The remaining 42 examples are used as test set [11]. The data shown in figure 3 are based on 1024 simulations we performed on a massively parallel computer (MasPar MP-1). The networks are trained for 10000 epochs where each epoch consists of the parallel presentation of 16 different examples (batch learning). The learning rate is $\varepsilon_k = 0.5/(1+0.001k)$ and the learning moment $\mu = 0.4$.

We can see from figure 3(a) that the FF-R classifier outperforms not only the standard feed-forward network (including FF-I), but it has also better classification rates than standard cluster algorithms [3] (nearest neighbor) with less parameters (only 1/10 of the floating values are necessary to store the FF-R network compared to nearest neighbor method, where each training pattern must be stored). Figure 3(b) shows the generalization error (i.e. the KL-difference between the empirical test set distribution and the approximated distribution). All curves show the typical course of training errors: at first decreasing to a minimum and then monotonic increase due to the overfitting effect. But there are some differences between

329

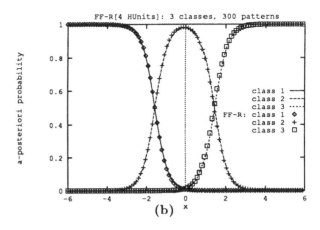

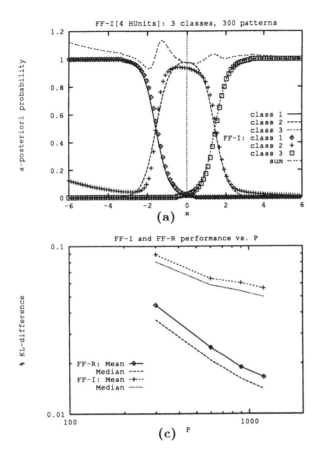

Figure 2: Approximation of the a-posteriori probabilities of the three gaussian class problem by **(a)** FF-I classifier and **(b)** FF-R classifier trained on 300 examples of the distribution. **(c)** Mean and median accuracy of approximation (percent of Kullback-Leibler difference) versus number of training patterns used. The results are based on 4096 trials.

the generalization error of the two classifiers. First of all, the generalization error of an FF-R network is smaller than that of a comparable network of FF-I type. The second phenomenon is that increasing the network size of a FF-R classifier reduces the minimum of generalization error but does not – contrary to what might be expected (and happens in case of FF-I networks) – accelerate the overfitting effect.

CONCLUSION

Standard multilayer perceptrons are used in statistical pattern recognition as 1-of-M classifiers. It has recently been proved that these networks really provide outputs which estimate a-posteriori probabilities – a fact which is only true for networks trained with asymptotically large training sets. In this paper we reversed the process. So, instead of a retrospective justification of the standard multilayer perceptron training, we specify the probabilistic constraints first and derive a network which fulfills these constraints. Therefore, the resulting networks estimate a-posteriori probabilities by construction. The described two step process of deriving networks which have a sound probabilistic interpretation can be applied within a number of different stochastic networks, e.g. Boltzmann machine, mean field approximation and stochastic feed-forward networks [4]. We explained the development process for feed-forward networks and derived a softmax normalized network as canonical classifier. The results of our simulations show an improved performance of the FF-R network compared with the standard multilayer perceptron classifiers.

The estimated a posteriori probabilities could be used in hybrid systems, i.e. combinations of expert systems and neural networks or neural networks and statistical pattern recognition systems. Moreover, one could think of a committee of classifiers to increase the overall classification performance. Future work will

Classifier	hidden nodes	% correct
Single-layer Perceptron	-	33
Multi-layer Perceptron	88	51
Multi-layer Perceptron	22	45
Multi-layer Perceptron	11	44
Radial Basis Functions	528	53
Radial Basis Functions	88	48
Gaussian Node Network	528	55
Square Node Network	88	55
Nearest Neighbour	-	56
FF-I classifier	16	54
FF-I classifier	8	52
FF-R classifier	32	57.9
FF-R classifier	16	56
FF-R classifier	8	54

(a)

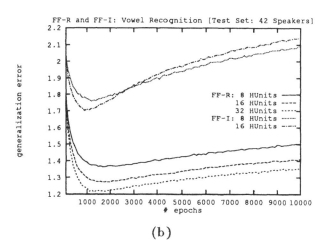

(b)

Figure 3: Vowel recognition using neural classifiers: (a) Percent of correctly classified vowels of the test set of 42 speakers according to Robinson [11] and our FF-I and FF-R results (averaged over 1024 trials). (b) Generalization error (KL-difference between empirical test set and the approximated distribution) of both types of neural classifiers and for a different number of hidden units.

also be dedicated to the application of our classification concept to other benchmark problems.

Acknowledgement

We wish to thank D.Pomerleau, M.Mozer and P.Smolensky for their critical review of this paper.

References

[1] J. Bridle, "Probabilistic Interpretation of Feedforward Classification Network Outputs, with Relationships to Statistical Pattern Recognition," in *Neurocomputing: Algorithms, Architectures and Applications* (F. F. Soulié and J. Hérault, eds.), Springer-Verlag, 1989.

[2] D. Deterding, *Speaker Normalisation for Automatic Speech Recognition*. PhD thesis, Cambridge University, 1988.

[3] R. Duda and P. Hart, eds., *Pattern Classification and Scene Analysis*. NY: Wiley Interscience, 1973.

[4] M. Finke, "Lernen in stochastischen neuronalen Netzen: Theorie und massiv parallele Implementierung." Masterthesis (in German), University of Karlsruhe, 1993.

[5] M. Finke and K.-R. Müller, "The use of stochastic neural network models for the estimation of probability distributions: Theory and applications," *in preparation*, 1993.

[6] H. Gish, "A Probabilistic Approach to the Understanding and Training of Neural Network Classifiers," in *Proc. IEEE Conf. on Acoustics, Speech and Signal Processing*, (Albuquerque), pp. 1361–1364, 1990.

[7] J. Hampshire and B. Perlmutter, "Equivalence Proof for Multilayer Perceptron Classifiers and the Bayesian Discriminant Function," in *Proceedings of the 1990 Connectionist Models Summer School*, (San Mateo, CA), Morgan Kaufmann, 1990.

[8] G. Hinton, "Connectionist Learning Procedures," in *Machine Learning: Paradigms and Methods*, pp. 185–234, Cambridge, MA: MIT Press, 1990.

[9] B. Lindgren, *Statistical Theory*. New York: Macmillan, 1976.

[10] M. Richard and R. Lippmann, "Neural Network Classifiers Estimate Bayesian a posteriori Probabilities," *Neural Computation*, vol. 3, pp. 461–483, 1991.

[11] A. Robinson, *Dynamic Error Propagation Networks*. PhD thesis, Cambridge University, 1989.

[12] D. Rumelhart, R. Durbin, R. Golden, and Y. Chauvin, "Backpropagation: The basic theory," Draft presented at Connectionist Models Summer School, Boulder, 1993.

LEARNING THEORY

ON OVERFITTING AND THE EFFECTIVE NUMBER OF HIDDEN UNITS

Andreas S. Weigend
Department of Computer Science and Institute of Cognitive Science
University of Colorado at Boulder
Boulder, CO 80309-0430
weigend@cs.colorado.edu

The problem of overfitting has drawn significant attention with sometimes apparently contradictory results, even about the mere presence or absence of the effect. In such experiments, the available data is split into two sets: a training set (used for the estimation of the parameters of the model; i.e., the weights and biases of the network), and a test set (used for the estimation of the generalization performance; i.e., the performance on out-of-sample data not used for fitting). An operational definition of overfitting is that the out-of-sample error starts to increase with training time after having gone through a minimum. A standard interpretation is that the network starts, at this point, to pick up idiosyncrasies of the training set that do not generalize to the test set.

This paper consists of two parts. In Part 1, we resolve the apparent contradiction by showing that the very presence (or absence) of overfitting can be related to the use of different test error measures. We also show that the relationship between network size and both shape and value of the overfitting curve is not as straightforward as it might seem: small networks start overfitting before they have learned all they could, and the best solutions are usually obtained with networks with a very large number of potential parameters. In Part 2, we characterize the activity of the hidden units, both individually and as an ensemble. This allows us to introduce an *effective* number of hidden units—in contrast to the *potential* number of hidden units considered in Part 1. All quantities are plotted as functions of the number of epochs; all learning is done with simple error backpropagation.

PART 1: HOW OVERFITTING DEPENDS ON THE ERROR MEASURE AND THE (POTENTIAL) NUMBER OF HIDDEN UNITS

We first briefly describe the architecture and the problem (phoneme classification). We then present three results:
1. *Overfitting can depend on the error measure used for testing. Specifically, we find that the cross-entropy error shows clear overfitting whereas the sum squared error does not.*
2. *Analyzing overfitting as a function of network size (the number of hidden units is varied), we find that fairly small networks (that never reach good performance) also, already, show overfitting.*
3. *Analyzing the performance as a function of network size, we find that large networks generalize better than small ones (the training is stopped in each case at the minimum of the test set).*

Data and Architecture

We illustrate our discussion with quantities obtained from a network trained to classify phonemes. The data is described in detail by Elman and Zipser (1988). The networks we use all have 160 inputs. The input units are fully connected to a varying number of sigmoids with a (0,1) range. The networks all have six outputs, corresponding to the six phonemes given by the task. We use normalized exponentials for the output activations (also called softmax). In order to estimate class probabilities, we choose cross-entropy error: the error for each pattern is chosen to be the logarithm of the activation value of the output unit that corresponds to the target class (Rumelhart et al., still in press). Training starts with small initial weights (uniformly distributed in [-0.01,0.01]). We choose a very small learning rate (a value of 0.01) and no momentum in order to avoid artifacts for the learning curves.

Result 1: **Overfitting depends on how the test error is measured.**

In recent years, conflicting claims have arisen on how prone to overfitting neural networks are when trained with error backpropagation. To clarify this issue, we describe results on a classification experiment (phoneme recognition). In the first setting, we train a network (with 15 hidden units) to minimize cross-entropy, and then test its out-of-sample performance by using several error measures.[1] The results are shown in Figure 1.

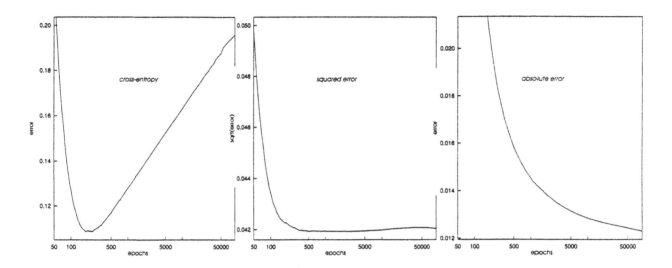

Figure 1. Out-of-sample errors as a function of training time for three error measures: cross-entropy, squared error, and absolute error. These three curves are from one and the same network that was trained with cross-entropy and tested (on the same data in each case) with different error measures.

Figure 1 shows that
*   the cross-entropy error *in*creases after passing though a minimum
*   the sum squared error remains essentially flat as training continues for a long time
*   the sum absolute error still *de*creases after 100,000 epochs.

It turns out that the number of false classifications (defined as the number of cases where the output with the largest activation does not correspond to the target class) remains constant after 500 epochs (at 0.4%). The network becomes overconfident: it moves the output of the target unit farther and farther away from the desired value of 1.0. This has the strongest effect on cross-entropy, since its logarithmic divergence at zero is the least forgiving. The squared error measure is less extreme, and absolute error, as the most robust measure of the three, penalizes large errors in comparison to small errors the least.

So far, we have considered the effect of different functional forms for the error evaluation and found these variations to be sufficient for producing the presence or absence of overfitting. From now on, we evaluate the performance only with cross-entropy. The quantity varied next is the number of hidden units.[2]

---

[1]In this first experiment, we keep the number of hidden units constant. Another variable, not discussed further in this paper, is the dependence of overfitting on the *size of the training set*. On the one extreme, if only very few training patterns are used (say, 20), no increase in the test error can be observed since the network quickly memorizes these few training patterns without any error. Because there is no error left, the weights do not change any more, and thus the test error does not change either. On the other extreme, if an infinite number of noise-free training patterns explores the test space completely, there would not be any overfitting either. The choice of a training set of 540 patterns throughout this paper corresponds to an intermediate regime where overfitting can occur.

[2]Since inputs and outputs are given by the problem, their numbers cannot be varied for a given problem. A degree of freedom that we did not explore is the number of hidden *layers*; we use throughout a single layer of hidden units.

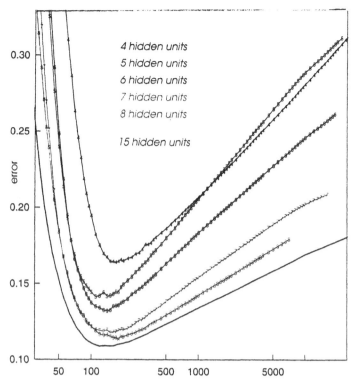

Figure 2. Out-of-sample errors for networks with different numbers of hidden units, plotted as a function of training time in epochs.

Figure 2 shows the test errors for networks with 4 to 15 hidden units. We also tried much larger networks (with up to 100 hidden units); their learning curves did not differ significantly from those of the network with 15 hidden units. Note that we did not average over different runs for each network size because averaging can wash out individually fairly sharp minima, and thus suggest erroneously the absence of overfitting.

What is not important in the figure is the number of epochs where the individual minima occur; the location of the minimum can always be moved by scaling the learning rate as a function of the number of hidden units. Two features, however, are important:

Result 2: **Small networks also overfit.**

We here consider the *shape* of the individual curves.

Perhaps surprisingly, even very small networks overfit. Rather than capturing (with their limited resources) as many properties as they can which do generalize, even very small networks begin to extract properties of the training set that do not generalize to the test set. This fact implies that heuristics such as "pick a network 'just large enough' and train it 'to convergence'" can be inappropriate. Another point that follows from the figure is that the existence of overfitting does not imply that the network size is sufficient for a given task, let alone too large.

We now turn to the value of the minimum of each curve in Figure 2.

Result 3: **There is no such thing as too large a network.**

The best performance on the test set is obtained by large networks, provided they are stopped early (at the minimum of the test set).[3] The out-of-sample error for the smallest network is significantly worse (by about 50%) than the error for the largest network.

This fact (that the largest networks are best) has a number of possible explanations. The first explanation focuses on the backpropagation search process (gradient descent): the higher dimensional the space, the easier it is to find a good solution. The

---

[3]To be methodologically clean, the final error should be reported on a *new* test set, and the present test set should be considered as a cross-validation set (see Weigend, Huberman, and Rumelhart, 1990). In the experiment reported here, no more data were available. As a simple test we divided the 540 test data points into two sets at random. The performance on both of them was comparable.

second explanation interprets a large network as a superposition of smaller networks. Let us draw the analogy to measuring a quantity (any quantity) T times: if the measurements are uncorrelated, the error on the true value of that quantity measured drops as $1/\sqrt{T}$. If all measurements are identical, there is neither gain nor harm. Similarly, the large network can be viewed as averaging several smaller networks, thus leading to possibly better (and in the worst case, equal) performance than a single, small network.[4] The third explanation views early stopping as a kind of regularizer; for linear networks (no hidden units), the regularizer corresponds to standard weight-decay (or ridge regression); see Guyon et al. (1992), and Moody (1992).

Summarizing Result 3, the heuristic of using large networks and stopping early can be useful. In our experience, this result is not limited to networks for classification but also holds for networks for regression.[5]

PART 2: **THE EFFECTIVE NUMBER OF HIDDEN UNITS**

In connectionist modeling, it is important to distinguish between potential network size and effective size. Whereas the potential size is fixed by the architecture, the effective size changes (usually increases) with training time. In Part 2 we present a measure that describes the effective number of hidden units of a network. Whereas Part 1 focused on the test errors, Part 2 focuses on the activation values of the hidden units and answers questions such as: How do the responses of hidden units change as a function of training time? Do all hidden units "get busy" at the same time in training, or one after the other? How correlated are their responses? And when they are all busy, do they do different things or not?
We first consider the hidden units individually (i) by plotting histograms of the activation values for each hidden unit (at certain points in the training process), and (ii) by computing the variances of the individual responses. We then analyze the ensemble of the hidden units by computing the eigenvalues of the covariance matrix of the activations, and by plotting them (again) against training time.

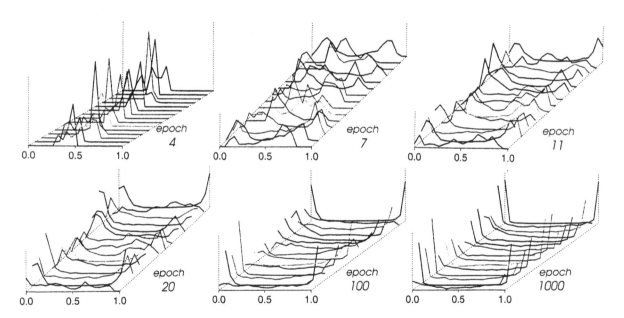

Figure 3. Histograms of hidden unit activations after 4, 7, 11, 20, 100, and 1000 epochs. In each of the six plots, we show the histograms of each of the 15 hidden units in different levels of gray.

---

[4]A more theoretical exposition can be found in the paper by Perrone (this volume). An alternative (Bayesian) perspective is offered by Buntine and Weigend (1991): rather than picking the maximum likelihood value, the various sub-nets can be interpreted as sampling the solution space, thus shifting the prediction towards a *maximum a posteriori* solution.
[5]The *Santa Fe Time Series Prediction and Analysis Competition* (Weigend and Gershenfeld, 1993) can be viewed as a comparison of different methods for regression. The best predictions for Data Set A (1,000 points) were obtained by a feed-forward network with 1,105 parameters (Wan, 1993)—more parameters than available data points! The training of the network was stopped early, and the stopping point was guided by the performance on a cross-validation set (a part of the available competition data that Wan had set aside). One example where we found the early stopping heuristic to be insufficient is the prediction of financial data: an explicit regularizer (such as *weight-elimination*) seems necessary to obtain forecasts better than chance (Weigend, Huberman and Rumelhart, 1992).

Focus 1: *Individual* hidden units: histograms and variances.

As a first attempt to describe the "busy-ness" of each hidden unit, we chop the (0,1) range into (evenly sized) bins and count how many input patterns produce a hidden unit activation that falls into that bin. (Such a plot is called a histogram.) For each epoch, we combine the 15 histograms of the 15 hidden units into one three-dimensional plot. (The order of the hidden units in the depth dimension is arbitrary.)

Early in training (after 4 epochs), all hidden units have activations around the central value of 0.5: the small weights and biases only allow for a small net-input, yielding activations around 0.5. As training continues, the range covered by the hidden unit activations broadens, and eventually the units show almost binary behavior; i.e., the activations tend to cluster around the extreme values of zero and one.

Such histograms only portray a snapshot in time (the state at a certain epoch). In order to visualize the changes in learning, it is desirable to characterize these 15 curves (in each plot) by one number each, such as the *variance* of hidden unit i,

$$VAR_i = 1/(N-1) \sum_p (x_i^{(p)} - \langle x_i \rangle)^2 \, ,$$

where the sum extends over the N patterns (indexed by (p)). The angular brackets $\langle \rangle$ denote the mean over patterns,

$$\langle x_i \rangle = 1/N \sum_p x_i^{(p)} \, .$$

The variance measures the amount of busy-ness: on the one hand, if the activations just hover around the mean, the variance is small. On the other hand, if the activation is zero for half of the patterns and one for the other half, the maximum of 0.25 for the variance is reached. In order to be able to express the busy-ness in the same mathematical units as the activations, it is convenient to use the square root of the variance, or *standard deviation*. The maximum value the standard deviation can take for signals limited to [0,1] is 0.5 (= $\sqrt{0.25}$). In Figure 4, we plot the standard deviation of each hidden unit against the epoch number.

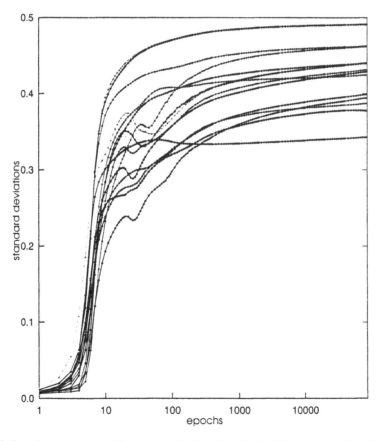

Figure 4. Standard deviations (square roots of the variances) of each individual hidden unit plotted against training time (in epochs on a logarithmic scale). Each curve corresponds to a hidden unit.

339

Figure 3 and Figure 4 both allow us to answer one of the questions: all hidden units "wake up" at the same time. To approach the next question (whether the units just duplicate each other or whether they do different things), we need to analyze them as an ensemble, rather than individually.

Focus 2: *Ensemble* of hidden units: eigenvalues of covariance matrix (principal components).

We begin this section with a geometrical interpretation of the hidden unit responses: each response can be viewed as a point in h-dimensional space. The 540 input patterns of the test set (presented as input, one after another) thus generate a set of 540 points in that space.[6] Potentially, these points could fill the entire h-dimensional space. However, let us consider the case where all the points lie on a one-dimensional straight line (in the h-dimensional space). This would allow us to re-express the network as a network with only one hidden unit. Similarly, if the points were on a two-dimensional (hyper-) plane, the effective number of hidden units would be two.[7]

We are interested in the dimensionality of the point cloud, but we do not care about its orientation in space. Ideally, we would like to rotate the original coordinates (corresponding to the hidden units in the network) to a new set of coordinates such that the first direction captures as much spread of the point cloud as possible, the second, while orthogonal to the first, as much of the remaining spread as possible, etc.

The mathematical approach consists of two steps. First, the correlational structure of the point cloud has to be captured. Considering only two-point interactions,[8] we use the *covariance* between hidden units i and j, given by

$$COV_{ij} = 1/(N-1) \sum_p (x_i^{(p)} - <x_i>) (x_j^{(p)} - <x_j>) .$$

The sum extends over the patterns. Angular brackets $<>$ denote the average over patterns. *COV* is by construction a symmetric matrix. Its main diagonal contains the h variances VAR_i introduced above. In addition, there are (at most) $h(h-1)/2$ different off-diagonal elements.[9]

Second, we have to find the effective dimension of the point cloud—it is given by the number of significantly non-zero *eigenvalues* of the covariance matrix. They describe the spreads along the new axes of the point cloud.[10] The square roots of the eigenvalues are called *principal components*.

In summary, the mathematical recipe to find the effective dimension consists of two steps:

1. Compute how responses of pairs of hidden units co-vary with each other (as patterns are presented at the input to the network). These numbers are combined in the covariance matrix.
2. Compute the eigenvalues of the covariance matrix. The number of significantly non-zero eigenvalues serves as *effective number of hidden units*.

The eigenvalues are computed after each epoch of learning. Numerically stable ways (such as singular value decomposition, implemented in most numerical and statistical packages) are available. In Figure 5, we plot the square roots of all the eigenvalues of the hidden unit ensemble as a function of training time.

---

[6]The distributions of the points of the test and the training set are very similar–differences between test and training set are on the 1% level of the hidden unit activations. Note that the effect of overfitting discussed in Part 1 lives off this small difference.

[7]We here consider only linear subspaces. The points might lie on a curved manifold of smaller dimension than the embedding space. If we were interested to find the number of degrees of freedom for a manifold of any shape, we could use the information theoretic measure of *redundancy*; see Gershenfeld and Weigend (1993). The generality of this measure, however, has a price: in order to estimate it reliably, several more orders of magnitude of data are needed than we have available in the present example. We thus restrict ourselves to the *linear effective* dimension of the hidden unit space. If the processing that follows the hidden units is strictly linear, the linear effective dimension is sufficiently general.

[8]By using the covariance matrix, we only explore two-point interactions (or second-order correlations). This is equivalent to assuming that the points are Gaussian distributed, since higher than second-order moments vanish for a Gaussian.

[9]When the covariance is normalized to lie between -1 and 1 (by dividing it by both of the standard deviations of the two individual hidden units), the (linear) correlation coefficient between hidden unit i and j is obtained.

[10]The eigen*vectors* of a matrix (or a linear operator) point in the directions that do not get rotated, but only contracted (if the absolute value of the corresponding eigenvalue is less than unity), or expanded (if it is larger than unity). The directions (also called principal directions) are not important to us, but the stretch of the point cloud along each axis is: its extension is given by the eigen*value* corresponding to the eigendirection.

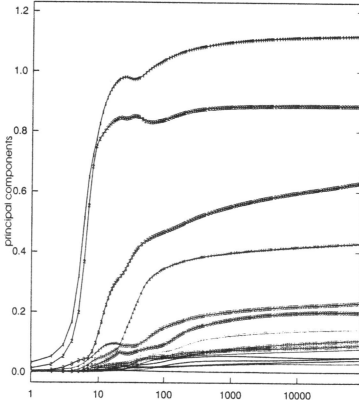

Figure 5. Evolution of principal components (square roots of the eigenvalues of the covariance matrix).

The network extracts the principal components sequentially. After 10 epochs, for example, only two eigenvalues have emerged; the remaining 13 are still dormant. Having two significant eigenvalues means that the hidden unit activation vectors (the responses to the input patterns) lie on a two-dimensional hyperplane in the 15-dimensional space. At this point in training, a third dimension is just slowly emerging. Compare this to Figure 4 where, also at epoch 10, all hidden units have already reached at least half of their final standard deviation.

Is this behavior surprising? Gradient descent with a simple cost function (such as cross-entropy or squared error) does not provide any incentive in for the hidden units to form an orthogonal representation. It is a "greedy algorithm:" the sole goal of the weight updates is to reduce the overall error. Thus, all hidden units go after the same features and only differentiate as much (or as little) as necessary to reduce the overall error. In other words, the hidden units form a distributed representation.

The information contained in Figures 4 and 5 is complementary. For example, an effective hidden unit dimension of one could be obtained either by a single active units and the rest sleeping, or by all of them busily doing the same. We know from Figure 4 that the latter is the case in backpropagation learning.

Summarizing Part 2, we saw that, on the one hand, all hidden units "wake up" at essentially the same time, as exhibited both by the histograms of their activation values (Figure 3) and by their individual variances (Figure 4). On the other hand, the units start off by doing the same thing and only later begin to differentiate: the effective number of hidden units (the number of significantly non-zero eigenvalues of the covariance matrix) grows slowly with training time (Figure 5). The effective number of hidden units is often very small compared to the potential number of hidden units given by the architecture of the network.

Acknowledgments

We thank Dave Rumelhart and the Stanford PDP group for all the discussions. We thank Jeff Elman for the data. We acknowledge the feedback of friends and colleagues when the figures of this paper were presented: at FAW (Ulm, Summer 1991; in particular Steve Hanson's comments), CLNL (Berkeley, Summer 1991), IJCNN (Singapore, Fall 1991), Neural Networks for Computing (Snowbird, Spring 1992), and at CMSS (Boulder, Summer 1993). We also thank Brian Bonnlander for his comments on this first written version. The analysis method of Part 2 was first presented in the context of time series prediction at INTERFACE (Seattle, Spring 1991; see Weigend and Rumelhart, 1991).

References

Buntine, W. L., and A. S. Weigend (1991) "Bayesian Backpropagation." *Complex Systems* **5**: 603–643.

Elman, J. L., and D. Zipser (1988) "Discovering the hidden structure of speech." *J. Acoust. Soc. Am.* **83**: 1615-1626.

Gershenfeld, N. A., and A. S. Weigend (1993) "The Future of Time Series." In *Time Series Prediction: Forecasting the Future and Understanding the Past,* edited by A. S. Weigend and N. A. Gershenfeld, pp. 1-70. Addison-Wesley.

Guyon, I., V. Vapnik, B. Boser, L. Bottou, and S. A. Solla (1992) "Structural Risk Minimization for Character Recognition." In *Advances in Neural Information Processing Systems 4,* edited by J. E. Moody, S. J. Hanson, and R. P. Lippmann, pp. 471–479. Morgan Kaufmann.

Moody, J. (1992) "The *Effective* Number of Parameters: An Analysis of Generalization and Regularization in Nonlinear Systems." In *Advances in Neural Information Processing Systems 4,* edited by J. E. Moody, S. J. Hanson, and R. P. Lippmann, pp. 847–854. Morgan Kaufmann.

Perrone, M. P. (1993) "General Averaging Results for Convex Optimization." This volume, pp. 364–371.

Rumelhart, D. E., R. Durbin, R. Golden, and Y. Chauvin (still in press) "Backpropagation: The Basic Theory." In *Backpropagation: Theory, Architectures and Applications,* edited by Y. Chauvin and D. E. Rumelhart. Lawrence Erlbaum.

Wan, E. A. (1993) "Time Series Prediction Using a Connectionist Network with Internal Delay Lines." In *Time Series Prediction: Forecasting the Future and Understanding the Past,* edited by A. S. Weigend and N. A. Gershenfeld, pp. 195-217. Addison-Wesley.

Weigend, A. S., B. A. Huberman, and D. E. Rumelhart (1990) "Predicting the Future: A Connectionist Approach." *International Journal of Neural Systems* **1**: 193–209.

Weigend, A. S., and D. E. Rumelhart (1991) "Generalization through Minimal Networks with Application to Forecasting." In *INTERFACE '91–23rd Symposium on the Interface: Computing Science and Statistics,* edited by E. M. Keramidas, pp. 362–370. Interface Foundation of North America.

Weigend, A. S., B. A. Huberman, and D. E. Rumelhart (1992) "Predicting Sunspots and Exchange Rates with Connectionist Networks." In *Nonlinear Modeling and Forecasting,* edited by M. Casdagli and S. Eubank, pp. 395–432. Addison-Wesley.

Weigend, A. S., and N. A. Gershenfeld, editors (1993) *Time Series Prediction: Forecasting the Future and Understanding the Past.* Addison-Wesley.

Increase of Apparent Complexity Is Due to
Decrease of Training Set Error

Robert Dodier
Dept. of Civil, Environmental, and Architectural Engineering
University of Colorado
Boulder, CO 80309
dodier@dendrite.cs.colorado.edu

What is Apparent Complexity?

We know that increasing the number of weights in a fully-trained neural network makes for better generalization, up to a point, and smaller training set error. In training, increasing the training time likewise makes for better generalization, up to a point, and smaller training set error. It seems as though extra weights sneak into the net during training. Certainly, complexity increases with number of weights, so we conclude that with training there is increasing "apparent complexity."

When generalization theory is expressed in concepts from statistical physics (Solla, 1993; Solla and Levin, 1992; Levin et al., 1990), there appears a free parameter β which corresponds to inverse physical temperature. As inverse computational temperature increases, average training set error decreases. An economical explanation of the quasi-mystical increase of apparent complexity of nonlinear feedforward, backpropagation networks seems to be

$$\beta = \frac{\text{architectural complexity}}{\text{training error above minimum}} \tag{1}$$

This relation is important because generalization error can be expressed as a function of β for special cases (Solla and Levin, 1992), and, it is hoped, for a broad class of neural networks. During training, architectural complexity is fixed while training error decreases, thus increasing β and giving rise to the increase of apparent complexity. So in practice, training set error is a free parameter, and β is derived.

The usual backpropagation with cross-validation ("early stopping") is a way to adjust β by reducing training set error. As training progresses, the validation set error at first decreases, then increases again, while training set error continues to fall; this simple but important observation is attributed to David Rumelhart (Michael Mozer, personal communication). Since decreasing training set error corresponds to increasing β, this seems to show that generalization error (estimated by validation set error) is a unimodal function of β. One would naturally want to find that optimal computational temperature which gives the least generalization error.

Pruning and varying the number of hidden units can be seen as methods to adjust temperature by changing the architectural complexity of a system. Regularization techniques and early stopping, on the other hand, adjust temperature by changing the training error. The two sets of methods are probably not equivalent, since the depth of the minimum of generalization error may well depend strongly on both architectural complexity and training error. To find a global minimum of generalization error, we must search both components of the architecture-training error space.

Incidentally, the so-called bias-variance dilemma can be described in terms of β. High bias gives a high error on the training set, which is equivalent to low β, and we are on the left branch of the "U"-shaped generalization error curve. High variance gives low error on the training set, which is equivalent to high β; we are on the right branch. The trick is to find that intermediate β for which generalization is optimal, that is, we seek the right balance of architectural complexity and training error.

Generalization in Physical Terms

Statistical thermodynamics begins with considering the probability that a system is in a given state (Kittel and Kroemer, 1980). It turns out that this probability depends on the energy level of the system, given the fundamental assumption that a system is in any accessible state with equal probability. Knowing the probability distribution, we can compute interesting quantities such as the mean kinetic energy per particle. Such computations are carried out by considering a set of identical systems, each with random behavior, called an ensemble, and mean values for a system are computed across members of its ensemble. Quantities such as mean energy are thus subject to fluctuations like any other statistic, but for large systems these fluctuations are extremely small, and actual values never vary far from the mean.

One can make arguments (Reif, 1967) that in an ordinary system[1] the number of accessible states $\Omega(E)$ in an energy interval between E and $E + \delta E$ increases extremely rapidly with the degrees of freedom of the system,

$$\Omega(E) \approx (E - E_0)^{df} \tag{2}$$

When temperature is defined in the usual way, $1/kT = \beta = \frac{\partial}{\partial E} \ln \Omega$ (where k is the Boltzmann constant), then to a rough approximation

$$\beta \approx \frac{df}{E - E_0} \tag{3}$$

At equilibrium, an ensemble will be uniformly distributed over the accessible states; in particular, for any pair of states that have the same energy level, there is no preference for either state.

We can also take a statistical approach to generalization (see, for example, Solla and Levin, 1992). Here an ensemble is a set of generalizers, all of the same architecture; the adjustable parameters of these are called weights, but the term is not meant to limit application of the theory to neural networks. Corresponding to the assertion mentioned above, it is assumed that there is no preference among weight vectors that give generalizers of the same error level. This condition holds for some methods of error minimization, such as simulated annealing. Unfortunately, it fails to hold for gradient descent since gradient descent is constrained to give weight samples only along a trajectory in the gradient field of the error function. There is hope: it may be possible to obtain "random enough" weight samples by starting at random weight vectors and applying gradient descent.

There is a natural and useful correspondence between the quantities found in statistical thermodynamics and those found in generalization theory.

apparent complexity, β	$\Leftrightarrow$	inverse temperature, β
weight space	$\Leftrightarrow$	state space
sum over weight space, Z	$\Leftrightarrow$	sum over state space, Z
error	$\Leftrightarrow$	energy

By requiring that minimization of error on the training set be equivalent to maximizing the likelihood of the training data (Solla and Levin, 1992), we find the likelihood of an input-output pair $\xi \equiv (x, y)$, given weights W, is

$$P(\xi | W) = \frac{1}{z(\beta)} \exp(-\beta \varepsilon(W, \xi)) \tag{4}$$

where the normalizing factor is

$$z(\beta) = \int d\xi \exp(-\beta \varepsilon(W, \xi)) \tag{5}$$

and the error $\varepsilon(W, \xi) \equiv d(y, f(x, W))$, where d can be any distance-like function, and f is the function implemented

---

1. The term is loosely applied to systems in which the total energy has no upper limit. For example, a sample of air.

by the generalizer with weights W. Introducing a prior distribution on the weights

$$\rho_0(W) \equiv P(W| \text{architecture}) \tag{6}$$

we find the posterior distribution after training with m examples is

$$\rho_m(W) = \frac{1}{Z}\rho_0(W)\exp(-\beta E(W)) \tag{7}$$

where $E(W)$ is the sum of errors on the training set, and Z is the all-important *partition function*,

$$Z = \int dW\, \rho_0(W)\exp(-\beta E(W)) \tag{8}$$

The posterior probability $\rho_m(W)\,dW$ can be considered the survival probability (Solla, 1993) of the generalizer which implements $f(x, W)$. Note that generalizers of low training error are favored by the term $\exp(-\beta E(W))$, just as states of low energy are favored in physical systems. As $\beta \to \infty$, generalizers with training error above the global minimum are completely excluded (their probabilities go to zero) and only minimum-error generalizers remain. Incidentally, the computational temperature must have units of error in order for expressions like $\exp(-\beta E(W))$ to make sense, just as in physics, $1/\beta$ has units of energy.

As stated elsewhere (Levin et al., 1990), the statistical formalism is applied only to generalizers of a specific architecture, with fixed numbers of weights. Yet we can broaden the application to generalizers of varying numbers of weights by starting from a suitable prior weight distribution, if the the class of generalizers we wish to consider are special cases of a certain architecture. The particular application of immediate interest is the class of neural networks with fixed numbers of inputs and outputs and varying numbers of hidden units. We can always set a reasonable upper limit M on the number of hidden units. The dimensionality of the weight vectors increases with the number of hidden units in an easily calculated way; for example, in a net with one hidden layer, five inputs, and one output, there are six more weights and a bias for each additional hidden unit. For $1, 2, 3 \ldots M$ hidden units there are $1, 6, 11, \ldots N_M$ weights. The weight vectors of dimension less than N_M can be embedded in $\mathbf{R}^{N_M}$ by appending zeros; thus the weight spaces of lower dimension form hyperplanes in the space of highest dimension, $\mathbf{R}^{N_M}$. An appropriate prior weight distribution has some mass associated with each of the hyperplanes, that is, with each architecture. Since the hyperplanes of dimension less than N_M have measure zero in $\mathbf{R}^{N_M}$, it is necessary to use delta functions to express the prior density over the "biggest" weight space in terms of prior densities over each of the hyperplanes.

$$\rho_0(W) = \alpha_1 \cdot \rho_{0,1}(W) \cdot \delta_{N_M-N_1}(W) + \ldots + \alpha_k \cdot \rho_{0,k}(W) \cdot \delta_{N_M-N_k}(W) + \ldots + \alpha_M \cdot \rho_{0,M}(W) \tag{9}$$

Each prior density $\rho_{0,k}$ integrates to 1 over its hyperplane; the k'th prior is only a function of the first N_k components of the weight vector. The weighting factors α_k sum to 1. The notation δ_{m-n} is meant to indicate a multi-dimensional delta function,

$$\delta_{m-n}(x_1, \ldots x_m) = \delta(x_{n+1}) \cdot \delta(x_{n+2}) \ldots \cdot \delta(x_m) \tag{10}$$

where $\delta(x)$ is the usual 1-dimensional delta function.

The prior density over the class of neural networks is then modified during learning to emphasize regions with lower training set error, just as in the case of an ensemble of nets with identical architectures. It is natural to consider architectural complexity as a function of the number of non-zero weights, since all nets in the class will have the same number of total weights. Expressing a density over a class of generalizers with similar but not identical architectures as a density over some larger parameter space makes this generalization theory applicable to *model selection* as well as training.

We can use the partition function to compute interesting averages over the ensemble. Levin et al. (1990) showed that

$$\langle E \rangle = \int dW\, E(W)\rho_m(W)$$

$$= \frac{1}{Z}\int dW\, E(W)\rho_0(W)\exp(-\beta E(W))$$

$$= \frac{1}{Z} \cdot -\frac{\partial}{\partial \beta} \int dW \, \rho_0(W) \exp(-\beta E(W))$$

$$= -\frac{1}{Z} \cdot \frac{\partial Z}{\partial \beta} = -\frac{\partial}{\partial \beta} \ln Z \tag{11}$$

Furthermore,

$$\frac{\partial}{\partial \beta} \langle E \rangle = \frac{\partial}{\partial \beta} \cdot -\frac{\partial}{\partial \beta} \ln Z = -\left(-\frac{1}{Z^2} \frac{\partial Z}{\partial \beta} \frac{\partial Z}{\partial \beta} + \frac{1}{Z} \frac{\partial^2 Z}{\partial \beta^2} \right) = \left(\frac{1}{Z} \frac{\partial Z}{\partial \beta} \right)^2 - \frac{1}{Z} \frac{\partial^2 Z}{\partial \beta^2}$$

$$= \langle E \rangle^2 - \langle E^2 \rangle = -\text{variance}(E) < 0, \tag{12}$$

that is, the average total training error is a strictly decreasing function of β. Since $E(W) \geq 0$ for all W, $\langle E \rangle \geq 0$. Since $\langle E \rangle$ is bounded below by 0, it has a greatest lower bound, which we can call E_0; since $\langle E \rangle$ is strictly decreasing, it tends to E_0. So $\beta \to \infty$ corresponds to *minimum-error* learning. In general, the minimum error E_0 is greater than 0, for example, in learning a noisy function. As for the behavior of $\langle E \rangle$ for small β,

$$\exp(-\beta E(W)) \to 1 \quad \text{as } \beta \to 0 \tag{13}$$

which implies

$$\langle E \rangle \to \frac{\int dW \, E(W) \rho_0(W)}{\int dW \, \rho_0(W)} = \int dW \, E(W) \rho_0(W) \quad \text{as } \beta \to 0 \tag{14}$$

This is the average error on the training set with respect to the prior density over the weight space, that is, the average error taking only preference into account, and not performance. This average may not exist. Linear generalizers that have a sum-of-squares error and an unbounded uniform weight space correspond to ordinary physical systems, and the total training set error and the total energy have no upper bound as temperature increases. But in other cases, for example a nonlinear neural network with a bounded weight space or bounded output activation, there exists a greatest possible error, hence even at infinite temperature the average training set error exists.

In summary,

At $\beta = 0$, $\langle E \rangle$ is the mean training set error with respect to prior density,

$\langle E \rangle$ is strictly decreasing with β,

$\langle E \rangle \to E_0$ as $\beta \to \infty$.

This means $\langle E \rangle$ is an invertible function of β, so we can always express β as a function of $\langle E \rangle$. We can model this dependence with the rational

$$\langle E \rangle = E_0 + \frac{c}{\beta} \tag{15a}$$

where c is some constant. Except for a term of order $1/m^2$, this is correct in the case of a linear generalizer (Levin et al., 1992), in which

$$c = N/2, \qquad \text{and} \tag{15b}$$

$$E_0 = (m-N) \cdot \sigma^2 \tag{15c}$$

where m is the number of patterns, N is the number of inputs (same as the number of weights), and σ^2 is the variance of the noise in the output. We can solve for β to give

$$\beta = \frac{c}{\langle E \rangle - E_0} \tag{16}$$

For the linear generalizer,

$$\beta = \frac{N/2}{\langle E \rangle - E_0} \tag{17}$$

thus

$$\beta \approx \frac{\text{architectural complexity}}{\text{training error above minimum}}$$

This is analogous to $\beta \approx df / (E - E_0)$ for ordinary physical systems.

For nonlinear generalizers, $\langle E \rangle = E_0 + c / \beta$ has the correct behavior for large β, but this expression is unbounded as $\beta \to 0$. For a neural net with squashing output and in other commonly encountered cases, this behavior is not appropriate, but of little consequence, since learning occurs at $\beta > 0$.

Experiments on the Relation Between Training and Generalization Error

For linear generalizers, there is an exact analogy between the physical and computational inverse temperatures. I suspect that a similar interpretation of β holds for nonlinear generalizers as well. To explore generalization ability as a function of training error, I created a target function F^* implemented by a 2-6-1 sigmoidal neural network $\overline{F}$ with additive noise of variance σ^2. The generalizers F were 2-6-1 nets with random initial weights. The input space A was the unit square $[0, 1] \times [0, 1]$, and the training set consisted of input-output pairs in which inputs were chosen uniformly at random from the input space, and outputs were computed as the target network's output plus noise.

I computed generalization error in what seems the natural way, integrating the error (here a squared difference) over the input space. This error is an extension of the usual validation error to an infinite sample.

$$E_G = \frac{1}{A} \cdot \int_A (F(x, y) - F^*(x, y))^2 dA \tag{18}$$

$$= \sigma^2 + \int_0^1 \int_0^1 (F(x, y) - \overline{F}(x, y))^2 dx dy \tag{19}$$

However, in contrast to the average training error which is easily expressed in terms of the partition function, the generalization error is an elusive quantity, and what is defined as the *prediction error* (Levin et al., 1990) is a rather different critter; the prediction error gauges the probability that a correct prediction is made. The prediction error of $F(x, y)$ given (x, y), averaged over all ways of choosing m examples in the training set, can be expressed in terms of the partition function as

$$-\ln p^{(m)}(F(x, y) | x, y) = -\frac{\partial}{\partial m} \langle\langle \ln Z \rangle\rangle + \langle\langle \ln z(\beta) \rangle\rangle \tag{20}$$

where the indicated averages are taken over all inputs and all ways of choosing a training set of m examples. For a linear net with no bias and normally distributed weights, inputs, and output noise, Solla and Levin (1990) showed that

$$-\ln p^{(m)} = \frac{N}{2m} + \beta \sigma^2 + \ln \sqrt{\frac{\pi}{\beta}} + O(1/m^2) \tag{21}$$

This function seems to have the wrong asymptotic behavior; it grows without bound as a minimum-error solution is approached, that is, as $\beta \to \infty$. However, Levin et al. (1990) showed that

$$-\frac{1}{\beta} \ln p^{(m)} \leq \langle \epsilon(W, x, y, F(x, y)) \rangle_{\rho_m} \tag{22}$$

That is, eq. 22 gives a lower bound for the average generalization error as computed using the same error definition as is used to compute training set error; thus this unnamed function is an estimate of generalization error as it is usually measured. Combining eq. 21 with eqs. 15, we can eliminate β and express generalization error in terms of training set error.

I constructed an ensemble of linear nets (2 inputs, 1 output, noise variance $\sigma^2 = 0.25$). These nets differed in some ways from those considered by Levin et al. in the derivation of $\ln p^{(m)}$; these nets have uniform weight, input, and noise distributions instead of normal distributions, and the output unit has a bias, but these differences should not affect the qualitative results. Also, in the ensemble I constructed, all nets shared the same training set, while Levin et al. take an average over all ways of choosing the training set. So in computing values of $\ln p^{(m)}$ I have essentially replaced a random variable by its mean value.

Figure 1 shows that $-\frac{1}{\beta}\ln p^{(m)}$ is a fair estimate of E_G as a function of the ensemble's per-pattern training set error. The generalization error estimate shows a weak minimum near the origin. This minimum may be lost in the noise of the linear ensemble, but a minimum near the origin is quite evident in a graph (Figure 2) made for a nonlinear ensemble of 2 inputs, 6 hidden units, 1 output, and noise variance $\sigma^2 = 0.25$. Intriguingly, the qualitative behavior observed for the nonlinear ensemble is the same as that predicted for the linear ensemble: a long near-linear region with a weak minimum near the origin. Note that the ensembles shown in Figures 1 and 2 are not trained.

In another experiment, I trained a set of 2-6-1 nets and computed E_G and E/m every 10 training epochs. Then I plotted E_G against E/m for each net, and also plotted E_G against the number of epochs. Figures 3 and 4 show how generalization evolves during training. Training finds the small region of weight space with solutions of low training error; overfitting occurs. Note that curves tend to pile up better when E_G is plotted against E/m than when plotted against number of epochs; in particular, the minima are more aligned, and the curves cross each other less. This is evidence that generalization error is more strongly determined by training error than by training epochs.

Discussion and Open Problems

Since generalization seems to depend on the learning error and not how a net arrived there, early-stopping methods are applicable to all learning methods, not just gradient descent. One might worry, for instance, that conjugate gradient methods are not suitable for early stopping since the solutions jump around in weight space. Yet the dynamics of learning don't matter; all that we need compare is validation set error against training set error, and stop when the former (considered as a function of the latter) increases. In fact, it seems we can likely extend early stopping to learning algorithms in which neither validation nor training error is monotonic across training epochs.

Note that $\beta = \frac{1}{2}N/(\langle E \rangle - E_0)$ is a statement about the way the size of the weight space grows with increasing error. This should not be surprising, given that the corresponding physical statement is based on the definition of temperature in terms of entropy. Since this growth depends on the way error is defined, a relation of the form given may not hold for definitions other than the usual sum-of-squares. Interestingly, Weigend (1993) has found that the behavior of test set error over training epochs depends on the error function used; this suggests relations between β, E_G, and E/m change qualitatively with the error definition.

Further work should yield β as a function of $\langle E \rangle$ for nonlinear nets, and establish the generic unimodality of generalization error. Then we can eliminate β and always express generalization error as a unimodal function of training error. The location and depth of the minimum is of interest, as are confidence bounds on the functions for average learning and generalization error.

Acknowledgments

I would like to thank Paul Smolensky, Mike Mozer, Franco Callari, Don Mathis, and Sara Solla for helpful discussions. I would also like to thank Mike Mozer for advice and patience above and beyond the call of duty. This research was supported by NSF PYI award IRI-9058450 and grant 90-21 from the James S. McDonnell Foundation. I urge the reader to use these results for peaceful purposes.

References

Kittel, C., and H. Kroemer, *Thermal Physics*. New York: W. H. Freeman and Co., 1980.

Levin, E., N. Tishby, and S. Solla, "A Statistical Approach to Learning and Generalization in Layered Neural Networks," *Proc. IEEE*, vol 78 no. 10, p. 1568, October 1990.

Solla, S. Connectionist Models Summer School lecture notes (unpublished). 1993.

Solla, S., and E. Levin, "Learning in linear neural networks: the validity of the annealed approximation." *Physical Review A*, vol 46 no. 4, p 2124, 1992.

Weigend, A. Connectionist Models Summer School lecture notes (unpublished). 1993.

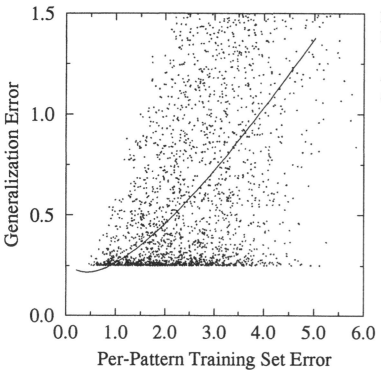

Figure 1. Generalization and Training Errors for an ensemble of linear nets.

An estimate of generalization error is also plotted.

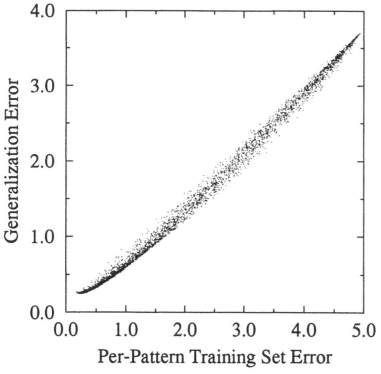

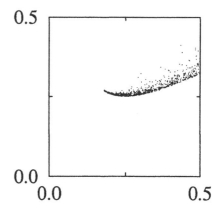

Figure 2. Generalization and Training Errors for an ensemble of nonlinear nets. Inset shows region near the origin.

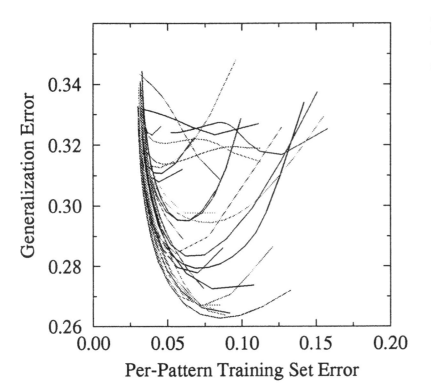

Figure 3. Generalization Error vs. Training Error. There is one curve per network.

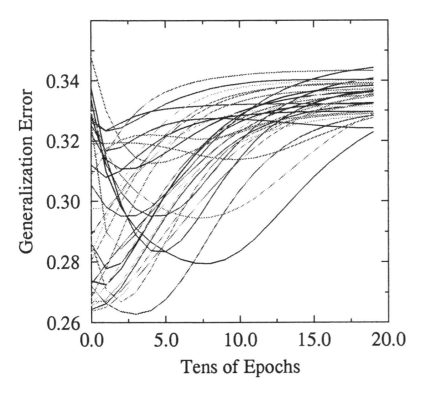

Figure 4. Generalization Error vs. Number of Training Epochs.

Momentum and Optimal Stochastic Search

Genevieve B. Orr, Todd K. Leen
Department of Computer Science and Engineering
Oregon Graduate Institute of Science & Technology
20000 Northwest Walker Road
PO Box 91000
Portland, OR 97291-1000
orr@cse.ogi.edu, tleen@cse.ogi.edu

INTRODUCTION

The rate of convergence for gradient descent algorithms, both batch and stochastic, can be improved by including in the weight update a "momentum" term proportional to the previous weight update. Several authors [1, 2] give conditions for convergence of the mean and covariance of the weight vector for momentum LMS with *constant learning rate*. However stochastic algorithms require that the learning rate decay over time in order to achieve true convergence of the weight (in probability, in mean square, or with probability one).

This paper uses the dynamics of weight space probabilities [3, 4] to address stochastic gradient algorithms with learning rate annealing and momentum. This theoretical framework provides a simple, unified treatment of asymptotic convergence rates and asymptotic normality. The results for algorithms without momentum have been previously discussed in the literature. Here we gather those results under a common theoretical structure and extend them to stochastic gradient descent with momentum.

DENSITY EVOLUTION AND ASYMPTOTICS

We consider stochastic optimization algorithms with weight $\omega \in R^N$. We confine attention to a neighborhood of a local optimum ω_* and express the dynamics in terms of the *weight error* $v \equiv \omega - \omega_*$. For simplicity we treat the continuous time algorithm [1]

$$\frac{dv(t)}{dt} = \mu(t) H[v(t), x(t)] \tag{1}$$

where $\mu(t)$ is the learning rate at time t, $H : R^N \times R^K \to R^N$ is the weight update function and $x(t)$ is the data fed to the algorithm at time t. For stochastic gradient algorithms $H = -\nabla_v \mathcal{E}(v, x(t))$, the gradient of the instantaneous cost function.

---

[1] Although algorithms are executed in discrete time, continuous time formulations are often advantagous for analysis. The passage from discrete to continuous time is treated in various ways depending on the needs of the theoretical exposition. Kushner and Clark [5] define continous time functions that interpolate the discrete time process in order to establish an equivalence between the asymptotic behavior of the discrete time stochastic process, and solutions of an associated deterministic differential equation. Heskes [6] draws on the results of Bedeaux *et al.* [7] that link (discrete time) random walk trajectories to the solution of a (continuous time) master equation. Heskes' master equation is equivalent to our Kramers-Moyal expansion (3) below.

Convergence (in mean square) to ω_* is characterized by the average squared norm of the weight error $E[\,|v|^2\,] =$ Trace C where

$$C \equiv \int d^N v \; v \, v^T \, P(v,t) \tag{2}$$

is the weight error correlation matrix and $P(v,t)$ is the probability density at v at time t. In [3] we show that the probability density evolves according to the Kramers-Moyal expansion

$$\frac{\partial P(v,t)}{\partial t} =$$

$$\sum_{i=1}^{\infty} \frac{(-1)^i}{i!} \sum_{j_1,\ldots j_i=1}^{N} \frac{\partial^i}{\partial v_{j_1} \partial v_{j_2} \ldots \partial v_{j_i}} \left\{ \left\langle \mu H_{j_1} \mu H_{j_2} \ldots \mu H_{j_i} \right\rangle_x P(v,t) \right\} , \tag{3}$$

where H_{j_k} denotes the j_k^{th} component of the N-component vector H, and $\langle \ldots \rangle_x$ denotes averaging over the density of inputs. Differentiating (2) with respect to time, using (3) and integrating by parts, we obtain the equation of motion for the weight error correlation

$$\frac{dC}{dt} = \mu(t) \int d^N v \; P(v,t) \left[v \left\langle H(v,x)^T \right\rangle_x + \left\langle H(v,x) \right\rangle_x v^T \right]$$

$$+ \; \mu(t)^2 \int d^N v \; P(v,t) \left\langle H(v,x) H(v,x)^T \right\rangle_x . \tag{4}$$

Asymptotics of the Weight Error Correlation

We wish to study the late time behavior of (4). Since the update function $H(v,x)$ is in general non-linear in v, the time evolution of the correlation matrix C_{ij} is coupled to higher moments $E[v_i v_j v_k \ldots]$ of the weight error. However, the learning rate is assumed to follow a schedule $\mu(t)$ that satisfies the requirements for convergence in mean square to a local optimum. Thus at late times the density becomes sharply peaked about $v = 0^2$. This suggests that we expand $H(v,x)$ in a power series about $v = 0$ and retain the lowest order non-trivial terms in (4) leaving:

$$\frac{dC}{dt} = -\mu(t) \left[(RC) + (CR^T) \right] + \mu(t)^2 D , \tag{5}$$

where R is the Hessian of the average cost function $\langle \mathcal{E} \rangle_x$, and

$$D \equiv \left\langle H(0,x) H(0,x)^T \right\rangle_x \tag{6}$$

is the diffusion matrix, both evaluated at the local optimum ω_*. (Note that $R^T = R$.) We use (5) with the understanding that it is valid for large t. The solution to (5) is

$$C(t) = U(t,t_0) C(t_0) U^T(t,t_0) + \int_{t_0}^{t} d\tau \; \mu(\tau)^2 \, U(t,\tau) \, D \, U^T(t,\tau) . \tag{7}$$

where the evolution operator $U(t_2,t_1)$ is

$$U(t_2,t_1) = \exp\left[-R \int_{t_1}^{t_2} d\tau \, \mu(\tau) \right] . \tag{8}$$

---

^{2}In general the density will have nonzero components outside the basin of ω_*. We are neglecting these, for the purpose of calculating the second moment of the the *local* density in the vicinity of ω_*.

We assume, without loss of generality, that the coordinates are chosen so that R is diagonal (D won't be) with eigenvalues λ_i, $i = 1 \ldots N$. Then with $\mu(t) = \mu_0/t$ we obtain

$$E[|v|^2] = \text{Trace}[C(t)] = \sum_{i=1}^{N} \left\{ C_{ii}(t_0) \left(\frac{t_0}{t} \right)^{2\mu_0\lambda_i} \right.$$

$$\left. + \frac{\mu_0^2 D_{ii}}{(2\mu_0\lambda_i - 1)} \left[\frac{1}{t} - \frac{1}{t_0} \left(\frac{t_0}{t} \right)^{2\mu_0\lambda_i} \right] \right\}. \tag{9}$$

We define

$$\mu_{crit} \equiv \frac{1}{2\lambda_{min}} \tag{10}$$

and identify two regimes for which the behavior of (9) is fundamentally different:

1. $\mu_0 > \mu_{crit}$: $E[|v|^2]$ drops off asymptotically as $1/t$.

2. $\mu_0 < \mu_{crit}$: $E[|v|^2]$ drops off asymptotically as

$$\left(\frac{1}{t} \right)^{(2\mu_0\lambda_{min})}$$

i.e. *more slowly than* $1/t$.

Figure 1 shows results from simulations of an ensemble of 2000 networks trained by LMS, and the prediction from (9). For the simulations, input data were drawn from a gaussian with zero mean and variance $R = 1.0$. The targets were generated by a noisy teacher neuron. The upper two curves in each plot (dotted) depict the behavior for $\mu_0 < \mu_{crit} = 0.5$. The remaining curves (solid) show the behavior for $\mu_0 > \mu_{crit}$.

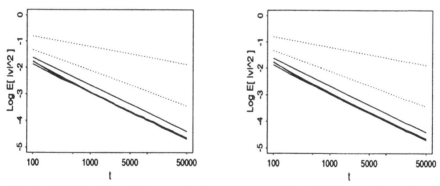

Fig.1: LEFT – Simulation results from an ensemble of 2000 one-dimensional LMS algorithms with $R = 1.0$, $D = 1.0$ and $\mu = \mu_0/t$. RIGHT – Theoretical predictions from equation (9). Curves correspond to (top to bottom) $\mu_0 = 0.2, 0.4, 0.6, 0.8, 1.0, 1.5$.

Asymptotic Normality

This formalism yields asymptotic normality rather simply. At late times, $\mu(t)$ becomes very small and one can truncate the Kramers-Moyal expansion (3) to second order in μ, leaving a Fokker-Planck equation. As the density becomes peaked up about $v = 0$, the linear part of the drift and the constant part of the diffusion dominate and the dynamics is governed by

353

$$\frac{\partial P(v,t)}{\partial t} = \mu(t) R_{ij} \frac{\partial}{\partial v_i} \left(v_j P(v,t) \right) + \frac{1}{2} \mu(t)^2 D_{ij} \frac{\partial^2 P(v,t)}{\partial v_i \partial v_j} \tag{11}$$

where repeated indices are summed over[3]. Next, we define a time-dependent coordinate transformation

$$y_i = h_{ij}(t) v_j \tag{12}$$

$$P(v,t) = \tilde{P}(y,t) h , \tag{13}$$

where $h = \mathrm{Det}\,[h_{ij}(t)]$. The Fokker-Planck equation, expressed in terms of the y variables, reads

$$\frac{\partial \tilde{P}}{\partial t} = \frac{\partial}{\partial y_j} \left\{ \left[\mu(t) h_{ji} R_{il} h_{lk}^{-1} - h'_{jl} h_{lk}^{-1} \right] y_k \tilde{P} \right\}$$
$$+ \frac{\mu(t)^2}{2} D_{ij} h_{ki} h_{lj} \frac{\partial^2}{\partial y_k \partial y_l} \tilde{P} . \tag{14}$$

Depending on μ_0 and R, different choices for h_{ij} are required to obtain stationary solutions. Summarizing the results (in one dimension for simplicity)

1. $\mu_0 > \mu_{crit}$:

    $y = v \sqrt{t}$ is asymptotically normal with variance $\mu_0^2 D/(2\mu_0 R - 1)$.

2. $\mu_0 = \mu_{crit}$:

    $y = v \sqrt{t/\mathrm{Ln}(t)}$ is asymptotically normal with variance $\mu_0^2 D$.

3. $\mu_0 < \mu_{crit}$:

    Using the new variable $y = v\,t^{(\mu_0 R)}$ the drift term in the Fokker-Planck equation (14) vanishes, leaving a pure diffusion process. The diffusion coefficient goes to zero as $t^{2(\mu_0 R - 1)}$. Thus the density $\tilde{P}(y)$ freezes at late times and we expect y to approach some non-trivial random variable. Though not rigorous, this argument is consistent with the results of Major and Revesz [9, and references therein].

The conditions for "optimal" (i.e. $1/t$) convergence of the weight error correlation, and the related results on asymptotic normality were previously discussed in the stochastic approximation literature [10, 11, and references therein]. The present formal structure provides the results with relative ease and facilitates the extension to stochastic gradient descent with momentum.

STOCHASTIC SEARCH WITH MOMENTUM

The discrete time algorithm for stochastic optimization with momentum is:

$$v(t + 1) = v(t) + \mu(t) H[v(t), x(t)] + \beta\,\Omega(t) \tag{15}$$

$$\Omega(t + 1) \equiv v(t + 1) - v(t)$$
$$= \Omega(t) + \mu(t) H[v(t), x(t)] + (\beta - 1)\,\Omega(t), \tag{16}$$

---

[3]Equation (11) can be derived rigorously by writing the weight error as the sum of deterministic and stochastic contributions $v = \phi + \sqrt{\mu}\,\xi$ and using these coordinates in the Kramers-Moyal expansion (3). This prescription corresponds to Van Kampen's system size expansion [6, 8]. The deterministic piece ϕ evolves by descent along the average or true gradient, approaching zero exponentially. The lowest order (in μ) piece of the Kramers-Moyal expansion for the density of the fluctuations $P(\xi, t)$ is equivalent to (11).

or in continuous time,

$$\frac{dv(t)}{dt} = \mu(t) \, H[v(t), x(t)] + \beta \, \Omega(t) \tag{17}$$

$$\frac{d\Omega(t)}{dt} = \mu(t) \, H[v(t), x(t)] + (\beta - 1) \, \Omega(t). \tag{18}$$

Weight Error Correlation

As before, we are interested in the late time behavior of $E[|v|^2]$. To this end, we define the $2N$-dimensional variable $Z \equiv (v, \Omega)^T$ and, following the arguments of the previous sections, expand $H[v(t), x(t)]$ in a power series about $v = 0$ retaining the linear part of the drift, and the constant part of the diffusion matrix. In this approximation the correlation matrix $\overline{C} \equiv E[ZZ^T]$ evolves according to

$$\frac{d\overline{C}}{dt} = K\overline{C} + \overline{C}K^T + \mu(t)^2 \, \overline{D} \tag{19}$$

with

$$K \equiv \begin{pmatrix} -\mu(t) \, R & \beta I \\ -\mu(t)R & (\beta - 1)I \end{pmatrix}, \quad \overline{D} \equiv \begin{pmatrix} D & D \\ D & D \end{pmatrix}, \tag{20}$$

I is the $N \times N$ identity matrix, and R and D are defined as before.

The evolution operator is now

$$\overline{U}(t_2, t_1) \equiv \exp\left[\int_{t_1}^{t_2} d\tau \, K(\tau)\right] \tag{21}$$

and the solution to (19) is

$$\overline{C} = \overline{U}(t, t_0) \, \overline{C}(t_0) \, \overline{U}^T(t, t_0) + \int_{t_0}^{t} d\tau \, \mu^2(\tau) \, \overline{U}(t, \tau) \, \overline{D} \, \overline{U}^T(t, \tau) \tag{22}$$

The squared norm of the weight error is the sum of first N diagonal elements of $\overline{C}$. In coordinates for which R is diagonal and with $\mu(t) = \mu_0/t$, we find that for $t \gg t_0$

$$E[|v|^2] \approx \sum_{i=1}^{N} \left\{ \overline{C}_{ii}(t_0) \left(\frac{t_0}{t}\right)^{\frac{2\mu_0\lambda_i}{1-\beta}} + \frac{\mu_0^2 \, D_{ii}}{(1-\beta)(2\mu_0\lambda_i - 1 + \beta)} \left(\frac{1}{t} - \frac{1}{t_0}\left(\frac{t_0}{t}\right)^{\frac{2\mu_0\lambda_i}{1-\beta}}\right) \right\}. \tag{23}$$

This reduces to (9) when $\beta = 0$. Equation (23) defines two regimes of interest:

1. $\mu_0/(1-\beta) > \mu_{crit}$: $E[|v|^2]$ drops off asymptotically as $1/t$.

2. $\mu_0/(1-\beta) < \mu_{crit}$: $E[|v|^2]$ drops off asymptotically as

$$\left(\frac{1}{t}\right)^{\frac{2\mu_0\lambda_{min}}{1-\beta}},$$

i.e. *more slowly than* $1/t$.

The form of (23) and the conditions following it show that the asymptotics of gradient descent with momentum are governed by the *effective learning rate*

$$\mu_{eff} \equiv \frac{\mu}{1-\beta} \, .$$

Figure 2 compares simulations with the predictions of (23) for fixed μ_0 and various β. The simulations were performed on an ensemble of 2000 networks trained by LMS as described previously but with an additional momentum term of the form given in (15). The upper three curves (dotted) show the behavior of $E[|v|^2]$ for $\mu_{eff} < \mu_{crit}$. The solid curves show the behavior for $\mu_{eff} > \mu_{crit}$.

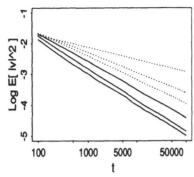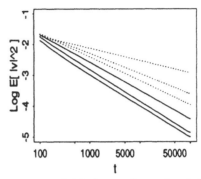

Fig.2: LEFT – Simulation results from an ensemble of 2000 one-dimensional LMS algorithms with momentum with $R = 1.0$, $D = 1.0$, and $\mu_0 = 0.2$. RIGHT – Theoretical predictions from equation (23). Curves correspond to (top to bottom) $\beta = 0.0, 0.4, 0.5, 0.6, 0.7, 0.8$.

Asymptotic Normality

The derivation of asymptotic normality proceeds similarly to the case without momentum. One first makes a (time-dependent) transformation into coordinates that diagonalize the drift K. The coefficients of the resulting Fokker-Planck equation are expanded in powers of $(1/t)$ and terms dominant at large t are retained. One finds that if

$$\mu_{eff_0} \equiv \frac{\mu_0}{1 - \beta} > \frac{1}{2\lambda_{min}}$$

then $\sqrt{t}\, v$ is asymptotically normal with variance

$$\frac{\mu_{eff_0}^2\, D}{2R\,\mu_{eff_0} - 1} \quad .$$

DISCUSSION

We have used the dynamics of the weight space probabilities to derive the asymptotic behavior of densities and weight error correlation for annealed stochastic gradient algorithms with momentum. The late time behavior is governed by the *effective* learning rate $\mu_{eff} \equiv \mu/(1 - \beta)$. For learning rate schedules μ_0/t, if $\mu_{0\,eff} > 1/(2\,\lambda_{min})$, then the squared norm of the weight error $v \equiv \omega - \omega_*$ falls off as $1/t$ and $\sqrt{t}\, v$ is asymptotically normal.

Acknowledgments This work was supported by grants from the Air Force Office of Scientific Research (F49620-93-1-0253) and the Electric Power Research Institute (RP8015-2).

References

[1] Mehmet Ali Tugay and Yalcin Tanik. Properties of the momentum LMS algorithm. *Signal Processing*, 18:117–127, 1989.

[2] John J. Shynk and Sumit Roy. The LMS algorithm with momentum updating. In *Proceedings of the IEEE International Symposium on Circuits and Systems*, pages 2651–2654. IEEE, 1988.

[3] Todd K. Leen and John E. Moody. Weight space probability densities in stochastic learning: I. Dynamics and equilibria. In Giles, Hanson, and Cowan, editors, *Advances in Neural Information Processing Systems, vol. 5*, San Mateo, CA, 1993. Morgan Kaufmann.

[4] Genevieve B. Orr and Todd K. Leen. Weight space probability densities in stochastic learning: II. Transients and basin hopping times. In Giles, Hanson, and Cowan, editors, *Advances in Neural Information Processing Systems, vol. 5*, San Mateo, CA, 1993. Morgan Kaufmann.

[5] H.J. Kushner and D.S. Clark. *Stochastic Approximation Methods for Constrained and Unconstrained Systems*. Springer-Verlag, New York, 1978.

[6] Tom M. Heskes, Eddy T.P. Slijpen, and Bert Kappen. Learning in neural networks with local minima. *Physical Review A*, 46(8):5221–5231, 1992.

[7] D. Bedeaux, K. Laktos-Lindenberg, and K. Shuler. On the relation between master equations and random walks and their solutions. *Journal of Mathematical Physics*, 12:2116–2123, 1971.

[8] C.W. Gardiner. *Handbook of Stochastic Methods, 2nd Ed*. Springer-Verlag, Berlin, 1990.

[9] Larry Goldstein. Mean square optimality in the continuous time Robbins Monro procedure. Technical Report DRB-306, Dept. of Mathematics, University of Southern California, LA, 1987.

[10] Christian Darken and John Moody. Towards faster stochastic gradient search. In J.E. Moody, S.J. Hanson, and R.P. Lipmann, editors, *Advances in Neural Information Processing Systems 4*. Morgan Kaufmann Publishers, San Mateo, CA, 1992.

[11] Halbert White. Learning in artificial neural networks: A statistical perspective. *Neural Computation*, 1:425–464, 1989.

Scheme to Improve the
Generalization Error

Rodrigo Garcés
Baskin Center for Computer Engineering and Information Sciences
University of California at Santa Cruz
Santa Cruz, CA 95064, USA
garces@cse.ucsc.edu

This paper introduces an algorithm to improve the generalization error of feedforward networks. It reduces the number of patterns needed to describe the classification function. Numerical results on a set of 1024 handwritten digits are provided where we manage to improve the generalization ability of our network by using this scheme.

1 Introduction

An interesting feature of neural networks lies in its ability to learn a classification function from examples. After a set of correctly classified instances has been presented during the training phase, the network is able to generalize new unseen instances. If the complexity of the system is large, the network will be able to learn the training data without error but in general its generalization error will be very poor. On the other hand if the number of parameters is reduced drastically, our system might not be able to learn the classification task at all. A central problem in neural networks is to find the optimal balance between the systems complexity (adjustable parameters) and the minimization of the generalization error[1]. This paper presents a simple algorithm to improve the generalization error by minimizing the the system complexity.

We will first briefly introduce the Perceptron problem and define the stability κ of the network. Next we will discuss its geometrical interpretation and define from it the Perceptron of optimal stability. We will make use of the AdaTron learning algorithm [2] to solve the Perceptron of optimal stability. Finally in the last sections we will present an algorithm to minimize the generalization error. The algorithm can even be applied for the case where the network is unable to correctly classified all of the training instances. Experimental results on a set of 1024 handwritten digits will be presented. We shall see that a cross validation curve can be plotted where a minimization of the generalization error is clearly recognize.

2 The Perceptron Problem

In order to introduce our algorithm, let us use a one layer feedforward network with N input neurons. This is the simplest model for neural network and it is known as the Perceptron. The Perceptron maps a N-dimensional input vector $\vec{\xi}^{\mu}$ to a binary output O^{μ}. μ is the index for the pattern.

---

[1] A good example of a reduction of the complexity to achieve a better generalization performance is the paper from Boser, Guyon and Vapnik [5].

The function is given by a $N-$dimensional weight vector $\vec{w}$:

$$O^\mu = \text{sign}\left(\vec{w}\vec{\xi}^\mu\right) = \begin{cases} +1 & \text{if } \vec{w}\vec{\xi}^\mu \geq 0 \\ -1 & \text{otherwise} \end{cases} \tag{1}$$

This equation is equivalent to the condition

$$\vec{w}\vec{\sigma}^\mu \geq 0 \quad \text{for all} \quad \mu = 1,\ldots,p, \quad \text{and} \quad \vec{\sigma}^\mu = O^\mu\vec{\xi}^\mu \tag{2}$$

Thus the problem of Perceptron learning can be expressed as the search for the weight vector $\vec{w}$ which satisfies the inequalities from equation (2) for a given set of p patterns. The vector weight $\vec{w}$ is a generalized description, also called hypotheses, of the target concept being learned. It is an approximation given the instances so far presented to the system. For a given $\vec{w}$ the input space is separated by a hyperplane into two parts $\vec{w}\vec{\xi}^\mu \geq 0$ and $\vec{w}\vec{\xi}^\mu < 0$, and the hyperplane is normal to the vector $\vec{w}$. The hypotheses weight vector $\vec{w}$ defines a $N-1$ dimensional dividing hyperplane in the N-dimensional space. The dividing hyperplane separates the $+1$ labels from the -1 labels. Each of the training patterns $\vec{\xi}^\mu$ has a distance to the dividing hyperplane. This margin is known as the stability κ^μ for pattern $\vec{\xi}^\mu$:

$$\kappa^\mu = \frac{\vec{w}\vec{\sigma}^\mu}{\|\vec{w}\|} \quad \text{where } \|\vec{w}\|^2 = \sum_j^N w_j^2 \text{ for } \quad \mu = 1,\ldots,p, \tag{3}$$

The stability of the system κ is defined as the distance between the closest training example and the dividing hyperplane:

$$\kappa = \min_\mu \left\{ \kappa^\mu = \frac{\vec{w}\vec{\sigma}^\mu}{\|\vec{w}\|} \right\} \tag{4}$$

3   The Perceptron of Optimal Stability

The system of inequalities in equation (2) in general do not have a unique solution. There will be a freedom of choice for the vector $\vec{w}$ and associated with it a different dividing hyperplane. Thus it would be useful to have some sort of criterion that defines the optimal solution. This criterion of course will depend on the task for which the network is being build. Apparently it is reasonable to aim for large distances between the dividing hyperplane and each of the μ patterns. This would enable us to differentiate with more accuracy the $+1$ labeled examples from the -1 labeled ones. In other words, what we need is to maximize this distance for all the p patterns in regard to the dividing hyperplane. This can be done by adding a new constraint to the Perceptron problem from equation (2). From all the weight vectors $\vec{w}$ that solve the Perceptron problem we will select the one that maximizes the stability κ. That is:

$$\max \kappa = \max \min_\mu \left\{ \kappa^\mu = \frac{\vec{w}\vec{\sigma}^\mu}{\|\vec{w}\|} \right\} \tag{5}$$

By maximizing κ we are maximizing the stability of the Perceptron. This is known as the Perceptron of optimal stability. The Perceptron of optimal stability is given by the weight vector $\vec{w}$ for which the stability κ is a maximum. The solution to this problem is unique (of course if a solution exists for the set of patterns). Proper scaling is required since the $\vec{w}\vec{\sigma}^\mu$ are linear in $\vec{w}$. The Perceptron of optimal stability problem can be written as:

$$\min\|\vec{w}\|^2 \quad \text{subject to the constraints} \quad \vec{w}\vec{\sigma}^\mu \geq c \geq 0 \quad \mu = 1,\ldots,p, \tag{6}$$

where c is a strictly positive threshold. This is a quadratic optimization problem with linear inequality constraints. This is a class of nonlinear problems termed as a convex programs. In the geometrical interpretation of the Perceptron problem there is a set of possible hyperplanes that divides the $+1$ from the -1 labels. The hyperplane whose distance to the nearest pattern is the greatest is the solution to the optimal stability problem. Actually the weight vector $\vec{w}$ perpendicular to this hyperplane is the solution to the problem. The Perceptron of optimal stability can be learned using various algorithms (see for example [1]). We used the AdaTron algorithm. [2]

---

[2]For a complete description of this algorithm see [2].

4 Brief Description of the AdaTron Algorithm

It is well known that the bonds of the Perceptron can be written as a linear combination of the pattern vectors:

$$\vec{w} = \frac{1}{N} \sum_{\mu=1}^{p} \chi^{\mu} \vec{\sigma^{\mu}} \tag{7}$$

where χ^{μ} is called the embedding strength of the pattern μ. χ^{μ} indicates how strongly pattern μ has been enforced during the construction of the weight vector $\vec{w}$. χ^{μ} can be define as the number of time steps that pattern μ has led to a change of the weight vector $\vec{w}$. The result of the Perceptron learning rule is something like a weighted hebbian learning rule, since hebbian terms corresponding to different patterns are added up with different weights, according to the number of times that they had to be activated before convergence was achieved. By means of an iteration learning rule it is possible to find the optimal bonds $\vec{w}$.

$$
\begin{aligned}
\vec{w}(t+1) &= \vec{w}(t) + \delta\chi^{\mu}\vec{\sigma^{\mu}} \text{ (sequentially)} \\
\text{or } \vec{w}(t+1) &= \vec{w}(t) + \sum_{\mu}^{p} \delta\chi^{\mu}\vec{\sigma^{\mu}} \text{ (in parallel).}
\end{aligned} \tag{8}
$$

where $\delta\chi^{\mu}$ is the update variable in the construction of the weight vector $\vec{w}$. $\delta\chi^{\mu}$ are our dynamical variables. Analytical calculations performed by [3] showed that the Perceptron divides the patterns into two subsets:

$$\text{either } (\chi^{\mu} > 0 \text{ and } \vec{w}\vec{\sigma^{\mu}} = 1) \text{ or } (\chi^{\mu} = 0 \text{ and } \vec{w}\vec{\sigma^{\mu}} \geq 1). \tag{9}$$

The patterns with the embedding strength $\chi^{\mu} = 0$ are automatically stabilized due to accidental correlations with the embedded ones. Now then, the idea of the AdaTron algorithm is to use the embedding strengths χ^{μ} as its dynamical variables. The AdaTron is a learning algorithm that relaxes exponentially towards the Perceptron of optimal stability. It uses the concept of adaptive learning known from Adaline to solve the Perceptron problem. The Adaline changes the embedding strength of each pattern according to the deviation from the desired value. That is:

$$\chi^{\mu}(t+1) = \chi^{\mu}(t) + \delta\chi^{\mu} \text{ for all } \mu = 1, \ldots, p. \tag{10}$$

The AdaTron performs Adaline learning for all of the patterns restricting the embedding strengths to positive values. Our update variable $\delta\chi^{\mu}$ can be written as:

$$\delta\chi^{\mu} = \max\{\gamma(1 - \vec{w}\vec{\sigma^{\mu}}), -\chi^{\mu}\} \quad (\Rightarrow \chi^{\mu} \geq 0 \text{ always}) \tag{11}$$

The parameter γ is the learning rate. Notice that the size of the gradient descending step varies at each iteration step. In order to guarantee its convergence γ should be $0 < \gamma < 2$ for the sequential version of the algorithm, while for the parallel version γ is similar to the parameter needed by the Adaline algorithm.

5 A Training Algorithm to Improve the Generalization Error

Up until now we have seen that the training instances of solvable problems are divided into two subsets, those with $\chi^{\mu} = 0$ and those with $\chi^{\mu} > 0$. But what happens if the target concept that we are trying to learn is non solvable? In this case we will have a third subset of instances with $\chi^{\mu} > 0$ and $\vec{w}\vec{\sigma^{\mu}} < 1$. Those are the instances that can not be correctly classified.

In this section we shall propose an algorithm to improve the generalization performance of our feedforward network under such circumstances. The algorithm is a very simple algorithm. We first divide a given set of patterns into two subsets. One will be use to train the network while the other subset will be use to test our hypothesis. We will be making use of the AdaTron learning algorithm to search for the weight vector $\vec{w}$, which is our initial hypothesis. As it is well known the one layer feedforward network is able classify correctly at most $p = 2N$ linear separable patterns.[3] We have included more instances in the training set as the network is able to classify correctly. The AdaTron algorithm is a batch learning algorithm that uses all the training instances to search for a hypothesis that best approximates the target concept. Those instances that have not been correctly classified by the hypothesis are characterized by having the largest embedding strength χ^μ and $\vec{w}\vec{\sigma}^\mu < 1$. So our initial hypothesis will be correct for a finite number of patterns while a couple of the patterns will be in the incorrect side of the hyperplane. They are those patterns that our hypothesis has not been able to classify correctly. If we take a look at the embedding strength χ^μ and the $\vec{w}\vec{\sigma}^\mu$ values for the training set, we observe three sets of patterns:

$$\text{either } (\chi^\mu > 0 \text{ and } \vec{w}\vec{\sigma}^\mu = 1)$$
$$\text{or } (\chi^\mu > 0 \text{ and } \vec{w}\vec{\sigma}^\mu < 1)$$
$$\text{or } (\chi^\mu = 0 \text{ and } \vec{w}\vec{\sigma}^\mu \geq 1). \tag{12}$$

Those patterns with $\chi^\mu = 0$ do not contribute to the hypothesis space[4]. The other two groups of patterns are known as the supporting patterns, where a distinction must be made between the correctly classified ones ($\chi^\mu > 0$ and $\vec{w}\vec{\sigma}^\mu = 1$) and those that are incorrectly classified ($\chi^\mu > 0$ and $\vec{w}\vec{\sigma}^\mu < 1$). The incorrectly classified supporting patterns have the largest embedding strength χ^μ values. This was to be expected since those are the patterns where the AdaTron algorithm spends the longest time trying to learn them.

In order to search a better hypothesis in the vector space, it is wise to get rid of the pattern for which the AdaTron algorithm has the hardest time learning, that is the pattern with the greatest χ^μ value.

So our algorithm follows the following iterative procedure:

1. Learn the perceptron of optimal stability using the AdaTron algorithm to find the hypothesis $\vec{w}$.

2. Remove only the pattern μ with the embedding strength χ^μ that has the biggest value.

3. Search for a new hypothesis $\vec{w}$ relearning the perceptron of optimal stability on the remaining patterns.

4. Test the generalization error of the new hypothesis using the instances of the testing set.

5. Iterate steps two, three and four until the smallest generalization error is reach.

6   Numerical Results

The experiments were run on a set of 1024 handwritten digits with a resolution of 16 by 16 pixels. We used a Perceptron with 256 input units and one output unit. The Perceptron was trained on a subset of 512 instances leaving the rest 512 handwritten digits for the testing set. The iterative procedure described above was followed recording the generalization error as well as the training error as a function of the number of supporting patterns. In the training error we included all of the 512 instances of the set, even those that were previously removed. As it can be seen from figure 1 there is a minimum in the generalization curve (upper curve). By using this scheme we manage to decrease the generalization error from 30.8% to 16.3%, which means that our hypothesis improved around 45% against its initial generalization error value. With the initial hypothesis $\vec{w}$, 12 out of the 512 training patterns were incorrectly classified. By just removing 2 of the training examples we were able to get a hypothesis $\vec{w}$ that could classify correctly all of the remaining instances of the training set.

At the beginning our initial hypothesis was composed of 512 instances out of which 308 did not contribute anything to the hypothesis, since there embedding strengths $\chi^\mu = 0$. These are the patterns that do not need to be learned since they are already correctly classified. We also had 204 supporting patterns ($\chi^\mu \geq 0$) where 12 of them were incorrectly classified. Their margin was negative indicating that they were on the wrong side of the dividing hyperplane. On the

---

[3]For more details see [4].

[4]See equation(7).

other hand, our optimal hypothesis (with the smallest generalization error) was composed of a total of 425 patterns' out of which 126 are supporting patterns all of which are correctly classified. the complexity of our hypothesis has been reduced drastically. We now need 126 patterns to described a better hypothesis vector weight $\vec{w}$ compared to the 204 patterns that we needed at the beginning. We manage to reduced the amount of instances describing the dividing hyperplane by 38%.

7 Conclusion

In this paper we have presented a simple algorithm to improve the generalization performance of feedforward networks. The algorithm has several interesting properties. First, it can be used to search for a hypothesis even when there does not exist a hypothesis that can correctly classified all of the instances in the training set. That is, we can use this algorithm on instances that are not linear separable. Second, this scheme has the ability to recognize those patterns that are incorrectly classified and are disturbing a proper selection of a good hypothesis weight vector $\vec{w}$. It is interesting to observe that it is not necessary to remove all the incorrectly classified instances from the set in order to get a perfect training error. We only need to remove a small fraction of the incorrectly classified patterns in order, not only to find a better hypothesis, but also one that is able to linearly separate those other patterns that were disturbing us at the beginning. Finally, the complexity of our hypothesis is reduce. The number of supporting patterns needed to described the weight vector $\vec{w}$ decreases drastically improving the generalization performance of our network. This scheme to improve the generalization error is not only limited to linear classifiers. The algorithm can also be used as a polynomial classifier if we recode the input space and search for the weight vector in a larger space.

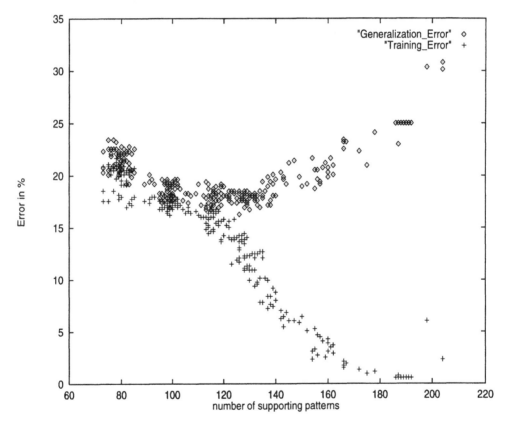

Figure 1: The training error (lower curve) and the generalization error (upper curve) as a function of the number of supporting patterns

Acknowledgements

Thanks to M. Warmuth for reading this paper and the Connectionist Models Summer School for two wonderful weeks of intense learning.

References

[1] Krauth W. and Mezard M., "Learning Algorithms with Optimal Stability in Neural Networks," *Journal of Physics A,* vol 20, p. L 745 , 1987.

[2] Anlauf J. K. and Biehl M., "The AdaTron an Adaptive Perceptron Algorithm," *Europhysic Letters,* vol 10, p. 687, 1989.

[3] Opper M., "Learning Times of Neural Networks: Exact Solution for a Perceptron Algorithm," *Physical Review A,* vol 38, pp. 3824-3826, 1988.

[4] Cover T. M., "Geometrical and Statistical Properties of Systems of Linear Inequalities with Applications in Pattern Recognition," *IEEE Transactions on Electronic Computers,* vol pp. 326-334, 1965.

[5] Boser B., Guyon I. M. and Vapnik V. N., "A Training Algorithm for Optimal Margin Classifiers," *Proceedings of the Fifth Annual ACM Workshop on Computational Learning Theory,* pp. 144-152, 1992.

GENERAL AVERAGING RESULTS FOR CONVEX OPTIMIZATION

Michael P. Perrone
Institute for Brain and Neural Systems
Brown University
Providence, RI 02912 USA
mpp@cns.brown.edu

INTRODUCTION

Recent neural network simulations have shown that averaging over the outputs of a population of neural network estimates can lead to improved network performance [3, 14, 19, 24, 27, 28, 26, 33, 39]. The perspective we will take in this paper is one of developing a firm theoretical basis for this observed phenomenon. This analysis will enable us to understand why averaging improves performance and to identify a wide class of common optimization tasks for which averaging can be used to improve performance.

Alternative methods to averaging exist for constructing more sophisticated, nonlinear combinations of networks. For example the Competing Expert algorithm [20] uses weighted averaging controlled by a non-linear gating network; while the Stacked Generalization [37], GENSEP [31] and Boosting [9] algorithms all attempt to improve performance by using successive networks to correct the errors of preceding networks. Although these methods have been shown to improve performance, these algorithms are motivated heuristically and currently do not lend themselves easily to theoretical analysis analogous to the that presented below for averaging. One very interesting line of research is to extend the analysis presented in this paper to these more sophisticated methods.

The paper begins with a presentation of a general averaging result for mean square error (MSE) optimization. It is then noted that averaging can be extended to l_p-norm optimization. Next, a basic result is derived which highlights the relation between convexity and averaging. The convexity result is then used to generalize the averaging method to a wide variety of optimization techniques. The paper closes with a discussion of how averaging methods and standard regularization techniques can be linked by showing that averaging is performing smoothing by variance reduction.

RELAXING THE ORTHOGONALITY ASSUMPTION

Given a population of n regression estimates of some function $f(x)$, the ith of which is denoted by $f_i(x)$, it can be shown [28], assuming the following orthogonality condition for $i \neq j$

$$E[(f_i(x) - f(x))(f_j(x) - f(x))] = 0, \tag{1}$$

that

$$\text{MSE}[\overline{f}] = \frac{1}{N}\overline{\text{MSE}[f]} \tag{2}$$

where a bar indicates an average over the population of regression estimates. For example, $\overline{f}$ is defined as

$$\overline{f} \equiv \frac{1}{n}\sum_i f_i(x). \tag{3}$$

This result implies that the MSE can be reduced arbitrarily small by increasing the size of the population sufficiently. Unfortunately, the orthogonality condition does not hold in general and must be relaxed to find a more realistic formulation. In what follows, a useful formulation of the effects of averaging is derived which does not rely on the previous orthogonality assumption.

From the *Cauchy inequality* [4],

$$\left(\sum_{i=1}^{n} x_i y_i\right)^2 \leq \left(\sum_{i=1}^{n} x_i^2\right)\left(\sum_{i=1}^{n} y_i^2\right),\tag{4}$$

we have, by setting $y_i = 1 \ \forall \ i$, that

$$\left(\sum_{i=1}^{n} x_i\right)^2 \leq n \sum_{i=1}^{n} x_i^2.\tag{5}$$

Replacing the x_i with $f_i(x) - f(x)$ and average over the data gives

$$\text{MSE}[\overline{f}] \leq \overline{\text{MSE}[f]}.\tag{6}$$

Equation (6) indicates that the average regressor is always better than the population average. Note however that by relaxing the orthogonality assumption, the $\frac{1}{N}$ behavior from Equation 2 is lost.

This result clearly extends to *generalized least mean squares* [7] where for some nonzero function $g(x)$ we minimize

$$\sum_{i=1}^{n} (y_i - f(x_i))^2 / g^2(x_i).\tag{7}$$

EXTENSIONS TO l_p-NORMS

The result of Eqn. (6) can be stated more generally: Optimization procedures which seek to minimize an l_2-norm cost function will always benefit from averaging. This is a powerful result due to the fact that most optimization done today is somehow related to a mean square error minimization problem. However since other l_p-norm minimization is not uncommon [12] particularly for $p = 1$ and $p = \infty$, it is interesting to consider the case when $p \neq 2$.

From *Hölder's inequality* [13] for $x_i, y_i \geq 0, 1/p + 1/q = 1$ and $p > 1$,

$$\sum_{i=1}^{n} x_i y_i \leq \left(\sum_{i=1}^{n} x_i^p\right)^{\frac{1}{p}} \left(\sum_{i=1}^{n} y_i^q\right)^{\frac{1}{q}},\tag{8}$$

we find by setting $y_i = 1 \ \forall \ i$ and using $|x_1 + \cdots + x_n| \leq |x_1| + \cdots + |x_n|$ that

$$\left|\frac{1}{n}\sum_{i=1}^{n} x_i\right|^p \leq \frac{1}{n}\sum_{i=1}^{n} |x_i|^p\tag{9}$$

for all x_i and $p > 1$. Equation (9) implies that any l_p-norm minimization procedure with $p \geq 1$ will benefit from the application of averaging.[1] In general we have that any cost function of the following form will benefit for averaging:

$$E(\{x_j\}) = \sum_{ij} \alpha_i |x_j|^{p_i},\tag{10}$$

where $\alpha_i \geq 0$ and $p_i \geq 1$.

Note that these results generalize in the natural way to L_p norms.

---

[1]The $p = 1$ case does not follow from the argument above; however its proof is trivial.

365

CONVEXITY AND AVERAGING

In this section we show that a sufficient condition for averaging to generate improved regression estimates is for the optimization measure to have the convexity property. Convexity is defined in the following way. A function, $h(x)$, is convex on an interval $[a, b]$ if $\forall \; x_1, x_2 \in [a, b]$

$$h\left(\frac{x_1 + x_2}{2}\right) \le \frac{h(x_1) + h(x_2)}{2}. \tag{11}$$

If $\Phi(u)$ is a convex function on the interval $\alpha \le u \le \beta$ and $f(x; \omega)$ and $g(\omega)$ defined on $[a, b]$ satisfy $\alpha \le f(x; \omega) \le \beta \; \forall \; x$ and $g(\omega) \ge 0$ then *Jensen's inequality* [13, 17] states

$$\Phi\left(\frac{\int_a^b f(x; \omega) g(\omega) d\omega}{\int_a^b g(\omega) d\omega}\right) \le \frac{\int_a^b \Phi(f(x; \omega)) g(\omega) d\omega}{\int_a^b g(\omega) d\omega}. \tag{12}$$

If we use a population of estimators, $\{f(x; \omega_j)\}$, to define

$$g(\omega) \equiv \frac{1}{n} \sum_{j=1}^n \delta(\omega - \omega_j), \tag{13}$$

where ω_j corresponds to the parameters of the jth regression estimate, then Eqn. (12) becomes

$$\Phi(\overline{f}) \le \overline{\Phi(f)} \tag{14}$$

where the equality holds only when all of the f_i are the same. Equation (14) is the discrete version of Jensen's Inequality. Thus, we have the following fundamental result:

Theorem 1 *Given a convex cost function $\Phi : \mathcal{R}^n \mapsto \mathcal{R}$ and a set of functions $f_i : \mathcal{R}^m \mapsto \mathcal{R}^n$ for some n and m, then the cost of the average of the functions, f_i, is always less than or equal to the average of the cost of the individual functions with equality only when all of the f_i are the same.*

This theorem, as stated, applies only to the simple average estimators; however a natural corollary which extends this result to the optimal weighted average estimator from the General Ensemble Method (GEM) [28], $f_{\text{GEM}}(x)$,

$$f_{\text{GEM}}(x) \equiv \sum_{i=1}^N \alpha_i f_i(x) \tag{15}$$

where

$$\alpha_i = \frac{\sum_j C_{ij}^{-1}}{\sum_k \sum_j C_{kj}^{-1}}, \tag{16}$$

and

$$C_{ij} \equiv E[(f_i(x) - f(x))(f_j(x) - f(x))], \tag{17}$$

is given below.

Corollary 1 *For any convex cost function $\Phi(x)$, the GEM estimator has a lower cost than the simple average estimator, i.e.*

$$\Phi(f_{\text{GEM}}) \le \Phi(\overline{f}) \le \overline{\Phi(f)}. \tag{18}$$

The proof of this corollary follows directly from the minimization of the cost $\Phi(f_{\text{GEM}})$ relative to the linear weights in the GEM estimator and the observation that the simple average estimator is a special case of the GEM estimator. In the case of the MSE, the cost function is quadratic and we can therefore find the optimal weights in closed form; however for general convex costs we will not be able to solve for the optimal weights in closed form. When closed form solutions do not exist, we can still find approximate solutions by using an iterative root finding algorithm or gradient descent.

With this theorem in hand, we can now go back to the l_p-norms. In the case of l_p-norms, Eqn. (14) implies that not only can we use $p \geq 1$ but that we can *not* use $p < 1$ unless we restrict $f(x)$ to be nonnegative in the case of $p < 0$ or in the case of $0 < p < 1$ additionally require that we maximize the cost (or minimize the negative cost for $0 < p < 1$. This restriction is not too severe as it still applies to optimizations that deal directly with probabilities. Thus for x_j nonnegative, we have a very wide selection of cost functions given by [2]

$$E(\{x_j\}) = \sum_{ij} (\alpha_i x_j^{p_{\alpha i}} - \beta_i x_j^{p_{\beta i}}), \tag{19}$$

where $\alpha_i, \beta_i \geq 0$ and $p_{\alpha i} \in (-\infty, 0) \cap [1, +\infty)$ and $p_{\beta i} \in (0, 1)$. Of course for $p \in (0, 1)$, the negative of the cost function is not bounded below. We can avoid this unboundedness be requiring a cost term with sufficiently large p. Also note that costs with $p < 0$ and negative costs with $0 < p < 1$ weight large errors more lightly than small errors!

EXTENDING AVERAGING TO OTHER COST FUNCTIONS

In the preceding sections, we have seen that averaging can be applied to a wide variety of cost functions. In this section we show how Maximum Entropy (ME), Maximum Mutual Information (MMI), Maximum Likelihood Estimation (MLE) and the Kullback-Leibler Information (KLI) can all benefit from averaging.

Suppose now that the functions that we are estimating are probability densities given by $p_j(x_i)$ where i is the index of the data and j is the index of the population of density function estimates.[3] In this case, the entropy of $p(x)$ is given by

$$H(p) = -\sum_i p(x_i) \ln p(x_i). \tag{20}$$

Note that $\Phi(z) \equiv z \ln z$ then $\Phi(z)$ is a convex function and therefore we can write for each data point that

$$\frac{1}{n} \sum_j p_j(x_i) \ln p_j(x_i) \geq \left(\frac{1}{n} \sum_j p_j(x_i)\right) \ln\left(\frac{1}{n} \sum_j p_j(x_i)\right) \tag{21}$$

which implies

$$H(\bar{p}) \geq \overline{H(p)}, \tag{22}$$

where the overline indicates an average over the population index j. From Eqn. (22), we see that averaging helps to *maximize* the entropy and should therefore be useful in ME optimization [34, 22]. Baldi [1] suggests that *minimizing* the entropy could also be useful in neural net learning; however averaging should not be used with this method as it would degrade performance. We must keep in mind that averaging will help minimize a convex function while it will help maximize a negative convex function such as entropy.

Mutual Information [5, 11, 25] can be defined in terms of the entropy as

$$I(a, b) = H(a) + H(b) - H(ab). \tag{23}$$

Therefore since $\Phi(u, v) \equiv u \ln u + v \ln v - uv \ln uv$ is a convex function[4] we can proceed as we did for entropy and to find that

$$I(\bar{p}, b) \geq \overline{I(p, b)}, \tag{24}$$

---

[2]The sum of two convex functions is convex.
[3]Note that since the p_j's are densities, the average over j is also a density.
[4]Consider $\Phi(u, v) = (1 - v)u \ln u + (1 - u)v \ln v$.

where $b(x)$ is some fixed reference density and the overline indicates an average over the population index j. Thus averaging should help MMI optimization.

We now turn to MLE which is probably the most commonly used alternative to LMS optimization. In MLE we attempt to maximize the *likelihood function* [36],

$$L(p) = \prod_i p(x_i), \tag{25}$$

where $p(x_i)$ is the probability of event x_i. We consider here the equivalent problem of maximizing the log-likelihood function, $\ln L(p)$. Starting with the *arithmetic-geometric mean inequality* [4],

$$\frac{a_1 + \cdots + a_n}{n} \geq (a_1 \cdots a_n)^{1/n}, \tag{26}$$

where $a_i \geq 0 \; \forall \; i$, we substitute $p_j(x_i)$ for a_i, take the log of both sides and sum over all of the data to get

$$\sum_i \ln(\frac{1}{n} \sum_j p_j(x_i)) \geq \frac{1}{n} \sum_{ij} \ln(p_j(x_i)), \tag{27}$$

where i is the data index and j is the population index. This result can be re-written as

$$\ln L(\bar{p}) \geq \overline{\ln L(p)}, \tag{28}$$

where the overline indicates an average over the population index j. Equation (28) demonstrates that averaging always increases MLE.

Finally, KLI is a commonly used measure in density estimation [23, 15, 8] and has been shown to be useful in neural network hand-written character recognition [38]. The KLI is given by

$$K(f,g) = \int f \ln(\frac{f}{g}), \tag{29}$$

and can be thought of as a distance between the two probability densities, f and g. Note that the KLI is not symmetric in f and g and is therefore not a proper distance. It can easily be symmetrized but this is rarely done. The KLI is sometimes know as the Cross Entropy or the Relative Entropy [6]. It has been shown that minimizing KLI subject to appropriate constraints leads to optimal learning rules [30].

From Equation (12) we have that $-\int f \ln(\frac{f}{g}) \leq \ln(\int f \frac{g}{f}) = 0$. Thus $K(f,g) \geq 0$. So we have that $K(p_i, \bar{p}) \geq 0$ which can be re-written as

$$\int p_j \ln(\frac{p_j}{g}) \geq \int p_j \ln \frac{\bar{p}}{g} \tag{30}$$

for some probability density g. If we sum over the population index j, we find

$$\overline{K(p,g)} \geq K(\bar{p}, g). \tag{31}$$

So the Kullback-Leibler Information between probability densities is reduced by averaging.

Smoothing by Variance Reduction

The averaging process is inherently a smoothing operation as can be seen by the following analysis. Fixing x, we can write that

$$E[(\hat{f}(x) - f(x))^2] = \text{VAR}(\hat{f}) + \text{BIAS}^2(\hat{f}) \tag{32}$$

where $\text{VAR}(\hat{f}) \equiv E[(\hat{f} - E[\hat{f}])^2]$ and $\text{BIAS}(\hat{f}) \equiv E[\hat{f}] - f(x)$. Now since $E[\overline{f}] = E[\hat{f}]$, we have that the bias term is the same for both $\text{MSE}[\hat{f}]$ and $\text{MSE}[\overline{f}]$ and therefore when we reduce the MSE by averaging it is

368

because we have reduced the variance term. This variance reduction corresponds to smoothing the estimate of $\hat{f}$.

Further, we observe that in the infinite limit the sum $\bar{f} = \frac{1}{n}\sum_i \hat{f}_i$ converges to $E[\hat{f}]$, i.e.

$$\lim_{n\to\infty} \bar{f}(x) = \int \hat{f}(x;\beta)p(\beta)d\beta \tag{33}$$

where β represents the weights of a network and $p(\beta)$ is the probability of generating a neural net with parameters β given some stochastic network generation process. Thus we can make the variance term as small as we like and we are essentially left only with the bias term. Note that if $p(\beta)$ corresponded to the true distribution of β and if $f(x;\beta)$ corresponded to the true model, then the averaging is equivalent to Monte Carlo Integration [21] and Bayesian Inference [10].

PENALIZED MLE, SMOOTHING SPLINES AND REGULARIZATION

Averaging can also be used with methods which explicitly try to avoid over-fitting through the use of penalty terms [2, 29, 32]. In the case of penalized MLE and smoothing splines [16, 18, 35] the penalty term takes the form of a regularizer which attempts to measure a solution's smoothness,

$$\ln \prod_i p(x_i) + \lambda \int (p'')^2 dx \tag{34}$$

$$\frac{1}{n}\sum_i (f(x_i) - f_i)^2 + \lambda \int (f'')^2 dx. \tag{35}$$

The smoothing parameter, λ, regulates how much smoothing is performed and can be estimated using cross-validation. Other regularizers can be used and in general they take the form

$$\int (D(p))^2 dx \tag{36}$$

where D is some linear differential operator corresponding to some *a priori* knowledge of the system to be fit. Regularizers of this form are convex; therefore averaging will reduce the regularizer penalty and therefore increase the smoothness of the solution.

SUMMARY

We have seen that for any optimization process involving a convex measure, the method of averaging is guaranteed to produce a network which has better performance than the average performance of a population of distinct networks from which it was generated. It is still possible, though not necessary, that there exists a network in the population which has better performance than the averaged network; however, it is not clear that there exists a reliable method for consistently selecting such a network. For example, one could use cross-validation to select the best network from a population; but there is no guarantee that this network will still be the best on new data. For the averaged network, we know that its better than average performance will hold for any data set. Further, cross-validation selection requires an additional independent data set whereas averaging can add this data to training data to generate better estimates. And finally, in the case where several networks all have the same performance, cross-validation is no better than guessing while averaging will still improve performance.

Acknowledgements

The author would like to thank the members of the Institute for Brain and Neural Systems at Brown University. This research was funded with grants from the Office of Naval Research, the National Science Foundation, and the Army Research Office.

369

References

[1] P. Baldi, "Computing with arrays of bell-shaped and sigmoid functions," in *Advances in Neural Information Processing Systems 3*, Morgan Kaufmann, 1991.

[2] A. R. Barron, "Complexity regularization with applications to artificial neural networks," in *Nonparametric Functional Estimation and Related Topics* (G. Roussas, ed.), pp. 561–576, Kluwer, 1991.

[3] W. G. Baxt, "Improving the accuracy of an artificial neural network using multiple differently trained networks," *Neural Computation*, vol. 4, no. 5, 1992.

[4] E. F. Beckenbach and R. Bellman, *Inequalities*. Springer-Verlag, 1965.

[5] J. S. Bridle, A. J. R. Heading, and D. J. C. MacKay, "Unsupervised classifiers, mutual information and 'phantom targets'," in *Advances in Neural Information Processing Systems 4* (J. E. Moody, S. J. Hanson, and R. P. Lippmann, eds.), pp. 1096–1101, Morgan Kaufmann, 1992.

[6] J. S. Bridle, "Training stochastic model recognition algorithms as networks can lead to maximum mutual information estimation of parameters," in *Advances in Neural Information Processing Systems 2* (D. S. Touretzky, ed.), pp. 211–217, Morgan Kaufmann, 1990.

[7] R. J. Carroll and D. Ruppert, *Transformation and weighting in regression*. Chapman and Hall, 1988.

[8] L. Devroye, *A Course in Density Estimation*. Birkhauser, 1987.

[9] H. Drucker, R. Schapire, and P. Simard, "Improving performance in neural networks using a boosting algorithm," in *Advances in Neural Information Processing Systems 5* (S. J. Hanson, J. D. Cowan, and C. L. Giles, eds.), pp. 42–49, Morgan Kaufmann, 1993.

[10] R. O. Duda and P. E. Hart, *Pattern Classification and Scene Analysis*. New York: John Wiley, 1973.

[11] C. C. Galland and G. E. Hinton, "Discovering high order features with mean field modules," in *Advances in Neural Information Processing Systems 2* (D. S. Touretzky, ed.), Morgan Kaufmann, 1990.

[12] R. Gonin and A. H. Money, *Nonlinear Lp-Norm Estimation*. Marcel Dekker, Inc., 1989.

[13] I. S. Gradshteyn and I. M. Ryzhik, *Table of Integrals, Series and Products*. Academic Press, Inc., 1980.

[14] L. K. Hansen, C. Liisberg, and P. Salamon, "Ensemble methods for handwritten digit recognition," in *Neural Networks for Signal Processing II: Proceedings of the 1992 IEEE Workshop* (S. Y. Kung, F. Fallside, and C. A. Kamm, eds.), pp. 333–342, IEEE, 1992.

[15] W. Härdle, *Applied Nonparametric Regression*, vol. 19 of *Econometric Society Monographs*. New York: Cambridge University Press, 1990.

[16] W. Härdle, *Smoothing Techniques with Implementation in S*. Springer Series in Statistics, New York, NY: Springer-Verlag, 1991.

[17] G. H. Hardy, J. E. Littlewood, and G. Polya, *Inequalities*. Cambridge University Press, 1952.

[18] H. J. Hastie and R. J. Tibshirani, *Generalized Additive Models*. New York, NY: Chapman and Hall, 1990.

[19] N. Intrator, D. Reisfeld, and Y. Yeshurun, "Face recognition using a hybrid supervised/unsupervised neural network," 1992. Preprint.

[20] R. A. Jacobs, M. I. Jordan, S. J. Nowlan, and G. E. Hinton, "Adaptive mixtures of local experts," *Neural Computation*, vol. 3, no. 2, 1991.

[21] M. H. Kalos and P. A. Whitlock, *Monte Carlo Methods: Basics*, vol. 1. John Wiley & Sons, 1986.

[22] J. N. Kapur and H. Kesavan, *Entropy Optimization Principles with applications*. Boston: Academic Press, 1992.

[23] S. Kullback and R. Leibler, "On information and sufficiency," *Annals of Statitstics*, vol. 22, pp. 79–86, 1951.

[24] W. P. Lincoln and J. Skrzypek, "Synergy of clustering multiple back propagation networks," in *Advances in Neural Information Processing Systems 2* (D. S. Touretzky, ed.), (San Mateo, CA), pp. 650–657, Morgan Kaufmann, 1990.

[25] R. Linkser, "An application of the principle of maximum information preservation to linear systems," in *Advances in Neural Information Processing Systems* (D. S. Touretzky, ed.), pp. 186–194, Morgan Kaufmann, 1989.

[26] R. M. Neal, "Bayesian learning via stochastic dynamics," in *Advances in Neural Information Processing Systems 5* (S. J. Hanson, J. D. Cowan, and C. L. Giles, eds.), vol. 5, San Mateo, CA: Morgan Kaufmann, 1993.

[27] M. P. Perrone, *Improving Regression Estimation: Averaging Methods for Variance Reduction with Extensions to General Convex Measure Optimization*. PhD thesis, Brown University, Institute for Brain and Neural Systems; Dr. Leon N Cooper, Thesis Supervisor, May 1993.

[28] M. P. Perrone and L. N. Cooper, "When networks disagree: Ensemble method for neural networks," in *Neural Networks for Speech and Image Processing* (R. J. Mammone, ed.), Chapman-Hall, 1993. [To Appear].

[29] T. Poggio and F. Girosi, "Regularization algorithms for learning that are equivalent to multilayer networks," *Science*, vol. 247, pp. 978–982, 1990.

[30] M. Qian, G. Gong, and J. Clark, "Relative entropy and learning rules," *Physical Review A*, vol. 43, no. 2, pp. 1061–1070, January 1991.

[31] D. L. Reilly, C. L. Scofield, L. N. Cooper, and C. Elbaum, "Gensep: A multiple neural network learning system with modifiable network topology," in *Abstracts of the First Annual International Neural Network Society Meeting*, INNS, 1988.

[32] J. Rissanen, "Stochastic complexity and modeling," *Annals of Statistics*, vol. 14, no. 3, pp. 1080–1100, 1986.

[33] C. Scofield, L. Kenton, and J.-C. Chang, "Multiple neural net architectures for character recognition," in *Proc. Compcon, San Francisco, CA, February 1991*, pp. 487–491, IEEE Comp. Soc. Press, 1991.

[34] J. Skilling, ed., *Maximum Entropy and Bayesian Methods*. Kluwer Academic Publishers, 1989.

[35] G. Wahba and S. Wold, "A completely automatic French curve: fitting spline functions by cross-validation," *Communications in Statistics, Series A*, vol. 4, pp. 1–17, 1975.

[36] S. S. Wilks, *Mathematical Statistics*. John Wiley and Sons, 1962.

[37] D. H. Wolpert, "Stacked generalization," *Neural Networks*, vol. 5, no. 2, pp. 241–260, 1992.

[38] L. Xu, A. Krzyzak, and C. Y. Suen, "Associative switch for combining classifiers," Department of Computer Science TR-X9011, Concordia University, Montreal, Canada, January 1990.

[39] L. Xu, A. Krzyzak, and C. Y. Suen, "Methods of combining multiple classifiers and their applications to handwriting recognition," *IEEE Transactions on Systems, Man, and Cybernetics*, vol. 22, no. 3, pp. 418–435, May/June 1992.

Multitask Connectionist Learning

Richard A. Caruana
School of Computer Science
Carnegie Mellon University
Pittsburgh, PA 15213
caruana@cs.cmu.edu

The standard methodology in connectionism is to break hard problems into simpler, reasonably independent subproblems, learn the subproblems separately, and then recombine the learned pieces [15]. This modularization can be counterproductive because it eliminates a potentially critical source of inductive bias: the inductive bias inherent in the similarity between different tasks drawn from the same domain. Hinton [5] proposed that generalization in artificial neural networks improves if networks learn to represent underlying regularities of the domain. A learner that learns related tasks *at the same time* can use these tasks as inductive bias for each other and thus better learn the the domain's regularities. This can make learning faster and more accurate and may allow some hard tasks to be learned that could not be learned in isolation. This paper explores the issue of enabling connectionist networks to learn domain regularities by training networks on multiple tasks drawn from the same domain.

MULTITASK LEARNING AND INDUCTIVE BIAS

We learn embedded in a world that simultaneously requires us to learn many related things. These things obey the same physical laws, derive from the same human culture, are preprocessed by the same sensory hardware.... Perhaps it is the similarity of the tasks we learn that enables us to learn so much with so little experience.

A child trained from birth on a single, isolated, complex task—and nothing else—would be unlikely to learn it. If you were trained from birth to play tennis—and nothing else—you would probably not learn tennis. Instead, you learn to play tennis in a world that asks you to learn many other things. You also learn to walk, to run, to jump, to exercise, to grasp, to throw, to swing, to recognize objects, to predict trajectories, to rest, to talk, to study, to practice, etc. These tasks are not the same—running in tennis is different from running on a track—yet they are related. Perhaps the similarities between the thousands of tasks you learn are what enable you to learn any one of them, including tennis, given so little training data.

An artificial neural network trained tabula rasa on a single, isolated, complex task is unlikely to learn it. A net with a 1000 by 1000 pixel input retina will be unlikely to learn to recognize complex objects in the real world given the number of training patterns and amount of training time we can afford. It may be better to embed the net in an environment that simultaneously tasks it to learn many related tasks. If these tasks can share computed subfeatures, the net may find that it is easier to learn the tasks together than to learn them in isolation. Thus if we simultaneously train the net to recognize objects and object outlines, shapes, edges, regions, subregions, textures, reflections, highlights, shadows, text, orientation, size, distance, etc., it may be better able to learn to recognize complex objects in the real world. This is Multitask Connectionist Learning.

Multitask Learning (MTL) is predicated on the notion that tasks can serve as mutual sources of inductive

372

bias[1] for each other. MTL is one particular kind of inductive bias. It uses the information contained in the training signal of related tasks to bias the learner to hypotheses that benefit multiple tasks. One does not usually think of training data as a bias; but when the training data contains the teaching signal for more than one task, it is easy to see that, from the point of view of any one task, the other tasks' training signal may serve as bias. For this multitask bias to exist, the inductive learner must also be biased (typically via a simplicity bias) to prefer hypotheses that have utility across multiple tasks.

AN EXAMPLE OF MULTITASK CONNECTIONIST LEARNING

Consider the following four boolean functions defined on 8 binary inputs:

```
Task 1  =   B1   OR    Parity(B2-B8)
Task 2  =  -B1   OR    Parity(B2-B8)
Task 3  =   B1   AND   Parity(B2-B8)
Task 4  =  -B1   AND   Parity(B2-B8)
```

where Bi represents the ith bit, "−" is logical negation, and Parity(B2–B8) is the parity of bits 2–8.

These tasks are related in several ways: 1) all are defined on the same inputs (eight binary bits); 2) each is defined using a common computed subfeature (Parity(B2-B8); and 3) on those inputs where Task 1 must compute Parity(B2-B8), Task 2 does not need to compute parity, and vice versa. (Tasks 3 and 4 are related similarly.)

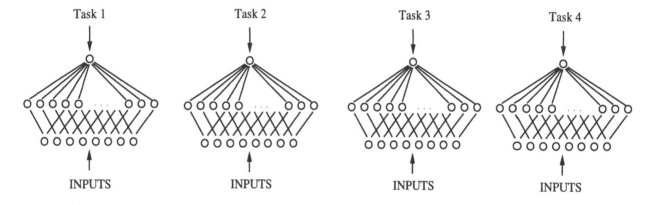

Figure 1: Single Task Learning (STL) of Four Functions Defined on the Same Inputs

Figure 1 shows the backprop nets one would typically train on these tasks. Since the tasks are independent, a separate net is used for each task. This is single task learning (STL). It is also possible, as shown in Figure 2, to use a single net to learn the four tasks at the same time. This is multitask learning (MTL).

The four graphs in Figure 3 show the generalization performance for single and multitask nets trained on Tasks 1–4. Each graph contains three generalization performance curves, one for that task trained in isolation, one for that task trained paired with another task (i.e., MTL with two tasks), and one for that task when all four tasks are trained together (i.e., MTL with four tasks). To simplify the presentation of the two-task multitask data, we present curves only for Tasks 1 and 2 trained together and for Tasks 3 and 4 trained together. Other task pairings yield similar results.

All runs used fully connected feed-forward nets with 8 input units, 160 hidden units, and 1–4 outputs. Nets were trained with backpropagation using MITRE's Aspirin/MIGRAINES 5.0 with learning rate = 0.1,

---

[1]Inductive bias is anything that causes an inductive learner to prefer some hypotheses over other hypotheses. Bias-free learning is impossible; in fact, much of the power of an inductive learner follows directly from the power of its inductive bias [7].

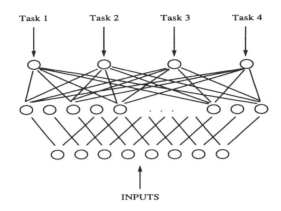

Figure 2: Multitask Learning (MTL) of Four Functions Defined on the Same Inputs

momentum = 0.9, and per-pattern updating. Training sets contained 64 patterns selected randomly from the 256 possible patterns. The remaining 192 patterns were used as a cross-validation hold-out set to measure generalization performance. Training sets were kept small to make generalization challenging. Each plot is the average of 20 runs.

The first graph in Figure 3 shows the average generalization performance during training for Task 1. The three curves represent the performance for Task 1 when trained alone, when trained with Task 2, and when trained with Tasks 2, 3, and 4. The poorest performance occurs when Task 1 is trained by itself (i.e., single task connectionist learning). Better generalization performance on Task 1 is achieved when a single net is trained on both Tasks 1 and 2 at the same time. And even better generalization performance is achieved by training all four tasks together on a single net. Similar results are found for the other tasks: for each task, better performance is achieved if that task is trained on a net that is trained simultaneously on the other tasks. (Note that better generalization performance is obtained without the need for additional training passes. The MTL run is computationally more efficient than the four STL runs it replaces.) To check the results presented graphically in Figure 3, an analysis of variance (ANOVA) of the peak generalization performances from each of the 20 training runs was also performed. This analysis confirms that MTL statistically outperforms STL at the .05 level.

Why is each task learned better if it is trained in the context of a net learning other related tasks at the same time? The MTL nets have sufficient capacity to learn each task independently—nets with less than 20 hidden units are adequate for these tasks. Other experiments confirm that backprop can separate unrelated tasks given sufficient net capacity and that excess capacity is not injurious to generalization on these tasks. We use large nets to minimize capacity effects when different *numbers* of tasks are trained on a net. Specifically, by using excess capacity we can be sure that the improved generalization performance is *not* due simply to multiple tasks constraining [2] the internal representation the hidden layer must learn—it must be a bias effect that arises from a beneficial summing of training signals in the aggregate gradient.

We have run two experiments to verify that the improved generalization performance of MTL is the result of a multitask inductive bias by ruling out two effects that do not depend on the tasks being related. The first effect is that adding noise to neural net learning sometimes improves generalization performance [6]. To the extent that the tasks are *uncorrelated*, their contribution to the aggregate gradient will appear as noise to other tasks and this might improve generalization. To test for this effect we trained nets on the tasks using random additional tasks. For example, we trained a four output net on Task 1 and three different random tasks. (Each random task was held constant during training—the random tasks are true functions.) Figure 4 shows the generalization performance for Task 1 multitask trained with three random functions. The performance for Task 1 when it is trained on nets simultaneously trained on random functions is similar to the performance for Task 1 trained alone. (When the other tasks are multitasked with random functions their performance drops slightly.) We conclude that it is unlikely that the MTL effect is due to the

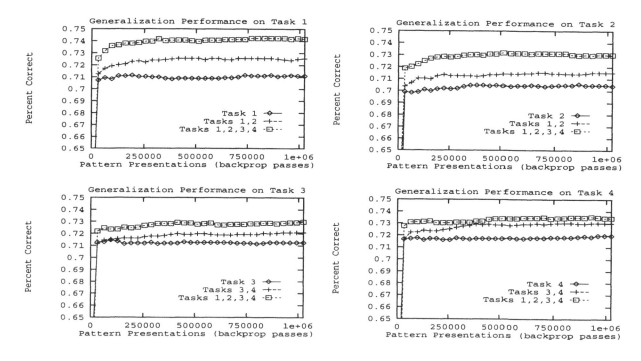

Figure 3: Generalization Performance of Single Task Learning and Multitask Learning on Tasks 1–4

uncorrelatedness of the multiple tasks serving as a beneficial source of noise. (Nets with 20 hidden units are able to train to 100 percent accuracy on one task and three random tasks, so net capacity is not artificially reducing performance with random functions.)

The second effect tested for is the possibility that adding tasks just changes the weight update dynamics to somehow favor nets with more tasks. To test for this we trained nets on "replicated" tasks. For example, a single net was trained on four copies of Task 1; each of its four outputs received exactly the same training signal. In this degenerate form of MTL each task correlates perfectly with the others and contributes no additional information and thus cannot serve as a source of knowledge-based inductive bias. Figure 4 also shows the performance of nets trained this way. (The performance for one output selected at random is shown.) Surprisingly, performance is better than for Task 1 trained in isolation. This improvement is gained without any additional information being given to the system. We can think of four explanations: 1) the extra copies increase the effective learning rate on the weights from the input layer to the hidden layer because their backpropagated error signals add; 2) the copies provide a better signal-to-noise ratio early in training when error signals are backpropagated through initially random weights because there are four times as many random weights from the output layer to the hidden layer; 3) having more weights connected to the same signal increases the odds that one of the weights will be close to a "good" value; and 4) the multiple connections to the hidden layer allow different hidden layer predictions to be averaged and thus act as a mechanism for combining multiple experts [8]. Work is currently underway to determine what mechanism(s) accounts for the observed performance increase. Fortunately, the replication effect is too small to explain all the MTL performance increase observed on Tasks 1–4 even if we assume it is somehow able to confer the same magnitude advantage for tasks as different as Tasks 1–4.

Is the MTL bias effect we observe large enough to be interesting? Probably. First, performance increased as the number of related tasks increased. In many domains it is surprisingly easy to add more tasks. The accumulated benefit of MTL might be significant in these domains. Second, generalization on small parity functions is hard. (Most studies learn parity by training on the complete set of patterns.) The fact that we see improved *generalization* on tasks that compute parity internally (but are not trained on any explicit

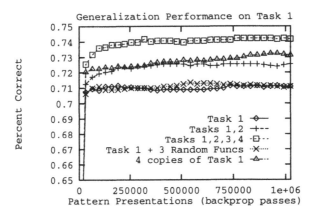

Figure 4: Performance of MTL Variants on Task 1

information about the parity function itself) is remarkable. Third, the networks have not been "told" that the tasks share a common computable subfeature and they differ significantly in how they use this subfeature. This represents a challenging case for MTL because the relationship between the tasks is buried deeply. Yet improvement occurs.

POTENTIAL DISADVANTAGES OF MTL

The advantages of MTL stem from the possibility that, if the tasks are related, information from the teaching signal of some task(s) might aid learning other tasks. But what are the potential disadvantages of using one net to learn several tasks?

1. Because the MTL net is learning several potentially competing tasks at the same time, the gradients computed from the error signal for each task may interfere. Fortunately, experiments suggest that backprop is able to separate uncorrelated tasks. The MTL aggregate gradients may still be flatter because they average several different error sources, but often they will point in directions beneficial to several tasks, i.e., towards more generally useful subfeatures.

2. The MTL net may begin to overtrain on different tasks at different times. If overtraining is prevented by halting training when the cross-validation generalization performance begins to drop, there will not be one place to stop training the MTL net to achieve peak generalization on all tasks. This is not really a problem, though. MTL requires that tasks are trained *in the context of other tasks,* not that learning produce a single net to use for all tasks. MTL can produce separate nets for each task, each representing the point where generalization performance peaked on that task. (We did this already for the ANOVA analysis.)

3. If the learning parameters (learning rate, momentum, etc.) must be set differently for different tasks, there may be no one setting appropriate to all the tasks. Where tasks require tweaking the learning parameters it may be impossible to train the tasks at one time. This may limit MTL's use in some domains.

HOW MTL CAN IMPROVE GENERALIZATION

There are several mechanisms by which MTL can improve generalization. MTL can provide a data amplification effect, can allow tasks to "eavesdrop" on features discovered for other tasks, and can bias the

376

net towards representations that might be overlooked or unlearnable if the tasks are learned separately.

The data amplification effect is best explained using Tasks 1–4. Both Task 1 and 2 need to compute the parity subfeature on half of the patterns, but Task 1 needs parity only on those patterns for which Task 2 does not, and vice versa. Thus the teaching signal for Task 1 provides information about parity half of the time and the teaching signal for Task 2 provides information about parity the other half of the time. A net trained on one of these tasks receives information about the parity subfeature only about half the time, whereas a net trained on both Tasks 1 and 2 gets information about the parity subfeature on every training pattern. *Both nets see exactly the same training patterns, but the multitask net is getting more information with each training pattern.* This can increase the effective sample size for a computed subfeature. To any one task, the other tasks are providing an inductive bias, i.e., a preference for hypotheses that more accurately compute common subfeatures. (This effect does not explain all the MTL performance observed on Tasks 1–4 because performance increases if Tasks 1 and 2 are trained with Tasks 3 and 4, yet Tasks 1 and 2 already "require" the parity subfeature for all patterns.)

"Eavesdropping" will be a common benefit of MTL. If tasks are related, it is likely that computed subfeatures needed by some tasks will sometimes be useful to other tasks. These subfeatures may not be learnable by the tasks that eavesdrop on them if they are trained separately, but might prove valuable sources of information when they are learned for other tasks.

MTL will sometimes bias nets to learn internal representations they would not learn if trained on tasks in isolation. For example, there are many representations nets can use for numeric quantities. If tasks require different properties of the representation (e.g., less sensitivity to noise like a Gray code or easy multiplication by powers of two like binary coding), these needs can influence the representation learned. Thus MTL may lead to the development of sophisticated representations that better capture the underlying structure of the domain [5] because they satisfy the needs of many tasks.

WHERE MULTIPLE TASKS COME FROM

Tasks 1–4 were carefully devised to be related in specific ways. Where will the additional tasks MTL requires come from for real-world problems? Often the real world gives us related tasks to learn at the same time if one avoids reductionism. For example, the Calendar Apprentice System (CAP) [3] learns to predict the location, time of day, day of the week, and duration of the meetings it schedules. These tasks are related; they are functions of the same data and share some common subfeatures. CAP currently learns these tasks independently. The MTL approach is to induce a single model for all four tasks at the same time.

It is not essential that a domain "naturally" present multiple related tasks to use MTL. MTL is a means of adding domain-specific inductive bias to an inductive system via additional teaching signal. For many domains it is surprisingly easy to devise additional related tasks. These might be semi-modular pieces of the larger task (e.g., tasking a robot to predict the trajectory of a ball when the full task requires the robot to catch the ball) or might be tasks that appear to require similar abilities as the given task(s). Acquiring the additional training signal is not trivial, but it is probably easier than asking domain experts to provide other forms of domain-specific inductive bias: domain experts excel at using their knowledge, but usually find codifying their knowledge difficult. MTL may be a convenient "pipe" through which to add domain-specific inductive bias. Note that MTL does not require that the training signals be available at run time. The training signals are needed only during training because they are outputs—not inputs—of the MTL net. Thus one is free to specify any feature or task that might be useful even if there will be no operational procedure to compute it later.

RELATED WORK

It is common to train artificial neural nets with many outputs. For example, in classification tasks it is common to use one output for each class. But using one net for a few strongly related tasks is also not new. The classic NETtalk [12] application uses one net to learn both phonemes and their stresses. *NETtalk is an example of multitask connectionist learning.* The multitask approach was natural for NETtalk because the goal was to learn to control a synthesizer that needed both phoneme and stress commands at the same time. (There is evidence that STL NETtalk performs far worse than MTL NETtalk [4].)

Work has been done to demonstrate that what is learned on one task can be used as a bias to aid other tasks learned later [10][11][13]. The key difficulties with these serial transfer approaches are: 1) it is difficult to scale the methods to long sequences of tasks; 2) the sequence in which the tasks will be learned must be defined manually; 3) learning tasks in sequence makes it harder for the net to devise complex representations satisfying the needs of many tasks; 4) if all the tasks are too hard to learn in isolation, sequential transfer will fail because it lacks the combined inductive bias at the most critical stage of learning: when it is first starting to develop an internal representation.

This work is most similar to Abu-Mostafa's catalytic hints [1][14]. We hope to advance the catalytic hints work in several ways:

1. by showing that tasks can be related in more diverse ways than hints yet still yield beneficial bias

2. by further exploring what mechanisms allow multiple tasks to serve as mutual sources of inductive bias

3. by demonstrating that creating new related tasks may be an efficient way of providing domain-specific inductive bias to learning systems

The empirical results for Tasks 1–4 begin to address these: Tasks 1–4 are not easily viewed as providing hints via constraints for each other, yet generalization performance increases when they are trained together.

SUMMARY

Acquiring domain-specific inductive bias is subject to the knowledge acquisition bottleneck. We suggest that one kind of domain-specific inductive bias is readily available if one avoids modularization, and that more can be acquired by collecting the teaching signal for additional tasks drawn from those domains. We describe several mechanisms by which this teaching signal can serve as an inductive bias when combined with a bias that prefers hypotheses benefiting several tasks. We provide an empirical demonstration that shows that even when the similarity between tasks is difficult to learn and recognize, MTL can improve generalization. We further demonstrate that this improvement is not easily attributed to capacity/constraint effects or to other effects not resulting from a mutual inductive bias due to similarity of the tasks.

We are currently applying MTL to other learning methods. For example, we have developed a multitask decision tree induction algorithm that automatically controls the strength of the multitask bias to prevent the decision trees from being so influenced by other tasks that they perform poorly on the main task(s). We are studying MTL in connectionist learning first, however, because there is an established methodology for training artificial neural networks with multiple outputs.

Precisely what is required for multitask connectionism to work is not known. We may have to devise new ways to help nets recognize common substructure and to "coerce" them to share representations for this substructure. We need to devise methods for detecting "eavesdropping" and for determining when new (or modified) internal representations have been learned. We need to understand better how tasks should be related for MTL to succeed. We need to demonstrate empirically that MTL can provide a strong enough inductive bias to be useful in complex tasks. (Work is currently underway to apply multitask connectionism to autonomous land-vehicle driving in ALVINN [9].) We conjecture that as the complexity of the domain increases, so too will the opportunity for creating additional related tasks. If this is true, MTL may provide a practical method of acquiring domain-specific inductive bias that scales naturally with the complexity of the task.

Acknowledgements

Thanks to Wray Buntine, Lonnie Chrisman, Jeff Jackson, Tom Mitchell, Jordan Pollack, Herb Simon, and Sebastian Thrun for their help in refining the ideas presented here.

This research was sponsored in part by the Avionics Lab, Wright Research and Development Center, Aeronautical Systems Division (AFSC), U. S. Air Force, Wright-Patterson AFB, OH 45433-6543 under Contract F33615-90-C-1465, Arpa Order No. 7597. The views and conclusions contained in this document are those of the authors and should not be interpreted as representing the official policies, either expressed or implied, of the U.S. Government.

References

[1] Y.S. Abu-Mostafa, "Learning From Hints in Neural Networks," *Journal of Complexity* 6:2, pp. 192–198, 1989.

[2] Y.S. Abu-Mostafa, "Hints and the VC Dimension," *Neural Computation,* 5:2, 1993.

[3] L. Dent, J. Boticario, J. McDermott, T. Mitchell, and D. Zabowski, "A Personal Learning Apprentice," *Proceedings of 1992 National Conference on Artificial Intelligence,* 1992.

[4] T.G. Dieterich, H. Hild, and G. Bakiri, "A Comparative Study of ID3 and Backpropagation for English Text-to-speech Mapping," *Proceedings of the Seventh International Conference on Artificial Intelligence,* pp. 24–31, 1990.

[5] G.E. Hinton, "Learning Distributed Representations of Concepts," *Proceedings of the Eight International Conference of The Cognitive Science Society,* pp. 1–12, 1986.

[6] L. Holmstrom, and P. Koistinen, "Using Additive Noise in Back-propagation Training," *IEEE Transactions on Neural Networks.* 3(1), pp. 24–38, 1992.

[7] T.M. Mitchell, "The Need for Biases in Learning Generalizations," Rutgers University: *CBM-TR-117,* 1980.

[8] M.P. Perrone, and L.N. Cooper, "When Networks Disagree: Ensemble Methods for Hybird Neural Networks," to appear in *Neural Networks for Speech and Image Processing,* 1993.

[9] D.A. Pomerleau, "Neural Network Perception for Mobile Robot Guidance," Carnegie Mellon University: *CMU-CS-92-115,* 1992.

[10] L.Y. Pratt, J. Mostow, and C.A. Kamm, "Direct Transfer of Learned Information Among Neural Networks," *Proceedings of AAAI-91,* 1991.

[11] L.Y. Pratt, "Non-literal Transfer Among Neural Network Learners," Colorado School of Mines: *MCS-92-04,* 1992.

[12] T.J. Sejnowski and C.R. Rosenberg, "NETtalk: A Parallel Network that Learns to Read Aloud," John Hopkins: *JHU/EECS-86/01,* 1986.

[13] N.E. Sharkey and A.J.C. Sharkey, "Adaptive Generalisation and the Transfer of Knowledge," University of Exeter: *R257,* 1992.

[14] S.C. Suddarth and A.D.C. Holden, "Symbolic-neural Systems and the Use of Hints for Developing Complex Systems," *International Journal of Max-Machine Studies* 35:3, pp. 291–311, 1991.

[15] A. Waibel, H. Sawai and K. Shikano, "Modularity and Scaling in Large Phonemic Neural Networks," *IEEE Transactions on Acoustics, Speech and Signal Processing,* 37(12), pp. 1888–98, 1989.

Estimating Learning Performance
Using Hints

Zehra Cataltepe and Yaser S. Abu-Mostafa
California Institute of Technology
Computer Science Department
Pasadena, CA 91125 USA
zehra@csvax.cs.caltech.edu

Learning from hints is a learning mechanism that unifies learning from examples and learning from explicit rules. Performance of the learning system on different hints may be used to estimate the learning performance of the system on the function. We develop a formula that estimates learning performance, without using a validation error, but only errors on hints. We give the derivation and test examples for this specific formula.

LEARNING FROM HINTS

Learning from hints [1], is a learning mechanism that unifies learning from examples and learning from explicit rules. It allows us to express rules in the form of examples and then use a learning-from-examples algorithm to teach this information to the system. Since usually we know more than just a finite set of input/output examples about a function, hints allow us to use the additional information, such as invariance properties, monotonicity, being binary, etc., in order to be able to achieve better solutions.

In the learning-from-examples paradigm, in order to measure how well a system has learned a function, the usual method is to set aside some examples of the function as a validation set, use the remaining examples as the training set and then test the performance using the validation set which is not used for training. Without a validation set, just accepting the performance on the training examples as the learning performance on the function usually does not give satisfactory results. The network sometime memorizes or overlearns those specific examples rather than the function we are trying to implement.

Being able to measure the learning performance without using a validation set would be useful. In this paper, using the idea that the learning performance can be measured by considering the performance on the hints that the function has as its properties, in addition to the performance of the function on training examples, we develop a formula for the learning performance of the function. We give the derivation, application example, and performance measurements for this formula.

TERMINOLOGY

We adopt the same terminology used in [2] in this paper. For the sake of completeness, we repeat what we need here.

The function that we are trying to implement using a learning-from-examples algorithm is $f : X \rightarrow Y$. In this paper we use $X = \mathcal{R}^n$ and $Y = [0, 1]$. The function being implemented by a given network is $g : X \rightarrow Y$, where X and Y are, usually, the same as in the definition of f. We consider the input/output pairs in the training set as a hint too and call it H_0. If we have N_0 examples in the training set, then H_0 is represented by the set of pairs $\{(x_i, f(x_i)) : 1 \leq i \leq N_0\}$. The error on the training set, or the hint H_0, is defined as:

$$E_0 = \frac{1}{N_0} \sum_{i=1}^{N_0} (f(x_i) - g(x_i))^2 \tag{1}$$

The validation or test error is defined in the same manner as:

$$E_t = \frac{1}{N_t} \sum_{i=1}^{N_t} (f(x_i) - g(x_i))^2 \tag{2}$$

where N_t is the number of test examples.

We use two types of invariance hints: H_1 is shift invariance, and H_2 is evenness in this paper. The estimates of error on these hints are given by:

$$E_1 = \frac{1}{N_1} \sum_{i=1}^{N_1} (g(x_i) - g(x_i'))^2 \tag{3}$$

$$E_2 = \frac{1}{N_2} \sum_{i=1}^{N_2} (g(x_i) - g(-x_i))^2 \tag{4}$$

for H_1 and H_2 respectively. In these formulas N_1 and N_2 are the number of examples we use to estimate the errors on H_1 and H_2 resp., x_i is any input to the network (not necessarily an example from the training set), and x_i' is a one-bit (cyclic) shifted version of the input vector x_i.

We define the learning error of the network on f as:

$$E = \mathcal{E}((f(x) - g(x))^2) \tag{5}$$

where $\mathcal{E}(.)$ denotes the expected value w.r.t. the probability distribution P of the input space. By the law of large numbers, E_t is very close in probability to E for large N_t. So throughout this paper, we take N_t to be large and treat E as the test error.

ESTIMATING LEARNING PERFORMANCE

In this section we give a derivation of a simple estimate of E for the case of binary functions. The ideas here can be generalized for non-binary functions.

Assume that we want to implement $f : \mathcal{R}^n \to \{0, 1\}$. Let's model the error of $g : \mathcal{R}^n \to [0, 1]$ on an example by a noise function n:

$$n(x_i) = |f(x_i) - g(x_i)| = \begin{cases} 1 - g(x_i), & \text{if } f(x_i) = 1; \\ g(x_i), & \text{if } f(x_i) = 0. \end{cases} \tag{6}$$

Assume that the noise function n has a mean μ and a variance σ^2. Then the learning performance of the network can be measured by:

$$E = \mathcal{E}((f(x) - g(x))^2) = \mathcal{E}(n^2(x)) = \mu^2 + \sigma^2 \tag{7}$$

Similarly, the error on any invariance hint can be measured by:

$$E_i' = \mathcal{E}((g(x) - g(x'))^2) = \mathcal{E}((n(x) - n(x'))^2) = 2\sigma^2 \tag{8}$$

assuming that $n(x)$ and $n(x')$ are independent random variables.

Since what we have are only estimates E_0 for E and E_1 and E_2 for E_1' and E_2' resp. we use these error estimates in formulas (7) and (8).

In order to get an estimate of μ, the mean of $n(x)$, we use the training set examples as follows:

$$[\mu^2] = \{ \frac{1}{N_0} \sum_{i=1}^{N_0} |f(x_i) - g(x_i)| \}^2 \tag{9}$$

Combining these formulas, we get an estimate of σ^2 as:

$$[\sigma^2] = \frac{2(E_0 - [\mu^2]) + E_1 + E_2}{6} \tag{10}$$

and finally, we get an estimate of E, using $E_i : (0 \le i \le 2)$ and $[\mu^2]$ as:

$$\hat{E} = [\sigma^2] + [\mu^2] \tag{11}$$

In order to give the reader a feel for how are E and E_0, E_1, and E_2 are related, we show E vs E_0, E_1, and E_2 for one specific run. For improving the visibility in the graph the points shown are averages over 10 actual points.

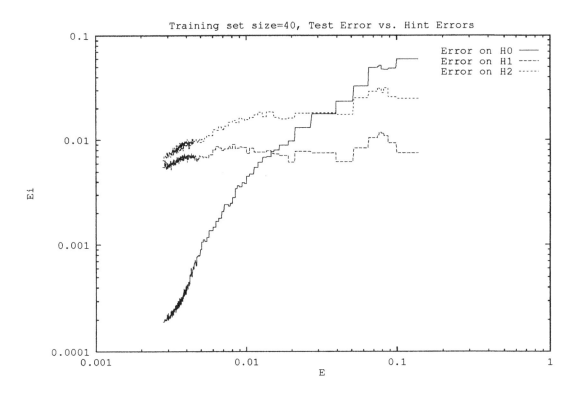

Figure 1: An Example of Test error vs. Errors on Hints.

In the following sections we give results of testing this formula $\hat{E}$.

EXPERIMENT

Functions to be Learned

In order to guarantee that the function we are trying to implement can be implemented by the neural network, we produce the function using a function-generating network. By imposing certain relationships between weights, we guarantee that the function generated by this network has the desired properties, such as being shift invariant, even, binary, etc. Then, we use this network to generate input/output examples of the function. In the learning phase, we begin with a network with random initial weights and the same architecture as the function generating network and use backpropagation learning [3].

Network Architecture

We used two layer feedforward networks with sigmoidal hidden and output units. All the functions were generated and taught by networks with 4 input, 8 hidden, and 1 output units.

Experimental Specifications

In this paper, we have experimented with three different functions, and a total of 27 runs with different initial conditions. The functions had two types of invariance properties, namely shift invariance(H_1) and evenness (H_2).

We chose the network inputs (i.e. input for function and hint examples) from the real numbers in the range [-1:1], the weights of the function-generating networks from [-3:+3], and the weights of the learning network from $[-1 : +1]$ uniformly. The reason why we chose larger range of weights for the generating network was to be able to cover a good portion of the output range of the sigmoid.

We generated 3 groups of training sets where each group contained training sets of size 20, 40, and 80. We trained each set using a specific set of initial weights. For each different training set, we taught the training examples (hint H_0) only.

We used backpropagation learning with a learning rate of 0.2, and momentum of 0.5. We trained the network for 5000 passes where at each pass we presented 20 examples from the training set. We used sequential mode of training, i.e. for each training example, we forwarded the inputs of the example, measured the training error, and then descended on this error.

EXPERIMENTAL RESULTS

Figures 2 through 4 show the pass number versus training error (E_0), test error (E), and the estimate of test error ($\hat{E}$) for training set sizes of 20, 40, 80. For the sake of improving visibility the points showed are averages of 20 pass intervals. These example runs have been chosen because they sample the kinds of behavior that we observed in all 27 different runs.

The most consistent observation for all these graphs is that, after the learning errors stabilize (i.e. after the first few hundred passes) $\hat{E}$ is always closer to E than E_0 is, and $\hat{E}$ roughly follows E by a nonincreasing difference. Since without $\hat{E}$ and E the only way of evaluating the learning error is E_0, in order to estimate how much better $\hat{E}$ is than E_0 we set the following criteria:

Find the test error, E, when minimum training error, E_0, is reached; and the test error when minimum $\hat{E}$ is reached; take the ratio of E at minimum E_0 over E at minimum $\hat{E}$. Let's call this ratio "**performance evaluation of the formula $\hat{E}$**". If the performance evaluation of the formula $\hat{E}$ is greater than 1, then $\hat{E}$ is performing better than E_0, and if it is less than 1, E_0 is better than $\hat{E}$.

Table 1 shows the minimum E_0, E at minimum E_0, minimum $\hat{E}$, E at minimum $\hat{E}$ and minimum E for different training set sizes. Figures 2 through 4, correspond to runs 1 through 3 in this table.

As it can be seen from Figure 2 and Figure 4, at runs 1 and 3 the network was "overtrained". By overtraining we mean "having an increase that survives, in the test error, E, while E_i is decreasing where H_i is a hint that is being taught to the network". In these runs E_0 kept decreasing, and when it was at its minimum value, E had a larger value than its minimum. However, $\hat{E}$ did not decrease as did E_0 at later passes, but followed E, and hence we have a better estimate of E using minimum $\hat{E}$ than using E_0.

In Figure 3, no overtraining took place, both E and E_0 were decreasing, and hence at the minimum of E_0, E had a small value too. $\hat{E}$ was outperformed in this case because it had small fluctuations that gave its global minimum before or after E reached its global minimum.

Table 2 shows the average performance evaluation of $\hat{E}$, for all runs we performed. On the average, $\hat{E}$ performed

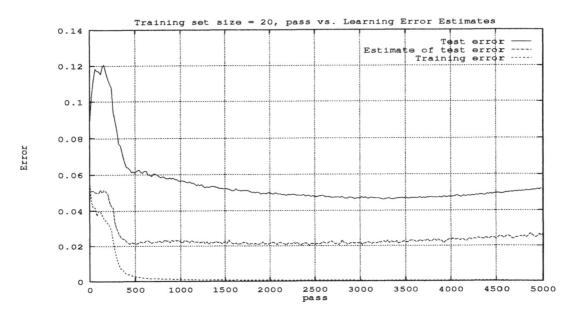

Figure 2: run 1

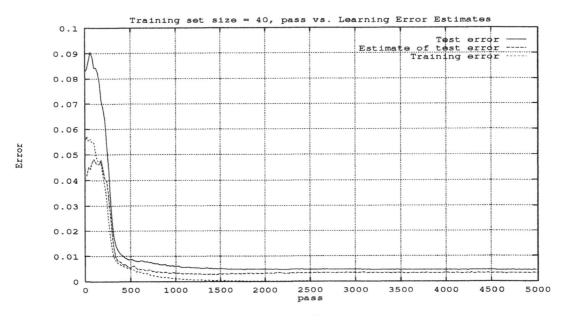

Figure 3: run 2

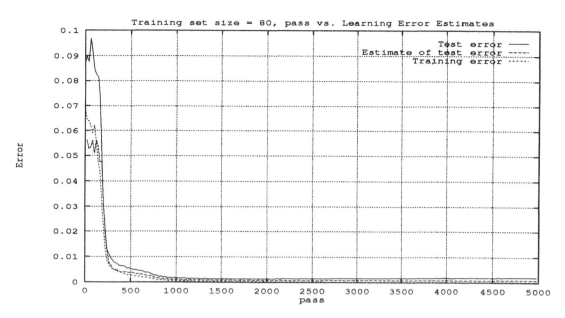

Figure 4: run 3

10% better than E_0. The second from last column of Table 2 shows the number of runs in which there was noticeable overtraining. Clearly, overtraining cases increase the performance of $\hat{E}$. Finally, the last column of Table 2 shows the number of cases in which performance of $\hat{E}$ was better than E_0, i.e. the number of cases where "performance evaluation" was greater than 1. $\hat{E}$ was better than E_0, 60% of the time in general.

Another statistic that can be obtained from Table 2 is the best and worst performance ratios for $\hat{E}$. At the worst case it was 10% poorer, and at the best case 84% better than E_0.

run	N_0	min E_0	E at min E_0	min $\hat{E}$	E at min $\hat{E}$	min E	performance
1	20	0.000071	0.050980	0.015157	0.046679	0.044892	1.092140
2	40	0.000031	0.004418	0.001676	0.004658	0.004343	0.948476
3	80	0.000075	0.001631	0.000394	0.001404	0.001224	1.161681

Table 1: Performance evaluation of formula $\hat{E}$ for runs in figures 2..4

Average	stddev	best	worst	no of runs	overtraining	better $\hat{E}$
1.099330	0.045083	1.837069	0.909091	27	8	16

Table 2: Average performance of formula $\hat{E}$

CONCLUSION

We have presented an example of derivation and test of a formula for the learning performance of an algorithm using hints. The formula we presented gave, in general, better approximation of learning error than the training error did. Different derivations with other types of hints, and different testing of formulas can be future research directions.

Acknowledgement

This work was supported by the AFOSR under grant number F49620-92-J-0398.

References

[1] Y.S. Abu-Mostafa, "Learning from Hints in Neural Networks," in *Journal of Complexity,* vol. 6, 1990, p. 192–198.

[2] Y.S. Abu-Mostafa, "A Method for Learning from Hints,", in *Advances in Neural and Information Processing Systems,* vol. 5, 1993, p. 73–80.

[3] D.E. Rumelhart, J.L. McClelland, R.J. Williams, "Learning Internal Representations by Error Propagation," in *"Parallel Distributed Processing,"* (D.E. Rumellhart *et al.,* Eds.) vol. 1, MIT Press, Cambridge, MA. 1986, pp. 318–362.

SIMULATION TOOLS

A Simulator for Asynchronous Hopfield Models

Arun Jagota
Department Of Computer Science
State University Of New York At Buffalo
Amherst, NY 14260 USA
jagota@cs.buffalo.edu

We describe a public-domain simulator specialized for discrete asynchronous Hopfield models. There is a careful efficient sequential implementation of asynchronous dynamics that is also well-suited to vector machines (the algorithm was implemented also on the Connection Machine CM-5 to confirm this). Any asynchronous dynamics and any on-line associative memory storage rule are supported. A symbolic input/output interface is provided: units are named; patterns are sets of ON units. Hashing is used for efficient symbol-to-unit mapping. The network grows during the training phase: units are automatically created for previously unseen symbols in the input. There is no inherent limit on the size of the network that may be created. The simulator has been instantiated for a special case of the discrete asynchronous Hopfield network proposed by the author. Over the last three years, it has been applied to associative memory problems (machine-printed word recognition; character restoration), knowledge representation, and combinatorial optimization (Approximating MAX-CLIQUE; Constraint Satisfaction Problems).

THE HOPFIELD MODEL

The discrete Hopfield network (HN) [5] (see [4] also) is a popular neural network model composed of units representing "neurons", connected pair-wise by symmetric real-valued weights representing "synapses". Each unit is ON or OFF and changes state based on input to it from other units. The power of HN lies in the demonstration that certain state update rules minimize an "energy" function, thereby guaranteeing convergence from any given initial state to some local energy minimum.

The appeal of HN also lies in its simplicity and hardware realizability (see [5, 6, 1, 4]). HN is also closely related to Ising spin models and has generated considerable interest in the statistical physics community (see [4]). It has also started receiving attention from the theoretical computer science community ([2, 18]). HN has found computational applications to associative memories and optimization problems (see [5, 7, 4]).

Formally, there are N units fully-connected by symmetric real-valued weights w_{ij}, with the self-weights $w_{ii} \geq 0$. Units have binary states: $S_i = 0$ (OFF) or $S_i = 1$ (ON) [1]. Unit S_i also has constant external input I_i. The input to unit S_i is:

$$n_i := \sum_j w_{ij} S_j + I_i \qquad (1)$$

Any asynchronous rule of the form: at time $t + 1$, pick one unit and update its state as follows:

$$S_i(t+1) := \begin{cases} 1 & \text{if } n_i(t) > 0 \\ 0 & \text{if } n_i(t) < 0 \\ S_i(t) & \text{otherwise} \end{cases} \qquad (2)$$

---

[1] An alternative formulation has $S_i \in \{-1, 1\}$

reduces the following energy function whenever a unit switches:

$$E = -\frac{1}{2} \sum_{ij} w_{ij} S_i S_j - \sum_i I_i S_i \tag{3}$$

thereby guaranteeing convergence from any initial state to some stable state [5]. Figure 1 shows a 5-unit HN (actually our special case).

SIMULATOR FEATURES

There is a need for a good simulator for the Hopfield model due to its popularity, applications, and the need to study its properties via simulation. In this article, we describe an efficient simulator (called **HS**) developed specifically for discrete asynchronous Hopfield models. This section describes its features; followed by a detailed example at the end. The next section discusses implementation details, the one following it presents an HN special case, and the final section summarizes applications of the special case on which the simulator has found serious use.

Input/Output Interface. Units have names. Binary patterns are represented by *sets* of ON units. Two modes are provided: *training* and *testing.*

Training Mode. A training pattern is represented by a set of the symbols representing the ON units (see examples at the end of this section). For a training set, the weights (or biases, for single-element sets) are adjusted according to the (on-line) storage rule. Individual sets may be preceeded by a nonnegative integer w (default 1) whose effect is as if the unweighted set were presented w times. This allows weighting of memories. The network starts off empty; as new symbols are seen in the input, new units are created. Any on-line rule—one that has access only to the current pattern and current weight values—may be implemented. The simulator is further optimized (see the next section) for a rule that adjusts *only* those weights connecting units that are *both* ON. We call such a rule *ON-triggered.* (The rule presented in the section introducing our Hopfield network special case is an example.)

Off-line Training. Some storage rules (e.g. the pseudo-inverse rule) are not suited for on-line implementation. Also, the weights for mapped optimization problems are usually derived directly from a hand-crafted energy function. Such off-line cases are handled as follows: (1) Design a rule that inputs binary (single-element) sets and increments the associated weight (bias) value by one; (2) Compute the weights (biases) off-line and transform the weights (biases) to integers; (3) Compute the minimum weight (bias) value and include it as the third (fourth) parameter in the configuration file (see paragraph: **Configuration**). All weights (biases) are initialized to this value; and (4) Compute the offset of each weight (bias) from this minimum value. Then train each weight (bias) as a binary (single-element) set and preceed the set by the offset of its weight (bias). See example.

Testing Mode. A test pattern is represented by a set of the symbols representing the units that are initially ON (the remaining units are initially OFF). Some elements of a test set may further be *clamped* (i.e, forced to remain ON during the dynamical evolution also). For each set, the (asynchronous) dynamics is invoked. It converges to a stable state which is then output as a set. Any symbols in the input not associated with units are ignored. The following options are provided: (1) Run dynamics for k cycles (instead of until convergence); (2) Output only stable state size (number of units ON); (3) Output the number of cycles to convergence; and (4) Perform energy-ascent (instead of energy-descent)

Configuration. The simulator uses a configuration file which must contain: (1) maximum number of units N, (2) weight learning rate (integer), (3) weight initial value (integer; same for all), (4) bias learning rate (integer), and (5) bias initial value (integer; same for all). **HS** allocates space for a fully-connected N-unit network, though running time of the dynamics depends only on the number of units currently in use. All weights and biases are integers for computational efficiency.

390

Debugging. Any submatrix of the weight matrix (subvector of the bias vector) may be displayed. A submatrix is identified by a set of row and a set of column indices; a subvector by a set of component indices.

Pre- and Post-processing. HS inputs from 'stdin' and outputs to 'stdout'. Unix pipes facilitate its convenient use, during training or testing, with pre- and post-processing programs. Two pairs of pre- and post-processing utilities are included in the package:

For Dictionaries. *'wrd_in'* inputs a collection of *strings* (on any alphabet) from 'stdin' and outputs a collection of *sets* to 'stdout'. *'wrd_out'* performs the reverse process. The string length is optionally included by *'wrd_in'* using the -s flag. For example:

```
wrd_in -s < input > output
wrd_out < output > new
cat input                  cat output                          cat new
dog dry                    { d1 o2 g3 3 } { d1 r2 y3 3 }       dog dry
```

An example of its use with **HS** , illustrating training of the words in the file 'input', followed by testing on the same words:

```
wrd_in -s < input | HS <network> -train
wrd_in < input | HS <network> -test | wrd_out > output
```

The file <network>.cfg must exist and is a configuration file (see Training and Testing example below).

For Binary Images. *'vis_in'* inputs a collection of two-dimensional binary *images* from 'stdin' and outputs a collection of *sets*. Each image is separated by a backslash. *'vis_out'* performs the reverse process. vis_in supports two options: either the output set contains the indices of all (black and white) pixels; or it contains the indices of only the black pixels. For these purposes, the image is interpreted as a vector rather than a matrix, in row-major convention. The following example illustrates the first option. The input file contains an image of the letter T.

```
vis_in < input > output
vis_out 3 < output > new
cat input        cat new          cat output
xxx              xxx              { x1 x2 x3 .4 x5 .6 .7 x8 .9 }
.x.              .x.
.x.              .x.
```

An example of its use with **HS** , illustrating training of the images in the file 'input', followed by testing on the same images:

```
vis_in < input | HS <network> -train
vis_in < input | HS <network> -test | vis_out 3 > output
```

Training and Testing Example. The following example uses the rooms example to illustrate the concepts discussed earlier. room.cfg is a configuration file, room.train is the training file, and room.test is a testing file. Invocations of HS for training, testing, and debugging are also shown. Symbols that are '*'-ed in room.test are clamped.

```
cat room.cfg
10 1 0 1 0

cat room.train
5 { ceiling walls fridge stove }  3 { ceiling walls tub toilet } 1 { ceiling walls bed dresser }
```

```
cat room.test
{ ceiling* walls* fridge }    { fridge tub bed* }

HS room -train < room.train
HS room -test < room.test > room.test.out
HS room -test
W { ceiling walls } { fridge stove }
W { ceiling } { walls fridge stove } I { ceiling walls }
```

The last invocation of **HS** illustrates use of debugging features: 'W' denotes "display the weight submatrix"; 'I' denotes "display the bias subvector".

Off-line Training Example. Consider storing the weight matrix $\begin{pmatrix} 0.0 & -0.5 & 0.4 \\ -0.5 & 0.0 & 0.3 \\ 0.4 & 0.3 & 0.0 \end{pmatrix}$ and the bias

vector $(-0.3, -0.2, 0.5)$. Note that the weights and biases are reals, however, we will store them using **HS** , using the method described earlier, as integers. As this involves only scaling by a constant, it affects neither the stable states nor the dynamical trajectories.

```
cat offline.cfg
3 1 -5 1 -3

cat offline.train
{ b }  8 { c } 5 { a a }  9 { a  c }  5 { b b }  8 { b c } 5 { c c }

HS offline -train < offline.train
HS offline
W { a b c } { a b c }
0 -5 4
-5 0 3
4  3 0
I { a b c }
-3 -2 5
```

IMPLEMENTATION DETAILS

Basic Data Structures. The set of ON unit indices V' is maintained as a linked list. Weight matrix $W \in Z^{N \times N}$ is maintained as a 2-d array; bias $I \in Z^N$ as a 1-d array.

Basic One-Set-Processing Algorithm. The simulator takes input from stdin, processing one set at a time as follows:

$V' \leftarrow$ Input_set_of_names_to_indices(mode);
if mode = training **then** storage_rule(V')   **else** { $V' \leftarrow$ Dynamics(V'); Display_as_names(V') }

Input_set_of_names_to_indices(mode) converts the unit names in an input set to their indices via hashing in very efficient constant time ($\leq$ 4 steps per conversion; independent of network size). If the mode is training then (1) a hash table entry is created for every name that does not map to an existing unit and (2) the weights of such a newly-created unit to other existing units (its bias) are initialized to the third (fifth) configuration parameter value. The indices of newly-created units are included in V'. If the mode is testing then names that do not map to existing units are ignored during the conversion.

Display_as_names converts the set of ON unit indices to a set of named units by direct indexing into an array of names, taking one step per conversion.

ON-triggered Storage Rule(V'). We ignore bias-learning and memory-weighting (w).

> for $i, j \in V'$ do $W[i,j] = W[j,i] \leftarrow f(i,j,W)$ endfor;

f is a user-supplied function. Though any on-line storage rule is supported, an ON-triggered rule, as described above, makes $\frac{|V'|(|V'|+1)}{2}$ f-evaluations. Any one of the following—a "naive" implementation of an ON-triggered rule, storage of non-sparse patterns ($|V'|$ is $\Theta(N)$) via a well-implemented ON-triggered rule, or an "all-pairs" on-line rule (such as the "generalized Hebb rule" of the Hopfield model)—require $\Theta(N^2)$ f-evaluations. To illustrate the time difference for sparse applications ($|V'| << N$), in one experiment, storage of 968 English words (sparse memories; $|V'| \leq 17$) in a 280-unit network via an ON-triggered rule took 15 seconds on a lightly loaded multi-macs encore 8-processor machine. Storage of 64 non-sparse memories ($|V'| = 280$) in a 280-unit network took 263 seconds under the same machine-load conditions.

Efficient Asynchronous Dynamics

Synchronous dynamics involves all the N^2 weights in each cycle; necessitating $\Theta(N^2)$ steps for a sequential implementation, or $\Theta(N^2)$ processors—one per weight—for an optimal parallel implementation.

Asynchronous dynamics however involves only the N weights connected to a switching unit (to propagate the effect of its switch to other units). Based on this observation, we develop an algorithm that realizes one asynchronous cycle (1) optimally (constant-time for "true" asynchronous updates) on a vector-machine with $O(N)$ processors and (2) in $\Theta(N)$ steps on a sequential machine.

Additional Data Structures. The following additional data structures may be realized as 1-d arrays on a sequential machine or as vector registers in a vector machine. Network state $S = (S_i) \in \{0,1\}^N$; vector of internal states $n = (n_i) \in Z^N$; vector of local unit energies $\Delta E = (\Delta E_i) \in Z^N$; vector of directions in which units can switch $V = (V_i) \in \{-1,0,1\}^N$; and the column-vector of unit i's weights: $W_i = (w_{ji})_i \in Z^N$.

Algorithm Dynamics(V').

$n \leftarrow I; \quad S \leftarrow \bar{0}$
for $i \in V'$ do $S_i \leftarrow 1; \quad n \leftarrow n + W_i$ endfor
loop

$$j:1,n \quad V_j \leftarrow \begin{cases} 1 & n_j > 0 \text{ and } S_j = 0 \\ -1 & n_j < 0 \text{ and } S_j = 1 \\ 0 & \text{otherwise} \end{cases}$$

$j:1,n \quad \Delta E_j \leftarrow -V_j n_j$
    $k \leftarrow F(\Delta E); \quad$ if $\Delta E_k \geq 0$ then exit
    if $V_k = 1$ then $\{ S_k \leftarrow 1; V' \leftarrow V' \cup \{k\}; n \leftarrow n + W_k \}$
    else $\{ S_k \leftarrow 0; V' \leftarrow V' \setminus \{k\}; n \leftarrow n - W_k \}$
endloop

F is a user-supplied function that returns the index of a unit that may switch (may return any index if no unit can switch). Let c denote the number of cycles to convergence.

Parallel Implementation Issues. A parallel implementation of this algorithm, with specialized hardware, requires only $O(N)$ processing elements. N^2 memory elements are needed however, to store the weights. The for loop may be implemented by a shift register which stores the *indices* of the units that are ON. The computation of F may require special circuitry. We assume that every vector operation—except the computation of F—takes one step each. An F-evaluation depends on the dynamical rule (constant time for the "weakest" stochastic rule; up to $\log N$ time for a "global" rule like steepest descent). The first *for* loop involves $O(|V'|)$ vector steps; the second *loop* $O(c)$ vector steps plus c F-evaluations. Hence the overall algorithm performs $O(|V'| + c)$ vector steps plus c F-evaluations. For "almost all" asynchronous Hopfield nets, c is $\Omega(|V'|)$. In this case, the algorithm running time is $O(c)$ vector steps plus c F-evaluations. This is asymptotically optimal (even $\Theta(N^2)$ processors do not reduce the time).

Sequential Implementation Issues. A sequential implementation of this algorithm is obtained by serializing every vector operation. For all reasonable F's, an F-evaluation takes $O(N)$ steps. Each vector operation takes $O(N)$ steps. Thus the sequential running time is $O(N(|V'| + c))$ steps. Again, since c is typically $\Omega(|V'|)$, the sequential running time in this case is $O(Nc)$. The sequential running time of a "naive" implementation is a much slower $\Omega(N^2 c)$.

Current Implementations. As of the time of writing, the simulator has been implemented in C, for sequential machines, and used extensively on the following machines: SUN Sparc-stations I, II, X, Multimacs Encore, and VAX 11/750. The simulator has also been implemented on the Connection Machine CM-5 in the language CM-Fortran. The Fortran 90 features of CM-Fortran were used to advantage to implement the vector operations employed in the above algorithm (**Algorithm Dynamics**). The CM-5 version of the simulator is still experimental and not very efficient.

Acquiring the Simulator. The simulator is available via anonymous ftp as follows:

```
ftp ftp.cs.buffalo.edu (or 128.205.32.9 subject-to-change)
Name : anonymous
> cd users/jagota
> get hsn.README
> binary
> get hsn.tar.Z
> quit
```

hsn.tar.Z contains the source code, examples, script sessions of test runs, and informal documentation. Neither binaries nor any documentation more detailed or clearer than the current paper are available at this time. The simulator is also available via e-mail from the author.

HOPFIELD-CLIQUE SPECIAL CASE

The simulator has been used primarily on a Hopfield model special case called the *Hopfield-clique Network* (HcN) [14, 13] which employs "binary" [2] weights: $w_{ij} = w_{ji} \in \{\rho, 1\}$ where $\rho << 0$. $w_{ii} = 0$. Units receive an equal positive bias $I_i = w_0 > 0$. Recently, it has been shown that a network implemented in optics [17] is in fact equivalent to HcN in its stable states [3]. Underlying HcN's weight matrix is an undirected graph $G_N = (V, E)$ whose vertices are the units and edges are the positive weights. Figure 1 shows an HcN weight matrix W and its underlying graph G_N.

Stable States. In a graph, a *clique* is a set of vertices such that every pair is connected by an edge. A clique is *maximal* if no strict superset is also a clique. For sufficiently small w_0 and for $\rho < -N$, the stable states of HcN are exactly the maximal cliques of its underlying graph G_N. With $\rho < -5$, the HcN of Figure 1 has two stable states: {a,b,d,e} and {c,d,e}. HcN's stable states as maximal cliques are the basis for graph-theoretic analyses of HcN (see [14, 13]) and all its applications (see [9, 15, 11]).

Storage Rule. HcN employs the following on-line ON-triggered memory storage rule, implemented in the simulator. Assume $\rho < -N$. Initial weights state: For all $i \neq j$, $w_{ij}(0) = \rho$. A set S of units (that are ON) defines a memory. S is stored as follows. For all $i \neq j$,

$$w_{ij}(t+1) := \begin{cases} 1 & \text{if units } i \text{ and } j \text{ are in the set } S \\ w_{ij}(t) & \text{otherwise} \end{cases} \qquad (4)$$

Upon storage of: {a,b,d,e} and {c,d,e}, HcN has the graph G_N of Figure 1. When $\rho < -5$, the stable states are the maximal cliques of G_N, the stored memories. Any graph may be stored via this rule by storing its edges as sets of two ON units. The storage rule provides **stable** storage to arbitrary collections of N-bit vectors (using $2N$ units) and to other discrete structures [14, 13].

---

[2] A continuous-weights version of HcN has also been used: $w_{ij} = w_{ji} \in \{\rho\} \cup (0, 1]$

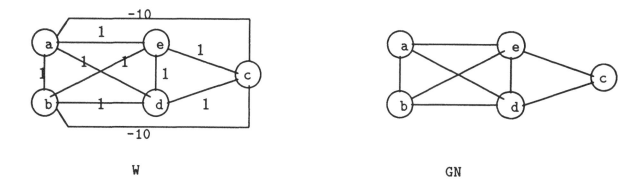

Figure 1: A 5-unit HcN instance and its underlying graph G_N

Steepest Descent Dynamics. HcN employs the following dynamics, implemented in the simulator. In a cycle, a unit whose switch reduces the energy maximally is switched. That is: Switch S_i: $\Delta E_i = \min_{S_j}(\Delta E_j)$. Steepest Descent on HcN has a useful graph-algorithmic characterization [14, 12, 11] and applications to associative memories [9] and optimization [11].

Additional Simulator Issues for HcN. Steepest descent on HcN has the following property: All switch-OFF's occur before any switch-ON's. The simulator provides an option to terminate its dynamics before the first switch-ON occurs. This is useful to perform only the "noise-removal" phase in associative memory error-correction. With any asynchronous dynamics, HcN converges in $O(N)$ cycles [13]. On sparse memories and sparse input ($|V'| << N$), HcN converges in $O(|V'|)$ cycles [14]. Hence, the sequential running time of the dynamics algorithm of Section is $O(N^2)$ and $O(N|V'|)$ for the non-sparse and sparse cases respectively, which is very efficient for a sequential simulation and also exploits sparse memories.

APPLICATIONS SUMMARY

Over the last few years, the HcN-instantiated simulator has been used on several applications. Training times of a network instance ranged from minutes to a few hours on SUN Sparc-station II machines.

Degraded printed word recognition given a dictionary [9]. HcN's stable storage has guaranteed that all stored words are "remembered"; noise-removal steepest descent (using only its switch-OFFs phase) has provided good partial error-correction even under overloaded conditions. Network size: 300 units. Memories sparse: ≤ 13 units each.

Degraded printed character restoration given perfect characters [8]. The network has exhibited some promise (good restorations) but also problems (restoration quality is sensitive to training set size/attributes). Network size: 512 units. Memories non-sparse: 256 units each.

Constraint Satisfaction Problems (see [16]) represented in HcN and N-queens solved approximately [10]. Maximum network size: 2500 units.

The NP-hard problem of finding the largest clique in a given graph approximately solved via HcN [11]. A given graph is stored in HcN by storing its edges using the HcN storage rule. Whereas several other HcN dynamics were evaluated on this problem, steepest descent remained competitive [11]. Maximum network size: 800 units.

All above applications use only the simulator features presented in this paper (chiefly HcN storage rule;

steepest descent dynamics).

References

[1] N. Farhat, D. Psaltis, A. Prata, and E. Paek, "Optical implementation of the Hopfield model," *Applied Optics*, vol. 24, 1985.

[2] P. Floreen and P. Orponen, "On the computational complexity of analyzing Hopfield nets," *Complex Systems*, vol. 3, pp. 577–587, 1989.

[3] T. Grossman and A. Jagota, "On the equivalence of two Hopfield-type networks," in *IEEE International Conference on Neural Networks*, pp. 1063–1068, IEEE, 1993.

[4] J. Hertz, A. Krogh, and R. Palmer, *Introduction to the Theory of Neural Computation*. Addison-Wesley, 1991.

[5] J. Hopfield, "Neural networks and physical systems with emergent collective computational abilities," *Proceedings of the National Academy of Sciences, USA*, vol. 79, 1982.

[6] J. Hopfield, "Neurons with graded responses have collective computational properties like those of two-state neurons," *Proceedings of the National Academy of Sciences, USA*, vol. 81, 1984.

[7] J. Hopfield and D. Tank, ""Neural" computation of decisions in optimization problems," *Biological Cybernetics*, vol. 52, pp. 141–152, 1985.

[8] A. Jagota, "Applying a Hopfield-style network to degraded printed text restoration," in *Conference on Neural Networks and PDP, Indiana-Purdue*, (West Lafayette, Indiana), pp. 20–30, Fort Wayne, April, Purdue Research Foundation, 1990.

[9] A. Jagota, "Applying a Hopfield-style network to degraded text recognition," in *International Joint Conference on Neural Networks*, vol. 1, (New York), San Diego, July, IEEE, 1990.

[10] A. Jagota, "Backtracking dynamics in a Hopfield-style network," in *International Joint Conference on Neural Networks*, (New York), Seattle, July, IEEE, 1991. Abstract in Proceedings.

[11] A. Jagota, "Efficiently approximating Max-Clique in a Hopfield-style network," in *International Joint Conference on Neural Networks*, vol. 2, (New York), pp. 248–253, Baltimore, June, IEEE, June 1992.

[12] A. Jagota, "A Hopfield-style network as a maximal clique graph machine," Tech. Rep. 90-25, Department of Computer Science, SUNY at Buffalo, Buffalo, NY, 1990.

[13] A. Jagota, "A Hopfield-style network with a graph-theoretic characterization," *Journal of Artificial Neural Networks*, 1992. To Appear.

[14] A. Jagota, "A new Hopfield-style network for content-addressable memories," Tech. Rep. 90-02, Department of Computer Science, SUNY at Buffalo, Buffalo, NY, 1990.

[15] A. Jagota, "Representing discrete structures in a Hopfield-style network," in *Neural Networks in Knowledge Representation and Inference* (D. Levine and M. Aparicio, eds.), Lawrence Erlbaum Associates, 1992. To be Published.

[16] A. Mackworth, "Constraint satisfaction," in *Encyclopedia of Artificial Intelligence, Second Edition* (S. Shapiro, ed.), (New York), pp. 285–290, John Wiley and Sons, 1992.

[17] I. Shariv, T. Grossman, E. Domany, and A. Friesem, "All-optical implementation of the inverted neural network model," in *Optics in Complex Systems*, vol. 1319, SPIE, 1990.

[18] J. Wiedermann, "On the computational efficiency of symmetric neural networks," *Theoretical Computer Science*, vol. 80, pp. 337–345, 1991.

An Object-Oriented Dataflow Approach for Better Designs of Neural Net Architectures

Alexander Linden
Adaptive Systems Research Group
German National Research Center for Computer Science
D-53 757 Sankt Augustin
Alexander.Linden@gmd.de

It is argued that the state-of-the-art for design and simulation tools for NN architectures is still not satisfactory. The approach presented in this paper is a very general block diagram approach formalized as data flow graphs. A prototype called SESAME[1] [10] has been implemented in C++. We show that SESAME improves the state-of-the-art in neurosimulation considerably. It allows elegant and extensible construction of multiple neural net paradigms and combinations thereof. The basic framework includes run-time parameterized multiple inheritance, nested parametrization and automated checks of wellformedness, which in practice turn out to be remarkably useful. For illustration it is shown how to specify arbitrary back propagation architectures. The presented framework conforms to the latest findings of software engineering with respect of reuse and extensibility [5].

MOTIVATION

Why are better programming environments for neural net architectures important? Their primary purpose is to increase the productivity of researchers and developers in the field. Research in neural networks is very experimental by nature. In practice, simulation is often the only way of analysis. Thus, the quality of the computer environment, i.e. the tool for specification and simulation, is of crucial importance. In addition to increasing the researchers' individual productivity, there are other benefits as well to having very powerful design and simulation tools. Designing neural networks is quite error-prone; errors may remain unrecognized, only causing a somewhat different system behavior. Widely used tools offer means of validation. Researchers can compare their new neural net architectures more thoroughly with others. World wide collaborations would be easier by exchange of modules, training algorithms, architectures and whole experiments.

I am not arguing here that *one* world wide standard would be a desirable or feasible goal. As in the domain of conventional programming languages, there probably will not be one simulation system equally appropriate to all different neural network paradigms. Nevertheless, better tools than existing ones have large potential.

The first section tries to capture some of the state-of-the-art and discusses the deficiencies of some of the most well-known approaches so far. In the second section, I will present the basic concepts of SESAME[1] [10] and recent advances. The approach is based on an object-oriented dataflow model and there exists a prototypical implementation in C++ which is freely obtainable (see end of this paper). I will illustrate the potential of this approach with several examples. Illustrations are given for supervised learning with multilayer nets. It is pointed out that other paradigms also fit nicely into the proposed framework. It is shown that arbitrary back propagation architectures can be constructed in a correct way. The paper concludes with a discussion about the advantages of this approach and a future perspective.

---

[1] Software Environment for the Simulation of Adaptive Modular systEms.

STATE OF THE ART

The state of the art is very diffuse and difficult to capture. A really serious evaluation of *all* approaches would involve several person-years and has not yet been done in the literature available to the author. There are various reasons for these difficulties.

- There exists several dozens of software systems called "neurosimulators", but also numerous packages in similar domains, like Khoros [16] for vision processing, or Simulink/Matlab^{TM} from Mathworks for control engineering, must be considered.
- There are other relevant research domains, which consider specification and simulation tools: Software engineering has invented *module interconnection languages*, having its roots in algebraic specification languages; VLSI-Design offers tools for the specification of integrated circuits.
- Software tools are difficult to evaluate in general.

Due to the flood of neurosimulation tools, many researchers are tired of hearing about "just yet another" simulator. However, the fact is that most researchers still use their own software, which underlines that the state-of-the-art is *not* satisfactory. I present a brief evaluation of some of the most well-known neurosimulators and point out some of their main deficiencies. I do not mean to imply that the simulation tools below are not useful or important — they certainly are. I will judge these systems along only a few dimensions. Emphasis is not put on their user interface or graphical abilities, rather on the clarity, expressive power, and extendibility of their description language.

Rochester-Simulator [2] has been the first serious neurosimulator and is a large library of C-Routines with X-Window-based run-time support. While being very flexible, it has no powerful language constructs. It requires the user to have good C programming capabilities and good knowledge of the internals if extending the simulator. The project stopped in early 1990.

SNNS [20] is clearly inspired by the Rochester-Simulator, also written in C, but offering a nicer graphics interface. Unfortunately, it does not have a systematic background. There are several deficiencies: Although it offers quite a lot of predefined NN architectures, it does not allow combinations thereof, thus limiting its expressive power. Also extension with new algorithms does not seem to be trivial. Clarity and flexibility suffers from the lack of encapsulated building blocks and object-orientation.

Aspirin/Migraines V6.0 [9], Planet [14], Xerion [19] are quite similar development environments. Their concepts are centered around building blocks, and all three use a nice description language. However, their building blocks are not very general. They seem unable to accept multiple typed data sinks and data sources. It is not easy to see how different learning paradigms can be integrated in a straightforward way. But the worst thing is that their expressive power is limited due to the fact that most of the functionality is handled in a hidden, implicit way. Planet seems in that context conceptually better organized than the other two. It allows one to define different flow of controls for a specific architecture. Instead Xerion and Aspirin define their control flow, by default, corresponding to the order in which elements are created. All three simulators handle back propagation, in a more implicit way, which limits their flexibility. Extensions still require a lot of understanding of the internals, but seem much easier than in SNNS.

Galatea [13], Khoros [16], Simulink/Matlab (from MathWorks) are more advanced. Their building blocks approach seems to be sufficiently general to support a wide variety of models. Flow of control is not handled implicitly. Despite the fact that they have much better conceptualization than the above, there are still severe drawbacks. Actually they have not yet begun to exploit the benefits of the building blocks approach, e.g. there is no multiple inheritance, automatic configuration, or nested parametrization (these concepts, which are more useful than one would believe, will be illustrated later in this paper). Even further, only Galetea is object-oriented. Another drawback is that all three environments are or will be commercial products. Finally all three are quite large compared to their functionality, which generally has negative effects on their extendibility; the documentation of Khoros, for example, has more than 2000 pages.

The four most severe disadvantages are: a) all approaches besides the last three offer either no or too specialized building block abstractions, b) no simulator is able to apply different training algorithms generically to arbitrary functional architectures, c) most of them require the user to learn about C, C++, or another complicated language. What is needed is a much more elegant description language, with only very few elements, while being very general and flexible, d) besides Galatea none of the other simulators are really object-oriented, which seems to be a must especially in neurosimulation. But Galatea does not allow (multiple) inheritance at run-time.

SESAME – ITS BASIC CONCEPTS

The objects studied in the field of neural nets are usually vectors, and the operations are mathematical functions of varying complexity. This abstraction facilitates a particular way of representing systems widely used in literature: namely *block diagrams*, which have been formalized as *data flow graphs (DFGs)* in computer science. The central idea of data flow graphs is the representation of programs as directed graphs (block diagrams). The nodes or blocks perform computations, whereas the arcs or connections specify the data dependencies. We distinguish between basic blocks and composite blocks.

A basic block consists of a) a list of data sinks, where it receives input data; b) a list of data sources to send internal data to other blocks; c) a list of built-in methods; d) internal data, e.g. activation vectors, and weight matrices; and e) a set of symbols or parameters such as learning rate, and size of activation vector. A method — in SESAME usually implemented as a C++ member function of the corresponding block class — reads data from the sinks, changes internal data via computational transformations, and makes (some of) its internal data visible to other blocks. Basic blocks can be class instances of different granularity. They can model neurons, whole layers of neuron, neural nets, or even full applications. Very often used building blocks are pattern sets, tapped delay line blocks, process simulations, and arbitrary mathematical transformations, e.g. the logistic function. But building blocks can also represent interfaces to I/O devices, as the filesystem, graphics windows, hardware drivers for robot arms. Also fuzzy-rule interpreters, and whole expert systems might be considered as building blocks.

Composite blocks are necessary for reuse but also for transparency when architectures grow larger. They also have lists of data sinks and sources, allowing them to get reused in even larger architectures. They may contain any interconnected set of smaller blocks, which can be either of basic or composite form. In that sense, composite blocks are block diagrams. Data sinks of a composite block can be connected with data sinks of subblocks, and data sources of subblocks can be connected to data sources of the composite block. The behaviors of composite blocks are described by scripts, which contain sequences of method calls to subblocks or simple control structures such as while-loops, if-then-else clauses, etc. Composite blocks can be used from the outside in the same way as basic ones. This framework is general enough to allow for universal computations. A proof is similar to a proof for Petri-nets. A formalization of the framework is in preparation.

Autoconfiguration is the process that can simplify the construction of large architectures quite a lot. It saves the users' time because it can automatically determine dataformats (e.g. sizes and ranges) of data sinks, data sources, and internal data, where possible. Also there are criteria for the wellformedness of block diagrams which lead to safer design. Inconsistencies and underspecifications can be detected automatically in the following way.

There are two different sources of dataformat constraints: the topology and the basic building blocks. Each connection between a source and a sink implies that the corresponding dataformats are identical. Basic block themselves define dataformats for or constraints between their sinks, sources and internal data. Consider, for example, a FileReader block, which simply looks up the dataformats from its pattern file, thus provides *initial* data format information. The same is true with various process simulation blocks, that define dataformats for state and control data sink and sources. On the other hand, a tapped delay line block, also called TimeWindow, defines a *constraint* on the sizes of its dataformats stating that the size of the incoming vector times the window size equals the size of the outgoing vector.

A resolving strategy now tries to determine dataformats from the global set of dataformat constraints. It yields one of three possible results (more details in [11]): **a)** *underspecification failure*, if format information is missing, e.g. the number of hidden units or a connection between blocks have been forgotten; **b)** *inconsistency failure*, if the design is inconsistent, e.g. if there is a wrong connection between two blocks, that require different dataformats; **c)** *success*, if every format has been determined correctly.

Parameterized Multiple Inheritance The strict division of any neural net experiment into three parts: a) topology of building blocks, b) flow of control between building blocks, and c) the C++-implementation of building blocks leads to a very simple and uniform design with only very few construction principles. Multiple inheritance is implemented in that framework by building the set-theoretic union of parameters, blocks, topology and scripts. Even further this can be accomplished during *run-time*, and thus provides a powerful way of building taxonomies without running into the combinatorical explosion of classes.

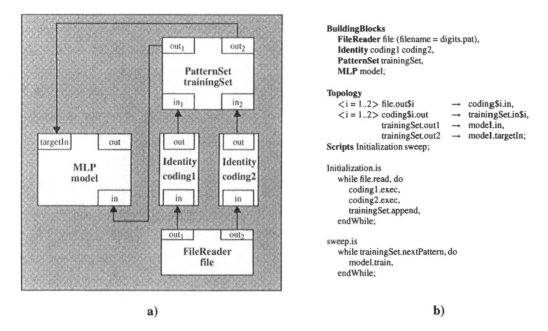

```
BuildingBlocks
    FileReader file (filename = digits.pat),
    Identity coding1 coding2,
    PatternSet trainingSet,
    MLP model;

Topology
    <i = 1..2> file.out$i          →  coding$i.in,
    <i = 1..2> coding$i.out        →  trainingSet.in$i,
                trainingSet.out1   →  model.in,
                trainingSet.out2   →  model.targetIn;
Scripts Initialization sweep;

Initialization.is
    while file.read, do
        coding1.exec,
        coding2.exec,
        trainingSet.append,
    endWhile;

sweep.is
    while trainingSet.nextPattern, do
        model.train,
    endWhile;
```

a)   b)

Figure 1: **a)** Is the block diagram representation of a simple supervised learning experiment in SESAME. Part **b)** shows the corresponding textual description.

EXAMPLES

Despite the generality of SESAME, this section will focus more on supervised learning and gradient descent because of their popularity. The next subsection presents a full example for a supervised learning experiment using the well-known multilayer net architecture. The second subsection shows how to construct arbitrary back propagation based gradient descent architectures in a provably correct way. Subsequent subsections will give brief discussions of other neural net paradigms.

Supervised Learning with Multilayer Perceptrons   SESAME offers a simple script language to define block diagrams. Fig. 1.a) shows the block diagram representation and 1.b) its corresponding textual description for a rudimentary supervised learning experiment. A *FileReader* block called *file* provides read-access to the filesystem to get the training patterns. Each pattern consists of an input and a target part. Coding blocks (here only the *Identity*) preprocess the different parts of a pattern coming from *file*. The *PatternSet*, named as *trainingSet*, receives and stores each (preprocessed) input and target vector. The composite building block of type *MLP*, named *model*, will receive these patterns successively from the *trainingSet*. The internal structure of an *MLP* is depicted in fig. 2.

The initialization phase is defined through a script called *Initialization*, which reads from file each pattern, and get each preprocessed and appended to the *trainingSet*. The *sweep*–script calls a method *nextPattern* on the *trainingSet*, causing an internal pointer to be incremented and the corresponding pattern to be sent to the *in*- and *targetIn*-sinks of the *MLP*. They are passed immediately to the corresponding sinks of the subblocks (see fig. 2.a). After that, the method *train* is called at the *MLP* causing a forward pass, a backward pass, and an update (see fig. 2.c).

Let us now define the semantics of each of the building blocks used in fig. 2.b) more thoroughly: The method *prop* of a building block of type *BPLinear* computes $A \cdot x + b$, where, in NN terminology, A is the internal "weight" matrix, b are the internal "biases", and x is the (input or hidden) vector to be received from the *in*-sink. The prefix BP of BPLinear means that it is able to backpropagate through incoming error signals according to the chain rule of differentiation (for a detailed discussion see below). The *prop* method of *BPLogistic* transforms incoming vectors with the logistic function. The whole script *prop* of composite block *MLP* defines $OUT = Logistic(A2 * Logistic(A1 * IN + b1) + b2)$. The script *propErr* defines the flow of control for corresponding error back propagation. See below for a much more detailed discussion.

400

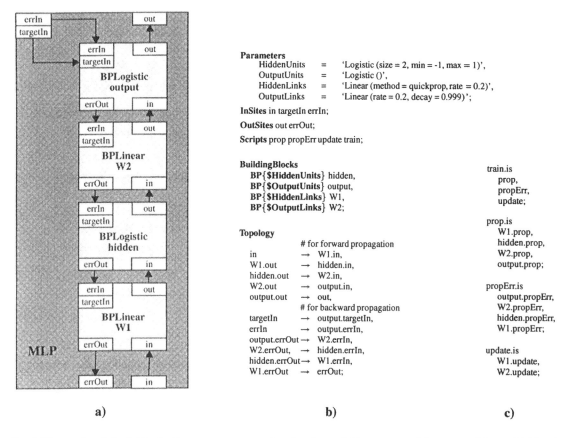

Parameters
HiddenUnits	=	'Logistic (size = 2, min = - 1, max = 1)',
OutputUnits	=	'Logistic ()',
HiddenLinks	=	'Linear (method = quickprop, rate = 0.2)',
OutputLinks	=	'Linear (rate = 0.2, decay = 0.999)';

InSites in targetIn errIn;

OutSites out errOut;

Scripts prop propErr update train;

BuildingBlocks
BP{$HiddenUnits} hidden,
BP{$OutputUnits} output,
BP{$HiddenLinks} W1,
BP{$OutputLinks} W2;

Topology

for forward propagation
in	→	W1.in,
W1.out	→	hidden.in,
hidden.out	→	W2.in,
W2.out	→	output.in,
output.out	→	out,

for backward propagation
targetIn	→	output.targetIn,
errIn	→	output.errIn,
output.errOut	→	W2.errIn,
W2.errOut,	→	hidden.errIn,
hidden.errOut	→	W1.errIn,
W1.errOut	→	errOut;

train.is
    prop,
    propErr,
    update;

prop.is
    W1.prop,
    hidden.prop,
    W2.prop,
    output.prop;

propErr.is
    output.propErr,
    W2.propErr,
    hidden.propErr,
    W1.propErr;

update.is
    W1.update,
    W2.update;

a)   **b)**   **c)**

Figure 2: **a)** Shows the default block diagram representation for the multilayer net architecture with one hidden layer of units. **b)** The corresponding textual representation for the topology, and **c)** for the flow of control.

Through *parametrization* a new type of multilayer net can be created having the *SoftMax* function as activation function at the output, which has been proven very good in the case of classification (e.g. see M. Finke and K.-R. M"uller, this volume). In order to change the architecture, the corresponding line in fig. 1.b) should read *MLP (OutputUnits = 'SoftMax ()') model;*. The parameter *OutputUnits* is expanded by {*$OutputUnits*} such that *'BPSoftMax ()'* becomes the string denoting the type of the *output* building block. There is no difference between composite or basic class names. Thus changing the line by *MLP (OutputLinks = 'MLP (OutputUnits = Identity)')* would create a multilayer perceptron within a multilayer perceptron, which results in this case in a two-hidden-layered MLP. Note that this is only an illustration of the concept of *nested parametrization* and not a recommended way here, but for committee learning architectures as the Hierarchy of Experts [6] this concept is of great utility.

Note also that by simple *inheritance* the standard MLP can be extended with direct links between the input and output layer, just adding a new building block (*BPLinear*), a few arcs, and extending existing scripts. An example of *multiple inheritance* from both an MLP and a radial basis function (RBF) network, yields a neural net where the MLP and the RBF process the input in parallel and the outputs can be either combined (e.g. added) or selected by competition.

Error Back Propagation for Arbitrary Nonrecurrent Architectures   This paragraph shows how to define back propagation on any nonrecurrent architecture in a *provably correct* way. Note that there is a large family of gradient descent algorithms which fit into the framework of back propagation (e.g. [1, 4, 8]). First let me bring you closer to the systematization of the data flow graph approach: Remember that a building block is a 5-tuple $(\mathcal{I}, \mathcal{O}, \mathcal{M}, \mathcal{D}, \mathcal{S})$, where $\mathcal{I}, \mathcal{O}, \mathcal{M}, \mathcal{D}, \mathcal{S}$ are sets of data sinks, data sources, methods, internal data, and symbols, respectively.

A building block performing some mathematical transformation F takes the form $(\{in\}, \{out\}, \{prop, ...\},$ $\{dataIn, dataOut, ...\}, \{inSize, outSize, ...\})$. There are additional components in that category, but they are not relevant here. The method *prop* works as follows: 1. it receives data from the *in*-sink and assigns it to *dataIn*; 2. it calculates $F(dataIn)$ and assigns the result to *dataOut*; 3. it sends *dataOut* to its *out*-source. Examples are *Logistic*, *SoftMax*, and *Linear*. From these kinds of building blocks BP-able blocks can be derived, by adding new ingredients (underlined here). BP-able blocks take the form ({*in*, <u>*errIn*</u>, <u>*targetIn*</u>}, {*out*, <u>*errOut*</u>}, {*prop*, <u>*propErr*</u>, ...}, {*dataIn*, *dataOut*, <u>*errorIn*</u>, <u>*target*</u>, <u>*errorOut*</u>, ...}, {*inSize*, *outSize*, <u>*weightTarget*</u>, *lbre* }). Examples are *BPLogistic* and *BPSoftMax*.

Let m and n be shorthands for *outSize* and *inSize*. The semantics of the single components are:

$$errorIn = (\delta_1, ..., \delta_m) \text{ with } \delta_k := \frac{\partial E}{\partial dataOut_k} \quad \text{and} \quad errorOut = (\theta_1, ..., \theta_n) \text{ with } \theta_l := \frac{\partial E}{\partial dataIn_l} \quad (1)$$

The vector *target* and its corresponding *targetIn*-sink are optional and allow intermediate target vectors. Let $\mathcal{S}^i$ be the set of indices j, for which there is a connection from $M^j.errOut$ to $M^i.errIn$.

The *propErr*-method of M^i has the following behavior:

1. sums up all *errorOut* vectors from follow-up blocks and adds the *target*, if available.

$$errorIn^i = \sum_{k \in \mathcal{S}^i} errorOut^k + weightTarget^i \cdot (target^i - dataOut^i) \quad (2)$$

2. computes the Jacobian G of F^i, with $g_{pq} = \partial dataOut_p^i / \partial dataIn_q^i$. $p = 1..m, q = 1..n$ (3)

3. computes $errorOut^i = G^T errorIn^i$

4. sends $errorOut^i$ via $errOut^i$ to predecessors of block M^i

A building block is *BP-trainable*, if it is BP-able and has another method called *update*, changing internal parameters, as weights or biases, according to incoming error signals. Most common example is *BPLinear*.

The *correctness* of any back propagation architecture can be assured, if for any BP-able block M^i and for each $j \in \mathcal{S}^i$ the following conditions must hold true:

1. *wellformedness of topology:* each block M^j is BP-able and there must exist a backward connection $M^i.out$ to $M^j.in$.

2. *wellformedness of flow of control:* the method $M^i.prop$ must be called before all method calls $M^j.prop$, and the method $M^i.propErr$ must be called after all method calls $M^j.propErr$. All *prop* methods must be called before the *propErr* methods.

3. *stochastic version of steepest descent:* all BP-Blocks that contain parameters to be trained, the *train*-method must be called exactly once during a training step.

The same framework can be applied also to functions that take the form $dataOut = F(dataIn_1, ..., dataIn_N)$, e.g. *ScalarProduct*, *TensorProduct*, etc.

A Back Propagation-Generator Due to the systematicity of this approach, any non-recurrent back propagation architecture can be generated automatically from arithmetic expressions. For example, a standard MLP with direct connections from input to output can be described with $OUT = \text{logistic}(BO + WIO * IN + WHO * \text{logistic}(BH + WIH * IN))$. Parsing this expression yields a syntactic derivation tree, which can be transformed into the appropriate block diagram representation. Building blocks are *BPAdder* (+), *BPMultiplier* (*) and *AdaptiveVector* for the biases *BH* and *BO*, *AdaptiveMatrix* for the matrices *WIH*, *WHO*, and *WIO*. The building block classes *AdaptiveVector* and *AdaptiveMatrix* offer methods for changing their internal state due to incoming error vectors or matrices. Quickprop, the Delta-Bar-Delta-Rule [4], or automatic rate adaption schemes [8], etc. , can be implemented *in a generic way*, regardless of the functional architecture. Also either all or only a fraction of parameters can be made subject to gradient descent. This schema results in developement times of minutes or hours rather than days or weeks.

Recurrent Networks In this framework, one simple way of training nets with recurrencies is unfolding-in-time, i.e. exploiting the transformation into an equivalent non-recurrent representation and proceed with regular back propagation. A dynamic implementation, capable of dealing with arbitrary long input sequences, can be obtained by augmenting each BP-able block with stacks of activation vectors and error vectors. A more detailed description would be beyond the scope of this paper.

Other Supervised Architectures   Fully connected recurrent nets as Hopfield nets, Boltzmann Machines, and others, can be specified in three different levels of granularity. 1. very fine grain: each neuron and each link is a building block 2. medium grain: the layer of neurons is one building block and the layer of links is the other, and both are connected with each other. 3. coarse grain: the whole neural network is one building block. The latter ansatz is always more efficient, especially if the training algorithm is *not local* in space. The deficiencies of having complicated large basic building blocks is the lack of reuse and weaker extensibility.

Unsupervised Architectures and Reinforcement Learning   Almost all architectures known from unsupervised learning and reinforcement learning can be represented elegantly as block diagrams. SESAME is also very appropriate in that context. Our research group has already done numerous experiments in that domain, e.g. speech recognition with cascaded self-organizing feature maps [7], look-ahead-planning applied to learning control [18], and selective sampling architectures for learning the kinematics of robot arms [12].

More complex experiments   SESAME's design is devoted to the construction of very complex neural net architectures. Specifying architectures, such as committee learning, e.g. MINOS [17] and the hierarchy of experts [6] does only involve a few number of lines ($\sim$ 30). Other designs in SESAME involving many building blocks include the bootstrap approach [15]. In our framework the application of this bootstrap approach to a hierarchy of experts would involve almost no extra line of code, but create hundreds of building blocks in a still very manageable way.

ADVANTAGES OF THIS APPROACH

The primary purpose of any design and simulation software tool is to increase productivity of its user, which has several different aspects, e.g. the *efficiency of the simulation*, the *transparency* of design, its *extensibility* and *flexibility*, and the possible degree of *reuse*, *safety*, support of *teamwork*.

In general, a block diagram approach is less efficient than direct programming. Nevertheless, the efficiency of SESAME can be further increased in several ways, i.e. by compiling a whole NN experiment or composite building blocks into one piece of rigid C++ Code without the whole run-time development system. This would also be of great interest for integrating successful architectures into other applications. Standard optimization methods can bring further speed-up. The data flow graph approach also facilitates the use of special purpose computers, e.g. data flow machines and vector pipeline computers. The ultimate speed-up will be obtained through VLSI design, where dataflow descriptions are compiled into chip designs and then put into silicon.

The strong modularization of that approach leads to the inclusion of new learning paradigms, graphics modules, without affecting the core of the simulator and without the necessity of understanding the internal of this simulator. This is of special importance for world wide exchange of code. The possibility of (parametrized) inclusion and (parametrized) (multiple) inheritance results in high levels of reuse. Its interactivity and the possibility of changing learning algorithms, or parts of the architecture within only a few keystrokes, allows easier modification to explore variations in learning algorithms. Based on observations of our research group, SESAME facilitates in general much shorter descriptions of experiments than other simulators. The correctness of design (safety) has been achieved by a) checking the consistency of the architecture by autoconfiguration with respect to its dataformats, b) the avoidance of unnecessary and redundant specifications helps to focus on the salient parts of an experiment, c) the usage of C++ modules that are so simple that they are correct with high probability.

Computations inside blocks are not restricted. This makes SESAME also appropriate for similar domains, e.g. time series prediction, control engineering, vision, signal processing, etc. Regarding all these advantages it seems quite safe to conclude that any successful approach must adopt a kind of building blocks approach as has been presented in this paper. Blocks can be made polymorphic, i.e. they adapt their functionality according to the type of data they receive or they have to send. Block diagrams can be made to create or delete internal blocks according to performance criterions (useful for pruning and growing algorithms). One big trend for the future might be the integration of symbolic and subsymbolic paradigms; here block diagrams offer a very good basis, too. They easily allow the construction of hybrid architectures, where an expert system can be treated as a block. The current state-of-the-art can be improved a lot. But this will still require more collaboration between both the neural net community and the software engineering community.

The software prototype and its preliminary documentation is available upon request to `sesame-request@gmd.de`.

Acknowledgments

I am very grateful to my colleagues Frank Weber, Christoph Tietz, Thomas Sudbrak, and Jörg Kindermann, who all helped developing and implementing SESAME. Many thanks also to Mike Mozer and Dave Touretzky for their useful comments on an earlier version of this paper.

References

[1] S. E. Fahlman, "An empirical sudy of learning speed in back-propagation networks," TR 162, CMU, 1988.

[2] N. Goddard, K. Lynne, T. Mintz, and L. Bukys, "Rochester connectionist simulator," Tech. Rep. TR-233 (revised), Comp. Science Dept, Rochester, 1989.

[3] S. J. Hanson, J. D. Cowan, and C. L. Giles, eds., *Advances in Neural Information Processing Systems 5: Proceedings of the 1992 Conference*, (San Mateo, Ca.), Morgan Kaufmann Publishers, 1993.

[4] R. A. Jacobs, "Increased rates of convergence through learning rate adaptation," *Neural Networks*, vol. 1, pp. 295–307, 1988.

[5] I. Jacobson, M. Christerson, P. Jonsson, and G. Övergaard, *Object-Oriented Software Engineering — A Use Case Driven Approach*, ACM Press and Addison-Wesley, 1992.

[6] M. I. Jordan and R. A. Jacobs, "Hierarchies of adaptive experts," in *Neural Information Systems 4* (J. Moody, S. Hanson, and R. Lippmann, eds.), (San Mateo, California), Morgan Kaufmann, 1992.

[7] J. Kindermann and C. Windheuser, "Unsupervised sequence classification," in *Neural Networks for Signal Processing 2 - Proc. of the 1992 IEEE Workshop*, pp. 184–193, IEEE, August 1992.

[8] Y. LeCun, P. Y. Simard, and B. Pearlmutter, "Automatic learning rate maximization by on-line estimation of the hessian's eigenvectors," in Hanson *et al.* [3], pp. 156–163.

[9] R. R. Leighton, *The Aspirin/MIGRAINES Neural Network Software*. User's Manual, Release V6.0. Oct. 1992

[10] A. Linden, T. Sudbrak, C. Tietz, and F. Weber, "An object-oriented framework for the simulation of neural nets," in Hanson *et al.* [3], pp. 797–804.

[11] A. Linden, T. Sudbrak, and C. Tietz, *The SESAME Handbook*. GMD, Sankt Augustin, 4.1 ed., 1993.

[12] A. Linden and F. Weber, "Implementing inner drive by competence reflection," in *Proc. of 2nd Int. Conf. on Sim. of Adapt. Behavior*, 1993.

[13] E. Marcade, *GALATEA II – User Manual ESPRIT III Project P7808*. Mimetics S. A., France, july 2 ed., 1993.

[14] Y. Miyata, *A User's Guide to PlaNet Version 5.6*. Comp. Science Dep., Univ. of Col. Boulder, jan 29, 1991.

[15] G. Paass, "Assessing and improving neural network predictions by the bootstrap algorithm," in Hanson *et al.* [3], pp. 196–203.

[16] J. R. Rasure and C. S. Williams, "An integrated data flow visual language and software development environment," *Journal of Visual Languages and Computing*, vol. 2, pp. 217–246, 1991.

[17] F. J. Śmieja, "Multiple network systems (MINOS) modules: Task division and module discrimination," in *Proc. of the 8th AISB Conf. on AI, Leeds, 16–19 April, 1991*, 1991.

[18] S. Thrun, K. Möller, and A. Linden, "Planning with an adaptive world model," in *Adv. in Neural Information Processing Systems 3* (R. P. Lippmann, J. E. Moody, and D. S. Touretzky, eds.), Morgan Kaufmann, 1991.

[19] D. van Camp, *The Xerion Neural Network Simulator — Version 3.1*. Dep. of Comp. Science, Toronto. 1993.

[20] A. Zell *et al.*, *SNNS Neural Network Simulator – User Manual Version 3.0*. Univ. of Stuttgart, Germany, 1993.

INDEX

event prediction 245
evolution 97
evolutionary programming 39
expectation maximization 122, 178, 316
experimental psychology 81
exponential memory 245

F

factorial codes 308
feature maps 31
feedforward architecture 280, 358
filtering 236
forward models 97
fractals 203
frequency 149
function approximation 255, 264
fuzzy neural networks 192

G

generalization 162, 170, 343, 358, 372, 380
global optimization 39
Good-Turing 122
graph algorithm 389

H

hard constraints 130
head direction cells 11
Hebbian learning 245, 291
hidden Markov models 122
hidden units
    effective number 335
    noise 48
high-level cognition 87
hints 380
hippocampus 11
holisitic transformation 162
Hopfield networks 389
horizontal connections 31
human cognition 228
hybrid
    learning 245
    systems 130

I

incomplete data 316
inductive bias 372
inflectional morphology 149
information
    maximization 291
    transmission 308
informed bias 157

interference patterns 57
internal representations 48
interpretation of neural networks 178, 184
inverse problems 316
iterated function systems 203

K

kinematics 316
Kullback-Leibler information 364

L

landmark learning 48
language 97, 113, 122, 130, 138, 149, 157
language acquisition device 97
lateral connections 31
learnability 255
learning
    from hints 380
        multiple tasks 372
        vector quantization 300
least mean squares 236, 351
lexical errors 73
linear classifier 358
linguistics 157
LISSOM 31
local view hypothesis 11

M

Markov models
    variable context 122
maximum likelihood estimation 316, 324, 364
mean field theory 73
mean square convergence 351
memory 228
mixture models 316
modularization 372
molecular biology 178, 184, 192
momentum 351
Morse code 57
motor control 97, 272, 316
multitask learning 372
music 228
mutual information 364

N

navigation 11
network capacity 372
neural network analysis 73
neural network classifiers 324
neurophysiology 57
neuroscience 20, 97

NofM algorithm 184
noise handling 236, 255
normalization 291
numerical
    constraints 130
    processing 73, 81
    transcoding 73

O

object localization 316
object-oriented design 397
ocular dominance 31
Oja 245
operating domain transition stability 280
optimality theory 138
optimization 364
overfitting 255, 335, 380

P

parameter drift 280
partial reinforcement extinction effect 65
part-of-speech tagging 122
past tense 149
path integration 11
pattern
    classification 178, 324
    recognition 87
perception 113
perceptron 358
phonology 113, 149
pitch 228
place cells 11
prediction 236, 245, 308
presubiculum 11
principal components 245, 335
productivity 162
promoters 184
protein structure prediction 178
pruning of networks 192
psychology 20, 57

Q

Q learning 264, 272

R

RAAM 162
radial basis functions 236
rate invariance 211
reaction time 81
recurrent choice 65
recurrent networks 97, 162, 170, 203, 211, 228

recursive auto-associative memory 162
redundancy reduction 308
regression 65, 324
reinforcement learning 65, 255, 264, 272
representation 20, 48, 87, 113, 170, 228
reversal in blocks 65
reversal learning 65
robot control 255, 272, 280
rules 149, 178, 184, 192

S

schemata 170
self-organization 31, 192, 300
semantics 138
sensory processing 97
sentence processing 130
sequence processing, see temporal pattern processing
sequential cascaded networks 203
SESAME 397
sigma pi 3
SIMD algorithm 389
simulation 389
singular value decomposition 335
soft competitive learning 291
soft weight-sharing 184
softmax normalization 324
software environments 389, 397
sonar 87
spatial cognition 11, 48
speech perception 316
speech production 272
spiking 3
splines 364
spreading activation 81
state-space analysis 170
statistical
    independence 308
    pattern recognition 324
stochastic
    approximation 300
    diffusion 39
    gradient descent 351
    models 324
strabismus 31
structure 162, 170
successive daily reversal 65
symbolic inference and learning 39, 157, 184
syntax
    ambiguity resolution 130
    categorization 122
    errors 73
systematicity 162

T

task decomposition 272
temporal
    clustering 291
    discounting 255
    locality 291
    pattern processing 211, 228, 236, 245, 308
    structure 211
time series 236
topographic relations 48
training time 335

U

unsupervised learning 291, 300, 308

V

validation error 380
variance reduction 364
vision at low SNR 39
visual cortex 31

W

weight elimination 335

410

411

Printed and bound by CPI Group (UK) Ltd, Croydon, CR0 4YY

17/10/2024

01775694-0017